T0213229

Lecture Notes in Computer Science   14110

Founding Editors

Gerhard Goos
Juris Hartmanis

Editorial Board Members

Elisa Bertino, *Purdue University, West Lafayette, IN, USA*
Wen Gao, *Peking University, Beijing, China*
Bernhard Steffen ⓘ, *TU Dortmund University, Dortmund, Germany*
Moti Yung ⓘ, *Columbia University, New York, NY, USA*

The series Lecture Notes in Computer Science (LNCS), including its subseries Lecture Notes in Artificial Intelligence (LNAI) and Lecture Notes in Bioinformatics (LNBI), has established itself as a medium for the publication of new developments in computer science and information technology research, teaching, and education.

LNCS enjoys close cooperation with the computer science R & D community, the series counts many renowned academics among its volume editors and paper authors, and collaborates with prestigious societies. Its mission is to serve this international community by providing an invaluable service, mainly focused on the publication of conference and workshop proceedings and postproceedings. LNCS commenced publication in 1973.

Welcome Message from Organizers

After the 2021 ICCSA in Cagliari, Italy and the 2022 ICCSA in Malaga, Spain, ICCSA continued its successful scientific endeavours in 2023, hosted again in the Mediterranean neighbourhood. This time, ICCSA 2023 moved a bit more to the east of the Mediterranean Region and was held in the metropolitan city of Athens, the capital of Greece and a vibrant urban environment endowed with a prominent cultural heritage that dates back to the ancient years. As a matter of fact, Athens is one of the oldest cities in the world, and the cradle of democracy. The city has a history of over 3,000 years and, according to the myth, it took its name from Athena, the Goddess of Wisdom and daughter of Zeus.

ICCSA 2023 took place in a secure environment, relieved from the immense stress of the COVID-19 pandemic. This gave us the chance to have a safe and vivid, in-person participation which, combined with the very active engagement of the ICCSA 2023 scientific community, set the ground for highly motivating discussions and interactions as to the latest developments of computer science and its applications in the real world for improving quality of life.

The National Technical University of Athens (NTUA), one of the most prestigious Greek academic institutions, had the honour of hosting ICCSA 2023. The Local Organizing Committee really feels the burden and responsibility of such a demanding task; and puts in all the necessary energy in order to meet participants' expectations and establish a friendly, creative and inspiring, scientific and social/cultural environment that allows for new ideas and perspectives to flourish.

Since all ICCSA participants, either informatics-oriented or application-driven, realize the tremendous steps and evolution of computer science during the last few decades and the huge potential these offer to cope with the enormous challenges of humanity in a globalized, 'wired' and highly competitive world, the expectations from ICCSA 2023 were set high in order for a successful matching between computer science progress and communities' aspirations to be attained, i.e., a progress that serves real, place- and people-based needs and can pave the way towards a visionary, smart, sustainable, resilient and inclusive future for both the current and the next generation.

On behalf of the Local Organizing Committee, I would like to sincerely thank all of you who have contributed to ICCSA 2023 and I cordially welcome you to my 'home', NTUA.

On behalf of the Local Organizing Committee.

Anastasia Stratigea

Organization

ICCSA 2023 was organized by the National Technical University of Athens (Greece), the University of the Aegean (Greece), the University of Perugia (Italy), the University of Basilicata (Italy), Monash University (Australia), Kyushu Sangyo University (Japan), the University of Minho (Portugal). The conference was supported by two NTUA Schools, namely the School of Rural, Surveying and Geoinformatics Engineering and the School of Electrical and Computer Engineering.

Honorary General Chairs

Norio Shiratori   Chuo University, Japan
Kenneth C. J. Tan   Sardina Systems, UK

General Chairs

Osvaldo Gervasi   University of Perugia, Italy
Anastasia Stratigea   National Technical University of Athens, Greece
Bernady O. Apduhan   Kyushu Sangyo University, Japan

Program Committee Chairs

Beniamino Murgante   University of Basilicata, Italy
Dimitris Kavroudakis   University of the Aegean, Greece
Ana Maria A. C. Rocha   University of Minho, Portugal
David Taniar   Monash University, Australia

International Advisory Committee

Jemal Abawajy   Deakin University, Australia
Dharma P. Agarwal   University of Cincinnati, USA
Rajkumar Buyya   Melbourne University, Australia
Claudia Bauzer Medeiros   University of Campinas, Brazil
Manfred M. Fisher   Vienna University of Economics and Business, Austria
Marina L. Gavrilova   University of Calgary, Canada

| Sumi Helal | University of Florida, USA and University of Lancaster, UK |
| Yee Leung | Chinese University of Hong Kong, China |

International Liaison Chairs

Ivan Blečić	University of Cagliari, Italy
Giuseppe Borruso	University of Trieste, Italy
Elise De Donker	Western Michigan University, USA
Maria Irene Falcão	University of Minho, Portugal
Inmaculada Garcia Fernandez	University of Malaga, Spain
Eligius Hendrix	University of Malaga, Spain
Robert C. H. Hsu	Chung Hua University, Taiwan
Tai-Hoon Kim	Beijing Jaotong University, China
Vladimir Korkhov	Saint Petersburg University, Russia
Takashi Naka	Kyushu Sangyo University, Japan
Rafael D. C. Santos	National Institute for Space Research, Brazil
Maribel Yasmina Santos	University of Minho, Portugal
Elena Stankova	Saint Petersburg University, Russia

Workshop and Session Organizing Chairs

| Beniamino Murgante | University of Basilicata, Italy |
| Chiara Garau | University of Cagliari, Italy |

Award Chair

| Wenny Rahayu | La Trobe University, Australia |

Publicity Committee Chairs

Elmer Dadios	De La Salle University, Philippines
Nataliia Kulabukhova	Saint Petersburg University, Russia
Daisuke Takahashi	Tsukuba University, Japan
Shangwang Wang	Beijing University of Posts and Telecommunications, China

Local Organizing Committee Chairs

Anastasia Stratigea	National Technical University of Athens, Greece
Dimitris Kavroudakis	University of the Aegean, Greece
Charalambos Ioannidis	National Technical University of Athens, Greece
Nectarios Koziris	National Technical University of Athens, Greece
Efthymios Bakogiannis	National Technical University of Athens, Greece
Yiota Theodora	National Technical University of Athens, Greece
Dimitris Fotakis	National Technical University of Athens, Greece
Apostolos Lagarias	National Technical University of Athens, Greece
Akrivi Leka	National Technical University of Athens, Greece
Dionisia Koutsi	National Technical University of Athens, Greece
Alkistis Dalkavouki	National Technical University of Athens, Greece
Maria Panagiotopoulou	National Technical University of Athens, Greece
Angeliki Papazoglou	National Technical University of Athens, Greece
Natalia Tsigarda	National Technical University of Athens, Greece
Konstantinos Athanasopoulos	National Technical University of Athens, Greece
Ioannis Xatziioannou	National Technical University of Athens, Greece
Vasiliki Krommyda	National Technical University of Athens, Greece
Panayiotis Patsilinakos	National Technical University of Athens, Greece
Sofia Kassiou	National Technical University of Athens, Greece

Technology Chair

Damiano Perri	University of Florence, Italy

Program Committee

Vera Afreixo	University of Aveiro, Portugal
Filipe Alvelos	University of Minho, Portugal
Hartmut Asche	University of Potsdam, Germany
Ginevra Balletto	University of Cagliari, Italy
Michela Bertolotto	University College Dublin, Ireland
Sandro Bimonte	CEMAGREF, TSCF, France
Rod Blais	University of Calgary, Canada
Ivan Blečić	University of Sassari, Italy
Giuseppe Borruso	University of Trieste, Italy
Ana Cristina Braga	University of Minho, Portugal
Massimo Cafaro	University of Salento, Italy
Yves Caniou	Lyon University, France

Ermanno Cardelli	University of Perugia, Italy
José A. Cardoso e Cunha	Universidade Nova de Lisboa, Portugal
Rui Cardoso	University of Beira Interior, Portugal
Leocadio G. Casado	University of Almeria, Spain
Carlo Cattani	University of Salerno, Italy
Mete Celik	Erciyes University, Turkey
Maria Cerreta	University of Naples "Federico II", Italy
Hyunseung Choo	Sungkyunkwan University, Korea
Rachel Chieng-Sing Lee	Sunway University, Malaysia
Min Young Chung	Sungkyunkwan University, Korea
Florbela Maria da Cruz Domingues Correia	Polytechnic Institute of Viana do Castelo, Portugal
Gilberto Corso Pereira	Federal University of Bahia, Brazil
Alessandro Costantini	INFN, Italy
Carla Dal Sasso Freitas	Universidade Federal do Rio Grande do Sul, Brazil
Pradesh Debba	The Council for Scientific and Industrial Research (CSIR), South Africa
Hendrik Decker	Instituto Tecnológico de Informática, Spain
Robertas Damaševičius	Kausan University of Technology, Lithuania
Frank Devai	London South Bank University, UK
Rodolphe Devillers	Memorial University of Newfoundland, Canada
Joana Matos Dias	University of Coimbra, Portugal
Paolino Di Felice	University of L'Aquila, Italy
Prabu Dorairaj	NetApp, India/USA
Noelia Faginas Lago	University of Perugia, Italy
M. Irene Falcao	University of Minho, Portugal
Cherry Liu Fang	U.S. DOE Ames Laboratory, USA
Florbela P. Fernandes	Polytechnic Institute of Bragança, Portugal
Jose-Jesus Fernandez	National Centre for Biotechnology, CSIS, Spain
Paula Odete Fernandes	Polytechnic Institute of Bragança, Portugal
Adelaide de Fátima Baptista Valente Freitas	University of Aveiro, Portugal
Manuel Carlos Figueiredo	University of Minho, Portugal
Maria Celia Furtado Rocha	PRODEB–PósCultura/UFBA, Brazil
Chiara Garau	University of Cagliari, Italy
Paulino Jose Garcia Nieto	University of Oviedo, Spain
Raffaele Garrisi	Polizia di Stato, Italy
Jerome Gensel	LSR-IMAG, France
Maria Giaoutzi	National Technical University, Athens, Greece
Arminda Manuela Andrade Pereira Gonçalves	University of Minho, Portugal

Andrzej M. Goscinski	Deakin University, Australia
Sevin Gümgüm	Izmir University of Economics, Turkey
Alex Hagen-Zanker	University of Cambridge, UK
Shanmugasundaram Hariharan	B.S. Abdur Rahman University, India
Eligius M. T. Hendrix	University of Malaga, Spain and Wageningen University, The Netherlands
Hisamoto Hiyoshi	Gunma University, Japan
Mustafa Inceoglu	EGE University, Turkey
Peter Jimack	University of Leeds, UK
Qun Jin	Waseda University, Japan
Yeliz Karaca	University of Massachusetts Medical School, Worcester, USA
Farid Karimipour	Vienna University of Technology, Austria
Baris Kazar	Oracle Corp., USA
Maulana Adhinugraha Kiki	Telkom University, Indonesia
DongSeong Kim	University of Canterbury, New Zealand
Taihoon Kim	Hannam University, Korea
Ivana Kolingerova	University of West Bohemia, Czech Republic
Nataliia Kulabukhova	St. Petersburg University, Russia
Vladimir Korkhov	St. Petersburg University, Russia
Rosa Lasaponara	National Research Council, Italy
Maurizio Lazzari	National Research Council, Italy
Cheng Siong Lee	Monash University, Australia
Sangyoun Lee	Yonsei University, Korea
Jongchan Lee	Kunsan National University, Korea
Chendong Li	University of Connecticut, USA
Gang Li	Deakin University, Australia
Fang Liu	AMES Laboratories, USA
Xin Liu	University of Calgary, Canada
Andrea Lombardi	University of Perugia, Italy
Savino Longo	University of Bari, Italy
Tinghuai Ma	Nanjing University of Information Science & Technology, China
Ernesto Marcheggiani	Katholieke Universiteit Leuven, Belgium
Antonino Marvuglia	Research Centre Henri Tudor, Luxembourg
Nicola Masini	National Research Council, Italy
Ilaria Matteucci	National Research Council, Italy
Nirvana Meratnia	University of Twente, The Netherlands
Fernando Miranda	University of Minho, Portugal
Giuseppe Modica	University of Reggio Calabria, Italy
Josè Luis Montaña	University of Cantabria, Spain
Maria Filipa Mourão	Instituto Politécnico de Viana do Castelo, Portugal

Louiza de Macedo Mourelle	State University of Rio de Janeiro, Brazil
Nadia Nedjah	State University of Rio de Janeiro, Brazil
Laszlo Neumann	University of Girona, Spain
Kok-Leong Ong	Deakin University, Australia
Belen Palop	Universidad de Valladolid, Spain
Marcin Paprzycki	Polish Academy of Sciences, Poland
Eric Pardede	La Trobe University, Australia
Kwangjin Park	Wonkwang University, Korea
Ana Isabel Pereira	Polytechnic Institute of Bragança, Portugal
Massimiliano Petri	University of Pisa, Italy
Telmo Pinto	University of Coimbra, Portugal
Maurizio Pollino	Italian National Agency for New Technologies, Energy and Sustainable Economic Development, Italy
Alenka Poplin	University of Hamburg, Germany
Vidyasagar Potdar	Curtin University of Technology, Australia
David C. Prosperi	Florida Atlantic University, USA
Wenny Rahayu	La Trobe University, Australia
Jerzy Respondek	Silesian University of Technology Poland
Humberto Rocha	INESC-Coimbra, Portugal
Jon Rokne	University of Calgary, Canada
Octavio Roncero	CSIC, Spain
Maytham Safar	Kuwait University, Kuwait
Chiara Saracino	A.O. Ospedale Niguarda Ca' Granda - Milano, Italy
Marco Paulo Seabra dos Reis	University of Coimbra, Portugal
Jie Shen	University of Michigan, USA
Qi Shi	Liverpool John Moores University, UK
Dale Shires	U.S. Army Research Laboratory, USA
Inês Soares	University of Coimbra, Portugal
Elena Stankova	St. Petersburg University, Russia
Takuo Suganuma	Tohoku University, Japan
Eufemia Tarantino	Polytechnic of Bari, Italy
Sergio Tasso	University of Perugia, Italy
Ana Paula Teixeira	University of Trás-os-Montes and Alto Douro, Portugal
M. Filomena Teodoro	Portuguese Naval Academy and University of Lisbon, Portugal
Parimala Thulasiraman	University of Manitoba, Canada
Carmelo Torre	Polytechnic of Bari, Italy
Javier Martinez Torres	Centro Universitario de la Defensa Zaragoza, Spain

Giuseppe A. Trunfio	University of Sassari, Italy
Pablo Vanegas	University of Cuenca, Equador
Marco Vizzari	University of Perugia, Italy
Varun Vohra	Merck Inc., USA
Koichi Wada	University of Tsukuba, Japan
Krzysztof Walkowiak	Wroclaw University of Technology, Poland
Zequn Wang	Intelligent Automation Inc, USA
Robert Weibel	University of Zurich, Switzerland
Frank Westad	Norwegian University of Science and Technology, Norway
Roland Wismüller	Universität Siegen, Germany
Mudasser Wyne	SOET National University, USA
Chung-Huang Yang	National Kaohsiung Normal University, Taiwan
Xin-She Yang	National Physical Laboratory, UK
Salim Zabir	France Telecom Japan Co., Japan
Haifeng Zhao	University of California, Davis, USA
Fabiana Zollo	University of Venice "Cà Foscari", Italy
Albert Y. Zomaya	University of Sydney, Australia

Workshop Organizers

Advanced Data Science Techniques with Applications in Industry and Environmental Sustainability (ATELIERS 2023)

Dario Torregrossa	Goodyear, Luxemburg
Antonino Marvuglia	Luxembourg Institute of Science and Technology, Luxemburg
Valeria Borodin	École des Mines de Saint-Étienne, Luxemburg
Mohamed Laib	Luxembourg Institute of Science and Technology, Luxemburg

Advances in Artificial Intelligence Learning Technologies: Blended Learning, STEM, Computational Thinking and Coding (AAILT 2023)

Alfredo Milani	University of Perugia, Italy
Valentina Franzoni	University of Perugia, Italy
Sergio Tasso	University of Perugia, Italy

Advanced Processes of Mathematics and Computing Models in Complex Computational Systems (ACMC 2023)

Yeliz Karaca	University of Massachusetts Chan Medical School and Massachusetts Institute of Technology, USA
Dumitru Baleanu	Cankaya University, Turkey
Osvaldo Gervasi	University of Perugia, Italy
Yudong Zhang	University of Leicester, UK
Majaz Moonis	University of Massachusetts Medical School, USA

Artificial Intelligence Supported Medical Data Examination (AIM 2023)

David Taniar	Monash University, Australia
Seifedine Kadry	Noroff University College, Norway
Venkatesan Rajinikanth	Saveetha School of Engineering, India

Advanced and Innovative Web Apps (AIWA 2023)

Damiano Perri	University of Perugia, Italy
Osvaldo Gervasi	University of Perugia, Italy

Assessing Urban Sustainability (ASUS 2023)

Elena Todella	Polytechnic of Turin, Italy
Marika Gaballo	Polytechnic of Turin, Italy
Beatrice Mecca	Polytechnic of Turin, Italy

Advances in Web Based Learning (AWBL 2023)

Birol Ciloglugil	Ege University, Turkey
Mustafa Inceoglu	Ege University, Turkey

Blockchain and Distributed Ledgers: Technologies and Applications (BDLTA 2023)

Vladimir Korkhov	Saint Petersburg State University, Russia
Elena Stankova	Saint Petersburg State University, Russia
Nataliia Kulabukhova	Saint Petersburg State University, Russia

Bio and Neuro Inspired Computing and Applications (BIONCA 2023)

Nadia Nedjah	State University of Rio De Janeiro, Brazil
Luiza De Macedo Mourelle	State University of Rio De Janeiro, Brazil

Choices and Actions for Human Scale Cities: Decision Support Systems (CAHSC–DSS 2023)

Giovanna Acampa	University of Florence and University of Enna Kore, Italy
Fabrizio Finucci	Roma Tre University, Italy
Luca S. Dacci	Polytechnic of Turin, Italy

Computational and Applied Mathematics (CAM 2023)

Maria Irene Falcao	University of Minho, Portugal
Fernando Miranda	University of Minho, Portugal

Computational and Applied Statistics (CAS 2023)

Ana Cristina Braga	University of Minho, Portugal

Cyber Intelligence and Applications (CIA 2023)

Gianni Dangelo	University of Salerno, Italy
Francesco Palmieri	University of Salerno, Italy
Massimo Ficco	University of Salerno, Italy

Conversations South-North on Climate Change Adaptation Towards Smarter and More Sustainable Cities (CLAPS 2023)

Chiara Garau	University of Cagliari, Italy
Cristina Trois	University of kwaZulu-Natal, South Africa
Claudia Loggia	University of kwaZulu-Natal, South Africa
John Östh	Faculty of Technology, Art and Design, Norway
Mauro Coni	University of Cagliari, Italy
Alessio Satta	MedSea Foundation, Italy

Computational Mathematics, Statistics and Information Management (CMSIM 2023)

Maria Filomena Teodoro	University of Lisbon and Portuguese Naval Academy, Portugal
Marina A. P. Andrade	University Institute of Lisbon, Portugal

Computational Optimization and Applications (COA 2023)

Ana Maria A. C. Rocha	University of Minho, Portugal
Humberto Rocha	University of Coimbra, Portugal

Computational Astrochemistry (CompAstro 2023)

Marzio Rosi	University of Perugia, Italy
Nadia Balucani	University of Perugia, Italy
Cecilia Ceccarelli	University of Grenoble Alpes and Institute for Planetary Sciences and Astrophysics, France
Stefano Falcinelli	University of Perugia, Italy

Computational Methods for Porous Geomaterials (CompPor 2023)

Vadim Lisitsa	Russian Academy of Science, Russia
Evgeniy Romenski	Russian Academy of Science, Russia

Workshop on Computational Science and HPC (CSHPC 2023)

Elise De Doncker	Western Michigan University, USA
Fukuko Yuasa	High Energy Accelerator Research Organization, Japan
Hideo Matsufuru	High Energy Accelerator Research Organization, Japan

Cities, Technologies and Planning (CTP 2023)

Giuseppe Borruso	University of Trieste, Italy
Beniamino Murgante	University of Basilicata, Italy
Malgorzata Hanzl	Lodz University of Technology, Poland
Anastasia Stratigea	National Technical University of Athens, Greece
Ljiljana Zivkovic	Republic Geodetic Authority, Serbia
Ginevra Balletto	University of Cagliari, Italy

Gender Equity/Equality in Transport and Mobility (DELIA 2023)

Tiziana Campisi	University of Enna Kore, Italy
Ines Charradi	Sousse University, Tunisia
Alexandros Nikitas	University of Huddersfield, UK
Kh Md Nahiduzzaman	University of British Columbia, Canada
Andreas Nikiforiadis	Aristotle University of Thessaloniki, Greece
Socrates Basbas	Aristotle University of Thessaloniki, Greece

International Workshop on Defense Technology and Security (DTS 2023)

Yeonseung Ryu	Myongji University, South Korea

Integrated Methods for the Ecosystem-Services Accounting in Urban Decision Process (Ecourbn 2023)

Maria Rosaria Guarini	Sapienza University of Rome, Italy
Francesco Sica	Sapienza University of Rome, Italy
Francesco Tajani	Sapienza University of Rome, Italy

Carmelo Maria Torre   Polytechnic University of Bari, Italy
Pierluigi Morano   Polytechnic University of Bari, Italy
Rossana Ranieri   Sapienza Università di Roma, Italy

Evaluating Inner Areas Potentials (EIAP 2023)

Diana Rolando   Politechnic of Turin, Italy
Manuela Rebaudengo   Politechnic of Turin, Italy
Alice Barreca   Politechnic of Turin, Italy
Giorgia Malavasi   Politechnic of Turin, Italy
Umberto Mecca   Politechnic of Turin, Italy

Sustainable Mobility Last Mile Logistic (ELLIOT 2023)

Tiziana Campisi   University of Enna Kore, Italy
Socrates Basbas   Aristotle University of Thessaloniki, Greece
Grigorios Fountas   Aristotle University of Thessaloniki, Greece
Paraskevas Nikolaou   University of Cyprus, Cyprus
Drazenko Glavic   University of Belgrade, Serbia
Antonio Russo   University of Enna Kore, Italy

Econometrics and Multidimensional Evaluation of Urban Environment (EMEUE 2023)

Maria Cerreta   University of Naples Federico II, Italy
Carmelo Maria Torre   Politechnic of Bari, Italy
Pierluigi Morano   Polytechnic of Bari, Italy
Debora Anelli   Polytechnic of Bari, Italy
Francesco Tajani   Sapienza University of Rome, Italy
Simona Panaro   University of Sussex, UK

Ecosystem Services in Spatial Planning for Resilient Urban and Rural Areas (ESSP 2023)

Sabrina Lai   University of Cagliari, Italy
Francesco Scorza   University of Basilicata, Italy
Corrado Zoppi   University of Cagliari, Italy

Gerardo Carpentieri   University of Naples Federico II, Italy
Floriana Zucaro   University of Naples Federico II, Italy
Ana Clara Mourão Moura   Federal University of Minas Gerais, Brazil

Ethical AI Applications for a Human-Centered Cyber Society (EthicAI 2023)

Valentina Franzoni   University of Perugia, Italy
Alfredo Milani   University of Perugia, Italy
Jordi Vallverdu   University Autonoma Barcelona, Spain
Roberto Capobianco   Sapienza University of Rome, Italy

13th International Workshop on Future Computing System Technologies and Applications (FiSTA 2023)

Bernady Apduhan   Kyushu Sangyo University, Japan
Rafael Santos   National Institute for Space Research, Brazil

Collaborative Planning and Designing for the Future with Geospatial Applications (GeoCollab 2023)

Alenka Poplin   Iowa State University, USA
Rosanna Rivero   University of Georgia, USA
Michele Campagna   University of Cagliari, Italy
Ana Clara Mourão Moura   Federal University of Minas Gerais, Brazil

Geomatics in Agriculture and Forestry: New Advances and Perspectives (GeoForAgr 2023)

Maurizio Pollino   Italian National Agency for New Technologies,
                             Energy and Sustainable Economic
                             Development, Italy
Giuseppe Modica   University of Reggio Calabria, Italy
Marco Vizzari   University of Perugia, Italy
Salvatore Praticò   University of Reggio Calabria, Italy

Geographical Analysis, Urban Modeling, Spatial Statistics (Geog-An-Mod 2023)

Giuseppe Borruso	University of Trieste, Italy
Beniamino Murgante	University of Basilicata, Italy
Harmut Asche	Hasso-Plattner-Institut für Digital Engineering Ggmbh, Germany

Geomatics for Resource Monitoring and Management (GRMM 2023)

Alessandra Capolupo	Polytechnic of Bari, Italy
Eufemia Tarantino	Polytechnic of Bari, Italy
Enrico Borgogno Mondino	University of Turin, Italy

International Workshop on Information and Knowledge in the Internet of Things (IKIT 2023)

Teresa Guarda	Peninsula State University of Santa Elena, Ecuador
Modestos Stavrakis	University of the Aegean, Greece

International Workshop on Collective, Massive and Evolutionary Systems (IWCES 2023)

Alfredo Milani	University of Perugia, Italy
Rajdeep Niyogi	Indian Institute of Technology, India
Valentina Franzoni	University of Perugia, Italy

Multidimensional Evolutionary Evaluations for Transformative Approaches (MEETA 2023)

Maria Cerreta	University of Naples Federico II, Italy
Giuliano Poli	University of Naples Federico II, Italy
Ludovica Larocca	University of Naples Federico II, Italy
Chiara Mazzarella	University of Naples Federico II, Italy

Stefania Regalbuto
Maria Somma

University of Naples Federico II, Italy
University of Naples Federico II, Italy

Building Multi-dimensional Models for Assessing Complex Environmental Systems (MES 2023)

Marta Dell'Ovo
Vanessa Assumma
Caterina Caprioli
Giulia Datola
Federico Dellanna
Marco Rossitti

Politechnic of Milan, Italy
University of Bologna, Italy
Politechnic of Turin, Italy
Politechnic of Turin, Italy
Politechnic of Turin, Italy
Politechnic of Milan, Italy

Metropolitan City Lab (Metro_City_Lab 2023)

Ginevra Balletto
Luigi Mundula
Giuseppe Borruso
Jacopo Torriti
Isabella Ligia

University of Cagliari, Italy
University for Foreigners of Perugia, Italy
University of Trieste, Italy
University of Reading, UK
Metropolitan City of Cagliari, Italy

Mathematical Methods for Image Processing and Understanding (MMIPU 2023)

Ivan Gerace
Gianluca Vinti
Arianna Travaglini

University of Perugia, Italy
University of Perugia, Italy
University of Florence, Italy

Models and Indicators for Assessing and Measuring the Urban Settlement Development in the View of ZERO Net Land Take by 2050 (MOVEto0 2023)

Lucia Saganeiti
Lorena Fiorini
Angela Pilogallo
Alessandro Marucci
Francesco Zullo

University of L'Aquila, Italy
University of L'Aquila, Italy
University of L'Aquila, Italy
University of L'Aquila, Italy
University of L'Aquila, Italy

Modelling Post-Covid Cities (MPCC 2023)

Giuseppe Borruso	University of Trieste, Italy
Beniamino Murgante	University of Basilicata, Italy
Ginevra Balletto	University of Cagliari, Italy
Lucia Saganeiti	University of L'Aquila, Italy
Marco Dettori	University of Sassari, Italy

3rd Workshop on Privacy in the Cloud/Edge/IoT World (PCEIoT 2023)

Michele Mastroianni	University of Salerno, Italy
Lelio Campanile	University of Campania Luigi Vanvitelli, Italy
Mauro Iacono	University of Campania Luigi Vanvitelli, Italy

Port City Interface: Land Use, Logistic and Rear Port Area Planning (PORTUNO 2023)

Tiziana Campisi	University of Enna Kore, Italy
Socrates Basbas	Aristotle University of Thessaloniki, Greece
Efstathios Bouhouras	Aristotle University of Thessaloniki, Greece
Giovanni Tesoriere	University of Enna Kore, Italy
Elena Cocuzza	University of Catania, Italy
Gianfranco Fancello	University of Cagliari, Italy

Scientific Computing Infrastructure (SCI 2023)

Elena Stankova	St. Petersburg State University, Russia
Vladimir Korkhov	St. Petersburg University, Russia

Supply Chains, IoT, and Smart Technologies (SCIS 2023)

Ha Jin Hwang	Sunway University, South Korea
Hangkon Kim	Daegu Catholic University, South Korea
Jan Seruga	Australian Catholic University, Australia

Spatial Cognition in Urban and Regional Planning Under Risk (SCOPUR23)

Domenico Camarda   Polytechnic of Bari, Italy
Giulia Mastrodonato   Polytechnic of Bari, Italy
Stefania Santoro   Polytechnic of Bari, Italy
Maria Rosaria Stufano Melone Polytechnic of Bari, Italy
Mauro Patano   Polytechnic of Bari, Italy

Socio-Economic and Environmental Models for Land Use Management (SEMLUM 2023)

Debora Anelli   Polytechnic of Bari, Italy
Pierluigi Morano   Polytechnic of Bari, Italy
Benedetto Manganelli   University of Basilicata, Italy
Francesco Tajani   Sapienza University of Rome, Italy
Marco Locurcio   Polytechnic of Bari, Italy
Felicia Di Liddo   Polytechnic of Bari, Italy

Ports of the Future - Smartness and Sustainability (SmartPorts 2023)

Ginevra Balletto   University of Cagliari, Italy
Gianfranco Fancello   University of Cagliari, Italy
Patrizia Serra   University of Cagliari, Italy
Agostino Bruzzone   University of Genoa, Italy
Alberto Camarero   Politechnic of Madrid, Spain
Thierry Vanelslander   University of Antwerp, Belgium

Smart Transport and Logistics - Smart Supply Chains (SmarTransLog 2023)

Giuseppe Borruso   University of Trieste, Italy
Marco Mazzarino   University of Venice, Italy
Marcello Tadini   University of Eastern Piedmont, Italy
Luigi Mundula   University for Foreigners of Perugia, Italy
Mara Ladu   University of Cagliari, Italy
Maria del Mar Munoz Leonisio University of Cadiz, Spain

Smart Tourism (SmartTourism 2023)

Giuseppe Borruso	University of Trieste, Italy
Silvia Battino	University of Sassari, Italy
Ainhoa Amaro Garcia	University of Alcala and University of Las Palmas, Spain
Francesca Krasna	University of Trieste, Italy
Ginevra Balletto	University of Cagliari, Italy
Maria del Mar Munoz Leonisio	University of Cadiz, Spain

Sustainability Performance Assessment: Models, Approaches, and Applications Toward Interdisciplinary and Integrated Solutions (SPA 2023)

Sabrina Lai	University of Cagliari, Italy
Francesco Scorza	University of Basilicata, Italy
Jolanta Dvarioniene	Kaunas University of Technology, Lithuania
Valentin Grecu	Lucian Blaga University of Sibiu, Romania
Georgia Pozoukidou	Aristotle University of Thessaloniki, Greece

Spatial Energy Planning, City and Urban Heritage (Spatial_Energy_City 2023)

Ginevra Balletto	University of Cagliari, Italy
Mara Ladu	University of Cagliari, Italy
Emilio Ghiani	University of Cagliari, Italy
Roberto De Lotto	University of Pavia, Italy
Roberto Gerundo	University of Salerno, Italy

Specifics of Smart Cities Development in Europe (SPEED 2023)

Chiara Garau	University of Cagliari, Italy
Katarína Vitálišová	Matej Bel University, Slovakia
Paolo Nesi	University of Florence, Italy
Anna Vaňová	Matej Bel University, Slovakia
Kamila Borsekova	Matej Bel University, Slovakia
Paola Zamperlin	University of Pisa, Italy

Smart, Safe and Health Cities (SSHC 2023)

Chiara Garau	University of Cagliari, Italy
Gerardo Carpentieri	University of Naples Federico II, Italy
Floriana Zucaro	University of Naples Federico II, Italy
Aynaz Lotfata	Chicago State University, USA
Alfonso Annunziata	University of Basilicata, Italy
Diego Altafini	University of Pisa, Italy

Smart and Sustainable Island Communities (SSIC_2023)

Chiara Garau	University of Cagliari, Italy
Anastasia Stratigea	National Technical University of Athens, Greece
Yiota Theodora	National Technical University of Athens, Greece
Giulia Desogus	University of Cagliari, Italy

Theoretical and Computational Chemistry and Its Applications (TCCMA 2023)

Noelia Faginas-Lago	University of Perugia, Italy
Andrea Lombardi	University of Perugia, Italy

Transport Infrastructures for Smart Cities (TISC 2023)

Francesca Maltinti	University of Cagliari, Italy
Mauro Coni	University of Cagliari, Italy
Francesco Pinna	University of Cagliari, Italy
Chiara Garau	University of Cagliari, Italy
Nicoletta Rassu	University of Cagliari, Italy
James Rombi	University of Cagliari, Italy

Urban Regeneration: Innovative Tools and Evaluation Model (URITEM 2023)

Fabrizio Battisti	University of Florence, Italy
Giovanna Acampa	University of Florence and University of Enna Kore, Italy
Orazio Campo	La Sapienza University of Rome, Italy

Urban Space Accessibility and Mobilities (USAM 2023)

Chiara Garau	University of Cagliari, Italy
Matteo Ignaccolo	University of Catania, Italy
Michela Tiboni	University of Brescia, Italy
Francesco Pinna	University of Cagliari, Italy
Silvia Rossetti	University of Parma, Italy
Vincenza Torrisi	University of Catania, Italy
Ilaria Delponte	University of Genoa, Italy

Virtual Reality and Augmented Reality and Applications (VRA 2023)

Osvaldo Gervasi	University of Perugia, Italy
Damiano Perri	University of Florence, Italy
Marco Simonetti	University of Florence, Italy
Sergio Tasso	University of Perugia, Italy

Workshop on Advanced and Computational Methods for Earth Science Applications (WACM4ES 2023)

Luca Piroddi	University of Malta, Malta
Sebastiano Damico	University of Malta, Malta
Marilena Cozzolino	Università del Molise, Italy
Adam Gauci	University of Malta, Italy
Giuseppina Vacca	University of Cagliari, Italy
Chiara Garau	University of Cagliari, Italy

Sponsoring Organizations

ICCSA 2023 would not have been possible without the tremendous support of many organizations and institutions, for which all organizers and participants of ICCSA 2023 express their sincere gratitude:

Springer Nature Switzerland AG, Switzerland
(https://www.springer.com)

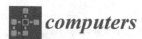

Computers Open Access Journal
(https://www.mdpi.com/journal/computers)

National Technical University of Athens, Greece
(https://www.ntua.gr/)

University of the Aegean, Greece
(https://www.aegean.edu/)

University of Perugia, Italy
(https://www.unipg.it)

University of Basilicata, Italy
(http://www.unibas.it)

 Monash University, Australia
(https://www.monash.edu/)

 Kyushu Sangyo University, Japan
(https://www.kyusan-u.ac.jp/)

 University of Minho, Portugal
(https://www.uminho.pt/)

Universidade do Minho
Escola de Engenharia

Referees

Francesca Abastante	Turin Polytechnic, Italy
Giovanna Acampa	University of Enna Kore, Italy
Adewole Adewumi	Algonquin College, Canada
Vera Afreixo	University of Aveiro, Portugal
Riad Aggoune	Luxembourg Institute of Science and Technology, Luxembourg
Akshat Agrawal	Amity University Haryana, India
Waseem Ahmad	National Institute of Technology Karnataka, India
Oylum Alatlı	Ege University, Turkey
Abraham Alfa	Federal University of Technology Minna, Nigeria
Diego Altafini	University of Pisa, Italy
Filipe Alvelos	University of Minho, Portugal
Marina Alexandra Pedro Andrade	University Institute of Lisbon, Portugal
Debora Anelli	Polytechnic University of Bari, Italy
Mariarosaria Angrisano	Pegaso University, Italy
Alfonso Annunziata	University of Cagliari, Italy
Magarò Antonio	Sapienza University of Rome, Italy
Bernady Apduhan	Kyushu Sangyo University, Japan
Jonathan Apeh	Covenant University, Nigeria
Daniela Ascenzi	University of Trento, Italy
Vanessa Assumma	University of Bologna, Italy
Maria Fernanda Augusto	Bitrum Research Center, Spain
Marco Baioletti	University of Perugia, Italy

Ginevra Balletto	University of Cagliari, Italy
Carlos Balsa	Polytechnic Institute of Bragança, Portugal
Benedetto Barabino	University of Brescia, Italy
Simona Barbaro	University of Palermo, Italy
Sebastiano Barbieri	Turin Polytechnic, Italy
Kousik Barik	University of Alcala, Spain
Alice Barreca	Turin Polytechnic, Italy
Socrates Basbas	Aristotle University of Thessaloniki, Greece
Rosaria Battarra	National Research Council, Italy
Silvia Battino	University of Sassari, Italy
Fabrizio Battisti	University of Florence, Italy
Yaroslav Bazaikin	Jan Evangelista Purkyne University, Czech Republic
Ranjan Kumar Behera	Indian Institute of Information Technology, India
Simone Belli	Complutense University of Madrid, Spain
Oscar Bellini	Polytechnic University of Milan, Italy
Giulio Biondi	University of Perugia, Italy
Adriano Bisello	Eurac Research, Italy
Semen Bochkov	Ulyanovsk State Technical University, Russia
Alexander Bogdanov	St. Petersburg State University, Russia
Letizia Bollini	Free University of Bozen, Italy
Giuseppe Borruso	University of Trieste, Italy
Marilisa Botte	University of Naples Federico II, Italy
Ana Cristina Braga	University of Minho, Portugal
Frederico Branco	University of Trás-os-Montes and Alto Douro, Portugal
Jorge Buele	Indoamérica Technological University, Ecuador
Datzania Lizeth Burgos	Peninsula State University of Santa Elena, Ecuador
Isabel Cacao	University of Aveiro, Portugal
Francesco Calabrò	Mediterranea University of Reggio Calabria, Italy
Rogerio Calazan	Institute of Sea Studies Almirante Paulo Moreira, Brazil
Lelio Campanile	University of Campania Luigi Vanvitelli, Italy
Tiziana Campisi	University of Enna Kore, Italy
Orazio Campo	University of Rome La Sapienza, Italy
Caterina Caprioli	Turin Polytechnic, Italy
Gerardo Carpentieri	University of Naples Federico II, Italy
Martina Carra	University of Brescia, Italy
Barbara Caselli	University of Parma, Italy
Danny Casprini	Politechnic of Milan, Italy

Omar Fernando Castellanos Balleteros	Peninsula State University of Santa Elena, Ecuador
Arcangelo Castiglione	University of Salerno, Italy
Giulio Cavana	Turin Polytechnic, Italy
Maria Cerreta	University of Naples Federico II, Italy
Sabarathinam Chockalingam	Institute for Energy Technology, Norway
Luis Enrique Chuquimarca Jimenez	Peninsula State University of Santa Elena, Ecuador
Birol Ciloglugil	Ege University, Turkey
Elena Cocuzza	Univesity of Catania, Italy
Emanuele Colica	University of Malta, Malta
Mauro Coni	University of Cagliari, Italy
Simone Corrado	University of Basilicata, Italy
Elisete Correia	University of Trás-os-Montes and Alto Douro, Portugal
Florbela Correia	Polytechnic Institute Viana do Castelo, Portugal
Paulo Cortez	University of Minho, Portugal
Martina Corti	Politechnic of Milan, Italy
Lino Costa	Universidade do Minho, Portugal
Cecília Maria Vasconcelos Costa e Castro	University of Minho, Portugal
Alfredo Cuzzocrea	University of Calabria, Italy
Sebastiano D'amico	University of Malta, Malta
Maria Danese	National Research Council, Italy
Gianni Dangelo	University of Salerno, Italy
Ana Daniel	Aveiro University, Portugal
Giulia Datola	Politechnic of Milan, Italy
Regina De Almeida	University of Trás-os-Montes and Alto Douro, Portugal
Maria Stella De Biase	University of Campania Luigi Vanvitelli, Italy
Elise De Doncker	Western Michigan University, USA
Luiza De Macedo Mourelle	State University of Rio de Janeiro, Brazil
Itamir De Morais Barroca Filho	Federal University of Rio Grande do Norte, Brazil
Pierfrancesco De Paola	University of Naples Federico II, Italy
Francesco De Pascale	University of Turin, Italy
Manuela De Ruggiero	University of Calabria, Italy
Alexander Degtyarev	St. Petersburg State University, Russia
Federico Dellanna	Turin Polytechnic, Italy
Marta Dellovo	Politechnic of Milan, Italy
Bashir Derradji	Sfax University, Tunisia
Giulia Desogus	University of Cagliari, Italy
Frank Devai	London South Bank University, UK

Piero Di Bonito	University of Campania Luigi Vanvitelli, Italy
Chiara Di Dato	University of L'Aquila, Italy
Michele Di Giovanni	University of Campania Luigi Vanvitelli, Italy
Felicia Di Liddo	Polytechnic University of Bari, Italy
Joana Dias	University of Coimbra, Portugal
Luigi Dolores	University of Salerno, Italy
Marco Donatelli	Università of Insubria, Italy
Aziz Dursun	Virginia Tech University, USA
Jaroslav Dvořak	Klaipeda University, Lithuania
Wolfgang Erb	University of Padova, Italy
Maurizio Francesco Errigo	University of Enna Kore, Italy
Noelia Faginas-Lago	University of Perugia, Italy
Maria Irene Falcao	University of Minho, Portugal
Stefano Falcinelli	University of Perugia, Italy
Grazia Fattoruso	Italian National Agency for New Technologies, Energy and Sustainable Economic Development, Italy
Sara Favargiotti	University of Trento, Italy
Marcin Feltynowski	University of Lodz, Poland
António Fernandes	Polytechnic Institute of Bragança, Portugal
Florbela P. Fernandes	Polytechnic Institute of Bragança, Portugal
Paula Odete Fernandes	Polytechnic Institute of Bragança, Portugal
Luis Fernandez-Sanz	University of Alcala, Spain
Maria Eugenia Ferrao	University of Beira Interior and University of Lisbon, Portugal
Luís Ferrás	University of Minho, Portugal
Angela Ferreira	Polytechnic Institute of Bragança, Portugal
Maddalena Ferretti	Politechnic of Marche, Italy
Manuel Carlos Figueiredo	University of Minho, Portugal
Fabrizio Finucci	Roma Tre University, Italy
Ugo Fiore	University Pathenope of Naples, Italy
Lorena Fiorini	University of L'Aquila, Italy
Valentina Franzoni	Perugia University, Italy
Adelaide Freitas	University of Aveiro, Portugal
Kirill Gadylshin	Russian Academy of Sciences, Russia
Andrea Gallo	University of Trieste, Italy
Luciano Galone	University of Malta, Malta
Chiara Garau	University of Cagliari, Italy
Ernesto Garcia Para	Universidad del País Vasco, Spain
Rachele Vanessa Gatto	Università della Basilicata, Italy
Marina Gavrilova	University of Calgary, Canada
Georgios Georgiadis	Aristotle University of Thessaloniki, Greece

Ivan Gerace	University of Perugia, Italy
Osvaldo Gervasi	University of Perugia, Italy
Alfonso Giancotti	Sapienza University of Rome, Italy
Andrea Gioia	Politechnic of Bari, Italy
Giacomo Giorgi	University of Perugia, Italy
Salvatore Giuffrida	Università di Catania, Italy
A. Manuela Gonçalves	University of Minho, Portugal
Angela Gorgoglione	University of the Republic, Uruguay
Yusuke Gotoh	Okayama University, Japan
Mariolina Grasso	University of Enna Kore, Italy
Silvana Grillo	University of Cagliari, Italy
Teresa Guarda	Universidad Estatal Peninsula de Santa Elena, Ecuador
Eduardo Guerra	Free University of Bozen-Bolzano, Italy
Carmen Guida	University of Napoli Federico II, Italy
Kemal Güven Gülen	Namık Kemal University, Turkey
Malgorzata Hanzl	Technical University of Lodz, Poland
Peter Hegedus	University of Szeged, Hungary
Syeda Sumbul Hossain	Daffodil International University, Bangladesh
Mustafa Inceoglu	Ege University, Turkey
Federica Isola	University of Cagliari, Italy
Seifedine Kadry	Noroff University College, Norway
Yeliz Karaca	University of Massachusetts Chan Medical School and Massachusetts Institute of Technology, USA
Harun Karsli	Bolu Abant Izzet Baysal University, Turkey
Tayana Khachkova	Russian Academy of Sciences, Russia
Manju Khari	Jawaharlal Nehru University, India
Vladimir Korkhov	Saint Petersburg State University, Russia
Dionisia Koutsi	National Technical University of Athens, Greece
Tomonori Kouya	Shizuoka Institute of Science and Technology, Japan
Nataliia Kulabukhova	Saint Petersburg State University, Russia
Anisha Kumari	National Institute of Technology, India
Ludovica La Rocca	University of Napoli Federico II, Italy
Mara Ladu	University of Cagliari, Italy
Sabrina Lai	University of Cagliari, Italy
Mohamed Laib	Luxembourg Institute of Science and Technology, Luxembourg
Giuseppe Francesco Cesare Lama	University of Napoli Federico II, Italy
Isabella Maria Lami	Turin Polytechnic, Italy
Chien Sing Lee	Sunway University, Malaysia

Marcelo Leon	Ecotec University, Ecuador
Federica Leone	University of Cagliari, Italy
Barbara Lino	University of Palermo, Italy
Vadim Lisitsa	Russian Academy of Sciences, Russia
Carla Lobo	Portucalense University, Portugal
Marco Locurcio	Polytechnic University of Bari, Italy
Claudia Loggia	University of KwaZulu-Natal, South Africa
Andrea Lombardi	University of Perugia, Italy
Isabel Lopes	Polytechnic Institut of Bragança, Portugal
Immacolata Lorè	Mediterranean University of Reggio Calabria, Italy
Vanda Lourenco	Nova University of Lisbon, Portugal
Giorgia Malavasi	Turin Polytechnic, Italy
Francesca Maltinti	University of Cagliari, Italy
Luca Mancini	University of Perugia, Italy
Marcos Mandado	University of Vigo, Spain
Benedetto Manganelli	University of Basilicata, Italy
Krassimir Markov	Institute of Electric Engineering and Informatics, Bulgaria
Enzo Martinelli	University of Salerno, Italy
Fiammetta Marulli	University of Campania Luigi Vanvitelli, Italy
Antonino Marvuglia	Luxembourg Institute of Science and Technology, Luxembourg
Rytis Maskeliunas	Kaunas University of Technology, Lithuania
Michele Mastroianni	University of Salerno, Italy
Hideo Matsufuru	High Energy Accelerator Research Organization, Japan
D'Apuzzo Mauro	University of Cassino and Southern Lazio, Italy
Luis Mazon	Bitrum Research Group, Spain
Chiara Mazzarella	University Federico II, Naples, Italy
Beatrice Mecca	Turin Polytechnic, Italy
Umberto Mecca	Turin Polytechnic, Italy
Paolo Mengoni	Hong Kong Baptist University, China
Gaetano Messina	Mediterranean University of Reggio Calabria, Italy
Alfredo Milani	University of Perugia, Italy
Alessandra Milesi	University of Cagliari, Italy
Richard Millham	Durban University of Technology, South Africa
Fernando Miranda	Universidade do Minho, Portugal
Biswajeeban Mishra	University of Szeged, Hungary
Giuseppe Modica	University of Reggio Calabria, Italy
Pierluigi Morano	Polytechnic University of Bari, Italy

Filipe Mota Pinto	Polytechnic Institute of Leiria, Portugal
Maria Mourao	Polytechnic Institute of Viana do Castelo, Portugal
Eugenio Muccio	University of Naples Federico II, Italy
Beniamino Murgante	University of Basilicata, Italy
Rocco Murro	Sapienza University of Rome, Italy
Giuseppe Musolino	Mediterranean University of Reggio Calabria, Italy
Nadia Nedjah	State University of Rio de Janeiro, Brazil
Juraj Nemec	Masaryk University, Czech Republic
Andreas Nikiforiadis	Aristotle University of Thessaloniki, Greece
Silvio Nocera	IUAV University of Venice, Italy
Roseline Ogundokun	Kaunas University of Technology, Lithuania
Emma Okewu	University of Alcala, Spain
Serena Olcuire	Sapienza University of Rome, Italy
Irene Oliveira	University Trás-os-Montes and Alto Douro, Portugal
Samson Oruma	Ostfold University College, Norway
Antonio Pala	University of Cagliari, Italy
Maria Panagiotopoulou	National Technical University of Athens, Greece
Simona Panaro	University of Sussex Business School, UK
Jay Pancham	Durban University of Technology, South Africa
Eric Pardede	La Trobe University, Australia
Hyun Kyoo Park	Ministry of National Defense, South Korea
Damiano Perri	University of Florence, Italy
Quoc Trung Pham	Ho Chi Minh City University of Technology, Vietnam
Claudio Piferi	University of Florence, Italy
Angela Pilogallo	University of L'Aquila, Italy
Francesco Pinna	University of Cagliari, Italy
Telmo Pinto	University of Coimbra, Portugal
Luca Piroddi	University of Malta, Malta
Francesco Pittau	Politechnic of Milan, Italy
Giuliano Poli	Università Federico II di Napoli, Italy
Maurizio Pollino	Italian National Agency for New Technologies, Energy and Sustainable Economic Development, Italy
Vijay Prakash	University of Malta, Malta
Salvatore Praticò	Mediterranean University of Reggio Calabria, Italy
Carlotta Quagliolo	Turin Polytechnic, Italy
Garrisi Raffaele	Operations Center for Cyber Security, Italy
Mariapia Raimondo	Università della Campania Luigi Vanvitelli, Italy

Bruna Ramos	Universidade Lusíada Norte, Portugal
Nicoletta Rassu	University of Cagliari, Italy
Roberta Ravanelli	University of Roma La Sapienza, Italy
Pier Francesco Recchi	University of Naples Federico II, Italy
Stefania Regalbuto	University of Naples Federico II, Italy
Rommel Regis	Saint Joseph's University, USA
Marco Reis	University of Coimbra, Portugal
Jerzy Respondek	Silesian University of Technology, Poland
Isabel Ribeiro	Polytechnic Institut of Bragança, Portugal
Albert Rimola	Autonomous University of Barcelona, Spain
Corrado Rindone	Mediterranean University of Reggio Calabria, Italy
Maria Rocco	Roma Tre University, Italy
Ana Maria A. C. Rocha	University of Minho, Portugal
Fabio Rocha	Universidade Federal de Sergipe, Brazil
Humberto Rocha	University of Coimbra, Portugal
Maria Clara Rocha	Politechnic Institut of Coimbra, Portual
Carlos Rodrigues	Polytechnic Institut of Bragança, Portugal
Diana Rolando	Turin Polytechnic, Italy
James Rombi	University of Cagliari, Italy
Evgeniy Romenskiy	Russian Academy of Sciences, Russia
Marzio Rosi	University of Perugia, Italy
Silvia Rossetti	University of Parma, Italy
Marco Rossitti	Politechnic of Milan, Italy
Antonio Russo	University of Enna, Italy
Insoo Ryu	MoaSoftware, South Korea
Yeonseung Ryu	Myongji University, South Korea
Lucia Saganeiti	University of L'Aquila, Italy
Valentina Santarsiero	University of Basilicata, Italy
Luigi Santopietro	University of Basilicata, Italy
Rafael Santos	National Institute for Space Research, Brazil
Valentino Santucci	University for Foreigners of Perugia, Italy
Alessandra Saponieri	University of Salento, Italy
Mattia Scalas	Turin Polytechnic, Italy
Francesco Scorza	University of Basilicata, Italy
Ester Scotto Di Perta	University of Napoli Federico II, Italy
Nicoletta Setola	University of Florence, Italy
Ricardo Severino	University of Minho, Portugal
Angela Silva	Polytechnic Institut of Viana do Castelo, Portugal
Carina Silva	Polytechnic of Lisbon, Portugal
Marco Simonetti	University of Florence, Italy
Sergey Solovyev	Russian Academy of Sciences, Russia

Maria Somma	University of Naples Federico II, Italy
Changgeun Son	Ministry of National Defense, South Korea
Alberico Sonnessa	Polytechnic of Bari, Italy
Inês Sousa	University of Minho, Portugal
Lisete Sousa	University of Lisbon, Portugal
Elena Stankova	Saint-Petersburg State University, Russia
Modestos Stavrakis	University of the Aegean, Greece
Flavio Stochino	University of Cagliari, Italy
Anastasia Stratigea	National Technical University of Athens, Greece
Yue Sun	European XFEL GmbH, Germany
Anthony Suppa	Turin Polytechnic, Italy
David Taniar	Monash University, Australia
Rodrigo Tapia McClung	Centre for Research in Geospatial Information Sciences, Mexico
Tarek Teba	University of Portsmouth, UK
Ana Paula Teixeira	University of Trás-os-Montes and Alto Douro, Portugal
Tengku Adil Tengku Izhar	Technological University MARA, Malaysia
Maria Filomena Teodoro	University of Lisbon and Portuguese Naval Academy, Portugal
Yiota Theodora	National Technical University of Athens, Greece
Elena Todella	Turin Polytechnic, Italy
Graça Tomaz	Polytechnic Institut of Guarda, Portugal
Anna Tonazzini	National Research Council, Italy
Dario Torregrossa	Goodyear, Luxembourg
Francesca Torrieri	University of Naples Federico II, Italy
Vincenza Torrisi	University of Catania, Italy
Nikola Tosic	Polytechnic University of Catalonia, Spain
Vincenzo Totaro	Polytechnic University of Bari, Italy
Arianna Travaglini	University of Florence, Italy
António Trigo	Polytechnic of Coimbra, Portugal
Giuseppe A. Trunfio	University of Sassari, Italy
Toshihiro Uchibayashi	Kyushu University, Japan
Piero Ugliengo	University of Torino, Italy
Jordi Vallverdu	University Autonoma Barcelona, Spain
Gianmarco Vanuzzo	University of Perugia, Italy
Dmitry Vasyunin	T-Systems, Russia
Laura Verde	University of Campania Luigi Vanvitelli, Italy
Giulio Vignoli	University of Cagliari, Italy
Gianluca Vinti	University of Perugia, Italy
Katarína Vitálišová	Matej Bel University, Slovak Republic
Daniel Mark Vitiello	University of Cagliari

Marco Vizzari	University of Perugia, Italy
Manuel Yañez	Autonomous University of Madrid, Spain
Fenghui Yao	Tennessee State University, USA
Fukuko Yuasa	High Energy Accelerator Research Organization, Japan
Milliam Maxime Zekeng Ndadji	University of Dschang, Cameroon
Ljiljana Zivkovic	Republic Geodetic Authority, Serbia
Camila Zyngier	IBMEC-BH, Brazil

Plenary Lectures

A Multiscale Planning Concept for Sustainable Metropolitan Development

Pierre Frankhauser

Théma, Université de Franche-Comté, 32, rue Mégevand, 20030 Besançon, France
pierre.frankhauser@univ-fcomte.fr

Keywords: Sustainable metropolitan development · Multiscale approach · Urban modelling

Urban sprawl has often been pointed out as having an important negative impact on environment and climate. Residential zones have grown up in what were initially rural areas, located far from employment areas and often lacking shopping opportunities, public services and public transportation. Hence urban sprawl increased car-traffic flows, generating pollution and increasing energy consumption. New road axes consume considerable space and weaken biodiversity by reducing and cutting natural areas. A return to "compact cities" or "dense cities" has often been contemplated as the most efficient way to limit urban sprawl. However, the real impact of density on car use is less clear-cut (Daneshpour and Shakibamanesh 2011). Let us emphasize that moreover climate change will increase the risk of heat islands on an intra-urban scale. This prompts a more nuanced reflection on how urban fabrics should be structured.

Moreover, urban planning cannot ignore social demand. Lower land prices in rural areas, often put forward by economists, is not the only reason of urban sprawl. The quality of the residential environment comes into play, too, through features like noise, pollution, landscape quality, density etc. Schwanen et al. (2004) observe for the Netherlands that households preferring a quiet residential environment and individual housing with a garden will not accept densification, which might even lead them to move to lower-density rural areas even farther away from jobs and shopping amenities. Many scholars emphasize the importance of green amenities for residential environments and report the importance of easy access to leisure areas (Guo and Bhat 2002). Vegetation in the residential environment has an important impact on health and well-being (Lafortezza et al. 2009).

We present here the Fractalopolis concept which we developed in the frame of several research projects and which aims reconciling environmental and social issues (Bonin et al., 2020; Frankhauser 2021; Frankhauser et al. 2018). This concept introduces a multiscale approach based on multifractal geometry for conceiving spatial development for metropolitan areas. For taking into account social demand we refer to the fundamental work of Max-Neef et al. (1991) based on Maslow's work about basic human needs. He introduces the concept of satisfiers assigned to meet the basic needs of "Subsistence, Protection, Affection, Understanding, Participation, Idleness, Creation, Identity and Freedom". Satisfiers thus become the link between the needs of everyone and society and may depend on the cultural context. We consider their importance, their location and their accessibility and we rank the needs according to their importance for individuals or households. In order to enjoy a good quality of life and to shorten trips and to reduce automobile use, it seems important for satisfiers of daily needs to be easily accessible. Hence, we consider the purchase rate when reflecting on the implementation of shops which is reminiscent of central place theory.

The second important feature is taking care of environment and biodiversity by avoiding fragmentation of green space (Ekren and Arslan 2022) which must benefit, moreover, of a good accessibility, as pointed out. These areas must, too, ply the role of cooling areas ensuring ventilation of urbanized areas (Kuttler et al. 1998).

For integrating these different objectives, we propose a concept for developing spatial configurations of metropolitan areas designed which is based on multifractal geometry. It allows combining different issues across a large range of scales in a coherent way. These issues include:

- providing easy access to a large array of amenities to meet social demand;
- promoting the use of public transportation and soft modes instead of automobile use;
- preserving biodiversity and improving the local climate.

The concept distinguishes development zones localized in the vicinity of a nested and hierarchized system of public transport axes. The highest ranked center offers all types of amenities, whereas lower ranked centers lack the highest ranked amenities. The lowest ranked centers just offer the amenities for daily needs. A coding system allows distinguishing the centers according to their rank.

Each subset of central places is in some sense autonomous, since they are not linked by transportation axes to subcenters of the same order. This allows to preserve a linked system of green corridors penetrating the development zones across scales avoiding the fragmentation of green areas and ensuring a good accessibility to recreational areas.

The spatial model is completed by a population distribution model which globally follows the same hierarchical logic. However, we weakened the strong fractal order what allows to conceive a more or less polycentric spatial system.

We can adapt the theoretical concept easily to real world situation without changing the underlying multiscale logic. A decision support system has been developed allowing to simulate development scenarios and to evaluate them. The evaluation procedure is based on fuzzy evaluation of distance acceptance for accessing to the different types of amenities according to the ranking of needs. We used for evaluation data issued from a great set of French planning documents like Master plans. We show an example how the software package can be used concretely.

References

Bonin, O., et al.: Projet SOFT sobriété énergétique par les formes urbaines et le transport (Research Report No. 1717C0003; p. 214). ADEME (2020)
Daneshpour, A., Shakibamanesh, A.: Compact city; dose it create an obligatory context for urban sustainability? Int. J. Archit. Eng. Urban Plann. 21(2), 110–118 (2011)

Ekren, E., Arslan, M.: Functions of greenways as an ecologically-based planning strategy. In: Çakır, M., Tuğluer, M., Fırat Örs, P.: Architectural Sciences and Ecology, pp. 134–156. Iksad Publications (2022)

Frankhauser, P.: Fractalopolis—a fractal concept for the sustainable development of metropolitan areas. In: Sajous, P., Bertelle, C. (eds.) Complex Systems, Smart Territories and Mobility, pp. 15–50. Springer, Cham (2021). https://doi.org/10.1007/978-3-030-59302-5_2

Frankhauser, P., Tannier, C., Vuidel, G., Houot, H.: An integrated multifractal modelling to urban and regional planning. Comput. Environ. Urban Syst. 67(1), 132–146 (2018). https://doi.org/10.1016/j.compenvurbsys.2017.09.011

Guo, J., Bhat, C.: Residential location modeling: accommodating sociodemographic, school quality and accessibility effects. University of Texas, Austin (2002)

Kuttler, W., Dütemeyer, D., Barlag, A.-B.: Influence of regional and local winds on urban ventilation in Cologne, Germany. Meteorologische Zeitschrift, 77–87 (1998) https://doi.org/10.1127/metz/7/1998/77

Lafortezza, R., Carrus, G., Sanesi, G., Davies, C.: Benefits and well-being perceived by people visiting green spaces in periods of heat stress. Urban For. Urban Green. 8(2), 97–108 (2009)

Max-Neef, M. A., Elizalde, A., Hopenhayn, M.: Human scale development: conception, application and further reflections. The Apex Press (1991)

Schwanen, T., Dijst, M., Dieleman, F. M.: Policies for urban form and their impact on travel: The Netherlands experience. Urban Stud. 41(3), 579–603 (2004)

Graph Drawing and Network Visualization – An Overview – (Keynote Speech)

Giuseppe Liotta

Dipartimento di Ingegneria, Università degli Studi di Perugia, Italy
giuseppe.liotta@unipg.it

Abstract. Graph Drawing and Network visualization supports the exploration, analysis, and communication of relational data arising in a variety of application domains: from bioinformatics to software engineering, from social media to cyber-security, from data bases to powergrid systems. Aim of this keynote speech is to introduce this thriving research area, highlighting some of its basic approaches and pointing to some promising research directions.

1 Introduction

Graph Drawing and Network Visualization is at the intersection of different disciplines and it combines topics that traditionally belong to theoretical computer science with methods and approaches that characterize more applied disciplines. Namely, it can be related to Graph Algorithms, Geometric Graph Theory and Geometric computing, Combinatorial Optimization, Experimental Analysis, User Studies, System Design and Development, and Human Computer Interaction. This combination of theory and practice is well reflected in the flagship conference of the area, the *International Symposium on Graph Drawing and Network Visualization*, that has two tracks, one focusing on combinatorial and algorithmic aspects and the other on the design of network visualization systems and interfaces. The conference is now at its 31st edition; a full list of the symposia and their proceedings, published by Springer in the LNCS series can be found at the URL: http://www.graphdrawing.org/.

Aim of this short paper is to outline the content of my Keynote Speech at ICCSA 2023, which will be referred to as the "Talk" in the rest of the paper. The talk will introduce the field of Graph Drawing and Network Visualization to a broad audience, with the goal to not only present some key methodological and technological aspects, but also point to some unexplored or partially explored research directions. The rest of this short paper briefly outlines the content of the talk and provides some references that can be a starting point for researchers interested in working on Graph Drawing and Network Visualization.

2 Why Visualize Networks?

Back in 1973 the famous statistician Francis Anscombe, gave a convincing example of why visualization is fundamental component of data analysis. The example is known as the *Anscombe's quartet* [3] and it consists of four sets of 11 points each that are almost identical in terms of the basic statistic properties of their x– and y– coordinates. Namely the mean values and the variance of x and y are exactly the same in the four sets, while the correlation of x and y and the linear regression are the same up to the second decimal. In spite of this statistical similarity, the data look very different when displayed in the Euclidean plane which leads to the conclusion that they correspond to significantly different phenomena. Figure 1 reports the four sets of Anscombe's quartet. After fifty years, with the arrival of AI-based technologies and the need of explaining and interpreting machine-driven suggestions before making strategic decision, the lesson of Anscombe's quartet has not just kept but even increased its relevance.

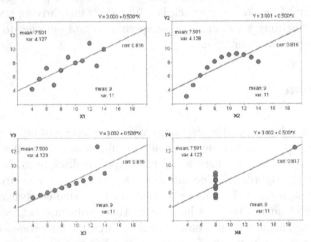

Fig. 1. The four point sets in Anscombe's quartet [3]; the figure also reports statistical values of the x and y variables.

As a matter of fact, nowadays the need of visualization systems goes beyond the verification of the accuracy of some statistical analysis on a set of scattered data. Recent technological advances have generated torrents of data that area relational in nature and typically modeled as networks: the nodes of the networks store the features of the data and the edges of the networks describe the semantic relationships between the data features. Such networked data sets (whose algebraic underlying structure is a called graph in discrete mathematics) arise in a variety of application domains including, for example, Systems Biology, Social Network Analysis, Software Engineering, Networking, Data Bases, Homeland Security, and Business Intelligence. In these (and many other) contexts, systems that support the visual analysis of networks and graphs play a central role in critical decision making processes. These are human-in-the-loop processes where the continuous interaction between humans (decision makers) and data mining or optimization algorithms (AI/ML components) supports the data exploration, the development of verifiable theories about the data, and the extraction of new knowledge that is used to make strategic choices. A seminal book by Keim et al. [33] schematically represents the human-in-the-loop approach to making sense of networked data sets as in Fig. 2. See also [46–49].

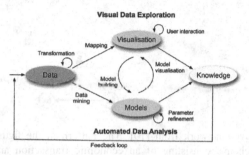

Fig. 2. Sense-making/knowledge generation loop. This conceptual interaction model between human analysts and network visualization system is at the basis of network visual analytics system design [33].

To make a concrete application example of the analysis of a network by interacting with its visualization, consider the problem of contrasting financial crimes such as money laundering or tax evasion. These crimes are based on relevant volumes of financial transactions to conceal the identity, the source, or the destination of illegally gained money. Also, the adopted patterns to pursue the illegal goals continuously change to conceal the crimes. Therefore, contrasting them requires special investigation units which must analyze very large and highly dynamic data sets and discover relationships between different subjects to untangle complex fraudulent plots. The investigative cycle begins with data collection and filtering; it is then followed by modeling the data as a social network (also called *financial activity network* in this context) to which different data mining and data analytic methods are applied, including graph pattern matching, social network analysis, machine learning, and information diffusion. By the network visualization system detectives can interactively explore the data, gain insight and make new hypotheses about possible criminal activities, verify the hypotheses by asking the system to provide more details about specific portions of the network, refine previous outputs, and eventually gain new knowledge. Figure 3 illustrates a small financial activity network where, by means of the interaction between an officer of the Italian Revenue Agency and the MALDIVE system described in [10] a fraudulent pattern has been identified. Precisely, the tax officer has encoded a risky relational scheme among taxpayers into a suspicious graph pattern; in response, the system has made a search in the taxpayer network and it has returned one such pattern. See, e.g., [9, 11, 14, 18, 38] for more papers and references about visual analytic applications to contrasting financial crimes.

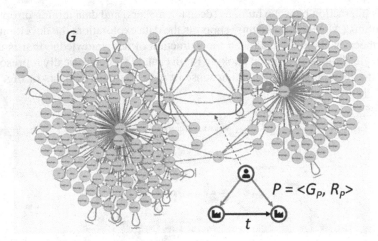

Fig. 3. A financial activity network from [10]. The pattern in the figure represents a Sup-pliesFromAssociated scheme, consisting of an economic transaction and two shareholding relationships.

3   Facets of Graph Drawing and Network Visualization

The Talk overviews some of the fundamental facets that characterize the research in Graph Drawing and Network Visualization. Namely:

- Graph drawing metaphors: Depending on the application context, different metaphors can be used to represent a relational data set modeled as a graph. The talk will briefly recall the matrix representation, the space filling representation, the contact representation, and the node-link representation which is, by far, the most commonly used (see, e.g., [43]).
- Interaction paradigms: Different interaction paradigms have different impacts on the sense-making process of the user about the visualized network. The Talk will go through the full-view, top-down, bottom-up, incremental, and narrative paradigms. Pros and cons will be highlighted for each approach, also by means of examples and applications. The discussion of the top-down interaction paradigm will also consider the hybrid visualization models (see, e.g., [2, 24, 26, 28, 39]) while the discussion about the incremental paradigm will focus on research about graph storyplans (see, e.g., [4, 6, 7]).
- Graph drawing algorithms: Three main algorithmic approaches will be reviewed, namely the force-directed, the layered), and the planarization-based approach; see, e.g., [5]. We shall also make some remarks about FPT algorithms for graph drawing (see, e.g., [8, 19, 20, 25, 27, 40, 53]) and about how the optimization challenges vary when it is assumed that the input has or does not have a fixed combinatorial embedding (see, e.g., [12, 13, 16, 17, 23]).
- Experimental analysis and user-studies: The Talk will mostly compare two models to define and experimentally validate those optimization goals that define a "readable"

network visualization, i.e. a visualization that in a given application context can easily convey the structure of a relational data set so to guarantee efficiency both in its visual exploration and in the elaboration of new knowledge. Special focus will be given to a set emerging optimization goals related to edge crossings that are currently investigated in the graph drawing and network visualization community unedr the name of "graph drawing beyond planarity" (see, e.g., [1, 15, 29, 35]).

The talk shall also point to some promising research directions, including: (i) Extend the body of papers devoted to user-studies that compare the impact of different graph drawing metaphors on the user perception. (ii) Extend the study of interaction paradigms to extended reality environments (see, e.g., [21, 30, 36, 37]); (iii) Engineer the FPT algorithms for graph drawing and experimentally compare their performances with exact or approximate solutions; and (iv) Develop new algorithmic fameworks in the context of graph drawing beyond planarity.

We conclude this short paper with pointers to publication venues and key references that can be browsed by researchers interested in the fascinating field of Graph Drawing and Network Visualization.

4   Pointers to Publication venues and Key References

A limited list of conferences where Graph Drawing and Network Visualization papers are regularly part of the program includes *IEEE VIS, EuroVis, SoCG, ISAAC, ACM-SIAM SODA, WADS,* and *WG.* Among the many journals where several Graph Drawing and Network Visualization papers have appeared during the last three decades we recall *IEEE Transactions on Visualization and Computer Graphs, SIAM Jounal of Computing, Computer Graphics Forum, Journal of Computer and System Sciences, Algorithmica, Journal of Graph Algorithms and Applications, Theoretical Computer Science, Information Sciences, Discrete and Computational Geometry, Computational Geometry: Theory and Applications, ACM Computing Surveys,* and *Computer Science Review.* A limited list of books, surveys, or papers that contain interesting algorithmic challenges on Graph Drawing and Network Visualization include [5, 15, 22, 29, 31–35, 41–45, 50–52].

References

1. Angelini, P., et al.: Simple k-planar graphs are simple (k+1)-quasiplanar. J. Comb. Theory, Ser. B, **142**, 1–35 (2020)
2. Angori, L., Didimo, W., Montecchiani, F., Pagliuca, D., Tappini, A.: Hybrid graph visualizations with chordlink: Algorithms, experiments, and applications. IEEE Trans. Vis. Comput. Graph. **28**(2), 1288–1300 (2022)
3. Anscombe, F.J.: Graphs in statistical analysis. Am. Stat. **27**(1), 17–21 (1973)
4. Di Battista, G., et al.: Small point-sets supporting graph stories. In: Angelini, P., von Hanxleden, R. (eds.) Graph Drawing and Network Visualization. GD 2022, LNCS, vol. 13764, pp. 289–303. Springer, Cham (2022). https://doi.org/10.1007/978-3-031-22203-0_21

5. Battista, G.D., Eades, P., Tamassia, R., Tollis, I.G.: Graph Drawing: Algorithms for the Visualization of Graphs. Prentice-Hall, Hoboken (1999)
6. Binucci, C., et al.: On the complexity of the storyplan problem. In: Angelini, P., von Hanxleden, R. (eds.) Graph Drawing and Network Visualization. GD 2022. LNCS, vol. 13764, pp. 304–318. Springer, Cham (2023). https://doi.org/10.1007/978-3-031-22203-0_22
7. Borrazzo, M., Lozzo, G.D., Battista, G.D., Frati, F., Patrignani, M.: Graph stories in small area. J. Graph Algorithms Appl. **24**(3), 269–292 (2020)
8. Chaplick, S., Giacomo, E.D., Frati, F., Ganian, R., Raftopoulou, C.N., Simonov, K.: Parameterized algorithms for upward planarity. In: Goaoc, X., Kerber, M. (eds.) 38th International Symposium on Computational Geometry, SoCG 2022, June 7–10, 2022, Berlin, Germany, LIPIcs, vol. 224, pp. 26:1–26:16. Schloss Dagstuhl - Leibniz-Zentrum für Informatik (2022)
9. Didimo, W., Giamminonni, L., Liotta, G., Montecchiani, F., Pagliuca, D.: A visual analytics system to support tax evasion discovery. Decis. Support Syst. **110**, 71–83 (2018)
10. Didimo, W., Grilli, L., Liotta, G., Menconi, L., Montecchiani, F., Pagliuca, D.: Combining network visualization and data mining for tax risk assessment. IEEE Access **8**, 16073–16086 (2020)
11. Didimo, W., Grilli, L., Liotta, G., Montecchiani, F., Pagliuca, D.: Visual querying and analysis of temporal fiscal networks. Inf. Sci. **505**, 406–421 (2019)
12. W. Didimo, M. Kaufmann, G. Liotta, and G. Ortali. Didimo, W., Kaufmann, M., Liotta, G., Ortali, G.: Rectilinear planarity testing of plane series-parallel graphs in linear time. In: Auber, D., Valtr, P. (eds.) Graph Drawing and Network Visualization. GD 2020. LNCS, vol. 12590, pp. 436–449. Springer, Cham (2020). https://doi.org/10.1007/978-3-030-68766-3_34
13. Didimo, W., Kaufmann, M., Liotta, G., Ortali, G.: Rectilinear planarity of partial 2-trees. In: Angelini, P., von Hanxleden, R. (eds.) Graph Drawing and Network Visualization. GD 2022. LNCS, vol. 13764, pp. 157–172. Springer, Cham (2023). https://doi.org/10.1007/978-3-031-22203-0_12
14. Didimo, W., Liotta, G., Montecchiani, F.: Network visualization for financial crime detection. J. Vis. Lang. Comput. **25**(4), 433–451 (2014)
15. Didimo, W., Liotta, G., Montecchiani, F.: A survey on graph drawing beyond planarity. ACM Comput. Surv. **52**(1), 4:1–4:37 (2019)
16. Didimo, W., Liotta, G., Ortali, G., Patrignani, M.: Optimal orthogonal drawings of planar 3-graphs in linear time. In: Chawla, S. (ed.) Proceedings of the 2020 ACM-SIAM Symposium on Discrete Algorithms, SODA 2020, Salt Lake City, UT, USA, January 5–8, 2020, pp. 806–825. SIAM (2020)
17. Didimo, W., Liotta, G., Patrignani, M.: HV-planarity: algorithms and complexity. J. Comput. Syst. Sci. **99**, 72–90 (2019)
18. Dilla, W.N., Raschke, R.L.: Data visualization for fraud detection: practice implications and a call for future research. Int. J. Acc. Inf. Syst. **16**, 1–22 (2015)
19. Dujmovic, V., et al.: A fixed-parameter approach to 2-layer planarization. Algorithmica **45**(2), 159–182 (2006)
20. Dujmovic, V., et al.: On the parameterized complexity of layered graph drawing. Algorithmica **52**(2), 267–292 (2008)

21. Dwyer, T., et al.: Immersive analytics: an introduction. In: Marriott, K., et al. (eds.) Immersive Analytics, LNCS, vol. 11190, pp. 1–23. Springer, Cham (2018)
22. Filipov, V., Arleo, A., Miksch, S.: Are we there yet? a roadmap of network visualization from surveys to task taxonomies. Computer Graphics Forum (2023, on print)
23. Garg, A., Tamassia, R.: On the computational complexity of upward and rectilinear planarity testing. SIAM J. Comput. **31**(2), 601–625 (2001)
24. Di Giacomo, E., Didimo, W., Montecchiani, F., Tappini, A.: A user study on hybrid graph visualizations. In: Purchase, H.C., Rutter, I. (eds.) Graph Drawing and Network Visualization. GD 2021. LNCS, vol. 12868, pp. 21–38. Springer, Cham (2021). https://doi.org/10.1007/978-3-030-92931-2_2
25. Giacomo, E.D., Giordano, F., Liotta, G.: Upward topological book embeddings of dags. SIAM J. Discret. Math. **25**(2), 479–489 (2011)
26. Giacomo, E.D., Lenhart, W.J., Liotta, G., Randolph, T.W., Tappini, A.: (k, p)-planarity: a relaxation of hybrid planarity. Theor. Comput. Sci. **896**, 19–30 (2021)
27. Giacomo, E.D., Liotta, G., Montecchiani, F.: Orthogonal planarity testing of bounded treewidth graphs. J. Comput. Syst. Sci. **125**, 129–148 (2022)
28. Giacomo, E.D., Liotta, G., Patrignani, M., Rutter, I., Tappini, A.: Nodetrix planarity testing with small clusters. Algorithmica **81**(9), 3464–3493 (2019)
29. Hong, S., Tokuyama, T. (eds.) Beyond Planar Graphs. Springer, Singapore (2020). https://doi.org/10.1007/978-981-15-6533-5
30. Joos, L., Jaeger-Honz, S., Schreiber, F., Keim, D.A., Klein, K.: Visual comparison of networks in VR. IEEE Trans. Vis. Comput. Graph. **28**(11), 3651–3661 (2022)
31. Jünger, M., Mutzel, P. (eds.) Graph Drawing Software. Springer, Berlin (2004). https://doi.org/10.1007/978-3-642-18638-7
32. Kaufmann, M., Wagner, D. (eds.): Drawing Graphs, Methods and Models (the book grow out of a Dagstuhl Seminar, April 1999), LNCS, vol. 2025. Springer, Berlin (2001). https://doi.org/10.1007/3-540-44969-8
33. Keim, D.A., Kohlhammer, J., Ellis, G.P., Mansmann, F.: Mastering the Information Age - Solving Problems with Visual Analytics. Eurographics Association, Saarbrücken (2010)
34. Keim, D.A., Mansmann, F., Stoffel, A., Ziegler, H.: Visual analytics. In: Liu, L., Özsu, M.T. (eds.) Encyclopedia of Database Systems, 2nd edn. Springer, Berlin (2018)
35. Kobourov, S.G., Liotta, G., Montecchiani, F.: An annotated bibliography on 1-planarity. Comput. Sci. Rev. **25**, 49–67 (2017)
36. Kraus, M., et al.: Immersive analytics with abstract 3D visualizations: a survey. Comput. Graph. Forum **41**(1), 201–229 (2022)
37. Kwon, O., Muelder, C., Lee, K., Ma, K.: A study of layout, rendering, and interaction methods for immersive graph visualization. IEEE Trans. Vis. Comput. Graph. **22**(7), 1802–1815 (2016)
38. Leite, R.A., Gschwandtner, T., Miksch, S., Gstrein, E., Kuntner, J.: NEVA: visual analytics to identify fraudulent networks. Comput. Graph. Forum **39**(6), 344–359 (2020)

39. Liotta, G., Rutter, I., Tappini, A.: Simultaneous FPQ-ordering and hybrid planarity testing. Theor. Comput. Sci. **874**, 59–79 (2021)
40. Liotta, G., Rutter, I., Tappini, A.: Parameterized complexity of graph planarity with restricted cyclic orders. J. Comput. Syst. Sci. **135**, 125–144 (2023)
41. Ma, K.: Pushing visualization research frontiers: essential topics not addressed by machine learning. IEEE Comput. Graphics Appl. **43**(1), 97–102 (2023)
42. McGee, F., et al.: Visual Analysis of Multilayer Networks. Synthesis Lectures on Visualization. Morgan & Claypool Publishers, San Rafael (2021)
43. Munzner, T.: Visualization Analysis and Design. A.K. Peters visualization series. A K Peters (2014)
44. Nishizeki, T., Rahman, M.S.: Planar Graph Drawing, vol. 12. World Scientific, Singapore (2004)
45. Nobre, C., Meyer, M.D., Streit, M., Lex, A.: The state of the art in visualizing multivariate networks. Comput. Graph. Forum **38**(3), 807–832 (2019)
46. Sacha, D.: Knowledge generation in visual analytics: Integrating human and machine intelligence for exploration of big data. In: Apel, S., et al. (eds.) Ausgezeichnete Informatikdissertationen 2018, LNI, vol. D-19, pp. 211–220. GI (2018)
47. Sacha, D., et al.: What you see is what you can change: human-centered machine learning by interactive visualization. Neurocomputing **268**, 164–175 (2017)
48. Sacha, D., Senaratne, H., Kwon, B.C., Ellis, G.P., Keim, D.A.: The role of uncertainty, awareness, and trust in visual analytics. IEEE Trans. Vis. Comput. Graph. **22**(1), 240–249 (2016)
49. Sacha, D., Stoffel, A., Stoffel, F., Kwon, B.C., Ellis, G.P., Keim, D.A.: Knowledge generation model for visual analytics. IEEE Trans. Vis. Comput. Graph. **20**(12), 1604–1613 (2014)
50. Tamassia, R.: Graph drawing. In: Sack, J., Urrutia, J. (eds.) Handbook of Computational Geometry, pp. 937–971. North Holland/Elsevier, Amsterdam (2000)
51. Tamassia, R. (ed.) Handbook on Graph Drawing and Visualization. Chapman and Hall/CRC, Boca Raton (2013)
52. Tamassia, R., Liotta, G.: Graph drawing. In: Goodman, J.E., O'Rourke, J. (eds.) Handbook of Discrete and Computational Geometry, 2nd edn., pp. 1163–1185. Chapman and Hall/CRC, Boca Raton (2004)
53. Zehavi, M.: Parameterized analysis and crossing minimization problems. Comput. Sci. Rev. **45**, 100490 (2022)

Understanding Non-Covalent Interactions in Biological Processes through QM/MM-EDA Dynamic Simulations

Marcos Mandado

Department of Physical Chemistry, University of Vigo, Lagoas-Marcosende s/n, 36310 Vigo, Spain
mandado@uvigo.es

Molecular dynamic simulations in biological environments such as proteins, DNA or lipids involves a large number of atoms, so classical models based on widely parametrized force fields are employed instead of more accurate quantum methods, whose high computational requirements preclude their application. The parametrization of appropriate force fields for classical molecular dynamics relies on the precise knowledge of the non-covalent inter and intramolecular interactions responsible for very important aspects, such as macromolecular arrangements, cell membrane permeation, ion solvation, etc. This implies, among other things, knowledge of the nature of the interaction, which may be governed by electrostatic, repulsion or dispersion forces. In order to know the balance between different forces, quantum calculations are frequently performed on simplified molecular models and the data obtained from these calculations are used to parametrize the force fields employed in classical simulations. These parameters are, among others, atomic charges, permanent electric dipole moments and atomic polarizabilities. However, it sometimes happens that the molecular models used for the quantum calculations are too simple and the results obtained can differ greatly from those of the extended system. As an alternative to classical and quantum methods, hybrid quantum/classical schemes (QM/MM) can be introduced, where the extended system is neither truncated nor simplified, but only the most important region is treated quantum mechanically.

In this presentation, molecular dynamic simulations and calculations with hybrid schemes are first introduced in a simple way for a broad and multidisciplinary audience. Then, a method developed in our group to investigate intermolecular interactions using hybrid quantum/classical schemes (QM/MM-EDA) is presented and some applications to the study of dynamic processes of ion solvation and membrane permeation are discussed [1–3]. Special attention is paid to the implementation details of the method in the EDA-NCI software [4].

References

1. Cárdenas, G., Pérez-Barcia, A., Mandado, M., Nogueira, J.J.: Phys. Chem. Chem. Phys. **23**, 20533 (2021)
2. Pérez-Barcia, A., Cárdenas, G., Nogueira, J.J., Mandado, M.: J. Chem. Inf. Model. **63**, 882 (2023)

3. Alvarado, R., Cárdenas, G., Nogueira, J.J., Ramos-Berdullas, N., Mandado, M.: Membranes **13**, 28 (2023)
4. Mandado, M., Van Alsenoy, C.: EDA-NCI: A program to perform energy decomposition analysis of non-covalent interactions. https://github.com/marcos-mandado/EDA-NCI

Contents – Part VII

Smart, Safe and Health Cities (SSHC 2023)

Smart and Sustainable Island Communities (SSIC 2023)

**Smart Transport and Logistics - Smart Supply Chains
(SmarTransLog 2023)**

Ports of the Future - Smartness and Sustainability (SmartPorts 2023)

Sustainability Performance Assessment: Models, Approaches, and Applications Toward Interdisciplinary and Integrated Solutions (SPA 2023)

"University Equity": Students' Facilities in Major Tourism Destination Towns

Miriam Capodiferro[1], Domenico Colonna[1], Michele Marvulli[1],
Giovanna Andrulli[1] (iD), Rachele Vanessa Gatto[2] (iD), Mariavaleria Mininni[1] (iD),
and Francesco Scorza[2(✉)] (iD)

[1] Department of European and Mediterranean Cultures, University of Basilicata, Via Lanera,
Matera, Italy
[2] School of Engineering, University of Basilicata, Viale dell'Ateneo Lucano, Potenza, Italy
francesco.scorza@unibas.it

Abstract. The paper discusses an experimental approach oriented to define urban regeneration strategies for the city of Matera (Basilicata, Italy) to address the strategic issues of the university students group intended as a specific city user category. A group of students in an urban planning course conducted the research, selecting measures to improve specific urban components such as green spaces, unused buildings, and pedestrian safety near schools. The study provides a draft masterplan for Matera, which can contribute to the public debate on "Child responsive" urban planning and support the city's cultural and tourism development strategy. The study highlights the advantages of the project, including a comprehensive view of specific problems and issues, a logical process to connect problems and solutions, and a reference matrix based on NUA principles. This research contributes to the development of tools and methodologies for NUA downscaling at the local level using innovative technologies and thematic components of urban design.

Keywords: New Urban Agenda · University City · Sustainable development

1 Introduction

The main objective of the Cohesion Policy is to promote greater equity and cohesion among the regions of the European Union through the allocation of funds to balance

The New Urban Agenda (NUA) [1, 2] represents the main list of global principles inspiring the design of the city of tomorrow. It comes from agreements among major stakeholder groups at global level involved in urban planning and territorial management. The NUA is closely linked to global sustainability targets, resulting in a new form of commitment in public decision-making [3]. The objective 11 of SDGs "Make cities and human settlements inclusive, safe, resilient and sustainable" is the mainframe of the NUA where the dimensions of contemporary urban living are explored in a people centered perspective [4–9]. According to the United Nations, the NUA is a global commitment to promote sustainable urban development. The current phase of implementation of

© The Author(s), under exclusive license to Springer Nature Switzerland AG 2023
O. Gervasi et al. (Eds.): ICCSA 2023 Workshops, LNCS 14110, pp. 3–13, 2023.
https://doi.org/10.1007/978-3-031-37123-3_1

the NUA makes it relevant to investigate how this global commitment may effectively generate local innovations in urban management practices [10, 11].

Scaling down the NUA principles and objectives to specific study areas is an ongoing process and is an emerging topic for urban studies [12]. Actually, the results of this process mainly go through the description of case studies or best practices due to the complexity to identify unique (or many) procedures of implementation. This is expectable due to the complexity of urban management in front of such ambitious and innovative goals, but the territorial professionals demand for more specific and operative guidance in order to apply locally [13].

Recent studies conducted at the University of Basilicata in Italy have shown that teaching sustainable development requires more and different tools, particularly in academia. The study involved students developing a project in Matera, which assessed the compliance of NUA principles in a specific sample area. The project analyzed the implementation of the principle of "AGE RESPONSIVE PLANNING" and proposed design hypotheses to improve the situation. This principle is included in the dimension of Social Sustainability and represents a challenging topic that opens urban studies towards new design perspectives applied to the city of the future. The case study target is represented by the University' students as a specific group of city users that demand for specific services and facilities.

The study demonstrated the effectiveness of an academic teaching approach on scaling down NUA principles and provided a preliminary structure for developing new tools to reinforce the new generation of territorial technicians, particularly engineers and architects. In conclusion, this paper highlights the key arguments and recommendations for future applications of the NUA in urban planning and territorial management, emphasizing the importance of sustainable development in urban areas.

2 Background and Scope of the Research

The UN's adoption of the Sustainable Development Goals (SDGs) has led to the integration of sustainable development into public policy making. The SDGs consist of 17 global goals and 169 targets aimed at achieving poverty reduction, protecting the planet, and ensuring peace and prosperity for all. One of the SDGs, SDG 11, focuses on making cities and human settlements inclusive, safe, resilient, and sustainable. The SDGs provide a framework for action on sustainable development and promote the integration of economic, social, and environmental policies.

Teaching sustainability in urban studies [14, 15] involves incorporating sustainable development concepts and practices into the study of cities and human settlements. This approach recognizes the interconnectedness of economic, social, and environmental issues in urban areas and aims to address them in a holistic and integrated way. Additionally, toward the principles and objectives of the New Urban Agenda (NUA), new specific tools and methodology should be provided in order to generate an alternative critical vision of the city in the young generation of university students, especially in the territorial technical degree curricula. Urban development and management principles didn't change but the way in which the new requirements identified by NUA has to be implemented in practices generated a new demand for tools and methods.

In this path, the research discussed in this paper shows an experiment of NUA downscaling in a specific case study simulating practical applications that allow students to experiment with the design of urban transformations through the lens of the NUA.

This research focuses on the city of Matera, a unique context that is a UNESCO site and was selected as the EU Capital of Culture in 2019 [16]. The study aims to verify the level of compliance of the "urban structure" with NUA specific objectives. The "urban structure" refers to the physical and social arrangement of a city, including its built environment, transportation networks, open spaces, and land uses. It can significantly impact a city's livability, sustainability, and economic vitality. An effective urban structure can support a high quality of life for residents, promote efficient use of resources, and facilitate economic growth and development.

In the specific case study the issue to improve the university city character of the place in order to enhance university students inclusion in the city has to be coupled with the tourism specialization of the place [17–19].

3 The Case Study and the Target

Planning and managing urban spaces in a sustainable way is critical for improving the quality of life of inhabitants and, as Goal 11 of the 2030 Agenda proposes, for making cities and human settlements inclusive, safe, and resilient. In particular, social sustainability requires that cities meet the needs of all inhabitants with equality for all in access to services and by promoting interaction among individuals and civic engagement. To achieve these goals, it is necessary to do targeted planning and define target assets by age. The target audience of young university students between the ages of 19 and 30 looks at programming of interventions related to gender equality, urban participatory process, wellness, and technological innovation, seeking to provide opportunities and services on par with students belonging to other Italian universities.

The project theme taken into analysis is that of university equity, and the area of intervention includes the Matera campus of the University of Basilicata and its conterminous areas, such as the Lanera district and the Piano area bordering the historic center and the Business Center with the central station [20].

The map describing the actual asset of the urban area highlights the university campus and the assessment of services closely related to students, namely the quality of residences, spaces and facilities for sports and wellness, and basic necessities and leisure services. In this regard we distinguish three different areas and routes:

- the area near the university is strongly residential and students find opportunities for rental housing, but the quality of the buildings is not always very good and we distinguish in good, mediocre and very bad the external state of preservation of the buildings. This area is affected by the red route to connect it to the transportation system and thus to the Matera Central and Matera South train stations and bus stops;
- the area related to sports includes the "Duni" School camp, the "Palasassi" sports center and the "Macamarda" Park, as well as public or private gyms and soccer fields, and is affected by the orange route to connect it to the university campus;

– the services and leisure area is located in the City Plan area and is affected by a
strong concentration of services related to commerce and food services that connect
the green route to the university.

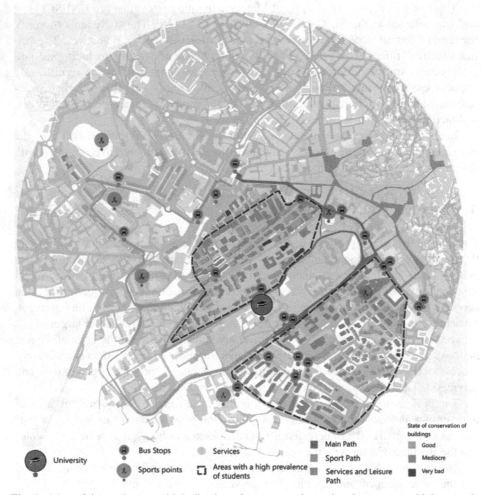

Fig. 1. Map of the study area with indication of routes, services related to sports and leisure and
the quality of residences for university students.

Finding the cross-relationships of the university site with the context allows us to
reflect on urban functions and urban land-use by combining the analysis of infrastructure,
greenery, and primary services and facilities and to question fundamental questions.
What is the role of the university in a city like Matera? Is it important that the hub
be located on one of the highest hills in the city? Is the system of proximity services
adequate to the needs of university students? The critical analysis of the results presented
in the next section highlights how new urban development strategies make it possible to
control and interpret the transformations of the territory and, at the same time, to provide
a clear and strong urban-oriented imaginary that is more organic and collaborative for
university students who will want to make qualified innovation.

4 "University Equity"

The critical study begins with a thorough examination of the conditions of the locations and services that make up the urban fabric. The emphasis is on the requirements, living arrangements, and inherent possibilities of locations associated with university students. By reconstructing the regular activities, nearby locations with thematic specification qualities have been mapped and classified in a predefined set of categories. This is in line with the descriptions of the three study areas, which are the major destination, the services and leisure area, and the sports area.

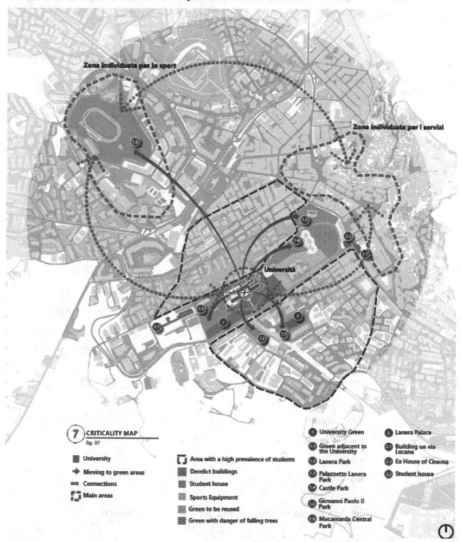

Fig. 2. Map of the study area with indication of critical points

The map shows how, in the close surrounding of the University Campus, a number of potential urban component are available for regeneration option in order to realize a sub-urban system oriented to satisfy the need of university users improving their quality of life and, consequently, enhancing the added value for the whole town from a socio-economic point of view.

The services provided by Italian universities with the highest levels of user satisfaction were analyzed in order to identify and define the framework of demands. In the next figure an overall comparison between the Campus in Matera and other Italian University City Campus is proposed referring to some general categories of university services and facilities. The survey, developed in a qualitative way, has not the ambition to be complete and to define a comprehensive assessment af such a complex system, but it is representative of the perception of a specific group of students.

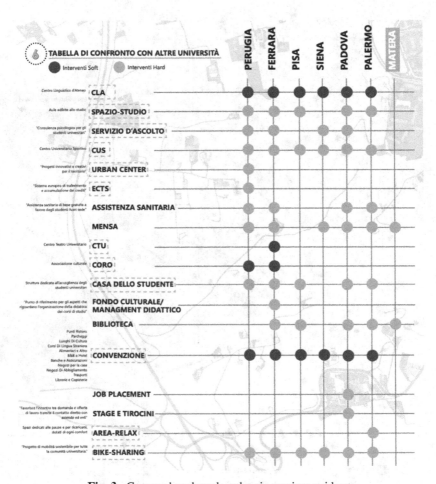

Fig. 3. Campus benchmark and main services evidence

It emerged a significant gap comparing the Matera Campus with selected benchmarks, in particular adequate recreation, cultural and sport facilities are missing.

The identified needs, represented as "the lack of" a specific service for the university students target, is a driver to identify a strategy and the consequent actions to improve the situation.

As can be seen, the supply basin is considerably smaller than the medium sized Italian University Campus, endangering the quality of service supply due to inefficiency and consequently the living experience of students during their university live in the Campus and in the city. The "soft" and "hard" acts used in the intervention method, which aims to improve quality of life, come together at the confluence of local crucial situations and identified requirements.

Moving from the deficit analysis and considering the specific place characteristics project actions was proposed in the design perspectives.

The project actions include:

– the creation of a ring that encourages sustainable mobility and represents a safe path that relates the previously identified thematic areas characterized by discontinuous segments for pedestrians;

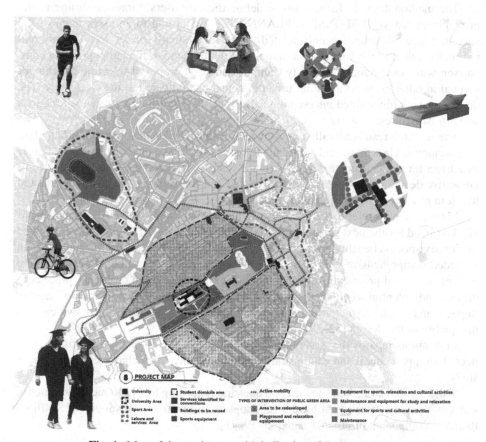

Fig. 4. Map of the study area with indication of design choices

- re-functionalization of selected abandoned buildings to be used as social-housing with price control;
- a hub dedicated to social welfare services for students integrating uses and practices revealed by the analysis of trends in other universities.

The previous Figure identifies main actions per intervention categories. This intervention scenario represents a draft masterplan to be discussed with local stakeholder in order to set priorities, responsibilities and operational dimension of the interventions.

5 Discussions and Conclusions

The paper discusses an experimental approach oriented to define urban regeneration strategies for the city of Matera (Basilicata, Italy) to address the strategic issues of the university students group intended as a specific city user category.

The approach was structured on NUA principles and follow the way of "downscaling" NUA at local level [17, 21–25].

The methodology, in facts, starts to define the city users' target according to the principle of "AGE RESPONSIVE PLANNING". According to an assessment of the specific place conditions, mainly related to the local supply of services directly and indirectly linked to the University Campus and the demand of the target group, a comparison with other Italian University Campus had been proposed selecting benchmark located in other cities with similar urban dimensions compared to the case study. The design process highlighted intervention categories distinguishing between soft actions and infrastructures.

The research results actually represent a draft master-plan developed in urban planning academic class that could contribute to the public debate on the university city role as a driver for strategic urban development in Matera. The recommendation to adopt collaborative design framework is widely accepted and robust approach has to be adopted to put in practice the operational implementation of such proposal [26– 31].

Main evidences refer to the topic of "teaching downscaling of NUA" as a new technical demand for the next generation of territorial technicians. The experiment allowed to identify specific benefits compared to the traditional urban regeneration approach: an extended comprehensive view of specific problems and issues to be addressed by the project; a rational process in verifying the logical nexus between problems, place conditions and potential solutions; a reference matrix based on NUA principle to measure impacts and results of the proposal as a robust accounting system to give evidence of the quality of the design [32–39].

Limitations regards the academic dimension of the laboratory, only partially connected with procedural and administrative rules and constraints characterizing the case study.

This research contributes to the open question regarding tools and methodologies to support NUA downscaling at local level adopting innovative technologies [25, 40] on thematic component of urban design [35–39, 41].

References

1. UN HABITAT: New Urban Agenda. United Nations (2016)
2. Las Casas, G., Scorza, F., Murgante, B.: New urban agenda and open challenges for urban and regional planning. In: Calabrò, F., Della Spina, L., Bevilacqua, C. (eds.) ISHT 2018. SIST, vol. 100, pp. 282–288. Springer, Cham (2019). https://doi.org/10.1007/978-3-319-92099-3_33
3. McCann, P., Ortega-Argilés, R.: Smart specialization, regional growth and applications to European union cohesion policy. Reg. Stud. **49**, 1291–1302 (2015). https://doi.org/10.1080/00343404.2013.799769
4. Vona, M., Harabaglia, P., Murgante, B.: Thinking about resilient cities: studying Italian earthquakes. Proc. Inst. Civ. Eng. Urban Des. Plann. **169**(4), 185–199 (2016). https://doi.org/10.1680/udap.14.00007
5. Murgante, B., Borruso, G., Lapucci, A.: Sustainable development: concepts and methods for its application in urban and environmental planning. Stud. Comput. Intell. **348**, 1–15 (2011). https://doi.org/10.1007/978-3-642-19733-8_1/COVER
6. Las Casas, G., Scorza, F., Murgante, B.: Razionalità a-priori: una proposta verso una pianificazione antifragile. Italian J. Reg. Sci. **18**, 329–338 (2019). https://doi.org/10.14650/93656
7. Murgante, B., Borruso, G., Lapucci, A.: Geocomputation and urban planning. Stud. Comput. Intell. **176**, 1–17 (2009). https://doi.org/10.1007/978-3-540-89930-3_1/COVER
8. Scorza, F., Pilogallo, A., Saganeiti, L., Murgante, B.: Natura 2000 areas and sites of national interest (SNI): measuring (un)integration between naturalness preservation and environmental remediation policies. Sustainability **12**(7), 2928 (2020). https://doi.org/10.3390/su12072928
9. Saganeiti, L., Mustafa, A., Teller, J., Murgante, B.: Modeling urban sprinkling with cellular automata. Sustain. Cities Soc. **65**, 102586 (2021). https://doi.org/10.1016/J.SCS.2020.102586
10. Scorza, F.: Training decision-makers: GEODESIGN workshop paving the way for new urban agenda. In: Gervasi, O., et al. (eds.) ICCSA 2020. LNCS, vol. 12252, pp. 310–316. Springer, Cham (2020). https://doi.org/10.1007/978-3-030-58811-3_22
11. Casas, G.L., Scorza, F.: From the UN new urban agenda to the local experiences of urban development: the case of Potenza. In: Gervasi, O., et al. (eds.) ICCSA 2018. LNCS, vol. 10964, pp. 734–743. Springer, Cham (2018). https://doi.org/10.1007/978-3-319-95174-4_56
12. Andersson, C.: Public space and the new urban agenda. J. Public Space. **1**, 5 (2016). https://doi.org/10.5204/JPS.V1I1.4
13. Tidball, K.G., Krasny, M.E.: Urban environmental education from a social-ecological perspective: conceptual framework for civic ecology education. Cities Environ. **3**(1), 1–20 (2010). https://doi.org/10.15365/cate.31112010
14. Bina, O., Balula, L., Varanda, M., Fokdal, J.: Urban studies and the challenge of embedding sustainability: a review of international master programmes. J. Clean Prod. **137**, 330–346 (2016). https://doi.org/10.1016/J.JCLEPRO.2016.07.034
15. Li, N., Chan, D., Mao, Q., Hsu, K., Fu, Z.: Urban sustainability education: challenges and pedagogical experiments. Habitat Int. **71**, 70–80 (2018). https://doi.org/10.1016/J.HABITATINT.2017.11.012
16. Mininni, M., Dicillo, C.: Urban policies and cultural policies for Matera en route to 2019 ǀ Politiche urbane e politiche culturali per Matera verso il 2019, Territorio (2015)
17. Scorza, F., Gatto, R.V.: Identifying territorial values for tourism development: the case study of Calabrian Greek area. Sustainability **15**(6), 5501 (2023). https://doi.org/10.3390/su1506 5501
18. Gatto, R., Santopietro, L., Scorza, F.: Tourism and abandoned inland areas development demand: a critical appraisal. In: Lecture Notes in Computer Science (including subseries Lecture Notes in Artificial Intelligence and Lecture Notes in Bioinformatics). 13382 LNCS, pp. 40–47 (2022). https://doi.org/10.1007/978-3-031-10592-0_4/COVER

19. Gatto, R., Santopietro, L., Scorza, F.: Roghudi: Developing knowledge of the places in an abandoned inland municipality. In: Lecture Notes in Computer Science (including subseries Lecture Notes in Artificial Intelligence and Lecture Notes in Bioinformatics), 13382 LNCS, pp. 48–53 (2022). https://doi.org/10.1007/978-3-031-10592-0_5/COVER

20. Mininni, M.: Matera Lucania 2017. Quodlibet (2017). https://doi.org/10.2307/j.ctv2gz3xk0

21. Lagonigro, D., et al.: Downscaling NUA: matera new urban structure. In: Gervasi, O., (ed.) Computational Science and Its Applications - ICCSA 2023. Springer (2023)

22. Florio, E., et al.: SuperABLE: Matera accessible for all. In: Gervasi, O. (ed.) Computational Science and its Applications - ICCSA 2023. Springer (2023)

23. Esposito Loscavo, B., et al.: Innovation ecosystem: the added value in a unique UNESCO city. In: Gervasi, O. (ed.) Computational Science and Its Applications - ICCSA 2023. Springer (2023)

24. Gatto, R.V., Corrado, S., Scorza, F.: Towards a definition of tourism ecosystem. In: 18th International Forum on Knowledge Asset Dynamics (IFKAD) - Managing Knowledge for Sustainability (2023)

25. Corrado, S., Scorza, F.: Machine learning based approach to assess territorial marginality. In: Gervasi, O., Murgante, B., Hendrix, E.M.T., Taniar, D., Apduhan, B.O. (eds.) Computational Science and Its Applications – ICCSA 2022. ICCSA 2022. Lecture Notes in Computer Science (including subseries Lecture Notes in Artificial Intelligence and Lecture Notes in Bioinformatics), vol. 13376. LNCS, pp. 292–302 (2022). https://doi.org/10.1007/978-3-031-10450-3_25/COVER

26. Campagna, M.: Metaplanning: about designing the geodesign process. Landsc. Urban Plan. **156**, 118–128 (2016).https://doi.org/10.1016/J.LANDURBPLAN.2015.08.019

27. Campagna, M.: Geodesign from theory to practice: from metaplanning to 2nd generation of planning support systems. Tema – J. Land Use Mob. Environ. (2014). https://doi.org/10.6092/1970-9870/2516

28. Scorza, F.: Sustainable urban regeneration in Gravina in Puglia, Italy. In: Fisher, T., Orland, B., Steinitz, C. (eds.) The International Geodesign Collaboration. Changing Geography by Design, pp. 112–113. ESRI Press, Redlands, California (2020)

29. Steinitz, C.: A Frame Work for Geodesign. Changing Geography by Design (2012)

30. Steinitz, C., Orland, B., Fisher, T., Campagna, M.: Geodesign to address global change. In: Intelligent Environments, pp. 193–242. Elsevier (2023). https://doi.org/10.1016/B978-0-12-820247-0.00016-3

31. Scorza, F., et al.: Training for territorial sstainable development design in basilicata remote areas: GEODESIGN workshop. In: Gervasi, O., Murgante, B., Misra, S., Rocha, A.M.A.C., Garau, C. (eds.) Computational Science and Its Applications – ICCSA 2022 Workshops. Lecture Notes in Computer Science (including subseries Lecture Notes in Artificial Intelligence and Lecture Notes in Bioinformatics). 13379 LNCS, pp. 242–252 (2022). https://doi.org/10.1007/978-3-031-10545-6_17

32. Las Casas, G., Scorza, F., Murgante, B.: Conflicts and sustainable planning: peculiar instances coming from Val D'agri structural inter-municipal plan. In: Papa, R., Fistola, R., Gargiulo, C. (eds.) Smart Planning: Sustainability and Mobility in the Age of Change. GET, pp. 163–177. Springer, Cham (2018). https://doi.org/10.1007/978-3-319-77682-8_10

33. Casas, G.L., Scorza, F.: Sustainable planning: a methodological toolkit. In: Gervasi, O., et al. (eds.) ICCSA 2016. LNCS, vol. 9786, pp. 627–635. Springer, Cham (2016). https://doi.org/10.1007/978-3-319-42085-1_53

34. Scorza, F.: Improving EU cohesion policy: the spatial distribution analysis of regional development investments funded by EU structural funds 2007/2013 in Italy. In: Murgante, B., et al. (eds.) ICCSA 2013. LNCS, vol. 7973, pp. 582–593. Springer, Heidelberg (2013). https://doi.org/10.1007/978-3-642-39646-5_42

35. Santopietro, L., Scorza, F.: The Italian experience of the covenant of mayors: a territorial evaluation. Sustainability **13**, 1289 (2021). https://doi.org/10.3390/su13031289
36. Scorza, F., Santopietro, L.: A systemic perspective for the sustainable energy and climate action plan (SECAP). Eur. Plann. Stud. 1–21 (2021). https://doi.org/10.1080/09654313.2021.1954603
37. Scorza, F., Fortunato, G.: Active mobility-oriented urban development: a morpho-syntactic scenario for a mid-sized town. Eur. Plann. Stud. 1–25 (2022). https://doi.org/10.1080/09654313.2022.2077094
38. Scorza, F., Fortunato, G.: Cyclable cities: building feasible scenario through urban space morphology assessment. J. Urban Plan Dev. **147**, 05021039 (2021). https://doi.org/10.1061/(ASCE)UP.1943-5444.0000713
39. Pilogallo, A., Scorza, F.: Mapping regulation ecosystem services specialization in Italy. J. Urban Plan Dev. **148**(1), 04021072 (2022). https://doi.org/10.1061/(ASCE)UP.1943-5444.0000801
40. Dastoli, P.S., Pontrandolfi, P., Scorza, F., Corrado, S., Azzato, A.: Applying geodesign towards an integrated local development strategy: the Val d'Agri case (Italy). In: Gervasi, O., Murgante, B., Misra, S., Rocha, A.M.A.C., Garau, C. (eds.) Computational Science and Its Applications – ICCSA 2022 Workshops. ICCSA 2022. Lecture Notes in Computer Science (including subseries Lecture Notes in Artificial Intelligence and Lecture Notes in Bioinformatics). 13379 LNCS, pp. 253–262 (2022). https://doi.org/10.1007/978-3-031-10545-6_18
41. Scorza, F., Saganeiti, L., Pilogallo, A., Murgante, B.: Ghost planning: the inefficiency of energy sector policies in a low population density region1. ARCHIVIO DI STUDI URBANI E REGIONALI, pp. 34–55 (2020). https://doi.org/10.3280/ASUR2020-127-S1003

Downscaling NUA: Matera New Urban Structure

Domenico Lagonigro[1], Vito Cazzati[1], Nicola Viggiano[1], Giovanna Andrulli[1] (iD),
Rachele Vanessa Gatto[2] (iD), Mariavaleria Mininni[1] (iD), and Francesco Scorza[2(✉)] (iD)

[1] Department of European and Mediterranean Cultures, University of Basilicata, via Lanera,
Matera, Italy
{domenico.lagonigro,vito.cazzati,nicola.viggiano,
giovanna.andrulli,mariavaleria.mininni}@unibas.it
[2] School of Engineering, University of Basilicata, Viale dell'Ateneo Lucano, Potenza, Italy
{rachelevanessa.Gatto,francesco.scorza}@unibas.it

Abstract. Downscale implementation of National Urban Environmental Technician (NUA) principles is an emerging topic in sustainable territorial development.
The approach has several advantages over traditional urban regeneration strategies, including a comprehensive view of problems and solutions, a rational process
to verify logical connections, and a reference matrix based on NUA principles to
measure impacts and results. The research focuses on laboratory design practice
results based on "age responsive planning" and "Child responsive" urban planning,
which aim to improve the safety and well-being of young people in urban areas.
A group of students in an Urban Planning course selected measures to enhance
urban fabric components such as green spaces, unused buildings, and pedestrian
safety near schools. The study provides a draft master-plan for Matera's future,
contributing to the "Child responsive" urban planning debate and supporting cultural and tourism development. The study offers advantages over traditional urban
regeneration approaches and contributes to developing tools and methodologies
for NUA downscaling at the local level, integrating innovative technologies and
thematic urban design components.

Keywords: New urban Agenda 2030 · Sustainability · Urban design

1 Downscaling NUA

The New Urban Agenda (NUA) [1] is a widely recognized concept that has led to the
development of new agreements among major stakeholder groups involved in urban
planning and territorial management. The NUA is linked to global sustainability targets,
which has resulted in a new form of commitment in public decision-making [2]. According to the United Nations, the NUA is a global commitment to promoting sustainable
urban development and ensuring that cities and human settlements are inclusive, safe,
resilient, and sustainable. The NUA is the result of a negotiation process involving various stakeholders, and it aims to address global issues by generating local innovations
in urban management practices.

© The Author(s), under exclusive license to Springer Nature Switzerland AG 2023
O. Gervasi et al. (Eds.): ICCSA 2023 Workshops, LNCS 14110, pp. 14–24, 2023.
https://doi.org/10.1007/978-3-031-37123-3_2

Scaling down the NUA principles and objectives to specific study areas is an ongoing process and one of the emerging topic for urban studies. Actually, it has not yet a comprehensive conceptualization including pre-designed procedures or rules. This has resulted in varying approaches in different case studies. However, recent studies conducted at the University of Basilicata in Italy showed that teaching sustainable development requires more and different tools, particularly in academia [3, 4]. The study involved students developing a project in Matera (EU Capital of Culture 2019) [5] that assessed the compliance of NUA principles in a specific sample area. The project titled "Matera new urban structure" analyzed the implementation of the principle of "AGE RESPONSIVE PLANNING," identified gaps and problems, and proposed design hypotheses to improve the situation. This principle is included in the dimension of Social Sustainability and represents a challenging topic that opens urban studies towards new design perspective applied to the city of the future.

The results of the study demonstrated the effectiveness of an academic teaching approach on scaling down NUA' principles and provided a preliminary structure for developing new tools to reinforce the new generation of territorial technicians, particularly engineers and architects. In conclusion, this paper highlights the key arguments and recommendations for future applications of the NUA in urban planning and territorial management [6].

2 Background and Scope of the Research

The adoption of SDGs by the UN has mainstreamed the concept of sustainable development in public policy making. The SDGs are a set of 17 global goals, with 169 targets, aimed at ending poverty, protecting the planet, and ensuring peace and prosperity for all. SDG 11 focuses on making cities and human settlements inclusive, safe, resilient, and sustainable. The SDGs provide a framework for action on sustainable development, promoting the integration of economic, social, and environmental policies.

Together with the diffusion and implementation of the SDGs, a new demand for education at all levels has emerged to verify the adequacy of current tools and approaches to meet the demands posed by the new global goals.

This statement highlights the importance of education and training to ensure that the implementation of the SDGs is successful. The United Nations recognizes the importance of education in achieving the SDGs and has made it a target under Goal 4: Quality Education. The report "Education for Sustainable Development Goals: Learning Objectives" by UNESCO provides guidelines for educators to incorporate sustainable development into their teaching practices. Additionally, "Transforming our world: the 2030 Agenda for Sustainable Development" outlines the importance of education as a means to empower individuals and communities to achieve sustainable development.

Teaching sustainable development needs more and different tools and a specific need emerges in academia, especially for those disciplines based on strong technical backgrounds. In fact, the traditional disciplinary approach to urban planning and territorial management is almost insufficient to address the complexity and interdependence of economic, social, environmental and spatial issues. The transdisciplinary approach, at the bases of former approaches, has to be re-oriented in order to better integrate knowledge domains including those specific contributions generated through the active participation of stakeholders. Furthermore, teaching sustainable development requires the adoption of critical thinking, ethical values, and practical skills [3].

The topic of downscaling NUA principles and objectives is still an open topic. The NUA is a global framework, and its principles and objectives need to be adapted to the local context. However, no pre-designed procedures or rules have been conceptualized. Single case studies produce different approaches, reflecting the diversity of local conditions and stakeholders. Therefore, a bottom-up approach, based on the participation of local communities and stakeholders, is needed [7–12]. Furthermore, the downscaling process requires the integration of different knowledge domains and the development of new tools and methods.

Young territorial technicians, such as Engineers and Architects, have the opportunity to gain competitiveness and readiness to develop solutions to the emerging problems in urban and territorial sustainable planning, by experimenting in practice the design of urban transformations by the lens of NUA [3, 4, 13].

The experience of this research benefits a peculiar case study area: the city of Matera. This specific and unique context is an UNESCO site and a city selected as EU Capital of Culture in 2019 [5, 14]. A place where the beauty of urban form, the valuable landscape, the current extreme tourism development conflict with the demand for economic development of the South Italy area and social concerns never solved by the local governments.

In particular the focus of the study is to verify the level of compliance of the "urban structure" with NUA specific objectives. We refer to "Urban structure" as the physical and social arrangement of a city, including its built environment, transportation networks, open spaces, and land uses. It encompasses the spatial organization of the city's various components and how they relate to each other. The urban structure of a city can have a significant impact on its livability, sustainability, and economic vitality. An effective urban structure can support a high quality of life for residents, promote efficient use of resources, and facilitate economic growth and development.

Those traditional urban development focuses have to be balanced, in the case of Matera, with the tourism specialization of the city and the way in which such specialization could be balanced with surrounding territory distributing added value and ensuring sustainable tourism pressure [10, 15–17].

3   The Case Study and the Target

According to the New Urban Agenda, it is necessary to foster a new path of sustainable urban development to improve the citizens' live according to social, economic, environmental and spatial dimensions. In a historical phase in which it is asked to work in territories in ecological, economic and social transition, it is necessary to find the ability to work in a context of consultation with local governments for the promotion of integrated actions, oriented to the energy transition and the fight against social inequalities to spread awareness and orient local communities towards new and complex paths of sustainability. Today, sustainability is the thickest lens through which urban planning is called to respond to change [13, 18], and the contamination capacity of this discipline allows for a deeper look at the question of responsibilities, skills and useful tools to address the challenges launched by the SDGs, starting with Goal 11 "Making inclusive, safe, durable and sustainable cities and human settlements," but expanding the reflection to the broad interconnections between all the goals [19].The target audience for the case study is "age responsive planning," i.e., planning for an age group between 3 and 27 years old, according to the "universal right to education" principle to support the right to quality education and counter the phenomenon of school dropout in the youngest age groups, considering also that knowledge and competence for high levels of education are crucial for entering the working world and determining one's future. The "Child responsive" principle highlights the need to ensure the safety and well-being of young people in urban planning. In order to implement this target, an area with a high concentration of educational institutions of all levels was selected, stretching from the center to the south of the city of Matera, from Piazza Mattcotti with the central train station to the Lanera district to the south of the city, one of the historic districts created as a result of Law No. 619 of May 17, 1952, "Risanamento dei rioni Sassi nell'abitato del Comune di Matera." Matera became in those years, thanks to the contribution of great architects and town planners, such as Adriano Olivetti, Luigi Piccinato, Ludovico Quaroni, the

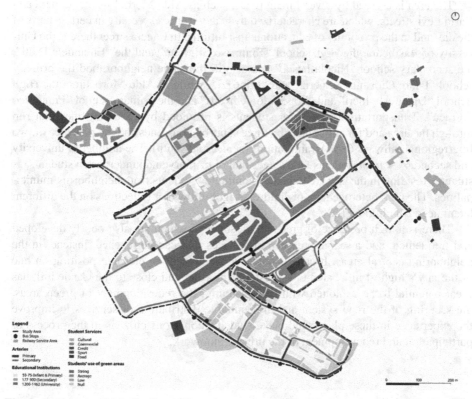

Fig. 1. Study area with indication of the green system, the education system, the mobility system and the service system for students.

center of experimentation of a new way of doing architecture, a new way of thinking of a city capable of taking into account the socio-economic peculiarities of communities and above all the wealth of millenary history, together with the customs and traditions of individuals. As in the past, Matera could become a laboratory of policies to help understand what the role of a medium-sized European city can be, whether the heritage of a city still has the capacity to structure larger territories, whether urban space can once again become a form of citizenship, conceived as an incubator of the city's civic value, and whether this value can be made legible in urban design and its forms [14]. It is therefore useful to define, as shown in the state of the art map, the urban framework, that is, the set of infrastructures (equipment, services and facilities) designed to meet the needs of the population settled in an urban area, in terms of education, health, leisure, transport, etc. Analyses were conducted on the basis of: - the green system with classification based on youth use; - the mobility system with main and secondary arteries and urban and suburban public transportation service with the identification of different stops and stations for buses and trains; - the education system with classification according to different grades (infant and primary, first and second level secondary school and university) and student enrollment numbers; - the system of student services (cultural, commercial, sports, etc.) (Fig. 1).

The area is crossed by several main roads, such as Aldo Moro, Lucana, Lanera and Carlo Levi streets, which are characterized by heavy traffic especially in certain parts of the day and in the proximity of educational institutions. In Lanera street there is the University of Basilicata, the High school "Tommaso Stigliani" and the "Emanuele Duni", the secondary school "Nicola Festa," and also in the same neighborhood the primary school "Padre Giovanni Semeria" and "Minozzi." while in Aldo Moro street the High School "Dante Alighieri" and "Loperfido - Olivetti" and the primary school "Francesco Torraca". Transportation service for students is provided by 15 urban lines that run through the area and for commuters by three suburban bus lines and the presence of two Interregional railways (FAL) train stations (center and south). The number of university and secondary school students far exceeds that of primary and kindergarten students, as students residing in the city are joined by commuter students from neighboring municipalities. The high heterogeneity of children's ages allows for reflections on the different latent needs of children [20].

There is a high presence of green areas, some of which are also poorly developed and frequented, and a scarce presence of services that can be reached, instead, in the neighboring central areas. It can be said that the area in an elevated position on one of the city's highest hills, along the western ring road and close to the Castle hill, has great potential to be exploited with new planning, the redevelopment of green areas, the securing of the road system and the equitable distribution of services to improve the experience in these places and make students conscious citizens in the process of participation and redevelopment of the urban framework.

4 Urban Planning Framework: An Institutional Care

The objectives of the NUA fit together with the urban analysis of a specific context where, through the reconstruction of the dynamics affected by users and the mapping of services and mobility, critical issues related to the sensitivity of places emerge with particular attention to collective life. Main critical urban fabric categories that emerged according to the study area analysis:

- Unused buildings, closed to public schools and other educational centers.
- The uncomplete university campus still missing the student canteen and other basic facilities
- The generalized problem regarding road safety especially during congestion hours.
- The state of maintenance of green space and their suitability to satisfy students and residents local needs.

The study on traffic congestion emphasizes key critical locations close to schools during peak hours and the consequent diminished usability of public spaces. The presence of the University Campus represents a structural component of the study area. There are significant academic functions in the Campus and therefore the study area becomes the destination of daily displacement (for residents and commuters) of the various groups of users mentioned in the context. The abandonment of green areas and school-oriented structures, which deny university students vital services, has an impact on the public space's quality. Ineffective traffic control and a lack of parking near primary schools, as illustrated in Table 2, cause a standstill in road flow (Fig. 2).

Among the proposals of the study, the introduction of "Pedibus," a mode of transportation for kindergarten and primary school students, replaces the use of private cars and public transportation or school bus services. This soft action, in addition to mediating problems relating to traffic, promotes moments of sharing between children after school. The sustainability of the proposal arises from the careful observation of the needs of the students and the potential present in situ. The green areas that act as a hinge between the various institutes, through a process of punctual and systematic enhancement, represent the scenario of daily life. Particular attention to urban furniture and the characterization of the pavement mark a leap towards new forms of socialization and inclusion (Fig. 3).

The project proposal was structured on the basis of the following general requirements:

- Sustainability intended as CO_2 emissions reduction depending on the modal shift from cars to active mobility (journey on foot);
- Safety for students moving around the study area based on punctual traffic management solutions favoring pedestrian mobility.
- Sociality, allowing children to socialize with each other during the journey time to and from school along green urban pathways improving the quality of the journey;
- Health, improving the childrens and students' capacity to have outdoor physical activities enjoying functional green spaces.

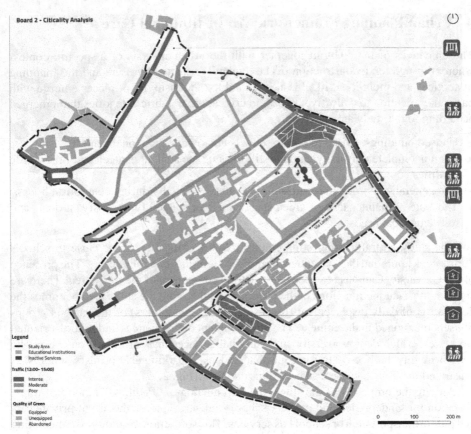

Fig. 2. Study area with indication of services and mobility

Proposed interventions include the main categories proposed by the New Urban Agenda: "hard" and "soft" measures considering both the infrastructural regeneration of specific parts of the case study areas and organizational actions to be (easily) implemented in the short term. The whole schema represents a draft masterplan to be discussed with local stakeholder in order to set priorities, responsibilities and operational dimension of the interventions.

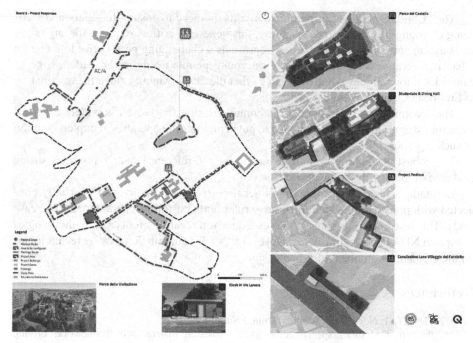

Fig. 3. Study area with indication of proposals

5 Conclusions

The paper discusses an experimental approach oriented to define urban regeneration strategies for the city of Matera (Basilicata, Italy) to address the strategic issues of a specific target of city users and a sub urban area selected according to specific requirements. The approach was structured on NUA principles and follows the way of "downscaling" NUA at local level.

Starting with Goal 11 "Making inclusive, safe, durable and sustainable cities and human settlements," but expanding the reflection to the broad interconnections between all the goals.The target audience for the case study is "age responsive planning," i.e., planning for an age group between 3 and 27 years old, according to the "universal right to education" principle to support the right to quality education and counter the phenomenon of school dropout in the youngest age groups.

The "Child responsive" principle highlights the need to ensure the safety and well-being of young people in urban planning.

The research demonstrated how Matera could become a laboratory of policies to help understand what the role of a medium-sized European, whether urban space can once again become a form of citizenship, conceived as an incubator of the city's civic value, and whether this value can be made legible in urban design and its forms.

The focus of the proposal goes to a set of infrastructures (equipment, services and facilities) designed to meet the needs of the population settled in an urban area, in terms of education, health, leisure, transport, etc.

The "Child responsive" principle highlights the need to ensure the safety and well-being of young people in urban planning, this generates critical remarks for any urban areas and in particular for Matera may represents a challenging perspective to integrate urban regeneration strategies centered on young people needs in the wider scope of cultural and tourism development strategy that the city is running since the nomination to European Capital of Culture 2019.

The recommendation to adopt collaborative design framework is widely accepted and a robust approach has to be adopted to put in practice the operational implementation of such a proposal [28–33].

The robust accounting system generated by the reference matrix provides strong evidence of the quality of the design.

Limitations regard the academic dimension of the laboratory, only partially connected with procedural and administrative rules and constraints characterizing the case study. This research contributes to the open question regarding tools and methodologies to support NUA downscaling at local level [15, 34–37] adopting innovative technologies on the thematic component of urban design.

References

1. UN HABITAT: New Urban Agenda. United Nations (2016)
2. Veldhuizen, C.: Smart specialisation as a transition management framework: driving sustainability-focused regional innovation policy? Res Policy. **49**, 103982 (2020). https://doi.org/10.1016/J.RESPOL.2020.103982
3. Li, N., Chan, D., Mao, Q., Hsu, K., Fu, Z.: Urban sustainability education: challenges and pedagogical experiments. Habitat Int. **71**, 70–80 (2018). https://doi.org/10.1016/J.HABITA TINT.2017.11.012
4. Scorza, F., Grecu, V.: Assessing sustainability: research directions and relevant issues. In: Gervasi, O., et al. (eds.) ICCSA 2016. LNCS, vol. 9786, pp. 642–647. Springer, Cham (2016). https://doi.org/10.1007/978-3-319-42085-1_55
5. Mininni, M., Dicillo, C.: Urban policies and cultural policies for Matera en route to 2019 | Politiche urbane e politiche culturali per Matera verso il 2019. Territorio (2015)
6. Las Casas, G., Scorza, F., Murgante, B.: New urban agenda and open challenges for urban and regional planning. In: Calabrò, F., Della Spina, L., Bevilacqua, C. (eds.) ISHT 2018. SIST, vol. 100, pp. 282–288. Springer, Cham (2019). https://doi.org/10.1007/978-3-319-92099-3_33
7. Steinitz, C.: A Frame Work for Geodesign. Changing Geography by Design (2012)
8. Campagna, M., Ervin, S., Sheppard, S.: How geodesign processes shaped outcomes. In: Fisher, T., Orland, B., Steinitz, C. (eds.) The International Geodesign Collaboration. Changing Geography by Design, pp. 145–148. ESRI Press, Redlands, California (2020)
9. Steinitz, C., Orland, B., Fisher, T., Campagna, M.: Geodesign to address global change. Intell. Environ. 193–242 (2023). https://doi.org/10.1016/B978-0-12-820247-0.00016-3
10. Scorza, F., et al.: Training for Territorial Sustainable Development Design in Basilicata Remote Areas: GEODESIGN Workshop. Lecture Notes in Computer Science (including subseries Lecture Notes in Artificial Intelligence and Lecture Notes in Bioinformatics). 13379 LNCS, 242–252 (2022). https://doi.org/10.1007/978-3-031-10545-6_17/COVER
11. Dastoli, P.S., Pontrandolfi, P., Scorza, F., Corrado, S., Azzato, A.: Applying Geodesign Towards an Integrated Local Development Strategy: The Val d'Agri Case (Italy). Lecture Notes in Computer Science (including subseries Lecture Notes in Artificial Intelligence and Lecture Notes in Bioinformatics). 13379 LNCS, 253–262 (2022). https://doi.org/10.1007/978-3-031-10545-6_18/COVER

12. Pietro, F., Angela, P., Angela Pilogallo, F.S.: Facing urban regeneration issues through geodesign approach. In: Leone, A., Gargiulo, C. (eds.) Environmental and territorial modelling for planning and design. FedOAPress. Gravina in Puglia. Italy (2018). https://doi.org/10.6093/978-88-6887-048-5

13. Liu, J., et al.: Systems integration for global sustainability (2015). https://doi.org/10.1126/science.1258832

14. Mininni, M.: Matera Lucania 2017. Quodlibet (2017). https://doi.org/10.2307/j.ctv2gz3xk0

15. Scorza, F., Gatto, R.V.: Identifying territorial values for tourism development: the case study of Calabrian Greek area. Sustainability 15, 5501 (2023). https://doi.org/10.3390/SU15065501

16. Gatto, R., Santopietro, L., Scorza, F.: Roghudi: developing knowledge of the places in an abandoned inland municipality. In: Gervasi, O., Murgante, B., Misra, S., Rocha, A.M.A.C., Garau, C. (eds.) Lecture Notes in Computer Science (including subseries Lecture Notes in Artificial Intelligence and Lecture Notes in Bioinformatics), vol. 13382 LNCS, pp. 48–53. Springer, Heidelberg (2022). https://doi.org/10.1007/978-3-031-10592-0_5/COVER

17. Gatto, R., Santopietro, L., Scorza, F.: Tourism and abandoned inland areas development demand. In: Gervasi, O., Murgante, B., Misra, S., Rocha, A.M.A.C., Garau, C. (eds.) A Critical Appraisal. Lecture Notes in Computer Science (including subseries Lecture Notes in Artificial Intelligence and Lecture Notes in Bioinformatics), vol. 13382 LNCS, pp. 40–47. Springer, Heidelberg (2022). https://doi.org/10.1007/978-3-031-10592-0_4/COVER

18. Haanes, K., et al.: Sustainability: The "Embracers" Seize Advantage. Boston, MA (2011)

19. Andersson, C.: Public space and the new urban agenda. J. Public Space 1, 5 (2016). https://doi.org/10.5204/JPS.V1I1.4

20. Scorza, F.: Sustainable urban regeneration in Gravina in Puglia, Italy. In: Fisher, T., Orland, B., and Steinitz, C. (eds.) The International Geodesign Collaboration. Changing Geography by Design, pp. 112–113. ESRI Press, Redlands, California (2020)

21. Corrado, S., Scorza, F.: Machine learning based approach to assess territorial marginality. In: Gervasi, O., Murgante, B., Hendrix, E.M.T., Taniar, D., Apduhan, B.O. (eds) Lecture Notes in Computer Science (including subseries Lecture Notes in Artificial Intelligence and Lecture Notes in Bioinformatics).vol. 13376 LNCS, pp. 292–302. Springer, Heidelberg (2022). https://doi.org/10.1007/978-3-031-10450-3_25/COVER

22. Pilogallo, A., Scorza, F.: Mapping regulation ecosystem services specialization in Italy. J. Urban Plan Dev. 148, (2022). https://doi.org/10.1061/(ASCE)UP.1943-5444.0000801

23. Scorza, F., Santopietro, L.: A systemic perspective for the sustainable energy and climate action plan (SECAP). Eur. Plann. Stud. 1–21 (2021). https://doi.org/10.1080/09654313.2021.1954603

24. Santopietro, L., Scorza, F.: The Italian experience of the covenant of mayors: a territorial evaluation. Sustainability. 13, 1289 (2021). https://doi.org/10.3390/su13031289

25. Scorza, F., Fortunato, G.: Active mobility-oriented urban development: a morpho-syntactic scenario for a mid-sized town. Eur. Plann. Stud. 1–25 (2022). https://doi.org/10.1080/09654313.2022.2077094

26. Scorza, F., Fortunato, G.: Cyclable cities: building feasible scenario through urban space morphology assessment. J Urban Plan Dev. 147, 05021039 (2021). https://doi.org/10.1061/(ASCE)UP.1943-5444.0000713

27. Scorza, F., Saganeiti, L., Pilogallo, A., Murgante, B.: Ghost planning: the inefficiency of energy sector policies in a low population density region1. Arch. di studi urbani e regionali. 34–55 (2020). https://doi.org/10.3280/ASUR2020-127-S1003

28. Vona, M., Harabaglia, P., Murgante, B.: Thinking about resilient cities: studying Italian earthquakes, vol. 169, pp. 185–199 (2016). https://doi.org/10.1680/UDAP.14.00007

29. Murgante, B., Borruso, G., Lapucci, A.: Sustainable development: concepts and methods for its application in urban and environmental planning. Stud. Comput. Intell. 348, 1–15 (2011). https://doi.org/10.1007/978-3-642-19733-8_1/COVER

30. Las Casas, G., Scorza, F., Murgante, B.: Razionalità a-priori: una proposta verso una pianificazione antifragile. Italian J. Reg. Sci. **18**, 329–338 (2019). https://doi.org/10.14650/93656
31. Murgante, B., Borruso, G., Lapucci, A.: Geocomputation and urban planning. Stud. Comput. Intell. **176**, 1–17 (2009). https://doi.org/10.1007/978-3-540-89930-3_1/COVER
32. Scorza, F., Pilogallo, A., Saganeiti, L., Murgante, B.: Natura 2000 areas and sites of national interest (SNI): Measuring (un)integration between naturalness preservation and environmental remediation policies. Sustainability (Switzerland). 12, (2020). https://doi.org/10.3390/SU12072928
33. Saganeiti, L., Mustafa, A., Teller, J., Murgante, B.: Modeling urban sprinkling with cellular automata. Sustain Cities Soc. **65**, 102586 (2021). https://doi.org/10.1016/J.SCS.2020.102586
34. Capodiferro, M., et al.: "University equity": students' facilities in major tourism destination towns. In: Gervasi, O. (ed.) Computational Science and Its Applications - ICCSA 2023 (2023)
35. Florio, E., et al.: SuperABLE: Matera accessible for all. In: Gervasi, O. (ed.) Computational Science and Its Applications - ICCSA 2023. Springer (2023)
36. Esposito Loscavo, B., et al.: Innovation ecosystem: the added value in a unique UNESCO city. In: Gervasi, O. (ed.) Computational Science and Its Applications - ICCSA 2023. Springer (2023)
37. Gatto, R.V., Corrado, S., Scorza, F.: Towards a definition of tourism ecosystem. In: 18th International Forum on Knowledge Asset Dynamics (IFKAD) - MANAGING KNOWLEDGE FOR SUSTAINABILITY (2023)

Enhancing Territorial and Community Resilience Through a Structured Institutional Governance: The Resilience HUB of the Province of Potenza

Rosalia Smaldone[1,2], Alessandro Attolico[1], and Francesco Scorza[2]([⊠]) [iD]

[1] Department of Territorial Planning, Innovation Development, Resilience, Province of Potenza, Potenza, Italy
{rosalia.smaldone,alessandro.attolico}@provinciapotenza.it
[2] School of Engineering, University of Basilicata, Viale dell'Ateneo Lucano 10, Potenza, Italy
francesco.scorza@unibas.it

Abstract. The Disasters are a threat to human security, as they cause many deaths and the destruction of livelihoods and assets. Over the last decade, over 700 thousand people globally lost their lives, over 1.4 million were injured, and approximately 23 million were made homeless as a result of disasters. Overall, more than 1.5 billion people were affected by disasters in various ways.

The Sendai Framework for Disaster Risk Reduction (2015–2030) emphasizes the necessity to strengthen competencies, management and implementation capacities at different governance levels as a necessary condition to progress in the reduction of disaster risk and associated loss at global, regional, and local level. The implementation at the local and urban level has been identified as a crucial breaking point for enhanced resilience and human security.

The Province of Potenza claims an experience that comes far back in time, and that is characterized by a strong institutional action on a territory that reflects the great fragility of the Italian peninsula and a high risks profile.

The Province has long played and is still playing a strong coordinating role within its regional government coverage made up of its 100 small and very small Municipalities. Within this process, it has distinguished itself over the years for a role of excellence at international level, playing an active role in disaster and disaster risks management, also offering expertise and know-how to other areas of Italy hit by disasters.

In force of this acknowledgement, at the last Global Platform on Disaster Risk Reduction in Bali Indonesia (May 2023), due to the strong commitment provided in following up it resilience implementation strategy and actions, the Province of Potenza has been appointed a MCR2030 Resilience HUB by the United Nations Disaster Risk Reduction Office and is building the basis for enhancing territorial and community resilience through a structured institutional governance built on a holistic multisectoral multistakeholder partnership.

Keywords: DRR · DRM · Governance · Resilience

© The Author(s), under exclusive license to Springer Nature Switzerland AG 2023
O. Gervasi et al. (Eds.): ICCSA 2023 Workshops, LNCS 14110, pp. 25–39, 2023.
https://doi.org/10.1007/978-3-031-37123-3_3

1   Disaster Risk Reduction and Disaster Risk Management: From the International Framework to Local (Provincial) Contest

1.1   Global State on Disaster Risk Reduction

Disasters are a threat to human security, as they cause many deaths and the destruction of livelihoods and assets [1]. Over the last decade, over 700 thousand people globally lost their lives, over 1.4 million were injured, and approximately 23 million were made homeless as a result of disasters. Overall, more than 1.5 billion people were affected by disasters in various ways. The total economic loss was more than $1.3 trillion.

Women, children, persons with disabilities and the elderly are particularly vulnerable to the negative effects of disasters. Worse, disaster impacts on human security goes far beyond the immediate effects, as disasters are often linked to health issues and pandemics, social and political unrest, displacement and migration and long-term destabilization of economic growth and prosperity, thus affecting threats across the seven identified areas within the human security approach.

Especially the most vulnerable lack the ability to recover quickly from disasters, and in many least developed countries development gains are lost for decades, directly impacting the human security of the affected communities.

Disaster risk was increasing globally, even before the advent of the coronavirus disease (COVID-19) pandemic. Intensive and extensive risks are growing at an unprecedented rate. Human action is creating greater and more dangerous risk. Disasters have increasing impacts on communities and whole systems as risk multiplies. Everyone is living downstream of something else. Global impacts become local, and vice versa. Impacts also cascade across sectors, creating new challenges.

Recent large-scale disasters – including the COVID-19 pandemic and major weather events that caused supply chain disruptions – have led many to conclude that something new is happening. Increasingly, people live in a world in which disaster risk manifests systemically, inflicting damage across the vital systems and infrastructure upon which human societies and economies depend. Despite commitments to build resilience, tackle climate change and create sustainable development pathways, current societal, political and economic choices are doing the reverse. Human actions continue to push the planet towards its existential and ecosystem limits. In the face of intensifying climate change impacts and increasing system threats, risk reduction efforts often seem too little and too late.

In the wake of the COVID-19 pandemic and the hottest decade on record, there is growing momentum to change how the global community manages risk, and a willingness to accelerate action on climate change.

While disasters are claiming lives annually, they are also costing more and increasing poverty. On a global level, the dollar value economic loss associated with all disasters –geophysical, climate- and weather-related – has averaged approximately $170 billion per year over the past decade, with peaks in 2011 and 2017 when losses soared to over $300 billion (Fig. 2). In 2011, the high losses were mainly due to the Tōhoku earthquake in Japan and floods in Thailand, both of which became complex and systemic disasters with cascading impacts across national, regional and international economies. In 2017, the losses were from intense hurricane/cyclone seasons in the North Atlantic and East

Asia. Such economic loss figures are likely underestimated, given the gaps in data for many countries, and the medium- and long-term economic losses that are not tracked. For example, a recent study of the losses to the tourism sector due to the Sunda Strait tsunami and COVID-19 in Indonesia highlighted that only by calculating indirect losses can disaster impact be assessed comprehensively and ultimately managed [2–4] (Fig. 1).

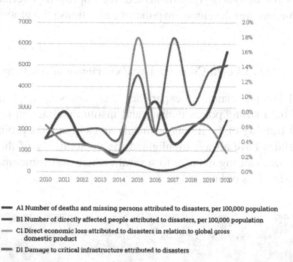

— A1 Number of deaths and missing persons attributed to disasters, per 100,000 population
— B1 Number of directly affected people attributed to disasters, per 100,000 population
— C1 Direct economic loss attributed to disasters in relation to global gross domestic product
— D1 Damage to critical infrastructure attributed to disasters

Fig. 1. A Number of deaths and missing persons attributed to disasters, actual data 2010–2020 and outlook 2021–2030 (Sendai Framework Target A) according to UNDRR analysis based on DesInventar [5].

The Sendai Framework for Disaster Risk Reduction 2015–2030 (SFDRR 2015–30) [1] outlines seven clear targets and four priorities for action to prevent new and reduce existing disaster risks: (i) Understanding disaster risk; (ii) Strengthening disaster risk governance to manage disaster risk; (iii) Investing in disaster reduction for resilience and; (iv) Enhancing disaster preparedness for effective response, and to "Build Back Better" in recovery, rehabilitation and reconstruction.

It aims to achieve the substantial reduction of disaster risk and losses in lives, livelihoods and health and in the economic, physical, social, cultural and environmental assets of persons, businesses, communities and countries over the next 15 years.

The Framework was adopted at the Third UN World Conference on Disaster Risk Reduction in Sendai, Japan, on March 18, 2015 and currently it is under the mid-term review process of its implementation.

SFDRR emphasizes the necessity to strengthen competencies, management and implementation capacities at different governance levels as a necessary condition to progress in the reduction of disaster risk and associated loss at global, regional, and local level [6]. The implementation at the local and urban level has been identified as a crucial breaking point for enhanced resilience and human security.

It also calls for a comprehensive approach to building resilient and security of people, including ensuring a comprehensive involvement of all affected, as well as comprehensive risk assessment evaluating all potential risks to an individual, a community, or a state.

Mainstreamed to the SFDRR, also the Global Agendas on Sustainable Development (SDGs) and on Climate (Paris Agreement) ask for improved governance mechanism integrating socio-economic development policies and actions with global human security and welfare [7].

1.2 The DRR/DRM at Local Contest: The Experience of the Province of Potenza

The Province of Potenza claims an experience that comes far back in time, and that is characterized by a strong policy-making and institutional action on a territory that reflects the great fragility of the Italian peninsula and a high risks profile [8].

Severe landslides have always highlighted the vulnerability of the territory of the Province of Potenza, causing damage to several centers and sometimes giving rise to catastrophes causing loss of human lives.

Fig. 2. Landslides on the provincial territory Source: Provincial Master Plan (2013)

As regards seismic exposure, the 1857 earthquake in the area of the Val d'Agri and that of November 23, 1980 (Irpinia and the province of Potenza) left their mark causing thousands of casualties, destruction of entire areas, damage to many urban centers and big ruins. Landslides, earthquakes and other disasters have not only sown death and devastation but have also contributed to forming a deep need for awareness and action towards DRR/DRM.

Since 2004 the Province of Potenza implemented a Provincial Civil Protection System working in particular with Municipalities, Volunteers and all local, regional and national actors of the civil protection system. At this regard, the provincial Civil Protection Office also produced two planning documents (Province of Potenza 2004) acting as organizational guiding tools for the entire "mechanism" [9].

Among the other instruments and tools for Disasters Risk Management (DRM), the implementation of a suited for purpose Geographic Information System (GIS) of the "Elements Exposed to Risks", that allows the collection and updating of information about the different variables on the territory, by integrating and putting them in relation to each other for producing *risks* and *damages* scenarios. The data implementation of the territorial monitoring activities and of the elements exposed to risks has been performed during the years. These are mainly finalized to the DRR actions aiming at giving a feature of the territorial risks, by integrating the static (buildings, handworks, etc.) and dynamic (calamitous phenomena and their space-time evolution) territorial information.

Infrastructure's vulnerability has been taken in consideration also in the assessment of the response of the disaster management structure to contrast the effects of disasters: the disaster management organization, the handling of the rescue machine to and from the affected areas, the availability of structures and areas for the operation activities, etc.

At the same time, the assessment of the social vulnerability has been provided on who and where people are more exposed to the risks, who could need particular assistance both during a disaster and in prevention activities.

In order to have a comprehensive knowledge of the risks at local level, it has been also important to typify all the social, economic, urban and territorial elements in order to better quantify the most probable effects of a disaster in terms of population and built environment involved and injured.

With a comprehensive knowledge of the vulnerability over the territory and of the exposed elements (population and assets), it has been possible to build different scenarios characterizing the overall territorial and urban risk.

On the basis of these deep assessments and studies, the organization of above mentioned the Provincial Civil Protection System and the drafting of the Provincial Civil Protection Plan have activated a permanent interconnection between the Provincial Authority and the territory, promoting forms of institutional cooperation and carrying out propulsion and coordination activities. Through these activities territorial data have been collected and revealed to be very useful for the outlining of the provincial planning, becoming a strategic knowledge framework for the whole territory, communities and citizens for the raising of awareness towards risks.

In this way, the Province of Potenza has distinguished itself over the years for a role of excellence at international level, playing an active role in disaster and disaster risks management, also offering expertise and know-how to other areas of Italy hit by disasters.

2 Structured Governance and Stakeholders and Communities' Involvement in the Territorial Strategy of the Province of Potenza

2.1 DRR/DRM Governance: The Strategy of the Province of Potenza

During the years, the Province of Potenza's institutional action in DRR policy-making has been characterized by a strong political will and public support, i.e. a great commitment that resulted in a strong governance enriched by evidence and accountability towards the involved institutions, stakeholders, major groups, local communities and citizens. The strategy used has been progressively shaped and adapted based on the specific and contingent needs and on the feedback from the accountability process, always keeping its vision and commitment at their highest potentials.

For this reason, the need for a radical reconsideration of the whole action derived. This change of strategy was felt as necessary for ensuring the territory, as a whole, being involved more actively and concretely in disaster risks reduction policies and actions, both at territorial and local levels. A long period of analysis and assessment has been performed, even on a global scale, to adjust and develop a different, unique and most effective/efficient strategy, with the goal of implementing DRR policies and actions throughout all the territory and at all levels.

Due to these considerations, the Province of Potenza placed then DRR in close connection with its territorial governance and planning institutional duties, thus transforming DRR and Resilience to disasters into real "structural" policy-making and actions to be implemented by coordinating territorial and urban development and land-use, with a wide area vision and approach [10, 11]. In this way, the Province intended also to provide a strong contribution for calibrating and optimizing the resources for the safe and sustainable development of the territory as a whole.

In this contest the Province of Potenza has long played and is still playing a strong coordinating role within its regional government coverage made up of 100 small and very small Municipalities ("secondary cities" that represent the vast majority of Italian municipalities on which a large part of the population is concentrated), through a complex action for the construction of an effective strategy for achieving an improved management of the territory and for combating the risks due to natural, climatic and human factors.

This action has resulted in the definition of specific regional strategies and planning tools carried out by capitalizing the experiences gained in the many years of experience in different fields of its institutional duties [12].

The Province - representing its network of municipalities - has contributed to the drafting of the new global agreement on disaster risk reduction (post-2015) adopted at the 3rd World Conference in Sendai (Japan). As coordinator of the local Resilience network, the Province of Potenza also actively participated to the consultations processes for the development and the adoption of the global agreements on SDGs, Climate and the New Urban Agenda, providing many experience-based inputs for the development of post-2015 territorial and urban actions as representative of "Local Governments" major group.

Following up the adoption of the aforementioned international agreements, it has been engaged in the review, follow-up and localization of the global goals and targets at the local level and it is providing strong support in exporting its experience to other regions and cities.

The Provincial Structural Plan (PSP/TCP, 2013) [13] represents a further milestone for defining the subsequent government actions for the territory. The TCP is a territorial coordination plan that outlines oriented objectives and future development scenarios according to a coordination approach of the different territorial vocations and local strategies. The TCP is qualified as a strategic tool for capturing and driving additional resources (allocated in particular on EU, national and regional programming as well as other derivation) and for assisting urban planning in the ongoing process of strong reorganization of territorial governance. During the TCP's drafting process, the engagement of all relevant and key-stakeholders has been performed as a critical requirement. This approach has ensured that all the stakeholders, and in particular those who have expertise in local and regional territorial policies (i.e. local, regional, national institutions - including authorities, agencies and other public and private-public bodies), scientific institutions, academia & research, professions, trade, industry, crafts, etc., have been informed, consulted, involved and have provided for their active contribution [14–17].

The local communities and social groups have been also involved in the process, through specific engagement processes. In this way, the relevant groups of interests and other stakeholders have been well integrated into the development of the planning process [18–21]. This contributed and is helping to facilitate the overall implementation process (based on the same multi-stakeholder and all-society inclusive approach) due to a broad sharing of objectives and related tangible actions (Fig. 3).

Fig. 3. Communities' involvement process carried out by the Province of Potenza

The policies and actions put in place are based on the so called #weResilient strategy that has been specifically outlined and defined for pursuing regional socio-economic development through a structural combination of environmental sustainability, territorial security and climate change contrasting polices to be implemented through specific actions at urban and local level.

The main objective of the #weResilient strategy consists in coordinating urban policies and planning and in assisting the local territory through a subsidiary engagement
process mainly addressed to municipalities, communities, social groups and citizens, for
pursuing an improved territorial governance and appropriate land use policies/actions
with wide area (regional) outlook.

A fundamental element of the strategy is the active engagement of communities in
local decision-making processes in the field of territorial policies (sustainable development, disaster risk reduction and climate changes adaptation/mitigation) and the coordi-
nating/driving action directed to the Municipalities in this inclusion process. Hence the
establishment of 'permanent platforms' focused on the implementation of a Resilience
of communities that is inclusive of the different categories/social groups.

This process of institutional "involvement" has the objective of strengthening the
capacity of individuals and communities to reduce risks of catastrophes and to pursue sustainable development by spreading knowledge and raising awareness about the
importance of prevention and risk mitigation and through their involvement in relevant
decision-making processes related to territorial policies. The involvement of relevant
"institutional" stakeholders completes and integrates all the participation process.

3   The Resilience HUB of the Province of Potenza

In the strategy implementation performed so far, most of the efforts have been devoted
to setting-up a complex system of progressive engagement having the main purpose of
entrusting and engaging key-actors in the institutional policy-making regarding territorial
and urban sustainable and resilient development. For reaching this goal, many actions
have been launched and performed including:

- the setting-up of a permanent network with Municipalities for outlining and development strategies and related actions by assuring adequate subsidiary support and
  coordination;
- the setting-up of permanent "platforms" with stakeholders and major groups for
  collecting needs, discussing problems and identify possible solution to be adopted;
- the setting-up of IT communication tools for providing wide evidence of the actions
  performed and the progresses made (accountability);
- the organization and implementation of specific capacity building activities, mostly
  addressed to institutional key-actors but with the enlargement also to civil society;
- the implementation of specific awareness-raising and information campaigns;
- facilitating involvement and raising support (not only financial) by the private sector,
  by means of specific engagement programs and initiatives;
- setting-up of practical processes of progressive confidence/trust building, outlined and
  calibrated on the specific and contingent needs of the different social components and
  on reciprocal cooperation and assistance.

Moreover, since DRR and Resilience building are holistic and multistakeholder processes where the role of the governments (at all level) is pivotal for transforming words
into actions, many actions (including evidence activities) have been performed also for
building and/or raising the public support and political will and for maintaining them at
the highest level for the upcoming phases.

A strategic step in this action is represented by the enrollment - as a whole territorial "system" - to the UNISDR "Making Cities Resilient" Campaign in 2014. The role of the Province of Potenza, with particular regards to territorial risk reduction and actions for adapting to climate change, supported such a massive active participation to the MCR global Campaign in order to better support local governments and municipalities to become more "resilient" in facing disasters. So, as part of the MCR global Campaign, the Province has become the leader of a distinctive action in the world: to constitute a wide territorial Network including all its 100 Municipalities through formal Statements of Commitments aiming at developing a common territorial development strategy covering the improvement of resilience to disasters with a wide-area strategic coordination and a multiscale and multilevel holistic implementation approach.

For this action, in 2015, the Province has been acknowledged as a UN world Champion for Inclusive Resilience and Territorial Safety.

Within the Campaign, a deeper process of downscaling the above described #weResilient strategy to the municipal contexts has been made more effective by means of specific voluntary agreements with some Municipalities of the provincial Network aimed at working on specific development topics identified as particularly relevant by the mayors and/or local communities.

The Province has committed to supporting these committed Municipalities on a voluntary basis in implementing actions aimed at consolidating a multi-stakeholder and communities-centered approach to pursue specific objectives of urban development into the general context of territorial resilience.

As illustrated, the Province of Potenza is playing a leading role providing by providing subsidiary assistance and support in developing specific urban/local strategies and actions fully integrated into the general outlined framework of #weResilient territorial sustainable and resilient development. On the other hand, the signatory Municipalities are committed of integrating more focused sustainable development and community resilience requirements within specific urban - including other relevant sectorial - planning and related actions.

By downscaling the model proposed by the Province of Potenza and with its support, these municipalities are locally implementing a "multi-stakeholder approach" based on the active involvement of institutions, organisms, associations representing the different professional and social categories that have now the possibility to be driving forces against risk of disasters.

Within the international contest, thanks to its networks, The Province is playing a very active role in connecting cities with cities in a learning and peer-to-peer processes of mutual exchange and cooperation.

In this context, the experience of the Province of Potenza as Champion for 'Inclusive Resilience and Territorial Safety' has been strategic in demonstrating commitment, achievements and good practice in DRR and resilience building to the involved cities in order to help them in identifying key themes and success factors.

Lots of the success factors identified are based on the UNDRR's 'Ten Essentials for Making Cities Resilient', suggesting that certain core priorities promote sustainability of resilience building [22–25].

The Province is concretizing these international mentoring activities in a structured path within a partnership with interested cities, materialized in a Pilot Action, carried out starting with the DDR assessment of the City and, after a sharing and learning ongoing process, drafting a Resilience strategy, as final result.

This pilot action has, as its aim, the improvement in understanding and in capacity to address disaster risks and build resilience at local levels.

Moreover, some "city-to-city" learning exchange workshops have been and are organized for the cities of its international networks,

The learning exchange is between the institutional and civil platform of the territory of the Province of Potenza (Basilicata Region, Italy) and the municipalities/cities involved.

The main Objectives of the workshops are:

- To promote a dialogue and exchange among the local governments by capitalizing on the large network of cities engaged in MCR2030 initiative;
- To share knowledge with and disseminate best practices on the development and implementation of comprehensive urban disaster risk reduction plans;
- To highlight the added value of the multistakeholder and community engagement approaches in implementing the Sendai Framework for Disaster Risk Reduction (2015–2030) on the local level;
- To showcase local efforts in finding and implementing innovative solutions to reduce disaster risk towards the achievement of sustainable and resilient development.

Due to the strong commitment provided so far in following up it resilience implementation strategy and actions, at the last Global Platform on Disaster Risk Reduction in Bali Indonesia, the Province of Potenza has been appointed a MCR2030 Resilience HUB by the United Nations Disaster Risk Reduction Office.

4 Steps Forward Enhancing Territorial and Community Resilience Through a Structured Institutional Governance

Based on the long-lasting experience achieved in implementing DRM/DRR from a governative side and on the progresses made in lay the foundations for local and global alliances for Resilience, through its Resilience HUB the Province of Potenza has started working on a holistic multisectoral multistakeholder partnership with the aim of structurally engaging stakeholders and communities in intergovernmental decision and policy making processes (stakeholder engagement mechanism).

Key functions of this new structured institutional governance include to:

- to build an inclusive and broad local action for downscaling the Sendai Framework objectives integrated to the SDGs and Climate goals in the New Urban Agenda framework;
- to create avenues to influence territorial policies design and implementation
- to strengthen citizen-led and social engagement mechanisms;

– to promote coordination, information exchange and harmonization between stakeholder groups.

The Province of Potenza Resilience Hub is working for establishing peer-to-peer specialized thematic relevant stakeholders' partnerships with the main objective to working together for focusing the actions and maximizing the effectiveness of the results [26–28].

Of strategic relevance, the renovated partnership established with the School of Engineering of the University of Basilicata on the definition of strategic actions for sustainable and resilient local development and the inclusive involvement of communities.

Under this focused framework, the mutual collaboration is being provided for the implementation of joint actions to increase territorial and urban resilience, in particular with the following actions:

- to contribute to the definition of shared technical-scientific approaches for the implementation of the #weResilient strategy at the local level, proposing innovative forms and contents within the objectives and local actions of transformation and intervention: among these are resilience, the fight against climate change, sustainable development and related innovations for land management with the active and continuous involvement of municipalities, institutions, communities and citizens;
- to jointly contribute to the definition and implementation of strategic and innovative territorial actions, in particular on the issues of sustainable and resilient territorial and urban development and territorial security also through the candidacy of projects directly funded by the EU and/or other institutions of national importance and international;
- to encourage the experimentation of innovative actions of institutional collaboration aimed at improving vertical and horizontal governance on the development of territorial and urban resilience;
- to participate through qualified technical-scientific contributions in the actions of participation and active involvement of stakeholders, communities, interest groups and citizens carried out jointly;
- to contribute, within their respective areas of responsibility, to strengthening and expanding the Resilience HUB, through operational collaboration in the related activities and the sharing of experiences, know-how and good practices available to them in favor of other global communities interested in increasing the own level of resilience, maintaining the role of coordination and facilitation for the Province of Potenza's Resilience HUB, with the aim of:

– to promote dialogue and exchanges between local governments by capitalizing on the network of cities involved in the international MCR2030 initiative;
– to share knowledge and disseminate best practices for the development and implementation of comprehensive spatial/urban disaster risk reduction plans;
– to highlight the added value of the human security approach in implementing the Sendai Framework for Disaster Risk Reduction (2015–2030) at the local level;
– to show local efforts in finding and implementing innovative solutions to reduce disaster risk and fight climate change (mitigation and adaptation) towards achieving sustainable and resilient development;
– to strengthen institutional collaboration with the stakeholders who will be identified as active partners of the HUB;

- tocontribute to the implementation and achievement of the objectives of the main global agendas SFDRR, SDGs, Paris Agreement, New Urban Agenda, in an integrated form, localizing them to individual contexts which will be the subject of joint work.

The goal is to pursue the following expected results:

- improving knowledge and understanding of risks and sharing tools to develop and implement local action plans for disaster risk reduction resilience;
- identifying best practices in local disaster risk reduction;
- supporting local authorities and governments to implement objective e) of the Sendai Framework;
- supporting local authorities and governments in implementing the objectives of the global agendas SFDRR, SDGs, Paris Agreement, New Urban Agenda, in an integrated form;
- jointly defining training, information and active involvement activities for local communities and citizens aimed at promoting a culture of resilience to disaster risk, contrast (mitigation and adaptation) to climate change and sustainable territorial and urban development, including through the joint organization of participatory and co-design workshops for key players;
- contributing to the innovation of strategic planning and impact monitoring tools with reference to the system of indicators defined at national and international level for the local implementation of the international objectives of sustainable and resilient development;
- cooperating for the innovation of methods and tools for territorial design and decision support for the local implementation of the global objectives defined in the global Agendas and relative follow-up through case-studies on specific territories [29, 30];
- contributing to the selecting and applying methodological approaches, analytical methodologies, public/private engagement procedures, validated in a qualified scientific context and jointly implemented on the territory;
- jointly engaging in effective dissemination of the results of shared activities within the international communities;
- exploring and sharing joint participation in regional, national, European and international research calls and programmes;
- contributing to activating and implementing qualified training and capacity building actions, the activation of training internships, scholarships, grants and research doctorates, etc., the active involvement of learners from other national and international realities interested in benefit from the cultural, scientific and professional exchange activities activated by the Resilience HUB [31].

One relevant achievement the establishment of a research doctorate course on harmonized downscaling of the global Agendas' objectives into territorial and urban planning addressed to technical staff of the Province of Potenza's Resilience HUB as a driving force for specialization and capacity building of government skills that are functional to the territory and communities [9, 32].

5 Conclusion

The appointment of MCR2030 Resilience HUB for the Province of Potenza represents the 'starting point' of a new and renewed commitment, that is seeing the Province of Potenza strengthening its institutional role as a wide area authority in supporting municipalities and local communities in implementing sustainable and resilient territorial development, as included in its multi-years action plan (as HUB).

Within these activities, the expected results are:

- enhancing beneficiary cities in understanding and equipping with tools for developing and implementing local DRR resilience action plans;
- identifying added value of the multistakeholder and community engagement approaches to strengthen disaster risk reduction planning in the involved munici-palities/cities;
- identifying best practices in local disaster risk reduction and risk assessment methods which have been developed to be capitalized and transferred over the territory;
- supporting local authorities/governments to enhance territorial and community resilience through a structured institutional governance based on holistic multisectoral multistakeholder partnerships (stakeholder engagement mechanism) [33].

References

1. United Nations Office for Disaster Risk Reduction: Global Assessment Report on Disaster Risk Reduction 2022: Our World at Risk: Transforming Governance for a Resilient Future, Geneva (2022)
2. Scorza, F., Gatto, R.V.: Identifying territorial values for tourism development: the case study of Calabrian Greek area. Sustainability 15, 5501 (2023). https://doi.org/10.3390/SU15065501
3. Gatto, R., Santopietro, L., Scorza, F.: Tourism and abandoned Inland areas development demand: a critical appraisal. In: Gervasi, O., Murgante, B., Misra, S., Rocha, A.M.A.C., Garau, C. (eds.) ICCSA 2022. LNCS, vol. 13382, pp. 40–47. Springer, Cham (2022). https://doi.org/10.1007/978-3-031-10592-0_4
4. Gatto, R.V., Corrado, S., Scorza, F.: Towards a definition of tourism ecosystem. In: 18th International Forum on Knowledge Asset Dynamics (IFKAD) - Managing Knowledge For Sustainability (2023)
5. UNDRR: Making Cities Resilient Report 2019: A snapshot of how local governments progress in reducing disaster risks in alignment with the Sendai Framework for Disaster Risk Reduction, Geneve (2019)
6. United Nations Development Programme (UNDP): Localizing The POST-2015 Development Agenda, Geneva (2014)
7. UNFCC: Adoption of the Paris agreement In: United Nations Framework Convention on Climate Change (UNFCCC), Paris, France, p. 31. (2015)
8. Attolico, A., Smaldone, R.: The #weResilient strategy for downscaling local resilience and sustainable development: the Potenza province and municipalities of Potenza and Pignola case. Disaster Prev. Manag. Int. J. 29, 793–810 (2020). https://doi.org/10.1108/DPM-04-2020-0130/FULL/XML
9. Attolico, A., et al.: Implementation of the "resilience of communities" policy in land use planning on the provincial territory of Potenza Province of Potenza (Italy)

10. Scorza, F., Saganeiti, L., Pilogallo, A., Murgante, B.: Ghost planning: the inefficiency of energy sector policies in a low population density region1. Archivio di studi urbani e regionali, 34–55 (2020). https://doi.org/10.3280/ASUR2020-127-S1003
11. Scorza, F., Pilogallo, A., Saganeiti, L., Murgante, B., Pontrandolfi, P.: Comparing the territorial performances of renewable energy sources' plants with an integrated ecosystem services loss assessment: a case study from the Basilicata region (Italy). Sustain. Cities Soc. 56, 102082 (2020). https://doi.org/10.1016/j.scs.2020.102082
12. Casas, G.L., Scorza, F.: Sustainable planning: a methodological toolkit. In: Gervasi, O., et al. (eds.) ICCSA 2016. LNCS, vol. 9786, pp. 627–635. Springer, Cham (2016). https://doi.org/10.1007/978-3-319-42085-1_53
13. Province of Potenza: Provincial Structural Master Plan (Provincial Territorial Coordination Plan - TCP), Potenza (2013)
14. Scorza, F., Pontrandolfi, P.: Citizen participation and technologies: the C.A.S.T. architecture. In: Gervasi, O., et al. (eds.) ICCSA 2015. LNCS, vol. 9156, pp. 747–755. Springer, Cham (2015). https://doi.org/10.1007/978-3-319-21407-8_53
15. Scorza, F., Fortunato, G., Carbone, R., Murgante, B., Pontrandolfi, P.: Increasing urban walkability through citizens' participation processes. Sustainability 13, 5835 (2021). https://doi.org/10.3390/su13115835
16. Carbone, R., Saganeiti, L., Scorza, F., Murgante, B.: Increasing the walkability level through a participation process. In: Gervasi, O., et al. (eds.) ICCSA 2018. LNCS, vol. 10964, pp. 113–124. Springer, Cham (2018). https://doi.org/10.1007/978-3-319-95174-4_9
17. Glass, J.J.: Citizen participation in planning: the relationship between objectives and techniques. J. Am. Plann. Assoc. 45, 180–189 (1979). https://doi.org/10.1080/01944367908976956
18. Rudd, A., Malone, K., Bartlett, M.: Participatory urban planning. Urban Environ. Educ. Rev. (2017). https://doi.org/10.7591/CORNELL/9781501705823.003.0030
19. Aichholzer, G., Strauß, S.: Evaluating e-participation: frameworks, practice, evidence. Presented at the (2016). https://doi.org/10.1007/978-3-319-25403-6_6
20. Conroy, M.M., Evans-Cowley, J.: E-participation in planning: an analysis of cities adopting on-line citizen participation tools. Eviron. Plann. C. Gov. Policy 24, 371–384 (2006). https://doi.org/10.1068/c1k
21. Soligno, R., Scorza, F., Amato, F., Casas, G.L., Murgante, B.: Citizens participation in improving rural communities quality of life. In: Gervasi, O., et al. (eds.) ICCSA 2015. LNCS, vol. 9156, pp. 731–746. Springer, Cham (2015). https://doi.org/10.1007/978-3-319-21407-8_52
22. Dvarioniene, J., Grecu, V., Lai, S., Scorza, F.: Four perspectives of applied sustainability: research implications and possible integrations. In: Gervasi, O., et al. (eds.) ICCSA 2017. LNCS, vol. 10409, pp. 554–563. Springer, Cham (2017). https://doi.org/10.1007/978-3-319-62407-5_39
23. Johnson, C., Blackburn, S.: Advocacy for urban resilience: UNISDR's making cities resilient campaign. Environ. Urban. 26, 29–52 (2014). https://doi.org/10.1177/0956247813518684
24. Frazier, T.G., Thompson, C.M., Dezzani, R.J., Butsick, D.: Spatial and temporal quantification of resilience at the community scale. Appl. Geogr. 42, 95–107 (2013). https://doi.org/10.1016/j.apgeog.2013.05.004
25. Viitanen, J., Kingston, R.: Smart cities and green growth: outsourcing democratic and environmental resilience to the global technology sector. Environ. Plan. Econ. Space 46, 803–819 (2014). https://doi.org/10.1068/a46242
26. Attolico, A., Scorza, F.: A transnational cooperation perspective for "low carbon economy." In: Gervasi, O., et al. (eds.) ICCSA 2016. LNCS, Part I, vol. 9786, pp. 636–641. Springer, Cham (2016). https://doi.org/10.1007/978-3-319-42085-1_54

27. Attolico, A., Smaldone, R., Scorza, F., De Marco, E., Pilogallo, A.: Investigating good practices for low carbon development perspectives in Basilicata. In: Gervasi, O., et al. (eds.) ICCSA 2018. LNCS, vol. 10964, pp. 763–775. Springer, Cham (2018). https://doi.org/10.1007/978-3-319-95174-4_58

28. Scorza, F., Attolico, A., Moretti, V., Smaldone, R., Donofrio, D., Laguardia, G.: Growing sustainable behaviors in local communities through smart monitoring systems for energy efficiency: renergy outcomes. In: Murgante, B., et al. (eds.) ICCSA 2014. LNCS, vol. 8580, pp. 787–793. Springer, Cham (2014). https://doi.org/10.1007/978-3-319-09129-7_57

29. Corrado, S., Scorza, F.: Machine learning based approach to assess territorial marginality. In: Gervasi, O., Murgante, B., Hendrix, E.M.T., Taniar, D., Apduhan, B.O. (eds.) ICCSA 2022. LNCS, vol. 13376, pp. 292–302. Springer, Cham (2022). https://doi.org/10.1007/978-3-031-10450-3_25

30. Dastoli, P.S., Pontrandolfi, P., Scorza, F., Corrado, S., Azzato, A.: Applying geodesign towards an integrated local development strategy. the Val d'Agri case (Italy). In: Gervasi, O., Murgante, B., Misra, S., Rocha, A.M.A.C., Garau, C. (eds.) ICCSA 2022. LNCS, vol. 13379, pp. 253–262. Springer, Cham (2022). https://doi.org/10.1007/978-3-031-10545-6_18

31. Scorza, F., Attolico, A.: Innovations in promoting sustainable development: the local implementation plan designed by the Province of Potenza. In: Gervasi, O., et al. (eds.) ICCSA 2015. LNCS, vol. 9156, pp. 756–766. Springer, Cham (2015). https://doi.org/10.1007/978-3-319-21407-8_54

32. Attolico, A., et al.: Engaged communities for low carbon development process. In: Gervasi, O., et al. (eds.) ICCSA 2017. LNCS, vol. 10409, pp. 573–584. Springer, Cham (2017). https://doi.org/10.1007/978-3-319-62407-5_41

33. Dvarioniene, J., et al.: Stakeholders involvement for energy conscious communities: the energy labs experience in 10 European communities. Renew. Energy 75, 512–518 (2015). https://doi.org/10.1016/j.renene.2014.10.017

Sustainable Approaches in Water Tariff Design to Reduce Water Service Divide

Luigi Dolores[✉] [iD], Maria Macchiaroli[iD], and Gianluigi De Mare[iD]

University of Salerno, Via Giovanni Paolo II, 132, Fisciano, SA, Italy
{ldolores,mmacchiaroli,gdemare}@unisa.it

Abstract. Inequality in access to water and the use of the water service is a global problem which requires an equitable distribution of the resource and its efficient management. Although universally recognized by the United Nations as an inviolable human right, access to water and sanitation is often characterized by inequalities which also manifest themselves through different levels of quality in the provision of water supply, purification and sewer.

Also in Italy, the Water Service Divide is significant and affects about a third of the population. The National Regulatory Authority for Energy, Networks and the Environment (ARERA) has introduced a simplified approach to defining water tariffs aimed at water operators with difficulty overcoming this problem. However, the scheme is not always easily applicable, especially in cases where it is also necessary to design the tariff structure and the related incremental blocks (or brackets). To remedy this criticality, in the present work a mathematical programming model is proposed, based on the simplex algorithm, which allows the estimation of water tariffs and consumption blocks also for water operators characterized by the absence of data on costs and revenues of water management. The proposed model, which guarantees compliance with all the economic constraints imposed by the national Authority, makes it possible to design consistent tariffs between the various water service operators, reducing management gaps. The model, easily applicable by the operators, can also represent a simplified scheme for the initial tariff planning which is independent of the knowledge of the data on operating costs and revenues.

Keywords: Water Service Divide · Water inequality · Water Tariff · Simplex Algorithm · Water Economics · Economic Evaluation of Projects

1 Introduction

Water is a fundamental resource for life and the development of human activities. Due to its use in multiple fields (mining, energy, agriculture, industry, domestic, etc.), water often becomes the object of conflict and different interests in terms of management and use. Because of this, situations of water inequality, unfortunately, occur, i.e. unequal distribution and scarce availability of the resource in some areas of the planet. Population

---

All authors contributed in equal parts to this work.

© The Author(s), under exclusive license to Springer Nature Switzerland AG 2023
O. Gervasi et al. (Eds.): ICCSA 2023 Workshops, LNCS 14110, pp. 40–51, 2023.
https://doi.org/10.1007/978-3-031-37123-3_4

growth, the climate crisis, consumerism and the expansion of markets have strongly contributed to the increase in water consumption, putting the poorest populations in a condition of scarcity above all and expanding the phenomenon of the Water Service Divide [1].

By Water Service Divide we mean the disparity in access to water resources by users, which manifests itself through different levels of quality guaranteed in the provision of the aqueduct, sewerage and purification services. In this regard, substantial imbalances regarding access to water resources and the methods of managing water services exist. This translates into the so-called "citizenship gap", i.e. an asymmetry in the delivery methods of services offered at a territorial or national level [2]. This water inequality, which implies a non-optimal and homogeneous resource allocation, is often caused by obsolete management methods that generate impartiality and further amplify social stratification [3, 4]. While on the one hand water and sanitation have been universally recognized by the United Nations as an inviolable human right (as enshrined in the Sustainable Development Goal 6—SDG6—of the 2030 Agency), On the other hand, huge challenges lie ahead in curbing the water inequality and ensuring effective safe access to water resources for all people [5]. In this sense, many studies have recently been conducted aimed at measuring inequality in access to water, even if specific and unambiguous metrics to be adopted to achieve the SDG6 sustainable development objective have not yet been identified [6]. Furthermore, this goal is still difficult to achieve, since about one in ten inhabitants of the planet still does not have safe access to water. It is estimated that 80% of people without access to safe drinking water live in rural areas. Serious inequalities are also recorded regarding access to sanitation. Only 55% of the world population lives in conditions of hygienic-sanitary security. Continuing with current consumption patterns, it is estimated that by 2025 around two-thirds of the planet's inhabitants will live in countries characterized by water stress [7]. Currently, North Africa, East Africa, Southern Africa, the Middle East, China, Mexico and India are the most water-poor countries in the world. Around 2 billion people for whom water stress is a serious problem are concentrated in these areas. Among the areas richest in water, we find South America, Oceania, Northern Asia and North America (in particular Canada, with a per capita availability of water ranging from 10,000 to 50,000 L per person). In Europe, there are inequalities between the northern and central-southern territories. Water availability varies between an average of 65,000 L for Great Britain, France, Italy, Spain, Portugal and Greece and an average of 5,000 L for Germany, Poland and Romania. In the Mediterranean basin, Italy is the richest country in water resources thanks to the presence of the Alps. However, there are important inequalities between the North and South [8]. According to ISTAT statistics for the years 2015–2018, Italy is in first place in the EU for withdrawals of water for drinking use: 428 L per inhabitant per day. However, just under half of the volume of water withdrawn from the source (47.9%) does not reach the end users due to water losses from supply and distribution networks. The daily supply for potable use is quantifiable in 220 L per inhabitant. 21.3% of families connected to the municipal water network consider themselves very satisfied with the service offered, while 63.3% are quite satisfied. The overall level of satisfaction varies significantly in the area. Very or fairly satisfied families are nine out of ten in the North, eight in the Center and in the South and down to seven in the Islands. The share of families who prefer not to consume tap water is still significant, despite the degree of trust showing a progressive improvement: from 40.1% in 2002 to 29.0% in 2018, for a total number of families equal to 7 million 500 thousand.

As regards the issue of the Water Service Divide in Italy, the most recent studies show that the infrastructural gap between the North and the South of the country is significant. In particular, in the face of a large area of the country, located mainly in the North and in the Center, in which the use of services, the implementation of investments, the regional legislative activity, the decision-making mechanisms of the government bodies of the field and the managerial and industrial capabilities of the operators appear to be in line with the achievement of the highest objectives in the sector, situations persist, mainly in the South and in the Islands, in which there are inefficiencies [9].

In fact, in the South water service providers are often subsidized by public institutions to mitigate the infrastructural gap with the North of the country and to improve the quality standards in the supply of the resource [10]. This gap is due both to the inefficiency of the distribution network since in some provinces of the South and Islands water losses exceed 50% [11], and to the inability of low-budget business management to ensure industrial management of the service, with the emergence of economies of scale that allow for compliance with the Italian and European principle regarding full cost recovery. Economies of scale and scope are pursued through the push towards the definition of supply basins of at least provincial size, as well as through the vertical integration of the water service, which provides for management by a single assignee of the aqueduct, sewerage and purification activities [12].

In Italy, today, there are over 8 million inhabitants of self-managed municipalities; of these, about 65% are in the south of the country.

To promote increasing levels of provision of water services in disadvantaged areas and to level the inequalities in terms of accessibility to water between areas of the country, the Regulatory Authority for Energy, Networks and Environment (ARERA), an Italian body that carries out regulation and control activities in various sectors, including the water sector, has promoted simplified forms of tariff regulation. The main objective is to strengthen the aggregation processes between the managements, highly fragmented throughout the country, and to overcome the Water Service Divide. To this end, with Resolution 580/2019/R/idr (Approval of the Water Tariff Method for the third regulatory period MTI–3), ARERA introduced the Convergence Regulatory Scheme to which those managements that have persistent levels of criticality in carrying out the planning and implementation of infrastructural interventions. The Convergence Regulatory Scheme introduces important simplifications that allow water tariffs to be determined on a parametric basis in the absence of significant technical and/or economic data [13]. In analogy to what is envisaged for managing entities in an ordinary state of operation (i.e. which do not present deficiencies in terms of technical-economic data), a structure of the respective for Increasing Block Tariffs (IBTs) [14]. This method of tariff articulation provides for the planning of water tariffs which progressively increase as consumption increases. Each tariff is made up of a fixed portion and a variable portion. The fixed portion is aimed at covering the fixed costs of supplying the service, while the variable portion has the objective of promoting sustainable use of water by associating progressively higher tariffs with increasing blocks of consumption. The IBT structure intends to reward the most virtuous users and, at the same time, penalize those who consume greater volumes of water [15]. In summary, the Convergence Regulatory Scheme allows for the definition of the water tariff for each consumption block for water operators for which deficiencies emerge in the deeds and data necessary for tariff purposes. In other words, the Convergence Regulatory Scheme allows operators with difficulty to plan the gradual achievement of specific regulatory objectives over four years. Nonetheless, the scheme in question does not eliminate some critical issues. In particular, in the case of total absence of tariff, cost and consumption data, a recurring situation for low-budget business management, it is difficult to estimate the tariffs and define the consumption blocks for those operators characterized, in fact, by persistent criticalities.

To make up for the structural gaps inherent in the Convergence Regulatory Scheme, this work proposes a mathematical programming model, based on the simplex algorithm, which allows the definition of water tariffs and consumption blocks also for those less virtuous companies that do not have enough data on tariffs, costs and volumes of water consumed. The model can guarantee compliance with all economic constraints imposed by the National Authority (ARERA). The ultimate goal is to level out inequalities in terms of accessibility to water and to align the less virtuous operators with the more efficient ones.

The work has the following structure: Sect. 2 is dedicated to the analysis of the reference literature; Sect. 3 describes the regulatory constraints established by ARERA; Sect. 4 presents the proposed model; Sect. 5 shows the main conclusions highlighting future research ideas.

2 State of Art

One of the most used methods to solve problems related to the management of water resources consists of the modelling and simulation of water systems [16]. For example, through simulation scenarios in the management of water resources, it is possible to identify water pricing and market mechanisms, i.e., policies and strategies that envisage the use of economic incentives to manage water demand and allocate water resources more efficiently. The water pricing approach is to set rates that reflect the true cost of water, including the costs of supply, treatment and distribution. This can incentivize users to save water and use it more efficiently. In some cases, water pricing can also be used to generate revenue to support water infrastructure and conservation efforts. The market-based approach is the creation of water markets, where water rights can be bought and sold and water can be allocated based on market demand. The market-based approach can help allocate water resources more efficiently and provide opportunities for water users to trade the resource, ensuring that water is distributed where it is most valued.

Another useful method in solving issues related to the planning and management of water resources is the application of optimization techniques. Over the years numerous studies have been conducted aimed at the conservation and correct allocation of water resources through optimization tools [17]. Indeed, optimization methods can be used to determine the best allocation of water resources in a complex water system. This can help ensure that water resources are used efficiently and sustainably. For example,

Yang et al. (2012) apply a decentralized optimization method to solve a water allocation problem in the context of a river basin [18]. Second, optimization methods can be used to plan long-term water resources management, taking into account different future scenarios. This can help identify the most effective management options to ensure the long-term availability of safe drinking water. For example, Maiolo et al. (2017) devised a model for optimizing drinking water distribution systems to the effects of climate change [19]. Finally, optimization methods can be used to determine optimal water rates that reflect the true cost of water. This can incentivize users to save water and use it more efficiently. To cite one example, Pulido-Velazquez et al. (2013) present a method for simulating water pricing policies related to resource availability and for designing efficient pricing policies that incorporate the marginal value of water. They then followed two approaches: priority-based simulation and economic optimization [20]. In another work, Abdulbaki et al. (2017) present an integer linear programming model for the optimal treatment and allocation of water resources. The model seeks to minimize the total cost of water, including the economic cost of treatment and distribution, as well as associated environmental costs [21]. Macchiaroli et al. (2023), propose an optimization model aimed at designing sustainable water tariffs for users and, at the same time, able to discourage excessive water consumption [22].

Also in the present work, a mathematical optimization model is used. In particular, the simplex algorithm is applied to design the water tariffs and to define the consumption blocks in compliance with the constraints envisaged in the Convergence Regulatory Scheme. The simplex algorithm is a linear programming (PL) method used in operations research to find solutions to an optimization problem. It was conceived by George Dantzig in 1947 [23]. It is often the most efficient algorithm for solving linear programming (LP) problems [24]. The simplex algorithm is an iterative optimization method used to solve linear programming problems. In particular, the simplex algorithm is used to find the maximum or minimum point of a linear function subject to linear constraints. This algorithm is based on the idea of moving along the boundary of the feasible domain of a linear programming problem until reaching the maximum or minimum point. The feasible domain is the set of all possible solutions that satisfy the linear constraints of the problem. The simplex algorithm starts with a feasible solution to the linear programming problem. This solution can be determined for example by using the Gauss elimination method to solve the system of linear equations associated with the problem. Next, the algorithm tries to improve the solution iteratively. At each iteration, the algorithm selects a basic variable and a non-basic variable and calculates the ratio of the objective function value to the coefficient of the basic variable in the corresponding row of the constraint matrix. The selected basic variable is then swapped with the non-basic variable, thus changing the solution to the problem. This process is repeated iteratively until the maximum or minimum point of the objective function is reached [25–27]. The simplex algorithm has been used in some studies for planning water resource management systems [28–30]. But there are no significant examples of application cases aimed at designing water tariffs in compliance with regulatory constraints.

The following section describes the proposed model starting from the definition of the basic economic constraints introduced for those operators that must refer to the Convergence Regulatory Scheme.

3 The Design of the Water Tariff

In Italy, ARERA, for each regulatory period, defines the cost component and updates the tariff method starting from regulatory schemes. During the last period the national Authority had to integrate the methodology for the recognition of electricity costs to protect the economic sustainability of service operators due to the particular volatility of energy prices [31–34].

The Resolution n. 580/2019/R/idr (Water Tariff Method for the third regulatory period MTI-3) introduces the new provisions concerning the determination of tariffs for the performance of aqueduct, sewerage and purification services for the years 2020–2023. Through the application of regulatory schemes, it is possible to define, for each management, the value of the tariff multiplier ϑ, i.e., the coefficient by which to multiply the tariffs in force to update them to the expected costs and revenues.

The applicable tariff rules are attributable to two schemes: (i) the Regulatory Schemes Matrix, where the operators in possession of all the required technical and economic data can select the most appropriate operating scheme based on the starting conditions of the management; (ii) the Convergence Regulatory Scheme that presents simplified rules for management where there is a lack of data necessary for the preparation of water tariffs.

The Convergence Regulatory Scheme applies to management companies with persistent criticalities in the performance of service planning activities, and investment implementation and which have conditions of exclusion. In the case of the convergence scheme, the cost items to be recognized in the tariff are parametrically reconstructed based on reference benchmarks. The simplified rules are applicable only for the current regulatory period, at the end of which the management must refer to the ordinary Regulatory Schemes Matrix.

The Convergence Regulatory Scheme shall apply to those operations covered by one more of the following cases:

1. Tariff revenues, costs and management quality data are known;
2. Only tariff revenues are known;
3. Neither tariff revenues nor operating costs are known.

In the first two cases, the tariff multiplier, for each a = {2020, 2021, 2022, 2023}, is calculated as follows:

$$\vartheta^a = (1+\alpha Y), \tag{1}$$

where (α) is the *aggregation factor*, equal to 1.5 for those managements that have started an aggregation process and equal to 1 in the absence of this process. The parameter (Y) is instead the *increment factor*, which represents the ability over time of the operator to adapt to current regulatory provisions. In particular, it is equal to 5% for the first year, 4% for the second, 3% for the third and 2% for the last year.

In the absence of both revenue and cost data, the tariff multiplier is a function of the Operator's Revenue Constraint (VRG), i.e. the maximum value of revenues that can normally be obtained from management, as established for ordinary operators that refer to the Regulatory Schemes Matrix.

However, in the case of the Convergence Regulatory Scheme, this constraint is calculated in a simplified manner, taking into account only two cost items estimated on a parametric basis. In particular, we have:

$$VRG_{conv}^{a} = \left(Capex_{conv}^{a} + CO_{conv}^{S} \right), \tag{2}$$

where VRG_{conv}^{a} is the Operator's Revenue Constraint who does not have the revenue and cost data, $Capex_{conv}^{a}$ is the cost of capital set equal to $16\% \cdot CO_{conv}^{S}$, and CO_{conv}^{S} are the operating costs also estimated on a parametric basis, following the provisions of art. 17 of Resolution 580/2019/R/idr, to which appropriate simplifications are applied, not illustrated here for obvious reasons of synthesis.

The Area Governing Body (EGA), to which the management for which the convergence regulatory scheme is applicable, refers is required to fulfil a series of obligations for each of the years of the regulatory period. In particular, the obligations to be fulfilled within the first year are as follows: to carry out the recognition of the level of availability and reliability of technical data, to assess whether the water distributed to users complies with the Quality-of-Service Regulation (RQTI), to adopt a program for achieving compliance with the Urban Waste Water Management (RQTI) legislation. The obligations of the second year consist in certifying the correct preparation of the technical-accounting registers and defining the structure of the fees for each service. For the third year, the EGA must verify whether the operator has fulfilled the contractual quality data reporting and recording obligations under the standard (RQSII). Finally, for the fourth year, monitoring obligations, the preparation of registers, and the communication of technical quality data must be attested and the reliability of measurement data must be verified [13].

From the obligations of the EGA, it emerges that the structure of the fees for water services must be defined within the second year of the regulatory period, following the indications of Annex A of Resolution 580/2019/R/idr (Integrated Text for Water Services Tariffs - TICSI).

The proposed work focuses precisely on the structure of water tariffs, in particular for domestic users; domestic use accounts for about 73% of the total volume of water supplied annually on the national territory [35]. In this regard, the National Authority in the TICSI defines a structure that contemplates a fixed tariff portion, not correlated to consumption, and a variable tariff portion, proportionate to consumption and variable by consumption range. The latter portion is determined once the consumption ranges have been established using the standard per-capita criterion, i.e. considering a typical domestic user made up of three people. In the articulation of the ranges, again the ARERA regulation provides for a consumption range at a reduced tariff (T_{red}), a range at a basic tariff (T_{bas}), and excess ranges which can vary from 1 to 3 ($T_{exc1}, T_{exc2}, T_{exc3}$). If the adoption of the standard pro-capita criterion is used, for each domestic user, the subsidized consumption range corresponds to the interval between 0.00 m³/year and 55.00 m³/year (minimum quantity of water to be guaranteed for a user made up of three people). T_{bas} is stable by updating the basic tariff previously in force using the multiplier ϑ, T_{red} must be between 50% and 80% of T_{bas} (in this regard, it is the EGA that imposes the percentage value to be adopted on the low-budget business management), the maximum overage fee must be less than or equal to six times T_{red}. Also, the overage tariffs must be incremental to each other. The fixed tariff portion must not exceed 20% of the total revenues obtainable from the aqueduct service. Finally, the TICSI requires that the following constraint be respected (iso-revenue):

$$\sum_u tarif_u^a \cdot \left(vs_u^{a-2}\right)^T = \sum_u tarif_u^{new,a} \cdot \left(vs_u^{new,a-2}\right)^T, \tag{3}$$

where $\sum_u tarif_u^a \cdot \left(vs_u^{a-2}\right)^T$ are the revenues derived from pre $-$ existing articulations, while $\sum_u tarif_u^{new,\, a} \cdot \left(vs_u^{new,a-2}\right)^T$ are the revenues obtainable by applying the new tariff structure to the new reclassification of volumes consumed (or scale variables, vs) defined according to the TICSI criteria [36].

However, the application of TICSI in the case of operators that refer to the Convergence Regulatory Scheme appears critical for the aspects illustrated below. This occurs above all for case 3, i.e. when the operator has neither the tariff data nor the cost data. As is often found, these operators do not even have suitable data measuring the actual consumption of each user, or in any case, the information kit is incomplete and fragmented. It, therefore, becomes complicated to use both the per capita criterion based on actual consumption and the standard type to establish consumption ranges. Therefore, it is not possible to define in Eq. (3) the values of vs_u^{a-2} and $vs_u^{new,a-2}$, condition essential to comply with the iso-cable constraint imposed by the Authority.

To find a solution to the problem, further simplifying hypotheses are introduced in the next paragraph and a mathematical programming model is proposed which makes it possible to define the tariffs to be applied to each consumption class, also for those managements which use the Convergence mechanism in the total absence of data.

4 The Proposed Model

In applying TICSII to operators that use the Convergence Regulatory Scheme, the following water tariff ranges were considered (Table 1):

Table 1. Minimum tariff ranges for the aqueduct service.

Tariffs	Consumption ranges	
	Min (m³/year)	Min (m³/year)
T_{red}	0	55
T_{bas}	56	220
T_{exc}	>220	

The definition of the size of the three consumption classes and the use of a single excess tariff derives from the observation from the national average data to municipal management in economics [35].

In the absence of information on previous revenues and consumption for each user, the proposed model opts for the replacement of the first member of (3) with the Operator's

Revenue Constraint as defined in the case of convergence through Eq. (2). In this way, we obtain the following equation of the iso-revenue:

$$VRG^a_{conv} = \sum_u tarif_u^{new,a} \cdot \left(vs_u^{new,a-2}\right)^T. \tag{4}$$

The second member of (4) is equal to:

$$\sum_u tarif_u^{new,a} \cdot \left(vs_u^{new,a-2}\right)^T = \sum_u T_{RES}^{new,a}, \tag{5}$$

where $T_{RES}^{new,a}$ is the fee for the aqueduct service for a resident user, equal to:

$$T_{RES}^{new,a} = QF_{ACQ}^{new,a} + T_{red}^{new,a}q_{red} + T_{bas}^{new,a}(q_{bas}) + T_{exc}^{new,a}(q_{exc}). \tag{6}$$

where $QF_{ACQ}^{new,a}$ is the fixed tariff portion of the aqueduct service and the components q represent the volumes annually consumed by a user in a year, divided by the respective consumption ranges. In the case in question, in the absence of data on annual consumption volumes per user due to management criticalities, a distribution of volumes in tariff ranges derived from national data is considered [35]; in particular, the tariff relating to the first range (T_{red}) is applied to 34% of resident domestic consumption, the tariff relating to the second range (T_{bas}) is applied to 60% of consumption, and the tariff relating to the third range (T_{exc}) is applied to 6% of consumption.

Having defined the multiplier ϑ with the convergence scheme, the T_{bas} is known. $QF_{ACQ}^{new,a}$ and $T_{exc}^{new,a}$ remain unknown. To estimate these unknowns, defining a tariff structure that respects the constraints set by the TICSI, it was decided to resort to mathematical optimization tools [37]. The objective function is represented by (5), which by (4) must tend to VRG^a_{conv}, respecting the following constraints to follow (7).

$$\begin{cases} T_{exc} \leq 6T_{red} \\ QF_{ACQ}^{new,a} \leq 20\% \cdot VRG^a_{conv}. \end{cases} \tag{7}$$

The first constraint of Eq. (7) is aimed at containing the progressiveness of the tariffs (with positive effects in favor of large families), while the second constraint derives from the application of a criterion recently elaborated by the EU jurisprudence, which requires relating the fixed tariff portion to the "burdens borne by the water distribution services to make it available to users, in sufficient quantity and quality, regardless of the actual consumption they make of it" (judgment of the Court of Justice in Case C-686/15) [35]. In particular, according to the National Authority, the charges connected to the activity of measurement, qualitative analysis and those relating to the safety of water supplies are covered by the fixed tariff portion.

Once the nature of the objective function is defined, it is clear that it is a linear programming problem. For its resolution, the simplex algorithm was used. This algorithm, which can be implemented with the Excel software using the "solver" command, makes it possible to estimate T_{exc} and $QF_{ACQ}^{new,a}$, and therefore to define the complete tariff breakdown even if the Convergence Regulatory Scheme is used.

5 Conclusions

In Italy, despite the efforts of the Regulatory Authority for Energy Networks and the Environment (ARERA) to improve the Integrated Water Service, a significant disparity in the management and implementation of investments still exists between certain areas, mainly located in the southern regions and islands, and the rest of the country. The inadequacies in the South are primarily due to limited management and organizational capabilities, rather than a lack of funding. This is especially true for those managements entrusted directly to municipalities that operate water services at an economic cost. Between 2016 and 2021, the per capita investments made by these economically managed systems showed an average value of €8 per inhabitant, with significant differences based on geographic location. While per capita investments in the Northwest and Northeast are significantly higher, with an average of €23 and €18 per inhabitant, respectively, the average per capita investment value in the central and southern regions is €7 per inhabitant [12].

To reduce the Water Service Divide, new regulatory provisions have recently been introduced. The National Authority introduced the Convergence Regulatory Scheme with the Water Tariff Methodology - MT3 to overcome the North-South differences and lead less efficient water operators towards the national standard. This scheme allows less efficient operators to apply a simplified system for defining the tariff multiplier ϑ. However, the introduced simplifications do not seem sufficient to carry out the complete articulation of the tariffs by consumption bands, as provided for by the Integrated Text for Water Services Tariffs (TICSI). To address this issue, a model is proposed to allow for the complete articulation of water tariffs and compliance with the constraints imposed by ARERA. The model, which uses the Simplex Method, makes it feasible to apply the provisions provided for by TICSI even to those managements that do not have tariff data or cost data. The proposed model aligns with the community objectives regarding the management of the water resource, which require water tariff schemes to fulfil four different and sometimes conflicting objectives: (i) ecological sustainability, (ii) economic efficiency, (iii) financial sustainability, and (iv) social equity/affordability. In particular, it allows the operator to adopt tariffs that encourage users to avoid wasting resources, in compliance with the "polluter pays" and "full cost recovery" principles.

In the context of sustainable urban projects and urban regeneration, sustainable water management practices are crucial [38]. These practices can help reduce the Water Service Divide and promote ecological sustainability, economic efficiency, financial sustainability, and social equity/affordability in urban areas [39].

The next goal of the research is to apply the model to a case study, quantifying with appropriate simulations both the financial effects on the operator of the water service as a result of the definition of tariff ranges carried out even in the absence of data and also by analyzing the sustainability of the model for the utilities.

References

1. Babuna, P., et al.: Modeling water inequality and water security: the role of water governance. J. Environ. Manag. **326**, 116815 (2023). https://doi.org/10.1016/j.jenvman.2022.116815

2. Marotta, S.: Una questione di governance. Il PNRR e il "Water Service Divide" tra Centro-Nord e Mezzogiorno/A question of governance. NRRP and the "Water Service Divide" between the Center-North and the South. Cartografie sociali. Rivista semestrale di sociologia e scienze umane **13**(8), 83–100 (2022)

3. Babuna, P., Yang, X., Bian, D.: Water use inequality and efficiency assessments in the Yangtze river economic delta of China. Water **12**(6), 1709 (2020). https://doi.org/10.3390/w12061709

4. Druckman, A., Jackson, T.: Measuring resource inequalities: development and application of an area-based Gini coefficient. Ecol. Econ. **65**(2), 242–252 (2008)

5. Yang, H., Bain, R., Bartram, J., Gundry, S., Pedley, S., Wright, J.: Water safety and inequality in access to drinking-water between rich and poor households. Environ. Sci. Technol. **47**(3), 1222–1230 (2013). https://doi.org/10.1021/es303345p

6. Cetrulo, T.B., Marques, R.C., Malheiros, T.F., Cetrulo, N.M.: Monitoring inequality in water access: challenges for the 2030 agenda for sustainable development. Sci. Total Environ. **727**, 138746 (2020). https://doi.org/10.1016/j.scitotenv.2020.138746

7. ASviS – Alleanza Italiana per lo Sviluppo Sostenibile. https://asvis.it/goal10

8. Gruppo CAP. https://acquadelrubinetto.gruppocap.it/ambiente/acqua-nel-mondo/

9. Fondazione Utilitatis: Blue Book 2022, Utilitalia, Roma, Italy (2022)

10. lo Storto C.: Performance evaluation of water services in Italy: a meta-frontier approach accounting for regional heterogeneities. Water **14**(18), 2882 (2022). https://doi.org/10.3390/w14182882

11. Bucci, M., Ivaldi, G., Messina, G., Moller, L., Gennari, E.: I divari infrastrutturali in Italia: una misurazione caso per caso [Infrastructure gaps in Italy: a case-by-case measurement]. Bank of Italy Occasional Paper (635), pp. 1–37 (2021). https://doi.org/10.2139/ssrn.3896357

12. Fondazione Utilitatis: Blue Book 2023, Utilitalia, Roma, Italy (2023)

13. ARERA: Delibera 580/2019/R/idr del 27/12/2019: Approvazione del Metodo Tariffario Idrico per il terzo Periodo Regolatorio (MTI-3) (2019)

14. Klassert, C., Sigel, K., Klauer, B., Gawel, E.: Increasing block tariffs in an arid developing country: a discrete/continuous choice model of residential water demand in Jordan. Water **10**, 248 (2018). https://doi.org/10.3390/w10030248

15. Suárez-Varela, M., Martinez-Espineira, R., González-Gómez, F.: An analysis of the price escalation of non-linear water tariffs for domestic uses in Spain. Utilities Policy **34**, 82–93 (2015). https://doi.org/10.1016/j.jup.2015.01.005

16. Zeinalie, M., Bozorg-Haddad, O., Chaplot, B.: Modeling and simulation in water resources management. In: Bozorg-Haddad, O. (ed.) Essential Tools for Water Resources Analysis, Planning, and Management. SW, pp. 1–31. Springer, Singapore (2021). https://doi.org/10.1007/978-981-33-4295-8_1

17. Zeinalie, M., Bozorg-Haddad, O., Azamathulla, H.M.: Optimization in water resources management. In: Bozorg-Haddad, O. (ed.) Essential Tools for Water Resources Analysis, Planning, and Management. SW, pp. 33–58. Springer, Singapore (2021). https://doi.org/10.1007/978-981-33-4295-8_2

18. Yang, Y.C.E., Zhao, J., Cai, X.: Decentralized optimization method for water allocation management in the Yellow River Basin. J. Water Resour. Plan. Manag. **138**(4), 313–325 (2012). https://doi.org/10.1061/(ASCE)WR.1943-5452.0000199

19. Maiolo, M., Mendicino, G., Pantusa, D., Senatore, A.: Optimization of drinking water distribution systems in relation to the effects of climate change. Water **9**(10), 803 (2017). https://doi.org/10.3390/w9100803

20. Pulido-Velazquez, M., Alvarez-Mendiola, E.D.U.A., Andreu, J.: Design of efficient water pricing policies integrating basinwide resource opportunity costs. J. Water Resour. Plan. Manag. **139**(5), 583–592 (2013). https://doi.org/10.1016/j.resconrec.2019.04.004

21. Abdulbaki, D., Al-Hindi, M., Yassine, A., Abou Najm, M.: An optimization model for the allocation of water resources. J. Clean. Prod. **164**, 994–1006 (2017). https://doi.org/10.1016/j.jclepro.2017.07.024

22. Macchiaroli, M., Dolores, L., De Mare, G.: Design the water tariff structure: application and assessment of a model to balance sustainability, cost recovery and wise use. Water **15**(7), 1309 (2023). https://doi.org/10.3390/w15071309

23. Nash, J.C.: The (Dantzig) simplex method for linear programming. Comput. Sci. Eng. **2**(1), 29–31 (2000). https://doi.org/10.1109/5992.814654

24. Hall, J.A.J.: Towards a practical parallelisation of the simplex method. Comput. Manag. Sci. **7**, 139–170 (2010). https://doi.org/10.1007/s10287-008-0080-5

25. Dantzig, G.B.: Inductive proof of the simplex method. IBM J. Res. Dev. **4**(5), 505–506 (1960). https://doi.org/10.1147/rd.45.0505

26. Shamir, R.: The efficiency of the simplex method: a survey. Manag. Sci. **33**(3), 301–334 (1987). https://doi.org/10.1287/mnsc.33.3.301

27. Gale, D.: Linear programming and the simplex method. Notices of the AMS **54**(3), 364–369 (2007)

28. Miao, D.Y., Li, Y.P., Huang, G.H., Yang, Z.F., Li, C.H.: Optimization model for planning regional water resource systems under uncertainty. J. Water Resour. Plan. Manag. **140**(2), 238–249 (2014)

29. Gupta, M., Rao, P., Jayakumar, K.: Optimization of integrated sewerage system by using simplex method. VFSTR J. STEM **3**, 2455–2062 (2017)

30. Feng, Z.K., Niu, W.J., Zhou, J.Z., Cheng, C.T.: Linking Nelder-Mead simplex direct search method into two-stage progressive optimality algorithm for optimal operation of cascade hydropower reservoirs. J. Water Resour. Plan. Manag. **146**(5), 04020019 (2020)

31. Macchiaroli, M., Dolores, L., Nicodemo, L., De Mare, G.: Energy efficiency in the management of the integrated water service. a case study on the white certificates incentive system. In: Gervasi, O., et al. (eds.) ICCSA 2021. LNCS, vol. 12956, pp. 202–217. Springer, Cham (2021). https://doi.org/10.1007/978-3-030-87010-2_14

32. ARERA: Delibera 639/2021/R/Idr, Criteri per l'aggiornamento biennale (2022–2023) delle predisposizioni tariffarie del servizio idrico integrato (2021)

33. Dolores, L., Macchiaroli, M., De Mare, G.: Financial impacts of the energy transition in housing. Sustainability **14**, 4876 (2022). https://doi.org/10.3390/su14094876

34. Macchiaroli, M., Dolores, L., De Mare, G., Nicodemo, L.: Tax policies for housing energy efficiency in italy: a risk analysis model for energy service companies. Buildings **13**, 582 (2023). https://doi.org/10.3390/buildings13030582

35. ARERA: Documento per la consultazione 251/2017/R/IDR (2017)

36. ARERA: Delibera 665/2017/R/IDR, Approvazione del testo integrato corrispettivi servizi idrici (TICSI), recante i criteri di articolazione tariffaria applicata agli utenti (2017)

37. Dolores, L., Macchiaroli, M., De Mare, G.: Financial targets for the sponsee and the sponsor in the restoration/recovery of the historical and architectural heritage. In: Bevilacqua, C., Calabrò, F., Della Spina, L. (eds.) NMP 2020. SIST, vol. 177, pp. 155–165. Springer, Cham (2020). https://doi.org/10.1007/978-3-030-52869-0_13

38. Sessa, M.R., Russo, A., Sica, F.: Opinion paper on green deal for the urban regeneration of industrial brownfield land in Europe. Land Use Policy **119**, 106198 (2022). https://doi.org/10.1016/j.landusepol.2022.106198

39. Morano, P., Tajani, F., Guarini, M.R., Sica, F.: A systematic review of the existing literature for the evaluation of sustainable urban projects. Sustainability **13**(9), 4782 (2021). https://doi.org/10.3390/su13094782

Identification of Patterns of Socio-Economic and Spatial Processes via Principal Component Analysis and Clustering Algorithms. The Case Study of Southern Italy

Alfonso Annunziata(✉) ⓘ, Francesco Scorzaⓘ, Simone Corradoⓘ, and Beniamino Murganteⓘ

University of Basilicata, Potenza, Italy
annunziata.alfonso@yahoo.it

Abstract. The Implementation of place-based strategies and governance procedures to intervene in inland regions presenting critical socio-economic conditions
is a central aspect of cohesion policies at the national and European level. The
identification of configurations of socio-economic and spatial conditions specific
to distinct areas is a central element for defining targeted policies that combine
mitigation and adaptation strategies. The study proposes a set of metrics, based
on validated open data set, and combines Principal Component Analysis (PCA)
and clustering functions to discerne regions presenting specific configurations of
social, economic and spatial conditions. Six Italian regions, including Abruzzo,
Basilicata, Calabria, Campania, Molise and Puglia are selected as study areas.
The Municipalities are selected as the unit of analysis. The aim of this study is
to define a set of variables to understand the social, economic and spatial conditions specific to distinct cluster of municipalities and to discern distinct types of
marginal declining areas. The findings of the study provide relevant information
for the definition of targeted policies and for balancing adaptation and mitigation
strategies.

Keywords: Inland Areas · Principal Component Analysis · Spatial Analysis ·
Clustering · Open Data

1 Introduction

The decline and marginalization of rural internal areas are emerging as a central issue
of European and national policies. The 2019 Politcal Guidelines for the European Commission underline the centrality of rural areas as the place of residence of more than 50%

This paper is the result of the joint work of the authors. In particular, the data collection and
analysis were conducted by Alfonso Annunziata and Simone Corrado and the methodological
approach was conceived by Beniamino Murgante and Francesco Scorza. 'Discussion and Conclusions' was written jointly by the authors. Simone Corrado wrote the 'Literature Review'. The
sections 'Introduction' and 'Results' were written by Alfonso Annunziata. Beniamino Murgante
and Francesco Scorza wrote the 'Methodology' section and supervised the study.

© The Author(s), under exclusive license to Springer Nature Switzerland AG 2023
O. Gervasi et al. (Eds.): ICCSA 2023 Workshops, LNCS 14110, pp. 52–69, 2023.
https://doi.org/10.1007/978-3-031-37123-3_5

of European population, as a central element of European identity, society and economy. As a result, the preservation of rural areas landscape, and cultural, social and economic structures, and investment in rural areas' development emerge as relevant aims of European policies [1]. Similarly, Italian strategy for internal areas underlines the centrality of policies aimed at increasing social inclusion, development, and quality of life of internal areas, due to their extension - accounting for 60% of the entire country's surface area, including 52% of the municipalities and 22% of the population - as well as the significance of the environmental and cultural resources located in the rural landscapes. European and National Institutions recognize depopulation, marginalization, locational disadvantage and decline of economic activities as the main issues facing rural areas, and as the target of cohesion policies.

Moreover, consensus emerges on the need of targeted and coordinated strategies, integrating adaptation and mitigation. This perspective is based on the conceptualization of rural decline as a multi-dimensional process resulting from combinations of social, economic and spatial trends specific to individual areas. Hence, the recognition of local specificity is a pre-condition for the formulation of policies. The study proposes a set of metrics, based on validated open data set, and combines Principal Component Analysis (PCA) and clustering functions to discern regions presenting specific configurations of social, economic and spatial conditions. The proposed article describes the preliminary stages of a study, conducted within the framework of the research Project Mitigo, and aimed at investigating the conditions of marginality in the municipalities of the Basilicata Region, resulting from recognizable spatial and socio-economic tendencies. Six Italian regions, including Abruzzo, Basilicata, Calabria, Campania, Molise and Puglia are selected as study areas. The Municipalities are selected as the unit of analysis. The aim of this study is to develop a set of metrics to discern the social, economic and spatial conditions specific to individual clusters of municipalities.

The article is articulated on five sections. After the introduction, the scientific literature on the topic of rural areas' decline and the research method are described in Sects. 2 and 3. Section 4 presents the results of the analysis. Lastly, the findings of the study, its limitations and its future development are presented in the Conclusions section.

2 Literature Review

Rural depopulation is a relevant topic of national and European policies, of the political debate and of studies in the field of social sciences, environmental science, engineering and agricultural and biological science.

The analysis of the scientific literature, conducted via the Web of Science database and the Bibliometrics tool, returns 273 items containing, in the field topic, the terms sequence 'rural depopulation'.

The selected corpus of articles is cited 7,693 times, excluding self-citations, by 6822 articles, resulting in an average number of citations per item equal to 28.89, and in a H-index of 35. The most frequent terms, in the keywords field, are rural depopulation (55), depopulation (31), agriculture (10), land abandonment (10), rural development (10), land use (7), migration (7), rural population (6), urbanization (6) and land use change (5). Moreover, the analysis of the co-occurrence structures, underline the significant relation among the terms rural depopulation, land abandonment, land use, migration, urbanization, farmland abandonment, school closure, soil erosion, abandoned hamlet, land degradation. These interdependencies underline an merging focus on the relation among migration, population decrease, closure of basic services, and the depopulation's impact on environmental structures, in terms of land abandonment and degradation and soil erosion. Yet, rural depopulation is a component of a multidimensional process of rural decline or of 'rural shrinkage' [2].

Grasland et al. [3] define rural shrinkage as a process resulting in a significant decrease of population over a period equal to or superior than a generation. A distinction is to be made discerning active shrinkage, as a result of out migration, and legacy shrinkage, intended as a consequence of natural population decrease and regions' age structure. Moreover, out-migration can be determined by regional rural-urban processes or by transnational, globalized movements. A more relevant distinction discerns simple shrinkage, related to simple population decrease, and complex shrinkage, resulting from the interaction of social, economic and spatial processes [4, 5]. Copus et al. [5] identify four types of complex decline. These types of shrinkage processes can be co-present and interact within a region, determining specific configurations of cumulative causation of rural depopulation and decline. The four identified types of complex shrinkage processes are denoted as: economic restructuring, locational disadvantage, peripherisation and disruptive events. More precisely, economic restructuring refers to the decline in traditional labour-intensive agricultural practices and in extractive and manufacturing activities, resulting in land abandonment. Land abandonment, in turns, is related to relevant impacts on social, cultural and economic structures and on environmental systems, including depopulation, land degradation and soil erosion, decrease in biodiversity, and loss of cultural landscapes [6–8]. Locational disadvantage refers to local negative conditions, including isolation, sparsity, scarcity of natural resources, fragmentation of agricultural land, minor land productivity, determining negative impacts on economic development [7, 9, 10]. Peripherisation regards the macro-scale processes of spatial reorganization of economic activities and globalization [4]. Lastly, disruptive events, include historical events, political regime transitions, or political integration process. The Eu integration process, and related transnational rural and agricultural policy initiatives, the end of the socialist regimes era, and wars in the Balkan and in Ukraine represent major disruptive events [5, 6, 11, 12].

The complex interaction of social, economic and cultural factors related to rural depopulation is recognized in the definition of internal areas proposed by the Italian National Strategies for Internal Areas (SNAI). Internal areas are defined as regions that present conditions of marginalisation, in terms of distance from services of education, healthcare, and transportation, and where trends of contraction of human presence are recognizable. These trends result in trends of depopulation, population ageing, unemployment, land abandonment and decrease in the use of local capital. Lastly, a further aspect concerns the evolution of European rural and agricultural policies. This evolution can be described in terms of a transition on two directions: from an exogenous paradigm based on outer inputs aimed at sustaining rural economies and favour population retention to endogenous and neo-endogenous solutions, aimed at supporting the valorization of the territorial capital; and from mitigation strategies, aimed at inverting depopulation tendencies, to adaptation strategies aimed at increasing residents' quality of life in the context of the inevitability of local processes of rural decline. A consensus emerges in the political debate and in the scientific discourse, on the need of targeted strategies that combine adaptation and mitigation policies [4, 5, 13–15]. In order to identify areas presenting specific socio-economic trend and spatial processes, the subsequent section presents a method for discerning spatial clusters based on socio-economic and spatial variables.

3 Methodology

The study develops a set of indicators of socio-economic and spatial variables and uti-lizes clustering algorithms and statistical analysis to identify clusters of municipalities presenting similar conditions. The study is articulated on seven stages: i) selection of the area of study and of the unit of analysis; ii) definition of categories of socio-economic and spatial variables; iii) definition and measurement of relevant indicators; iv) Implementa-tion of Principal Component Analysis (PCA) to reduce the dimensionality of the variable space; v) Construction of the elbow plot and determination of the optimal k-number of clusters, applied for implementing the K-means clustering function; vi) implementation of the K-means clustering function and categorization of the units of analysis into k distinct clusters; vii) exploratory statistical analysis of the distribution of the values of a sub-set of indicators within each cluster (see Fig. 1). The area of study includes six Italian region – Abruzzo, Basilicata, Calabria, Campania, Molise and Puglia - comprised in the macro-area South Italy defined by the Italian National Institute for Statistics. The 1783 Municipalities comprised in the study area, are selected as the unit of analysis. The focus on the municipal scale is aimed at recognizing broad regional processes and configurations of socio-economic and spatial variables, and at the same time, at provid-ing a detailed description of the area of study that captures local specific conditions and trends. The socio-economic and spatial conditions investigated include conditions of access to services, education, Residential buildings, individual socio-economic status, digital infrastructure, Municipal infrastructures, Agriculture, Service and Industry sec-tors, and population (see Table 1). In particular, Access to basic services is measured via indicators of proximity to four categories of services: rail stations, hospitals, educational facilities, pharmacies.

Proximity is formalized as the number, weighted by distance, of services of the i-th category, located within a pre-determined distance from the centroid of the administrative area of each municipality. The radius is equal to 40 km. This value is identified as a relevant distance limit for evaluating proximity to occasionally accessed functions [16]. The four indicators of access to services AR40ST, AR40ED, AR40OSP, AR40FAR are calculated via the Attraction reach function of the Place Syntax Tool (PST) [17]. The Education system is described in terms of Percentage of resident population with a secondary education degree and in terms of Percentage of resident population with a tertiary education degree, measured for the year 2020. These data are retrieved from ISTAT open dataset. Moreover, the Quantity of services offered by the municipality compared to the average of municipalities comparable in terms of population, is utilized as a metric of public investment in reducing inequality in the education sector.

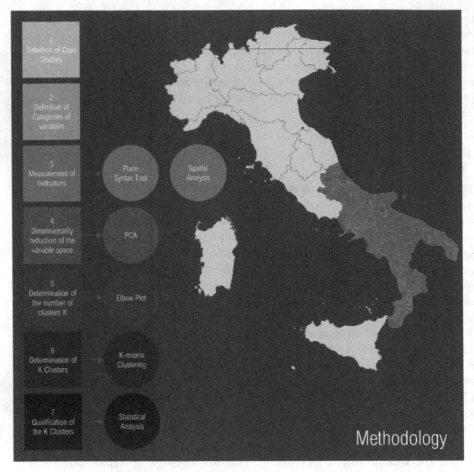

Fig. 1. Methodology and organization of the study

Table 1. Indicators of socio-economic and spatial tendencies in the area of study

Category	Indicator Code	Indicator Definition
Access to Service	AR40ST	Coverage of transportation services (RFI Stations), Radius 40 km
	AR40ED	Coverage of Education facilities, Radius 40 km
	AR40OSP	Coverage of healthcare services (Hospitals), Radius 40 km
	AR40FAR	Coverage of healthcare services (Pharmacies), Radius 40 km

(continued)

Table 1. (*continued*)

Category	Indicator Code	Indicator Definition
Population	RP6520	Proportion of the Population over 65 years of age, in 2020
	DPOP	Variation of the resident population over the 1981–2020 period
	P1000ED	Number of residents per 1000 housing units
	SMI_19_02	Aggregated Internal Migration Balance over the 2002–2019 period
	SME_19_02	Aggregated External Migration Balance over the 2002–2019 period
	SN_19_02	Aggregated Natural Balance over the 2002–2019 period
Socio-economic Status	R_C_10	Proportion of resident population with annual income in the range 0–10000 € - 2020
	R_IMP	Average annual income per taxpayer - 2020
	R_INAT	Proportion of inactive people to the resident population
Access to Internet	SP_GRE	Average Maximum download speed
	SP30HH	Number of Households served by internet network with speed in the range 0–30 Mbps
Municipal Infrastructures and Facilities	D_OUTGN	Amount of services offered by the municipality compared to the average of municipalities with equivalent resident population - 2018
	SSTDABGN	Standard Expenditure per resident for the provision of basic services - 2018
	SSTOABGN	Historical Expenditure per resident for the provision of basic services - 2018
Building Stock	P_ED_DIS	Proportion of available housing unitis to total housing units - average 2015,2016,2017,2018 (%)
	QIR22	Average Quotation of Housing units - 2022

(*continued*)

Table 1. (*continued*)

Category	Indicator Code	Indicator Definition
Education	D_OUT_IS	Amount of educational services offered by the municipality compared to the average of municipalities with equivalent resident population - 2018
	SSSG	Percentage of resident population with a secondary education degree - 2020
	TSTRZ	Percentage of resident population with a tertiary education degree - 2020
Agriculture	N_FARM_D20	Number of Agricultural Enterprise per Km^2 - 2020
	R_AGR18	Proportion of Agricultural land to the total surface area of the municipality - 2018
Local Economy – Industrial and Service sectors	VA_ADD	Value added per employee of local units (apparent labor productivity)
	ADD_MOL+	Percentage of employees in local units with a non-negative corrected Gross Operating Margin
	TUR1000A	Tourist presences - average 2015,2016,2017,2018 – Number of tourists per 1,000 residents

Lastly, demographic factors include population variation over the 1981–2021 period, percentage of population of age superior to 65 years, internal migration balance, external migration balance, and natural balance, calculated over the 2002–2021 period. Data related to population trends, level of education and to productivity of industrial activities are retrieved from the ISTAT open data set. Data related to investment for services at the municipal scale are retrieved from the Open Civitas data set. Data related to the number of farms are retrieved from the Italian Agricultural Accounting Information Network (RICA) data set. Lastly, data related to individual income are retrieved from the open data set of the Italian Ministry of economy and finance. For each variable, the most recent data, or the data covering the broadest time span are considered.

The dimensionality of the variable space is then reduced via techniques of principal component analysis, implemented via the GeoDa tool. The singular value decomposition, and the z-transformation are selected as the method and the standardization functions for the determination of the Principal components. Each principal component is calculated as a linear combination of the original variables, of the i-th category, that maximizes the explained variance of the set of the original variables [18]. The principal components are selected as the input variables for grouping the 1783 municipalities into k clusters, via partitioning clustering functions. The objective of Clustering functions is to determine compact set of similar observation, such that the intra-cluster similarity is maximized and the similarity among cluster is minimized. Similarity is formalized in terms of distance, in the multi-dimensional variable space, among each pair of observations i and j. A distinction is made between the distances of each observation in the j-th cluster from the other observations contained in the same cluster (intra cluster dissimilarity) and the distances of each observation in cluster j-th from the observations not contained in the j-th cluster (between-cluster dissimilarity). In the case of K-means clustering functions, which are utilized for this study, dissimilarity is formalized as the sum of squared Euclidean distances across the p-dimensions of the variable space. As a consequence, the objective of minimizing the loss function, is formalized as minimizing the sum of squared distances among observations within each cluster or, alternatively, as reducing the sum of squared deviations from the mean in each cluster, the within sum of squared errors. The compactness of the clusters is then assessed by calculating the ratio of the between clusters sum of squared errors to the total sum of squared errors. This measure is denoted as the Sum of Squares Ratio. Superior values denote an improved separation of the clusters. The value of the sum of squares ratio increases with the number of clusters, k. As a result, the definition of the optimal number k of clusters is a central aspect for the implementation of the k-means clustering function. An elbow-plot is calculated for representing the variation of the sum of squares ratio against the value of k. The rationale is that the optimal value of k is indicated by the point of the curve at which the improvement of the fit decreases. In the last stage, a set of measures of central tendency and variability of the original variables is calculated for each cluster and scatter-plots and probability distributions are used to model the distribution of data values of the original variables within each cluster. The objective is to infer spatial and socio-economic tendencies, specific to each cluster of municipalities.

4 Results

The Principal component analysis, reduces the dimensions of the variable spaces to 13 principal components. The set of principal components is selected by using the 95% limit criterion, that is, by selecting the minimum set of principal components required to explain the 95% of variance in the set of the original variables. The determination of the optimal number k of clusters returns a k equal to 7. As a consequence, The K-means clustering function is implemented to group the 1783 units of analysis into seven clusters, based on the similarity of the social, economic and spatial conditions, represented by the 13 principal components. A second clustering is implemented, considering a number of clusters equal to 8. The results, for k = 7 presents a sum of squares ratio equal to 0.499, thus indicating an adequate level of separation of the sets of units of analysis. For k = 8, the sum of squares ratio is equal to 0.517 (Table 2).

A preliminary interpretation of the results underlines the emergence of a compact cluster of municipalities contiguous to the City of Naples as a recognizable set (see Fig. 2). A second cluster, consisting of 202 municipalities, include the metropolitan area of Bari, and major urbanized areas, including the cities of Avellino, Battipaglia, Campobasso, Catanzaro, Chieti, Foggia, Isernia, L'Aquila, Lecce, Matera, Pescara, Potenza, Reggio Calabria, Salerno, Vibo Valentia, and industrial poles, including Melfi. Moreover, compact sub-sets comprised in cluster 3 can be recognized, including municipalities in the plain areas of the Apulia Region and of the Calabria Region. More precisely,

Table 2. Centroids of the Clusters

Principal Components	Clusters						
	CL 1	CL 2	CL 3	CL 4	CL 5	CL 6	CL 7
PC1_SPA	−0.83	−0.51	−0.27	0.40	−0.86	6.72	−0.45
PC1_EDU	−0.89	0.68	−0.29	1.56	−0.40	−0.20	0.88
PC2_EDU	0.20	0.39	−0.44	−0.24	0.46	−0.93	0.10
PC1_DIG	−0.60	−0.73	0.94	0.77	−0.94	1.87	−0.16
PC1_SERV	−0.05	0.12	−0.57	−0.26	2.35	−0.78	0.98
PC1_BLD	−0.55	−0.27	0.02	1.04	−0.91	1.90	2.25
PC1_SES	−1,33	0.66	−0.11	2.26	−0.98	0.74	0.32
PC1_AGR	−0.29	−0.13	0.63	0.29	−0.75	0.15	−0.80
PC1_ECO	−0.36	0.46	−0.18	0.27	−0.48	0.22	1.42
PC2_ECO	−0.10	−0.13	−0.04	−0.12	0.02	−0.27	5.82
PC1_POP	1.25	0.39	−0.97	−1.99	2.92	−3.19	−0.52
PC2_POP	−0.38	0.27	−0.22	0.42	0.84	−0.43	0.47
PC3_POP	0.00	−0.18	0.27	−0.61	0.04	0.75	−0.04

Within Cluster Sum of Squares							
	CL 1	CL 2	CL 3	CL 4	CL 5	CL 6	CL 7
	4023.08	3828.89	3671.93	2828.34	2277.98	1991.59	811.66

Sum of Squares Ratio	
SSR	0.499024

areas comprised in Cluster 3 can be qualified as areas of agricultural production. The municipalities comprised in cluster 3 present, in fact, a superior average density of farms. Mountain areas, presenting a median average elevation of 551.86 and of 502.36 m above sea level, are comprised in cluster 1, 2 and 5. Lastly, Cluster 7 comprises 30 municipalities presenting a significant tourism potential, denoted by values of the indicator average number of tourists per 1000 residents, ranging from 83.79 to 602.15 and resulting in a mean value of 254.99. Decrease of population is more significant in municipalities comprised in clusters 1,2 and 5. More precisely, the mean and median variation of population over the 1981–2021 period are equal to −0.311 and −0.322 for cluster 1 municipalities, to −0.119 and to −0.127 for cluster 2 municipalities and −0.473 and −0.489 for area comprised in Cluster 5. Population is stable in plain areas (mean equal to 0.036 and median equal to 0.010) and in the 30 municipalities comprised in Cluster 7 (mean equal to 0.057 and median equal to 0.064 respectively). A significant increase of population is observed in urbanized areas comprised in Cluster 4 and 5.

The mean is equal to 0.363 and the median to 0.280 in regional-scale poles included in Cluster 4 and to 0.351 and to 0.258 respectively in the Municipalities comprised in the Naples metropolitan area (see Table 3).

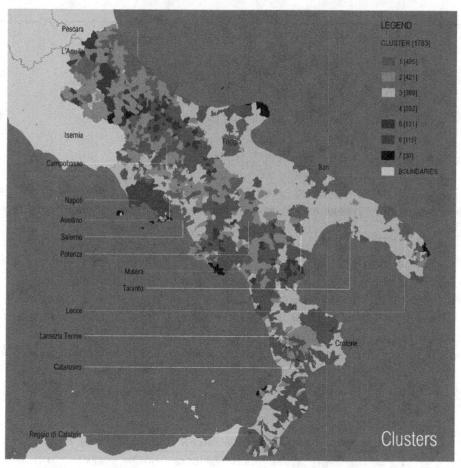

Fig. 2. Visualization of the seven clusters determined via a K-means Clustering algorithm

Table 3. Measures of Central tendency and of variance

D_POP							
CLUSTER	MIN	MAX	RANGE	MEAN	MEDIAN	STDDEV	IQR
1	−0.660	0.221	0.881	−0.311	−0.322	0.138	0.187
2	−0.653	0.450	1.103	−0.119	−0.128	0.170	0.242
3	−0.407	2.573	2.980	0.037	0.010	0.223	0.195
4	−0.389	2.588	2.977	0.364	0.281	0.414	0.453
5	−0.770	0.078	0.848	−0.473	−0.490	0.140	0.175
6	−0.338	1.718	2.056	0.352	0.258	0.417	0.450

(continued)

Table 3. (*continued*)

D_POP

CLUSTER	MIN	MAX	RANGE	MEAN	MEDIAN	STDDEV	IQR
7	−0.299	0.792	1.091	0.058	0.065	0.222	0.296

RP6520

CLUSTER	MIN	MAX	RANGE	MEAN	MEDIAN	STDDEV	IQR
1	0.192	0.442	0.250	0.280	0.276	0.039	0.052
2	0.178	0.361	0.183	0.258	0.257	0.033	0.043
3	0.142	0.303	0.161	0.220	0.220	0.028	0.040
4	0.119	0.287	0.168	0.212	0.212	0.028	0.038
5	0.230	0.564	0.334	0.349	0.339	0.065	0.073
6	0.096	0.245	0.149	0.169	0.167	0.028	0.041
7	0.185	0.287	0.102	0.234	0.235	0.024	0.030

SN_19_02

CLUSTER	MIN	MAX	RANGE	MEAN	MEDIAN	STDDEV	IQR
1	−320.65	30.61	351.26	−111.47	−107.93	56.72	75.08
2	−230.97	38.71	269.68	−89.09	−86.55	49.17	68.31
3	−122.20	168.85	291.05	−7.22	−10.68	43.97	61.17
4	−132.72	228.75	361.47	8.06	6.55	49.01	64.24
5	−560.10	−20.35	539.74	−232.59	−217.76	90.93	117.08
6	−38.66	379.64	418.30	74.66	68.60	56.64	71.63
7	−146.63	60.40	207.03	−26.67	−31.07	47.60	67.84

SMI_19_02

CLUSTER	MIN	MAX	RANGE	MEAN	MEDIAN	STDDEV	IQR
1	−399.41	126.81	526.21	−108.88	−108.38	59.85	74.07
2	−213.10	313.50	526.60	−49.59	−58.78	65.71	71.87
3	−310.13	246.43	556.56	−61.71	−62.28	64.52	67.98
4	−144.35	492.37	636.71	42.29	28.70	104.60	135.85
5	−914.29	245.49	1159.77	−116.50	−117.81	126.11	120.78
6	−238.52	677.69	916.21	−47.66	−67.65	107.72	99.25
7	−153.18	64.52	217.69	−34.70	−39.38	48.28	76.39

AR_40_0SP

CLUSTER	MIN	MAX	RANGE	MEAN	MEDIAN	STDDEV	IQR
1	0.00	10.90	10.90	1.97	1.63	1.57	1.96
2	0.00	24.23	24.23	3.92	2.90	3.14	3.74
3	0.00	25.59	25.59	5.24	4.03	4.51	4.93

(*continued*)

Table 3. (*continued*)

AR_40_0SP

CLUSTER	MIN	MAX	RANGE	MEAN	MEDIAN	STDDEV	IQR
4	0.04	36.89	36.85	9.61	8.81	6.29	9.02
5	0.00	9.89	9.89	1.81	1.32	1.73	1.56
6	20.76	70.45	49.70	43.96	43.94	13.55	22.39
7	0.00	9.51	9.51	4.04	3.22	2.99	5.38

AR_40_EDU

CLUSTER	MIN	MAX	RANGE	MEAN	MEDIAN	STDDEV	IQR
1	0.00	56.14	56.14	8.43	6.08	8.04	7.11
2	0.00	119.53	119.53	18.07	13.75	15.39	18.86
3	0.00	117.71	117.71	25.27	18.35	22.07	25.75
4	0.00	156.69	156.69	45.86	37.92	29.71	41.49
5	0.00	40.05	40.05	6.41	4.45	6.26	4.48
6	108.64	348.57	239.93	217.96	218.12	64.89	112.69
7	0.00	47.22	47.22	19.51	19.93	15.67	28.31

In terms of proportion of the elderly population on the total population, the measures of central tendency for individual clusters underlines the critical conditions of munici-palities comprised in cluster 5. In these areas, in fact, the mean value of the proportion of the elderly population is equal to 0.348 and the median to 0.339. Values, in particular, range from 0.23, observed in Monteleone di Puglia to 0.564, measured in San Benedetto in Perillis. As a result, 105 out of 131 municipalities comprised in cluster 5 present a proportion of elderly population superior to 0.3. This value represents a critical point, indicating the loss of the municipality's endogenous capacity to maintain adequate levels of demographic vitality. Critical conditions are also observed in municipalities comprised in Clusters 1 and 2. The mean and median values of the proportion of the elderly popula-tion are equal, respectively, to 0.280 and 0.276 in Cluster 1 municipalities, and to 0.258 and to 0.257 in Cluster 2 areas. Values are comprised in the ranges 0.192–0.442 and 0.178–0.361. A distinct condition is observed in the Metropolitan areas of Naples. The mean and median values are equal to 0.167, and the proportion of the elderly population ranges from 0.096 to 0.245. A significant component of population decrease is repre-sented by the natural balance. This is measured via an aggregated natural balance metric, calculated as the proportion of the aggregated natural balance over the 2002–2019 period on the total population measured in the year 2002 (see Table 3). A significant, negative trend is observed in the municipalities comprised in Clusters 1,2 and 5 representing mountain internal areas. In particular the mean and the median are equal to −0.232 and to −0.217 in Cluster 5 municipalities. Viceversa, urbanized areas comprised in Cluster 4 present a stationary condition (mean equal to 0.008 and median equal 0.006) and the Naples metropolitan area present a moderate positive natural trend (mean equal to 0.074 and median equal to 0.068). A significant variance of values of the internal migration balance is observed for all clusters. Yet, a relevant negative trend can be recognized in Cluster 5 and in Cluster 1: In cluster 5 74 out of 131 municipalities (56%) present an Internal migration inferior than −0.100. In cluster 1 275 municipalities out of 495 present a significant negative internal migration balance. Lastly, the external migration balance underlines a general positive trend, in particular in the Naples metropolitan area (mean equal to 0.048 and median equal to 0.038, in Cluster 3 areas (mean and median are respectively equal to 0.050 and 0.041), in urbanized areas included in Cluster 4 (mean equal to 0.056 and median equal to 0.048) and in internal areas comprised in Cluster 5 (mean equal to 0.093 and median equal to 0.072). Clusters 1, 2 and 5 present also critical conditions in terms of access to basic services. In particular, the average number of hospital in a 40 km range is equal to 1.97 for Cluster 1 Municipalities, to 3.92 for cluster 2 areas and to 1.81 for municipalities comprised in Cluster 5. Municipalities comprised in the Naples metropolitan area present the most favorable conditions of access to hospital. The average number of destinations in the 40 km range is equal, in fact, to 43.96. Lastly, a similar condition emerges regarding educational facilities. The average number of destinations is equal to 8.43 for areas in cluster 1, to 18.06 for municipalities in cluster 2, to 6.41 for areas included in Cluster 5. Viceversa, favorable conditions of access to education is observed in the Naples metropolitan area (mean equal to 217.96) and in urbanized areas in Cluster 4 (mean equal to 45.86).

5 Discussion and Conclusion

Clustering functions emerge as relevant tools for investigating processes that incorporate a spatial dimension. In particular, the analysis demonstrates the relevance of the proposed metrics and of k-means clustering functions as a tool for preliminary analyses aimed at discerning specific socio-economic processes co-present in a region.

The results, in fact, underline seven specific configurations of spatial and socio-economic conditions: i) a vast metropolitan area, emerging as a supra-local centrality; ii) a set of urbanized regions, emerging as local poles of services, and presenting co-presence of agricultural and industrial activities; iii) municipalities presenting a significant tourism potential; iv) areas presenting a significant concentration of agricultural activities; v) internal areas presenting distinct forms of decline and marginalisation.

As a result, the clustering functions, based on the principal components derived from the set of socio-economic and spatial variables, discern as specific clusters the declining rural areas, and, more precisely, identifies three distinct forms of decline. Municipalities comprised in cluster 5, in particular, present the most significant trends of population decrease and ageing. The decrease and ageing of population is reflected by economic conditions: Economic metrics, in fact, underline the superior incidence of income deriving from retirement pensions in cluster 5 areas (mean proportion of pension income equal to 0.397) and in cluster 1 area (mean equal to 0.358). Similarly, proportion of inactive individual is significant in cluster 5 areas, and is equal to 0.592. Viceversa, the proportion of income deriving from employment is inferior, and equal, on average, to 0.279 in cluster 5 municipalities and to 0.326 in Cluster 1 areas.

Moreover, areas comprised in clusters 1 and 5 present inferior average income, equal, respectively, to 12827.31 € per year and to 13585.70 € per year, and a superior proportion of residents earning an income of less than 10000 euros per year, equal, on average, to 0.442 in Cluster 5 municipalities and to 0.472 in Cluster 1 municipalities. Lastly, the level of productivity is inferior in Clusters 1 and 5, and is equal, on average, to 23.01 and to 23.45.

Viceversa, Cluster 2 municipalities present a moderate decrease of population (mean value equal to -0.118), combined with a relevant proportion of the elderly population (mean value of 0.258), and, compared to Clusters 1 and 5 areas, moderately inferior proportion of residents earning less than 10000 € per year, minor proportion of pension income (mean of 0.304), superior average income, equal to 15579.63 € per year, and productivity (equal to 27.15).

A preliminary interpretation of the results can lead to the qualification of the clusters of internal mountain areas in terms of distinct levels of decline: Cluster 5 municipalities reveal a condition of decline considerable as non-reversible, Cluster 1 areas reveal an advanced level of decline, and Cluster 2 a condition of mild decline. The discerning of distinct forms of decline underlines the need for targeted policies, based on specific combinations of adaptation and mitigation strategies. Considerations based on these preliminary results indicate the prevailing need, in Cluster 5 areas, for adaptation strategies, hence, for policies aimed at increasing the quality of life of residents. In Clusters 1 and 2 a combination of actions aimed at increasing quality of life and of mitigation strategies aimed at promoting economic development at limiting tendencies to depopulation can be considered as favorable. In particular, mitigation interventions in municipalities comprised in Cluster 2 and in Cluster 3 could privilege mitigation strategies aimed at valorizing the local cultural, natural and landscape capital and the residual economic potential, related to the agricultural and tourism sectors.

Inadequate conditions of access to basic services emerges as a relevant critical aspect of municipalities included in Clusters 1, 2 and 5, and as a significant element of marginalization and decrease in quality of life. Consequently, the implementation of alternative forms of provision of basic services emerges as a central aspect of adaptation strategies. For instance, the Italian National Strategy for Internal Areas (SNAI) prefigures a reorganization of the healthcare system based on a decentralized infrastructure of local facilities, including pharmacies, general practitioners, and alternative forms of service provision, including health homes, mobile health services, integrated home care.

Moreover, the SNAI prefigures the improvement of telemedicine services. Concerning transport services, the modest transport demand, locational disadvantages, and dispersed urbanization of internal rural areas, determine the need for the development of a multi-modal transport model that integrates public transit [19], active mobility and flexible and semi-flexible demand responsive shared transport services [20]. These solutions can include car-sharing and split car-sharing services, carpooling solutions based on autonomous driving vehicles [21], ride-hailing and shared ride-hailing [22]. A relevant aspect, central to the implementation of mitigation and adaptation strategies, concerns the improvement of the internet infrastructures. In clusters 1, 2 and 5 areas, in fact, the average proportion of households served by an internet infrastructure providing speeds ranging from 0 to 30 Mbps is equal, respectively, to 0.836, 0.884 and 0.953, and the maximum average download speed is equal to, respectively, 24.722 Mbps, 20.459 Mbps and 12.624 Mbps. Mitigation strategies, and in general terms actions aimed at promoting economic development, are frequently related to the valorization of sustainable forms of tourism, including eco-tourism and smart tourism, and to the incentivization of agricultural practices. In this perspective, the development of an agricultural production model based on multifunctional farms emerges as a relevant policy. Multifunctional farms are recognized as fundamental elements for the conservation and valorisation of the local capital and of traditional, sustainable forms of production [23–26]. The emergence of multifunctional entrepreneurial strategies in the primary production sector is considered a form of resilience and resistance to the crisis in the agriculture industry, and a valuable element for the conservation and maintenance of environmental and socio-cultural landscape values. The adoption of multifunctional strategies results in the diversification of agricultural production, particularly based on traditional crops and on conservation, organic, and biological farming practices. It aims at integrating agricultural production and complementary functions, including transformation and distribution of products, catering, accommodation, environmental education, nature experience, cultural services and maintenance of the rural landscape components. The notion of multifunctionality underlines the diverse potential functions of the agricultural sector in contemporary society, and in particular in marginalized areas: maintaining the vitality and adequate conditions for socio-economic development of rural areas, ensuring food security for the population, diversifying food production, and preserving the landscape. Moreover, the concept of multifunctionality in agricultural practices is related to the concept of sustainable tourism. Multifunctional farms, in fact, emerge as tourism experience providers in the context of alternative forms of sustainable tourism, including eco-tourism, geo-tourism and smart tourism. Eco-tourism refers to a form of responsible travel based on sustainable practices of nature experience, and aimed at promoting the local economic and social development, while minimizing the impact on the environment. It focuses primarily on experiencing and understanding the landscape, its flora, fauna and the cultural artifacts from the locality [27], and it aims to foster the involvement of local enterprises and service providers.

Tourism economy development can also be enable by strategies of tourism informatization, and in particular, by smart tourism; Smart tourism, in fact, refers to the integration of digital platforms and tools for improving the tourist's experience - by providing personalized and engaging experiences for tourists - and for enabling the instant integration of data related to tourist activities, product consumption, and tourism and social resources [28, 29]. Final consideration concerns the relevance of selected indicators. In particular, a main limitation to this study regards the limited availability of complete, integrated and open data set. In particular, data on the structure of economic activities, in the manufacturing and tourism sectors is provided at NUTS-3 regions level, thus not providing useful information for discerning social and economic trends specific to compact service poles, intermediate urbanized areas, areas of dispersed urbanization and marginal rural areas. Moreover, variations in the definition of categories, or in the procedures for the calculation of indicators, prevent the comparison of data related to distinct periods and, consequently, the reconstruction of trends at the municipal level. For instance, due to a revised definition of active enterprise, the data related to the Number of employees of local units of active enterprises calculated from the year 2019, are not comparable to data related to previous years. Lastly, the number of employees itself is defined as a continuous variable in surveys from 2012, and as a discrete variable in 2001 and 2011 census data. Moreover, privacy regulations require that data related to the structure of agricultural production at the municipal scale – including Net labor productivity, Net productivity of land, Incidence of public support, Net labor profitability, Net value added of labor and Net value added of land - are not available for municipalities where less than 5 enterprises are located. Similar criteria limit the availability of data relevant to the understanding of patterns of educational poverty: data, aggregated at the municipal level, related to the results of the Invalsi test, for the measurement of students' competences, are available for municipalities where two or more schools are located. As a consequence, the future development of this study will focus on the definition of metrics for understanding the socio-economic tendencies at the local scale, and for qualifying the clusters of declining rural areas in terms of specific social and economic conditions [30, 31]. The relevance of studies aimed at defining metrics for the analysis of the spatial distribution of social and economic trends and of conditions of access to basic services relies in their contribution in increasing the transparency and impact of public policies. Spatial information, in fact, can facilitate informed decisions in the context of the definition and implementation of cohesion policies [32]. In particular, spatial and statistical analysis techniques can assist public agencies and local governments in identifying distinct forms of complex rural shrinkage, defining adaptation and mitigation objectives, formulating targeted strategies, and measuring the outcomes of public interventions.

Acknowledgements. The study was supported by the Italian National Operational Programme on Research and Innovation ('PON', MIUR, 2014-2020) through the Research Project "MitiGO - Mitigazione dei rischi naturali per la sicurezza e la mobilità nelle aree montane del Mezzogiorno", ARS01_00964; CUP B44I20000300005.

References

1. European Commission, Directorate-General for Communication, Leyen, U.: A union that strives for more: my agenda for Europe: political guidelines for the next European Commission 2019–2024. Publications Office (2019). https://doi.org/10.2775/018127
2. European Committee of the Regions: The impact of demographic change on European regions. Publications Office (2016). https://doi.org/10.2863/26932
3. Grasland, C., et al.: Shrinking regions: a paradigm shift in demography and territorial development. Parlement Européen; Direction Générale des politiques internes de l'Union (2008)
4. Dolton-Thornton, N.: Viewpoint: how should policy respond to land abandonment in Europe? Land Use Policy **102**, 105269 (2021). https://doi.org/10.1016/j.landusepol.2020.105269
5. Copus, A., et al.: ESCAPE. European shrinking rural areas: challenges, actions and perspectives for territorial governance: applied research. Final report. Version. 21, 2020 (2020)
6. Lasanta, T., Arnáez, J., Pascual, N., Ruiz-Flaño, P., Errea, M.P., Lana-Renault, N.: Space–time process and drivers of land abandonment in Europe. CATENA **149**, 810–823 (2017). https://doi.org/10.1016/j.catena.2016.02.024
7. MacDonald, D., et al.: Agricultural abandonment in mountain areas of Europe: environmental consequences and policy response. J. Environ. Manag. **59**, 47–69 (2000). https://doi.org/10.1006/jema.1999.0335

8. Rizzo, A.: Declining, transition and slow rural territories in southern Italy characterizing the intra-rural divides. Eur. Plan. Stud. **24**, 231–253 (2016). https://doi.org/10.1080/09654313.2015.1079588
9. Alamá-Sabater, L., Budí, V., Álvarez-Coque, J.M.G., Roig-Tierno, N.: Using mixed research approaches to understand rural depopulation. Economía Agraria y Recursos Naturales Agric. Resour. Econ. **19**, 99–120 (2019)
10. Reynaud, C., Miccoli, S., Benassi, F., Naccarato, A., Salvati, L.: Unravelling a demographic 'Mosaic': spatial patterns and contextual factors of depopulation in Italian municipalities, 1981–2011. Ecol. Ind. **115**, 106356 (2020). https://doi.org/10.1016/j.ecolind.2020.106356
11. Pašakarnis, G., Morley, D., Malienė, V.: Rural development and challenges establishing sustainable land use in Eastern European countries. Land Use Policy **30**, 703–710 (2013). https://doi.org/10.1016/j.landusepol.2012.05.011
12. Ioffe, G., Nefedova, T., Kirsten, D.B.: Land abandonment in Russia. Eurasian Geogr. Econ. **53**, 527–549 (2012). https://doi.org/10.2747/1539-7216.53.4.527
13. Syssner, J.: Arguments for a local adaptation policy. In: Syssner, J. (ed.) Pathways to Demographic Adaptation: Perspectives on Policy and Planning in Depopulating Areas in Northern Europe, pp. 69–86. Springer, Cham (2020). https://doi.org/10.1007/978-3-030-34046-9_6
14. Dax, T., Fischer, M.: An alternative policy approach to rural development in regions facing population decline. Eur. Plan. Stud. **26**, 297–315 (2018). https://doi.org/10.1080/09654313.2017.1361596
15. Horlings, L.G., Marsden, T.K.: Exploring the 'new rural paradigm' in Europe: eco-economic strategies as a counterforce to the global competitiveness agenda. Eur. Urban Reg. Stud. **21**, 4–20 (2014). https://doi.org/10.1177/0969776412441934
16. Yamu, C., Frankhauser, P.: Spatial accessibility to amenities, natural areas and urban green spaces: using a multiscale, multifractal simulation model for managing urban sprawl. Environ. Plann. B Plann. Des. **42**, 1054–1078 (2015). https://doi.org/10.1068/b130171p
17. Stahle, A., Marcus, L., Karlström, A.: Place syntax tool — GIS software for analysing geographic accessibility with axial lines. Presented at the New Developments in Space Syntax Software, pp. 35–42 (2007)
18. Anselin, L.: A local indicator of multivariate spatial association: extending Geary's c. Geogr. Anal. **51**, 133–150 (2019). https://doi.org/10.1111/gean.12164
19. Harz, J., Sommer, C.: Determinants of success and constraints of integrated ridesharing in rural areas. Transp. Res. Interdiscip. Perspect. (2020)
20. Bruzzone, F., Scorrano, M., Nocera, S.: The combination of e-bike-sharing and demand-responsive transport systems in rural areas: a case study of Velenje. Res. Transp. Bus. Manag. **40**, 100570 (2021). https://doi.org/10.1016/j.rtbm.2020.100570
21. von Mörner, M.: 4 - Demand-oriented mobility solutions for rural areas using autonomous vehicles. In: Coppola, P., Esztergár-Kiss, D. (eds.) Autonomous Vehicles and Future Mobility, pp. 43–56. Elsevier (2019). https://doi.org/10.1016/B978-0-12-817696-2.00004-4
22. Elting, S., Ehmke, J.F.: Potential of shared taxi services in rural areas – a case study. Transp. Res. Procedia **52**, 661–668 (2021). https://doi.org/10.1016/j.trpro.2021.01.079
23. Organisation for Economic Co-operation and Development: Multifunctionality: Towards an Analytical Framework. OECD Publishing, Paris (2001)
24. Organisation for Economic Co-operation and Development: The New Rural Paradigm: Policies and Governance. OECD Publishing, Paris (2006)
25. Belletti, G., Brunori, G., Marescotti, A., Rossi, A.: Individual and Collective Levels in Multifunctional Agriculture. University of Florence, Florence (2002)
26. Meloni, B., Pulina, P. (eds.): Turismo sostenibile e sistemi rurali: multifunzionalità, reti di impresa e percorsi. Rosenberg & Sellier, Torino (2020)
27. Kiper, T.: Role of ecotourism in sustainable development. In: Özyavuz, M. (ed.) Advances in Landscape Architecture, Ch. 31. IntechOpen, Rijeka (2013). https://doi.org/10.5772/55749

28. Annunziata, A., Desogus, G., Garau, C.: Smart tourism governance for urban bioregion: an evaluating approach to the relationship between coastal and inland areas of South Sardinia. In: Building the Urban Bioregion Governance Scenarios for Urban and Territorial Planning, p. 290. SdT Edizioni, Firenze, Italy (2022)

29. Wang, D., Wang, F.: Contributions of the usage and affective experience of the residential environment to residential satisfaction. Null. **31**, 42–60 (2016). https://doi.org/10.1080/026 73037.2015.1025372

30. Corrado, S., Scorza, F.: Machine learning based approach to assess territorial marginality. In: Gervasi, O., Murgante, B., Hendrix, E.M.T., Taniar, D., Apduhan, B.O. (eds.) ICCSA 2022. LNCS, vol. 13376, pp. 292–302. Springer, Cham (2022). https://doi.org/10.1007/978-3-031-10450-3_25

31. Santarsiero, V., Nolè, G., Scorza, F., Murgante, B.: Geographic information and socio-economic indicators: a reading of recent territorial processes in the test area of Basilicata region. In: Calabrò, F., Della Spina, L., Piñeira Mantiñán, M.J. (eds.) NMP 2022. LNNS, vol. 482, pp. 2104–2111. Springer, Cham (2022). https://doi.org/10.1007/978-3-031-06825-6_202

32. Murgante, B., Borruso, G., Lapucci, A.: Geocomputation and urban planning. In: Murgante, B., Borruso, G., Lapucci, A. (eds.) Geocomputation and Urban Planning. SCI vol. 176, pp. 1–17. Springer, Heidelberg (2009). https://doi.org/10.1007/978-3-540-89930-3_1

Modeling of Landscape for the Integration of Agrivoltaics Using a GIS Approach

Grazia Fattoruso[1]([⊠]) [iD], Alessandra Scognamiglio[2] [iD], Andrea Venturo[3],
Domenico Toscano[4] [iD], Giulia Nardella[3], and Massimiliano Fabbricino[3]

[1] Photovoltaic and Sensor Applications Laboratory, ENEA RC Portici, P.le E. Fermi 1,
80055 Naples, Italy
`grazia.fattoruso@enea.it`
[2] Innovative Devices Laboratory, ENEA RC Portici, P.le E. Fermi 1, 80055 Naples, Italy
[3] Department of Civil, Architectural and Environmental Engineering, University of Naples
Federico II, Via Claudio 21, 80125 Naples, Italy
[4] Department of Chemical, Materials and Production Engineering, University of Naples
Federico II, P.le V. Tecchio 80, 80125 Naples, Italy

Abstract. Italy, with the highest number of UNESCO heritage sites worldwide
and among the countries with the most ambitious renewable (i.e., photovoltaic)
energy targets in Europe, is a living lab for experimenting with contradictions
and synergies between a traditional idea of landscape preservation, and the new
challenges offered by the introduction of photovoltaics in the landscape. The agrivoltaics has been emerging as a novel paradigm of integrated PV, making dual and
synergic use of land for agriculture and PV generation. However, the design of
agrivoltaic systems follows criteria that do not explicitly consider the landscape
features. The landscape preservation is mainly conceived as protection of certain
areas, and many projects only consider normative limits to realize the systems.
The objective of this research work has been to develop a GIS-based tool able to
implement the commonly descriptive approach used to address the integration of
agrivoltaics into the landscape pattern. Metrics have been properly defined and
evaluated to describe the landscape structure, its composition and spatial arrangement. They are applied to describe single landscape elements by such features as
size, shape, number or for whole landscape by describing the arrangement of landscape elements. A quantitative analysis of the landscape, given by this spatially
explicit approach, will provide preliminary inputs for the design of the agrivoltaic
patterns in order to achieve the most relevant landscape integration criteria based
on archetypes. This GIS tool is targeted at the policy makers as well as PV project
developers.

Keywords: Sustainable Agrivoltaics · Landscape · GIS tools

1 Introduction

Achieving energy transition goals to address global climate change and increasing energy
needs requires significant investments in solar energy. The expansion of utility-scale
solar development across the globe has increased the pressure on land resources for

© The Author(s), under exclusive license to Springer Nature Switzerland AG 2023
O. Gervasi et al. (Eds.): ICCSA 2023 Workshops, LNCS 14110, pp. 70–80, 2023.
https://doi.org/10.1007/978-3-031-37123-3_6

energy generation and other land uses (e.g., agriculture, biodiversity conservation) [1]. To address this growing issue, greater emphasis has been placed on integrated solar development strategies such as the development of agrivoltaic systems that co-locate solar energy production and agricultural land uses.

Originally, developing agrivoltaics meant merely dividing a piece of land for agriculture and energy [2]. Only in the last decades, the concept of agrivoltaics, making dual and synergic use of land for agriculture and photovoltaic (PV) generation has been emerging, with a large variety of novel agrivoltaic systems.

Beyond achieving the renewable energy goals in the near future, the agrivoltaics development might meet the effort to mitigate the climate change's impacts on the agriculture. In fact, it has also been emerging as a promising approach to improve the land productivity, achieve water saving, more generally increase the resilience to climate change.

Here, we refer to agrivoltaic systems as the co-location in synergy of ground-mounted photovoltaic development, though with specific configurations (i.e. raised PV panels, high porosity, etc.) and one or more of the following agricultural activities: crop cultivation, animal husbandry (e.g., livestock grazing, apiaries), or habitat enhancement to improve ecosystem services [3–5].

Ecosystem services are the direct and indirect benefits that ecosystems provide to humans. Agrivoltaic systems have the potential to influence positively different ecosystem services depending on priorities and implementation goals. Most clearly, agrivoltaic systems produce electricity and thus contribute directly to energy and economy. Their configurations can also support other services. Crops and livestock can be grown or supported on land co-located with agrivoltaic systems; natural habitat implemented at agrivoltaic systems can support plant and animal biodiversity, achieving conservation goals; thoughtful management can also result in beneficial regulating services, including carbon sequestration and water and soil conservation [1].

Thought, the large expansion of agrivoltaic systems is cause of concern and debate for the impact on the landscape in terms of landscape transformation and ecosystem services.

Italy, with the highest number of UNESCO heritage sites worldwide and among the countries with the most ambitious renewable (i.e., photovoltaic) energy targets in Europe, is a living lab for experimenting with contradictions and synergies between a traditional idea of landscape preservation, and the new challenges offered by the introduction of agrivoltaics in the landscape.

The authors are promoters at national and European level of a new idea of agrivoltaics, termed sustainable agrivoltaics [6, 7], aimed at maximizing the synergies among energy, food and landscape. Sustainable agrivoltaic systems have to optimize on the same unit of land energy and agriculture achievements making sustainable and harmonious the integration of them within the landscape.

However, the design of these systems follows criteria that do not explicitly consider the landscape features. The landscape preservation is mainly conceived as protection of certain areas, and many projects only consider normative limits to realize the agrivoltaic systems.

To meet the proposed sustainable agrivoltaics paradigm, the design of agrivoltaic systems has to be within-landscape scale including local ecosystems along with agriculture and photovoltaic systems.

At this scope, a spatially centric tool has been developed able to evaluate quantitatively the landscape structure, its composition and spatial arrangement, for supporting a sustainable and harmonious inclusion of agrivoltaic systems into the landscape pattern. This GIS tool is targeted at the policy makers as well as PV project developers.

The objective of this research is to bring together the large-scale deployment of agrivoltaics and landscape preservation. To do that, landscape analysis and management tools, such as that here proposed, are needed for supporting the development of agrivoltaic projects within-landscape scale so that they can be not only efficient but also *beautiful* and sustainable.

2   Material and Methods

2.1   Study Area

The study area is the Region of Campania. It is located in South Italy and lies between longitudes 13 e 16 E and latitudes 39 e 42 N (Fig. 1).

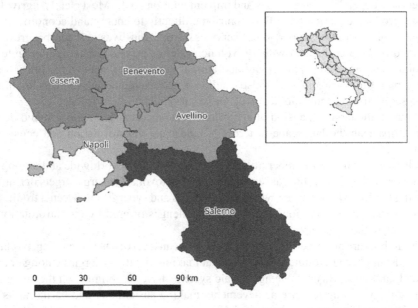

Fig. 1. Location map of the study area – Region of Campania (Southern Italy).

It extends over an area of 13.670 km² with a population of about 5.6 million inhabitants and a density of 424,4 inhabitants/km².

Its territory consists of 51% hills of 34%, mountains and of 15% plains. The highest mountain has an altitude of 1898 m s.l.m while the largest flat areas are the Plain of Sele and the plain of Volturno. Its climate is mild. Its annual average temperature is about 5 °C in winter and 18 °C in summer with cold winters and dry summers. The annual average precipitation is around 1000 mm. The annual global solar radiation value across this Region varies between 997 kWh/m²/year and 1664 kWh/m²/year. The annual average electricity demand is about 18414 GWh covered entirely from national production including only about 5% of photovoltaic energy.

According to the Corine Land Cover Classification, agricultural areas in Campania correspond to about 54% (5555 km²) of the total available are, followed by forest and seminatural areas with 3953 km² (38%). In the category of agricultural areas, permanent crops account for approximately 21% of the total, divided into 9.7% for fruit trees and berry plantations, 10.9% for olive groves and 0.7% for Vineyards. Also, in the category of agricultural areas a significant percentage is covered by non-irrigated arable land and Complex cultivation patterns, which cover about 20% and 32% respectively.

A site suitability map for agrivoltaic systems was performed by the authors for the Campania [8]. It returns that the eligible regional area is 342,305 ha, with 52% of the agricultural land being highly suitable for agrivoltaic systems and 47% being moderately suitable.

For the scope of this work, two study areas have been selected. The first study area is within the Basso Volturno Landscape Unit as identified by the Landscape Plan of the Campania Region. The second area is within the Vallo di Diano Landscape Unit as identified by the "Landscape Plan" of the Campania Region [9]. These study areas cover a surface of about 220 ha and 80 ha, respectively.

These landscapes have been selected due to their different structure, one with small land parcels and the other one with larger land parcels. They have been characterized evaluating the patches geometry and density.

2.2 Methodology

The objective of this research work has been to develop a spatial pattern analysis tool able to quantify the landscape structure in order to support a sustainable and harmonious introduction of agrivoltaics into the landscape pattern.

This approach aims to support the sustainable agrivoltaics development making dual and synergic use of land for agriculture and photovoltaic generation and minimizing the impact on the landscape pattern.

There is no a priori way to ensure that the integration of an agrivoltaic system into the landscape is effective i.e., sustainable, and harmonious, as this is mediated by the quality of the agrivoltaic project, which must be not only a technical project but also a landscape project.

What this means? It may occur that: (1) the land area occupied by the agrivoltaic system is too large with respect to the other elements of the landscape; (2) the orientation of the modules towards the Sun (South in the Northern hemisphere and North in the Southern one) determines a pattern with a single predominant direction (namely the

East West) determined by the parallel rows, and this can be striking with respect to the other geometric features of the landscape; (3) the density of the photovoltaic pattern (Land Area Occupation Ratio- LAOR) can be too high compared to the landscape pattern, resulting a strong sense of artificiality that does not suit the features of the landscape, especially when natural or agrarian [10].

So, keeping that in mind, a set of landscape metrics has properly been defined for evaluating quantitatively the landscape composition and configuration.

These metrics will have to provide preliminary inputs for the design of the agrivoltaic patterns to fulfill the most relevant landscape integration criteria (e.g., shape and size of the whole agrivoltaic systems, porosity of the systems, etc.), based on archetypes.

Defining Metrics

The landscape ecology [11–13] has provided the conceptual and theoretical framework for defining the landscape metrics for analyzing the landscape patterns to be applied in the agrivoltaic projects.

Landscape ecologists view landscapes as an heterogeneous spatial mosaic of discrete patches (i.e. basic elements that make up a landscape), each representing a zone of relatively homogeneous conditions, where the size, shape and configuration of patches can affects key ecosystem functions (i.e. biodiversity and fluxes of organisms and materials) as well as visual attractiveness of landscape [14].

The patches comprising the landscape are not self-evident; they are defined relative to the phenomenon under investigation. For our scopes, the patches are essentially identified as agricultural land parcel and they are extracted from remote sensing images. The patches are generally grouped by class according to the category of land cover and use.

Of these patches, the matrix is the most extensive and most connected landscape element type and therefore plays the dominant role in the functioning of the landscape (Fig. 2). The corridor is a linear connection unit between patches [15].

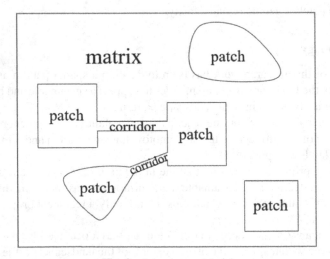

Fig. 2. A landscape Model

A landscape can be characterized by both its composition and configuration (or pattern). These two aspects of the landscape represent the landscape structure.

Landscape composition refers to features associated with the presence and amount of each patch type within the landscape but without being spatially explicit. In other words, landscape composition encompasses the variety and abundance of patch types within a landscape but not the placement or location of patches within the landscape mosaic (Fig. 2).

Landscape configuration refers to the physical distribution or spatial character of patches within the landscape. Some aspects of configuration are measures of the placement of patch types relative to other patch types, the landscape boundary, or other features of interest. Other aspects of configuration, such as shape and core area, are measures of the spatial character of the patches.

A first set of metrics, capturing patch geometry (i.e., shape and size) as well as patch density, has been selected. They are shown in Table 1. They are evaluated at patch and class level, though here the main class is agricultural.

Table 1. Landscape metrics

Metrics	Description	Formula
Area Class (CA)	Area of the patches of the corresponding class within the statistical zone	$CA = \sum_{i=1}^{n} az_{ij}$
Number of patches per class (NPC)	Number of patches for each corresponding class within the statistical zone	$NPC = nz_i$
Zone Area (ZA)	Area of the statistical zone in which landscape metrics are calculated	$ZA = TA_z$
Mean Area (MA)	Average patch area of a given class within the statistical zone	$MA = \frac{CA}{NPC}$
Largest Patch Index (LPI)	Look for the patch covering the largest area within the statistical zone, calculates the area of this patch and identifies the class of that patch	$LPI = \max(az_{ij})$
Total Class Edge (TCE)	Calculates Class Edge length for edges of all patches of the selected class within the statistical zone	$TCE = \sum_{k=1}^{m} ez_{ik}$
Edge Density (ED)	The length of the edges within the statistical zone per area defined by the user	$ED = \frac{TCE}{ZA} \cdot DA$

Evaluating the Metrics

Once defining the set of metrics, a zonal and statistical-vector based approach has been developed for evaluating these metrics [15]. It allows to evaluate the metrics within comparable areas, identifying, through these, any spatial patterns across the entire study area. As recommended in literature, hexagons have been selected as statistical zones for better analyzing the landscape for agrivoltaics development.

For evaluating the metrics, the following steps have been performed. First, the vector layer of land cover and use of the landscape unit has been extracted from remote sensing image by using *image segmentation* algorithms. Then, the extracted layer has been classified according to a specified set of land cover and use classes by *spatially based supervised classification algorithms*. Finally, a vector layer of regular statistical zones has been generated and the selected landscape metrics have been calculated for each class and statistical zone by using ZonalMetrics toolbox [16]. Two options of the ZonalMetric tool have been selected: 1) selecting the hexagons as statistical zones for better analyzing the landscape for agrivoltaics development; 2) performing the "select by centroid" method for selecting only the patches within the statistical zone having the centroid that falls within the zone, in order to guarantee the unique calculation of each patch within the study area. All these steps have been implemented within the ESRI ArcGIS Pro platform.

3 Results

The set of metrics, above defined, aims to characterize the structure of the agricultural landscape, previously evaluated suitable for the agrivoltaic systems with respect to solar and agriculture criteria (e.g., global horizontal radiation, annual average temperature, land slope and orientation, elevation, water deficit, land capability, Corine land cover and reduction percentage of irradiation) [8].

The developed methodology has been applied to two different landscapes falling into land areas evaluated highly suitable for agrivoltaic systems in the site suitability analysis performed by the authors for the entire regional territory of the Campania [8]. The selected landscapes are the Basso Volturno and Vallo Di Diano, in the North-West and South-Eastern of the regional territory respectively. From remote sensing images, the vector layers of the patches has been extracted and classified in 4 land cover and use classes: planted/cultivated, developed, water bodies, vegetation strips (Fig. 3, Fig. 4).

By calculating the selected metrics for the planted/cultivated class and for statistical zones, we have observed that the Basso Volturno landscape is characterized by patches with mean area less than 2 ha and a patch density of least of 10 on a statistical zone of 14 ha.

Fig. 3. Map of the agrivoltaics (high) suitable area of Basso Volturno (South Italy) including land cover and use layer and landscape structure layer.

Fig. 4. Map of agrivoltaics (high) suitable area of Vallo Di Diano (South Italy) including land cover and use layer and landscape structure layer.

For the Vallo Di Diano landscape, we have observed that it is characterized by patches with very low mean area (i.e. values between 0,1–0,2 ha) and a high patch density on a statistical zone of 3,5 ha (30–50 patches).

The zonal approach has allowed to evaluate the spatial pattern of the calculated metrics for the planted/cultivated class at landscape level.

In particular, for the Basso Volturno landscape, the Figs. 4a shows two continuity profiles related to the landscape feature *total area*, located in the central-south area of the landscape. They are characterized by a total area between 10–15 ha and 15–21 ha respectively.

The Fig. 6a shows that the zones with a lower number of patches (≤ 10) are mainly at North and East of the landscape while the zones with higher number of patches are located in the South-West of the landscape,

Therefore, 94% of the statistical zones are characterized by an average patch area of less than 2 ha. Patches with an average area greater than 2 ha are located in a single statistical area in the North-West of the landscape (Fig. 5a).

For the Vallo Di Diano landscape, the Fig. 5b shows that the landscape area at West of Tanagro River is characterized by zones with higher total patch area values between 3–3.5 ha. Figure 6b shows that the landscape is mainly characterized by zones with a low number of patches (≤ 30). Then, the zones with a higher number of patches (between 30 and 50 patches) are located mainly at West of Tanagro River.

Finally, the Fig. 7b shows that the landscape is characterized by patches with a very low average area, between 0.1–0.2 ha and by a very high patch density at the zone level (30–50 patches in 3.5 ha).

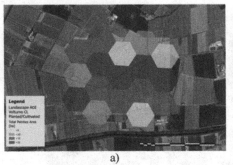 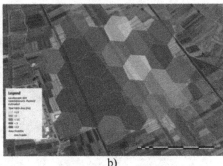

a)   b)

Fig. 5. Map of the landscape feature *total patch area* calculated for the planted/cultivated class and for each statistical zone. a) Basso Volturno landscape. b) Vallo di Diano landscape

Fig. 6. Map of the landscape feature *average patch area* calculated for the planted/cultivated class for each statistical zone. a) Basso Volturno landscape. b) Vallo di Diano landscape.

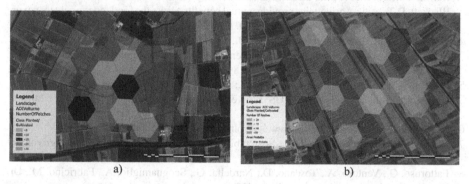

Fig. 7. Map of Map of the landscape feature *number of patches* calculated for the planted/cultivated class and for each statistical zone. a) Basso Volturno landscape. b) Vallo di Diano landscape.

4 Conclusion

The structure of the landscapes of Basso Volturno and Vallo di Diano has been quantitatively evaluated through specific landscape metrics here properly defined aimed at providing preliminary inputs for the design of sustainable agrivoltaic projects.

These landscapes have represented the study case for the development of a spatial pattern analysis tool able to evaluate quantitatively the landscape structure for sustainable agrivoltaics development. A preliminary set of landscape metrics has been properly defined for evaluating landscape features such as size and number of patches within-zone scale as well as their spatial arrangement across the whole landscape. The innovative vector/zonal based approach proposed allows to evaluate the metrics within comparable areas and to identify any spatial patterns on the entire landscape. The investigated approach aims to support the analysis of the landscape transformation can be inducted by the agrivoltaics expansion within the landscapes as well as support an inclusive and sustainable process of the agrivoltaics development in the surrounding landscape.

Funding. This research is funded by the ongoing projects: Ricerca del Sistema Elettrico - Progetto Integrato Fotovoltaico ad alta efficienza National Project PTR 22-24 and EU HORIZON Project SYMBIOSYST Create a Symbiosis where PV and agriculture can have a mutually beneficial relationship. Prj. N.101096352 - GAP-101096352.

References

1. Walston, L.J., et al.: Opportunities for agrivoltaic systems to achieve synergistic food-energy environmental needs and address sustainability goals. Front. Sustain. Food Syst. **6**, 374 (2022). https://doi.org/10.3389/fsufs.2022.932018
2. Goetzberger, A., Zastrow, A.: On the coexistence of solar-energy conversion and plant cultivation. Int. J. Sol. Energy **1**(1), 55–69 (1982). https://doi.org/10.1080/01425918208909875
3. Barron-Gafford, G.A., Pavao-Zuckerman, M.A., Minor, R.L., Sutter, L.F., Barnett-Moreno, I., Blackett, D.T., et al.: Agrivoltaics provide mutual benefits across the food–energy–water nexus in drylands. Nat. Sustain. **2**, 848–855 (2019). https://doi.org/10.1038/s41893-019-0364-5
4. Hernandez, R.R., Armstrong, A., Burney, J., Ryan, G., Moore-O'Leary, K., Diédhiou, I., et al.: Techno-ecological synergies of solar energy for global sustainability. Nat. Sustain. **2**, 560–568 (2019). https://doi.org/10.1038/s41893-019-0309-z
5. Proctor, K.W., Murthy, G.S., Higgins, C.W.: Agrivoltaics align with green new deal goals while supporting investment in the US' rural economy. Sustainability **13**, 137 (2021). https://doi.org/10.3390/su13010137
6. Agrivoltaico Sostenibile. https://www.agrivoltaicosostenibile.com/
7. Associazione Italiana Agrivoltaico Sostenibile. https://www.associazioneitalianagrivoltaicosostenibile.com
8. Fattoruso, G., Venturo, A., Toscano, D., Nardella, G., Scognamiglio, A., Fabricino, M., Di Francia, G.: Manuscript in preparation (2023)
9. Piano Paesaggistico Regionale (PPR). https://www.territorio.regione.campania.it/paesaggio-blog/piano-paesaggistico-regionale-ppr
10. Scognamiglio, A.: 'Photovoltaic landscapes': design and assessment. A critical review for a new transdisciplinary design vision. Renew. Sustain. Energy Rev. **55**, 629–661 (2016). https://doi.org/10.1016/j.rser.2015.10.072
11. Forman, R.T.T., Godron, M.: Landscape Ecology. Wiley, New York (1986)
12. Turner, M.G.: Landscape ecology: the effect of pattern on process. Annu. Rev. Ecol. Syst. **20**(1), 171–197 (1989). https://doi.org/10.1146/annurev.es.20.110189.001131
13. Urban D.L., O'Neill R.V., Shugart Jr., H.H.: Landscape ecology. A hierarchical perspective can help scientists understand spatial patterns. Bioscience **37**, 119–127 (1987)
14. McGarigal, K., Cushman, S.A., Neel, M.C., Ene, E.: Spatial pattern analysis program for categorical maps (2002). www.umass.edu/landeco/research/fragstats/fragstats.html
15. Forman, R.T.T.: Land Mosaics: the Ecology of Landscapes and Regions. Cambridge University Press, Cambridge (1995)
16. Adamczyk, J., Tiede, D.: ZonalMetrics-a Python toolbox for zonal landscape structure analysis. Comput. Geosci. **99**, 91–99 (2017). https://doi.org/10.1016/j.cageo.2016.11.005

Tourism Ecosystem Domains

Rachele Vanessa Gatto⬛ and Francesco Scorza(✉)⬛

School of Engineering, Laboratory of Urban and Regional Systems Engineering (LISUT),
University of Basilicata, Potenza, Italy
{rachelevanessa.gatto,francesco.scorza}@unibas.it

Abstract. The study deals with the effects of tourism promoted by European Union public investment policies. Tourism is considered as a cross-cutting area topic that receives strategies and funds aimed at promoting socio-economic development and enhancing resources in marginal areas. While it is true that an increase in attractiveness leads to an increase in tourist flows and demand for goods and services, the actual positive impact in terms of territorial capital growth and increased quality of life for residents remains uncertain. Following significant funding and the implementation of a specialized tourism policy, the current indicators used to monitor investment reconstruct a scenario that is poorly articulated with regard to potential externalities. The paper argues that tourism cannot be evaluated solely from an economic or environmental point of view, but has to be considered as a relational phenomenon involving different actors and disciplines. The use of an integrated and multidisciplinary framework based on the network of relationships between the interested parties allow for a more precise and complete assessment of the impact of tourism on the territory, thus providing a solid basis for the development of tourism policies and strategies based on sustainability principles.

Keywords: Sustainable tourism · rural areas · tourism policies · tourism ecosystem

1 Introduction

The main objective of the Cohesion Policy is to promote greater equity and cohesion among the regions of the European Union through the allocation of funds to balance economic and social differences between these areas. This means that economically less developed regions receive greater financial support to develop and improve their economies, in order to reach a level of development closer to that of the more developed regions of the EU. The regional cohesion policy contributes to promote the economic and social growth of the European Union, by fostering the balanced development of regions and ensuring cohesion among them. It represents a main component in regional development programs and policies [1] and, according to the perspective of the authors, the place-based criteria still remains a major objective in order to improve the effectiveness in local implementation [2–7].

The main financial instruments of the cohesion policy are the European Regional Development Fund (ERDF), the European Social Fund (ESF), and the Cohesion Fund.

© The Author(s), under exclusive license to Springer Nature Switzerland AG 2023
O. Gervasi et al. (Eds.): ICCSA 2023 Workshops, LNCS 14110, pp. 81–89, 2023.
https://doi.org/10.1007/978-3-031-37123-3_7

The ERDF provides funding for projects related to research and innovation, competitiveness of enterprises, environment, sustainable mobility, and energy. Tourism as an investment sector represents a potential driver for the integration of funding and local programming to lead the sustainable development of marginalized areas and, sometimes the local implementation experiences not clearly demonstrate the effectiveness of public investments against the general territorial development objectives [8–10].

The benefits generated by tourism in terms of job creation and income generation can also help to preserve and promote local cultural heritage and natural resources [11].

One of the key strategies for rural tourism development is the creation of attractive and high-quality tourism products that are tailored to the needs and interests of different types of tourists. This can be achieved through the development of specialized tourism services and products that are designed to showcase the unique characteristics and resources of the rural area integrating prominent tangible and immaterial tourism assets (natural, cultural, social) [12]. For example, rural areas with rich cultural heritage can develop cultural tourism products [13], while those with natural resources such as forests and lakes can focus on outdoor and nature-based tourism [14].

Another important strategy for tourism development is the establishment of partnerships and networks among local stakeholders, including tourism service providers, local communities, and public authorities. It has to be intended as a network of interrelated and interdependent players, resources, and processes [15]. Collaboration and cooperation can help to ensure that tourism development is sustainable, benefits local communities, and minimizes negative impacts on the environment.

Infrastructure development is also crucial for rural tourism development. This includes not only traditional infrastructure such as transportation and accommodation facilities but also digital infrastructure such as broadband internet access and online marketing platforms. Capacity building and training programs for local residents and tourism service providers can help to enhance the quality of tourism services and products, as well as improve the overall competitiveness of the rural tourism sector.

Tourism can be an effective tool for rural development [14], and the strategic components outlined above can help to ensure that rural tourism development could be characterized by an high sustainability level, benefits local communities, and could effectively contribute to the preservation of local cultural and natural resources. The strategic effort in ensuring that tourism development represent and effective and sustainable development model benefitting local communities, while minimizing negative impacts on the environment, represents the general policy making thinking but more efforts have to be paied in order to design place based strategy integrating local values.

The New 2030 Urban Agenda, supports planning practices addressing effective objectives for the development of rural and marginalized areas aiming to improve the quality of life and to promote sustainable development in rural and marginal areas. The NUA, the agenda aims to protect the environment and ecosystems of rural and marginal territories, promote local culture and heritage and improve the energy efficiency and environmental sustainability of the territories themselves. Those principles fit with the generalized understanding of tourism development in EU Regional development programs. What seems to be weak is the downscaling process of those principles, and according to the evidences of recent researches [16–20], specialized knowledge is needed to improve the current planning and programming practices in order to manage the local dimension of NUA.

The organization focuses on encouraging responsible resource consumption, conserving cultural and natural heritage, and ensuring respect for local communities and their interests. In addition, the UNWTO emphasizes the use of sustainable tourism indicators and certification schemes to measure and enhance the sustainability performance of tourism businesses and destinations.

2 Specialized Tourism in Inland Rural Areas and Assessment

The development of tourism in in-land rural areas is closely related to sustainable development objectives. Sustainable tourism is defined as *"tourism that takes full account of its current and future economic, social, and environmental impacts, addressing the needs of visitors, the industry, the environment, and host communities"* [21]. In this context, the development of tourism in in-land rural areas can contribute to the achievement of several sustainable development goals.

Assessing the impact of tourism on the territory is a crucial activity for understanding the effective sustainability of the tourism industry and for adopting the necessary measures to minimize negative impacts and maximize economic, social and environmental benefits.

In this sense, various tools have been developed in recent years to monitor the impact of tourism on the territory and to adopt the necessary countermeasures [22]. Among the main tools for evaluating the impact of tourism on the territory we find indicators of tourism sustainability, which have been developed to evaluate the impact of tourism on various aspects of sustainability, such as the environment, the economy and society. The tourism sustainability indicators are based on quantitative and qualitative data collected through field surveys, public policy analyzes and stakeholder interviews.

However, it is important to underline that the assessment of the impact of tourism on the territory can be influenced by various factors, such as the specific characteristics of tourist destinations, the size of the tourism industry and the public policies adopted by local authorities. Furthermore, data collection can be difficult and costly, necessitating the adoption of innovative methods and advanced technologies for data collection and information analysis. In summary, the evaluation of the impact of tourism on the territory is a complex activity.

The European Commission uses a number of indicators to assess the impact of tourism on sustainability. Among these, there are economic indicators that measure the contribution of tourism to GDP, employment and exports. In addition, social indicators are also used, which evaluate the accessibility of tourism to different social groups, cultural impact and visitor satisfaction. Environmental indicators, on the other hand, measure the impact of tourism on the use of water and energy, on CO_2 emissions and on the waste produced. However, these indicators do not yet represent a complete assessment of the impact of tourism on sustainability in a robust framework.

The fragmented disciplinary approach to tourism analysis often leads to an inadequate evaluation of tourism strategies. Tourism is a complex phenomenon that involves different dimensions, such as economic, social, cultural, environmental, and political aspects. However, the disciplinary approach tends to focus on a single dimension, neglecting the others and failing to capture the complexity of tourism impacts.

For example, an economic analysis of tourism may only consider the financial benefits generated by tourist activities without examining their social and environmental impacts. Similarly, a cultural analysis of tourism may only focus on the preservation of cultural heritage without considering the economic and environmental consequences of tourism development. It is a challenging task to evaluate the effectiveness of tourist public funding, and many approaches have been put out to measure its influence. Utilizing economic metrics like job growth, income generation, and tax receipts is one strategy [22]. Another strategy is to consider social and environmental indicators including participation in the community, preserving the environment and cultural preservation [23, 24] the metrics of visitors and residents satisfaction represent a valuable indicator to inform decision making process in front to the management of current tourism policies and strategic decision making [25].

This fragmented approach can lead to incomplete and biased assessments of tourism impacts and policies, potentially resulting in negative consequences for local communities and the environment. Therefore, a more comprehensive and integrated approach is needed to evaluate the sustainability and effectiveness of tourism strategies. This approach should involve interdisciplinary collaboration and the use of multiple evaluation tools and indicators that capture the various dimensions of tourism impacts.

Thus, more comprehensive and context-specific monitoring frameworks are needed to reflect the multidimensional nature of sustainable tourism, allowing for effective decision-making and policy implementation.

3 Tourism Ecosystem

The tourism industry is often seen as a purely economic activity that revolves around providing services to tourists and generating revenue for the local economy [26]. However, this perspective fails to recognize the relational nature of tourism [27].

Tourism involves the interaction between tourists and the host community, which includes not only businesses but also residents and other stakeholders. Tourists visit a destination to experience its culture, environment, and people. The host community, in turn, provides the necessary infrastructure and services for tourists to enjoy their stay. Thus, tourism is a complex reciprocal relationship that involves the exchange of goods, services, and experiences between tourists and the host community [15].

Furthermore, tourism can have a significant impact on the relationship between tourists and the host community. Tourists can bring new perspectives and ideas to a destination, while the host community can offer unique cultural experiences and traditions. However, if not managed properly, tourism can also lead to conflicts between tourists and locals over issues such as overcrowding, environmental degradation, and cultural exploitation such as over-tourism phenomena.

Therefore, it is important to view tourism as a relational activity and to consider the needs and interests of all stakeholders involved in tourism development. This includes involving the local community in decision-making processes, promoting sustainable tourism practices, and fostering a positive relationship between tourists and the host community.

According with those considerations the proposed definition of "tourism ecosystem" is: *A tourist ecosystem is defined as a network of interrelated and interdependent nodes that characterize a tourist destination area providing benefits in a territorial development scenario* (ref. [20]).

The tourism ecosystem is made up of multiple actors and disciplines that interact with each other to create a satisfying travel experience for tourists and to support the development of the local tourism sector. In this ecosystem, there are many interdisciplinary functions that allow the creation and optimization of the tourist offer. For example, marketing activities require close collaboration between marketing experts, tourism professionals, social scientists and hotel industry specialists, in order to identify the needs of tourists and promote the territory effectively.

Furthermore, tourism destination management requires collaboration between urban planners, architects, landscapers and local authorities in order to create quality and sustainable tourism infrastructures that considers the needs of tourists and local residents. Environmental management of the tourism ecosystem requires cooperation between experts in biology, ecology and environmental sciences, to ensure that the tourism activity does not damage local ecosystems and that sustainable management practices are adopted. Finally, staff training and management requires collaboration between training experts, tourism professionals and local authority representatives, in order to ensure that tourism staff have the necessary skills and knowledge to deliver a quality service to tourists. In summary, the interdisciplinary function (Fig. 1) of the tourist ecosystem is essential to guarantee a quality and sustainable tourist offer, which satisfies the needs of tourists and supports the development of the territory.

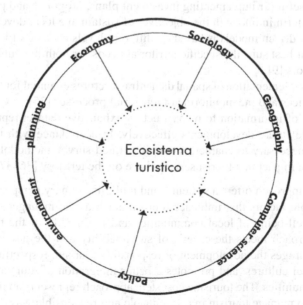

Fig. 1. Interdisciplinary tourism function

4 Final Remarks

According to the concept of "tourism ecosystem", the emerging approach in tourism development based represents a promising prospect for enhancing local approaches and applications within the paradigms of the NUA 2030 agenda. Compatibly with the objectives of the PNRR - tourism transition 4.0 - the outcome of the evaluation structures the network relationship between the actors of the tourism chain involved. The general issues in planning for tourism development: anticipating and monitoring the results of governance choices through measuring the impact on the social, environmental and economic components; could be organized in an operative dimension and supported by effective information tools. In particular, this research is grounded in the wider research project called "Tech4You" and will benefit of an extensive effort in developing spatial knowledge infrastructure for tourism development strategies for rebalancing the growth of Southern areas of Italy.

The "tourist ecosystem" approach remakes the fundamental characteristics of tourism as a complex relational phenomena. In this view, the research perspective adopts an operative approach based on data driven model for territorial tourism stock assessment defining minimum requirement for a "tourism ecosystem" according to a comparative analysis benchmarking minor and major tourist destinations. Implications regards several territorial planning domains [28–34] directly and indirectly connected with tourism sector.

Future implications include:

– the development of territorial models in order to provide decision support systems (DSS) useful for implementing investment plans, programs and projects in the medium-long term in line with the objectives of sustainable local development. The design of data-driven models is based on different levels capable of identifying the alternative that best suits the specific territorial needs for both the public sector and private operators [9];
– analysis and implementation of spatial data infrastructures essential for the evaluation of tourist services and the monitoring of territorial processes [35];
– the collection of information to reconstruct an exhaustive dataset represents a first phase to guide future developments effectively. In accordance with the envisaged models, it is necessary to characterize an integrated survey methodology aimed at illustrating the impact that tourist services have on the territory [36, 37].

Finally, this approach offers a systemic and multidisciplinary perspective that considers the multiple factors that influence tourism, such as the management of natural resources, the well-being of local communities and the quality of the tourism experience. This approach meets the criteria of sustainability and the new urban agenda 2030, as it encourages the development of responsible tourism, respectful of the environment and local cultures, and promotes a better integration of tourism into the life of the host communities. The tourism ecosystem approach represents an innovative and promising way to manage tourism in a sustainable and responsible way, improving the quality of tourism experiences and contributing to the sustainable development of local communities and their territories.

Acknowledgment. This work was granted by Next Generation UE - PNRR Tech4You Project funds assigned to Basilicata University (PP4.2.2 -SDI for Tourism ecosystems innovation and development based on cultural heritage. Scientific Coordinator prof. Daniela Carlucci; Responsible for the Action: Strategic sustainable development model for micro/macro tourism systems through the implementation of AI models at territorial scale, prof. Francesco Scorza).

References

1. Brandano, M.G., Crociata, A.: Cohesion policy, tourism and culture in Italy: a regional policy evaluation (2022). https://doi.org/10.1080/00343404.2022.2106365
2. Barca, F.: An agenda for a reformed cohesion policy (2009)
3. Casas, G.L., Scorza, F.: From the UN new urban agenda to the local experiences of urban development: the case of Potenza. In: Gervasi, O., et al. (eds.) ICCSA 2018. LNCS, vol. 10964, pp. 734–743. Springer, Cham (2018). https://doi.org/10.1007/978-3-319-95174-4_56
4. Las Casas, G., Scorza, F.: Comprehensive evaluation and context based approach for the future of European regional operative programming. In: ERSA 48th European Regional Science Association Congress, Liverpool, pp. 1–17 (2008)
5. Scorza, F., Casas, G.L.: Territorial specialization in attracting local development funds: an assessment procedure based on open data and open tools. In: Murgante, B., et al. (eds.) ICCSA 2014. LNCS, vol. 8580, pp. 750–757. Springer, Cham (2014). https://doi.org/10.1007/978-3-319-09129-7_54
6. Las Casas, G., Scorza, F.: A renewed rational approach from liquid society towards anti-fragile planning. In: Gervasi, O., et al. (eds.) ICCSA 2017. LNCS, vol. 10409, pp. 517–526. Springer, Cham (2017). https://doi.org/10.1007/978-3-319-62407-5_36
7. Casas, G.L., Scorza, F.: Sustainable planning: a methodological toolkit. In: Gervasi, O., et al. (eds.) ICCSA 2016. LNCS, vol. 9786, pp. 627–635. Springer, Cham (2016). https://doi.org/10.1007/978-3-319-42085-1_53
8. Gatto, R., Santopietro, L., Scorza, F.: Tourism and abandoned inland areas development demand: a critical appraisal. In: Gervasi, O., Murgante, B., Misra, S., Rocha, A.M.A.C., Garau, C. (eds.) ICCSA 2022. LNCS, vol. 13382, pp. 40–47. Springer, Cham (2022). https://doi.org/10.1007/978-3-031-10592-0_4
9. Corrado, S., Gatto, R.V., Scorza, F.: The European digital decade and the tourism ecosystem: a methodological approach to improve tourism analytics. In: 18th International Forum on Knowledge Asset Dynamics (IFKAD) - Managing Knowledge For Sustainability, Matera (2023)
10. Scorza, F., Gatto, R.V.: Identifying territorial values for tourism development: the case study of Calabrian Greek area. Sustainability **15**, 5501 (2023). https://doi.org/10.3390/SU15065501
11. Croes, R., Ridderstaat, J., Bąk, M., Zientara, P.: Tourism specialization, economic growth, human development and transition economies: the case of Poland. Tour. Manag. **82** (2021). https://doi.org/10.1016/j.tourman.2020.104181
12. Andreoli, A., Silvestri, F.: Tourism as a driver of development in the inner areas. Italian J. Plan. Pract. **7**, 80–99 (2017)
13. Carneiro, M.J., Lima, J., Silva, A.L.: Landscape and the rural tourism experience: identifying key elements, addressing potential, and implications for the future. J. Sustain. Tour. **23**, 1217–1235 (2015). https://doi.org/10.1080/09669582.2015.1037840
14. Sharpley, R.: Rural tourism and the challenge of tourism diversification: the case of cyprus. Tour Manag. **23**, 233–244 (2002). https://doi.org/10.1016/S0261-5177(01)00078-4
15. Hillebrand, B.: An ecosystem perspective on tourism: the implications for tourism organizations. Int. J. Tour. Res. **24**, 517–524 (2022). https://doi.org/10.1002/jtr.2518

16. Capodiferro, M., et al.: "University equity": students' facilities in major tourism destination towns. In: Gervasi, O. (ed.) Computational Science and Its Applications - ICCSA 2023 (2023)
17. Lagonigro, D., et al.: Downscaling NUA: matera new urban structure. In: Gervasi, O. (ed.) Computational Science and Its Applications - ICCSA 2023. LNCS, pp. 14–24. Springer, Heidelberg (2023)
18. Florio, E., et al.: SuperABLE: matera accessible for all. In: Gervasi, O. (ed.) Computational Science and Its Applications - ICCSA 2023. LNCS, pp. 152–161. Springer, Heidelberg (2023)
19. Esposito Loscavo, B., et al.: Innovation ecosystem: the added value in a unique UNESCO city. In: Gervasi, O. (ed.) Computational Science and Its Applications - ICCSA 2023. LNCS, pp. 129–137. Springer, Heidelberg (2023)
20. Gatto, R.V., Corrado, S., Scorza, F.: Towards a definition of tourism ecosystem. In: 18th International Forum on Knowledge Asset Dynamics (IFKAD) - Managing Knowledge For Sustainability (2023)
21. Romão, J., Neuts, B.: Territorial capital, smart tourism specialization and sustainable regional development: experiences from Europe. Habitat Int. **68**, 64–74 (2017). https://doi.org/10.1016/J.HABITATINT.2017.04.006
22. Plzakova, L.: Evaluation of investments in the tourism sector with a local focus. Eval. Program. Plan. **94**, 102151 (2022). https://doi.org/10.1016/J.EVALPROGPLAN.2022.102151
23. Andereck, K.L., Nyaupane, G.P.: Exploring the nature of tourism and quality of life perceptions among residents. J. Travel Res. **50**, 248–260 (2011). https://doi.org/10.1177/0047287510362918
24. Jepson, D., Sharpley, R.: More than sense of place? Exploring the emotional dimension of rural tourism experiences. J. Sustain. Tour. **23**, 1157–1178 (2015). https://doi.org/10.1080/09669582.2014.953543
25. Buhalis, D.: Tourism and information technologies: past, present and future. Tour. Recreat. Res. **25**, 41–58 (2000). https://doi.org/10.1080/02508281.2000.11014899
26. Merinero-Rodríguez, R., Pulido-Fernández, J.I.: Analysing relationships in tourism: a review. Tour Manag. **54**, 122–135 (2016). https://doi.org/10.1016/j.tourman.2015.10.010
27. Picaud-bello, K., Stevens, E., Cloutier, L.M., Renard, L.: Coordinating service ecosystems for innovation : the case of tourism destination innovation projects. Ind. Mark. Manag. **106**, 444–460 (2022). https://doi.org/10.1016/j.indmarman.2022.08.013
28. Scorza, F., Santopietro, L.: A systemic perspective for the sustainable energy and climate action plan (SECAP). Eur. Plan. Stud., 1–21 (2021). https://doi.org/10.1080/09654313.2021.1954603
29. Santopietro, L., Scorza, F.: The Italian experience of the covenant of mayors: a territorial evaluation. Sustainability **13**, 1289 (2021). https://doi.org/10.3390/su13031289
30. Scorza, F., Fortunato, G.: Cyclable cities: building feasible scenario through urban space morphology assessment. J. Urban Plan. Dev. **147**, 05021039 (2021). https://doi.org/10.1061/(ASCE)UP.1943-5444.0000713
31. Scorza, F., Fortunato, G.: Active mobility-oriented urban development: a morpho-syntactic scenario for a mid-sized town. Eur. Plan. Stud., 1–25 (2022). https://doi.org/10.1080/09654313.2022.2077094
32. Scorza, F., Saganeiti, L., Pilogallo, A., Murgante, B.: Ghost planning: the inefficiency of energy sector policies in a low population density region1. Archivio di Studi Urbani e Regionali, 34–55 (2020). https://doi.org/10.3280/ASUR2020-127-S1003
33. Pilogallo, A., Scorza, F.: Mapping regulation ecosystem services specialization in Italy. J. Urban Plan. Dev. **148** (2022). https://doi.org/10.1061/(ASCE)UP.1943-5444.0000801
34. Scorza, F., Pilogallo, A., Saganeiti, L., Murgante, B., Pontrandolfi, P.: Comparing the territorial performances of renewable energy sources' plants with an integrated ecosystem services loss assessment: a case study from the Basilicata region (Italy). Sustain. Cities Soc. **56**, 102082 (2020). https://doi.org/10.1016/j.scs.2020.102082

35. Scorza, F., Casas, G.L., Murgante, B.: Overcoming interoperability weaknesses in e-government processes: organizing and sharing knowledge in regional development programs using ontologies. In: Lytras, M.D., Ordonez de Pablos, P., Ziderman, A., Roulstone, A., Maurer, H., Imber, J.B. (eds.) WSKS 2010. CCIS, vol. 112, pp. 243–253. Springer, Heidelberg (2010). https://doi.org/10.1007/978-3-642-16324-1_26

36. Scorza, F., Pilogallo, A., Las Casas, G.: Investigating tourism attractiveness in inland areas: ecosystem services, open data and smart specializations. In: Calabrò, F., Della Spina, L., Bevilacqua, C. (eds.) ISHT 2018. SIST, vol. 100, pp. 30–38. Springer, Cham (2019). https://doi.org/10.1007/978-3-319-92099-3_4

37. Bachtler, J., McMaster, I.: EU cohesion policy and the role of the regions: investigating the influence of Structural Funds in the new member states. Environ. Plan. C Gov. Policy **26**, 398–427 (2008). https://doi.org/10.1068/c0662

Sustainable Tourism Ecosystem Balancing Territorial Values: A Place-Based Perspective

Rachele Vanessa Gatto[ID] and Francesco Scorza[(✉)] [ID]

School of Engineering, Laboratory of Urban and Regional Systems Engineering (LISUT),
University of Basilicata, Potenza, Italy
{rachelevanessa.gatto,francesco.scorza}@unibas.it

Abstract. Specialized tourism based on investments for the construction of main attractors does not represent an effective generalized regeneration strategy for the recovery of European inland rural areas. Remarking on the expected results of national policies and the relative effectiveness of the investment in tourist carriers through the evaluation of case studies, this research argues that the hypothesis to invert abandonment trends through generalized tourism development strategies may not be considered a suitable option in the decision-making process. Instead, the paper proposes a territorial analysis structure that explores socio-ecological dimensions to build knowledge for sustainable strategic plans. The study identifies territorial values in abandoned settlements in Calabrian Greek Area (southern Italy), and presents a new scenario for tourism development that prioritizes investment in supporting local informal tourism welcoming systems as an alternative to large infrastructural investment. Such investment is expected to produce long-term benefits for resident communities in abandoned inland rural areas. The study concludes with general recommendations to improve tourism development policies in a place-based approach.

Keywords: tourism ecosystem · sustainable development · inner areas

1 Introduction

Tourism is considered a catalyst for the social and economic development of any destination area [1]. When considering rural and peripheral territories, it becomes evident that national development policies and local programs assign a structural role to tourism development in improving territorial competitiveness. In fact, tourism is positioned as a primary option for rehabilitating areas that have suffered from the crisis in rural economies and the growing abandonment of the countryside [2]. The significance of the tourism component in a territorial development strategy is derived from its ability to mobilize flows of people, capital, and goods and generate a positive impact on the areas of interest [3]. In many instances, rural tourism development is funded by public investments that involve the construction of significant infrastructure projects, which are referred to as "tourism attractors" and are designed to offer a range of recreational activities for potential tourists [4]. This approach is often viewed as a "standard model" for

© The Author(s), under exclusive license to Springer Nature Switzerland AG 2023
O. Gervasi et al. (Eds.): ICCSA 2023 Workshops, LNCS 14110, pp. 90–103, 2023.
https://doi.org/10.1007/978-3-031-37123-3_8

local development planning, despite the fact that there is still uncertainty surrounding the ability to accurately measure the potential benefits of such intervention policies [5]. As a result, a critical perspective has emerged regarding the planning of territorial development throughout all phases of the planning cycle, including ex ante evaluation, problems and needs assessment, logic nexus evaluation of actions and expected outcomes, evaluation and decision making regarding investments, ongoing evaluation, final evaluation, and ex post evaluation [6]. In addition to its overall development role, there are distinct structural differences between the two primary tourism models that exist worldwide: mainstream tourism and slow tourism [7]. Within the spectrum of tourism development, we specifically examine the role of "specialized tourism" [1] in the rural scenario as a key driver for policymaking in inland peripheral areas. It has often been promoted, increasingly as a counterpoint to mass, package-type tourism in destination areas [8], and to obtain alternative sources of income where the agricultural sector has declined [2]. Although specialized tourism is mainly based on sustainability and the enhancement of the values of places, developing new services aimed at a specific category of users, has in many cases not demonstrated effectiveness in generating a context-based growth.

This research focuses on the relevance of territorial values in inland rural areas as a precondition to design local low-investment territorial strategies for tourism enhancement as an alternative to the widespread approach based on huge public infrastructure investments. In order to base a critical perspective on the effectiveness of the current approach toward tourism development in inland rural areas, this paper introduces an ongoing evaluation of two selected projects' past beneficiaries of relevant public/private investment. The analysis of demographic data represents the main monitoring indicator of the growth to achieve the goal reported in the national guidelines "National Strategy for in land rural areas" (Strategia Nazionale Aree Interne, hereafter SNAI). Remarking the expected results of SNAI and the relative effectiveness of the investment in tourist carriers, two fundamental questions arise: is it really possible to imagine a future tourism-based repopulation of these areas? Does the growth of seasonal presences in relation to the public infrastructure investments effectively improve the quality of life of the permanent population compared with the preservation of the existing territorial values? To respond to these questions, an overview of selected consolidated intervention referring to mainstream design approaches to local inland rural areas development is proposed: intervention addressed towards a specific target of users in a completely abandoned town; and large scale recovery operation. Additionally, a critical point arose: strategies implementing public tourism development policies, mostly based on public investments in temporary devices/events, appear to be ineffective in contrasting structural territorial weaknesses such as depopulation of the permanently resident inhabited area.

The present analysis offers a critique of the use of public investments in tourism infrastructures as central components of development/regenerative policies aimed at promoting inland tourism. This critique stems from an examination of how the issue is framed and how the distinctive characteristics of these areas are considered when formulating policies for urban and territorial development. A critical evaluation of the cases reviewed in this study supports this argument.

Therefore, the objective of the research is to open-up a new path-line to identify local values in the phase of context evaluation of the planning cycle [9] in order to support coherent actions in a long-term perspective. In our view, development programs favor targeted actions that can stimulate the endogenous forces of the local system in order to encourage sustainable development, mitigate the social and economic costs of abandonment, and improve the quality of life for both residents and visitors.

This paper aims to contribute to the ongoing debate surrounding sustainable tourism development in rural areas, operating on two levels. Firstly, as a contribution to policy-making, it draws attention to the conflicts that arise between the general trends in current design approaches, which are based on the public's capacity to invest in infrastructure. Secondly, in the academic debate, it proposes a preliminary pathway for integrating multidisciplinary components. This approach will benefit scholars who are focusing on rural sustainable development, tourism management, place-making, territorial analysis, and territorial values niches investigation. Through a territorial analysis that identifies abandoned or neglected places in local systems, a frame-vision [10] of the study area is returned. Specialized tourism is not considered a valid hypothesis for the enhancement of current marginal uses and practices. In this context, new tourism attractors oriented to generate exogenous tourism flows appear not to be compatible with the capacity of the local system to gain economic and social advantages. Thus, the research recommends focusing on local inhabitants' capacity to play a role in the process of tourism development and consequently to plan exploitation actions centered on their potentials. The results are a tourism model base on a small number of guests maximizing the income for those inhabitants who take care of them guiding those groups through territorial experiences.

In the next section the case study analysis is discussed. The discussion section refers to the main argument supporting the research thesis to balance tourism development on specific place based values recognition more than to generalized investment policy oriented to generate effective tourism attractors structure. The conclusions suggest main policies recommendations, and future possible scenarios of research based on enhancing weaknesses and strengths of the discussed results.

2   Greek Area in Calabria Region: A Laboratory for Sustainable Tourism Design

The Greek area in the Calabria region (Italy) is a territory that includes 13 municipalities according to the taxonomy proposed by the implementation of territorial governance and landscape protection policies "quadro territoriale regionale paesaggistico" (hereafter QTRP). Among these, Bova, Roccaforte del Greco and Roghudi are strictly related to each other and affected by severe depopulation. The ancient settlement of old Roghudi has been completely abandoned for more than 50 years. The area falls within the SNAI-72 pilot projects, where with the support of public funds equal to EUR 25,869,716.00, a massive infrastructure investment is planned with the general objective to *"Increase the number of inhabitants by 17.8% in the next decade 2018–2028, with an average annual rate of increase in the resident population equal to 1.5%, which should make it possible to bring the number of inhabitants from 9125 (as of 31 December 2016) to 10,750 with an increase of 1625 people"* [11]. As highlighted by the document, the strategy consists of a widespread intervention on a large scale and most of the funds will be destined to the improvement of mobility as well as to the creation of tourist services such as widespread hotels and urban welfare.

Among the municipalities selected by the pilot strategy and the regional planning tool, the analysis focuses on the completely abandoned urban settlement of Roghudi vecchio and the referring local system.4.1. Abandonment: An Irreversible Trend.

The centers with less than a thousand inhabitants in the system of reference are Bova, Roghudi and Roccaforte del Greco, located at high altitudes (Table 1).

Table 1. Resident population of the minor centers included in the territorial system as selected case study area in the year 2020. Fonts: ISTAT.

Roghudi Nuovo	Bova	Roccaforte del Greco
952 inhabitants	402 inhabitants	387 inhabitants

These small towns have undergone a gradual and slow process of depopulation due to various factors presented by the analysis of the permanent population loss in the period 1971–2015. The most important changes took place in Bova and Roccaforte del Greco with the decrease, respectively, of 67.95% and 64.27% of inhabitants. The result of migration affected Roghudi Nuovo, which registers a population loss of 30.54%. Negative local trends and aging of population are worse conditions for imagining future scenarios, considering, moreover, negative generational change is underway, comprising a cycle of decline [12]. The irreversibility is also enhanced by the absence, at the national level, of demographic and economic growth margins. Indeed, according to Istat report [13], in 2048, there will be more deaths than births within the country.

Table 2. Roghudi demographic index in 2019. Fonts: ISTAT.

Old Age	Structural Dependence	Ex-Change Rate of Active Population	Mortality	Birth Rate
170.5	50.5	114.8	12.3	9.2

In 2019, in Roghudi Nuovo, the old age index, which expresses the ratio of the population over 65 to the population under 14, shows that there are 170 elderly people for every 100 young people. Even more critical is the comparison between births and deaths correlated by the structural dependency index which expresses dependents for every 100 working inhabitants, registering about one dependent for every two working users. Furthermore, the exchange rate data reveal the very elderly working age population (Table 2). The demographic structure represents a barrier for investments in local development. The exodus from inland rural areas began in the 1960s, in correspondence with the economic boom. The industrial revolution, technology innovation in the production of products and exchange of goods/services in global market [12] induced municipalities to redesign their urban layout, taking advantage of the coast, which is seen as a more accessible place (Fig. 3. Condofuri, Bova, Roghudi and San Lorenzo move part of their urban scenario in other sites structuring, essentially compacting the development line (Fig. 1).

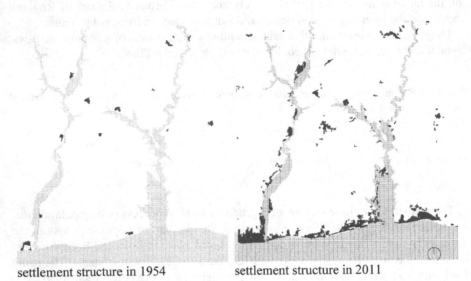

settlement structure in 1954   settlement structure in 2011

Fig. 1. Urban settlement evolution between 1954–2011. The black areas represent the residential settlement system.

Future scenario predicts for rural areas a non-replacement of aging population; hence, the negative trend is projected to continue into the next decades [12]. The influence is provided not only by economic reasons but also by other factors: local and external. Local factors can include complex landforms that make the development of activities hostile, while external factors such as changes on a global scale are equally decisive for settlement dynamics [14].

The Calabrian Greek area identified by the QTPR identifies a portion of territory historically inhabited by Greek-speaking populations that reaches its greatest concentration in the river Amendolea basin. The complex morphology of this area with accentuated differences in altitude and the presence of rivers represents one aspect of the identity of the landscape (Fig. 4). The QRTP, in identifying resources of regional importance, recognizes priority intervention policies. A first general map classifies land cover and protected areas, municipalities and national or regional parks in order to protect and preserve the autochthonous flora–fauna. Further lines of development are traced by the existing anthropological resources such as the characteristics of the built structure which is distinguished by the common disposition on the slopes and agropastoral activities. Roghudi ancient settlement and Roccaforte del Greco are situated in the boundaries of Aspromonte National Park and this is considered an attribute to identify in naturalistic tourism development [15].

Roghudi, Bova, and Roccaforte del Greco are small urban agglomerations that serve as nodes within a territorial system that shares common features, values, and services.

These nodes and the roads connecting them comprise a closed infrastructural ring encircling the basin of the Amendolea River. The diagram depicted in Fig. 2 illustrates the relationships between these urban agglomerations and their connection network. The hierarchy of the road network linking these nodes varies according to the morphology and characteristics of the roads, which influence travel speed. The axis between Roccaforte del Greco and Roghudi Vecchio, where the natural environment is wild, is associated with slow travel, and ordinary vehicles are no longer able to travel. Within the network, trekking circuits have developed along traditional sheep-farming itineraries, connecting isolated rural houses with the main nodes.

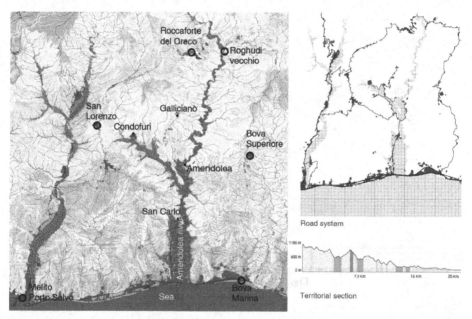

Fig. 2. Territorial map of the study area highlighting main orographically characters, the system of settlement and main infrastructural connections.

It has become apparent that the case of Roghudi cannot be classified within the traditional archetype of abandoned villages, but rather should be regarded as a unique component of a broader territorial system that provides an appropriate scale for designing a tourism development strategy.

Through travel within the study area, it was possible to produce a qualitative report on social practices by examining the uses, historical development, and current dynamics of the urban structure. As a result, territorial values (TV) are associated with specific locations on the map represented by points or lines, which are linked to a scenario of urban interaction.

The significance of TV depends on:

1. Physical attribute: hot spot intervention that is not expected in a completely abandonment place, in contrast with the surrounding assessment.

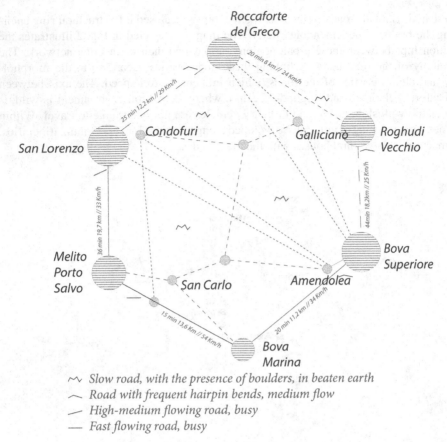

Roccaforte
del Greco

20 min 8 km // 24 Km/h

25 min 12,2 km // 29 Km/h

Condofuri

San Lorenzo

Galliciano

Roghudi
Vecchio

36 min 19,7 km // 33 Km/h

44min 18,2km // 25 Km/h

Melito
Porto
Salvo

San Carlo

Amendolea

Bova
Superiore

15 min 13,6 Km // 54 Km/h

20 min 11,2 km // 34 Km/h

Bova
Marina

∿ Slow road, with the presence of boulders, in beaten earth
⌒ Road with frequent hairpin bends, medium flow
⁓ High-medium flowing road, busy
— Fast flowing road, busy

Fig. 3. Local area network.

2. Unexpected practices or activity related to specific places.

Along the Roccaforte del Greco–Roghudi Vecchio axis, flows of people who spo-radically inhabit the public space have been observed. As illustrated in Fig. 6, the abandoned village is undergoing a naturalization process characterized by the prolifer-ation of vegetation that grows to adapt to the morphology of the buildings. Meanwhile, the municipalities have provided facilities oriented towards the enhancement and preser-vation of public structures, such as the recently restored church or the solar panel lights above the old public lighting system that is no longer in use. Certain current activities define collective perception, such as recreational practices that involve interacting with the environment. The uninhabited town square becomes a suitable meeting place for spending community moments linked to events such as the local festival and family travel experiences. Along the route, there are informal niche tourism practices where local people with extensive knowledge of the area attend to tourists and offer itineraries to discover remote places and sample slow food. Inventories could offer new dimensions for promoting sustainable tourism in order to preserve cultural and landscape features

without requiring significant investment in infrastructure. As a result, the challenges facing rural communities could represent an opportunity for inhabitants to better organize
their offering of products and services.

Fig. 4. A selection of images collected during the territorial visit.

The places of territorial identity define a map where two categories of cultural points
can be identified in relation to the observed social practices: meeting points and leisure
activities.

3 Discussions

The case of Roghudi highlights how tourism based on identity values can represent an
alternative to large investments through systematic reorganization of territorial supply.
Abandoned towns and internal area settlements with fewer than a thousand inhabitants
do not meet the minimum conditions necessary to observe a change in demographic
trends following investments in services targeting a specific user base in the tourism
sector.

Current European policies focus on mitigating the abandonment of rural areas, while
a policy of adaptation to this phenomenon could be adopted [16]. The objective focuses
on the well-being of the permanent population by directing useful resources towards the

re-organization of territorial supply. Through the exploration of the territory, informal processes are observed that contribute to the subsistence economy of the place [17].

The nature of the phenomenon implies a lack of statistical data to detect the extent of the flows [18, 19], but their trace in the system allows the recognition of a territorial matrix defined by interdependence characteristics. These data are potential resources for intercepting tourist ecosystems [19–21] and contributing to the sustainable development of tourism. Current European and national policies overlook territorial values for the economic and social growth of rural areas, comparing this model to urban reality [16]. The hypotheses considered are those of a connection with the places that defines the dimensions of the tourist offer, which in contexts as the one considered is divided into small categories of services often organized through informal actions based on the skills and availability of residents. This cannot be classified through a traditional economic model, but rather is configured as a phenomenon to be monitored over time through public support programs linked to micro-entrepreneurship, specific professional training, and technical and scientific support to social groups engaged as actors in this process [22, 23].

Monitoring will be useful to verify those minimum requirements necessary to project this territorial organization into a formalized territorial development process through the tools of EU development policies [24].

4 Conclusions

Territorial system explores different forms of niche activities that informally involve local populations [25]. To guide future sustainable and effective developments, it is crucial to identify informal processes and collect data to construct a comprehensive knowledge framework. The problem of abandonment cannot be attributed solely to depopulation, which creates conditions of uninhabited municipalities, but is also linked to the socio-ecological realities characterizing the case study area. In planning for sustainable development of abandoned municipalities, it is recommended to extend the territorial analysis to a wider functional area to identify relevant relationships among nodes of the inland settlement network, rather than relying solely on a single pole as the only focus of the strategic design process. Thus, a polycentric structure should be adopted to formulate vision frameworks that seek appropriate solutions. Consequently, the common approach of identifying major infrastructural investments as tourism attractors/facilities to reverse abandonment trends may not be the suitable option in the decision-making process.

The argument in support of this statement is that the construction of large tourist attractions often requires huge financial investments and the creation of infrastructure that can have a negative impact on the environment and local communities. Moreover, these large-scale tourism projects may only attract seasonal tourists, without promoting sustainable long-term tourism development. On the other hand, it could be more effective to use a low-cost, medium-term approach to tourism development planning, with greater participation and involvement of the local community in the design and implementation of development initiatives. This way, there could be greater involvement of local resources and the implementation of sustainable and integrated tourism development strategies into the local reality. After an in-depth understanding of the context (empirical and quantitative), identifying hidden social processes becomes increasingly relevant, and the hypothesis of pointing out the value of unofficial experiential tourism itineraries has emerged as the primary focus of the regeneration strategy.

Therefore, the generalized approach of considering tourism as the core driver for inland and abandoned areas' development oriented to the repopulation objective (as proposed recently in the SNAI) results in a weak scenario. Seasonal tourism generated through significant tourism infrastructural investments (attractions, accommodation facilities, specific services) is an exogenous factor that activates only partially the endogenous potential of local communities in the target areas.

It can be inferred that there will be a proactive approach to seeking to harmonize future initiatives and objectives with the 2030 urban agenda for urban sustainability. Overall, all the objectives of the 2030 Urban Agenda [26] are aimed at promoting sustainable urban growth through the promotion of sustainable practices and technologies, efficient resource management, the adoption of inclusive policies, and the promotion of collaboration among all urban sector stakeholders. Additionally, the topic of downscaling NUA [27–30] represents an operative research dimension to cover new knowledge demand in applied planning for tourism development. What is relevant to highlight are the following objectives, which assume an operational character to guide the developments of this research:

1. Objective 7: Sustainable and Resilient Cities—This objective aims to promote safe, inclusive, resilient, and sustainable urban cities and communities.
2. Objective 11: Sustainable Cities and Communities—This objective aims to make urban cities and communities more inclusive, safe, resilient, and sustainable by promoting sustainable mobility, waste management, efficient use of resources, and the adoption of innovative technologies.
3. Objective 13: Climate Action—This objective aims to promote action to address climate change and mitigate its effects in urban cities and communities through the adoption of low-carbon emission technologies and the promotion of renewable energies.
4. Objective 17: Partnerships for the Goals—This objective aims to promote collaboration among all urban sector stakeholders, including local governments, civil society organizations, and the private sector, to achieve the goals of the 2030 Urban Agenda.

However, the study's weakness lies in the partial capacity to analyze social niches capital according to the short investigation terms. The complexity of social relations and structures, even in depopulated and remote areas characterized by small numbers of inhabitants, is a time-consuming process based on the interaction between the researcher and the local community.

Another critical issue is related to the weaknesses of the spatial planning system operating for territorial development, which does not offer an effective reference framework to formulate a development proposal. The only spatial planning tools that include tourism enhancement as a driver for local development is the Calabrian Greek Area Strategy that mainly proposes a territorial classification according to landscape structures. It is weak in the proposal of exploitation options.

Future research on the case study area of the Roghudi polycentric system in Calabria (Italy) should include structured interactions with local groups, involving them in co-design practices [22]. Regarding the general issue of territorial development in inland areas based on tourism, low-investment territorial strategies in the medium term represent an option to be deeply assessed according to the recommendation to better direct resources by actively involving the local population. The hypothesis is that intangible investment in forms of governance and incentives can lead to a better result in terms of cost-benefit [15].

The problem of abandonment cannot be considered only as the cause of depopulation-generating conditions of uninhabited municipalities, but a phenomenon linked to the socio-ecological realities characterizing the case study area. The first recommendation for improving the strategic approach in planning the sustainable development of abandoned municipality is not to consider a single pole as the only focus of the strategic design process but to extend the territorial analysis to a wider area functional to identify relevant relations among nodes of the inland settlement network.

Hence, the need to formulate vision frameworks seeking appropriate solutions has to be developed in a polycentric structure. As a consequence, the common approach that is based on identifying major infrastructural investment as tourism attractor/facility as a solution to invert abandonment trends will probably not be a suitable option in the decision-making process [6].

In order to plan for the growth of tourism, and economic and social capital in ways that utilize environmental capital in a sustainable way, after an in-depth understanding of the context (empirical and quantitative), the identification of hidden social processes became more and more relevant and the hypothesis to point out the value of unofficial experiential tourism itineraries emerged as the main focus of the regeneration strategy [31].

Hence, it can be argued that the widespread perception of tourism as the main catalyst for the development and repopulation of inland and abandoned areas, as recently suggested in the SNAI, is a flawed approach. The reason being that seasonal tourism, which is generated through large-scale investments in tourism infrastructure (such as attractions, accommodation facilities, and specialized services) [32–35], only partially activates the endogenous potential of the local communities residing in these regions [36]. Concerning the general issue of territorial development in inland areas based on tourism, the low-investment territorial strategies in the medium term represents an option to be deeply assessed according to the recommendation to better direct resources by actively involving the local population [37]. The hypothesis is that the intangible investment in forms of governance and incentives can lead to a better result in terms of cost–benefit.

The emerging approach in tourism development based on the concept of "tourism ecosystems" [38] represents a promising perspective to improve local approaches and applications under the NUA and 2030 agenda paradigms. The main academic position on optimizing the management of tourism development in rural areas is that rural tourism development should be sustainable and community-based [39, 40]. This entails careful planning, significant involvement of local communities, constant evaluation of impacts, and rigorous monitoring of tourism activities, in order to ensure that tourism development is environmentally, socially, and culturally sustainable and responsible.

Studies [41–46] indicate that rural communities can benefit from tourism through increased employment, access to services, and increased cultural awareness. However, these benefits can be threatened by uncontrolled tourism growth and a lack of participation of local communities in tourism planning and management.

Acknowledgement. This paper is extracted from a wider research work already published in Sustainability Journal by the same authors:

Scorza, F.; Gatto, R.V. Identifying Territorial Values for Tourism Development: The Case Study of Calabrian Greek Area. *Sustainability 2023, Vol. 15, Page 5501* **2023**, *15*, 5501, https://doi.org/10.3390/SU15065501.

References

1. Croes, R., Ridderstaat, J., Bąk, M., Zientara, P.: Tourism specialization, economic growth, human development and transition economies: The case of Poland. Tour Manag. **82** (2021). https://doi.org/10.1016/j.tourman.2020.104181
2. Sharpley, R.: Rural tourism and the challenge of tourism diversification: the case of Cyprus. Tour Manag. **23**, 233–244 (2002). https://doi.org/10.1016/S0261-5177(01)00078-4
3. Brau, R., Di Liberto, A., Pigliaru, F.: Tourism and development: a recent phenomenon built on old (institutional) roots? World Econ. **34**, 444–472 (2011). https://doi.org/10.1111/j.1467-9701.2010.01320.x
4. Gatto, R., Santopietro, L., Scorza, F.: Tourism and Abandoned Inland Areas Development Demand: A Critical Appraisal. Lecture Notes in Computer Science (including subseries Lecture Notes in Artificial Intelligence and Lecture Notes in Bioinformatics). 13382 LNCS, pp. 40–47 (2022). https://doi.org/10.1007/978-3-031-10592-0_4
5. Andreoli, A., Silvestri, F.: Tourism as a driver of development in the inner areas. Italian J. Planning Pract. **7**, 80–99 (2017)
6. Scorza, F., Santopietro, L., Giuzio, B., Amato, F., Murgante, B., Casas, G.L.: Conflicts between environmental protection and energy regeneration of the historic heritage in the case of the city of matera: tools for assessing and dimensioning of sustainable energy action plans (SEAP). In: Gervasi, O., et al. (eds.) ICCSA 2017. LNCS, vol. 10409, pp. 527–539. Springer, Cham (2017). https://doi.org/10.1007/978-3-319-62407-5_37
7. Lumsdon, L.M., McGrath, P.: Developing a conceptual framework for slow travel: a grounded theory approach. J. Sustain. Tour. **19**, 265–279 (2011). https://doi.org/10.1080/09669582.2010.519438
8. Getz, D.: Developing rural tourism: the potential of beach resort hinterlands. In: Faulkner, B., Tidswell, C., Weaver, D. (eds.), Progress in tourism and hospitality research: Proceedings of the eighth Australian Tourism and Hospitality Research Conference, pp. 700–714. Bureau of Tourism Research, Canberra, A.C.T. (1998)
9. Casas, G.L., Scorza, F.: Sustainable planning: a methodological toolkit. In: Gervasi, O., et al. (eds.) ICCSA 2016. LNCS, vol. 9786, pp. 627–635. Springer, Cham (2016). https://doi.org/10.1007/978-3-319-42085-1_53
10. Faludi, A.: Cohesion, Coherence, Cooperation: European Spatial Planning Coming of Age ?
11. Grecanica agenzia di sviluppo locale: SNAI Area Grecanica (2021)
12. Navarro, L.M., Pereira, H.M.: Rewilding Abandoned Landscapes in Europe, pp. 900–912 (2012). https://doi.org/10.1007/s10021-012-9558-7
13. Istat: PREVISIONI DELLA POPOLAZIONE RESIDENTE E DELLE FAMIGLIE 2 Calo graduale ma continuo della popolazione, pp. 1–32 (2021)

14. Lasanta, T., Arnáez, J., Pascual, N., Ruiz-flaño, P., Errea, M.P., Lana-renault, N.: Catena space – time process and drivers of land abandonment in Europe. Catena (Amst). (2016). https://doi.org/10.1016/j.catena.2016.02.024
15. Duglio, S., Bonadonna, A., Letey, M., Peira, G., Zavattaro, L., Lombardi, G.: Tourism development in inner mountain areas-the local stakeholders' point of view through a mixed method approach. Sustainability (Switzerland), **11**(21), (2019). https://doi.org/10.3390/su11215997
16. Brandano, M.G., Crociata, A.: Cohesion policy, tourism and culture in Italy: a regional policy evaluation. Reg. Stud. pp. 1–17 (2022). https://doi.org/10.1080/00343404.2022.2106365
17. Garrod, B., Wornell, R., Youell, R.: Re-conceptualising rural resources as countryside capital: The case of rural tourism. J. Rural. Stud. **22**, 117–128 (2006). https://doi.org/10.1016/j.jrurstud.2005.08.001
18. Corrado, S., Scorza, F.: Machine Learning Based Approach to Assess Territorial Marginality. Lecture Notes in Computer Science (including subseries Lecture Notes in Artificial Intelligence and Lecture Notes in Bioinformatics). 13376 LNCS, pp. 292–302 (2022). https://doi.org/10.1007/978-3-031-10450-3_25/COVER
19. Corrado, S., Gatto, R.V., Scorza, F.: The European digital decade and the tourism ecosystem: a methodological approach to improve tourism analytics. In: 18th International Forum on Knowledge Asset Dynamics (IFKAD) - MANAGING KNOWLEDGE FOR SUSTAINABILITY., Matera (2023)
20. Gatto, R.V., Corrado, S., Scorza, F.: Towards a definition of tourism ecosystem. In: 18th International Forum on Knowledge Asset Dynamics (IFKAD) - MANAGING KNOWLEDGE FOR SUSTAINABILITY (2023)
21. Scorza, F., Pilogallo, A., Las Casas, G.: Investigating tourism attractiveness in inland areas: ecosystem services, open data and smart specializations. In: Calabrò, F., Della Spina, L., Bevilacqua, C. (eds.) ISHT 2018. SIST, vol. 100, pp. 30–38. Springer, Cham (2019). https://doi.org/10.1007/978-3-319-92099-3_4
22. Scorza, F., et al.: Training for Territorial Sustainable Development Design in Basilicata Remote Areas: GEODESIGN Workshop. Lecture Notes in Computer Science (including subseries Lecture Notes in Artificial Intelligence and Lecture Notes in Bioinformatics). 13379 LNCS, pp. 242–252 (2022). https://doi.org/10.1007/978-3-031-10545-6_17/COVER
23. Scorza, F., Pontrandolfi, P.: Citizen participation and technologies: the C.A.S.T. architecture. In: Gervasi, O., et al. (eds.) ICCSA 2015. LNCS, vol. 9156, pp. 747–755. Springer, Cham (2015). https://doi.org/10.1007/978-3-319-21407-8_53
24. Scorza, F.: Improving EU cohesion policy: the spatial distribution analysis of regional development investments funded by EU structural funds 2007/2013 in Italy. In: Murgante, B., et al. (eds.) ICCSA 2013. LNCS, vol. 7973, pp. 582–593. Springer, Heidelberg (2013). https://doi.org/10.1007/978-3-642-39646-5_42
25. Gatto, R., Santopietro, L., Scorza, F.: Roghudi: Developing Knowledge of the Places in an Abandoned Inland Municipality. Lecture Notes in Computer Science (including subseries Lecture Notes in Artificial Intelligence and Lecture Notes in Bioinformatics). 13382 LNCS, pp. 48–53 (2022). https://doi.org/10.1007/978-3-031-10592-0_5
26. UNhabitat: The New Urban Agenda (2016). https://doi.org/10.18356/4665f6fb-en
27. Capodiferro, M., et al.: "University equity": students' facilities in major tourism destination towns. In: Gervasi, O. (ed.) Computational Science and Its Applications - ICCSA 2023 (2023)
28. Lagonigro, D., et al.: Downscaling NUA: Matera new urban structure. In: Gervasi, O. (ed.) Computational Science and Its Applications - ICCSA 2023. Springer (2023)
29. Florio, E., et al.: SuperABLE: matera accessible for all. In: Gervasi, O. (ed.) Computational Science and Its Applications - ICCSA 2023. Springer (2023)
30. Esposito Loscavo, B., et al.: Innovation ecosystem: the added value in a unique UNESCO city. In: Gervasi, O. (ed.) Computational Science and Its Applications - ICCSA 2023. Springer (2023)

31. Kim, H., Stepchenkova, S., Babalou, V.: Branding destination co-creatively: a case study of tourists' involvement in the naming of a local attraction. Tour Manag. Perspect. **28**, 189–200 (2018). https://doi.org/10.1016/j.tmp.2018.09.003

32. Scorza, F., Saganeiti, L., Pilogallo, A., Murgante, B.: Ghost planning: the inefficiency of energy sector policies in a low population density region1. ARCHIVIO DI STUDI URBANI E REGIONALI. 34–55 (2020). https://doi.org/10.3280/ASUR2020-127-S1003

33. Scorza, F., Pilogallo, A., Saganeiti, L., Murgante, B., Pontrandolfi, P.: Comparing the territorial performances of renewable energy sources' plants with an integrated ecosystem services loss assessment: a case study from the Basilicata region (Italy). Sustain Cities Soc. **56**, 102082 (2020). https://doi.org/10.1016/j.scs.2020.102082

34. Scorza, F., Fortunato, G.: Active mobility-oriented urban development: a morpho-syntactic scenario for a mid-sized town. European Planning Studies, pp. 1–25 (2022). https://doi.org/10.1080/09654313.2022.2077094

35. Scorza, F., Fortunato, G.: Cyclable cities: building feasible scenario through urban space morphology assessment. J. Urban Plan Dev. **147**, 05021039 (2021). https://doi.org/10.1061/(ASCE)UP.1943-5444.0000713

36. Cai, L.A.: Cooperative branding for rural destinations. Ann. Tour Res. **29**, 720–742 (2002). https://doi.org/10.1016/S0160-7383(01)00080-9

37. Dastoli, P.S., Pontrandolfi, P., Scorza, F., Corrado, S., Azzato, A.: Applying geodesign towards an integrated local development strategy: the Val d'Agri Case (Italy). Lecture Notes in Computer Science (including subseries Lecture Notes in Artificial Intelligence and Lecture Notes in Bioinformatics). 13379 LNCS, pp. 253–262 (2022). https://doi.org/10.1007/978-3-031-10545-6_18/COVER

38. Hillebrand, B.: An ecosystem perspective on tourism: the implications for tourism organizations. Int. J. Tour. Res. **24**, 517–524 (2022). https://doi.org/10.1002/jtr.2518

39. Soligno, R., Scorza, F., Amato, F., Las Casas, G., Murgante, B.: Smart Solutions for the development of rural communities. In: Plan Together – Right Now – Overall: From Vision to Reality for Vibrant Cities and Regions, pp. 861–874 (2015)

40. Soligno, R., Scorza, F., Amato, F., Casas, G.L., Murgante, B.: Citizens participation in improving rural communities quality of life. In: Gervasi, O., et al. (eds.) ICCSA 2015. LNCS, vol. 9156, pp. 731–746. Springer, Cham (2015). https://doi.org/10.1007/978-3-319-21407-8_52

41. Vona, M., Harabaglia, P., Murgante, B.: Thinking about resilient cities: studying Italian earthquakes. **169**, 185–199 (2016). https://doi.org/10.1680/UDAP.14.00007

42. Murgante, B., Borruso, G., Lapucci, A.: Sustainable development: concepts and methods for its application in urban and environmental planning. Studies in Comput. Intelligence. **348**, 1–15 (2011). https://doi.org/10.1007/978-3-642-19733-8_1/COVER

43. Las Casas, G., Scorza, F., Murgante, B.: Razionalità a-priori: una proposta verso una pianificazione antifragile. Italian J. Regional Sci. **18**, 329–338 (2019). https://doi.org/10.14650/93656

44. Murgante, B., Borruso, G., Lapucci, A.: Geocomputation and urban planning. Studies in Comput. Intell. **176**, 1–17 (2009). https://doi.org/10.1007/978-3-540-89930-3_1/COVER

45. Scorza, F., Pilogallo, A., Saganeiti, L., Murgante, B.: Natura 2000 areas and sites of national interest (SNI): measuring (un)integration between naturalness preservation and environmental remediation policies. Sustainability (Switzerland) **12**, (2020). https://doi.org/10.3390/SU12072928

46. Saganeiti, L., Mustafa, A., Teller, J., Murgante, B.: Modeling urban sprinkling with cellular automata. Sustain Cities Soc. **65**, 102586 (2021). https://doi.org/10.1016/J.SCS.2020.102586

The Design of Local Actions Toward EU2050 Targets Performed on Municipal Budgets

Luigi Santopietro[1]($\boxtimes$) (iD), Silvia Solimene[2] (iD), Ferdinando Di Carlo[3] (iD),
Manuela Lucchese[4] (iD), and Francesco Scorza[1] (iD)

[1] School of Engineering, Laboratory of Urban and Regional Systems Engineering (LISUT), University of Basilicata, Viale dell'Ateneo Lucano 10, 85100 Potenza, Italy
`{luigi.santopietro,francesco.scorza}@unibas.it`
[2] School of Engineering, University of Basilicata, Viale dell'Ateneo Lucano 10, 85100 Potenza, Italy
`silvia.solimene@unibas.it`
[3] Department of Mathematics, Computer Science and Economics, University of Basilicata, Viale dell'Ateneo Lucano 10, 85100 Potenza, Italy
`ferdinando.dicarlo@unibas.it`
[4] Department of Economics, University of Campania "Luigi Vanvitelli", Capua, Italy
`manuela.lucchese@unicampania.it`

Abstract. The pathways in designing local interventions toward climate neutrality can be declined according to several approaches such as energy efficiency, climate adaptation/mitigation or the reduction of GHG emissions. In this research, the authors explored an economic approach oriented by sustainability criteria according to the Sustainable Development Goals provided by the Agenda 2030. In this scenario, the European initiative of the Covenant of Mayors (CoM) was selected because each CoM signatory develops an Action Plan, designing energy efficiency and climate interventions for climate change. The methodological proposal is based on the analysis of the investment expenditures related to the public energy efficiency interventions retrieved from the Municipal budget. This allows for the addressing of effective support in designing interventions oriented to couple the economics with climate neutrality. As a sample study area, the Basilicata Region was selected, where out of 131 Municipalities, 92 are CoM Signatories, that have designed energy efficiency interventions through their Sustainable Energy Action Plans (SEAP). The methodological proposal was applied to the CoM Municipality group and non-CoM ones to highlight the differences. The results achieved have been compared so as to remark: 1. The differences in terms of expenditure allocated and interventions planned by Municipalities' sample according to the methodological proposal and 2. The impact of the CoM initiative and whether SEAP represents an effective driver to boost energy transition in small municipalities.

Keywords: SEAP · Municipal budget · energy efficiency · small municipalities

© The Author(s), under exclusive license to Springer Nature Switzerland AG 2023
O. Gervasi et al. (Eds.): ICCSA 2023 Workshops, LNCS 14110, pp. 104–116, 2023.
https://doi.org/10.1007/978-3-031-37123-3_9

1 Introduction

Climate neutrality is the current target addressed globally through numerous sustainability initiatives, including different approaches such as energy efficiency, the reduction of GHG emissions or adaptation/mitigation to climate change [1–4]. Among these approaches, energy efficiency is the most adopted, with a wide range of measures, including reducing energy consumption, decreasing dependence on non-renewable energy sources, and limiting greenhouse gas emissions. In Europe, the framework related to energy efficiency was harmonized in 2008 with the "20–20–20 package" [5] a set of laws passed to ensure the EU meets its climate and energy targets for the year 2020 on three key targets: 20% cut in greenhouse gas emissions (from 1990 levels), 20% of EU energy from renewables and 20% improvement in energy efficiency.

In 2019, the EU presented the European Green Deal [6], striving to be the first climate-neutral continent. From the perspective of becoming a resource-efficient and competitive economy, ensuring no net emissions of greenhouse gases by 2050, the European Green Deal also represents a way out of the COVID-19 pandemic [7].

Implementing energy efficiency measures poses several challenges, that cities and municipalities must address, to achieve the sustainability goals provided by the UN Agenda 2030 [8, 9]. The UN Agenda 2030 for Sustainable Development was presented in 2015, including the ambitious goal of developing "an action plan for people, planet and prosperity". The approach promoted by the UN Agenda is integrated and aims to address the social, environmental and economic challenges facing present and future generations. The 2030 Agenda includes 17 Sustainable Development Goals (SDGs), divided into 169 indivisible targets and which balance the three popular dimensions of sustainable development: economic, social and environmental. Nowadays, SDGs represent a challenge for both public and private organizations [10]. In particular, the 2030 Agenda emphasized the key role that national, regional and local public administration plays in achieving sustainability goals. Many authors and policymakers have focused their attention on this phenomenon [11, 12].

In this scenario, Municipalities and cities play a crucial role in promoting energy efficiency by encouraging and supporting businesses and residents to adopt sustainable practices. Public Administration (PA) is also a critical factor in facilitating and implementing sustainable policies and practices [13–16]. PA must ensure that sustainable policies are developed, implemented, and monitored effectively to reduce greenhouse gas emissions and limit energy consumption. Additionally, it can provide incentives to encourage citizens and organizations to adopt energy-efficient practices, such as offering tax credits and rebates.

The authors among the initiatives related to energy and climate issues selected a European one, the Covenant of Mayors (CoM) started in 2008, gathering mayors and local administrators with the ambition to tackle the "20–20–20" targets provided by 2020 climate & energy package [5]. It is possible divide the initiative by two different commitment period: the first (2008–2020) pursued the targets provided by the 2020 climate & energy package, while the second (2020-ongoing) is pursuing the targets provided by the European Green Deal [6]. Previous researches [17, 18] remarked the relevant engagement within the CoM signatories of "small" Municipalities (i.e. under 10.000 inhabitants) classified as XS Signatories by CoM; coming mainly from Italy and Spain. CoM

Signatories translated their commitment in interventions with the Sustainable Energy Action Plan (SEAP) during the first period and now are developing a Sustainable Energy and Climate Action Plan (SECAP) including climate related interventions. These plans contain structured public and private interventions, related to energy efficiency and climate adaptation/mitigation related to a set of sectors (for example residential buildings, transport, and public lighting). They represent an opportunity to boost the local implementation of the Sustainable Development Goals provided by the UN Agenda 2030 [8], improve the resilience of the territories and support the technical skill weakness of the small municipalities.

The aim of this research is to provide a means of support for the design of energy efficiency interventions by way of economic analysis through the evaluation of Municipalities' budgets, coupling the 2050 climate targets with the economics issue.

The methodological proposal was applied to the Basilicata Region, which was selected because it has 92 CoM Signatories, that have developed 81 approved SEAPs, containing energy efficiency actions. These plans are suitable to define a sample where the methodological proposal has been applied, and compare the results achieved with non-CoM Municipalities.

The results achieved reveal the usefulness of the methodological proposal in design interventions according to a context-based approach and the replication of it in other contexts.

Moreover, the research contributes to the investigation concerning the impact of the CoM initiative on Municipalities compared to non-CoM ones, in supporting and developing public energy efficiency investments (see also [19]).

The structure of the research provided in Sect. 2, details the databases investigated for the analysis of the Municipal budgets, highlighting the share of public investments according to the CoM membership; Sect. 3 is related to the description of the study area; Sect. 4 the main outcomes which have presented an opening to the future perspectives of the research.

2 Dataset Investigated

In Italy, the government structure is divided into three levels: a national, a regional and a local government [11]. In recent years, the public accounting system has undergone numerous changes. In particular, Decree 118/2011 has decisively revised the accounting rules for local governments (LGs). Italian LGs, which include municipalities, provinces, mountain communities or consortia, draft their budgets every year to authorize expenditure [10].

This municipal budget consists of two main components: revenue and expenditure. Revenue comprises all financial resources available to the authority and is divided into current and capital revenue. Expenditure represents the financial resources to be allocated for the provision of services to citizens, for the ordinary functioning of the entity and for the realization of investments. Expenditure is divided into current expenditure, capital expenditure, expenditure for the repayment of loans, and expenditure for services on behalf of third parties.

For the purpose of this article, the authors chose to evaluate the energy efficiency initiatives proposed in the SEAP through the analysis of investment expenditure, in order to assess the allocation of financial resources by municipalities. In particular, the investment expenditure item details the payments made for each mission or intervention, i.e., it consists of all the costs that the municipality incurs for the purchase of real estate or the construction of infrastructure and long-term projects in the municipality. The result also includes the so-called *residual liabilities*, which represent the debts of the municipal authority, i.e. expenditure committed but not paid during the year (see also [20]).

The authors investigated budget data in two different time frames: the first for the years 2005–2015 and the second for the period 2016–2021. Even though the reform changed the presentation of budget items to a large extent, we identified some similarities between macro-categories, allowing comparisons to be easily made (see Table 1).

Table 1. Comparison of Municipalities budget items (Source: "Open Bilanci" Database)

Categories in the first-time frame (2005–2015)		Categories in the second time frame (2016–2021)	
Education	Expenditure for school services and maintenance of buildings owned - excluding kindergartens	*Education and the right to study*	Amount of all expenditure on education and school buildings (excluding kindergartens)
Public lighting	Expenses for public lighting installations	*Energy and diversification of energy sources*	Expenditure on administration and operation of activities and services relating to the use of energy sources, including electricity and natural gas
Public buildings	Expenditure on public housing, on the operation of offices, on the provision of benefits to citizens in need, and on the construction and maintenance of facilities	*Public and local housing and social housing plans*	Expenses for the construction, purchase and renovation of public and social housing

The authors selected two databases detailing the public interventions and investments for the Municipalities of Basilicata Region. Databases are:

1. "Open Bilanci" a public web-database with a temporal coverage from 2005–2021 where Italian municipal budgets are collected and detailed in terms of investments, expenditure and interventions related to several sectors (road maintenance, public lighting and public buildings).

2. CoM dataset, provided by the Global Covenant of Mayors for Climate and Energy (GCoM) containing a collection of action plans and monitoring reports from MyCovenant platform in the context of the GCoM initiative.

'Open Bilanci' database was examined in order to collect budget data useful for our analysis. The principle of cash management was chosen, which considers the income and expenditure that the municipality has received (receipts) and paid (payments) during the year, regardless of the year in which receivables (assessments) and payables (commitments) arose.

Analyzing the complete collection of plans and monitoring reports provided by the EU Joint Research Centre [21], in April 2023, it counts 10425 Signatory and 68% of them have submitted to CoM an Action Plan. Considering the Signatories with an Action Plan submitted, 67% of them are classified by CoM as XS Municipalities (i.e. with a resident population under 10000 inhabitants). This majority of XS Municipalities is proved considering that Italy is at first place among CoM Countries in terms of XS CoM Signatories (no. 2545), followed by Spain (no.1492). Italy and Spain both represent over 90% of the whole XS Municipality class. However, this relevant engagement of XS Municipalities has set a CO_2 emissions target reduction in the range of 20–30%, close to the 20% of 20–20-20 target, but far from the current target (55%) provided by the European Green Deal. In order to understand how the relevance of public interventions is planned by the CoM signatories, the authors evaluated the occurrences of the SEAP/SECAP sectors. Results from the CoM database, highlight that XS Signatories have a preferential interest in developing actions related to sectors basically "public" like public lighting or municipal building equipment facilities. Instead, considering "private" sectors (involving not only public actors but also a private company, stakeholders etc..), there is a relevant development of interventions related to the improvement of the energy production (including r.e.s. technologies) and energy efficiency of the buildings toward the green transition.

3 Study Area

The authors selected the Basilicata Region in the South of Italy (see Fig. 1) be-cause of 92 Municipalities on 131 are CoM Signatories. Among them, 81 have developed a SEAP including interventions related to the energy efficiency and represent a suitable sample to be compared to non-CoM in order to validate the methodological proposal. CoM provide for its signatories, three typologies of adhesions:

- As an individual signatory;
- As a group of signatories committing individually (joint SEAP - option 1), where each signatory in the group individually commits to reducing CO_2 emissions;
- As a group of signatories committing collectively (joint SEAP - option 2), where the group of signatories collectively commits to reducing CO_2 emissions.

It is relevant that considering the two Provinces (Matera and Potenza), all Municipalities from Matera Province are CoM signatories submitting a joint SEAP committing individually while for Potenza Province the whole of CoM Signatories are individual ones.

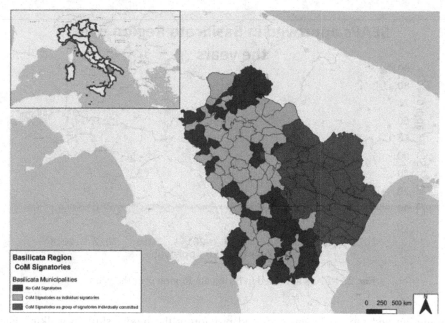

Fig. 1. Study area

Analyzing SEAPs submitted over the years by the Signatories (see Fig. 2), the times-pan between 2014 and 2017, registered a significative increase in terms of SEAPs submitted. This increase had a boost also by European and international legislation framework on energy and climate issues as Paris Agreement, Pact of Amsterdam or Urban Agenda for EU [22, 23].

In detail actions developed within the SEAPs can be categorized into four sectors: Local Electricity Production, Municipal Buildings, Residential Buildings, and Transport. A detailed explanation of the recurrent actions developed in each sector is:

- Local Electricity Production Sector: the actions in this sector are mainly focused on the installation of photovoltaic systems to generate electricity locally.
- Municipal Buildings Sector: in this sector, the actions are geared towards improving the energy efficiency of the buildings owned by the municipality. The approach is to replace and improve the building envelope and lighting systems with more efficient LED technologies.
- Residential Buildings Sector: the actions in this sector are geared towards reducing electricity and thermal consumption in residential buildings. The approach is to improve the energy efficiency of buildings by replacing the building envelope, increasing energy efficiency in space heating and hot water systems, and improving lighting systems with LED technologies.
- Transport Sector: the actions in this sector are focused on reducing the carbon footprint of the transport system. This is achieved by replacing the vehicle fleet with less

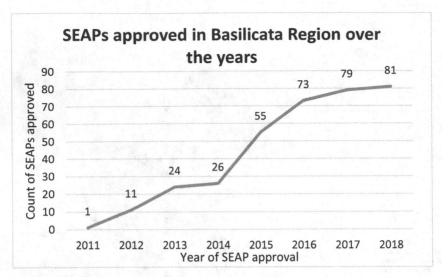

Fig. 2. SEAPs approved in Basilicata Region over the years.

polluting and more efficient ones and promoting the modal shift to walking and cycling.

The authors classified SEAPs interventions concerning data related to investments in Municipal budgets in the three macro-categories previously defined: education, public lighting and public buildings. Education includes investments in energy efficiency interventions in schools related to the installation of Renewable Energy Sources (RES) technologies and improvements in building energy performance; public lighting is referred to as the expenditure's investment of streetlamps and public buildings are related to the investments on the renovation (including energy efficiency interventions) of the public buildings. All these technological solutions produce a territorial impact, that should be taken into account in order to balance the different interventions sector according to territorial characteristics [24–26].

4   Results and Discussions

Several considerations can be made by analyzing the budget data of the municipalities of the Basilicata Region. The sample was divided into two categories: in the first category, investment expenditure in the three sectors selected (public lighting, education and public building) for municipalities in the province of Potenza was analyzed; in the second category, expenditure by municipalities in the province of Matera was examined. In addition, the two categories were divided into municipalities that joined the CoM and municipalities that did not join the CoM, in order to assess the general impact of joining the initiative.

The first analysis was conducted on investment expenditure expressed in absolute terms in the three selected sectors for the municipalities of the province of Potenza. There are 62 signatory municipalities and 38 non-signatory ones in this province. From the graph on average, the investment expenditure of signatory municipalities is higher than that of non-signatory municipalities in the public lighting sector (see Fig. 3).

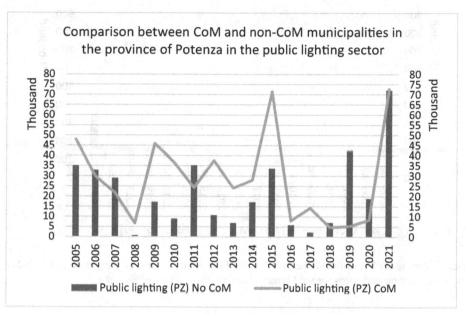

Fig. 3. Averages of investments per year in the public lighting sector (for the period 2005–2021) expressed in thousand euros for the Municipalities in the province of Potenza.

In the Education sector, this increase is even more pronounced (see Fig. 4). In the public building sector, in contrast, there has been a decrease in investment expenditure in recent years. The education sector stands out as the most advantageous investment opportunity for municipalities participating in the CoM initiative. In terms of budget analysis, CoM member municipalities in the province of Potenza and Matera tend to invest more in this sector on average. This could be attributed to the spatial planning aspect, as the Basilicata Region comprises areas with low-density housing, where public education buildings and administrative offices are the primary public buildings. As a result, municipal governance prioritizes energy efficiency investments in buildings associated with public education. The public lighting sector also seems to confirm the positive role of CoM in investment. However, in recent years, a decrease in investments is noted, only to be increased in 2021 (Fig. 5).

The province of Matera is composed of 31 municipalities and all of them have joined the CoM, which is why the analysis conducted did not include a comparison between CoM and non-CoM, but rather an exploratory analysis by assessing the trend of investment expenditure in the three selected sectors (see Fig. 6).

The initial evaluation of investments related to public energy efficiency measures has revealed the positive impact of the initiative on small municipalities. This impact is evidenced by increased investments in education and public lighting. Moreover, the

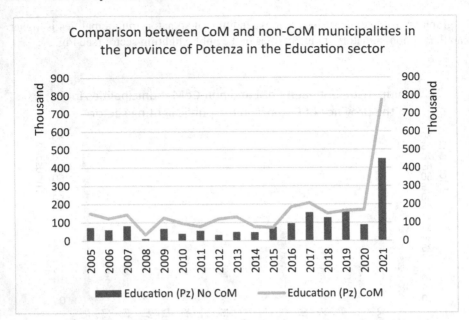

Fig. 4. Averages of investments per year in the Education sector (for the period 2005–2021) expressed in thousand euros for the Municipalities in the province of Potenza.

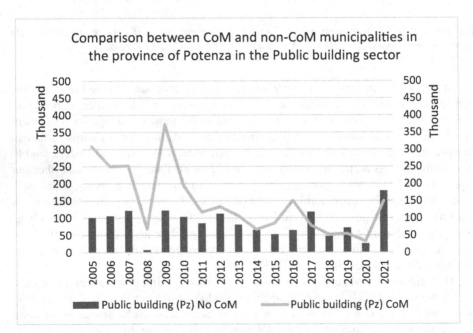

Fig. 5. Averages of investments per year in the Public Building sector (for the period 2005–2021) expressed in thousand euros for the Municipalities in the province of Potenza.

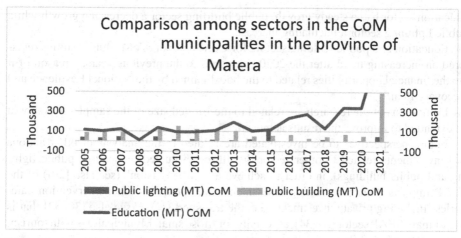

Fig. 6. Averages of investments per year in the three sectors (for the period 2005–2021) expressed in thousand euros for the Municipalities in the province of Matera.

initiative has encouraged investment policies in energy efficiency, addressing the technical capacity weaknesses of small municipalities and implementing measures to reduce CO_2 emissions in line with EU 2050 targets. The voluntary approach adopted by CoM has resulted in increased investments, promoting the incentive to plan interventions for reducing energy consumption and supporting the development of a "green conscience" among citizens through these interventions [27, 28]. Additionally, municipal budget data can be a useful tool to monitor the implementation of the SEAP and could be considered as an additional indicator for inclusion in the CoM monitoring reports.

5   Conclusions

The research has provided a methodological proposal as means of support for the design of energy efficiency interventions by way of economic analysis through the evaluation of Municipalities' budgets, coupling the 2050 climate targets with the economics issue.

The methodological proposal was applied to the Basilicata Region, on a sample of energy efficiency interventions deriving from 131 Municipalities, where 81 of them have developed energy efficiency interventions within their SEAPs. A comparison on the economic performance of the energy efficiency interventions between CoM and non-CoM Municipalities was performed.

The results achieved reveal the usefulness of the methodological proposal in design interventions according to a context-based approach and the replication of it in other contexts.

Moreover, the research contributed to the assessment of the effective and positive impact of the CoM initiative on Municipalities compared to non-CoM ones, in supporting and developing public energy efficiency investments.

The three sectors for CoM Municipalities during the timespan considered have a stock in investment over than no-CoM ones. However, they had different trends in investments:

education sector had a steady growth, public building sector a decreasing growth while public lightning sector a fluctuating increase.

Education and public building sectors for CoM and non-CoM Municipalities registered an increasing trend after the 2020 compared to the previous years, a reason of it are the financial opportunities related to the boost gained by the National Resilience and Recovery Plan.

Limitations of the research are related to the limited size of the sample, that should be extended to improve the results achieved.

Future perspectives to be investigated are related to the analysis of other actions and investments related to other sector than three evaluated (education, public lighting and public buildings), in order to achieve an "urban vision" (see also [29]) of the SEAP impacts. Other interesting assessments are related to other intervention categories (including private investments (i.e. the transport sector (see also [30–32] that is one of main SEAP sector [33, 34], especially for those small Municipalities with tourism specialization [35–37]).

This assessment can be extended to other CoM and non-CoM Municipalities in order to understand what categories (public or private) drive the investments toward the EU2050 targets and whether other EU funded programs contributes [19, 38].

References

1. Mazzariello, A., Pilogallo, A., Scorza, F., Murgante, B., Las Casas, G.: Carbon stock as an indicator for the estimation of anthropic pressure on territorial components. In: Gervasi, O., et al. (eds.) ICCSA 2018. LNCS, vol. 10964, pp. 697–711. Springer, Cham (2018). https://doi.org/10.1007/978-3-319-95174-4_53

2. Pietrapertosa, F., Salvia, M., De Gregorio Hurtado, S., Geneletti, D., D'Alonzo, V., Reckien, D.: Multi-level climate change planning: an analysis of the Italian case. J Environ Manage. **289**, 112469 (2021). https://doi.org/10.1016/j.jenvman.2021.112469

3. Di Leo, S., Pietrapertosa, F., Salvia, M., Cosmi, C.: Contribution of the basilicata region to decarbonisation of the energy system: results of a scenario analysis. Renew. Sustain. Energy Rev. **138**, 110544 (2021). https://doi.org/10.1016/j.rser.2020.110544

4. Salvia, M., et al.: Understanding the motivations and implications of climate emergency declarations in cities: the case of Italy. Renew. Sustain. Energy Rev. **178**, 113236 (2023). https://doi.org/10.1016/j.rser.2023.113236

5. European Commission: 2020 climate & energy package | Climate Action. https://ec.europa.eu/clima/policies/strategies/2020_en. Accessed 01 Dec 2020

6. European Commission: The European Green Deal., Brussels (2020)

7. Becchetti, L., Piscitelli, P., Distante, A., Miani, A., Uricchio, A.F.: European green deal as social vaccine to overcome COVID-19 health & economic crisis. The Lancet Regional Health - Europe. **2**, 100032 (2021). https://doi.org/10.1016/j.lanepe.2021.100032

8. United Nations: Transforming our world: the 2030 Agenda for Sustainable Development. In: Sustainable Development Goals, pp. 333–374. Wiley (2019). https://doi.org/10.1002/9781119541851.app1

9. Las Casas, G., Scorza, F., Murgante, B.: New urban agenda and open challenges for urban and regional planning. In: Calabrò, F., Della Spina, L., Bevilacqua, C. (eds.) ISHT 2018. SIST, vol. 100, pp. 282–288. Springer, Cham (2019). https://doi.org/10.1007/978-3-319-92099-3_33

10. Bisogno, M., Cuadrado-Ballesteros, B., Rossi, F.M., Peña-Miguel, N.: Sustainable development goals in public administrations: enabling conditions in local governments. International Review of Administrative Sciences. 002085232211464 (2023). https://doi.org/10.1177/002 08523221146458

11. Saha, D., Paterson, R.G.: Local government efforts to promote the "three Es" of sustainable development. J. Plan. Educ. Res. **28**, 21–37 (2008). https://doi.org/10.1177/0739456X0832 1803

12. Wang, X., Hawkins, C. V., Lebredo, N., Berman, E.M.: Capacity to sustain sustainability: a study of U.S. cities. Public Administration Rev. **72**, 841–853 (2012). https://doi.org/10.1111/j.1540-6210.2012.02566.x

13. Kaur, A., Lodhia, S.K.: Key issues and challenges in stakeholder engagement in sustainability reporting. Pac. Account. Rev. **31**, 2–18 (2019). https://doi.org/10.1108/PAR-11-2017-0092

14. Grubnic, S., Ball, A.: Sustainability accounting and accountability in the public sector. In: Sustainability Accounting and Accountability, pp. 243–265. Routledge (2007). https://doi.org/10.4324/NOE0415384889.ch13

15. Martínez-Córdoba, P.-J., Amor-Esteban, V., Benito, B., García-Sánchez, I.-M.: The commitment of spanish local governments to sustainable development goal 11 from a multivariate perspective. Sustainability **13**, 1222 (2021). https://doi.org/10.3390/su13031222

16. Las Casas, G., Scorza, F., Murgante, B.: Conflicts and sustainable planning: peculiar instances coming from Val D'agri structural inter-municipal plan. In: Papa, R., Fistola, R., Gargiulo, C. (eds.) Smart Planning: Sustainability and Mobility in the Age of Change. GET, pp. 163–177. Springer, Cham (2018). https://doi.org/10.1007/978-3-319-77682-8_10

17. Santopietro, L., Scorza, F., Rossi, A.: Small municipalities engaged in sustainable and climate responsive planning: evidences from UE-CoM. In: Gervasi, O., et al. (eds.) ICCSA 2021. LNCS, vol. 12957, pp. 615–620. Springer, Cham (2021). https://doi.org/10.1007/978-3-030-87013-3_47

18. Santopietro, L., Scorza, F.: The Italian experience of the covenant of mayors: a territorial evaluation. Sustainability (Switzerland) **13**, 1–23 (2021). https://doi.org/10.3390/su13031289

19. Scorza, F.: Improving EU cohesion policy: the spatial distribution analysis of regional development investments funded by EU structural funds 2007/2013 in Italy. In: Murgante, B., et al. (eds.) ICCSA 2013. LNCS, vol. 7973, pp. 582–593. Springer, Heidelberg (2013). https://doi.org/10.1007/978-3-642-39646-5_42

20. Santopietro, L., Solimene, S., Di Carlo, F., Lucchese, M., Scorza, F., Murgante, B.: A first financial assessment of SEAP public energy interventions performance through municipal budget. Presented at the (2022). https://doi.org/10.1007/978-3-031-10592-0_6.

21. Melica, G., et al.: Covenant of Mayors: 2021 assessment. Climate change mitigation and adaptation at local level (2022). https://doi.org/10.2760/58412

22. United Nations: Paris Agreement. In: Conference of the Parties on its twenty-first session, p. 32. Paris (2015)

23. European Commission: Urban agenda for the EU - Pact of Amsterdam., Amsterdam (2016)

24. Saganeiti, L., Pilogallo, A., Faruolo, G., Scorza, F., Murgante, B.: Energy landscape fragmentation: basilicata region (Italy) study case. In: Misra, S., et al. (eds.) ICCSA 2019. LNCS, vol. 11621, pp. 692–700. Springer, Cham (2019). https://doi.org/10.1007/978-3-030-24302-9_50

25. Saganeiti, L., Pilogallo, A., Faruolo, G., Scorza, F., Murgante, B.: Territorial fragmentation and renewable energy source plants: which relationship? Sustainability **12**, 1828 (2020). https://doi.org/10.3390/su12051828

26. Scorza, F., Saganeiti, L., Pilogallo, A., Murgante, B.: GHOST PLANNING: the inefficiency of energy sector policies in a low population density region. ARCHIVIO DI STUDI URBANI E REGIONALI (2020)

27. Scorza, F., Pontrandolfi, P.: Citizen participation and technologies: the C.A.S.T. architecture. In: Gervasi, O., et al. (eds.) ICCSA 2015. LNCS, vol. 9156, pp. 747–755. Springer, Cham (2015). https://doi.org/10.1007/978-3-319-21407-8_53

28. Pietrapertosa, F., et al.: An educational awareness program to reduce energy consumption in schools. J Clean Prod. **278**, 123949 (2021). https://doi.org/10.1016/j.jclepro.2020.123949

29. Scorza, F., Santopietro, L.: A systemic perspective for the sustainable energy and climate action plan (SECAP). European Planning Studies, pp. 1–21 (2021). https://doi.org/10.1080/09654313.2021.1954603

30. Scorza, F., Fortunato, G.: Active mobility oriented urban development: a morpho-syntactic scenario for mid-sized town. European Planning Studies (2022). https://doi.org/10.1080/09654313.2022.2077094

31. Scorza, F., Fortunato, G.: Cyclable cities: building feasible scenario through urban space morphology assessment. J. Urban Planning Dev. **147**, 05021039 (2021). https://doi.org/10.1061/(asce)up.1943-5444.0000713

32. Fortunato, G., Scorza, F., Murgante, B.: Cyclable city: a territorial assessment procedure for disruptive policy-making on urban mobility. In: Misra, S., et al. (eds.) ICCSA 2019. LNCS, vol. 11624, pp. 291–307. Springer, Cham (2019). https://doi.org/10.1007/978-3-030-24311-1_21

33. Croci, E., Lucchitta, B., Janssens-Maenhout, G., Martelli, S., Molteni, T.: Urban CO2 mitigation strategies under the covenant of mayors: an assessment of 124 European cities. J. Clean. Prod. **169**, 161–177 (2017). https://doi.org/10.1016/j.jclepro.2017.05.165

34. Kona, A., et al.: Covenant of Mayors in figures: 8-year assessment. Publications Office of the European Union, Luxembourg (2017). https://doi.org/10.2760/64731

35. Santopietro, L., Scorza, F., Murgante, B.: Multiple components in GHG stock of transport sector: technical improvements for SECAP baseline emissions inventory assessment. TeMA – J. Land Use, Mobility Environ. **15**, 5–24 (2022). https://doi.org/10.6092/1970-9870/8391

36. Pilogallo, A., Saganeiti, L., Scorza, F., Las Casas, G.: Tourism attractiveness: main components for a spacial appraisal of major destinations according with ecosystem services approach. In: Gervasi, O., et al. (eds.) ICCSA 2018. LNCS, vol. 10964, pp. 712–724. Springer, Cham (2018). https://doi.org/10.1007/978-3-319-95174-4_54

37. Scorza, F., Gatto, R.V.: Identifying territorial values for tourism development: the case study of calabrian greek area. Sustainability **15**, 5501 (2023). https://doi.org/10.3390/su15065501

38. Scorza, F., Casas, G.L.: Territorial specialization in attracting local development funds: an assessment procedure based on open data and open tools. In: Murgante, B., et al. (eds.) ICCSA 2014. LNCS, vol. 8580, pp. 750–757. Springer, Cham (2014). https://doi.org/10.1007/978-3-319-09129-7_54

An Assessment of Built-Up Areas Trend Among EU27 Small Municipalities

Luigi Santopietro[1]([✉]) [iD], Valentina Palermo[2] [iD], and Francesco Scorza[1] [iD]

[1] School of Engineering, Laboratory of Urban and Regional Systems Engineering (LISUT), University of Basilicata, Viale dell'Ateneo Lucano 10, 85100 Potenza, Italy
{luigi.santopietro, francesco.scorza}@unibas.it
[2] Joint Research Centre, European Commission, Ispra, VA, Italy
valentina.palermo@ec.europa.eu

Abstract. Land use, land use change and forestry (LULCF) were included by the Regulation (EU) 2018/841, in the 2030 climate and energy framework, as a sector accounting green-house gas emission. In this perspective, EU has established a comprehensive framework (such as European Landscape Convention, EU's Common Agricultural Policy or EU's Urban Agenda) aimed at reducing land consumption and promoting sustainable land use practices, facing climate change. Sustainable land use practices are also addressed by the UN Sustainable Development Goals (SDGs) with specific targets related to land consumption. In the EU perspective of achieving "net zero land consumption by 2050" target, the authors examined the trend of built-up areas in small Italian municipalities (those with a population below 10,000 inhabitants) and compared it with population growth. Results are oriented to understand if the built-up areas trend is related to a densification process or land consumption compared to the population growth. Data was retrieved from the Global Human Settlement Layer and Eurostat. Results remarked that demographic dynamics and land urbanization are two intertwined processes, but in the last decade, the increase of built-up areas overcame the decreasing population growth. Moreover, it is relevant that land consumption processes involved small municipalities as well as bigger ones.

Keywords: small municipalities · land consumption · built-up growth · EU 2050 targets

1 Introduction

The Regulation (EU) 2018/841 on the inclusion of greenhouse gas emissions and removals from land use, land use change and forestry (LULCF) [1], considered LULCF as a sector contributing to the EU's 2030 emission reduction target (Agreement between EU leaders, October 2004 [2]). This commitment is in line with the Paris Agreement [3], which also focuses on the critical role of the land use sector in reaching long-term climate mitigation objectives. The EU has established a comprehensive framework aimed

© The Author(s), under exclusive license to Springer Nature Switzerland AG 2023
O. Gervasi et al. (Eds.): ICCSA 2023 Workshops, LNCS 14110, pp. 117–128, 2023.
https://doi.org/10.1007/978-3-031-37123-3_10

at reducing land consumption and promoting sustainable land use. The key legislation includes:

- The European Landscape Convention (ELC) [4]: This convention was established in 2000 and aims to protect, manage and plan landscapes throughout Europe. It promotes sustainable land use practices and aims to ensure that any changes to the landscape are carried out in a way that respects its cultural, natural and visual value;
- The EU Biodiversity Strategy for 2030 [5]: This strategy was adopted in 2020 and sets out the EU's commitment to halt the loss of biodiversity and ecosystem services. One of its main objectives is to reduce the impact of land use on biodiversity, including by reducing land take and increasing the land area under restoration, improved management, and sustainable use;
- The EU's Common Agricultural Policy (CAP) [6]: The CAP provides financial support to farmers to promote sustainable land use practices, such as agroforestry, organic farming, and biodiversity-friendly farming. The new CAP, which entered into force in 2023, puts more emphasis on environmental and climate goals;
- The EU's Urban Agenda [7]: The EU's Urban Agenda aims to promote sustainable urban development and reduce land consumption. It encourages the development of compact and connected cities, the reuse of brownfield sites, and the protection of green and blue infrastructure;
- The EU's Circular Economy Action Plan [8]: The Action Plan, adopted in 2020, aims to promote a circular economy in which resources are kept in use for as long as possible. One of the key objectives is to reduce the use of primary raw materials, including land.

Moreover, the relevance of sustainable land use practices and integrated land-use planning (including the restoration of degraded land) is addressed by the UN Sustainable Development Goals (SDGs) with specific targets related to land consumption. In detail, SDG 15, Target 15.1: by 2030, ensure the conservation, restoration and sustainable use of terrestrial and inland freshwater ecosystems and their services, in particular forests, wetlands, mountains and drylands; target 15.2: by 2020, promote the implementation of sustainable management of all types of forests, halt deforestation, restore degraded forests, and increase afforestation and reforestation; SDG3.target 11.3: by 2030, enhance inclusive and sustainable urbanization and capacity for participatory, integrated and sustainable human settlement planning and management in all countries. In the EU perspective of achieving "net zero land consumption by 2050" target, the authors examined the trend of built-up areas in small Italian municipalities (those with a population below 10,000 inhabitants) and compared it with population growth. Results are oriented to understand if the built-up areas trend is related to a densification processes or land consumption compared to the population growth. To this aim, data was extracted from the built-up surface statistics in EU LAU2[1] of the Global Human Settlement Layer (GHSL) and assessed by the indicator Land Consumption Ratio (LCR).

---

[1] Local Administrative Unit level (LAU 2) consisted of a system of municipalities or equivalent units in the 28 EU Member States maintained by Eurostat (see also https://ec.europa.eu/eur ostat/web/nuts/background).

The research is structured as follows: Sect. 2 explains the dataset and research tools selected, Sect. 3 shows the results achieved and discuss the main highlights while Sect. 4 concludes and includes future perspectives of the research.

2 Materials and Research Tools

Built-up surface statistics [9] are retrieved by the summary statistics of GHS-BUILT-S multi-temporal (1975–2020) at LAU level from the 2020 polygon layer provided by the Geographic Information System of the Commission (GISCO). The definition of 'built-up area' according to the GHSL framework is *the union of all the satellite data samples that corresponds to a roofed construction above ground which is intended or used for the shelter of humans, animals, things, the production of economic goods or the delivery of services*. For each LAU2 data related to the country code and built-up in square kilometers is provided for the period 1975 and 2020 in 5 years intervals, according to the concept and methodology of Schiavina et al. (2022) [10].

The trend of built up-areas was assessed by the land consumption ratio (LCR) [11] as:[2]

$$LCR = \frac{LN((Built - uparea_{t+n}/Built - uparea_t))}{y}$$

where:

- *Built-up area* $_t$ is the Built-up area of LAU2 in t (initial year) in square kilometers;
- *Built-up area* $_{t+n}$ is the Built-up Area of the LAU2 in $t + n$ (final year) in square kilometers;
- y is the number of years between the two measurement periods.

Demographic data was retrieved by the Eurostat database at LAU 2 level. In detail, the historical population data from 1961 to 2011 (collected for one year in each decade) was selected. The demographic trend of the municipalities of the sample was assessed with the population density computed as:

$$Population density : \frac{LAU2Population}{LAU2Surface[\text{Km}^2]}$$

Population density is expressed as the ratio between the annual population of each country or within LAU 2 provided by Geographic Information System of the Commission (GISCO) and corresponding LAU 2 surface expressed in square kilometres.

3 Results and Discussions

The authors designed the sample, selecting those Municipalities with a population below 10000 inhabitants in 2020 within the EU27 countries. The sample includes 71988 municipalities from 16 EU27 countries (Austria, Belgium, Cyprus, Czech Republic, Estonia,

---

[2] LCR equation here selected presents a logarithmic built-up growth that may be used for developing countries and it requires further specific study in describing European built-up growth.

Finland, France, Germany, Italy, Latvia, Lithuania, Luxembourg, Malta, Romania, Spain, Slovakia) with a population of less than 10000 inhabitants that are signatories to the Covenant of Mayors.

The authors employed two different approaches to depict the changes in built-up areas and support the obtained results: a snapshot approach using built-up areas to provide a static picture, and a trend-based approach using LCR to show the dynamic changes over time.

The first step was the evaluation of the built-up areas among the countries of the sample for the years 1975–2020 (see Fig. 1), where France, Germany, Italy and Romania registered a relevant increase in term of built-up areas (on average 230%). However, focusing on the last 10 years, the built-up areas increase had a tangible reduction, with an average of 56%. Suggesting a decrease of the built-up area expansion.

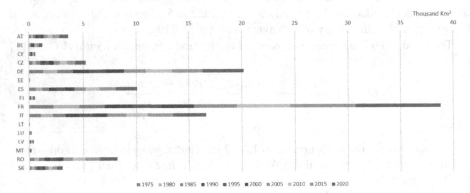

Fig. 1. Built-up areas of selected municipalities within EU for the years 1975–2020

The growth trend of the built-up area was also assessed by the LCR.

LCR represents the rate at which land occupied by a city/urban area change during a period of time (usually one year), expressed as a percentage of the land occupied by the city/urban area at the start of that time. Figure 2 shows the distribution of the average LCR for the EU countries of the sample, highlighting that with the exception of Latvia and Malta, all countries doubled LCR, particularly in the last 10 years.

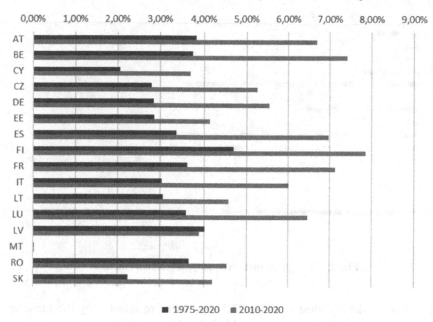

Fig. 2. Distribution of average LCR in the selected countries

From the analysis on the average population density (see Fig. 3), a demand in housing until 2011could be assumed leading to a potential increase of built-up areas. However, the trend reversed in the last 10 years with a reduction of population density opposite to an increase of built-up. Demographic changes and urban land use are closely linked processes, usually, as the population grows and its activities increase, human settlements expand their physical footprint to accommodate them. However, these two elements decouple with diverging trajectories of demography and land consumption (Kroll & Kabisch, 2012).

The study focuses on Italy, which shows a high share (84%) of small municipalities. The methodology explained in the previous paragraph has been applied and results have been reported through a classification according to NUTS3[3], aiming at understanding of the dynamics occurred for built-up areas and population density Fig. 4 shows the Italian NUTS3 regions included into the sample. Figure 5 shows data related to the expansion of built-up areas from 1975 to 2020 shows a relatively small gap between the North and South regions, with an average increase of 334% for the North and 279% for the South, with a significant increase (over 600%) in settlements in 12 NUTS3 regions (ITC33, ITF46, ITF47, ITF48, ITF51, ITH10, ITH54, ITI11, ITI14, ITI1A, ITI22, ITI45) are recorded. This phenomenon is not evenly distributed throughout the regions as it is

---

[3] Nomenclature of Territorial Unit Statistics (NUTS) is the classification with three levels of a single, coherent system for dividing up the EU's territory set up by Eurostat. In Italy NUTS3 Regions correspond to the Provinces.

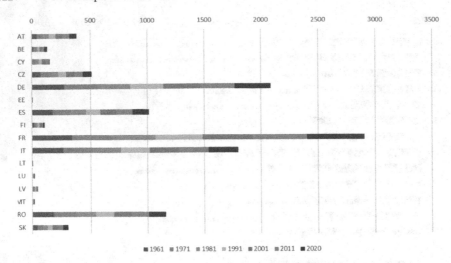

■ 1961 ■ 1971 ■ 1981 ■ 1991 ■ 2001 ■ 2011 ■ 2020

Fig. 3. Average population density in selected countries

not possible to identify clusters of NUTS3 regions more affected by the increase of built areas. Indeed, in the last decade (2010–2020) Italian NUTS3 regions experienced an average of built-up areas increase of 61% compared to 2010, equal to 10 square kilometers of new built-up areas.

NUTS3 CODE	NUTS level 3	NUTS3 CODE	NUTS level 3	NUTS3 CODE	NUTS level 3	NUTS3 CODE	NUTS level 3	NUTS3 CODE	NUTS level 3	NUTS3 CODE	NUTS level 3
ITC11	Torino	ITC47	Brescia	ITF43	Taranto	ITG16	Enna	ITH42	Udine	ITI17	Pisa
ITC12	Vercelli	ITC48	Pavia	ITF44	Brindisi	ITG17	Catania	ITH43	Gorizia	ITI18	Arezzo
ITC13	Biella	ITC49	Lodi	ITF45	Lecce	ITG18	Ragusa	ITH44	Trieste	ITI19	Siena
ITC14	Verbano-Cusio	ITC4A	Cremona	ITF46	Foggia	ITG19	Siracusa	ITH51	Piacenza	ITI1A	Grosseto
ITC15	Novara	ITC4B	Mantova	ITF47	Bari	ITG25	Sassari	ITH52	Parma	ITI21	Perugia
ITC16	Cuneo	ITC4C	Milano	ITF48	Barletta-Andria	ITG26	Nuoro	ITH53	Reggio nell'Em	ITI22	Terni
ITC17	Asti	ITC4D	Monza e della	ITF51	Potenza	ITG27	Cagliari	ITH54	Modena	ITI31	Pesaro e Urbi
ITC18	Alessandria	ITF11	LiAquila	ITF52	Matera	ITG28	Oristano	ITH55	Bologna	ITI32	Ancona
ITC20	Valle diAosta/	ITF12	Teramo	ITF61	Cosenza	ITH10	Bolzano-Bozer	ITH56	Ferrara	ITI33	Macerata
ITC31	Imperia	ITF13	Pescara	ITF62	Crotone	ITH20	Trento	ITH57	Ravenna	ITI34	Ascoli Piceno
ITC32	Savona	ITF14	Chieti	ITF63	Catanzaro	ITH31	Verona	ITH58	Forlì-Cesena	ITI35	Fermo
ITC33	Genova	ITF21	Isernia	ITF64	Vibo Valentia	ITH32	Vicenza	ITH59	Rimini	ITI41	Viterbo
ITC34	La Spezia	ITF22	Campobasso	ITF65	Reggio di Cala	ITH33	Belluno	ITI11	Massa-Carrara	ITI42	Rieti
ITC41	Varese	ITF31	Caserta	ITG11	Trapani	ITH34	Treviso	ITI12	Lucca	ITI43	Roma
ITC42	Como	ITF32	Benevento	ITG12	Palermo	ITH35	Venezia	ITI13	Pistoia	ITI44	Latina
ITC43	Lecco	ITF33	Napoli	ITG13	Messina	ITH36	Padova	ITI14	Firenze	ITI45	Frosinone
ITC44	Sondrio	ITF34	Avellino	ITG14	Agrigento	ITH37	Rovigo	ITI15	Prato		
ITC46	Bergamo	ITF35	Salerno	ITG15	Caltanissetta	ITH41	Pordenone	ITI16	Livorno		

Fig. 4. Italian NUTS3 included in the sample

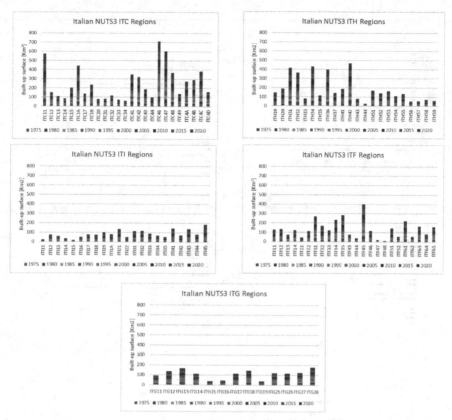

Fig. 5. Built-up areas from 1975 to 2020 for Italian NUTS3 Regions

These 12 regions experienced a relevant increase of average population density between 1975 and 2020, as shown in Fig. 6. The Built-up area increase could be related to the increase of average population density, justified by the housing demand. In Fig. 7 the distribution of average LCR for NUTS3 regions, shows that all NUTS3 regions in Italy increased their built-up areas. It is also relevant that within ITC and ITH regions, only four NUTS3 regions (ITC4D, ITH34, ITH43, ITH44) increased their population density with a limited increase of LCR for the years 2010–2020 compared to 1975–2020. On the contrary, the other regions had no significant changes in population density but have doubled or tripled the LCR for the years 2010–2020 compared to 1975–2020.

Fig. 6. Average population density of the Italian NUTS3 Regions

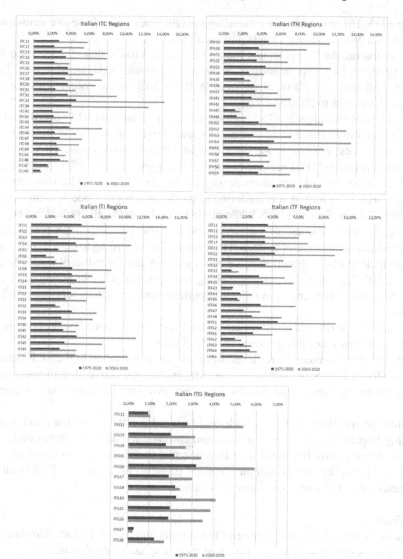

Fig. 7. Distribution of average LCR for NUTS3 Regions

4 Conclusions

This research has quantified built-up area changes and population density for small municipalities in EU countries in selected timeframes. Despite their population size and limited increase in population density, these municipalities registered relevant increase of built-up areas with irreversible land consumption processes.

These processes should be monitored with specific indicators as suggested in previous works [12–14], by quantifying built-up area changes and demographic dynamics over time [15, 16] or specifically estimating the efficiency of land use as a consequence of population growth and new land consumed [17].

By comparing the European and Italian LCR, it was found that all EU27 countries, excluding Malta, have experienced an increase in their built-up areas. Moreover, Italy's trend of doubling its built-up areas from 2010 to 2020 is consistent with the trend observed from 1975 to 2020.

The analysis on Italian NUTS3 regions, returns a scenario of widespread land consumption, not only related to historically industrialized and urbanized Italian regions (as ITC, ITH ones) but also to the ones with low-density settlements. This is the case of Potenza province (ITF51 region) that registered a growth of 654% of built-up areas and a decrease of 46% of population density for the period 1975–2020. However, these processes need to be looked at considering also other anthropic processes, such as large Renewable Energy System plants while aiming to achieve the EU policy targets, have stimulated the anthropic use of the territories (see also [18, 19]). RES plants are not considered as a component of territorial transformation according to current urban planning and their spatial distribution came about without any formal territorial scheme or provision [20–22]. Therefore, policy making tools should consider potential conflicts arising between carbon emission reduction policies and ecosystem services provisions [23–28].

Furthermore, territorial transformations are currently influenced by the combination of multi-scale processes that generate complex changes.

Relevant insights could be retrieved from specific formulation of the LCR equation, according to the European built-up area growth, in the perspective of implementing and monitoring the land consumption reduction in achieving the EU zero land consumption target.

Future perspectives of this research could extend the sample of the municipalities including larger ones, in order to analyze and compare the different trends on built-up areas. Moreover, territorial transformations oriented to the low carbon transition could be assessed including other anthropic elements (see also [29]), such as RES plants and also preservation of natural and ecosystem values.

Disclaimer
The views expressed are purely those of the authors and may not in any circumstances be regarded as stating an official position of the European Commission.

References

1. European Parliament, Council of the European Union: Regulation (EU) 2018/841 of the European Parliament and of the Council of 30 May 2018 on the inclusion of greenhouse gas emissions and removals from land use, land use change and forestry in the 2030 climate and energy framework, and amending Regulation (2018)
2. European Union: Regulation (EU) 2021/1119 of the European Parliament and of the Council of 30 June 2021 establishing the framework for achieving climate neutrality and amending Regulations (EC) No 401/2009 and (EU) 2018/1999 ('European Climate Law')., Brussels (2021)

3. United Nations: Paris Agreement. In: Conference of the Parties on its twenty-first session. p. 32., Paris (2015)
4. European Council: Council of Europe Landscape Convention (2000)
5. European Commission: EU biodiversity strategy for 2030., Luxembourg (2021). https://doi.org/10.2779/677548
6. European Council: Regulation (EU) 2021/2115 of the European Parliament and of the European Council of 2 December 2021 laying down rules concerning support for the strategic plans to be drawn up by the Member States under the common agricultural policy (CAP strategic plans). Diario Oficial de la Unión Europea. 2021, pp. 1–186 (2021)
7. European Commission: Urban agenda for the EU - Pact of Amsterdam., Amsterdam (2016)
8. European Commission: Communication from the Commission to the European Parliament, the Council, the European Economic and Social Committee and the Committee of the Regions. A new Circular Economy Action Plan For a cleaner and more competitive Europe COM/2020/98 final (2020)
9. Schiavina, M., Melchiorri, M.: GHS-BUILT-LAU2STAT R2022A - GHS built-up surface statistics in European LAU2, multitemporal (1975–2020) (2022). https://doi.org/10.2905/94D62A61-25D0-42FD-9E1E-A41F877CF788
10. Schiavina, M., Melchiorri, M., Corbane, C., Freire, S., Batista e Silva, F.: Built-up areas are expanding faster than population growth: regional patterns and trajectories in Europe. J Land Use Sci. **17**, 591–608 (2022). https://doi.org/10.1080/1747423X.2022.2055184
11. UN-Habitat: SDG Indicator 11.3.1 Training Module: Land Use Efficiency., Nairobi (2018)
12. Saganeiti, L., Mustafa, A., Teller, J., Murgante, B.: Modeling urban sprinkling with cellular automata. Sustain Cities Soc. **65**, 102586 (2021). https://doi.org/10.1016/j.scs.2020.102586
13. Saganeiti, L., Pilogallo, A., Scorza, F., Mussuto, G., Murgante, B.: Spatial indicators to evaluate urban fragmentation in basilicata region. In: Gervasi, O., et al. (eds.) ICCSA 2018. LNCS, vol. 10964, pp. 100–112. Springer, Cham (2018). https://doi.org/10.1007/978-3-319-95174-4_8
14. Nolè, G., Lasaponara, R., Lanorte, A., Murgante, B.: Quantifying urban sprawl with spatial autocorrelation techniques using multi-temporal satellite data. Int. J. Agri. Environ. Inf. Syst. **5**, 20–38 (2014). https://doi.org/10.4018/IJAEIS.2014040102
15. Wolff, M., Haase, D., Haase, A.: Compact or spread? a quantitative spatial model of urban areas in Europe since 1990. PLoS ONE **13**, e0192326 (2018). https://doi.org/10.1371/journal.pone.0192326
16. Sharma, L., Pandey, P.C., Nathawat, M.S.: Assessment of land consumption rate with urban dynamics change using geospatial techniques. J. Land Use Sci. **7**, 135–148 (2012). https://doi.org/10.1080/1747423X.2010.537790
17. Kalnay, E., Cai, M.: Impact of urbanization and land-use change on climate. Nature **423**, 528–531 (2003). https://doi.org/10.1038/nature01675
18. Di Leo, S., Pietrapertosa, F., Salvia, M., Cosmi, C.: Contribution of the Basilicata region to decarbonisation of the energy system: results of a scenario analysis. Renew. Sustain. Energy Rev. **138**, 110544 (2021). https://doi.org/10.1016/j.rser.2020.110544
19. Mazzariello, A., Pilogallo, A., Scorza, F., Murgante, B., Las Casas, G.: Carbon stock as an indicator for the estimation of anthropic pressure on territorial components. In: Gervasi, O., et al. (eds.) ICCSA 2018. LNCS, vol. 10964, pp. 697–711. Springer, Cham (2018). https://doi.org/10.1007/978-3-319-95174-4_53
20. Saganeiti, L., Pilogallo, A., Faruolo, G., Scorza, F., Murgante, B.: Territorial fragmentation and renewable energy source plants: which relationship? Sustainability **12**, 1828 (2020). https://doi.org/10.3390/su12051828

21. Faruolo, G., Santopietro, L., Saganeiti, L., Pilogallo, A., Scorza, F., Murgante, B.: The design of an urban atlas to spread information concerning the growth of anthropic settlements in basilicata region. In: Gervasi, O., et al. (eds.) ICCSA 2020. LNCS, vol. 12255, pp. 214–225. Springer, Cham (2020). https://doi.org/10.1007/978-3-030-58820-5_17

22. Saganeiti, L., Pilogallo, A., Faruolo, G., Scorza, F., Murgante, B.: Energy landscape fragmentation: basilicata region (Italy) study case. In: Misra, S., et al. (eds.) ICCSA 2019. LNCS, vol. 11621, pp. 692–700. Springer, Cham (2019). https://doi.org/10.1007/978-3-030-24302-9_50

23. Scorza, F., Pilogallo, A., Saganeiti, L., Murgante, B., Pontrandolfi, P.: Comparing the territorial performances of renewable energy sources' plants with an integrated ecosystem services loss assessment: a case study from the Basilicata region (Italy). Sustain Cities Soc. **56**, 102082 (2020). https://doi.org/10.1016/j.scs.2020.102082

24. Scorza, F., Pilogallo, A., Saganeiti, L., Murgante, B.: Natura 2000 areas and sites of national interest (SNI): Measuring (un) integration between naturalness preservation and environmental remediation policies. Sustainability **12**, 2928 (2020). https://doi.org/10.3390/su1207 2928

25. Pilogallo, A., Saganeiti, L., Scorza, F., Murgante, B.: ECOSYSTEM SERVICES' BASED IMPACT ASSESSMENT FOR LOW CARBON TRANSITION PROCESSES. TEMA-JOURNAL OF LAND USE MOBILITY AND ENVIRONMENT (2019)

26. Pilogallo, A., Saganeiti, L., Scorza, F., Murgante, B.: Ecosystem services approach to evaluate renewable energy plants effects. In: Misra, S., et al. (eds.) ICCSA 2019. LNCS, vol. 11624, pp. 281–290. Springer, Cham (2019). https://doi.org/10.1007/978-3-030-24311-1_20

27. Scorza, F., Saganeiti, L., Pilogallo, A., Murgante, B.: GHOST PLANNING: the inefficiency of energy sector policies in a low population density region. ARCHIVIO DI STUDI URBANI E REGIONALI (2020)

28. Las Casas, G., Scorza, F., Murgante, B.: Conflicts and sustainable planning: peculiar instances coming from Val D'agri structural inter-municipal plan. In: Papa, R., Fistola, R., Gargiulo, C. (eds.) Smart Planning: Sustainability and Mobility in the Age of Change. GET, pp. 163–177. Springer, Cham (2018). https://doi.org/10.1007/978-3-319-77682-8_10

29. Corrado, S., Scorza, F.: Machine learning based approach to assess territorial marginality. In: Lecture Notes in Computer Science. Springer (2022). https://doi.org/10.1007/978-3-031-10450-3_25

Innovation Ecosystem: The Added Value in a Unique UNESCO City

Bidemi Esposito Loscavo[1], Nunzio Patimisco[1], Gianluca Pietrafesa[1],
Giovanna Andrulli[1] (iD), Rachele Vanessa Gatto[2] (iD), Mariavaleria Mininni[1] (iD),
and Francesco Scorza[2]([✉]) (iD)

[1] Department of European and Mediterranean Cultures, University of Basilicata, Via Lanera,
Matera, Italy
[2] School of Engineering, University of Basilicata, Viale dell'Ateneo Lucano, Potenza, Italy
francesco.scorza@unibas.it

Abstract. The paper discusses an experimental approach oriented to define urban regeneration strategies for the city of Matera (Basilicata, Italy) to address the strategic issues of developing an "innovation ecosystem" as a high value urban development strategy. A group of students in an urban planning course conducted the research, selecting measures to improve specific urban components in a comprehensive view. The study provides a draft master-plan for a specific area of the city of Matera. It may contribute to the public debate on public investments in technological innovations for the strategic development of the former EU Capital of Culture 2019. The study highlights the advantages of the project, including a comprehensive view of specific problems and issues, a logical process to connect problems and solutions, and a reference matrix based on NUA principles. This research contributes to the development of tools and methodologies for NUA downscaling at the local level using innovative technologies and thematic components of urban design.

Keywords: New urban Agenda 2030 · Sustainability · Urban design · innovation ecosystem

1 Introduction

The concept of innovation in urban governance refers to the use of new ideas, methods, and technologies to improve the efficiency, effectiveness, and responsiveness of urban governance. The New Urban Agenda (NUA) [1, 2] represents the main list of global principles inspiring the design of the city of tomorrow getting on shoulders the principle of livability in urban areas, inclusiveness and sustainability.

Innovation HUB represents quite a common intervention category in urban regeneration as it represents a way to include the contribution of innovative SME and start-up in the design of urban fabric combining the benefits of functional regeneration with the strategic perspective of added value for the local socio-economic system. Innovation HUB are, in fact, an invariant of smart city strategy [3, 4], and realized different effects according to the implementation features.

© The Author(s), under exclusive license to Springer Nature Switzerland AG 2023
O. Gervasi et al. (Eds.): ICCSA 2023 Workshops, LNCS 14110, pp. 129–137, 2023.
https://doi.org/10.1007/978-3-031-37123-3_11

According to the NUA structure, the project analyzed the implementation of the principle of "AGE RESPONSIVE PLANNING" and proposed design hypotheses to improve the actual situation. In particular the target of the study was the young people between 20 and 35. It means students or young professionals facing the market and proposing innovation also in terms of new start-ups.

This is connected with the idea of Innovation HUB as a physical repository for innovative ideas and innovative business models but the students identify a distributed functional and infrastructural system in the center of Matera town where to approach urban innovation by the concept of innovation ecosystem.

Recent studies conducted at the University of Basilicata in Italy have shown that teaching sustainable development requires more and different tools, particularly in academia. The study involved students developing a project in Matera, which assessed the compliance of NUA principles in a specific sample area [5–12].

The study demonstrated the effectiveness of an academic teaching approach on scaling down NUA principles and provided a preliminary structure for developing new tools to reinforce the new generation of territorial technicians, particularly engineers and architects. In conclusion, this paper highlights the key arguments and recommendations for future applications of the NUA in urban planning and territorial management, emphasizing the importance of sustainable development in urban areas.

2 Background and Scope of the Research

The term "innovation ecosystem" refers to the interconnected network of various individuals, organizations, institutions, and resources that collectively contribute to the development, implementation, and diffusion of innovative ideas, products, and services. This includes entrepreneurs, researchers, investors, policymakers, and other stakeholders who work together to create an environment that fosters innovation and supports its growth. The innovation ecosystem involves both formal and informal mechanisms, such as research institutions, incubators, accelerators, funding sources, regulatory frameworks, and cultural attitudes towards risk-taking and entrepreneurship. A thriving innovation ecosystem can have significant positive effects on economic growth, job creation, and social progress.

Innovation ecosystems and urban regeneration are closely connected, as innovation can play a key role in driving urban regeneration efforts. By fostering collaboration between actors within an innovation ecosystem, new technologies and approaches can be developed that support the goals of urban regeneration. For example, new businesses and industries can be attracted to an area, generating economic growth and creating new jobs. In addition, innovative solutions can be developed to address social and environmental challenges, such as reducing carbon emissions, improving public health, or increasing access to affordable housing.

Overall, innovation ecosystems and urban regeneration are mutually reinforcing concepts that can support each other's goals. By creating an environment that fosters innovation, urban regeneration efforts can be more effective, and by supporting urban regeneration, innovation ecosystems can generate economic, social, and environmental benefits for communities.

In this case we adapt the concept of innovation ecosystem to a peculiar urban context: the City of Matera. Matera was the EU Capital of CUlture in 2019 and it is actually recognized worldwide for its unique urban fabric marked by "Sassi" districts, an ancient settlement climbing a natural canyon (the "Gravina").

The identity of the place is linked to the historical capital combined with a number of rural traditions influencing social habits, foods, arts etc.

The city benefits from Matera 2019 EU COC in terms of tourism flows and the local tourism system developed extensively. Actually, the debate about the future of the city opens a question about a new effective strategy integrating tourism marked with a high added value sector.

The presence of the University and research center in the town combined with other key business operators opens a perspective to realize an innovation ecosystem in the core of the town.

This proposal, coherently with NUA recommendations, opens a qualitative studio experience with architectural MSc students, synthetically reported in this paper.

3 The Case Study and the Target

In the sustainability criteria of the New Urban Agenda, it is important to consider planning that is age-appropriate and responsive to the needs of each citizen. Taking into account the preservation and protection of the environment and proactive planning to ensure a better future for the population, it is intended to promote quality growth and social cohesion. In particular, there is a need for a connection between the world of work and young people, creating new opportunities in urban planning to enhance skills and abilities in the world of work. The development of new emerging enterprises is essential to ensure a long-term economic future and to prevent young people from being uneducated, formed and employed.

The ISTAT permanent business census in 2019 shows that the local business system compared to the national system is weak, both in terms of numbers and scope. It shows a low capacity for internationalization, collaboration and financing, but also for investment in digital technologies.

The 'age responsive planning' target relative to a population bracket between 20 and 35 years of age was applied to an area of the city of Matera where most of the economic life takes place, i.e. between the business center and the Piano, and extends from the Macamarda Park to the Province Palace, involving Don Minzoni Street, Vittorio Veneto Square, S. Biagio Street, S. Giovanni Square, Corso Street, S. Francesco Square, Ridola Street, part of Lucana Street and Lanera Street (Fig. 1).

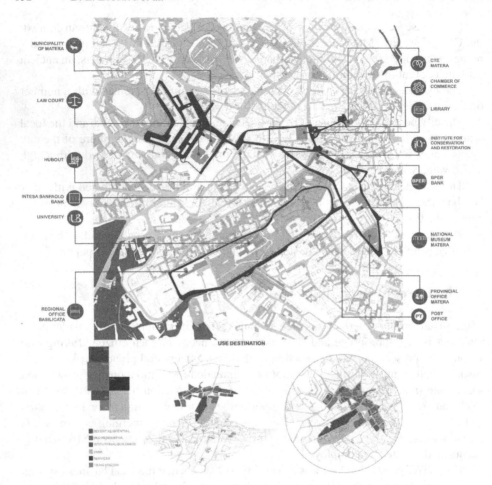

Fig. 1. Study area with indication of social incubators and composition of destination use.

Analyzing the urban framework and thus the set of services offered to citizens, we have a composition of the area's destination use consisting of the historical fabric (31%) and parks (28%), while services (13%), institutional and residential buildings account for 8% and 15% of the total respectively and the remaining 5% is occupied by the train station.

For the project theme 'ecosystem of innovations', all the enclosures where working life takes place were identified, as shown on the map: the Inland Revenue Agency, Intesa Sanpaolo Bank, the National Library, BPER Bank, the Chamber of Commerce, the House of Technology, the Municipality of Matera, the HubOut, the Institute for Conservation and Restoration, the National Museum, the Italian Post Office, the Prefecture, the Province, the Region, the Law Court and the University of Basilicata. These are linked by principles of proximity and interrelationships which, if functionally linked, can constitute a balanced, renewed and sustainable ecosystem of innovation production. The capacity of the innovation ecosystem is to create a network of individuals, entities, resources and structures that unite intentions, thereby catalyzing the emergence of new products, ideas, methods and systems.

These principles have been applied in various contexts and we can take as reference successful ecosystems such as Apple park, Googleplex and Nvidia Headquarters located in California (USA) or in Italy LUISSenlab and PoliHub that through start-ups, university laboratories and companies redesign the future through technological innovation in co-working spaces.

The intention is to create a network for sharing projects in places and spaces to innovate and redevelop in an excellent location, the heart of the city of Matera, in order to attract ideas and funding for young people from Lucania and not only.

4   Defining an Ecosystem

The limited job offer in digital services assumes relevant characteristics for young people under 35 in cities distant from the nation's main infrastructure system. The study conducted emphasizes the absence of employment in high-tech industries, and Fig. 2 illustrates how this weak sector is concentrated in a 15-min radius. The system that has been discovered includes a number of institutional and non-institutional actors that, when connected, can create the possibility of creating a network of support for widespread initiatives and skills. The proximity condition represents an added value to encourage the exchange of ideas. San Rocco Hub is part of the localized services which, in comparison

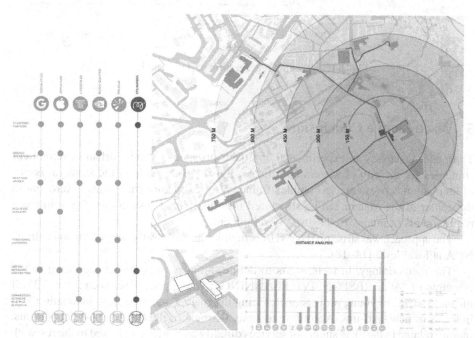

Fig. 2. Study area with indication of distance from the ecosystem center and services benchmark analysis

with other similar realities that have distinguished themselves internationally for being incubators of innovation, fails to have a significant impact on urban realities.

Within the thematic area identified, two buildings in a strategic position in a state of abandonment are undergoing redevelopment in order to implement the services and offer a meeting space and Co-Working spaces (Fig. 3).

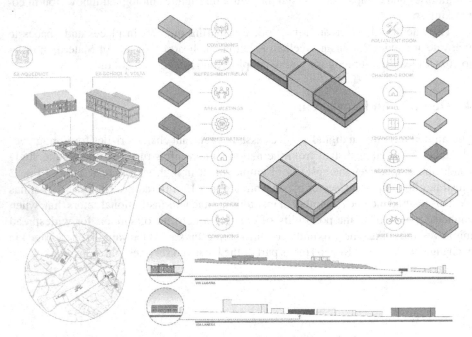

Fig. 3. Co-working regeneration design hypothesis

5 Discussioni e Conclusioni

The paper discusses an experimental approach oriented to define urban development strategies for the city of Matera (Basilicata, Italy) [13] to address the strategic issues of innovation ecosystem as a complex framework of structure and infrastructure that in the center of the Matera can be structured in a distributed system ensuring minimum requirements of innovative business development.

The approach was structured on NUA principles and follow the way of "downscaling" NUA at local level [14–18].

The methodology, in facts, starts to define the city users' target according to the principle of "AGE RESPONSIVE PLANNING": young people between 20 and 35. It means students or young professionals facing the market and proposing innovation also in terms of new start-ups. According to an assessment of the specific place conditions, mainly related to the local supply of services directly and indirectly linked to the research topic. The design process highlighted intervention categories distinguishing between soft actions and infrastructures.

The research results actually represent a draft master-plan developed in urban planning academic class that could contribute to the public debate on the university city role as a driver for strategic urban development in Matera. The recommendation to adopt collaborative design framework is widely accepted and robust approach has to be adopted to put in practice the operational implementation of such proposal [19–23].

Main evidences refer to the topic of "teaching downscaling of NUA" as a new technical demand for the next generation of territorial technicians. The experiment allowed to identify specific benefits compared to the traditional urban regeneration approach: an extended comprehensive view of specific problems and issues to be addressed by the project; a rational process in verifying the logical nexus between problems, place conditions and potential solutions; a reference matrix based on NUA principle to measure impacts and results of the proposal as a robust accounting system to give evidence of the quality of the design.

Limitations regards the academic dimension of the laboratory, only partially connected with procedural and administrative rules and constraints characterizing the case study.

This research contributes to the open question [17, 18, 24, 25] regarding tools and methodologies to support NUA downscaling at local level [26–31] adopting innovative technologies [22, 32] on thematic component of urban design [33, 34].

References

1. UN HABITAT: New Urban Agenda. United Nations (2016)
2. Caprotti, F., et al.: The new urban agenda: key opportunities and challenges for policy and practice. Urban Res Pract. **10**, 367–378 (2017). https://doi.org/10.1080/17535069.2016.127 5618
3. Garau, C., Annunziata, A.: A method for assessing the vitality potential of urban areas. the case study of the metropolitan city of Cagliari, Italy. City, Territory and Architecture **9**(1), 1–23 (2022). https://doi.org/10.1186/s40410-022-00153-6
4. Garau, C., Annunziata, A., Yamu, C.: A walkability assessment tool coupling multi-criteria analysis and space syntax: the case study of Iglesias, Italy. Eur. Plann. Stud., 1–23 (2020). https://doi.org/10.1080/09654313.2020.1761947
5. Scorza, F., Fortunato, G.: Active mobility-oriented urban development: a morpho-syntactic scenario for a mid-sized town. Eur. Plann. Stud., 1–25 (2022). https://doi.org/10.1080/096 54313.2022.2077094
6. Scorza, F., Fortunato, G.: Cyclable cities: building feasible scenario through urban space morphology assessment. J. Urban Plan. Dev. **147**, 05021039 (2021). https://doi.org/10.1061/(ASCE)UP.1943-5444.0000713
7. Scorza, F., Santopietro, L.: A systemic perspective for the Sustainable Energy and Climate Action Plan (SECAP). Eur. Plann. Stud., 1–21 (2021). https://doi.org/10.1080/09654313.2021.1954603
8. Santopietro, L., Scorza, F.: The Italian experience of the covenant of mayors: a territorial evaluation. Sustainability. **13**, 1289 (2021). https://doi.org/10.3390/su13031289
9. Gatto, R., Santopietro, L., Scorza, F.: Roghudi: Developing knowledge of the places in an abandoned inland municipality. Lecture Notes in Computer Science (including subseries Lecture Notes in Artificial Intelligence and Lecture Notes in Bioinformatics). LNCS, vol. 13382, pp. 48–53 (2022). https://doi.org/10.1007/978-3-031-10592-0_5/COVER

10. Gatto, R., Santopietro, L., Scorza, F.: Tourism and Abandoned Inland Areas Development Demand: A Critical Appraisal. Lecture Notes in Computer Science (including subseries Lecture Notes in Artificial Intelligence and Lecture Notes in Bioinformatics). LNCS, vol. 13382, pp. 40–47 (2022). https://doi.org/10.1007/978-3-031-10592-0_4/COVER
11. Santopietro, L., Scorza, F., Murgante, B.: Multiple components in GHG stock of transport sector: technical improvements for SECAP Baseline Emissions Inventory assessment. TeMA – J. Land Use, Mobility Environ. **15**, 5–24 (2022). https://doi.org/10.6092/1970-9870/8391
12. Corrado, S., Giannini, B., Santopietro, L., Oliveto, G., Scorza, F.: Water management and municipal climate adaptation plans: a preliminary assessment for flood risks management at urban scale. In: Gervasi, O., et al. (eds.) ICCSA 2020. LNCS, vol. 12255, pp. 184–192. Springer, Cham (2020). https://doi.org/10.1007/978-3-030-58820-5_14
13. Mininni, M.: Matera Lucania 2017. Quodlibet (2017).https://doi.org/10.2307/j.ctv2gz3xk0
14. Capodiferro, M., et al.: "University equity": students' facilities in major tourism destination towns. In: Gervasi, O. (ed.) Computational Science and Its Applications - ICCSA 2023 (2023)
15. Lagonigro, D., et al.: Downscaling NUA: Matera new urban structure. In: Gervasi, O. (ed.) Computational Science and Its Applications - ICCSA 2023. Springer (2023)
16. Florio, E., et al.: SuperABLE: Matera accessible for all. In: Gervasi, O. (ed.) Computational Science and Its Applications - ICCSA 2023. Springer (2023)
17. Gatto, R.V., Corrado, S., Scorza, F.: Towards a definition of tourism ecosystem. In: 18th International Forum on Knowledge Asset Dynamics (IFKAD) - Managing Knowledge for Sustainability (2023)
18. Corrado, S., Gatto, R.V., Scorza, F.: The European digital decade and the tourism ecosystem: a methodological approach to improve tourism analytics. In: 18th International Forum on Knowledge Asset Dynamics (IFKAD) - Managing Knowledge for Sustainability, Matera (2023)
19. Campagna, M.: Metaplanning: about designing the geodesign process. Landsc. Urban Plan. **156**, 118–128 (2016). https://doi.org/10.1016/J.LANDURBPLAN.2015.08.019
20. Steinitz, C., Orland, B., Fisher, T., Campagna, M.: Geodesign to address global change. Intelligent Environments, 193–242 (2023). https://doi.org/10.1016/B978-0-12-820247-0.00016-3
21. Fiore, P., Padula, A., Angela Pilogallo, F.S.: Facing urban regeneration issues through geodesign approach. The case of Gravina in Puglia. In: Leone, A., Gargiulo, C. (eds.) Environmental and Territorial Modelling for Planning and Design. FedOAPress (2018). https://doi.org/10.6093/978-88-6887-048-5
22. Dastoli, P.S., Pontrandolfi, P., Scorza, F., Corrado, S., Azzato, A.: Applying geodesign towards an integrated local development strategy: the Val d'Agri Case (Italy). Lecture Notes in Computer Science (including subseries Lecture Notes in Artificial Intelligence and Lecture Notes in Bioinformatics). LNCS, vol. 13379, pp. 253–262 (2022). https://doi.org/10.1007/978-3-031-10545-6_18/COVER
23. Padula, A., Fiore, P., Pilogallo, A., Scorza, F.: Collaborative approach in strategic development planning for small municipalities. applying geodesign methodology and tools for a new municipal strategy in Scanzano Jonico. In: Leone, A., Gargiulo, C. (eds.) Environmental and Territorial Modelling for Planning and Design, pp. 665–672. FedOApress (2018). https://doi.org/10.6093/978-88-6887-048-5
24. Casas, G.L., Scorza, F.: Sustainable planning: a methodological toolkit. In: Gervasi, O., et al. (eds.) ICCSA 2016. LNCS, vol. 9786, pp. 627–635. Springer, Cham (2016). https://doi.org/10.1007/978-3-319-42085-1_53
25. Scorza, F., Gatto, R.V.: Identifying territorial values for tourism development: the case study of calabrian greek area. Sustainability **15**, 5501 (2023). https://doi.org/10.3390/SU15065501
26. Vona, M., Harabaglia, P., Murgante, B.: Thinking about resilient cities: studying Italian earthquakes **169**, 185–199 (2016). https://doi.org/10.1680/UDAP.14.00007

27. Murgante, B., Borruso, G., Lapucci, A.: Sustainable development: concepts and methods for its application in urban and environmental planning. Stud. Comput. Intell. **348**, 1–15 (2011). https://doi.org/10.1007/978-3-642-19733-8_1/COVER
28. Las Casas, G., Scorza, F., Murgante, B.: Razionalità a-priori: una proposta verso una pianificazione antifragile. Italian J. Reg. Sci. **18**, 329–338 (2019). https://doi.org/10.14650/93656
29. Murgante, B., Borruso, G., Lapucci, A.: Geocomputation and urban planning. Stud. Comput. Intell. **176**, 1–17 (2009). https://doi.org/10.1007/978-3-540-89930-3_1/COVER
30. Scorza, F., Pilogallo, A., Saganeiti, L., Murgante, B.: Natura 2000 areas and sites of national interest (SNI): measuring (un) integration between naturalness preservation and environmental remediation policies. Sustainability (Switzerland) **12**, 2928 (2020). https://doi.org/10.3390/SU12072928
31. Saganeiti, L., Mustafa, A., Teller, J., Murgante, B.: Modeling urban sprinkling with cellular automata. Sustain. Cities Soc. **65**, 102586 (2021). https://doi.org/10.1016/J.SCS.2020.102586
32. Corrado, S., Scorza, F.: Machine learning based approach to assess territorial marginality. Lecture Notes in Computer Science (including subseries Lecture Notes in Artificial Intelligence and Lecture Notes in Bioinformatics). LNCS, vol. 13376, pp. 292–302 (2022). https://doi.org/10.1007/978-3-031-10450-3_25/COVER
33. Pilogallo, A., Scorza, F.: Mapping regulation ecosystem services specialization in Italy. J. Urban Plan. Dev. **148**, 04021072 (2022). https://doi.org/10.1061/(ASCE)UP.1943-5444.0000801
34. Scorza, F., Saganeiti, L., Pilogallo, A., Murgante, B.: Ghost planning: the inefficiency of energy sector policies in a low population density region1. Archivio di Studi Urbani e Regionali, 34–55 (2020). https://doi.org/10.3280/ASUR2020-127-S1003

Strategic Development Scenarios in Inland Areas: Logical Framework Approach Preparing Collaborative Design

Barbara Castellaneta⬦, Priscilla Sofia Dastoli(✉)⬦, Simone Corrado⬦,
Rachele Gatto⬦, Rossella Scorzelli⬦, Shiva Rahmani⬦, and Francesco Scorza⬦

School of Engineering, Laboratory of Urban and Regional Systems Engineering,
University of Basilicata, 10, Viale dell'Ateneo Lucano, 85100 Potenza, Italy
`barbara.castellaneta@studenti.unibas.it`,
`{priscillasofia.dastoli,simone.corrado,rachelevanessa.gatto,`
`rossella.scorzelli,shiva.rahmani,francesco.scorza}@unibas.it`

Abstract. Inland areas in Italy are experiencing an increasing trend of depopulation and a critical lack of territorial competitiveness. A "place-based" spatial development policy is seen as an effective way to address this structural weakness, reducing the social and economic exclusion of resident communities. The paper's aim is to apply a study method based on the Logical Framework Approach (LFA) structured methodology that, at the outset, requires an in-depth knowledge of the local context. The study area is located in the Basilicata Region's hinterland and displays the same features of Italian inland areas, far from the centres offering essential services and a fragmented settlement system. The study is composed of a first analysis phase, through the geoSWOT definition. This is followed by a problem analysis and the consequent objective identification phase. Finally, the strategy organised in the Logical Framework Matrix (LFM) is set out, which highlights the rational link between the structure levels. The conclusions highlight the method's robustness as a teaching strategy in urban and regional studies. The specific results achieved are closely in line with the New Urban Agenda (NUA) goals and represent a downscaling to specific case studies.

Keywords: Local development strategy · Inland Area · New Urban Agenda

1 Introduction

The paper presents the results of an educational workshop held at the University of Basilicata's School of Engineering. The research objective was to define a robust framework integrating local context knowledge with a structured methodology based on the Logical Framework Approach, as a preliminary step to the organisation of a participatory workshop with local stakeholders.

The methodological structure of the work is based on the Logical Framework Approach adopted since the 1970s as a reference for the Territorial Engineering course in the master's degree in Environmental Engineering.

© The Author(s), under exclusive license to Springer Nature Switzerland AG 2023
O. Gervasi et al. (Eds.): ICCSA 2023 Workshops, LNCS 14110, pp. 138–151, 2023.
https://doi.org/10.1007/978-3-031-37123-3_12

The research is linked to a wider research project funded by the Italian national government and co-funded by the European Union (ERDF, PON Research and Innovation 2014–2020), which investigates the relationships between environmental risks and fragmented settlement systems in inland areas. The MITIGO project (Mitigation of Natural Risks for Safety and Mobility in the Mountain Areas of Southern Italy)[1] includes several disciplinary contributions and takes urban studies into account in terms of planning sustainable local development strategies [1].

The study area (Fig. 1) is located in the inland area of the Basilicata Region (Italy), between the cities of Potenza and Matera and between the Basento and Bradano valleys. In particular, the following municipalities are included in the study area: Albano di Lucania, Campomaggiore, Castelmezzano and Pietrapertosa.

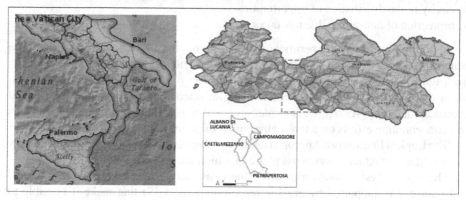

Fig. 1. On the left, in red, the boundaries of the MITIGO Project pilot area. On the right, a physical map of the thirty municipalities showing the study area consisting of four municipalities [2]. (Color figure online)

In the following sections, the special features of the study area are described and the methodological approach is briefly outlined to highlight the main stages of the research.

The geoSWOT is then discussed as the first output of the LFA methodology to highlight the spatial attributes that characterise the processing. The analysis of the problems and the consequent phase of identification of the objectives are represented through two synthetic graphs that describe the strategic branches to be considered in order to proceed to the final phase of spatial planning. At this stage, a brief reference is made to best practices that can also be adapted and repeated in the study area.

Finally, a part of the LFM is presented to give evidence of the rational link between the programme's structure levels. The conclusions highlight the robustness of the method as a teaching strategy in urban and regional studies. This work is the preliminary step to organizing a participatory workshop with local stakeholders, using the Geodesign methodology [3–7]. The specific results achieved are closely in keeping with the NUA [8, 9] objectives and represent an example of downscaling to specific case studies. Furthermore, the application's spatial scope covers an inter-municipal area, thus going

---

[1] "Progetto MITIGO". https://www.mitigoinbasilicata.it/ (accessed Apr. 04, 2023).

beyond the consolidated urban area, by addressing issues related to urban development management in regions with low settlement density.

2 Methodology

A rational approach [10, 11] was chosen to achieve an optimal analysis of the territory system, which is in itself complex, with an analysis aimed at understanding characteristic processes.

This approach pursues the three safeguarding principles as the logical basis of the proposal:

- efficient allocation of resources
- equity in the distribution of opportunities
- protection of non-renewable resources.

In addition, it plans to experiment with the search for a rational 'a-priori' logic, in which the objectives-products-activities-meanings connection becomes clear, starting from the problems and through the implementation of the Logical Framework Approach (LFA). This methodology is based on an operational view of the 'procedural approach' and proposes a process for defining and monitoring objectives and strategies and concentrating efforts on a few well-defined directions.

The Logical Framework Approach takes two phases: a first analysis phase, necessary to know the context and a synthesis phase in which the process is defined.

The first analysis operation involved the construction of a geoSwot [12], defined so because it is supported by graphic representations (GIS) that make it possible to geographically identify what is available on the territory.

Once the critical issues on which to focus were defined, there was a move to the use of the Problem Tree and Objective Tree techniques. All the problems are related with an arrow that makes the cause-effect relationship explicit, forming a hierarchy in which all the branches flow into the key-problem or core-problem; from the key-problem spring the effects, making explicit the causal links between the problems identified, in cause-effect logic.

The objective tree will have the same structure as the problem tree, in that it represents its transformation into a positive one; common objectives can be grouped together, unrealistic and/or unrealisable ones eliminated and new ones inserted if, in the transition from problem to objective, it is useful to better argue specific aspects. The objectives represent future positive wishes. The positive translation changes the cause-effect logic, and here the arrows follow the means-ends logic, i.e. it defines what is needed to achieve the goal.

In the objective tree, identification of strategic lines is possible, provided that the means-ends relationship is correctly verified. In this case, this results in a representation of 'clusters', which are thematically and sectorial consistent with the intervention assumed in the development program. The selection of 'clusters' enables the identification of action strategies which are categorised for a specific intervention sector.

2.1   geoSwot

The SWOT analysis makes it possible to identify strengths, to be exploited and enhanced; weaknesses, on which to focus recovery activities; threats, to be understood and fought against with targeted actions; and finally, opportunities, to be captured and cultivated. The study area's geoSwot (Fig. 2) shows how the weaknesses of the area under examination fall largely into structural problem categories common to inland and mountainous areas.

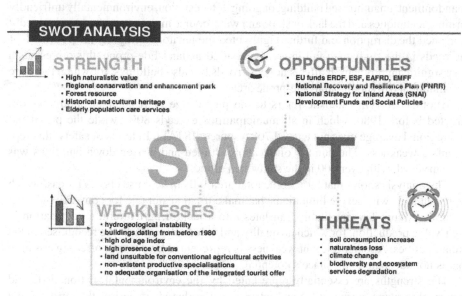

SWOT ANALYSIS

STRENGTH
- High naturalistic value
- Regional conservation and enhancement park
- Forest resource
- Historical and cultural heritage
- Elderly population care services

OPPORTUNITIES
- EU funds ERDF, ESF, EAFRD, EMFF
- National Recovery and Resilience Plan (PNRR)
- National Strategy for Inland Areas (SNAI)
- Development Funds and Social Policies

WEAKNESSES
- hydrogeological instability
- buildings dating from before 1980
- high old age index
- high presence of ruins
- land unsuitable for conventional agricultural activities
- non-existent productive specialisations
- no adequate organisation of the integrated tourist offer

THREATS
- soil consumption increase
- naturalness loss
- climate change
- biodiversity and ecosystem services degradation

Fig. 2. GeoSWOT's main contents for the study area.

National data show how, from 1951 to 2019, the Mezzogiorno's Inner Areas lost 1.2 million residents ($-2.5‰$ on average per year; Italy $-1.6‰$) and one in three municipalities has systematically lost population since 1951 [13]. Moreover, the average value

Table 1. Some background data on the MITIGO area

	Old-age index	Births per 1000 inhabitants	Ruins unit	Percentage wooded area
Albano di Lucania	223,6	6,6	93	51,6%
Campomaggiore	326,2	5,4	42	62,1%
Castelmezzano	408,6	4,1	115	67,7%
Pietrapertosa	314,6	4,3	174	68,4%
Basilicata	214,1	6,1		

of the old-age index[2] found in the municipalities of the MITIGO area (318) exceeds the regional (214) and national (187) values (Table 1).

Another weakness concerns hydrogeological instability, which is widespread in Basilicata and represents a significant problem. Among the natural factors that make the territory susceptible to hydrogeological instability is undoubtedly its geological and geomorphological layout, characterised by a young orography and rising relief. Hydrogeological risk is also strongly influenced by human action. The mountainous land abandonment, unauthorised building, ongoing deforestation, environmentally unfriendly farming techniques and the lack of slope and watercourse maintenance have undoubtedly worsened the disruption and further highlighted the territory's fragility [14]. As 18% of the roads in the study area fall in areas classified as landslide-prone, this represents a very significant problem. It affects not only roads but also buildings, for which there are 670 inhabitants living in landslide-prone areas.

Another worrying statistic refers to the percentage of residential buildings constructed before 1980, which in all municipalities exceeds 80%, while the provincial and regional average does not exceed 70% (source: ISTAT). In terms of safety, this represents a weakness. The number of decaying, ruined and broken down buildings was also surveyed, with over 400 in the study area alone.

The analysis shows that 59% of the total area falls in land use class VI areas, which represent soils with severe limitations that make them unsuitable for conventional agricultural activity. This inevitably translates into a lack of agricultural specialisation in high-value production, for which no quality and valorisation marks are recognised in the municipalities. Another relevant weakness is represented by a tourist offer organisation that is not adequate to the place's potential.

The strengths are essentially represented by the environmental, nationalistic and historical heritage, a true added and intrinsic value that characterises the territory in a special and unique way. The territory includes protected areas of high naturalistic value, in particular, Special Areas of Conservation (SAC), which have been recognised by the European Commission: Dolomiti di Pietrapertosa, Bosco di Montepiano, Foresta Gallipoli-Cognato, Bosco Cupolicchio [15]. Also significant is the presence of the Gallipoli Cognato Regional Park, a protected natural area established in 1997, which also includes Pietrapertosa and Castelmezzano municipalities.

The data referring to the woodland resource is representative, in all the municipalities the percentage of woodland compared to the total extension exceeds 50%, which represents an added value for the area's valorisation. Another strong point is the historical and cultural heritage, and the numerous events linked to local identity. Events linked to religious worship and tradition are numerous and represent a tourist attraction to be exploited, such as the Mascio rite in Pietrapertosa.

The threats are mainly climate change and increasing land take [16]. The 2007 Fourth Assessment Report of the Intergovernmental Panel on Climate Change (IPCC) and numerous following studies state that climate change is producing significant impacts on plant and animal communities, biodiversity and ecosystem services [17]. As far as

---

[2] The old-age index is a synthetic but very dynamic indicator of a population's ageing status. It is obtained by relating the amount of the elderly population (65 years and over) to the youth population (0–14 years), multiplied by 100.

land take and loss of naturalness are concerned, Basilicata today has lower values than the average, but the trend is growing. This growth is not justified since Basilicata is a region with low population density and a decreasing demographic trend [18]. The most important opportunities are represented by ordinary and extraordinary funds, including the National Recovery and Resilience Plan (PNRR), the National Strategy for Inner Areas (SNAI) and EU cohesion funds.

2.2   From Problem Analysis to Objective Definition

The problem tree (Fig. 3) illustrates the critical issues, placed in connection upon the basis of the cause-effect relationship, structured according to a hierarchy that makes it possible to identify the specific fields on which to act.

From the analysis carried out, it emerged that the decline and the lack of territorial valorisation represent the central problem, the system's fulcrum from which the effects observed in the study area spring. This leads to a disadvantaged and vulnerable condition both economically and environmentally.

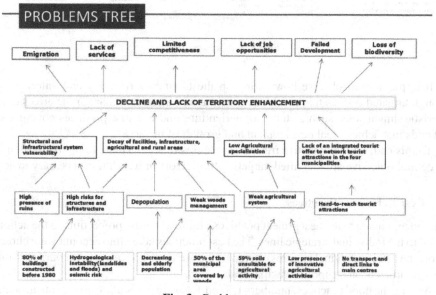

Fig. 3. Problems tree.

The causes identification and the subsequent actions for their removal or containment are the starting point to avoid the induced effects, including significant emigration and biodiversity loss before they become irreversible conditions for the territory.

The problems found in the previous diagram, let us transport these to the positive, identifying future desirable positive conditions. This modifies the logic, so we move from cause-effect to means-ends logic. Thus to define what is needed to achieve the ends, the objectives (Fig. 4).

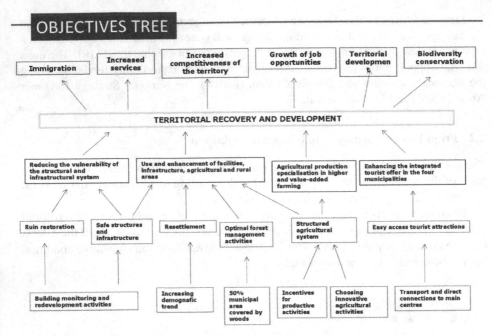

Fig. 4. Objectives tree.

It is possible to observe how acting on the territory's recovery and valorisation, through targeted actions that touch in a synergic and integrated manner the area's characteristic dimensions, such as tourism, agriculture and forestry, produces conclusions and ends that achieve real development and growth of the area.

To this end, on the objective tree, the strategies that contribute to the realisation of the central objective are identified, targeting the sectors in which it is necessary to act.

2.3 Best Reference Practices

Reference is made to the best project practices (Table 2) before proceeding to the actions linked to the individual strategic lines. The best practices taken into account were chosen according to the individual features offered by the area and, above all, to encourage strong synergy projects on a supra-municipal scale.

Among the good practices, numbers 1.1 and 1.4 were particularly taken into account. In the first case, the municipalities taking part in the project identified an area in the Local Government Plan to experiment with collective functions in line with environmental protection and conservation. The second one, on the other hand, is a practical experience of conservation agriculture, with medicinal herb cultivation combined with honey production as an environmentally and ecosystem-friendly solution.

2.4 Logical Framework Matrix (LFM)

The proposal, outlined in the Logical Framework Matrix (Fig. 5), aims to emphasise the effectiveness and efficiency principles and to clarify the coherence and relevance

Table 2. Best reference practices on the project area MITIGO

N°	Practice	Actors	Activities	Location	Outcomes and Products	link
1.1	Shared Soils Project	Municipalities / Cariplo Foundation	*Educational and practical activities with citizens; municipal technician training*	Albino, Nembro, Ponte San Pietro, Pradalunga municipalities (Piedmont)	Setting up soil valorisation paths for social and naturalistic functions	https:// www. fondaz ioneca riplo. it/it/ index. html
1.2	SOS4Life European project initiative	Municipalities	*Assessment and mapping of seven soil ecosystem services, and impact analysis of the services' consumption*	Forlì, San Lazzaro di Savena and Carpi Municipalities (Emilia Romagna)	Environmental planning and evaluation process based on Ecosystem Services	http:// www. sos4li fe.it/
1.3	Life HelpSoil	Municipalities	*Setting up conservation agriculture activities for sustainable and stable productivity*	Po Valley (Northern Italy)	Promoting the dissemination of improved solutions that increase agricultural sustainability and competitiveness	https:// www. lifehe lps oil.eu/
1.4	Herbalist	Farms	*The project aims to develop product micro-supply chains from officinal plants*	Project at the Villiago di Sedico biological farm (Veneto Region)	Development of a officinal plant product chain to be sponsored by farms	
1.5	The Cerreto Brigantes	Community cooperation	*Accommodation and tourist services, educational programmes, chestnut recovery, and chestnut production rediscovery*	Emilia-Romagna	Local partnership processes and tools for sustainable and long-lasting forest management	https:// www. ibriga ntidic erreto. com/

of choices to the implementation context, according to the search for a context- or place-based policy.

Logical Framework Matrix "MITIGO area"				
INTERVENTION LOGIC	**OBJECTIVELY VERIFIABLE INDICATORS**			**MEANS OF VERIFICATION**
OVERALL OBJECTIVE	**PERFORMANCE INDICATORS**	**EFFICIENCY INDICATORS**		
GO: Territorial Recovery and Enhancement				
SO1: Exploitation of structural, agricultural and forestry heritage	No. of monitoring-adaptation and enhancement activities	No. of monitoring-adaptation and valorisation/investment activities		Municipal Offices
SO2: Agricultural production specialisation in higher value-added crops	No. of agricultural activities in higher value-added crops	No. of agricultural activities in higher value-added crops/investment		Municipal Offices ISTAT
SO3: Strengthening integrated tourism offer in the four municipalities	tourist presences	Tourist presences/investments		ISTAT
R1.1: Suitable facilities and infrastructure	No. of adequate facilities and infrastructure	No. of adequate facilities and infrastructure/investment		Municipal Technical Offices
R1.2: New residents	No. of residents	No. of residents / investment and facilities		Municipal Offices ISTAT
R1.3: Forest management partnerships	Hectares of managed woodland	Hectares of woods managed/investments		Municipal Offices
R2.1: Agricultural system specialisation in high-value medicinal herbs	Hectares cultivated with officinal herbs	Hectares cultivated with officinal herbs/investments		Municipal Offices
R2.2: High-quality honey production	Kg honey produced	Kg honey produced/investment		Municipal Offices
R2.3: High Value Production	Revenue from product sales	Revenue from the product/ investment sales		ISTAT
R2.4: Increased companies' income	Companies' income	Companies' income/investment		ISTAT
R3.1: Tourist presences in all municipalities	Balanced tourist presences in municipalities	Balanced tourist presences in municipalities / investment		ISTAT
R3.2: Non-seasonal flows	Tourist presences in winter months	Tourist presence in winter months / investment		ISTAT
A1.1) Building monitoring and redevelopment	INPUT			
A1.1) Hydrogeological instability monitoring	Public funding (PNRR, EU funds ERDF, ESF, EAFRD, EMFF) Specialised equipment and human resources			
A1.2) Economic and tax benefits for home buyers in municipalities	CONDITIONS			
A1.2) Economic and tax advantages for starting new businesses	Cooperation between municipalities			
A1.3) Establishing forest management cooperatives	Entrepreneurs and workers to be employed in new businesses in the area			
A1.3) Making available areas of municipal woods	Cooperation between public and private partners			
A 2.1) Training and coaching for innovative agricultural activities for officinal herb production	Cooperation between service providers			
A 2.2) Training and promotion of techniques for herb-based flavoured honey production	Training institutions and personnel to be employed			
A 2.3) Establishment of product processing, valorisation and distribution chains	Specialised staff			
A 3.1) All-inclusive tourism packages spread across all municipalities	Availability of free properties			
A 3.2) Tour operators' training	PRECONDITIONS			
A 3.2) Exploitation of mountain outdoor activities	Collaboration agreement between the four municipalities			

Fig. 5. Logical Framework Matrix "MITIGO area".

The Logical Framework Approach adopted is an 'aid to thinking' [19] rather than a set of procedures. This approach represents a working tool with the goal of streamlining the design process. It does not focus on the discussion of what needs to be made, but rather on the problems and needs to be solved, and only consequently of the goals to be achieved.

In the first section, which contains the intervention logic, the objectives are set out, starting with the general one, i.e. 'recovery and enhancement of the territory' identified in the previous analysis phase. This represents the central and general objective, which is realised through the definition of secondary objectives. These objectives specifically define the various fields of application and contribute to its realisation. By analysing the strategies identified within the objective tree, the following specific objectives were defined:

1. enhancement of structural, agricultural and forestry heritage;
2. agricultural production focus on crops with a higher added value;
3. enhancement of the integrated tourist offer in the four municipalities [20–24].

Through the results definition, the objectives are pursued. This section, therefore, includes the specific, measurable and concrete results associated with each specific objective. These objectives are achieved by deploying targeted and defined actions.

A representative example can be related to specific objective No. 3, i.e. "enhancement of the integrated tourist offer in the four municipalities". The objective is achieved if results are observed, such as an increase in tourist presence in all municipalities and the non-seasonality of flows. Consequently, results are achieved if the specific actions described are put into practice, such as the creation of all-inclusive tourist packages, the promotion of social marketing, tourist operator training, and the enhancement of outdoor activities in mountain areas.

Next to the section containing the logic behind the process, we find the indicators section, which must be objective and verifiable, providing actual evidence of context, effectiveness and efficiency. The definition of context indicators makes it possible to demonstrate how the central objective relating to "recovery and enhancement of the territory", represents the process' fulcrum and the most significant point for the MITIGO Area municipalities. In fact, the territory is characterised by a high value of biodiversity, naturalness and a potential tourist attractiveness that is high, but not equally exploited in the four municipalities. The decreasing demographic trend, combined with a precarious economic system, has led to a progressive exodus from the area. This is emblematic in the high presence of ruins, which are a symptom of marked landscape degradation. This underlines the suitability and relevance of the objective identified, and how much it is a priority.

The efficiency and effectiveness indicators identified make it possible to measure the objectives' realisation and specific results' achievement.

With regard to the verification means identified, in addition to Istat, municipal offices were considered authoritative and certified information sources. To this end, the authorities' collaboration in the process will be indispensable.

The necessary inputs were mainly identified in public funds with which human resources, equipment and specialised personnel could be associated.

3 Discussion and Conclusions

It is difficult to reverse the trend of depopulation and the increase in the elderly population with single, punctual actions. A "place-based" spatial development policy must be implemented; therefore, a long-term strategy has been proposed to tackle the resource under-exploitation and to reduce the social and economic exclusion of these marginal places. The more this strategy is specific and linked to the MITIGO area, the more effective and appropriate it will be for achieving improvement in the local socio-economic condition.

A strategy made up of targeted actions that start from elements that currently represent weaknesses, through the valorisation of strengths and by seizing the opportunities found, can make a difference.

In the Logframe Matrix, activities with improved solutions to enhance the sustainability and competitiveness of agricultural activities were indicated. An example of conservative and sustainable soil use is the medicinal herb crops associated with beekeeping. At the same time, the focus was on protecting and ensuring the sustainable use of soil while preserving its functions. In particular, the focus has been on conservative farming activities, which can play an important role in restoring soil functionality and enhancing soil ecosystem services. On a wide scale, the strategy outlined contributes to increasing resilience and climate change adaptation capacity [25–28].

The 17 Sustainable Development Goals of the 2030 Agenda, adopted by all United Nations Member State, and the Paris Climate Agreement (2015) consider the three dimensions of sustainable development, i.e. economic, social and ecological, in a balanced manner.

Taking into account the municipalities in the area under analysis, the work aims to find opportunities for development and valorisation, so that the NUA principles can be applied to the rural context. If we consider the topic of environmental sustainability, it is present throughout the NUA, as biodiversity and ecosystems conservation are essential aspects for sustainable development, both in urban and rural contexts. This is also central to the 2030 agenda, which has as its Goal 15, "life on earth".

The conservation of natural areas and assets that provide ecosystem services through land management and spatial planning is a central theme that is reflected in the spatial analysis carried out. Other fundamental themes are represented by the shared planning process, which must consider the stakeholders' voices, especially those who are directly involved with the given ecosystems [29, 30].

All this is in order to identify integrated solutions and multi-sectorial planning, taking into account all sectors of society with respect for the environment, conservation of biodiversity and respect for ecosystems at the centre. Based on this, with reference to individual activities, there are several actions that could be taken by the four municipalities with the aim of protecting biodiversity and conserving ecosystems, thus realizing the principles expressed within the NUA.

The compliance NUA framework [31–35] reinforce the proposal linking local objectives and proposed actions to a global framework addressing the contemporary planning perspective a mean to achieve global sustainability in the urban perspective [36–38].

This work is the preliminary step to organizing a participatory workshop [39–41] with local stakeholders. The goal is to use the Geodesign methodology to create proposals for change and assess their impacts, sharing information with stakeholders involved in this context.

References

1. Scorza, F., Santopietro, L., Corrado, S., Dastoli, P.S., Santarsiero, V., Gatto, R., Murgante, B.: Training for territorial sustainable development design in Basilicata remote areas: geodesign workshop. In: Gervasi, O., Murgante, B., Misra, S., Ana, M.A., Rocha, C., Garau, C. (eds.) Computational Science and Its Applications – ICCSA 2022 Workshops: Malaga, Spain, July 4–7, 2022, Proceedings, Part III, pp. 242–252. Springer International Publishing, Cham (2022). https://doi.org/10.1007/978-3-031-10545-6_17
2. Villani, V., Barbato, G., Rianna, G., Mercogliano, P.: Profilo climatico per un'area compresa fra le città di Potenza e Matera, e fra le valli dei fiumi Basento e Bradano. (2022)
3. Steinitz, C., Orland, B., Fisher, T., Campagna, M.: Geodesign to address global change. In: Intelligent Environments, pp. 193–242 (2023). https://doi.org/10.1016/B978-0-12-820247-0.00016-3
4. Scorza, F.: Sustainable urban regeneration in Gravina in Puglia, Italy. In: Fisher, T., Orland, B., Steinitz, C. (eds.) The International Geodesign Collaboration. Changing Geography by Design, pp. 112–113. ESRI Press, Redlands, California (2020)
5. Padula, A., Fiore, P., Pilogallo, A., Scorza, F.: Collaborative approach in strategic development planning for small municipalities. Applying geodesign methodology and tools for a new municipal strategy in Scanzano Jonico. In: Leone, A., Gargiulo, C. (eds.) Environmental and territorial modelling for planning and design, pp. 665–672. FedOApress (2018). https://doi.org/10.6093/978-88-6887-048-5
6. Dastoli, P.S., Pontrandolfi, P., Scorza, F., Corrado, S., Azzato, A.: Applying geodesign towards an integrated local development strategy: the Val d'Agri Case (Italy), BT - Computational Science and Its Applications – ICCSA 2022 Workshops, pp. 253–262 (2022). https://doi.org/10.1007/978-3-031-10545-6_18
7. Scorza, F.: Training decision-makers: GEODESIGN workshop paving the way for new urban agenda. In: Gervasi, O., et al. (eds.) ICCSA 2020. LNCS, vol. 12252, pp. 310–316. Springer, Cham (2020). https://doi.org/10.1007/978-3-030-58811-3_22
8. UN HABITAT: New Urban Agenda. United Nations (2016)
9. Pontrandolfi, P., Dastoli, P.S.: Comparing impact evaluation evidence of EU and local development policies with new urban Agenda themes: the Agri Valley case in Basilicata (Italy).https://doi.org/10.3390/su13169376
10. Casas, G.L., Scorza, F.: Sustainable planning: a methodological toolkit. In: Gervasi, O., et al. (eds.) ICCSA 2016. LNCS, vol. 9786, pp. 627–635. Springer, Cham (2016). https://doi.org/10.1007/978-3-319-42085-1_53
11. Dastoli, P.S., Pontrandolfi, P.: Strategic guidelines to increase the resilience of inland areas: the case of the Alta Val d'Agri (Basilicata-Italy). In: Gervasi, O., et al. (eds.) ICCSA 2021. LNCS, vol. 12958, pp. 119–130. Springer, Cham (2021). https://doi.org/10.1007/978-3-030-87016-4_9
12. Helms, M.M., Nixon, J.: Exploring SWOT analysis – where are we now?: a review of academic research from the last decade. J. Strateg. Manag. 3, 215–251 (2010). https://doi.org/10.1108/17554251011064837
13. Bianchino, A., Carbonara, M., Carucci, A.M., Tebala, D.: Le aree interne tra spopolamento e povertà. https://www.istat.it/it/files/2022/09/31_ISTAT_MILeS2022_Bianchino_Carbonara_Carucci_Tebala.pdf

14. Rischio idrogeologico in Basilicata. http://www.protezionecivilebasilicata.it/protcivbas/sec tion.jsp?sec=100053
15. Regione Basilicata: Siti Rete Natura 2000. https://rsdi.regione.basilicata.it/siti-rete-natura-2000/
16. ISPRA: Consumo di suolo, dinamiche territoriali e servizi ecosistemici (2022)
17. Pilogallo, A., Saganeiti, L., Scorza, F., Murgante, B.: Assessing the impact of land use changes on ecosystem services value. In: Gervasi, O., et al. (eds.) ICCSA 2020. LNCS, vol. 12253, pp. 606–616. Springer, Cham (2020). https://doi.org/10.1007/978-3-030-58814-4_47
18. Saganeiti, L., Pilogallo, A., Scorza, F., Mussuto, G., Murgante, B.: Spatial indicators to evaluate urban fragmentation in basilicata region. In: Gervasi, O., et al. (eds.) ICCSA 2018. LNCS, vol. 10964, pp. 100–112. Springer, Cham (2018). https://doi.org/10.1007/978-3-319-95174-4_8
19. Coleman, G.: Logical framework approach to the monitoring and evaluation of agricultural and rural development projects. Project Appraisal **2**, 251–259 (1987). https://doi.org/10.1080/02688867.1987.9726638
20. Scorza, F., Gatto, R.V.: Identifying territorial values for tourism development: the case study of Calabrian Greek area. Sustainability **15**, 5501 (2023). https://doi.org/10.3390/SU15065501
21. Gatto, R., Santopietro, L., Scorza, F.: Roghudi: developing knowledge of the places in an abandoned inland municipality. Lecture Notes in Computer Science (including subseries Lecture Notes in Artificial Intelligence and Lecture Notes in Bioinformatics). LNCS, vol. 13382, pp. 48–53 (2022). https://doi.org/10.1007/978-3-031-10592-0_5/COVER
22. Séraphin, H., Platania, M., Spencer, P., Modica, G.: Events and tourism development within a local community: the case of winchester (UK). Sustainability **10**(10), 3728 (2018). https://doi.org/10.3390/su10103728
23. Murgante, B., Borruso, G., Lapucci, A.: Sustainable development: concepts and methods for its application in urban and environmental planning. In: Murgante, B., Borruso, G., Lapucci, A. (eds.) Geocomputation, Sustainability and Environmental Planning, pp. 1–15. Springer Berlin Heidelberg, Berlin, Heidelberg (2011). https://doi.org/10.1007/978-3-642-19733-8_1
24. Corrado, S., Gatto, R.V., Scorza, F.: The European digital decade and the tourism ecosystem: a methodological approach to improve tourism analytics. In: 18th International Forum on Knowledge Asset Dynamics (IFKAD) - Managing Knowledge for Sustainability, Matera (2023)
25. Scorza, F., Santopietro, L.: A systemic perspective for the Sustainable Energy and Climate Action Plan (SECAP). Eur. Plann. Stud., 1–21 (2021).https://doi.org/10.1080/09654313.2021.1954603
26. Santopietro, L., Scorza, F.: The Italian experience of the covenant of mayors: a territorial evaluation. Sustainability **13**, 1289 (2021). https://doi.org/10.3390/su13031289
27. Scorza, F., Fortunato, G.: Active mobility-oriented urban development: a morpho-syntactic scenario for a mid-sized town. Eur. Plann. Stud., 1–25 (2022). https://doi.org/10.1080/09654313.2022.2077094
28. Scorza, F., Fortunato, G.: Cyclable cities: building feasible scenario through urban space morphology assessment. J Urban Plan Dev. **147**, 05021039 (2021). https://doi.org/10.1061/(ASCE)UP.1943-5444.0000713
29. Daley, J.M., Angulo, J.: People-centered community planning. J. Community Dev. Soc. **21**, 88–103 (1990). https://doi.org/10.1080/15575339009489963
30. Dastoli, P.S., Pontrandolfi, P.: Methods and tools for a participatory local development strategy - new metropolitan perspectives. Calabrò, F., Della Spina, L., Piñeira Mantiñán, M.J. (eds.), pp. 2112–2121. Springer International Publishing, Cham (2022). https://doi.org/10.1007/978-3-031-06825-6_203

31. Pilogallo, A., Saganeiti, L., Scorza, F., Murgante, B.: Ecosystem services approach to evaluate renewable energy plants effects. In: Misra, S., et al. (eds.) ICCSA 2019. LNCS, vol. 11624, pp. 281–290. Springer, Cham (2019). https://doi.org/10.1007/978-3-030-24311-1_20

32. Scorza, F., Murgante, B., Las Casas, G., Fortino, Y., Pilogallo, A.: Investigating territorial specialization in tourism sector by ecosystem services approach. In: Stratigea, A., Kavroudakis, D. (eds.) Mediterranean Cities and Island Communities. PI, pp. 161–179. Springer, Cham (2019). https://doi.org/10.1007/978-3-319-99444-4_7

33. Pilogallo, A., Scorza, F.: Ecosystem services multifunctionality: an analytical framework to support sustainable spatial planning in Italy. Sustainability. 14, 3346 (2022). https://doi.org/10.3390/SU14063346

34. Pilogallo, A., Saganeiti, L., Scorza, F., Las Casas, G.: Tourism attractiveness: main components for a spacial appraisal of major destinations according with ecosystem services approach. In: Gervasi, O., et al. (eds.) ICCSA 2018. LNCS, vol. 10964, pp. 712–724. Springer, Cham (2018). https://doi.org/10.1007/978-3-319-95174-4_54

35. Pilogallo, A., Scorza, F.: Mapping regulation ecosystem services specialization in Italy. J. Urban Plann. Dev. 148 (2022). https://doi.org/10.1061/(ASCE)UP.1943-5444.0000801

36. Garau, C., Annunziata, A.: A method for assessing the vitality potential of urban areas. The case study of the metropolitan city of Cagliari, Italy. City, Territory and Architecture 9(1), 1–23 (2022). https://doi.org/10.1186/s40410-022-00153-6

37. Garau, C., Annunziata, A., Yamu, C.: A walkability assessment tool coupling multi-criteria analysis and space syntax: the case study of Iglesias, Italy. Eur. Plann. Stud., 1–23 (2020). https://doi.org/10.1080/09654313.2020.1761947

38. Francini, M., Chieffallo, L., Palermo, A., Viapiana, M.F.: A method for the definition of local vulnerability domains to climate change and relate mapping. Two case studies in southern Italy. Sustainability 12(22), 9454 (2020). https://doi.org/10.3390/su12229454

39. Conroy, M.M., Evans-Cowley, J.: E-Participation in planning: an analysis of cities adopting on-line citizen participation tools. Eviron. Plann. C. Gov. Policy 24, 371–384 (2006). https://doi.org/10.1068/c1k

40. Scorza, F., Fortunato, G., Carbone, R., Murgante, B., Pontrandolfi, P.: Increasing urban walkability through citizens' participation processes. Sustainability 13, 5835 (2021). https://doi.org/10.3390/su13115835

41. Scorza, F., Pontrandolfi, P.: Citizen participation and technologies: the CAST architecture. In: Gervasi, O., et al. (eds.) ICCSA 2015. LNCS, vol. 9156, pp. 747–755. Springer, Cham (2015). https://doi.org/10.1007/978-3-319-21407-8_53

SuperABLE: Matera Accessible for All

Eularia Florio[1], Simone Rocco Marcosano[1], Raffaele Parrulli[1], Giovanna Andrulli[1] (iD),
Rachele Vanessa Gatto[2] (iD), Mariavaleria Mininni[1] (iD), and Francesco Scorza[2](✉) (iD)

[1] Department of European and Mediterranean Cultures, University of Basilicata, Via Lanera,
Matera, Italy
[2] School of Engineering, University of Basilicata, Viale Dell'Ateneo Lucano, Potenza, Italy
francesco.scorza@unibas.it

Abstract. The article describes an experimental approach focused on developing urban regeneration strategies for Matera, Italy, with a particular emphasis on addressing the needs of all, including people with different kinds of impediment. The study was conducted by a group of students in an urban planning course who selected measures to improve various urban components, including heritage, urban regulation and pedestrian safety. The result was a draft guidelines for the city that can inform public debate on "Planning for migrants, ethnic, minorities and persons with disabilities" and support the city's cultural and tourism development strategy. The study's strengths include its comprehensive view of specific problems and issues, a logical process for connecting problems and solutions, and a reference matrix based on NUA principles. The research contributes to the development of tools and methodologies for NUA downscaling at the local level, leveraging innovative technologies and thematic components of urban design.

Keywords: New urban Agenda 2030 · Sustainability · Urban design · universal design

1 Introduction

The New Urban Agenda (NUA) is a widely accepted concept that has led to the development of new agreements among key stakeholder groups involved in urban planning and territorial management. The NUA is associated with global sustainability targets and has resulted in a new form of commitment in public decision-making. The United Nations describes the NUA [1] as a global commitment to promoting sustainable urban development, ensuring that cities and human settlements are inclusive, safe, resilient, and sustainable. The NUA aims to address global issues by generating local innovations in urban management practices. Although there is no comprehensive conceptualization of how to downscale NUA principles and objectives, recent studies have shown that teaching sustainable development requires more and different tools, particularly in academia [2–4]. The study conducted by a student class at the University of Basilicata demonstrated the effectiveness of an academic approach in scaling down NUA principles and provided a preliminary structure for developing new tools to reinforce

© The Author(s), under exclusive license to Springer Nature Switzerland AG 2023
O. Gervasi et al. (Eds.): ICCSA 2023 Workshops, LNCS 14110, pp. 152–161, 2023.
https://doi.org/10.1007/978-3-031-37123-3_13

the new generation of territorial technicians, particularly engineers and architects. The study involved students developing a project in Matera (EU Capital of Culture 2019) that assessed the compliance of NUA principles in a specific sample area. The project is titled "SuperABLE" and it analyzed the implementation of the principle of "PLANNING FOR MIGRANTS, ETHNIC MINORITIES AND PERSONS WITH DISABILITIES" identified gaps and problems, and proposed design hypotheses to improve the situation. The topic overcomes traditional approaches to avoid local barriers for disabilities in specific buildings or public spaces through a comprehensive approach oriented to offer an integrated vision of a city where people with limited mobility capacity can access and benefit city services and public facilities through inclusive approach. The results of the study demonstrated the effectiveness of an academic teaching approach on scaling down NUA' principles [5–7] and provided a preliminary structure for developing new tools to reinforce the new generation of territorial technicians, particularly engineers and architects [8]. In conclusion, this paper highlights the key arguments and recommendations for future applications of the NUA in urban planning and territorial management.

2 Downscaling NUA

The United Nations has adopted the [9] (SDGs), which consist of 17 global goals with 169 targets aimed at ending poverty, protecting the planet, and ensuring peace and prosperity for all. The adoption of the SDGs has brought sustainable development into public policy making. SDG 11 focuses on making cities and human settlements inclusive, safe, resilient, and sustainable, and provides a framework for action on sustainable development. Education and training are essential to ensure the successful implementation of the SDGs. The UN recognizes the importance of education in achieving the SDGs, and UNESCO provides guidelines for educators to incorporate sustainable development into their teaching practices. However, teaching sustainable development requires new tools and approaches, especially in technical disciplines such as urban planning and territorial management. The downscaling of the New Urban Agenda (NUA) principles and objectives to the local context is an open topic, and a bottom-up approach based on the participation of local communities and stakeholders is needed [10–13].

The research focuses on verifying the level of compliance of the principle of universal accessibility in the specific context of Matera addressing the general research question: "how to improve city accessibility for all?". In particular, the city which represents a unique tourist destination site, is an open laboratory in order to experiment with innovative forms of places accessibility within an integrated tourism offer targeted on limited mobility people or other specific weaker groups of city users [14–16].

In particular the focus is on the concept of "right to the city" that according to NUA must be reinforced through explicit inclusion and integration efforts.

Accessible and disability inclusive urban planning is usually called "universal design" and it should represent a driver to enhance the quality of urban design in the ordinary process of urban management and mainly in urban regeneration projects. When we "design for the margins", we "design for all", and it benefits everyone (United Nations Department of Economic and Social Affairs). Participation of disability stakeholders is essential. Persons with disabilities and the organizations that they lead are stakeholders, rights holders and agents in the urban development process Young territorial technicians, such as Engineers and Architects, have the opportunity to gain competitiveness and readiness to develop solutions to the emerging problems in urban and territorial sustainable planning, by experimenting, in practice, the design of urban transformations through the lens of NUA.

3   The Case Study and the Target

Through social, economic, environmental and cultural considerations, the complexity of urbanization underscores the innate interconnections between what is the New Urban Agenda and the Sustainable Development Goals: an equitable and just world for present and future generations, where no one and no place is left behind.

Some connections between the two global agendas are evident, especially with regard to SDGs 11 on sustainable cities to "Make cities and human settlements inclusive, safe, resilient and sustainable." Cities are where new societies develop and must be able to accommodate diversity. This includes having to provide access to places in a safe and sustainable way while paying attention to the needs of those in vulnerable situations such as the elderly and disabled. The target audience for the project is "Planning for migrants, ethnic, minorities and persons with disabilities" which involves respecting the principles of equality, welcome, inclusion and integration with participatory and conscious urban planning that benefits everyone. Hence the importance of transit accessibility for connections and services and the creation of community spaces for cultural exchange. The New Urban Agenda promotes initiatives that benefit all of society, especially the most fragile with access to transportation, health and education facilities, and even historical, architectural and artistic heritage. The area of intervention identified includes the historic center of the city of Matera, such as the Sassi and the Piano, which in its conformation of urban fabric closely related to the surrounding landscape unique in the world, presents peculiarities in terms of accessibility. In fact, the first nucleus of the built-up area of Matera was built on a rocky spur jutting out with steep walls into the Gravina, and to the north and south of this one can distinguish two suspended valleys, dug into the calcarenite bank and furrowed by two incisions called Grabiglioni, now covered and no longer visible. These morphological conditions, linked to the decisive presence in the calcarenite bench, favored the formation of the Sasso Caveoso and the Sasso Barisano on this site, and in the 1600s there was the expansion of the town center and thus the realization of ecclesiastical structures, government and residence of the bourgeois and aristocratic classes in the Plan [17, 18]. Taking into account the singular characteristics of the context and Law No. 13 of January 9, 1989, which contains the provisions of the Minister of Public Works to eliminate and promote the overcoming of architectural barriers in public buildings, private homes and public transportation and Ministerial Decree No. 236 of 1989 by which the technical prescriptions necessary to ensure accessibility, adaptability and visitability are established, a gold route accessible to all has been traced that connects U.N.E.S.C.O. cultural heritage sites and includes: Square San Giovanni; the "Luigi Guerricchio" viewpoint known as the "Three Arches"; Vittorio Veneto Square; Beccherie Street, Cathedral Square viewpoint; Sedile Square; San Francesco Street; D. Ridola and the Piazzetta Pascoli viewpoint (Fig. 1).

Fig. 1. Study area with indication of available and accessible U.N.E.S.C.O. cultural assets and gold route.

The Sassi have an urban line called "Linea Sassi" and parking spaces for the disabled that make it possible to reach the cultural sites present, but difficulties are encountered for Piazza San Pietro Caveoso, Convento di Sant' Agostino and Casa Grotta because of their location. In particular, we can state that access to the Sassi district is characterized by stairways and ramps with a suboptimal slope of more than 8 percent, and bus stops are difficult to reach and do not allow safe boarding and alighting from public transportation for people with mobility disabilities. The paths along Fiorentini Street, Madonna delle Virtù Street, and Caesarea Street have uneven paving and often lack sidewalks or are smaller in size than required by regulations.

The node of accessibility has been addressed by the Municipality of Matera and there are partially implemented or unapproved projects that have found rejection by the Superintendence of the Basilicata Region and non-compliance with Law 11/11/1986 No. 771 bearing "Conservation and Recovery of the Sassi districts of Matera." In particular, taking into consideration the technical report on the infrastructural mesh of the Municipality of Matera for the implementation of a program for pedestrian accessibility in the Sassi districts, it is necessary to take into account the fragility of the context and the heritage of very high architectural, historical, monumental, landscape and archaeological value. Therefore, the implementation of mechanized vertical paths appears to be inconsistent with the context and the existing road system and accessibility, and it will be necessary to implement soft design solutions more in line with the context of reference.

Carrying out a careful reflection for the accessibility of the city of Matera is a great opportunity to create new landscape and cultural itineraries and make the most fragile people tell about the territories in a logic of slow rediscovery of their identities.

4   Towards a Measurable Boundary

In a consolidated settlement bound by the presence of sites of cultural interest of international importance, the design of fully accessible routes represents a challenge for the current field of urban design. Public organizations have proposed numerous measures to address the topic over the years.

Problems related to the impact of too invasive hard solutions as considered by the appropriate authorities emerge from the analyzed documents. Conflicts and issues that positively detailed and influenced the intervention approach in accordance with the genius loci developed from the elaboration of and suggestions put forth.

A first step in identifying the issues in the area is to analyze the cultural assets and the standards established to ensure accessibility to locations. In fact, part of the previously identified golden route is characterized by slopes and lift systems that are unsuitable for the transit of people with reduced mobility. As highlighted in figure two, the two main systems oriented towards tourist usability are marked by points of discontinuity and morphological characteristics which constitute a barrier to exploring the historical center. In particular, there are drop-off points of the "Sassi line" bus stop that are incompatible with fragile users.

In order to encourage inclusive mobility, the proposed scenario focuses on the redefinition of the existing itineraries according to a public circular route. Along with the rental with driver system, the mobility as stated above provides the opportunity to reach the gates of the historic core from a variety of locations and adds additional, adequately designated bus stops (Figs. 2 and 3).

The rental of specific chairs will be guaranteed with electric wheels with a number of advanced features, such as the self-balancing wheels allow the user to always maintain a correct position while driving, the third wheel and two tracks ensure users to drive on uneven terrain with ease, and above all it offers the possibility of climbing stairs thanks to the elevation of the seat. These are just a few of the planned soft actions, in the added information points whose absence was complained of. Additionally, the chair can balance on two wheels and face slopes of up to 34° thanks to gyroscope technology.

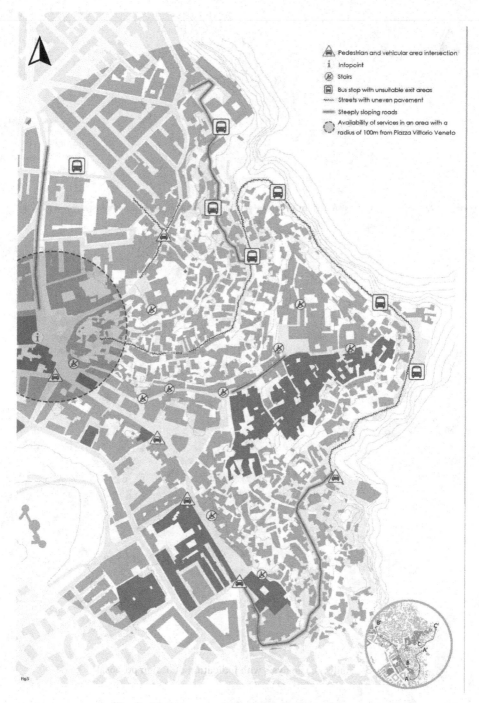

Fig. 2. Study area analysis with indication of issues.

Fig. 3. Study area analysis with indication of design proposal

5 Discussions and Conclusions

The article explores a novel experimental method aimed at developing strategies for reviving urban areas in Matera, a city in the Basilicata region of Italy. The goal is to address the strategic concerns of a specific group of city users and a selected suburban area in accordance with specific criteria. The approach is founded on the principles of the National Urban Agenda (NUA), which are "downscaled" to the local level [5–7, 19–21]. The methodology commences by defining the target population of city users using the "Planning for Migrants, Ethnic Minorities, and Persons with Disabilities" principle [16]. Collaborative design frameworks are highly recommended [4, 12, 22–25], and a strong approach is required to implement such a proposal effectively. The primary focus of this study is on the emerging technical requirements of teaching the downscaled implementation of NUA principles to the next generation of territorial technicians. The research experiment has exposed several distinct advantages compared to traditional urban regeneration methods [21, 26–31]. Specifically, the project enables a more comprehensive and expansive outlook on the specific problems and issues that must be addressed, a logical process for verifying the links between problems, place conditions, and potential solutions, and a reference matrix founded on NUA principles to measure the impacts and outcomes of the proposal [32, 33]. The reference matrix's robust accounting system provides strong evidence of the design's quality. However, the study's limitations relate to the laboratory's academic dimension, which is only partially related to the procedural and administrative rules and constraints that characterize the case study. This research makes a significant contribution to the ongoing discussion on tools and methodologies [19, 20, 27, 28, 34–37] to support the downscaling of NUA to the local level, using innovative technologies in the thematic domain of urban design.

References

1. UN HABITAT: New Urban Agenda. United Nations (2016)
2. Parker, P.: From sustainable development objectives to indicators of progress. N Z Geog. **51**, 50–57 (1995). https://doi.org/10.1111/j.1745-7939.1995.tb02051.x
3. Scorza, F., Attolico, A.: Innovations in promoting sustainable development: the local implementation plan designed by the province of Potenza. In: Gervasi, O., et al. (eds.) ICCSA 2015. LNCS, vol. 9156, pp. 756–766. Springer, Cham (2015). https://doi.org/10.1007/978-3-319-21407-8_54
4. Scorza, F., et al.: Training for territorial sustainable development design in basilicata remote areas: GEODESIGN workshop. In: Gervasi, O., Murgante, B., Misra, S., Rocha, A.M.A.C., Garau, C. (eds.) Computational Science and Its Applications – ICCSA 2022 Workshops. ICCSA 2022. LNCS, vol. 13379, pp. 242–252. Springer, Cham (2022). https://doi.org/10.1007/978-3-031-10545-6_17/COVER
5. Capodiferro, M., et al.: "University equity": students' facilities in major tourism destination towns. In: Gervasi, O. (ed.) Computational Science and Its Applications - ICCSA 2023 (2023)
6. Lagonigro, D., et al.: Downscaling NUA: Matera new urban structure. In: Gervasi, O. (ed.) Computational Science and Its Applications - ICCSA 2023. Springer (2023)
7. Esposito Loscavo, B., et al.: Innovation ecosystem: the added value in a unique UNESCO city. In: Gervasi, O. (ed.) Computational Science and Its Applications - ICCSA 2023. Springer (2023)

8. Melikov, P., et al.: Characterizing urban mobility patterns: a case study of Mexico City. In: Shi, W., Goodchild, M.F., Batty, M., Kwan, M.-P., Zhang, A. (eds.) Urban Informatics. TUBS, pp. 153–170. Springer, Singapore (2021). https://doi.org/10.1007/978-981-15-8983-6_11

9. UN: Sustainable Development Goals (2014). http://www.igbp.net/download/18.62dc35801 456272b46d51/1399290813740/NL82-SDGs.pdf, https://doi.org/10.1038/505587a

10. Aichholzer, G., Strauß, S.: Collaborative forms of citizen (e-)Participation. In: Aichholzer, G., Kubicek, H., Torres, L. (eds.) Evaluating e-Participation. PAIT, vol. 19, pp. 109–122. Springer, Cham (2016). https://doi.org/10.1007/978-3-319-25403-6_6

11. Conroy, M.M., Evans-Cowley, J.: E-participation in planning: an analysis of cities adopting on-line citizen participation tools. Eviron. Plann. C. Gov. Policy 24, 371–384 (2006). https://doi.org/10.1068/c1k

12. Scorza, F., Pontrandolfi, P.: Citizen participation and technologies: the C.A.S.T. architecture. In: Gervasi, O., et al. (eds.) ICCSA 2015. LNCS, vol. 9156, pp. 747–755. Springer, Cham (2015). https://doi.org/10.1007/978-3-319-21407-8_53

13. Pontrandolfi, P., Scorza, F.: Sustainable urban regeneration policy making: inclusive participation practice. In: Gervasi, O., et al. (eds.) ICCSA 2016. LNCS, vol. 9788, pp. 552–560. Springer, Cham (2016). https://doi.org/10.1007/978-3-319-42111-7_44

14. Scardaccione, G., Scorza, F., Las Casas, G., Murgante, B.: Analyzing migration flows in Italy with spatial autocorrelation techniques. In: ECQTG2011 17th European Colloquium on Quantitative and Theoretical Geography (2011)

15. Las Casas, G.B., et al.: Spatial assessment of migration flows in Italy to enhance urban and regional policies. Urbanistica Informazioni 257, 38–42 (2014)

16. Scardaccione, G., Scorza, F., Casas, G. Las, Murgante, B.: Spatial autocorrelation analysis for the evaluation of migration flows: the Italian case. In: Taniar, D., Gervasi, O., Murgante, B., Pardede, E., Apduhan, B.O. (eds.) Computational Science and Its Applications – ICCSA 2010. ICCSA 2010. LNCS, vol. 6016, pp. 62–76. Springer, Berlin, Heidelberg (2010). https://doi.org/10.1007/978-3-642-12156-2_5. https://doi.org/10.1007/978-3-642-12156-2-5

17. Mininni, M., Dicillo, C.: Urban policies and cultural policies for Matera en route to 2019 I Politiche urbane e politiche culturali per Matera verso il 2019. Territorio (2015)

18. Mininni, M.: Matera Lucania 2017. Quodlibet (2017). https://doi.org/10.2307/j.ctv2gz3xk0

19. Casas, G.L., Scorza, F.: Sustainable planning: a methodological toolkit. In: Gervasi, O., et al. (eds.) ICCSA 2016. LNCS, vol. 9786, pp. 627–635. Springer, Cham (2016). https://doi.org/10.1007/978-3-319-42085-1_53

20. Gatto, R.V., Corrado, S., Scorza, F.: Towards a definition of tourism ecosystem. In: 18th International Forum on Knowledge Asset Dynamics (IFKAD) - MANAGING KNOWLEDGE FOR SUSTAINABILITY (2023)

21. Scorza, F., Gatto, R.V.: Identifying territorial values for tourism development: the case study of Calabrian Greek Area. Sustainability 15(6), 5501 (2023). https://doi.org/10.3390/su1506 5501

22. Scorza, F.: Training decision-makers: GEODESIGN workshop paving the way for New Urban Agenda. In: Gervasi, O., et al. (eds.) ICCSA 2020. LNCS, vol. 12252, pp. 310–316. Springer, Cham (2020). https://doi.org/10.1007/978-3-030-58811-3_22

23. Fiore, P., Padula, A., Pilogallo, F.S.A.: Facing urban regeneration issues through geodesign approach. The case of Gravina in Puglia. In: Leone, A., Gargiulo, C. (eds.) Environmental and Territorial Modelling for Planning and Design. FedOAPress (2018). https://doi.org/10.6093/978-88-6887-048-5

24. Padula, A., Fiore, P., Pilogallo, A., Scorza, F.: Collaborative approach in strategic development planning for small municipalities. Applying geodesign methodology and tools for a new municipal strategy in Scanzano Jonico. In: Leone, A. and Gargiulo, C. (eds.) Environmental and Territorial Modelling for Planning and Design, pp. 665–672. FedOApress (2018). https://doi.org/10.6093/978-88-6887-048-5

25. Scorza, F.: Sustainable urban regeneration in Gravina in Puglia, Italy. In: Fisher, T., Orland, B., and Steinitz, C. (eds.) The International Geodesign Collaboration. Changing Geography by Design, pp. 112–113. ESRI Press, Redlands, California (2020)
26. Pilogallo, A., Scorza, F.: Ecosystem services multifunctionality: an analytical framework to support sustainable spatial planning in Italy. Sustainability **14**, 3346 (2022). https://doi.org/10.3390/SU14063346
27. Scorza, F., Santopietro, L.: A systemic perspective for the Sustainable Energy and Climate Action Plan (SECAP). European Planning Studies, pp. 1–21 (2021). https://doi.org/10.1080/09654313.2021.1954603
28. Corrado, S., Scorza, F.: Machine learning based approach to assess territorial marginality. In: Gervasi, O., Murgante, B., Hendrix, E.M.T., Taniar, D., Apduhan, B.O. (eds.) Computational Science and Its Applications – ICCSA 2022. ICCSA 2022. LNCS, vol. 13376. Springer, Cham (2022). https://doi.org/10.1007/978-3-031-10450-3_25
29. Scorza, F., Saganeiti, L., Pilogallo, A., Murgante, B.: Ghost planning: the inefficiency of energy sector policies in a low population density region1. Archivio di Studi Urbani e Regionali (127), 34–55 (2020). https://doi.org/10.3280/ASUR2020-127-S1003
30. Scorza, F., Fortunato, G.: Active mobility-oriented urban development: a morpho-syntactic scenario for a mid-sized town. Eur. Plan. Stud. 1–25 (2022). https://doi.org/10.1080/09654313.2022.2077094
31. Scorza, F., Fortunato, G.: Cyclable Cities: building feasible scenario through urban space morphology assessment. J. Urban Plan. Dev. **147**, 05021039 (2021). https://doi.org/10.1061/(ASCE)UP.1943-5444.0000713
32. Scorza, F.: Improving EU cohesion policy: the spatial distribution analysis of regional development investments funded by EU structural funds 2007/2013 in Italy. In: Murgante, B., et al. (eds.) ICCSA 2013. LNCS, vol. 7973, pp. 582–593. Springer, Heidelberg (2013). https://doi.org/10.1007/978-3-642-39646-5_42
33. Scorza, F., Casas, G.B.L., Murgante, B.: That's ReDO: ontologies and regional development planning. In: Murgante, B., et al. (eds.) ICCSA 2012. LNCS, vol. 7334, pp. 640–652. Springer, Heidelberg (2012). https://doi.org/10.1007/978-3-642-31075-1_48
34. Santopietro, L., Scorza, F.: The italian experience of the covenant of mayors: a territorial evaluation. Sustainability **13**, 1289 (2021). https://doi.org/10.3390/su13031289
35. Gatto, R., Santopietro, L., Scorza, F.: Tourism and abandoned inland areas development demand: a critical appraisal. In: Gervasi, O., Murgante, B., Misra, S., Rocha, A.M.A.C., Garau, C. (eds.) Computational Science and Its Applications – ICCSA 2022 Workshops. ICCSA 2022. LNCS, vol. 13382. Springer, Cham (2022). https://doi.org/10.1007/978-3-031-10592-0_4. https://doi.org/10.1007/978-3-031-10592-0_4/COVER
36. Gatto, R., Santopietro, L., Scorza, F.: Roghudi: Developing knowledge of the places in an abandoned inland municipality. In: Gervasi, O., Murgante, B., Misra, S., Rocha, A.M.A.C., Garau, C. (eds.) Computational Science and Its Applications – ICCSA 2022 Workshops. ICCSA 2022. LNCS, vol. 13382. Springer, Cham (2022). https://doi.org/10.1007/978-3-031-10592-0_5
37. Scorza, F., Santopietro, L., Giuzio, B., Amato, F., Murgante, B., Casas, G.L.: Conflicts between environmental protection and energy regeneration of the historic heritage in the case of the city of matera: tools for assessing and dimensioning of sustainable energy action plans (SEAP). In: Gervasi, O., et al. (eds.) ICCSA 2017. LNCS, vol. 10409, pp. 527–539. Springer, Cham (2017). https://doi.org/10.1007/978-3-319-62407-5_37

"Back to the Villages": Design Sustainable Development Scenarios for In-Land Areas

Antonia Lacerenza, Velia Terminio, Valeria Lacidogna, Verdiana Parente, Rachele Gatto[ID], Rossella Scorzelli[ID], Simone Corrado[ID], Schiva Rahmani[ID], Priscilla Sofia Dastoli[ID], and Francesco Scorza[✉][ID]

School of Engineering, Laboratory of Urban and Regional Systems Engineering, University of Basilicata, 10, Viale dell'Ateneo Lucano, 85100 Potenza, Italy

{antonia.lacerenza,velia.terminio,valeria.lacidogna,
verdiana.parente,rachele.gatto,rossella.scorzelli,
simone.corrado,schiva.rahmani,priscillasofia.dastoli,
francesco.scorza}@unibas.it

Abstract. In-land Areas refers to territories that are farther from cities, often located in mountainous contexts, where job opportunities are less frequent. The National Strategy for Internal Areas (SNAI) represents an innovative national policy for development and territorial cohesion that aims to counter the marginalization and demographic decline phenomena specific to the In-land areas Italy and ultimately countering their "demographic negative trend". This paper aims to structure a strategic planning process aimed at answering those critical issues within a specific marginal area of Basilicata including four municipalities: Albano di Lucania, Campomaggiore, Castelmezzano, and Pietrapertosa. The methodological framework is based on the Logical Framework Approach as a preliminary analytical-knowledge phase to a co-design exercise that will be carried out with the main actors of the context within a specific Geodesign workshop. The LFA main output are discussed in the paper pointing out the rational process of strategic planning development.

Keywords: Logical Framework Approach · Strategic Planning · In-land area development

1 Introduction

In-land Areas (IA) are defined as municipalities that are distant from essential services, particularly schools, healthcare, and railway transportation. We are referring to territories that are farther from cities, often located in mountainous contexts, where job opportunities are less frequent. IA are mainly present in the regions of Southern Italy: a total of 1,718 municipalities (67.4%) are part of them, with significant incidence rates in Basilicata, Sicily, Molise, and Sardinia (all exceeding 70%). The IA of Southern Italy represent 44.8% of the national total [1–3]. As a consequence, large areas of the country are less livable for families. This leads to the progressive depopulation that has characterized peripheral municipalities since the post-war period.

© The Author(s), under exclusive license to Springer Nature Switzerland AG 2023
O. Gervasi et al. (Eds.): ICCSA 2023 Workshops, LNCS 14110, pp. 162–176, 2023.
https://doi.org/10.1007/978-3-031-37123-3_14

The National Strategy for Internal Areas (SNAI) represents an innovative national policy for development and territorial cohesion that aims to counter the marginalization and demographic decline phenomena specific to the In-land areas Italy. This is an ambitious place-based policy project, which has developed new multilevel local governance modalities aimed at addressing, through the adoption of an integrated approach oriented towards promoting and local development, the demographic challenges and responding to the needs of territories characterized by significant disadvantages of a geographical or demographic nature. The National Strategy aims to intervene in such places, investing in the promotion and protection of the wealth of the territory and local communities, enhancing their natural and cultural resources, creating new job opportunities and new opportunities, and ultimately countering their "demographic negative trend."

However, in-land areas are also characterized by high vulnerability of the territory to natural risks, influenced by geomorphological characteristics typical of mountainous territories. Overall greater fragility of the territory and difficult accessibility often linked to morphology may contribute to the causes of the progressive abandonment of these territories [4, 5].

This research, developed mainly within the framework of the course of Territory Engineering - Master's Degree in Environmental Engineering, aims to structure a strategic planning process aimed at answering the previously mentioned critical issues within a marginal area of Basilicata between the cities of Potenza and Matera and the Basento and Bradano valleys: the municipalities of Albano di Lucania, Campomaggiore, Castelmezzano, and Pietrapertosa.

The methodological framework of reference adopts the Logical Framework Approach as a preliminary analytical-knowledge phase to a co-design exercise that will be carried out with the main actors of the context within a specific Geodesign workshop [6–11].

In addition to reporting evaluation elements of the case study through a rigorous territorial analysis procedure, the work proposes development strategies and exemplifies design solutions derived from an evaluation of best practices.

"This work contributes to the wider MITIGO research project - Mitigation of natural risks for safety and mobility in the mountainous areas of Southern Italy - co-financed by the European Union - ERDF, PON Research and Innovation 2014–2020," which is led by the University of Basilicata. In order to offer a contribution to the improvement of the social and economic conditions of Southern Italy, the Mitigo project proposes approaches for mitigating hydrogeological and seismic risks for road connections and strategic structures in mountainous urban areas affected by landslides and earthquakes, lack of services, mobility difficulties, and depopulation phenomena [12–14].

The following section describes the reference principles, derived from the NUA, to which the study contributes in the process of downscaling to the local scale. This is followed by a discussion of the main elaborations of the Logical Framework Approach [15], from the construction of the geo-SWOT to the identification of the main intervention strategies. The last section indicates possible selected design strategy.

2   NUA Inspiring the Future of Local Development

The 2030 Agenda was born in 2015 from an agreement signed by the United Nations to address the great challenges of the planet through a common approach, defining 17 Sustainable Development Goals which are incorporated into a major action program for a total of 169 targets. The main target of the NUA is represented by cities intended as engines of sustainable development and areas for experimenting with innovative solutions to overcome the challenges of sustainability [16–19]. It is an important document since it renews and strengthens the global commitment to sustainable urban development, and it is an operational document, in fact it is considered as the accelerator of the Sustainable Development Goals defined in the 2030 Agenda [20–22]. In addition, urbanization, defined as a tool and engine of development, it is a cross-cutting theme within the SDGs. In particular, Objective 11 of the 2030 Agenda, which aims to "Make cities and human settlements inclusive, safe, resilient and sustainable", is central to the challenges of improving the quality of life in human settlements and shows connections with numerous other objectives affecting specific sectors. In the following figure we therefore report the diagram representing the connections identified with objective 11 and their respective description (Fig. 1).

Fig. 1. NUA themes

4.4: By 2030, substantially increase the number of youth and adults who have relevant skills, including technical and vocational skills, for employment, decent jobs and entrepreneurship.

8.3: Promote development-oriented policies that support productive activities, decent job creation, entrepreneurship, creativity and innovation, and encourage the formalization and growth of micro-, small-and medium-sized enterprises, including through access to financial services.

8.9: By 2030, devise and implement policies to promote sustainable tourism that creates jobs and promotes local culture and products.

9.1: Develop quality, reliable, sustainable and resilient infrastructure, including regional and transborder infrastructure, to support economic development and human well-being, with a focus on affordable and equitable access for all.

10.2: By 2030, empower and promote the social, economic and political inclusion of all, irrespective of age, sex, disability, race, ethnicity, origin, religion or economic or other status.

15.4: By 2030, ensure the conservation of mountain ecosystems, including their biodiversity, in order to enhance their capacity to provide benefits that are essential for sustainable development.

These general purposes certainly have value if considered within a properly urban context but, in the perspective of this work, they are projected towards a domain of application that must be characterized as rural. However, the New Urban Agenda was born in a context in which the focus is on large cities and once again we see urban planning projected towards growth, towards urban agglomeration, neglecting abandonment in these processes, a phenomenon which is happening in 60% of the global territory, representative of a rural context. But rural areas are functional to cities, therefore a process of downscaling, i.e. resizing the process envisaged by the application of the New Urban Agenda [23, 24] at the local level, is therefore necessary. However, it is a fairly complex process as there are no predefined procedures that ensure the efficiency of the planning actions, because to date the monitoring of the implementation of the NUA mainly passes through the selection of good implementation practices rather than through indicators that make the contexts of application. These instances, and the research demand linked to the downscaling of the NUA represent new dimensions for the disciplines of urban and territorial planning and bring out a demand for innovation to refer to new tools, new methodologies and frameworks for monitoring the effects [25–27].

3 The Logical Framework Approach for NUA Downscaling

The LFA is an analytical tool for communicating the complexity of the project in a clear and comprehensible way in a single tabular document, which contains all the relevant objectives and aspects that must be pursued. Two distinct stages are recognized:

1. Phase of Analysis: elaborated in analysis of the context, of the problems, of the objectives, of the strategies;
2. Synthesis phase: involves the construction of the Logframe matrix and the implementation of the project.

3.1 SWOT, GEOSWOT and Context Analysis

The context analysis was carried out using the SWOT ANALYSIS methodology, considering the following systems:

1. Demographics and population structure,
2. Natural and environmental resources,
3. Historical-cultural resources,
4. Settlement system,
5. Production and employment system,
6. Infrastructural system (Table 1).

Table 1. Swot Analysis points

STRENGHTS	WEAKNESSES
• Presence of highly valuable areas from the perspective of nature and biodiversity (SIC, ZPS, ZSC): 15.97% in Pietrapertosa, 12.29% in Castelmezzano, 1.73% in Campomaggiore, 7.61% in Albano Di Lucania • Greater tourist attractiveness in Castelmezzano and Pietrapertosa due to the presence of the following practicable sites and activities: parco regionale di Gallipoli-Cognato, volo dell'angelo, percorso delle pietre, via ferrata Salemm, via ferrata Marcirosa, il ponte nepalese, la gradinata normanna • Agricultural specialization of the Albano Di Lucania territory in terms of productive system • Presence of considerable cultural heritage characterized by artistic and architectural-monumental values	• Various natural hazards affect the territory: 94% of it falls in seismic zone 2; 26% falls in landslide risk zone; 5 km of ss407 Basentana in hydraulic risk zone • Population decreased by 21% since 2002 • Old age index (65+ /0–14) is 318, higher than the provincial (214) and regional (207) figures as of 2021 • A non- integrated touristic proposal • Poor level of accessibility • 22% reduction in active enterprises in the territory since 2002 • Limited offer of outreach services in terms of quantity and sectoral diversification
OPPORTUNITIES	THREATS
• National strategy for internal areas • Outright grants for tourism in 2023, provided by Invitalia agency • Program for environment and climate action (life 2021–2027) • PNRR fundings	• Climate change • 2% increase in interest rates on business credit expected between 2022 and 2023 that may affect entrepreneurship development • Economic crisis aggravated by health emergency and geopolitical uncertainties with deteriorating employment indicators • Underestimate the specific needs of Regions and rural areas due to a program based on a single Strategic Plan

This elaboration, in addition to representing the synthesis that derives from the analysis of the socio-demographic variables of the context, was constructed through an exclusively spatial approach respecting the rules according to which each statement contained in the matrix finds correspondence in a cartography which gives an account of the intensity of the phenomena and their territorial location in explicit form (Figs. 2 and 3).

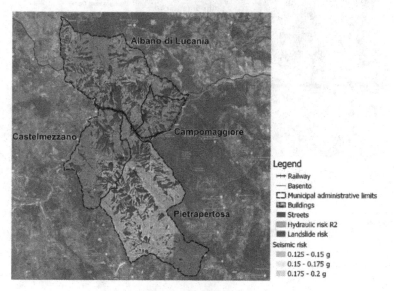

Fig. 2. Weaknesses.

As shown in the previous figures, strengths and weaknesses allow an overview of the territory under study and favor the comparison between the two main territorial portions coinciding with the municipalities to the north (Albano di Lucania and Campomaggiore) and to the south (Castelmezzano and Pietrapertosa) of the Basento river.

4   The Design of Development Strategies (LFM)

The problem tree is a diagram that offers an overall representation of the critical issues highlighted in the context analysis phase It is the result of a process analytical through which the causes and effects that determine a territorial condition of underdevelopment are identified and organized in a hierarchical form (Fig. 4).

The Logical Framework Approach, following the identification of the criticalities of the context, requires the elaboration of the tree of objectives which is achieved by transforming each problem ("current negative situation") into possible objectives to be achieved ("future positive situation") (Fig. 5).

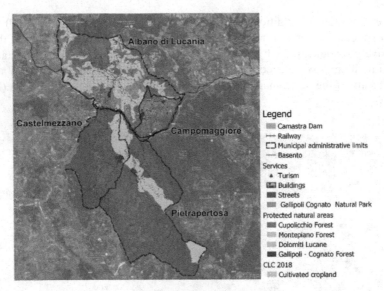

Fig. 3. Strenghts.

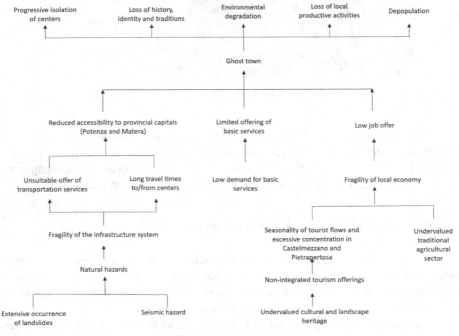

Fig. 4. Problems tree.

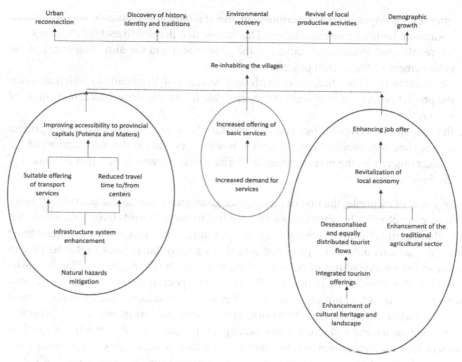

Fig. 5. Objectives tree.

It makes it possible to identify three coherent strategies with respect to a single sector of intervention. Three main areas emerge in the case study:

1. Enhancement of the job offer, through the development of the tourism and primary sector, supported by incentives or funds for companies and for the training of personnel to be employed. These activities will lead to the creation of new jobs, new tourist attractions and consequent seasonal adjustment and fair distribution of tourist flows;
2. Enhancement of the offer of services in the area, taking advantage of incentives aimed at opening new commercial activities and primary services that are absent or underdeveloped (e.g. school services);
3. Improve territorial accessibility, using funds for infrastructural and mobility interventions, acting on the one hand on the infrastructure system by improving the road network, on the other on the mobility service by increasing transport services; this objective supports activities that promote inclusive use for all, placing the needs of people with disabilities at the center.

From the analysis of the strategies we move on to the synthesis phase with the Logical Frame Matrix. From an operational point of view, "The Logical Framework matrix [28]" involves the construction of a table that summarizes the key elements of the project:

1. the hierarchy of the project Objectives, the specific Objectives, the expected Results and the Activities, with the necessary Resources,

2. Intervention logic, ie the description of the fundamental elements according to a bottom-up logic of cause and effect. This means that the activities lead to the results, the results lead to the achievement of the project aim and the aim contributes to the achievement of the overall objectives;
3. Objectively verifiable Indicators (with their Sources of Verification) which describe the project objectives in objectively measurable terms and prove the achievement of each result.
4. the Conditions (Hypothesis, assumption), i.e. those factors external to the project and beyond management control which, however, condition the achievement of the project objectives, the non-occurrence of which may prevent the correct execution of the intervention.

By way of example, the first of the selected strategies is discussed below: "strengthening the job offer". The activities with the relative expected results have been associated with the specific objective (see Table 2). For example, to achieve the goal of generating new jobs, actions have been proposed aimed at opening businesses in the hospitality sector in the municipalities of Albano di Lucania and Campomaggiore. This is consistent with what is indicated in the geo-SWOT with respect to the need to balance tourist supply and demand within the study area. For a more equitable distribution of tourist flows on a territorial scale, the activity of creating integrated tourist packages is proposed to enhance the natural and monumental heritage, supported by outdoor activities such as birdwatching and trekking routes to counteract the tourist seasonality. To promote more inclusive forms of tourism, actions have been proposed for the organization of nature trails accessible to people with disabilities.

In the agri-food tourism sector, the enhancement of the production and valorisation of the products of the primary sector are associated with agri-food chain projects which close the production, transformation, distribution and marketing process of local products within the territorial system. Below is an extract of the matrix relating to the specific objective "Enhancement of the job offer".

Table 2. Enhancement of job offer

ACTIVITIES	RESULTS
A1.1.1 Organise training internships with tourism enterprises **A1.1.2** Opening of activities in the hospitality sector in Albano di Lucania and Campomaggiore **A1.2.1** Opening local production activities specialising in forestry (chestnut), arboreal (lavender), beekeeping	**R1.1** New jobs in the tourism sector
A1.2.2 Organise training programmes	**R1.2** New jobs in the agro-food sector

(*continued*)

Table 2. (*continued*)

ACTIVITIES	RESULTS
A1.3.1 Enhancement of the natural, landscape and monumental heritage by offering integrated packages **A1.3.2** Organise outdoor activities in equipped areas (birdwatching, trekking routes..)	**R1.3** Deseasonalised and equally distributed tourist flows
A1.4.1 Planning guided tours of agri-food companies with product tasting **A.1.4.2** Organise nature trails accessible to the differently abled	**R1.4** New tourist attractors
A1.5.1 Production, processing, distribution and marketing of local products (honey, jams, infusions…)	**R1.5** New agro-food chains

5 Pilot Actions and Reference Projects

Good practices have been selected to give an operational perspective to the proposed strategic framework and to suggest typical actions for the Geodesign debate that will follow according to the MITIGO research project program with the direct involvement of local actors. The selection criteria refer to: applicability to the context in question, consistency with the principles selected by the NUA; a significant efficiency in the comparison between expected results and resources used. These good practices mainly pertain to the social and environmental sphere of sustainability. These are examples that make it possible to put the principles of sustainable development into practice and to stimulate actors to implement further projects on the basis of other positive experiences. In relation to the environmental sphere, the theme of "Resilience and adaptation to climate change" was selected, as it is closely linked to the natural risks (seismic and hydrogeological) present in the area which require mitigation actions. The best practices identified are the following:

- Reforestation: provides for the extension of the green forest area by planting coniferous and deciduous trees in areas at risk of landslides or floods, adjacent to existing woods, to reduce or prevent this risk;

- Information campaigns: fall within the so-called Soft Measures described within the NUA, mainly concerning the organization of services and in this case information campaigns, as it is necessary to make citizens aware of the risks to which they are exposed.

With regard to the social sphere, the theme of "Strengthening marginalized groups" was selected. The project is unique:

- "The neighborhood butler", an activity that aims to place, following a training period, the professional figure who is trained, in the economic-productive sectors linked to personal services and support to businesses, for example as a family assistant, since the professional figure of the neighborhood butler can be defined as a light home assistance to support families in simple and daily needs.

Per il tema relativo alla "Pianificazione sensibile all'età" la buona pratica selezionata è:

- "La Farmacia dei servizi", un'evoluzione dell'attività professionale nell'ambito delle cure primarie, che nasce dalla volontà di ampliare i servizi territoriali, sia per favorire la deospedalizzazione della sanità, sia per ampliare il ruolo che le farmacie devono assolvere nell'ambito del Sistema Sanitario Nazionale, avvicinando la sanità ai cittadini e riducendo i costi.

For the topic related to "Planning for migrants, ethnic minorities and people with disabilities" the proposal is:

- "Accessible Dolomites" which provides for the creation of paths accessible to people with motor disabilities with the support of specialized personnel for accompaniment, to guarantee the universal right to enjoy an equally universal beauty.

6 Conclusions

This paper describes a strategic approach for sustainable development planning in In-land Areas. In particular it aims to structure a strategic planning process aimed at answering those critical issues within a specific marginal area of Basilicata including four municipalities: Albano di Lucania, Campomaggiore, Castelmezzano, and Pietrapertosa. The methodological framework is based on the Logical Framework Approach as a preliminary analytical-knowledge phase to a co-design exercise that will be carried out with the main actors of the context within a specific Geodesign workshop.

The case study area is characterized by high vulnerability of the territory to natural risks, influenced by geomorphological characteristics typical of mountainous territories [29–31]. Overall greater fragility of the [32–34] territory and difficult accessibility often linked to morphology may contribute to the causes of the progressive abandonment of these territories [35–40].

This research was developed mainly within the framework of the course of Territory Engineering - Master's Degree in Engineering as a results of a semester laboratory actively engaging students in Environmental and Civil Engineering.

The methodological framework of reference adopts the Logical Framework Approach as a preliminary analytical-knowledge phase to a co-design exercise that will be carried out with the main actors of the context within a specific Geodesign workshop.

This work contributes to the wider MITIGO research project - Mitigation of natural risks for safety and mobility in the mountainous areas of Southern Italy" which is led by the University of Basilicata.

The LFA methodology, already applied by the research group in a number of operational territorial application [41–47], was intended as a formalized and robust structure to deliver a process o downscaling NUA principles in the case study context also referring to tourism development perspective [30, 48–51].

The comparison with selected good practices makes the strategic design obtained with LFA more expressive of specific actions and suitable intervention solutions.

References

1. Dastoli, P.S., Pontrandolfi, P., Scorza, F., Corrado, S., Azzato, A.: Applying Geodesign Towards an Integrated Local Development Strategy: The Val d'Agri Case (Italy). In: Gervasi, O., Murgante, B., Misra, S., Rocha, A.M.A.C., Garau, C. (eds.) Computational Science and Its Applications – ICCSA 2022 Workshops. ICCSA 2022. LNCS, vol. 13379. Springer, Cham (2022). https://doi.org/10.1007/978-3-031-10545-6_18
2. Scorza, F., et al.: Training for territorial sustainable development design in basilicata remote areas: GEODESIGN workshop. In: Gervasi, O., Murgante, B., Misra, S., Rocha, A.M.A.C., Garau, C. (eds.) Computational Science and Its Applications – ICCSA 2022 Workshops. ICCSA 2022. LNCS, vol. 13379, pp. 242–252. Springer, Cham (2022). https://doi.org/10.1007/978-3-031-10545-6_17/COVER
3. Curatella, L., Scorza, F.: Polycentrism and insularity metrics for in-land areas. In: Gervasi, O., et al. (eds.) ICCSA 2020. LNCS, vol. 12255, pp. 253–261. Springer, Cham (2020). https://doi.org/10.1007/978-3-030-58820-5_20
4. Las Casas, G., Scorza, F., Murgante, B.: Conflicts and sustainable planning: peculiar instances coming from Val D'agri structural inter-municipal plan. In: Papa, R., Fistola, R., Gargiulo, C. (eds.) Smart Planning: Sustainability and Mobility in the Age of Change. GET, pp. 163–177. Springer, Cham (2018). https://doi.org/10.1007/978-3-319-77682-8_10
5. Scorza, F., Santopietro, L., Giuzio, B., Amato, F., Murgante, B., Casas, G.L.: Conflicts between environmental protection and energy regeneration of the historic heritage in the case of the city of Matera: tools for assessing and dimensioning of sustainable energy action plans (SEAP). In: Gervasi, O., et al. (eds.) ICCSA 2017. LNCS, vol. 10409, pp. 527–539. Springer, Cham (2017). https://doi.org/10.1007/978-3-319-62407-5_37
6. Fiore, P., Padula, A., Pilogallo, F.S.A.: Facing urban regeneration issues through geodesign approach. The case of Gravina in Puglia. In: Leone, A. and Gargiulo, C. (eds.) Environmental and Territorial Modelling for Planning and Design. FedOAPress (2018). https://doi.org/10.6093/978-88-6887-048-5
7. Padula, A., Fiore, P., Pilogallo, A., Scorza, F.: Collaborative approach in strategic development planning for small municipalities. Applying geodesign methodology and tools for a new municipal strategy in Scanzano Jonico. In: Leone, A. and Gargiulo, C. (eds.) Environmental and Territorial Modelling for Planning and Design, pp. 665–672. FedOApress (2018). https://doi.org/10.6093/978-88-6887-048-5
8. Scorza, F.: Sustainable urban regeneration in Gravina in Puglia, Italy. In: Fisher, T., Orland, B., and Steinitz, C. (eds.) The International Geodesign Collaboration. Changing Geography by Design, pp. 112–113. ESRI Press, Redlands, California (2020)
9. Campagna, M., Ervin, S., Sheppard, S.: How geodesign processes shaped outcomes. In: Fisher, T., Orland, B., and Steinitz, C. (eds.) The International Geodesign Collaboration. Changing Geography by Design, pp. 145–148. ESRI Press, Redlands, California (2020)

10. Campagna, M.: Metaplanning: about designing the Geodesign process. Landsc Urban Plan. **156**, 118–128 (2016). https://doi.org/10.1016/J.LANDURBPLAN.2015.08.019
11. Steinitz, C., Orland, B., Fisher, T., Campagna, M.: Geodesign to address global change. Intell. Environ. 193–242 (2023). https://doi.org/10.1016/B978-0-12-820247-0.00016-3
12. Scorza, F.: Improving EU cohesion policy: the spatial distribution analysis of regional development investments funded by EU structural funds 2007/2013 in Italy. In: Murgante, B., et al. (eds.) ICCSA 2013. LNCS, vol. 7973, pp. 582–593. Springer, Heidelberg (2013). https://doi.org/10.1007/978-3-642-39646-5_42
13. Brandano, M.G., Crociata, A.: Cohesion Policy, tourism and culture in Italy: a regional policy evaluation (2022). https://doi.org/10.1080/00343404.2022.2106365
14. Garau, C., Annunziata, A.: A method for assessing the vitality potential of urban areas. The case study of the Metropolitan City of Cagliari, Italy. City, Territ. Architect. **9**(1), 1–23 (2022). https://doi.org/10.1186/s40410-022-00153-6
15. Vagnby, B.H.: Logical framework approach, vol. 64 (2000)
16. Capodiferro, M., et al.: "University equity": students' facilities in major tourism destination towns. In: Gervasi, O. (ed.) Computational Science and Its Applications - ICCSA 2023 (2023)
17. Lagonigro, D., et al.: Downscaling NUA: Matera new urban structure. In: Gervasi, O. (ed.) Computational Science and Its Applications - ICCSA 2023. Springer (2023)
18. Florio, E., et al.: SuperABLE: Matera accessible for all. In: Gervasi, O. (ed.) Computational Science and Its Applications - ICCSA 2023. Springer (2023)
19. Esposito Loscavo, B., et al.: Innovation ecosystem: the added value in a unique UNESCO city. In: Gervasi, O. (ed.) Computational Science and Its Applications - ICCSA 2023. Springer (2023)
20. UN: Sustainable Development Goals (2014). http://www.igbp.net/download/18.62dc35801456272b46d51/1399290813740/NL82-SDGs.pdf, https://doi.org/10.1038/505587a
21. Hák, T., Janoušková, S., Moldan, B.: Sustainable Development Goals: a need for relevant indicators. Ecol Indic. **60**, 565–573 (2016). https://doi.org/10.1016/j.ecolind.2015.08.003
22. Wood, S.L.R., et al.: Distilling the role of ecosystem services in the Sustainable Development Goals. Ecosyst. Serv. **29**, 70–82 (2018). https://doi.org/10.1016/j.ecoser.2017.10.010
23. UN HABITAT: New Urban Agenda. United Nations (2016)
24. Caprotti, F., et al.: The New Urban Agenda: key opportunities and challenges for policy and practice. Urban Res. Pract. **10**, 367–378 (2017). https://doi.org/10.1080/17535069.2016.1275618
25. Caprotti, F., et al.: The New Urban Agenda: key opportunities and challenges for policy and practice **10**, 367–378 (2017). https://doi.org/10.1080/17535069.2016.1275618
26. Andersson, C.: Public space and the new Urban Agenda. J. Public Space **1**, 5 (2016). https://doi.org/10.5204/JPS.V1I1.4
27. Casas, G.L., Scorza, F.: From the UN New Urban Agenda to the local experiences of urban development: the case of Potenza. In: Gervasi, O., et al. (eds.) ICCSA 2018. LNCS, vol. 10964, pp. 734–743. Springer, Cham (2018). https://doi.org/10.1007/978-3-319-95174-4_56
28. Casas, G.L., Scorza, F.: Sustainable planning: a methodological toolkit. In: Gervasi, O., et al. (eds.) ICCSA 2016. LNCS, vol. 9786, pp. 627–635. Springer, Cham (2016). https://doi.org/10.1007/978-3-319-42085-1_53
29. Corrado, S., Giannini, B., Santopietro, L., Oliveto, G., Scorza, F.: Water management and municipal climate adaptation plans: a preliminary assessment for flood risks management at urban scale. In: Gervasi, O., et al. (eds.) ICCSA 2020. LNCS, vol. 12255, pp. 184–192. Springer, Cham (2020). https://doi.org/10.1007/978-3-030-58820-5_14
30. Gatto, R.V., Corrado, S., Scorza, F.: Towards a definition of tourism ecosystem. In: 18th International Forum on Knowledge Asset Dynamics (IFKAD) - MANAGING KNOWLEDGE FOR SUSTAINABILITY (2023)

31. Corrado, S., Scorza, F.: Machine learning based approach to assess territorial marginality. In: Gervasi, O., Murgante, B., Hendrix, E.M.T., Taniar, D., Apduhan, B.O. (eds.) Computational Science and Its Applications – ICCSA 2022. ICCSA 2022. LNCS, vol. 13376. Springer, Cham (2022). https://doi.org/10.1007/978-3-031-10450-3_25

32. Lombardini, G., Scorza, F.: Resilience and smartness of coastal regions. a tool for spatial evaluation. In: Gervasi, O., et al. (eds.) ICCSA 2016. LNCS, vol. 9788, pp. 530–541. Springer, Cham (2016). https://doi.org/10.1007/978-3-319-42111-7_42

33. Lai, S., Lombardini, G.: Regional drivers of land take: a comparative analysis in two Italian regions. Land Use Policy **56**, 262–273 (2016)

34. Zoppi, C.: Governance, pianificazione e valutazione strategica. Sviluppo sostenibile e governence nella pianificazione urbanistica, Gangemi Editore, Roma (2008)

35. Vona, M., Harabaglia, P., Murgante, B.: Thinking about resilient cities: studying Italian earthquakes. Proc. Inst. Civil Eng. Urban Design Plan. **169**(4), 185–199 (2016). https://doi.org/10.1680/udap.14.00007

36. Murgante, B., Borruso, G., Lapucci, A.: Sustainable development: Concepts and methods for its application in urban and environmental planning. Stud. Comput. Intell. **348**, 1–15 (2011). https://doi.org/10.1007/978-3-642-19733-8_1/COVER

37. Las Casas, G., Scorza, F., Murgante, B.: Razionalità a-priori: una proposta verso una pianificazione antifragile. Italian J. Region. Sci. **18**, 329–338 (2019). https://doi.org/10.14650/93656

38. Murgante, B., Borruso, G., Lapucci, A.: Geocomputation and urban planning. Stud. Comput. Intell. **176**, 1–17 (2009). https://doi.org/10.1007/978-3-540-89930-3_1/COVER

39. Scorza, F., Pilogallo, A., Saganeiti, L., Murgante, B.: Natura 2000 areas and sites of national interest (SNI): Measuring (un)integration between naturalness preservation and environmental remediation policies. Sustainability (Switzerland). **12** (2020). https://doi.org/10.3390/SU12072928

40. Saganeiti, L., Mustafa, A., Teller, J., Murgante, B.: Modeling urban sprinkling with cellular automata. Sustain. Cities Soc. **65**, 102586 (2021). https://doi.org/10.1016/J.SCS.2020.102586

41. Scorza, F.: Towards self energy-management and sustainable citizens' engagement in local energy efficiency Agenda. Int. J. Agricul. Environ. Inform. Syst. **7**, 44–53 (2016). https://doi.org/10.4018/ijaeis.2016010103

42. Scorza, F.: Smart monitoring system for energy performance in public building. In: Gervasi, O., et al. (eds.) ICCSA 2015. LNCS, vol. 9156, pp. 767–774. Springer, Cham (2015). https://doi.org/10.1007/978-3-319-21407-8_55

43. Scorza, F., Saganeiti, L., Pilogallo, A., Murgante, B.: Ghost planning: the inefficiency of energy sector policies in a low population density region1. Archivio di Studi Urbani e Regionali, pp. 34–55 (2020). https://doi.org/10.3280/ASUR2020-127-S1003

44. Scorza, F., Fortunato, G.: Active mobility-oriented urban development: a morpho-syntactic scenario for a mid-sized town. Eur. Plan. Stud. 1–25 (2022). https://doi.org/10.1080/09654313.2022.2077094

45. Scorza, F., Fortunato, G.: Cyclable Cities: building feasible scenario through urban space morphology assessment. J. Urban Plan. Dev. **147**, 05021039 (2021). https://doi.org/10.1061/(ASCE)UP.1943-5444.0000713

46. Pilogallo, A., Scorza, F.: Mapping regulation ecosystem services specialization in Italy. J. Urban Plan. Dev. **148** (2022). https://doi.org/10.1061/(ASCE)UP.1943-5444.0000801

47. Scorza, F., Pilogallo, A., Saganeiti, L., Murgante, B., Pontrandolfi, P.: Comparing the territorial performances of renewable energy sources' plants with an integrated ecosystem services loss assessment: a case study from the Basilicata region (Italy). Sustain. Cities Soc. **56**, 102082 (2020). https://doi.org/10.1016/j.scs.2020.102082

48. Gatto, R., Santopietro, L., Scorza, F.: Roghudi: Developing knowledge of the places in an abandoned inland municipality. In: Gervasi, O., Murgante, B., Misra, S., Rocha, A.M.A.C., Garau, C. (eds.) Computational Science and Its Applications – ICCSA 2022 Workshops. ICCSA 2022. LNCS, vol. 13382. Springer, Cham (2022). https://doi.org/10.1007/978-3-031-10592-0_5
49. Gatto, R., Santopietro, L., Scorza, F.: Tourism and abandoned inland areas development demand: a critical appraisal. In:Gervasi,O., Murgante,B., Misra, S.,Rocha,A.M.A.C., Garau, C. (eds.) Computational Science and Its Applications – ICCSA 2022 Workshops. ICCSA 2022. LNCS, vol. 13382. Springer, Cham (2022). https://doi.org/10.1007/978-3-031-105 92-0_4
50. Corrado, S., Gatto, R.V., Scorza, F.: The European digital decade and the tourism ecosystem: a methodological approach to improve tourism analytics. In: 18th International Forum on Knowledge Asset Dynamics (IFKAD) - MANAGING KNOWLEDGE FOR SUSTAINABILITY. , Matera (2023)
51. Scorza, F., Gatto, R.V.: Identifying territorial values for tourism development: the case study of Calabrian Greek Area. Sustainability 15(6), 5501 (2023). https://doi.org/10.3390/su1506 5501

Smart, Safe and Health Cities (SSHC 2023)

Towards an Urban Smart Mobility: Preliminary Results of an Experimental Investigation in Artena

Mauro D'Apuzzo[1](✉) , Azzurra Evangelisti[1] , Giuseppe Cappelli[1,2],
Sofia Nardoianni[1], Stefano Buzzi[1], and Vittorio Nicolosi[3]

[1] University of Cassino and Southern Lazio, Via G. Di Biasio 43, 03043 Cassino, Italy
{dapuzzo,giuseppe.cappelli1,sofia.nardoianni,buzzi}@unicas.it
[2] University School for Advanced Studies, IUSS, Piazza della Vittoria n.15, 27100 Pavia, Italy
giuseppe.cappelli@iusspavia.it
[3] University of Rome "Tor Vergata", Via del Politecnico, 1, 00133 Rome, Italy
nicolosi@uniroma2.it

Abstract. With a higher awareness of sustainable development issues, the social costs of externalities of urban mobility have become unbearable. Whether in major cities improvement of transit may mitigate some of these drawbacks, in small municipalities countermeasures can be very challenging. Within this context, the "Smart Urban Mobility Management" (SUMMa) project it is trying to implement new technologies by making use of modern digital technologies and 5G communication networks for managing transportation systems in a small town. In this paper an application of a smart mobility paradigm based on a digital platform employing an enhanced Mobile Broadband, massive Machine Type Communications and Mobile Edge Computing, is presented. The digital platform has been conceived to help Artificial Intelligence algorithms for recognition image and interpretation of traffic field data, collected by H-D cameras. The system has been used to evaluate Origin-Destination flows on a real time basis. The estimated O/D matrix together with the collected traffic counts can be used in order to develop and calibrate a travel demand prediction model that will allow to evaluate urban mobility externalities. Preliminary results obtained on a test site located in the city of Artena seem to indicate that the proposed system is promising in capturing vehicular traffic pattern.

Keywords: Smart Mobility · Smart Road · SUMMa Project · 5G communication technology · AI technology · O/D matrix

1 Background

With the increasingly number of travels from rural areas to cities, especially with an increase of global population, several cities, all over the world, have the ambition to became more sustainable and smarter [1]. Recently, first with Agenda 30 and its 17 UN Sustainable Development Goals [2, 3] for 2030, and secondly with the Next Generation

© The Author(s), under exclusive license to Springer Nature Switzerland AG 2023
O. Gervasi et al. (Eds.): ICCSA 2023 Workshops, LNCS 14110, pp. 179–193, 2023.
https://doi.org/10.1007/978-3-031-37123-3_15

EU in Europe [4] that give a great impulse to address the problem of the urban mobility, the problem of create smart and sustainable cities is more critical than ever [5]. However, these two adjectives seem to be very related and somehow exchangeable because Smart Cities have the urgent need of new technological and digital transportation infrastructures [6] to offer accessible and intermodal mobility solutions and services [7]. According to Lai et al. [8], the problem to identify uniquely a definition of Smart Mobility is due to the several identities involved in this process and the different technologies that a city may offers [9]. According to the European Commission [10], "A smart city is a place where traditional networks and services are made more efficient with the use of digital solutions for the benefit of its inhabitants and business".

But how to evaluate how smart and sustainable is a city? According to Garau et al. [11], six variables need to be tackled in account (public transport, cycle lane, bike sharing, car sharing, private mobility support system, public transport support system) to generate a smart mobility synthetic indicator, that allows to compare cities among them to assess how smart and sustainable they are [12].

To transform a city in a Smart City, IoT technologies need to be adopted [13, 14] and this is possible today with the digitalization [15], with implementation of the maximum performance of digital infrastructure (such as 5G) and the recent development and spread of Artificial Intelligence and machine learning technologies [13] for transport automation and intelligent transport system (ITS) [16–18]. Although the improved technologies play a fundamental role in collect and analyzed a huge amount of data, this launch to digitalization and modernization of infrastructures and mode of transport, need to be assisted by strong Sustainable Urban Mobility Plan (SUMP) that have to offer a clear vision in the long period time [19].

Given this new impulse to re-think the European cities in a smarter way (in Italy great effort are made with the MIT Decree 70/2018 of the Italian Ministry of Infrastructures and Transports [20]), the city of Artena has become the protagonist in the hosting of the Smart Urban Mobility Management or S.U.M.Ma National project, within the Smarter Italy Project [21]. With the aim to enhance new digital technologies such as IoT (Internet of Things), AI, Blockchain and the use of 5G communication networks, to improve the competitiveness of the transportation systems through new services for the management and modernization of both urban and rural mobility systems, in this paper the preliminary results are shown.

1.1 Smart Urban Mobility Management (SUMMa) Project

The goal of the project "Smart Urban Mobility Management" (Summa) is to make the most of the performance of a 5G network in terms of bandwidth and available power compared to Smart Mobility scenarios. Specific studies and tests will be carried out to optimize mobile communication and obtain trade-off curves. The project proposal involves the creation of a system for the analysis of mobility thanks to the use of sensors and advanced cameras that exploit specific algorithms based on Neural Networks to recognize subjects and objects framed.

A simplified representation of the Summa platform architecture is shown in Fig. 1.

This project is aimed at the enhancement of the Digital Technologies promoted by the Government Call as an enabling factor and necessary to increase the complexity and

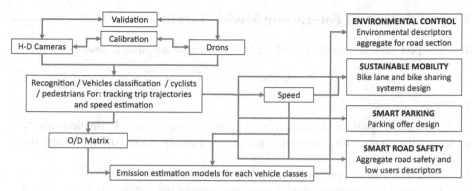

Fig. 1. Simplified SUMMa platform architecture.

competitiveness of the Italian Logistics system, considering the importance of human and commodity flows that affect the entire national supply chain, from tourism to exports of Made in Italy.

Digital technologies such as iot (Internet of Things), AI (Artificial Intelligence), Blockchain and the use of new 5G communication networks, as well as making logistics processes more efficient, may contribute to the structuring of new services for the management and modernization of transport systems.

The project idea involves the creation of a modular architecture in which to experiment with the simultaneous implementation of enhanced connections Mobile Broadband (eMBB), massive Machine Type Communications (mmtc) and Ultra-Reliable Low-Latency Communications (URLLC) in a 5G network to support Sustainable Mobility, and the implementation of services that exploit the potential of Mobile Edge Computing. Mobile Edge Computing allows to implement low latency and location-based services; it is an essential technology for the realization of the services proposed by the project, which will offer the computing platform for the implementation of AI algorithms combined with image recognition and interpretation of data from the field. Therefore, it will be possible to estimate the flows close to the camera detection sections and to process an O/D matrix for a given standard day and a certain time slot.

This allows us to estimate possible congestion effects and, being within the reach of citizens, allow them to choose any alternative routes avoiding long queues and possible delays.

Moreover, the platform allows to estimate, averaged data in the 24 h of a typical day, of environmental pollution that allow to realize of the best ones to mitigate such problem.

However, to concretize the data provided by the platform, in terms of traffic counts and O/D matrices, there is a need to know the municipal territory of Artena and then to determine a model for travel demand and for the corresponding transport supply model.

2 Travel Demand Forecasting Model, TDFM

The transport demand model (TDFM) [22] can be summarized as follows:

$$d_{od}[K] = d(SE, T) \tag{1}$$

Where

- d_{od} is the average traffic flows between the origin zone "o" and destination zone "d";
- K are all features such as activities and mode of transportation of the specific study area
- SE is a vector that represent features (K) of socioeconomics variables;
- T is a vector that represent service level attributes of the transport delivery system.

Therefore, it aims to associate to the mean value of the travel flows the characteristics K, which can be summarized in:

- The purpose of the trip;
- Time interval in which the trip takes place;
- The area of origin and destination of the trip;
- The mode of transport used during the trip;
- The routes chosen.

The TDFM consists of four sub models by virtue of the characteristics listed above. It results to be a cascade model where the data of input of the successive sub model are the data of output of the previous sub model. Such sub-models are divided as in Fig. 2.

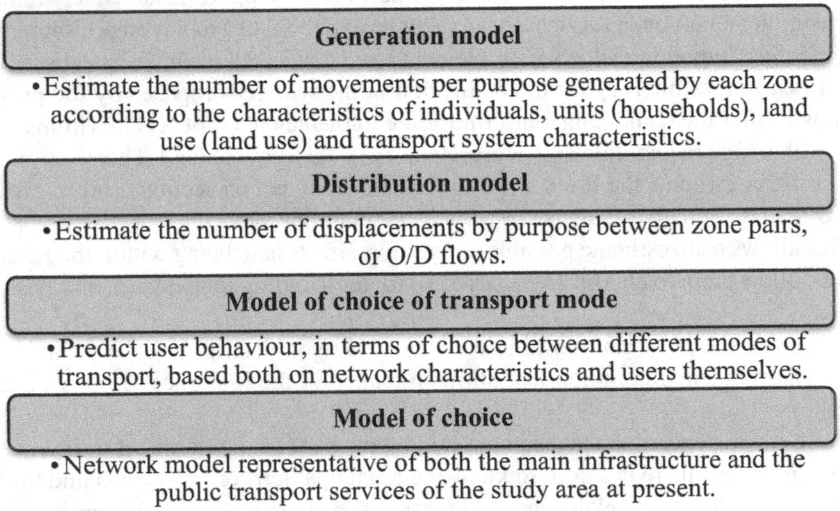

Generation model

• Estimate the number of movements per purpose generated by each zone according to the characteristics of individuals, units (households), land use (land use) and transport system characteristics.

Distribution model

• Estimate the number of displacements by purpose between zone pairs, or O/D flows.

Model of choice of transport mode

• Predict user behaviour, in terms of choice between different modes of transport, based both on network characteristics and users themselves.

Model of choice

• Network model representative of both the main infrastructure and the public transport services of the study area at present.

Fig. 2. Simplified TDFM architecture.

This model can therefore be represented in the following way:

$$d^i_{od}(s, h, m, k) = d^i_o(sh)p^i(d/osh)p^i(m/dosh)p^i(k/mdosh) \tag{2}$$

Where:

- s is a specific purpose for the trip;
- h is the time taken to make the trip;
- m is the mode used to carry out the trip;
- k is the path chosen by the user to make the trip;
- $d_o^i(sh)$ is the generation model;
- $p^i(d/osh)$ is the distribution model;
- $p^i(m/dosh)$ is the modal of choice of transport mode;
- $p^i(k/mdosh)$ is the model of choice.

3 Case Study - Traffic Modeling

3.1 Zoning and Road Network Structure

For this case study, having carried out preliminary studies [26] on the distribution of the population and the relative productive activities, an aggregation of the internal traffic zones is proposed equal to 11, compared to the microzoning proposed by ISTAT [23], represented in Fig. 3.

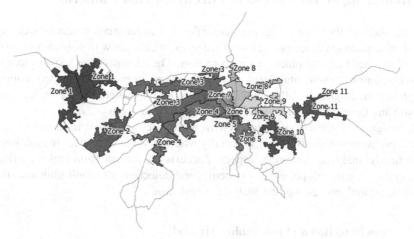

Fig. 3. Zoning of Artena [24]

To define the basic road network, in Fig. 4, the types of roads considered are:

- State roads;
- Municipal roads;
- Local roads.

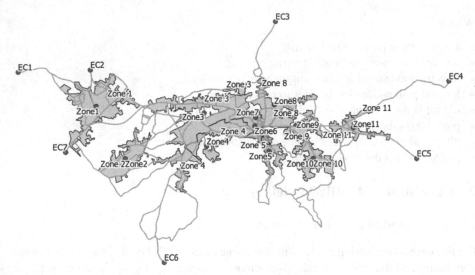

Fig. 4. Graph of Artena's Road network [24]

4   Monitoring of Vehicle Flows Through Fixed Cameras

The study foresees the monitoring of vehicular flows with automatic detection techniques through video images based on the use of cameras, which allow to continuously detect the traffic scenes that take place on a road section. The cameras offer a spatio-temporal representation of the vehicular flows, so it is necessary to process the video sequences through methodologies that allow an interpretation of the content of each image (spatial analysis) and their correlation in time sequences (time analysis).

To design an automatic detection system with video images it is necessary to use specialized hardware and software, especially whether video sequences in real time are automatically analyzed, important aspects concern the transmission and reception of data, number of cameras per control system, zone detection for monitoring and finally "image detection" processing and analysis in real time.

4.1   Camera Detection and Positioning Method

The proposed method of traffic detection is based on the use of a video monitoring system through the presence of cameras, which allow the continuous detection of traffic scenarios that take place on a section or at a road intersection. Cameras with artificial intelligence algorithms on board - installed in strategic points of the city - can recognize, classify, and count vehicles, track their movements, and detect their speed.

In more detail, the latest generation of cameras can extract precise data on vehicles (type, color, mark, number plate, direction, speed) from the images and, based on the algorithms adopted, detect anomalies in their behavior (vehicle stopped or wrong-handed) and locate their movements within the city. In addition, they automatically detect traffic jams, accidents, abnormal events and provide statistics in temporal (and real-time) succession of traffic conditions.

Intelligent image processing allows to send event notifications and alert operators in real time. In addition, all the data collected by the cameras gives a timely picture of city mobility, with the consequent planning of an efficient management of vehicular. The European Commission is currently working on a proposal for a Council Directive on the approximation of the laws of the Member States relating to the protection of the environment.

After analyzing the internal road network of the municipality of Artena and its external connections, 7 strategic points were identified: 4 refer to the perimeter area of the urban center and then detect traffic in or out of Artena to neighboring municipalities external sections, and 3 are arranged internally to the municipality. The identification of these strategic points allows to optimally place the cameras to be allocated.

Fig. 5. Location of the cameras [25].

In Fig. 5 are shown in blue traffic detection cameras, in Fig. 6 there is in yellow the camera that serves as an environmental station.

Fig. 6. Location of the environmental station. [25]

4.2 Algorithm for the Study of the Movements Intercepted by the Cameras

Once the position of the cameras had been defined, it was necessary to identify the relevant traffic data intercepted by them, which are divided into:

Trips within the municipality of Artena;
Trips from the municipality of Artena outwards;
Trips from the outside towards the town of Artena;
Through-traffic trips (from outside the Artena area to outside the Artena area).

A post-processing algorithm has been developed and implemented to gain relevant traffic information by the network of automatic detection cameras. In Fig. 7 and Fig. 8, the structure of the algorithm, by means of a schematic representation, is proposed in the two cases of streams intercepted by a camera on the cordon section and by a camera located in the inner urban area.

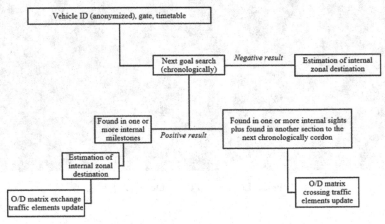

Fig. 7. Structure of the algorithm for the study of the streams intercepted by a camera on the cordon section.

All these relevant traffic information has been reported within a single Origin/Destination matrix in which trips within a single traffic zone (the so-called intra-zonal trips) have been neglected.

The structure of this matrix provides information on the probability that a vehicle, intercepted by the internal cameras and by those placed in the external sections, can reach a certain traffic area or another. All this is expressed in probabilistic terms as the number of cameras is insufficient to cover the entire Municipality of Artena: if this had been possible, the destination of a vehicle would have been identified in deterministic terms.

4.3 SUMMA Platform for Algorithm Implementation

The platform SUMMA has been implemented in a specific Dashboard that allows to obtain the necessary data to carry out studies on the mobility of the municipality of Artena.

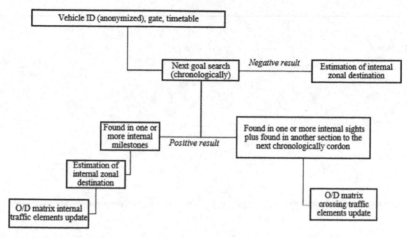

Fig. 8. Structure of the algorithm for the study of the streams intercepted by a camera on the internal section.

The home screen is defined as follows in Fig. 9.

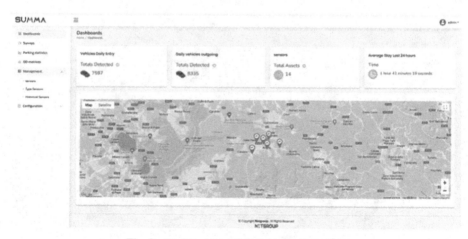

Fig. 9. Dashboard of SUMMA platform [26]

This platform allows, for a typical day and a user-defined time slot (Fig. 10a), to obtain the estimated traffic counts from the cameras and to derive the relevant O/D matrix, (Fig. 10b).

a)

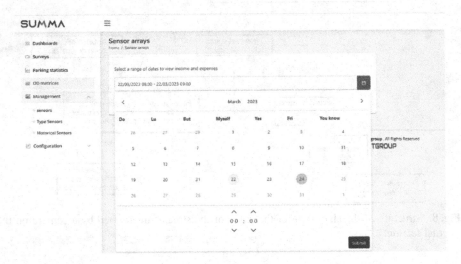

b)

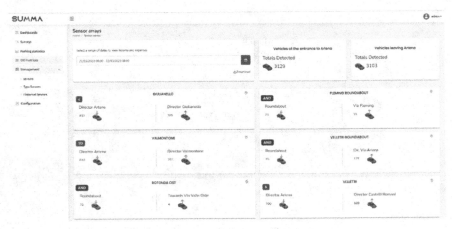

Fig. 10. a) Selection of day and time slot to extract data from, b) extracted data [25].

This traffic data will then be implemented on the development of a Travel Demand Forecasting Model by means of a macro-modelling approach. In detail O/D estimates have been used as information basis for a macroscopic analysis, to perform a traffic assignment, and to calibrate a traffic forecasting model at urban level.

The platform also allows, thanks to the presence of the environmental station, to obtain measurements on the environmental impacts averaged in the 24h period of a typical day as follows in Fig. 11.

Environmental Report Data

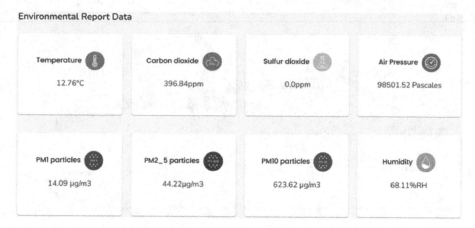

Fig. 11. Environmental Report Data [25]

5 Results Obtained: Route Choice and Traffic Assignment

To define the intervention measures aimed to improve the sustainability of the munic-ipality of Artena in terms of mobility, the traffic model previously described, has been developed. With the data elaborated by the aforementioned SUMMA platform, several O/D matrix have been obtained. In addition, with the traffic counts available, the model was calibrated, and several analyses was carried out on specific time windows (peak hours) on a typical working day.

Below are the results of a typical day in the morning time slot (07.15 - 08.15) in terms of vehicular flow and saturation rate in Fig. 12a) and b).

As it can be easily detected by the analysis of the obtained results from Figs. 12a and 12b, road sections connecting city of Artena with the nearest municipalities are those affected by more high traffic flows compared with those pertaining the internal roads of the municipality themselves.

5.1 Calibration

Following the assignment of traffic by means of the User Equilibrium method the model needs to be calibrated with traffic counts provided by the cameras.

A comparison has been made between the calibration based on the O/D matrix derived by commuting traffic provided by National Statistical Office (ISTAT) within the Census data collection activities that is referring to the morning peak time 7.15–8.15 (see Fig. 13a) and the calibration based on the estimated O/D matrix obtained from the automatic detection cameras within the SUMMA platform (see Fig. 13b).

a)

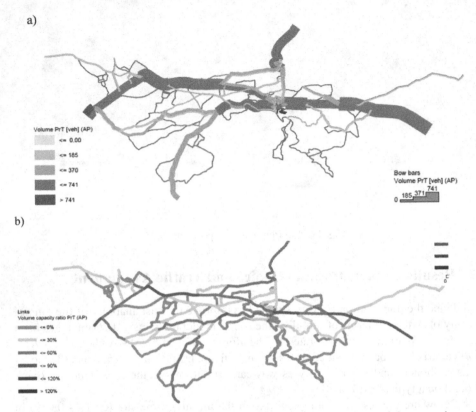

b)

Fig. 12. Car and motorcycle mode traffic flow distribution for a) morning peak hour matrix and b) Volume capacity ratio.

As it can be clearly highlighted by these preliminary results, the calibration of traffic prediction macroscopic model performed on the estimated O/D matrix obtained from the SUMMA platform shows a better agreement between predicted and measured traffic flows than that obtained on the ISTAT matrix, exhibiting a higher Coefficient of Determination (R^2). It therefore seems that the proposed post-processing algorithm seems to better capture the mobility pattern in the examined urban area.

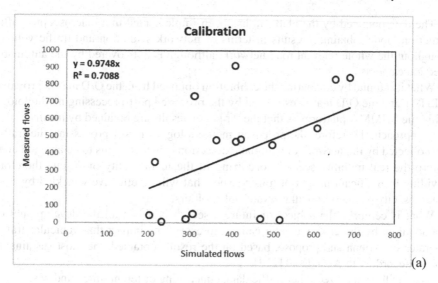

(a)

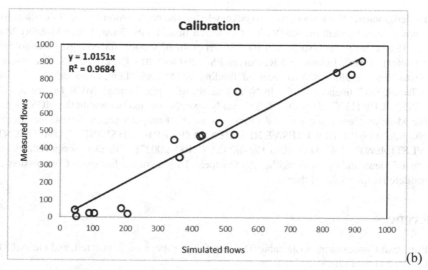

(b)

Fig. 13. Model calibration based on ISTAT O/D matrix a) and on estimated O/D matrix provided by the SUMMA platform b).

6   Conclusion

This article presents some results related to the development of the SUMMA project, promoted within the Smarter Italy project funded by Italian Ministry of Economic Development. The pilot project took place in the municipality of Artena and involved the design and development of a digital platform system for mobility analysis using advanced sensors, cameras that leverage specific AI algorithms and 5G communication infrastructure.

The data obtained by the platform has been implemented in a macroscopic traffic prediction model obtaining results in terms of network saturation and traffic volume throughout the whole relevant road network, although is not covered by the automatic detection cameras.

What it is found by comparing the calibration obtained from the O/D matrix provided by ISTAT and the O/D matrix estimated by the proposed post-processing methodology within the SUMMA platform, is that the far better results are obtained by means of this latter approach. Therefore, the proposed methodology for post-processing the traffic data collected by the network of automatic detection cameras seems to be able to better capture the real mobility scenario occurring in the municipality of Artena therefore providing a significant insight of traffic issues that will be effectively tackled by road managers, city planners and all relevant stakeholders.

What is certainly the subject of future research is above all the development of data acquired by the environmental camera to assess the impact that vehicular traffic generates on Artena and propose, based on the results obtained, the most sustainable choices according to Agenda 30 [2, 3].

Also, will be analyzed other traffic data, concerning different time windows.

Acknowledgments. The authors wish to acknowledge the contribution by the Italian Ministry of Economic Development (MiSE-DGSCERP) which financed the Smart Urban Mobility Management (SUMMa) project, sponsored by the "Program of support for emerging technologies in the context of 5G", Economical Resources FSC 2014–2020 - CIPE 61/2018. The research leading to these results has also received funding by Project "Ecosistema dell'innovazione Rome Technopole" financed by EU in NextGenerationEU plan through MUR Decree n. 1051 23.06.2022 - CUP H33C22000420001. This study was also carried out within the MOST – Sustainable Mobility Center and received funding from the European Union Next-GenerationEU (PIANO NAZIONALE DI RIPRESA E RESILIENZA (PNRR) – MISSIONE 4 COMPONENTE 2, INVESTIMENTO 1.4 – D.D. 1033 17/06/2022, CN00000023). This manuscript reflects only the authors' views and opinions, neither the European Union nor the European Commission can be considered responsible for them.

References

1. European Commission. Sustainable Mobility for Europe: safe, connected, and clean. COM (2018) 293 final (2018)
2. UN Sustainable Development Goals, Agenda 30. https://sdgs.un.org/goals. Access April 2023
3. Paiva, S., Ahad, M.A., Tripathi, G., Feroz, N., Casalino, G.: Technologies for Urban Smart Mobility: Recent Trends, Opportunities and Challenges. Sensors **21**(6), 2143 (2021). https://doi.org/10.3390/s21062143
4. Next Generation EU. https://next-generation-eu.europa.eu/index_en. Access April 2023)
5. Chiordi, S., Desogus, G., Garau, C., Nesi, P., Zamperlin, P.: A preliminary survey on smart specialization platforms: evaluation of european best practices. In: Gervasi, O., Murgante, B., Misra, S., Ana, M.A., Rocha, C., Garau, C. (eds.) Computational Science and Its Applications – ICCSA 2022 Workshops: Malaga, Spain, July 4–7, 2022, Proceedings, Part VI, pp. 67–84. Springer International Publishing, Cham (2022). https://doi.org/10.1007/978-3-031-10592-0_7
6. Maldonado Silveira Alonso Munhoz, P.A., et al.: Smart mobility: the main drivers for increasing the intelligence of urban mobility. Sustainability **12**(24), 10675. https://doi.org/10.3390/su122410675. (2020)

7. Flügge, B. (ed.): Smart Mobility – Connecting Everyone. Springer, Wiesbaden (2017). https://doi.org/10.1007/978-3-658-15622-0
8. Lai, C.S., et al.: A review of technical standards for smart cities. Clean Technol. **2**(3), 290–310 (2020)
9. Ghazal, T.M., et al.: IoT for smart cities: Machine learning approaches in smart healthcare—a review. Future Internet **13**(8), 218 (2021)
10. European Commission. https://commission.europa.eu/eu-regional-and-urban-development/topics/cities-and-urban-development/city-initiatives/smart-cities_en. Access April 2023
11. Garau, C., Masala, F., Pinna, F.: Cagliari and smart urban mobility: analysis and comparison. Cities **56**, 35–46 (2016)
12. Pinna, F., Masala, F., Garau, C.: Urban policies and mobility trends in Italian smart cities. Sustainability **9**(4), 494 (2017)
13. Allam, Z., Dhunny, Z.A.: On big data, artificial intelligence and smart cities. Cities **89**, 80–91 (2019)
14. Garau, C., Nesi, P., Paoli, I., Paolucci, M., Zamperlin, P.: A big data platform for smart and sustainable cities: environmental monitoring case studies in Europe. In: Gervasi, O., et al. (eds.) ICCSA 2020. LNCS, vol. 12255, pp. 393–406. Springer, Cham (2020). https://doi.org/10.1007/978-3-030-58820-5_30
15. Alvalez, R.: The relevance of informational infrastructures in future cities. Field actions science reports (2017)
16. European Commission. Sustainable and Smart Mobility Strategy – putting European transport on track for the future. COM (2020) 789 final (2020)
17. DIRECTIVE 2010/40/EU OF THE EUROPEAN PARLIAMENT AND OF THE COUNCIL on the framework for the deployment of Intelligent Transport Systems in the field of road transport and for interfaces with other modes of transport (2010)
18. Coni, M., Garau, C., Pinna, F.: How has cagliari changed its citizens in smart citizens? exploring the influence of ITS technology on urban social interactions. In: Gervasi, O., et al. (eds.) ICCSA 2018. LNCS, vol. 10962, pp. 573–588. Springer, Cham (2018). https://doi.org/10.1007/978-3-319-95168-3_39
19. Torrisi, V., Garau, C., Inturri, G., Ignaccolo, M.: Strategies and actions towards sustainability: encouraging good ITS practices in the SUMP vision. In: AIP Conference Proceedings, vol. 2343, no. 1, p. 090008. AIP Publishing LLC (2021)
20. G.U. 18/04/2018, n. 90. Modalità attuative e strumenti operativi della sperimentazione su strada delle soluzioni di Smart Road e di guida connessa e automatica. D. MIN. INFRASTRUTTURE E TRASP. 28/02/2018. English version "Implementation methods and operational tools of road testing of Smart Road solutions and connected and automatic driving" (2018)
21. MITD Homepage. https://innovazione.gov.it/argomenti/smarter-italy/. Accessed 7 March 2021
22. Cascetta, E.: Transportation Systems Analysis. Models and Applications. 2nd Edn. pp. 1–752, Springer (2009). https://doi.org/10.1007/978-0-387-75857-2
23. ISTAT Homepage. https://www.istat.it/en/censuses/population-and-housing. Accessed 7 March 2021
24. QGIS Development Team, 2017. QGIS Geographic Information System. Open-Source Geospatial Foundation Project. http://qgis.osgeo.org
25. SUMMA platform. https://summa.netgroup.it/dashboard
26. D'Apuzzo, M., Evangelisti, A., Santilli, D., Buzzi, S., Mazzei, M., Bietoni, V.: New smart mobility applications: preliminary findings on a pilot study in the municipality of Artena. In: Gervasi, O., et al. (eds.) ICCSA 2021. LNCS, vol. 12954, pp. 21–36. Springer, Cham (2021). https://doi.org/10.1007/978-3-030-86979-3_2

A Preliminary Effort to Develop a Framework of Distance Decay Functions for New Urban Active Mobility

Mauro D'Apuzzo[1]([✉]) [iD], Giuseppe Cappelli[1,2], Sofia Nardoianni[1], Vittorio Nicolosi[3], and Azzurra Evangelisti[1] [iD]

[1] University of Cassino and Southern Lazio, Via G. Di Biasio 43, 03043 Cassino, Italy
{dapuzzo,sofia.nardoianni}@unicas.it,
giuseppe.cappelli@iusspavia.it
[2] University School for Advanced Studies, IUSS, Piazza della Vittoria n.15, 27100 Pavia, Italy
[3] University of Rome "Tor Vergata", Via del Politecnico, 1, 00133 Rome, Italy
nicolosi@uniroma2.it

Abstract. Sustainable mobility in urban areas has made a giant leap forward with the widespread diffusion of muscular bike, e-bike and e-scooter in the last years. There is therefore the need to provide new modelling tools for urban transport planners in order to manage the increase of these new transport users as far as the safety issues are concerned. Following a risk-based approach to urban road safety, evaluating the road network exposure to the new active modes (especially cycling ones), implies the use of suitable Distance Decay Functions (DDFs) that can be easily implemented in a travel demand prediction model. In this paper, a new methodology to develop DDFs is proposed. The method has been calibrated and applied to a dataset of over 90 Italian cities where land use and terrain data have been collected and regressed in order to evaluate a combined model taking into account modal split and trip distance. It is believed that the use of this method may help urban road designers and city planners in identifying critical traffic scenarios induced by new active mobility and in studying suitable countermeasures to improve traffic safety.

Keywords: Sustainable Mobility · Impedance Function · Modal Split · e-Bike

1 Introduction

Although cycling is one of the most used mode of transport, according to the existing international literature on cycling mode choice and route choice modelling, cycling users follow some specific rules than other users not do [1].

In the last years, according to several national and European sources [2, 3], bikes sales are increased, and this can be addressed to the lower cost for transportation for road users [4]. The most frequent factors that encouraged cycling are physical health and fitness (38%), contribution to environmental sustainability (14%), economy (13%) and

© The Author(s), under exclusive license to Springer Nature Switzerland AG 2023
O. Gervasi et al. (Eds.): ICCSA 2023 Workshops, LNCS 14110, pp. 194–208, 2023.
https://doi.org/10.1007/978-3-031-37123-3_16

time saving (10%), and the antagonist factors are perceived crash risk (17%), adverse weather conditions (17%) and lack of safety (16%) [5].

Cycling and in general bike commuting have huge health benefits, such as a 16% increase in VO_{2max} (maximum oxygen consumption) and a 15% increase in HDL cholesterol [6] and improve also the cardiorespiratory system by 30% in low fitness adults [7]: the thresholds for cardiorespiratory fitness improvements is reached for approximately for 170 (women) and 250 (men) min/week at moderate intensity [8]. According to Matthews et al. [9] a daily cycling activity leads to a 20% risk reduction of all-cause mortality with an activity of less than 60 min, and with 100 min to a 30% (among women): a moderate cycling activity reduces also the risk of colon cancer of 20% and 45% for respectively 90 min and 2h cycling for women and men [10].

Often cycling is described as a way to reduce the congestion in urban areas for several reason, from environmental to safety aspects. But recently the desire to introduce cycling demand analysis in traffic plan and design has become very strong. Assessing the cycling demand is not easy and this type of analysis are also in an early stage because the variables that play a fundamental role are several but also difficult to retrieve somehow. As it is possible to read in the works of Maldonado-Hinarejos et al. [11], two approaches are often used to assess the cycling demand, and in particular references are made to: aggregate level method and discrete choice model.

The concept of finding an accurate form of the cycling travel choice models is strictly connected with the accessibility, which reflect the personal ability to reach a destination [12]: this is a crucial aspect to bear in mind because it is correlated with cycling (but also walking) behaviors [36–40]. In general, the distance (but also other land variables, such as slope and the energy expenditure) between home/office and a transport terminal is one on the major barrier to the promotion of active mobility [13, 14] and if this distance is very high or not very accessible in term of land characteristics, the use of motorized mean of transport is encouraged [15]: according to Pucher et al.[16], half of the trip made with private vehicle shorter than 5 km could be replaced by cycling trips.

In this paper, the role of the cycle lane equipment (that is related with safety issues), slope and travel distances characteristics during cycling activity will be explored. A model that give information on bike share by comparing data among 90 Italian cities is proposed and several Distance Decay Functions (DDFs) are obtained in order to assess the modal split to new and sustainable mode of transport.

2 Framework of the Methodology

2.1 Description of the Methodology

The aim of this paper is to find a correlation among the main explanatory variables that affect the choice to cycle. To better understand the reason behind this choice, the main step is to identify an optimal sample size for each class of population. For this purpose, (see Fig. 1), a flow chart of the proposed methodology is reported here below, in order to highlight the main step of the procedure and to simplify the total understanding of the method proposed.

Going to sample design, the layout of the procedure can be split into two main steps: development of a travel choice model at municipal level, on one hand, and the development of a calibrated distance probability density function for each investigated travel mode.

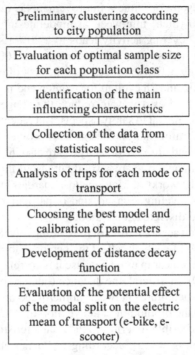

Fig. 1. Flow chart of the proposed methodology [41].

2.2 Travel Choice Model: Identification of the Explanatory Variables

Travel mode choice models allow to study how many transport users will move in a certain area of interest. The bike demand follows rules that other modes do not and so is essential to study which characteristics or which determinants influence in a positive or a negative way bike commuting [17], very different from car and public transport use [18]. People that use bike for recreational matter have other motivation than people that use bike for commuting and these characteristics are proposed here. In the monolithic study of Heinen et al. (2009) [1], the authors give a systematic review on the current scientific literature in this field. They divided the main determinants into five groups:

1. Built environment.
2. Natural environment
3. Socio-economic factors
4. Psychological Factors

5. Cost Aspects.

Travel behaviors are very influenced by built environment and several investigations have been carried out in order to discover these relationships. A fundamental role, that is common also to other mode of transport, is played by the trip distance between the origin and the destination [19]. In a study on cycling behaviors in 17 countries across the whole world [20], the authors show that the distance distribution is unrelated to the diffusion in a particular country of the cycling phenomena and there is a high likelihood that a bicycle-related trip is shorter than 5 km.

It essential also to recognize that the cycling demand is also influenced by the surrounding landscape, hilliness and weather. Heinen et al. [1] state that hilliness and landscape are rarely considered in mode choice model. According to Parking et al.[21], hilliness is expected to have a very predominant role in the proportion of users that cycle to work.

Among the socio-economic factors, it is possible to find household characteristics, age, gender, income, car and bicycle ownership, employment status [18] that are strictly related. Several studies highlight that men cycle more than women [22, 23], and women who bicycle are more likely to bicycle by choice [24].

Psychological factors are also introduced in mode choice studies in recent years, and references are made to the Theory of Planned Behaviors [1, 25]. Personal attitude, perceived social norms and habits influence commuters' decisions to use bike as a mode of transport.

Travel time and related costs, safety and efforts influence the most cycling than other mode of transport [1]. Muñoz et al. [26], show that with an increasing sidewalk width, total length of bike lane, and proportion of protected bike lane, users are more likely to use active transportation mode.

As a matter of fact, for each single trip it is possible to associate a generalized cost, affected by the length of trips, the travel time, the internal and external cost of movement. In a heterogeneous territory, such as Italy, all these aspects may affect the different choices that road users make. In order to highlight these characteristics, a careful experimental design has to be carried out and urban areas must be selected in a way they will represent the whole territory and the population's behaviors in modal choice at national level.

2.3 Collection of the Data and Disaggregation Process

In order to collect adequate data on commuting for several mode of transport, references are made to the Italian Census [27], that store freely downloadable commuting data. The main problem with this type of data is that they are organized in an "aggregate" form. As a matter of fact, if c is a homogeneous group of people that makes a trip, with these type of data it is impossible to retrieve information on the exact movement of a single individual, but only the transportation mode used and the interval time in which every class of movement c is in. Although other important information are not available in these type of data, for each mode of transport, a common value of operational speed is chosen in order to calculate the distance of the movements of single c homogeneous group of individuals (it is essential to highlight that Italian Census data do not give the exact duration of the trip, but a specific range of time in which the trip of the specific group is completed).

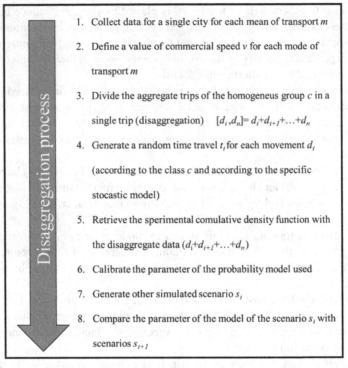

Disaggregation process

1. Collect data for a single city for each mean of transport m

2. Define a value of commercial speed v for each mode of transport m

3. Divide the aggregate trips of the homogeneus group c in a single trip (disaggregation) $[d_i, d_n] = d_i + d_{i+1} + \ldots + d_n$

4. Generate a random time travel t_i for each movement d_i (according to the class c and according to the specific stocastic model)

5. Retrieve the sperimental comulative density function with the disaggregate data $(d_i + d_{i+1} + \ldots + d_n)$

6. Calibrate the parameter of the probability model used

7. Generate other simulated scenario s_i

8. Compare the parameter of the model of the scenario s_i with scenarios s_{i+1}

Fig. 2. Disaggregation process: the main steps [41].

The main drawback is that this way to proceed is a simplification of the reality because the assumption that a group of individuals make a movement with the same amount of time is a rough hypothesis: each individual will complete a single trip according to some specific factors and/or conditions that will influence his own travel time with a determinate mode of transport. In order to use data in a more useful and also realistic way, a "disaggregation" process is proposed, that consists in assigning a random time for each movement in the single homogeneous group, to replicate the human behaviours that will be translated in a different travel time for each single individual analysed: the "disaggregation process" allows to move from a global to a particular point of view (see Fig. 2).

2.4   Analysis of the Movements and Development of Distance Decay Functions

As discussed previously, the "disaggregation" process allows to elaborate in a more realistic and punctual way the aggregated data, available for several mode of transport (pedestrian, bike, motorbike, car passenger, car driver, train, public transport). After applying the "disaggregation" procedure for each mode of transport analysed (not only for bike but also the for other ones, since there is the need to assess the relationship among them), a set of probability density distribution of trip length is obtained by means of an Erlang model, expressed as follows (1):

$$f_d(d) = \frac{\lambda e^{-\lambda d}(\lambda d)^{k-1}}{(k-1)!} \tag{1}$$

Where:

- d is the distance [km];
- k is the shape parameter (mainly expressed as a natural number);
- λ is the rate parameter.

By comparing the cumulative probability function, according to the Erlang model proposed and the experimental one, obtained by disaggregating the available data with the aforementioned process, the two parameter of the model can be estimated (2):

$$F_d(d) = 1 - e^{-\lambda d} \sum_{n=0}^{k-1} \frac{(\lambda d)^n}{n!} \tag{2}$$

Where:

- d is the distance [km];
- k is the shape parameter;
- λ is the rate parameter.

The best value of k (a natural number) and λ are evaluated after the calibration phase. Once the value of k is defined and a corresponding λ is evaluated, a new value of k is defined and a new λ is evaluated: this process will stop until the best agreement in terms of Pearson coefficient between the values of experimental cumulative probability distribution function and the values of the cumulative probability distribution of the Erlang model expressed is reached.

3 Case Study

3.1 Experimental Design and Travel Choice Models

According to the aforementioned technical literature reported in the Sect. 2.2, land use variables (such as cycle lane equipment), socio-economic variables (car insurance, average income, and parking fee) and terrain-related variables (such as the elevation gain, expressed as the maximum difference between the elevation of a randomly sampled set of points within an defined study area or also slope parameter) can greatly affect the transport modal choice. It is therefore necessary to collect relevant data in order to develop sound statistical models allowing to evaluate the proportion of trips for each transport mode.

As a preliminary step of this procedure, 90 cities from different regions across Italy are selected: the philosophy behind this process is to highlight the differences in terms of different descriptor that could influence commuting behaviours. Within the sampling design process, it is essential to guarantee that cities have different main characteristics such as different altitude, different terrain characteristics, mean income, car insurance, cycle lanes, parking fee, area of the municipality and of the city centre and number of inhabitants. These main characteristics may have strong influence on bike-commuting uses: some of them could facilitate the use of the bikes, other may not encourage the travel-to-work or travel-to-study trips. In the Table 1, the main characteristics collected are reported and arranged for each territorial unit (North, Centre, and South Italy) and for three selected population range values within small and middle-size Italian cities (namely, <10'000 inhabitants, between 10'000 and 50'000 inhabitants and between 50'000 and 100'000 inhabitants). It is important also to highlight that the Italian territory is not very uniform in terms of terrain characteristic, socio-economic descriptors such as work occupancy and average income, due to some historical and cultural matters that are difficult to evaluate.

Table 1. Mean Values of the Attributes in Cycling choice model at Municipal level [41].

City Size	0-10000 Inhabitants			10000-50000 Inhabitants			50000-100000 Inhabitants		
Mean Value	North	Centre	South	North	Centre	South	North	Centre	South
Car Insurance [Euro]	292	357	364	290	351	363.	299	353	330
Parking Fee [Euro]	0.93	-	1.25	1.21	1.01	0.89	1.27	1.01	1.15
Income [Euro]	19992	16145	14503	21872	18815	17469	21326	21009	18164
Cycle lane Equipment [m/inhab]	0.022	0	0	0.012	0.004	0	32.59	21.12	8.48
Elevation Gain [m]	177	83	89	55	157	76	55	53	134
Bike Proportion [%]	2.43	0.46	0.71	5.15	1.99	1.15	10.45	5.11	1.05

As it was seen, several studies tend to summarize and classify in specific determinants the reason why a movement is made with bike or using another mode of transport. In this study particular attention is paied to cycle lane equipment and slope parameter that are not very addressed in the current scientific literature review.

Generally speaking, cycle lanes are specific infrastructure dedicated to the cycling flows, but they interact with motorized traffic within a wider transport supply system. According to the European Guideline PRESTO [28], cycle infrastructures need five main requirements: they must be safe, direct, cohesive, attractive, comfortable, but, among them, the author highlight that safety is "undeniably the basic requirement and must to be overriding concern". Rietveld et al. [29] found that safety constitutes a component in the generalized cost (defined by some authors [30] as resistance) and it explains also the amount of cycling proportion in municipalities: for these reasons Cycle Lane Equipment is considered in this study as a vital factor in forecasting cycling demand at national level.

As discussed before, the topography of the territory influences the reason why to cycle or not for commuting purpose, but it is less likely to influences recreational cyclists' attitudes. As it plays a fundamental role, hilliness and the effect of slope on cycling demand need to be studied in greater depth. According to Meeder et al.[31], few studies account for topography in travel choice model. With these strong scientific evidences, a Travel Choice Model is here proposed by collecting the information required for the three class of dimensionality:

$$BS = a * CLE + b * e^{-c*s} \tag{3}$$

Where:

- BS is the Bike Share;
- CLE is cycle lane equipment;
- s is the value of the slope parameter;
- a,b,c are the estimated parameter of the model (as can be seen in Table 2).

Table 2. Estimated parameters of the three models and main statistics.

City Size (no. Inhabitants)	Variable	Value	Std. Error	t-ratio	Prob(t)	Adj-R^2
0-10000	a	8.437784	8.098035	1.041955	0.30667	0.55
	b	5.01E-02	9.27E-03	5.401254	0.00001	
	c	64.59339	18.05094	3.578395	0.00133	
10000-50000	a	134.173	23.8274	5.631037	0.00001	0.62
	b	5.63E-02	1.22E-02	4.598703	0.00009	
	c	56.25408	24.24962	2.319792	0.02815	
50000-100000	a	91.12659	30.23564	3.01388	0.00555	0.51
	b	0.124859	3.39E-02	3.687348	0.00101	
	c	38.78388	19.27888	2.011729	0.05433	

It is also essential to highlight that for the model for a city size between 50'000 and 100'000 inhabitants, the max value of the slope parameter is considered (in agreement with some technical evidence [32]), while for the other size class the mean value of the slope parameter has been used. As it possible to see in Fig. 3, a graphical output of the model is proposed.

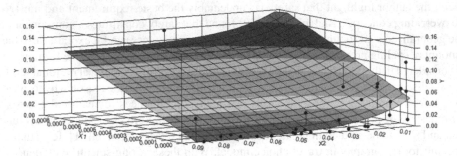

Fig. 3. Graphical output of the model for a city size between 10'000 and 50'000 inhabitants, where Y is BS, $X1$ is CLE and $X2$ is s.

3.2   Development of Distance Decay Functions

The methodology above described is applied on a real case study (a city in Northern Italy has been chosen falling within the size range 50 k to 100 k number of inhabitants). It is essential to remember that the "disaggregation" process (by simulating different scenarios starting from a random generation by a uniform random variable of the travel time) is also tested.

In order to understand how reliable and accurate is this procedure, 10 different scenarios are generated and a benchmark among them is made: as it possible to see in Table 3, the dispersion coefficient is used as main metric to compare the 10 different simulated scenarios, providing so good results, yielding an error related to a simulated scenario of about 1%. As a graphical mode of comparison (see Fig. 4), an experimental cumulative probability function and a cumulative function according to the Erlang model is shown. A fairly good agreement between experimental and theoretical cumulative distribution can be highlighte confirming the statements before.

The fitting criterion used, within an optimisation process to calibrate the parameters of the described Erlang model, is based on the evaluation of the Pearson coefficient, assessed by comparing the cumulated probability generated by the disaggregation process (in this study a uniform random variable is used) and the cumulated probability of the Erlang model. Given a defined value of k, the best λ is estimated when the maximum value of the correlation Pearson coefficient is obtained for different mode of transport. In Fig. 5, several density probability functions are shown: the main information given is how the probability to use a defined mode of transport, m, for a specific trip's length range will be. This modal split model is essential to evaluate traffic flows on the road network, within a Travel Demand Prediction Model (TDPM).

By combining the information of the density probability function with the number of trip that have a common distance, seven Distance Decay Functions, DDF (for each

Table 3. Simulation of different scenarios after the disaggregation process: comparison of different value of λ and dispersion coefficient (DC) calculated [41].

s_i	k	λ	$E[\lambda]$	$\sigma[\lambda]$	$DC[\lambda]$	$DC\%[\lambda]$
1	2	0.670598				
2	2	0.673344				
3	2	0.671799				
4	2	0.683659				
5	2	0.676874				
6	2	0.672633	0.675645	0.00552	0.00817	0.816995
7	2	0.676854				
8	2	0.670984				
9	2	0.671923				
10	2	0.687781				

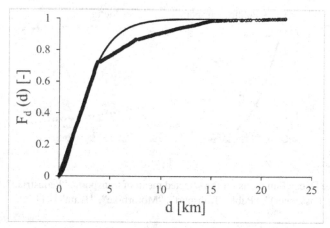

Fig. 4. Comparison between an experimental cumulative probability function and a cumulative function according to the Erlang (the transport mode selected is "Bike") [41].

mode of transport), can be obtained. In Fig. 6, for a defined distance range, the modal proportion among the different mode of transport is shown and, in turn, the corresponding amount of trips that are carried out.

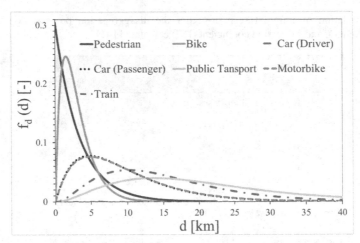

Fig. 5. Erlang density probability functions for the selected mean of transport: "Pedestrian", "Bike", "Car (Driver)", "Car (Passenger)", "Public Transport", "Motorbike", "Train" [41].

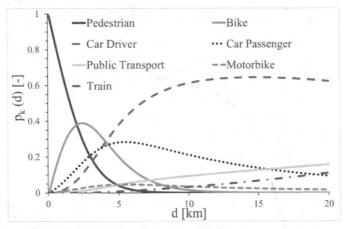

Fig. 6. Distance Decay Functions for the selected mean of transports: "Pedestrian", "Bike", "Car (Driver)", "Car (Passenger)", "Public Transport", "Motorbike", "Train" [41].

3.3   An Application to Assess the Modal Split to e-bike

A potential aspect of a DDFs framework is that it is possible to assess the modal split behaviours after the adoption of alternative mode of transport. One particular effect that can be studied is the modal split to electric mode of transport, and in the present case, the e-bike. As it was highlighted in the current scientific literature review, physical activity is similar for e-bikers and cyclists that use a conventional bike [33], but the main difference is that e-bikes trips are faster than c-bike trips [34] and that could impact the length of the trip that an user is willing to do.

After the adoption of e-bike, as it is been studied by Sun et al. [35], car users will use the new mode of transport and the amount of this modal split depends on the length of the trip. Although no studies has been performed in the Italian context, given also the difficulty to create a relationship by which assessing how the modal split will be, such type of information could be derived in a very simple and effective way within a DDFs framework. Combining the information of the aforementioned work [35] on the percentage of the modal split according to a specific trip length with the information retrieved by the DDFs here developed for a specific case study, new DDFs are calibrated for the all mode of transport. With this methodology, new relationships among the mode of transport on a defined trip distance are obtained: in Fig. 7, an example of modified DDF framework taking into account the modal split from car to e-bike is provided.

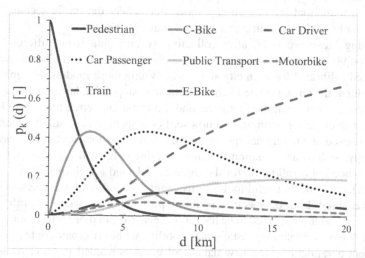

Fig. 7. Distance Decay Functions for the selected mean of transports after the modal split from "Car" to "E-Bike": "Pedestrian", "C-Bike", "Car (Driver)", "Car (Passenger)", "Public Transport", "Motorbike", "Train", "E-Bike" [41].

4 Conclusions

Travel mode choice models allow to study how many transport users will move in a certain area of interest and it is essential to study which characteristics or which determinants influence in a positive or a negative way bike commuting [16]. People that use bike for recreational matter have motivation other than people using bike for commuting and these latter characteristics are proposed here in this paper. After the collection of several data regarding the main characteristic that may influence bike share (with a specific focus on Cycle Lane Equipment and slope characteristics), three demand models are obtained. Within this context, also several DDFs for a specific case study are retrieved for different mode of transport and finally, using this tool, an example on how use these functions is proposed in order to evaluate modal split from cars to e-bike.

According to the scientific literature, it seems that some terrain-related variables such as slope may affect travel mode choice behaviour as far as urban commuting on bike is concerned. However, several cities in Italy are located on Alps and Apennines, so users have to spend a lot of energy and resources in order to make even a simple movement of few meters. Therefore, in these cities, the elevate value of the slope parameter may play an impeding role compared with those cities with low or null elevation gain. However, it has to be underlined that, other than this aspect that is more related to the field of "energetic" issues, the presence of cycle lane could influence the modal choice, based on a principle of perceived and quantifiable safety [30]: users will follow a route if they feel themselves in a safety condition and so cycle lane equipment play a fundamental role in commuting choices. In addition, it has to be acknowledged that municipal size, expressed in terms of population, may also play a critical role on travel model choice behaviour at municipal level since city's size may affect the traffic scenario and the transport supply model operating in a specific analysis area.

Following these premises, after collecting several data from different national databases on 90 Italian cities of different dimensions, three Travel Choice Models are obtained and calibrated for each city size class. Within these models, two main aspect are highlighted: the terrain related variables, such as slope, that have not enough investigated in the current scientific literature, and the cycle lane equipment may influence the decision to cycle for commuting purpose. For a specific case study, several DDFs are also proposed and the modal split to new mode of transport has been assessed. This methodology, with some limitation (for instance, due to the low numerosity of the city studied, the need of a validation for the three models and a lack of Italian data on the modal split), could be an useful tool for city managers and road designers to improve, for instance, safety level on specific corridors, promote new sustainable infrastructure where the demand it is expected to be higher and also to gain more information to tackle accessibility issues related to sustainable mobility within a urban context. As future development a validation on a new dataset of cities is needed in order to assess the efficiency and efficacy of the methodology and, as a future research step, the aim is to explore the influences of safety and energy expenditure parameters on cycling Travel Choice Models.

Acknowledgements. This study was carried out within the MOST – Sustainable Mobility Center and received funding from the European Union Next-GenerationEU (PIANO NAZIONALE DI RIPRESA E RESILIENZA (PNRR) – MISSIONE 4 COMPONENTE 2, INVESTIMENTO 1.4 – D.D. 1033 17/06/2022, CN00000023). The research leading to these results has also received funding by Project "Ecosistema dell'innovazione Rome Technopole" financed by EU in NextGenerationEU plan through MUR Decree n. 1051 23.06.2022 - CUP H33C22000420001. This manuscript reflects only the authors' views and opinions, neither the European Union nor the European Commission can be considered responsible for them.

References

1. Heinen, E., Van Wee, B., Maat, K.: Commuting by bicycle: an overview of the literature. Transp. Rev. **30**(1), 59–96 (2010)
2. Isfort. 17° Rapporto sulla mobilità degli italiani. Tra gestione del presente e strategie per il futuro. https://www.isfort.it/wp-content/uploads/2020/12/RapportoMobilita2020.pdf

3. CONEBI. Confederation of the European Bicycle Industry. https://www.conebi.eu/
4. Fishman, E., Schepers, P., Kamphuis, C.B.M.: Dutch cycling: quantifying the health and related economic benefits. Am. J. Public Health **105**(8), e13–e15 (2015)
5. Useche, S.A., Montoro, L., Sanmartin, J., Alonso, F.: Healthy but risky: a descriptive study on cyclists' encouraging and discouraging factors for using bicycles, habits and safety outcomes. Transport. Res. F: Traffic Psychol. Behav. **62**, 587–598 (2019)
6. Oja, P., et al.: Health benefits of cycling: a systematic review. Scand. J. Med. Sci. Sports **21**, 496–509 (2011). https://doi.org/10.1111/j.1600-0838.2011.01299.x
7. Hendriksen, I.J., Zuiderveld, B.O.B., Kemper, H.C., Bezemer, P.D.: Effect of commuter cycling on physical performance of male and female employees. Med. Sci. Sports Exerc. **32**(2), 504–510 (2000)
8. De Geus, B., Joncheere, J., Meeusen, R.: Commuter cycling effect on physical performance in untrained men and women in Flanders: minimum dose to improve indexes of fitness. Scand. J. Med. Sci. Sports **19**(2), 179–187 (2009)
9. Matthews, C.E., et al.: Influence of exercise, walking, cycling, and overall nonexercise physical activity on mortality in Chinese women. Am. J. Epidemiol. **165**(12), 1343–1350 (2007)
10. Hou, L., Ji, B.T., Blair, A., Dai, Q., Gao, Y.T., Chow, W.H.: Commuting physical activity and risk of colon cancer in Shanghai China. Am. J. Epidemiol. **160**(9), 860–867 (2004)
11. Hitge, G., Joubert, J.W.: A nodal approach for estimating potential cycling demand. J. Transp. Geogr. **90**, 102943 (2021)
12. Wu, X., Lu, Y., Lin, Y., Yang, Y.: Measuring the destination accessibility of cycling transfer trips in metro station areas: a big data approach. Int. J. Environ. Res. Public Health **16**(15), 2641 (2019)
13. Nian, G., Chen, F., Li, Z., Zhu, Y., Sun, D.: Evaluating the alignment of new metro line considering network vulnerability with passenger ridership. Transp. A Transp. Sci. **15**, 1402–1418 (2019)
14. Sun, D., Guan, S.: Measuring vulnerability of urban metro network from line operation perspective. Transp. Res. Part A Policy Pract. **94**, 348–359 (2016)
15. Zhao, P., Li, S.: Bicycle-metro integration in a growing city: the determinants of cycling as a transfer mode in metro station areas in Beijing. Transp. Res. Part A Policy Pract. **99**, 46–60 (2017)
16. Pucher, J., Buehler, R.: Cycling for everyone: lessons from Europe. Transp. Res. Rec. **2074**, 58–65 (2008)
17. Ton, D., Duives, D.C., Cats, O., Hoogendoorn-Lanser, S., Hoogendoorn, S.P.: Cycling or walking? Determinants of mode choice in the Netherlands. Transport. Res. Part A: Policy Pract. **123**, 7–23 (2019)
18. Wardman, M., Hatfield, R., Page, M.: The UK national cycling strategy: can improved facilities meet the targets? Transp. Policy **4**(2), 123–133 (1997)
19. Pucher, J., Buehler, R.: Why Canadians cycle more than Americans: a comparative analysis of bicycling trends and policies. Transp. Policy **13**(3), 265–279 (2006)
20. Goel, R., et al.: Cycling behaviour in 17 countries across 6 continents: levels of cycling, who cycles, for what purpose, and how far? Transp. Rev. **42**(1), 58–81 (2022)
21. Parkin, J., Wardman, M., Page, M.: Estimation of the determinants of bicycle mode share for the journey to work using census data. Transportation **35**, 93–109 (2008)
22. Dill, J., Voros, K.: Factors affecting bicycling demand: initial survey findings from the Portland, Oregon, region. Transp. Res. Rec. **2031**(1), 9–17 (2007)
23. Ji, Y., Fan, Y., Ermagun, A., Cao, X., Wang, W., Das, K.: Public bicycle as a feeder mode to rail transit in China: the role of gender, age, income, trip purpose, and bicycle theft experience. Int. J. Sustain. Transp. **11**(4), 308–317 (2017)

24. Singleton, P.A., Goddard, T.: Cycling by choice or necessity? Exploring the gender gap in bicycling in Oregon. Transp. Res. Rec. **2598**(1), 110–118 (2016)
25. Ajzen, I.: The theory of planned behaviour: reactions and reflections. Psychol. Health **26**(9), 1113–1127 (2011)
26. Muñoz, B., Monzon, A., Daziano, R.A.: The increasing role of latent variables in modelling bicycle mode choice. Transp. Rev. **36**(6), 737–771 (2016)
27. ISTAT: Basi territoriali e variabili censuarie. https://www.istat.it/it/archivio/104317. Access April 2022
28. Dufour, D.: PRESTO Cycling policy guide. Cycling infrastructure (2010)
29. Rietveld, A.P., Daniel, V.: Determinants of bicycle use: do municipal policies matter? Transport. Res. Part A: Policy Pract. **38**(7), 531–550 (2004)
30. Schepers, P., Hagenzieker, M., Methorst, R., van Wee, B., Wegman, F.: A conceptual framework for road safety and mobility applied to cycling safety. Accid. Anal. Prev. **62**, 331–340 (2014)
31. Meeder, M., Aebi, T., Weidmann, U.: The influence of slope on walking activity and the pedestrian modal share. Transport. Res. Procedia **27**, 141–147 (2017)
32. Menghini, G., Carrasco, N., Schüssler, N., Axhausen, K.: Route choice of cyclists in Zurich. Transp. Res. A **44**, 754 (2010)
33. Castro, A., et al.: Physical activity of electric bicycle users compared to conventional bicycle users and non-cyclists: insights based on health and transport data from an online survey in seven European cities. Transport. Res. Interdiscipl. Perspect. **1**, 100017 (2019)
34. Otero, I., Nieuwenhuijsen, M.J., Rojas-Rueda, D.: Health impacts of bike sharing systems in Europe. Environ. Int. **115**, 387–394 (2018)
35. Sun, Q., Feng, T., Kemperman, A., Spahn, A.: Modal shift implications of e-bike use in the Netherlands: Moving towards sustainability? Transp. Res. Part D Transp. Environ. **78**, 102202 (2020)
36. Santilli, D., D'Apuzzo, M., Evangelisti, A., Nicolosi, V.: Towards sustainability: new tools for planning urban pedestrian mobility. Sustainability **13**(16), 9371 (2021). https://doi.org/10.3390/su13169371
37. D'Apuzzo, M., Santilli, D., Evangelisti, A., Nicolosi, V.: A conceptual framework for risk assessment in road safety of vulnerable users. In: Gervasi, O., et al. (eds.) ICCSA 2021. LNCS, vol. 12958, pp. 542–556. Springer, Cham (2021). https://doi.org/10.1007/978-3-030-87016-4_39
38. D'Apuzzo, M., Santilli, D., Evangelisti, A., Nicolosi, V.: Some remarks on soft mobility: a new engineered approach to the cycling infrastructure design. In: Gervasi, O., et al. (eds.) ICCSA 2021. LNCS, vol. 12958, pp. 441–456. Springer, Cham (2021). https://doi.org/10.1007/978-3-030-87016-4_33
39. D'Apuzzo, M., Santilli, D., Evangelisti, A., Di Cosmo, L., Nicolosi, V.: Towards a better understanding of vulnerability in pedestrian-vehicle collision. In: Gervasi, O., et al. (eds.) ICCSA 2021. LNCS, vol. 12958, pp. 557–572. Springer, Cham (2021). https://doi.org/10.1007/978-3-030-87016-4_40
40. D'Apuzzo, M., Cappelli, G., Evangelisti, A., Santilli, D.: A design method for pedestrian areas by a simplified approach to predict the future traffic scenarios. In: Gervasi, O., Murgante, B., Misra, S., Ana, M.A., Rocha, C., Garau, C. (eds.) Computational Science and Its Applications – ICCSA 2022 Workshops: Malaga, Spain, July 4–7, 2022, Proceedings, Part IV, pp. 360–373. Springer International Publishing, Cham (2022). https://doi.org/10.1007/978-3-031-10542-5_25
41. D'Apuzzo, M., Evangelisti, A., Cappelli, G., Nicolosi, V.: An introductory step to develop Distance Decay Functions in the Italian context to assess the modal split to e-bike and e-scooter. In: 2022 Second International Conference on Sustainable Mobility Applications, Renewables and Technology (SMART), pp. 1–8. IEEE (2022)

How to Ensure Walkable Pedestrian Paths?
An Assessment in the Largo Felice Area
of Cagliari (Italy)

Federica Stabile[1] [ID], Chiara Garau[2] [ID], Silvia Rossetti[1]([✉]) [ID], and Vincenza Torrisi[3] [ID]

[1] Department of Engineering and Architecture, University of Parma, Parco Area delle Scienze, 181/A, 43124 Parma, Italy
silvia.rossetti@unipr.it

[2] Department of Civil and Environmental Engineering and Architecture, University of Cagliari, 09129 Cagliari, Italy

[3] Department of Electrical, Electronic and Computer Engineering, University of Catania, 95125 Catania, Italy

Abstract. Improve walkability, and therefore the capacity to provide safe and accessible walking opportunities, has emerged as a crucial topic especially for post-pandemic cities, seeking to create inclusive and liveable urban spaces. In this direction, a user-centred planning approach prioritises the creation of pleasant and accessible walking environments, which are essential for achieving a sustainable urban development. The physical features of the urban areas must be carefully designed and implemented to enhance the living standards, safety, and inclusiveness, also for vulnerable users. Based on the Geographic Information System (GIS) tools, this paper provides an analytical-assessment approach for evaluating walkability in urban settings, in order to identify the significant properties of urban infrastructures. The methodology is characterised by an integrated approach based on a survey process, including remote observations. The evaluation of pedestrian paths' performances considers the most influencing attributes (e.g., sidewalk width; visibility; crosswalk provision) which have been identified and evaluated for the case study of Largo Felice in Cagliari, Italy. To obtain an overall assessment in terms of safety, approachability, and enjoyment, each of these indicators has been analysed by aggregating and cross-referencing the detected attributes. The results highlight critical issues associated with the study area, that hinder the approachability and safety of pedestrian pathways, e.g., architectural barriers, discontinuities, poor visibility. Finally, the paper provides some recommendations for improving walkability in urban areas. Future research developments will include the assessment of further walkability attributes to perform a comprehensive analysis of an extended study area and in-field survey to validate the results.

Keywords: Urban planning · Walkability · Active Mobility · Pedestrian Paths · Sustainable Mobility · GIS · Cagliari (Italy)

© The Author(s), under exclusive license to Springer Nature Switzerland AG 2023
O. Gervasi et al. (Eds.): ICCSA 2023 Workshops, LNCS 14110, pp. 209–226, 2023.
https://doi.org/10.1007/978-3-031-37123-3_17

1   Introduction

Within the urban planning perspective, urban mobility represents one of the most important factors in ensuring a high quality of life in cities and walking is the primary transport mode at the neighbourhood level, offering access to services and amenities. The scientific literature is well established on the topic of active mobility, promoting the paradigm shift to reduce car dependency in favour of sustainable transport mobility alternatives, i.e., shared mobility [1–3], but even more active mobility [4–7], i.e., walking and cycling. Urban environments should support and encourage walking, which is the most important asset for communities, as most origin-destination pairs are within a range of distance suitable for walkability [8, 9]. The requirement for adequate pedestrian infrastructure is closely influenced by the morphological and functional organisation of urban activities and public services. In this regard, urban mobility is one of the main issues that must be extensively addressed to foster a broader democratisation of the city, promoting socialisation and an all-encompassing use of urban services. Many cities still continue to be characterised by low performance levels of pedestrian and bicycle infrastructure networks, especially for vulnerable users [10–13]. Thus, the creation of pedestrian-friendly environments constitutes a key research concept on how to correctly plan and design pedestrian pathways [14]. Moving towards a more sustainable framework focused of a and user-centred perspective, cities can achieve high infrastructural performance levels related to liveability, safety and inclusion [15–17]. Several studies on walkability provided appropriate criteria and tools for investigating, analysing and assessing the walkability of pedestrian network [18–22]. Nowadays, cities have become extremely complex entities and public administrations need effective tools to collect and evaluate several attributes related to the existing infrastructure in an effective way. Based on this premise, the paper proposes an analytical-assessment methodology of walkability applied to a real case study, coinciding with the area of Largo Felice in Cagliari (Italy), to identify a clear performance level of pedestrian paths. To provide a detailed assessment, attributes related to pedestrian approachability, safety and enjoyment, have been considered for pedestrian paths and crossings. The performed evaluation associates a qualitative assessment to each attribute, describing the characteristics of the infrastructure, and a quantitative value, based on the associated characteristics above mentioned. The analysis procedure is characterized by a series of research steps, including surveys with remote observations and mapping techniques, aiming at identifying weaknesses and critical points and providing a prioritization of interventions to ensure a more walkable pedestrian environment [23]. The results of the assessment showed that the Largo Felice area has several challenges hindering pedestrian paths, e.g., the presence of obstacles along the sidewalks, discontinuity, zebra crossings with excessive lengths. Therefore, the study provides valuable insights to improve the walkability of the Largo Felice area and offers useful methods to be replicated within other contexts. The paper is structured as follows: Sect. 2 presents the case study of Largo Felice in Cagliari; Sect. 3 focuses on the proposed methodology to assess walkability indicators within the analysed area; Sect. 4 describes the outcomes of the methodology application based on calculation of walkability composite indicators and their geographical representation through chromatic, and finally Sect. 5 provides conclusions and possible further developments of the research.

2   Case Study

The research area is located in southern Cagliari and encompasses a portion of Cagliari's historical centre (Fig. 1), with Largo Carlo Felice serving as its main street. This boulevard leads to the renowned Piazza Yenne. The selected area is characterised by a strategic location and high accessibility levels, close to both the seaport and the railway station, involving a high volume of activities. Furthermore, the extensive vehicular and pedestrian network characterising Largo Carlo Felice also played a key role in the selection of this area as case study. Specifically, it includes portions of three different neighbourhoods, namely Stampace, Marina and Castello. This area presents a significant impact due to vehicular traffic and hight motorisation rate. It is also characterised by different POIs (point of interests) such as cultural and historical elements, e.g., monuments, churches, theatres, and municipal buildings, as well as commercial activities, e.g., stores, restaurants and cafes as essential attraction for tourists visiting the city. These elements are situated along pedestrian links, including Corso Vittorio Emanuele II, newly pedestrianised road. Stampace and Marina are two neighbourhoods located respectively in the southwest and east of the historic centre of Cagliari, identified as the study area with the red border in Fig. 2.

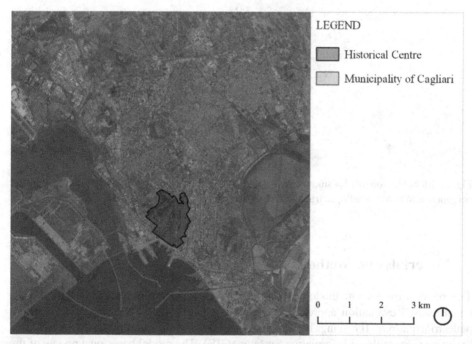

Fig. 1. Position of the historic center in relation to the Municipality of Cagliari. Source: Bing Aerial map processed in QGIS (authors elaboration).

The neighbourhoods are distinguished for the large number of artisans' and artists' boutiques, and are home to significant Baroque churches, e.g., San Michele and

Sant'Anna. The expansion of the Stampace district led to the gradual formation of modern districts in western Cagliari. Lastly, the Castello district is considered the main historical quarter of Cagliari. The neighbourhood has a high altitude compared to the rest of the city and it is characterised by cultural and architectural heritage. Castello currently hosts important institutions. Among the neighbourhoods, Stampace is one of the most densely populated in the municipality, considering approximately 7,200 inhabitants in 2021 [24], then Castello and Marina, respectively populated by approximately 1,300 and 2,600 inhabitants.

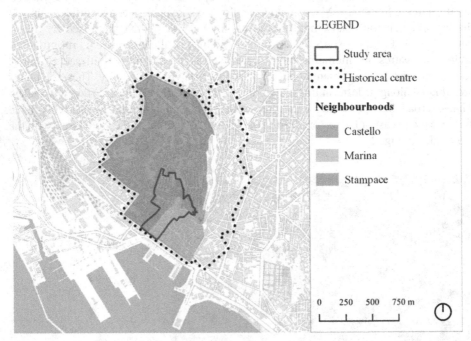

Fig. 2. Identification of the study area located in the historical center of Cagliari within the neighbourhoods of Castello, Marina and Stampace (authors elaboration).

3   Materials and Methods

This paper provides a methodology combining an integrated survey, mapping and well-encompassed evaluation approach of pedestrian networks. In the proposed research, pedestrian paths and crossings have been evaluated using an analytical-assessment model based on Geographical Information Systems (GIS). The model bases on a review of the existing literature, to identify and evaluate appropriate criteria for the acquisition and management of a large amounts of information on road infrastructures. Based on the objectives and guidelines identified in the pedestrian network survey, the main action is to specify the user group for planning purposes: the user group focuses on pedestrians also including vulnerable users [25]. In the GIS environment, the geometries used belongs to two different information layers, corresponding to pedestrian paths in a linear geometry and to pedestrian crossings in point geometry. The survey phase involved searching for data from official sources and carrying on remote inspections. Data sources include Open Data portals, i.e., the Cagliari Municipality's Geoportal [26], with information layers and interactive WebGIS maps, to identify relevant areas and infrastructures for preserving pedestrian mobility, i.e., restricted traffic zones and 30 zones. Furthermore, remote observations were useful to comprehend infrastructures features, enabling the identification of vulnerabilities and peculiarities of paths at different scales, to achieve growingly desirable streets [27, 28]. Several applications and models exist to collect and manage attributes associated with pedestrian infrastructures [29–39]. In this research, the pedestrian network is assessed by considering the most influential attributes of walkability, which have emerged during a literature review and that are also consistent with the study area. These attributes contributed to the calculation of composite indicators, useful for analysing complex phenomena and making them more understandable. The topics that emerge most in the literature and provide a detailed assessment related to walkability correspond to the following indicators of approachability, safety and enjoyment, respectively (see Table 1).

Table 1. Literature review on walkability indicators

INDICATORS	DESCRIPTION	REF.
Approachability	Refer to how easily pedestrians can walk, ensuring equal and safe accessibility for all. It is also associated with intermodality, allowing the pedestrian's modal shift from walking to the bus in a connected and continuous path	[6, 40–46]
Safety	Related to pedestrian safety which is a set of preventive measures to avoid accidents and ensure a protected environment for footpaths and pedestrian crossings	[47–51]
Enjoyment	Create pleasant, attractive, and comfortable environments for pedestrians, using elements, e.g., vegetation, street lighting or benches	[34, 52–58]

3.1 Quantitative and Qualitative Attributes Evaluation

Data related to the pedestrian movement are associated to sidewalks and crossings with selected attributes, based on evaluation of the literature and urban context. Qualitative and quantitative values have been collected and assigned to each attribute. It is important to underline that an in-depth study has been performed, considering these attributes for both sides of the road. Criteria used for attribute selection differ depending on the type of the road the examined segment is on. Thus, the evaluation is characterised by values ranging from pedestrian space to high-speed road. The evaluated attributes for sidewalks and crossings for each infrastructure level are shown in Table 2 below.

Table 2. Attributes involved in the indicator calculation.

Indicators	Attributes	Criteria		
		Pedestrian Space	30 km/h	Above 50 km/h
Approachability	Sidewalk provision (*sidewalks*)		X	X
	Continuity (*sidewalks*)		X	X
	Surface quality and maintenance (*sidewalks*)	X	X	X
	Ramp provision (*crossings*)		X	X
	Access ramp provision (*sidewalks*)		X	X
	Width of sidewalk (*sidewalks*)		X	X
	Bottlenecks/obstacle (*sidewalks*)	X	X	X
	LPT stops (*sidewalks*)		X	X
Safety	Sidewalk provision (*sidewalks*)		X	X
	Bottlenecks/obstacle (*sidewalks*)	X	X	X
	Lighting (*sidewalks*)	X	X	X
	Illuminated crossings (*crossings*)		X	X
	Excessive length (*crossings*)		X	X
	Presence of crossing devices (*crossings*)		X	X
	Presence of tactile signage on the curb access ramp (*sidewalks*)	X	X	X
	Crossing visibility (*crossings*)		X	X
	Crossing type (*crossings*)		X	X
Enjoyment	Sidewalk provision (*sidewalks*)		X	X
	Seats (*sidewalks*)	X	X	
	Width of sidewalk (*sidewalks*)		X	X
	Greenery (*sidewalks*)	X	X	X

Tables 3 and 4 summarise the selected attributes to perform the indicators assessment, also reporting the qualitative and quantitative evaluation for each of them. The first set of attributes is associated with the sidewalks, e.g., pavement quality, continuity, sidewalk provision and width, lighting, and tactile signage. The second set relates to pedestrian crossings, e.g., presence of access ramps, obstacles, visibility, and excessive length.

Table 3. Attributes involved for sidewalks assessment.

Attribute	Evaluation	Value
*Sidewalk provision	Both sides, only one side, Absent	2, 1, −1
*Continuity	Continuous paving along the sidewalk, Discontinuous paving along the sidewalk	1, −1
Surface quality and maintenance	Insufficient, Sufficient	−1, 1
*Width of sidewalk	<90 cm, 90 cm-150 cm, >150 cm	−1, 1, 2
*Access ramp provision	Present, Absent	1, −1
Bottlenecks/obstacle	Present, Absent	−1, 1
Lighting	Present, Absent	1, −1
**Seats	Present, Absent	2, 1
Presence of tactile signage on the curb access ramp	Present, Absent	1, −1
*LPT stops	Present, Absent	2, 1
Greenery	Present, Absent	2, 1

*Only Pedestrian link, ** Vehicular link

Table 4. Attributes involved for crossings assessment.

Attribute	Evaluation	Value
*Crossing type	Pedestrian crossings with traffic lights, pedestrian crossings	−1, 1 (30 km/h) 1, −1 (50–70 km/h)
*Ramp provision	Present, Absent	1, −1
Bottlenecks/obstacle	Present, Absent	−1, 1
Illuminated crossings	Present, Absent	1, −1
*Excessive length	Present, Absent	−1, 1
*Presence of crossing devices	Present, Absent	1, −1
*Crossing visibility	Clear view with raised/coloured crossings, Sidewalk extension, Distance to parking spaces, Reduced visibility	2, 1.5, 1, −1

*Only Pedestrian link, ** Vehicular link

3.2 Calculation of Composite Indicators

To perform a composite walkability assessment, the study proposes an analysis of the pedestrian network through an aggregate and cross-attribute evaluation. With the combination of different weighted attributes, specific values are calculated for the three indicators, as described in Table 1. They constitute key composite indicators of the pedestrian network performances, and their calculation is performed following the equations (Eq. 1–3):

$$I_V = a_{sidewalk\ provision} \cdot \left(1 + \frac{\sum_{i=1}^{n} a_n}{N}\right) \tag{1}$$

$$I_P = \sum_{i=1}^{n} a_n \tag{2}$$

$$I_C = \sum_{i=1}^{n} a_n \tag{3}$$

where:

- I_V = Indicator for vehicular links;
- I_P = Indicator for pedestrian links;
- I_C = Indicator for crossings;
- $a_{sidewalk\ provision}$ = value assigned to the attribute sidewalk provision (Table 2);
- $\sum_{i=1}^{n} a_n$ = Sum of the all-attribute values included in the evaluation of "Approachability", "Safety" and "Enjoyment" indicators (Table 1);
- n = number of considered attributes to calculate each of the three indicators;
- N = maximum value obtained by the sum of quantitative evaluation for the considered attributes.

The normalization of the obtained values for the indicators is achieved by following this formulation (Eq. 4), to obtain values between 0 and 1:

$$I_{V;P;C}^{Norm} = \frac{\left|I_{V;P;C} - I_{V;P;Cmin}\right|}{\left|I_{V;P;Cmax} - I_{V;P;Cmin}\right|} \tag{4}$$

4   Results and Discussion

The study conducted through data processing produced two types of results. First, thematic maps representing the most relevant individual attributes of the pedestrian network; second, the calculation of specific walkability indices, i.e., approachability, safety and enjoyment indicators.

The following thematic maps show the most significant individual attributes found in the preliminary analysis phase. Figure 3 considers the presence of continuous or discontinuous paving on sidewalks in vehicular links, as well as whether there is an access ramp at pedestrian crossings. From this map emerges a clear discontinuity above all in the northern part of the considered study area and specific criticalities in correspondence with some sidewalks. Figure 4 highlights the sidewalk provision (evaluated only for vehicular links) and how visible pedestrian crossings are from motor vehicles. In this case, there is a widespread reduced visibility at crossings and many road links without sidewalk provision or only on one side.

Figure 5 shows the presence of bottlenecks in the footpaths or obstacles along them, considering elements e.g., artificial lighting, rubbish bins and road signs. It is noticeable that there are obstacles along some pedestrian paths, which in some cases could be removed. Finally, Fig. 6 highlights attributes such as the presence of tactile signs and electronic crossing devices on pedestrian crossings, considered relevant to safety for the visually impaired. Tactile signs are present only along some sidewalks, while they are completely absent at crossing.

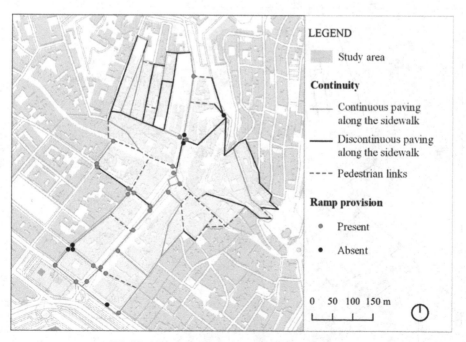

Fig. 3. Continuity and ramp provision attributes.

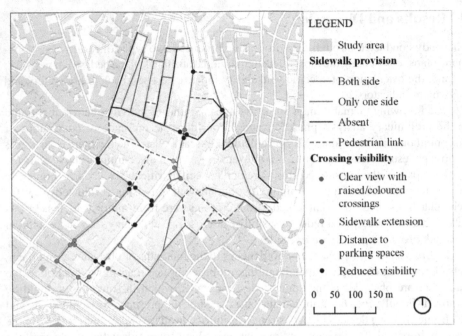

Fig. 4. Sidewalk provision and crossing visibility.

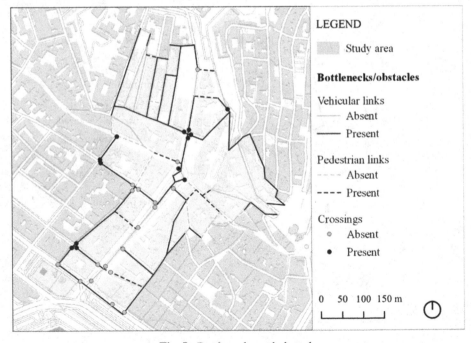

Fig. 5. Bottlenecks and obstacles

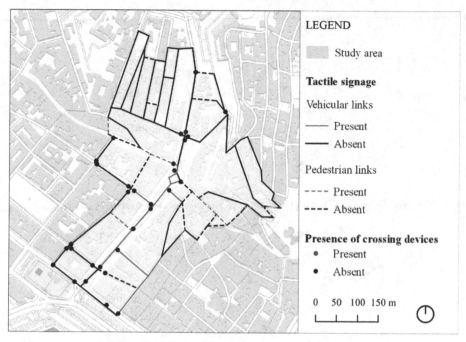

Fig. 6. Tactile signage and presence of crossing devices

According to the results of the performed analysis, the Largo Felice area presents some criticalities that affect the overall walkability level. Following the criteria provided in 2, the assessment has been considered more detailed and focused on issues of approachability, safety and enjoyment. Figures 7, 8 and 9 shows the maps derived from the calculation of each composite indicator.

The results demonstrate the close correspondence of the indicators to the actual physical configuration of the pedestrian paths, considering strengths and weaknesses. Links associated with low values of these indicators are generally characterized by pedestrian paths with poor functionality or not accessible for all users. Many of the critical links are related to the presence of obstacles and the reduced width of sidewalks, thus compromising approachability, especially in the northern part of the study area. Pedestrian paths are discontinuous due to pavement changes in level and steps, without ramp provision, also common in the southern part of the study area. The presence of numerous obstacles, e.g., lighting poles, garbage bins, and parking stalls close to crosswalks obstruct the pedestrian flow and reduce their visibility by drivers. Thus, pedestrians are often exposed to risks, also due to the excessive length of crossings and high vehicular traffic flows. As a result, it is advisable to limit vehicle speeds through traffic calming interventions and incentivize the implementation of pedestrian areas.

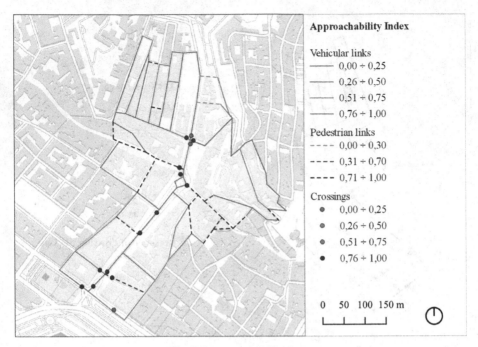

Fig. 7. Approachability index

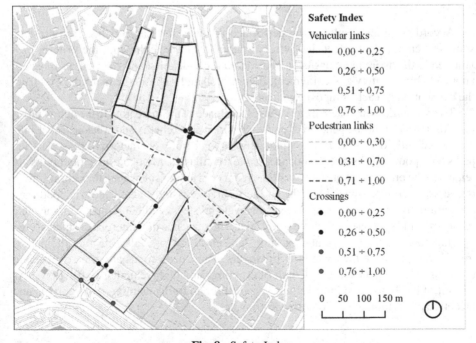

Fig. 8. Safety Index

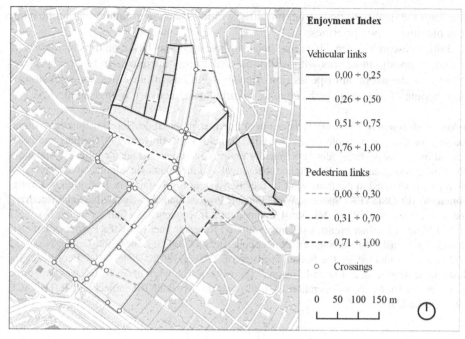

Fig. 9. Enjoyment Index

5 Conclusions

Nowadays, one of the main worldwide challenges within cities is to pursue a user-centred planning approach, that ensures a pleasant pedestrian experience, an opportunity of interaction with the urban environment and society, and thus promote sustainability.

In this direction, the current urban design paradigms require increasingly specific analyses. Furthermore, local authorities, must embrace an urban planning capable of guaranteeing approachability and safety of pedestrian paths for each user's category through priority, timely and rapid interventions. First of all, for the strengthening of pedestrian networks, urban spaces requalification interventions are needed. Simple analytical models are required to identify a priority of interventions and to incentivize active mobility in cities, thus the fundamental contribution of urban planning is to act through practical applications.

Within this context, the paper focused on the issue of walkability, evaluating the approachability, safety, and enjoyment of pedestrian paths in the area of Largo Felice in Cagliari and identifying potentialities and criticalities. With an extension of 15,52 hectares, the research area addressed in this work corresponds to an important central section of pedestrian flows in the historic centre. Through the calculation of composite indicators and the subsequent graphical processing of the obtained results, evident evaluations emerged. The choice of specific attributes for the calculation of these indicators has proved to be important for the research purposes, since the pedestrian network must provide adequate performance levels to meet of all user needs, even the vulnerable ones. The performed analysis can provide the public administration with a useful tool for assessing the quality of pedestrian mobility within urban environment and identifying possible intervention priorities.

Future research can involve more detailed investigations based on the calculation of further composite indicators with additional walkability attributes. In this perspective, to enhance the adoption of pedestrian-friendly solutions in our cities, an extension of the mapping of pedestrian paths beyond the urban road network is envisaged.

Acknowledgements. This work is the result of a project proposal developed within the doctoral course Smart and Sustainable Cities (3rd edition) held at the University of Cagliari and coordinated by C. Garau (https://dottorati.unica.it/dotticar/smart-and-sustainable-cities-3-edizione/). The course was attended by FS to refine theoretical and methodological tools with reference to the topics researched in the framework of the "Ecosystem for Sustainable Transition in Emilia-Romagna" (ECOSISTER) Spoke 4, WP1. Funder: Project funded under the National Recovery and Resilience Plan (NRRP), Mission 4 Component 2 Investment 1.5 - Call for tender No. 3277 of 30/12/2021 of Italian Ministry of University and Research funded by the European Union – NextGenerationEU. Award Number: Project code ECS00000033, Concession Decree No. 1052 of 23/06/2022 adopted by the Italian Ministry of, CUP D93C22000460001, "Ecosystem for Sustainable Transition in Emilia-Romagna" (Ecosister). The work of V. Torrisi was supported by European Union (NextGeneration EU), through the MUR-PNRR project SAMOTHRACE (ECS00000022).

Author Contributions. This paper is the result of the joint work of the authors. 'Abstract', 'Introduction' and 'Conclusions' were written jointly by the authors. FS wrote the 'Case Study'; VT and FS wrote "Materials and Methods" and "Results and discussion"; SR, CG and VT coordinated and supervised the paper.

References

1. Torrisi, V., Campisi, T., Ignaccolo, M., Inturri, G., Tesoriere, G.: Assessing the propensity to car sharing services in university cities: some insights for developing the co-creation process. Travel and tourism studies in transport development. Communications **24**(3), G1–G14 (2022)
2. Tiboni, M., Rossetti, S., Vetturi, D., Torrisi, V., Botticini, F., Schaefer, M.D.: Urban policies and planning approaches for a safer and climate friendlier mobility in cities: strategies, initiatives and some analysis. Sustainability **13**(4), 1778 (2021)
3. Campisi, T., et al.: A new vision on smart and resilient urban mobility in the aftermath of the pandemic: key factors on european transport policies. In: Gervasi, O., et al. (eds.) ICCSA 2021. LNCS, vol. 12958, pp. 603–618. Springer, Cham (2021). https://doi.org/10.1007/978-3-030-87016-4_43
4. Mezoued, A. M., Letesson, Q., Kaufmann, V.: Making the slow metropolis by designing walkability: a methodology for the evaluation of public space design and prioritizing pedestrian mobility. Urban Res. Pract. **15**(4), 584–603 (2022). https://doi.org/10.1080/17535069.2021.1875038
5. Morar, Tudor, Bertolini, Luca: Planning for pedestrians: a way out of traffic congestion. Procedia – Soc. Behav. Sci. **81**, 600–608 (2013). https://doi.org/10.1016/j.sbspro.2013.06.483
6. Moreno, C., Allam, Z., Chabaud, D., Gall, C., & Pratlong, F.: Introducing the "15-Minute City": sustainability, resilience and place identity in future post-pandemic cities. Smart Cities **4**(1), 93–111 (2021). https://doi.org/10.3390/smartcities4010006

7. Pucci, P., Colleoni, M. (eds.): Understanding Mobilities for Designing Contemporary Cities. RD, Springer, Cham (2016). https://doi.org/10.1007/978-3-319-22578-4

8. Annunziata, A., Garau, C.: A literature review on walkability and its theoretical framework. emerging perspectives for research developments. In: Gervasi, O., et al. (eds.) ICCSA 2020. LNCS, vol. 12255, pp. 422–437. Springer, Cham (2020). https://doi.org/10.1007/978-3-030-58820-5_32

9. Carra, M., Rossetti, S., Tiboni, M., Vetturi, D.: Urban regeneration effects on walkability scenarios. An application of space-time assessment for the people-and-climate oriented perspective. Tema. J. Land Use Mobil. Environ 101–114 (2022). https://doi.org/10.6092/1970-9870/8644

10. Campisi, T., Ignaccolo, M., Inturri, G., Tesoriere, G., Torrisi, V.: Evaluation of walkability and mobility requirements of visually impaired people in urban spaces. Res. Transp. Bus. Manag. **40**, 100592 (2021). https://doi.org/10.1016/j.rtbm.2020.100592

11. Pinna, F., Garau, C., Maltinti, F., Coni, M.: Beyond architectural barriers: building a bridge between disability and universal design. In: Gervasi, O., et al. (eds.) ICCSA 2020. LNCS, vol. 12255, pp. 706–721. Springer, Cham (2020). https://doi.org/10.1007/978-3-030-58820-5_51

12. Pinna, F., Garau, C., Annunziata, A.: A literature review on urban usability and accessibility to investigate the related criteria for equality in the city. In: Gervasi, O., et al. (eds.) ICCSA 2021. LNCS, vol. 12958, pp. 525–541. Springer, Cham (2021). https://doi.org/10.1007/978-3-030-87016-4_38

13. Nicoletta, R., et al.: Accessibility to local public transport in cagliari with focus on the elderly. In: Gervasi, O., et al. (eds.) ICCSA 2020. LNCS, vol. 12255, pp. 690–705. Springer, Cham (2020). https://doi.org/10.1007/978-3-030-58820-5_50

14. Forsyth, A.: What is a walkable place? The walkability debate in urban design. URBAN DESIGN Int. **20**(4), 274–292 (2015). https://doi.org/10.1057/udi.2015.22

15. Caselli, B., Rossetti, S., Ignaccolo, M., Zazzi, M., Torrisi, V.: Towards the definition of a comprehensive walkability index for historical centres. In: Gervasi, O., et al. (eds.) ICCSA 2021. LNCS, vol. 12958, pp. 493–508. Springer, Cham (2021). https://doi.org/10.1007/978-3-030-87016-4_36

16. Fonseca, F., et al.: Smart pedestrian network: an integrated conceptual model for improving walkability. In: Pereira, P., Ribeiro, R., Oliveira, I., Novais, P. (eds.) SC4Life 2019. LNIC-SSITE, vol. 318, pp. 125–142. Springer, Cham (2020). https://doi.org/10.1007/978-3-030-45293-3_10

17. Tira, M., Pezzagno, M., Richiedei, A.: Pedestrians, Urban Spaces and Health: Proceedings of the XXIV International Conference on Living and Walking in Cities (LWC, September 12–13, 2019, Brescia, Italy). CRC Press (2020)

18. Garau, C., Annunziata, A., Yamu, C.: A walkability assessment tool coupling multi-criteria analysis and space syntax: the case study of Iglesias, Italy. Eur. Plan. Stud. 1–23 (2020)

19. Yamu, C., Garau, C.: The 15-Min City: a configurational approach for understanding the spatial, economic, and cognitive context of walkability in Vienna. In: Gervasi, O., Murgante, B., Misra, S., Rocha, A.M.A.C., Garau, C. (eds.) Computational Science and Its Applications – ICCSA 2022 Workshops. ICCSA 2022. LNCS, vol. 13377. Springer, Cham (2022). https://doi.org/10.1007/978-3-031-10536-4_26

20. Pellicelli, G., Caselli, B., Garau, C., Torrisi, V., Rossetti, S.: Sustainable mobility and accessibility to essential services. an assessment of the san benedetto neighbourhood in Cagliari (Italy). In: Gervasi, O., Murgante, B., Misra, S., Rocha, A.M.A.C., Garau, C. (eds.) Computational Science and Its Applications – ICCSA 2022 Workshops. ICCSA 2022. LNCS, vol. 13382. Springer, Cham (2022). https://doi.org/10.1007/978-3-031-10592-0_31

21. Russo, A., Campisi, T., Tesoriere, G., Annunziata, A., Garau, C.: Accessibility and mobility in the small mountain municipality of Zafferana Etnea (Sicily): coupling of walkability assessment and space syntax. In: Gervasi, O., Murgante, B., Misra, S., Rocha, A.M.A.C., Garau, C. (eds.) Computational Science and Its Applications – ICCSA 2022 Workshops. ICCSA 2022. LNCS, vol. 13377. Springer, Cham (2022). https://doi.org/10.1007/978-3-031-10536-4_23

22. Blečić, I., Cecchini, A., Congiu, T., Fancello, G., Talu, V., Trunfio, G.A.: Capability-wise walkability evaluation as an indicator of urban peripherality. Environ. Plan. B Urban Anal. City Sci. **48**(4), 895–911 (2021)

23. European Transport Safety Council (ETSC).: How safe is walking and cycling in Eu-rope?. PIN Flash Report 38. ETSC: Brussels (2020). https://etsc.eu/how-safe-is-walking-and-cycling-in-europe-pin-flash-38/. Accessed 24 April 2023

24. Comune di Cagliari - Servizio Smart City e Innovazione Tecnologica -Atlante demografico di Cagliari (2021). https://www.comune.cagliari.it/portale/page/it/atlante_demografico_2021?contentId=DOC112641. Accessed 24 April 2023

25. Guida, C., Carpentieri, G., Masoumi, H.: Measuring spatial accessibility to urban services for older adults: an application to healthcare facilities in Milan. Eur. Transp. Res. Rev. **14**(1), 23 (2022). https://doi.org/10.1186/s12544-022-00544-3

26. Geoportale Comune di Cagliari. https://geoportale.comune.cagliari.it/. Accessed 24 April 2023

27. Campisi, T., Caselli, B., Rossetti, S., Torrisi, V.: The evolution of sustainable mobility and urban space planning: exploring the factors contributing to the regeneration of car parking in living spaces. Transport. Res. Procedia **60**, 76–83 (2022). https://doi.org/10.1016/j.trpro.2021.12.011

28. Guzman, L.A., Arellana, J., Castro, W.F.: Desirable streets for pedestrians: using a street-level index to assess walkability. Transp. Res. Part D: Transp. Environ. **111**, 103462 (2022). https://doi.org/10.1016/j.trd.2022.103462

29. Allen, D., Clark, S.: New directions in street auditing: lessons from the PERS audits. In: International Conference on Walking and Liveable Communities, Toronto, Ontario, Canada (2007)

30. Appolloni, L., Corazza, M.V., D'Alessandro, D.: The pleasure of walking: an innovative methodology to assess appropriate walkable performance in urban areas to support transport planning. Sustainability, **11**(12), Article 12 (2019). https://doi.org/10.3390/su11123467

31. Clifton, K.J., Livi Smith, A.D., Rodriguez, D.: The development and testing of an audit for the pedestrian environment. Landscape Urban Plan. **80**(1–2), 95–110 (2007). https://doi.org/10.1016/j.landurbplan.2006.06.008

32. D'Orso, G., Migliore, M.: A GIS-based method for evaluating the walkability of a pedestrian environment and prioritised investments. J. Transp. Geogr. **82**, 102555 (2020). https://doi.org/10.1016/j.jtrangeo.2019.102555

33. Duncan, D.T., Aldstadt, J., Whalen, J., Melly, S.J., Gortmaker, S.L.: Validation of Walk Score® for estimating neighborhood walkability: an analysis of four US Metropolitan Areas. Int. J. Environ. Res. Public Health **8**(11), 4160–4179 (2011). https://doi.org/10.3390/ijerph8114160

34. Ewing, R., Hajrasouliha, A., Neckerman, K.M., Purciel-Hill, M., Greene, W.: Streetscape features related to pedestrian activity. J. Plan. Educ. Res. **36**(1), 5–15 (2016). https://doi.org/10.1177/0739456X15591585

35. Fina, S., et al.: OS-WALK-EU: an open-source tool to assess health-promoting residential walkability of European city structures. J. Transp. Health **27**, 101486 (2022). https://doi.org/10.1016/j.jth.2022.101486

36. Gorrini, A., Bandini, S.: Elderly Walkability Index through GIS: Towards Advanced AI-based Simulation Models (2019)

37. Leslie, E., Coffee, N., Frank, L., Owen, N., Bauman, A., Hugo, G.: Walkability of local communities: using geographic information systems to objectively assess relevant environmental attributes. Health Place, 13(1), 111–122 (2007). https://doi.org/10.1016/j.healthplace.2005. 11.001
38. Moura, F., Cambra, P., Gonçalves, A.B.: Measuring walkability for distinct pedestrian groups with a participatory assessment method: a case study in Lisbon. Landscape Urban Plan. 157, 282–296 (2017). https://doi.org/10.1016/j.landurbplan.2016.07.002
39. Pucci, P., Carboni, L., Lanza, G.: Accessibilità di prossimità per una città più equa. Sperimentazione in un quartiere di Milano. TERRITORIO 99, 40–52 (2022). https://doi.org/10. 3280/TR2021-099006
40. Carr, L.J., Dunsiger, S.I., Marcus, B.H.: Walk ScoreTM as a global estimate of neighborhood walkability. Am. J. Prevent. Med. 39(5), 460–463 (2010). https://doi.org/10.1016/j.amepre. 2010.07.007
41. Castrignano, M., Colleoni, M., Pronello, C., Boffi, M. (eds.) :Muoversi in città. Accessibilità e mobilità nella metropoli contemporanea. FrancoAngeli (2012)
42. Dovey, K., Pafka, E.: What is walkability? The urban DMA. Urban Stud. 57(1), 93–108 (2020). https://doi.org/10.1177/0042098018819727
43. Garau, C., Pavan, V.M.: Evaluating urban quality: indicators and assessment tools for smart sustainable cities. Sustainability 10(3), Article 3 (2018). https://doi.org/10.3390/su10030575
44. Ignaccolo, M., Torrisi, V., Le Pira, M., Calabrò, G.: A step towards walkable environments: Spatial analysis of pedestrian compatibility in an urban context. Eur. Transp. Tra-sporti Europei, 76(6), 1–12 (2020)
45. Pajares, E., Büttner, B., Jehle, U., Nichols, A., Wulfhorst, G.: Accessibility by proximity: addressing the lack of interactive accessibility instruments for active mobility. J. Transp. Geogr. 93, 103080 (2021). https://doi.org/10.1016/j.jtrangeo.2021.103080
46. Rossetti, S., Tiboni, M., Vetturi, D., Zazzi, M., Caselli, B.: Measuring pedestrian accessibility to public transport in urban areas: A GIS-based discretisation approach. Eur. Transp. Trasp. Eur. 76(2) (2020)
47. Gargiulo, C., Zucaro, F., Gaglione, F.: A set of variables for the elderly accessibility in urban areas. TeMA-J. Land Use Mobil. Environ. 53–66 (2018). https://doi.org/10.6092/1970-9870/ 5738
48. Grossman, A., Rodgers, M.O., Xu, Y., Guensler, R., Watkins, K.: If safety matters, let's measure it: nationwide survey results for bicycle and pedestrian treatment prioritization. J. Transport. Eng. Part A: Syst. 145(1) (2019). https://doi.org/10.1061/JTEPBS.0000205
49. Rossetti, S.: Planning for Accessibility and Safety. Maggioli Editore (2020)
50. Schneider, R.J., Wiers, H., Schmitz, A.: Perceived safety and security barriers to walking and bicycling: insights from milwaukee. Transport. Res. Record 2676(9), 325–338 Scopus. (2022). https://doi.org/10.1177/03611981221086646
51. Tiboni, M., Rossetti, S.: Achieving people friendly accessibility. key concepts and a case study overview. TeMA – J. Land Use Mobil. Environ. (2014). https://doi.org/10.6092/1970- 9870/2487
52. Gehl, J.: Cities for people. Island Press (2010). https://gehlpeople.com/
53. Gubbels, J.S., et al.: The impact of greenery on physical activity and mental health of adolescent and adult residents of deprived neighborhoods: a longitudinal study. Health Place 40, 153–160 (2016). https://doi.org/10.1016/j.healthplace.2016.06.002
54. Guzman, L.A., Arellana, J., Castro, W.F.: Desirable streets for pedestrians: using a street-level index to assess walkability. Transport. Res. Part D Transp. Environ. 111, 103462 (2022). https://doi.org/10.1016/j.trd.2022.103462
55. Jacobs, A. B.: Great streets (4. print). MIT Pr. (1993)
56. Jaskiewicz, F.: Pedestrian level of service based on trip quality. Transportation Research Circular, TRB (2000)

57. Garau, C., Annunziata, A.: A method for assessing the vitality potential of urban areas. The case study of the Metropolitan City of Cagliari, Italy City. Territory Architect. **9**(1), 1–23 (2022). https://doi.org/10.1186/s40410-022-00153-6

58. Annunziata, A., Garau, C.: A literature review on the assessment of vitality and its theoretical framework. emerging perspectives for geodesign in the urban context. In: Gervasi, O., et al. (eds.) ICCSA 2021. LNCS, vol. 12958, pp. 305–322. Springer, Cham (2021). https://doi.org/ 10.1007/978-3-030-87016-4_23

Modelling Crime Dynamics and Risky Places: A Basic Combination of Crime Theories and Space Syntax to Evaluate Spatial Crime Impedance

Federico Mara(✉) 🄳 and Valerio Cutini 🄳

University of Pisa, Pisa, Italy
federico.mara@phd.unipi.it, valerio.cutini@unipi.it

Abstract. Effectively modelling urban systems is challenging but necessary to obtain appropriate tools to consciously intervene in cities. Among urban subsystems, urban security plays a fundamental role – since it is closely linked to the concepts of sustainability and liveability – and it is characterised by two specificities from the modelling standpoint. The first is that it requires considerable multidisciplinary integration between neighbouring fields including criminology, sociology and urban planning. The second is the specific need to include human logic and consequently human behaviour to some extent to be able to depict crime distribution dynamics. These two aspects are crucial in the environmental approach to security, which seeks the origins of criminal behaviour in the environment. In the logic of crime prevention through environmental design, it is therefore necessary to build models with the above-mentioned characteristics. In particular, this study represents a preliminary step of a modelling investigation aiming to show how even a few simple proven assumptions – in this specific case Crime Triangle and Rational Choice Perspective – and *ad hoc* urban modelling tools – the Space Syntax theory – can provide effective modelling. What emerges specifically in this paper is the central role, at least in light of the specific assumptions made, of pedestrian movement and the concepts of visibility and controllability, which can be interpreted through Space Syntax via *Axial Analysis* and *Visibility Graph Analysis*. This proposed basic modelling is then schematically applied to the historical centre of Grosseto with reference to robbery, drug dealing and pickpocketing to offer a first spatial recognition of the inner predisposition to host certain types of crime, which we refer to as 'spatial crime impedance'.

Keywords: Environmental approach to security · Crime prevention · Space Syntax · Pedestrian flow · Visibility · Urban modelling · Spatial crime impedance · Criminological environmental theories · Decision Support System

1 Introduction

Cities are complicated and complex systems, characterised by numerous factors interacting with each other according to non-linear rules. It is therefore extremely difficult to understand the cause-effect relationships between the various phenomena occurring

© The Author(s), under exclusive license to Springer Nature Switzerland AG 2023
O. Gervasi et al. (Eds.): ICCSA 2023 Workshops, LNCS 14110, pp. 227–243, 2023.
https://doi.org/10.1007/978-3-031-37123-3_18

in them and, consequently, to understand what interventions should be made in the city to achieve a predetermined desired effect. This complexity has also increased over the years due to the growing needs of inhabitants and increasing urbanisation [1]. In this chaotic scenario, the role of the urban planner – who, like a 'demiurge in process', has to plan interventions in the city while trying to modify and improve the environment around us – is as difficult as it is fundamental. Considering all the sub-systems into which the city can be analysed, the minimum unit is represented by the individual to whom all implemented policies are ultimately directed and on whom they must be measured. Individual considered in his 'universality', as a representative of all the needs of today's and tomorrow's citizens – while respecting the principles of sustainability – in the awareness that planning has a decisive role for both current and future generations. Therefore, more than a demiurge, the urban planner (with the partnership of the involved stakeholders) represents a technician at the service of the community. It follows that the reflections and interventions proposed must be aimed at maximising human well-being [2]. Among the various aspects related to human well-being is certainly present – and indeed represents one of the fundamental aspects to be satisfied – the security issue. Security is intended in a wide variety of meanings but its basic dimension is represented by physical safety, as described by Maslow [3] who identified it as the second primary need for man and a fundamental component of the primordial aggregating principles of men that led first to the formation of the early tribes and then of cities [4]. Even limiting the urban investigation to crime-related dynamics, the problem of the complexity of the system to be analysed persists. Then, the first goal of urban planners must be the realization of a model able to 'schematise' reality by achieving a degree of 'acceptable' simplification. Specifically, the search for the simplest possible model able to capture the dynamics being investigated, aid analysis and ultimately provide the answers sought, considering the 'perspective' with which the problem is addressed. However, modelling applied to the field of urban security – and in particular aimed at crime prevention – brings out some specificities.

First and foremost, the multidisciplinary nature of the topic. Various fields of investigation have been interested in the topic over time, developing different and rarely effectively integrated approaches and terminologies [5, 6]. These include criminologists, sociologists, psychologists, urban planners and architects, particularly concerning the environmental approach to security, the focus of this paper. Contributions coming from different fields show how their integration is indispensable to provide plausible models capable of interpreting crime dynamics – and, consequently, crime distribution – and the impact of the urban environment on these dynamics.

Secondly, the presence and the importance of human component. Compared to other geographical models, it is here necessary to include a real human behavioural model, however simplified. This is needed to understand how individuals behave in space and according to which decision-making process crime is carried out. In general, this second aspect is strongly influenced by the scale of investigation, as is the case with most modelling problems.

The question of which characteristics spatially most influence criminal or non-criminal behaviour and, spatially, which areas are most likely to 'host' a certain crime – in relation to human behaviour – is as intriguing as it is complex. This paper constitutes a preliminary investigation of the modelling aspects – with some preliminary results – of crime prevention through urban design topic, faced in a multidisciplinary logic. In particular, the interest of this paper is to illustrate the power of these interpretative models in understanding how, given a certain behavioural pattern, the impact of the spatial component can be assessed. Or rather, talking in configurational terms, the spatial impedance [7] that a certain environment interposes on the realisation of a specific crime. The result is a study that reduces crime dynamics interpretation to a few quantities and – as Space Syntax shows – closely related to the urban configuration: pedestrian flow and visibility. The objectives of the paper are thus to bring out the importance of crime prevention, to highlight the 'strength' of the configurational approach in the study of elements that have a strong impact on crime distribution, and to make readers reflect on how even simple models can provide very useful information on crime dynamics – hence the possibility of using these models as useful decision-support tools and preliminary studies on the urban environment in terms of 'predisposition' to crime. This is achieved through an initial theoretical discussion, the presentation of the quantities useful for such interpretations and, finally, the realisation of a basic case study applied to the historical centre of Grosseto.

2   Concepts and Methods

As anticipated, the paper is divided into two macro-sections. The first is 'revisional' (Sects. 3.1 to 3.4) while the second is 'applicative' (Sect. 3.5). The first offers a brief review of the criminological environmental approaches (Sect. 3.1): fundamental tools for interpreting criminal dynamics, with a particular focus on the rational choice perspective and the crime triangle (Sect. 3.2), chosen in this paper as a specific criminological theoretical model. Subsequently, a brief framework on Space Syntax theory analyse why and how Space Syntax represents an optimal tool for modelling flows and people behaviour in urban spaces also from a multi-scalar (urban, micro-urban, architectural) investigation perspective. Instead, in the second section (Sect. 3.5), once this multidisciplinary contextualisation has been provided, the practical applicability of these models will be discussed through the discussion of a simple case study on the historical centre of Grosseto.

3   Results and Discussion

3.1   Crime Theories

Among the interpretative models of crime distributions and human behaviour in criminal dynamics, environmental criminological theories play a key role. They represent models suitable for understanding criminal behaviour and how environmental components influence the occurrence of criminal events. Although they're different, the theories are not in contradiction but rather have several points of contact. They propose different perspectives and scales of analysis, so the choice of the crime theory that is most functional to the specific research question represents an important step. For this reason, this section offers a very quick overview of the main crime theories (for further details and discussions see [8]) to let the reader understand the different ways in which they approach the topic. This is followed by the choice of a specific interpretative 'set', which is further explored in Sect. 3.2.

Among the main environmental criminological theories are:

- Crime Prevention Through Environmental Design (CPTED);
- Defensible Space;
- Situational crime prevention (SCP);
- Rational choice perspective (RCP);
- Routine activities approach (RAA);
- Crime pattern theory (CPT);
- Broken Windows Theory (BWT);
- Problem-oriented policing (POP).

Defensible Space and CPTED – although very different in their concept – constitute the first real scientific reflections, made in the 1970s, in the field of the environmental approach to security, after the decisive contribution of the Ecology School of Chicago first and the important studies of Wood, Jacobs and Angel later [5]. **Crime Prevention Through Environmental Design (CPTED)**, coined by the psychologist Jeffery [9] although it became known thanks to Newman [10], introduces systems thinking to the analysis of criminal behaviour in relation to the environmental inputs humans receive, combining both organic and physical sciences. In particular, he dwells on the need to focus on the brain as the centre of elaboration of external inputs and the command centre for enacted behaviour, including criminal acts. Due to the high complexity this approach proposes, it was initially neglected and then recovered over time.

In opposition, the **Defensible Space**, coined by architect Newman [10] found immediate success due to its relative simplicity and the short timeframe in which concrete results could be achieved. Newman's was a practical approach in which general considerations were drawn from some general observations of reality. This led him to the definition of four principles: territoriality, surveillance, image and milieu and geographical juxtaposition, which were identified as key aspects capable of determining safe environments and thus to which analyses, plans and interventions must be targeted.

Situational Crime Prevention (SCP), born in 1976 [11], takes up Jeffery's studies and introduces the concept of benefit-cost in the criminal field, whereby by intervening in the environment it is possible to reduce the desirability of that place in the eyes of the potential criminal. This logic is also taken up by later approaches. The basis of this approach is the implicit assumption of the reasonableness of the criminal, specified by the **Rational Choice Perspective (RCP)** formally introduced in 1985 [12], according to which the criminal objectively assesses risks and possible gains. Furthermore, in the wake of this assumption, so-called 'scripts' to fight crimes have been proposed over time [13]. Assuming the RCP and the lack of precise spatiotemporal coordinates for a certain crime occurrence, it is possible to intervene at several moments in the 'storyline' by interrupting – through environmental modifications – the chain of events that would lead to that crime, in order to prevent it from taking place. In this sense, therefore, each of the steps leading to the crime occurrence represents an opportunity for the planner to counter and remove that possibility, interrupting the 'path to crime occurrence'.

Routine Activities Approach (RAA) coined by Cohen and Felson [14] shares some aspects with the SCP, however, being characterised by a wider scale of analysis. The key principle underlying the RAA is that a crime occurs where there is a convergence of a motivated offender, a suitable target and the absence of an 'active' (i.e., able to intervene) guardian. **Crime Pattern Theory (CPT)** [15], on the other hand, focuses on the concept of opportunities considered through (and generated by) the patterns that the everyday life of each of us, collectively, generates. According to this approach, some places are more 'risky' than others – *a priori* variable with the specific classes of crime – depending on their intended use, the daily dynamics that take place there and the concentration of people. The concept of 'awareness spaces' is also introduced: well-known and frequently travelled places in the daily routine where potential criminals make assessments of the existing potential opportunities.

Broken Windows Theory (BWT), introduced in 1982 by Wilson and Kelling [16] dwells on the impact that urban disorder and soft crimes can have on fear of crime and future crime occurrences, implying a kind of self-fulfilling prediction that starting with a diminished sense of belonging to the place leads, in turn, to abandonment and to the consequent perception of those areas as 'lawless', hence the propensity to host crime.

Finally, **Problem-Oriented Policing (POP)** introduced by Goldstein [17] is more of a kind of guide that promotes a proactive approach (situational approach) to the police force system, rather than a proper theory. POP thus promotes a problem-solving and democratic approach to crime prevention, shifting the focus from the exclusively repressive realm – which had characterised the police forces until then – to the preventive one.

The approaches just described have been extensively discussed over the years and this has led to their development and updating over time (for more details see [8]). As can be deduced from the albeit brief discussion, the approaches that refer to an interpretative behavioural model of individuals or a methodology aimed at the determination of recurrences and/or situations underlying criminal actions are those shown in Table 1, namely the SCP, RCP, RAA, CPT and, in a different way, the BWT. In particular, the investigation proposed in this paper specifically deals with the Routine Activities Approach and the Rational Choice Perspective, while excluding the more advanced concept of script. This is to demonstrate how even a very basic assumption – accompanied by specific and effective tools – can help in interpreting the social impact of urban space. This combination was decided on the basis of the scale of the investigation: the urban/micro-urban scale. For this scale these approaches are particularly suitable, as they do not envisage an analysis centred on the criminal and thus too close, nor do they imply a structured analysis of activities and temporal routines, which would have required more complicated modelling (but anyway feasible). The following section delves into these 'approaches'.

Table 1. Summary of the criminological environmental theories characterized by a specific methodology or interpretative model of crime occurrences.

Theory	Seminal work and authors	Description
Situational Crime Prevention (SCP)	*Crime as Opportunity* Mayhew, Clarke, Sturman and Hough 1976	It analyses the opportunities that the environment offers to a potential offender and it focuses on environmental modifications to reduce the benefit/cost of criminal offences
Rational Choice Perspective (RCP)	*Modelling Offenders' Decisions: A Framework for Research and Policy* Clarke and Cornish 1985	It considers the offender as 'rationality-driven', who therefore decides whether or not to commit a crime by weighing possible gains and risks
Routine Activities Approach (RAA)	*Social Change and Crime Rate Trends: A Routine Activity Approach* Cohen Felson 1979	It analyses criminal opportunities based on emergence phenomena resulting from the routine habits of the inhabitants. It also introduces the crime triangle
Crime Pattern Theory (CPT)	*Environmental Criminology* Brantingham Brantingham 1981	It analyses specific classes of crime based on the inhabitants' daily patterns
Broken Windows Theory (BWT)	*Broken Windows: The Police and Neighborhood Safety* Wilson Kelling 1982	It analyses the effect that urban disorder and soft crimes may have on the actual increase in crime occurrences

3.2 Crime Triangle and Rational Choice Theory

As already said, the Routine Activities Approach (RAA) is an environmental criminological theory that explains how criminal behaviour is influenced by everyday activities and routines. According to the RAA, crime is caused by "the convergence in space and time of [...]: (1) motivated offenders; (2) suitable targets; and (3) the absence of capable guardians against a violation" [14, p. 589]. This therefore suggests how crime occurrences are not solely determined by the offender's motivation but are also influenced by situational factors. When discussing this principle, the 'crime triangle' (Fig. 1) is usually taken into account.

The 'motivated offender' is an individual who has the desire and willingness to commit a crime. RAA proposes that offenders are more likely to commit crimes when they perceive the benefits to outweigh the risks. So, offenders may be deterred from committing crimes if they perceive a high risk of getting caught or facing severe consequences. The rational component of the individual is already implicitly included here.

The 'suitable target' is instead an object or person that the offender perceives as valuable or vulnerable and the RAA suggests that potential targets are more likely to be victimized if they are visible, accessible, and valuable. Please note that visibility and accessibility, key aspects according to the RAA, are two pivotal concepts of urban analysis, which will be discussed in more detail below. Targets may be objects, such as cars or electronic devices, or individuals; in particular much research [18, 19] outlines how people with poor self-defence skills such as women, the elderly, ethnic minorities, and lower-class people are more likely to be targets of crime.

Lastly, the 'absence of a capable guardian' represents the third key element of the RAA. It refers to the lack of individuals or systems that can prevent or deter criminal behaviour. The RAA proposes that capable guardians can include formal actors, such as police officers and security guards, or informal actors, such as friends and family members. This clarification of 'capable' specifies how guardians need to be proactive and have the capacity for effective immediate intervention. This therefore excludes the whole set of devices that refer to formal digital surveillance, i.e. all the various types of sensors and CCTV. The difference between 'on-field' control and digital control is a very interesting topic that will be explored in depth in the near future. Instead, in this discussion, we merely point out how the presence of CCTV combined with the offender's rationality principle should act as a deterrent – where it is common ground that CCTV is actually and effectively used for investigative and repressive purposes. In any case, there is no question that the lack of a 'capable' guardian makes a big difference in the realisation of the crime. It should be noted, therefore, how the presence of a capable guardian is related to the flows and to the compresence of people in the environment. This, when studied at the urban or neighbourhood scale – as is the intention of this study – directly refers to the study of transit pedestrian flows.

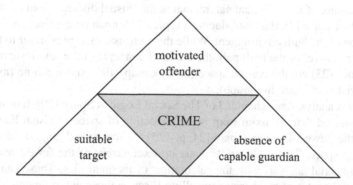

Fig. 1. Schematic representation of the crime triangle.

So, what are the assumptions of the above analysis from a modelling point of view? We assumed a simplifying law: crime occurs if there is the convergence of three elements. Then, full rationality of the offender was assumed. Then, the importance of flows – namely the co-presence of people who can potentially intervene and foil an attempted crime, thus making the crime commitment less attractive – in assessing the predisposition of an environment to crime emerged. The fundamental importance of visibility also emerged, as large flows in an area with visual barriers do not allow the crowd, the suitable guardians, to guarantee a possible 'defensive' intervention able to foil the crime and thus perform the deterrent function mentioned above. The importance, therefore, of being able to detect flows and visibility as characters capable of giving a measure of spatial crime impedance in the analysed environment emerged. It is therefore necessary to analyse the modelling tools that can be useful in interpreting the environmental component and thus provide useful information on the interventions to be made on the environment to deter specific criminal actions. In our case, therefore, all that remains is to choose a modelling tool from the toolbox that allows us to evaluate the aforementioned aspects, and Space Syntax perfectly meets our needs, as will be discussed in the following paragraphs.

3.3   A Matter of Flow and Visibility: Space Syntax

Space Syntax represents an optimal tool for investigating the aforementioned measures. It analyses the immaterial variables of a physical space through the reading of the various elements that compose it and their reciprocal relationships, thus enabling the understanding of otherwise hidden phenomena [7]. Space Syntax overturns the logic according to which space is the inert scenario in which things happen; it is instead the configuration of urban space that defines "the material preconditions for the pattern of movement, encounter and avoidance which are the material realization – as well as sometimes the generator – of social relations" [20, pag. ix]. Leaving aside an appropriate in-depth study of configurational theory, only a very brief reminder of the underlying logic, which is intrinsically linked to the concepts of flow and visibility, is provided here. For more in-depth information on the theory, the reader could refer to [20–22].

Space Syntax, which refers at the same time to the theory of interpretation of urban space and to the set of measures that allow for it, traces evaluations of spatial impedance back to a measure of a topological nature, that is the 'visual distance' that connects two points in urban space [7], thus introducing a typically human perceptive measure in the interpretation of the built environment. While the 'intrinsic measures' refer to the urban grid as the 'negative' of the built part, the cardinal concepts of the 'extrinsic measures' of urban space [23] are the convex space (convex map), the axial sightline (axial map) and the isovist field (visibility graph).

For convex analysis, see chapter 3 of The Social Logic of Space [20]. It is interesting to observe instead that the **axial map** is the reduction of space to visual lines, and in the case of the 'fewest-line axial map' [24, p. 425] the fewest and longest lines capable of describing space. This 'new grid', made up exclusively of the fewest and longest lines, permits axial analysis with the calculation of its quantities. These can describe the preferential routes of pedestrians travelling through those environments. The main ones are Integration (closeness) and Choice (betweenness), being also the ones with the greatest capacity for estimating pedestrian flow [25]. A strong correlation between sightline and movement thus emerges, as if this grid of optical axes represented a very reliable measure of spatial impedance in the interpretation of human behaviour. It is clear how a user's movement in urban space is determined by the way the user visually perceives urban space. Thus, the concept of the isovist field, linked to the concept of viewshed, is perhaps even more immediate due to its even more intuitive representation. However, the key to understanding both the **visibility graph** and, consequently, visibility graph analysis, is to realise that the essential element to which the grid is reduced is neither a convex space nor a linear element, but a vertex [26]. According to this logic, therefore, for each vertex of the urban grid a set of points in direct visual connection will be identifiable, which takes on the name of isovist [27–29]. Visibility graph analysis also develops a set of measures, largely shared with axial analysis but also with some specific quantities [30]. Furthermore, among the differences that can be found there is, for example, the VGA's characteristic of being able to give a visually more impactful representation – which is more detailed due to the possibility of defining the vertex dimension [31, 32] – and in some cases even outperforming axial analysis in the analysis of pedestrian movement [33].

With these few basics, the next section aims to shed light on the significant variables in assessing the susceptibility of the urban environment to certain crimes based on the assumptions made in the previous paragraphs.

3.4 More Than It Appears: Discussing Space Syntax Tools

With reference to the chosen environmental criminological theory, the Space Syntax theory with its set of measures proves very useful. In fact, we have said that the crime triangle is based on flows and visibility, and Space Syntax proves capable of effectively analysing these two pieces of information from space, extracting these intrinsic characteristics implicitly contained therein. The useful quantities to assess the spatial and configurational (so, natural) aptitude to host certain types of crimes, under specific assumptions, are now presented.

We understood in the previous section the different nature of axial maps versus visibility graphs and the different types of information they provide. As already mentioned, in this study we are interested in the flow and visibility aspects. However, we also have two additional important pieces of information to take into account when choosing the most functional analyses and measures. First, we are referring to a space of limited extension, at a scale that could be defined as micro-urban or, at most, urban. Second, we are interested in investigating the distribution of pedestrian flows.

With reference to the first point, the literature shows that VGA has historically been used specifically in the architectural field. However, under certain conditions - such as the presence of orography with negligible slopes and the realisation of a particularly detailed origin map that includes all 'visual obstacles' - VGA can be used at a micro-urban or urban scale [34] given also its 'finer granularity' of analysis compared to the other analyses offered by Space Syntax [32]. Thus, in terms of scale, both axial analysis and visibility graph analysis are usable and appropriate.

With regard to the second point, on the other hand, it is necessary to evaluate which types of analysis can best represent pedestrian movement. As testified by numerous studies [35–37] the configurational approach proved valid in estimating pedestrian movement, showing correlations between 55 and 75 per cent. In particular, it is believed that angular analysis (introduced by Turner [22] can more accurately estimate pedestrian movement. We therefore opt in this preliminary study for *Angular Segment Analysis* (ASA) and *Visibility Graph Analysis* (VGA) wanting to refer to the urban scale or below.

The quantities useful for detecting the above-mentioned information of interest are now specifically presented, indicating what exactly they represent from a mathematical and interpretative point of view. In particular, the quantities useful for assessing movement are integration (closeness) – obtained from mean depth – and choice (betweenness), which can be calculated, as mentioned, from both the axial map and the visual graph. However, connectivity could also be logically significant in the interpretation of criminal incidents, especially if weighed in some way with integration/choice (that is to say, with existing pedestrian flows). In fact, connectivity represents the number of segments connected to each segment of the network, which can therefore be interpreted as possible escape routes for a possible criminal, being then a crime incentivator index. On the other hand, it can also be interpreted as probable gateway for the arrival of new unforeseen 'guardians', which could therefore discourage crime commitment. This specific investigation, however, is postponed to future studies. As far as the VGA is concerned, the significant quantities of visual control and visual controllability are also presented, which are directly linked to the concepts of visibility and surveillance, as well as through vision, which is instead linked to the determination of the potentially busiest areas – and can therefore be used to support Integration. Summarising, then, the quantities taken into consideration here are:

- Angular segment integration/total depth;
- Angular segment choice;
- Visual integration/mean depth;
- Through vision;
- Visual controllability;
- Visual control.

We will omit here the in-depth explanation of the differences between axial analysis and angular analysis (for which please refer to [7, 22, 25], just remembering that angular analysis, taking into account the angle generated between the various axes into which space is decomposed, also 'weighs' the paths with respect to angular spatial impedance, then interpreting human behaviour whereby between two alternative paths a person would choose the one characterised by a 'smoother', less angular course [7]. The following is a quick comparison between visual mean depth (and consequently visual integration), through vision, visual control and visual controllability.

The **visual mean depth** represents the spatial impedance, that is the effort that has to be made to reach a given point in space from an origin point in space following the shortest path. This measure can be calculated in terms of visual, metric or angular distance [30]. However, like axial mean depth, visual mean depth depends on the size of the system. This makes comparisons between different systems problematic. In order to overcome this problem, Integration measures were created by calculating Relative Asymmetry (RA) and Real Relative Asymmetry (RRA), for which we refer to [20]. In particular, there are three different integration quantities: Visual Integration [HH], Visual Integration [P-value] and Visual Integration [Tekl]. Although Visual Mean Depth showed a higher correlation with pedestrian movement in the study by Koutsolampros et al. [30], Visual Integration [Tekl] – which in any case showed a very good correlation in the aforementioned study – will be used in this study (Sect. 3.5) for similarities and simplicity of visual comparison with Segment angular Integration. In particular, the greater the Integration [Tekl] values of a given space, the greater the pedestrian flows.

The **through vision**, introduced by Turner [25], represents the number of visual lines that cross a given vertex – and thus, by extension, location. It offers a hierarchisation of existing spaces on the basis of the number of isovists passing through them, thus also being interpretable as a magnitude of movement potential [30]. It highlights the vertexes (locations) that are most likely to be crossed because they find themselves in many paths.

The **visual control** was defined by Turner in 2001 [38] from the Control measure coined by Hillier and Hanson 1984 [20]. It consists of the value obtained by "summing the reciprocals of the neighbourhood sizes adjoining the vertex" [39, p. 6]. Specifically, the greater the number of cells visible from a given cell compared to the cells visible from the cells within the visual field of the former, the higher the value of the control. In this way, the space is hierarchised according to the potential of control over the surrounding neighbourhoods, thus highlighting the visually dominant areas [39].

The **visual controllability**, also introduced by Turner [38], is expressed by the ratio between immediate visible cells and the sum of all visible cells from immediate neighbourhood cells. This translates into a metric of how much space a cell sees in comparison to the isovist of its immediate neighbourhood cells, in which the more controllable a cell is, the higher the controllability value will be. Ultimately, therefore, space is hierarchised according to how much each of its vertices (and, by extension, locations) is 'naturally' controllable in comparison to the surrounding environment. For a detailed summary of these measures please refer to [30].

At this point, it is clear the framework and the information that the chosen Space Syntax analysis and measures can provide. Next paragraph will show how they can help the interpretation of areas naturally predisposed to host certain types of crime.

3.5   A Basic Spatial Crime Impedance Evaluation Tool

The preceding paragraphs drew all the necessary references. We chose a criminological interpretation key: the RAA, and in particular the crime triangle, together with the RCP. We selected the appropriate tools to assess the aspects suggested by the chosen criminological approaches (namely flow and visibility): *Angular Segment Analysis* and *Visibility Graph Analysis*, and in particular the Integration, Visual control and Visual controllability measures. Let us now see how these measures can provide important information on the 'susceptibility' of an environment to host crime occurrences or, using the configurational background, the spatial crime impedance. An inescapable premise: each type of crime follows a certain logic, always assuming the rationality of the offender. Although each crime is always linked to the combination of suitable target and guardian absence, it must be said that a crime such as pickpocketing and robbery, for example, have different 'boundary' conditions. In fact, the pick-pocketer will recognise in the crowd a possible hiding place and an opportunity to approach the target in an almost unsuspected manner. So, in that case, the lack of control will be given by the large number of people, for example. Vice versa for robbery, where the offender will look for isolated places with low flows of people so that he can easily avoid potential unexpected 'guardians'. According to this logic the analysis of the selected environment are conducted (Fig. 2).

The environment represents the historical centre of Grosseto, which corresponds to the portion of the city within the walls (Fig. 2a, b). The analyses were carried out with the software Depthmap X 0.8 and *Axial Analysis* and *Visibility Graph Analysis* were processed. Regarding the grid reduction of the system, for the Axial Analysis the *Angular Segment Analysis* obtained from the Fewest-Line Map (Minimal) was used. For the *Visibility Graph Analysis*, on the other hand, a 1*1 m eye-level grid (visibility) was chosen. In particular, angular integration, angular depth and angular choice as regards ASA and visual integration, visual depth, through vision, visual control and visual controllability as regards VGA were calculated and analysed. However, the measures chosen for discussion were reduced to those in Fig. 2. As discussed in the previous paragraphs, both ASA integration and choice and VGA integration and depth offer a measure of pedestrian flows. The hierarchy of the network emerges clearly, highlighting which sections are affected by greater or lower flows. ASA Choice (Fig. 2c) highlights how the largest flows are concentrated along three segments: Corso Giosuè Carducci, Via degli Aldobrandeschi and the continuation Via dell'Unione, Via Garibaldi. ASA Integration (Fig. 2d) confirms this hierarchy, even if the final stretch of Via Garibaldi acquires greater weight together with the Stretto Corsini, which cuts it crosswise. Consequently, by analysing the thinner segments of the network, the segments characterised by lower flows are identified and thus, from the perspective of the chosen theoretical model, characterised by the presence of fewer potential 'guardians'. The VGA reaffirms the aforementioned hierarchies in a more readable manner: it makes the streets of the urban agglomeration more evident – thanks to the vertex representation, as already mentioned – and let the interstitial spaces and squares emerge here, which are difficult to perceive in the ASA. The hierarchies are confirmed and further clarified by the Visual Depth (Fig. 2e) and Visual Integration [Tekl] (Fig. 2f), bringing out even more the areas affected by large or scarce pedestrian flows. However, the VGA is also able to provide a picture of the best areas for efficient control through the measurement of visual control (Fig. 2g), which could be used in the evaluation of interventions aimed.

at security (CCTV arrangement, police patrols, location of activities…) or at least surveillance. However, we will omit these aspects in this discussion. In fact, the measure of greatest interest for the model constructed above is the visual controllability (Fig. 2h), which highlights which areas are naturally – exclusively due to the way the space is constructed – subject to poor visibility, i.e. more 'hidden'. It emerges how large open spaces have high controllability values as much as a clear hierarchy. With that, locations with lower controllability values are highlighted, which are of particular interest for understanding crime dynamics.

Let us assume, for example, that we want to evaluate three specific classes of crime: robbery, drug dealing and pickpocketing. While assuming for each of them the logic described by the crime triangle and the full rationality of the offender, it is necessary to note that the specific rationales for each crime are different insofar as they are linked to the concepts of copresence and visibility (Fig. 3). Particularly suitable locations for a **robbery** will in fact be those characterised by low pedestrian flows, i.e. a low possibility of running into 'guardians', and low controllability values, i.e. locations that are naturally not visible from the surrounding areas. As already mentioned, in the case of robbery the measure of connectivity could be a further useful element in assessing the environment. The rationale and then the expected distribution is different for **drug dealing**, for which it is generally necessary to locate oneself in the vicinity of large flows of people that allow the offender to intercept the demand and, subsequently, identify an area sufficiently

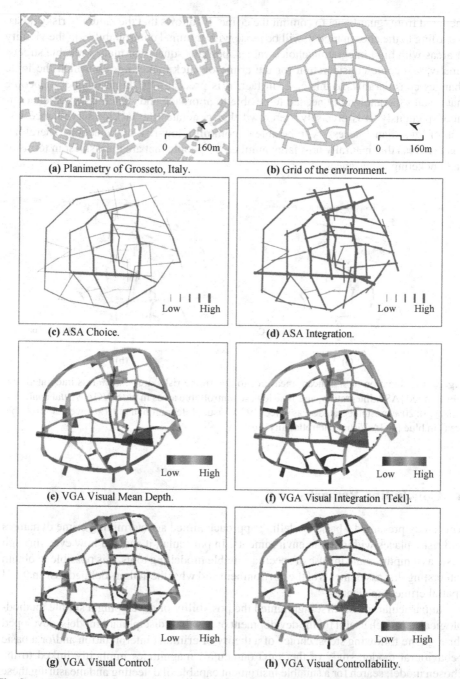

Fig. 2. **a**. Planimetry of Grosseto, Italy. **b**. Grid of the environment. **c**. ASA Choice. **d**. ASA Integration. **e**. VGA Visual Mean Depth. **f**. VGA Visual Integration [Tekl]. **g**. VGA Visual Control. **h**. VGA Visual Controllability.

sheltered from 'guardians' to commit the crime. It follows that the naturally risky areas, according to the chosen model, will be those with minimal controllability in the vicinity of areas with high integration/choice values, perhaps squares or main walkable streets. Finally, a specific consideration for the crime of **pickpocketing**, for which the logic changes considerably. In this case, in fact, it is precisely the large number of people that creates the anonymity needed to be able to approach and snatch a 'suitable target' inconspicuously. It is precisely the crowd that generates the lack of surveillance, the lack of 'guardians' necessary to be able to commit a low-risk crime action. Therefore, it is the areas that naturally host large numbers of people that are the riskiest in terms of pickpocketing occurrences.

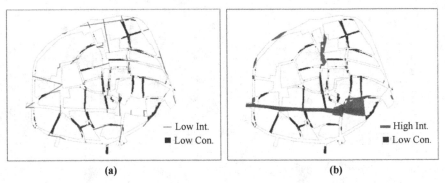

Fig. 3. Combination of significant measures to determine risky areas: 10% less integrated segments in red [ASA Integration] and 10% lowest controllable areas in blue [VGA Visual controllability] (a); 20% most integrated areas in red [VGA Visual Integration] and 10% lowest controllable areas in blue [VGA Visual controllability] (b).

4 Concluding Remarks

This study presented a basic modelling approach aimed at determining crime dynamics and risky places within urban environments. In particular, it showed how even through basic assumptions and the use of specific suitable modelling tools, it is possible to obtain interesting first assessments of the environment and what the authors defined as its natural spatial crime impedance.

In particular, it was first highlighted the possibility of developing a simple methodological approach useful for the development of new interdisciplinary models, developed through the following steps: choice of a theory of criminal interpretation and/or a basic behavioural model; study of the 'environmental' magnitudes implicitly linked to the chosen model; search for a suitable instrument capable of detecting and measuring these magnitudes; evaluation of risky places. Of course, this is only a rough outline, which may vary according to the specific choices made: for instance, in the case of this paper, it was necessary to distinguish the specific logics that guides the commission of certain crimes. This model also shows how through a conscious 'assemblage' of knowledge from different fields it is possible to create innovative basic effective modelling tools that can serve as very useful decision support tools in preventive terms, for the evaluation of future alternative design scenarios or as a guide for the optimisation of the layout of CCTV or sensors to obtain data on cities and citizens in the perspective of an integrated safe-smart city.

Secondly, the power of the model in assessing spatial crime impedance on the basis of two fundamental quantities such as pedestrian movement and visibility emerged, which can be optimally interpreted with the aid of Space Syntax theory from the urban form alone.

This paper, however, represents only a first step of a broader modelling investigation. The application to the historic city centre of Grosseto is a schematic demonstration that needs further investigation, such as: verifying the results of the spatial crime impedance with the real crime distribution in Grosseto; repeating this approach on other urban environments and comparing the results; evaluating the impact of the integration with further spatial information that is theoretically correlated with the crime distribution, such as the distribution of activities, the presence of physical barriers or CCTV, and night lighting, from which the need for an inter-scalar approach to the problem of urban security emerges. This model also lacks the temporal component - similarly to what was highlighted last year here at ICCSA by the authors [29] – although it remains to be seen whether in this case this refinement can generate better responses in modelling terms, taking into account the KISS modelling rule. In general, these types of tools are often undervalued, relying instead on numerical or aggregate data. However, appropriate models in this field have numerous advantages with a considerable impact on decision-making administrations and, consequently, on communities, such as: eliminating or at least mitigating perceptual aspects of the environment in the determination of risky places and the prioritisation of interventions, reducing subjectivity and working towards the real resolution of problems; allowing the evaluation of alternative scenarios and the fallout of planning choices in terms of security, as well as the optimisation of the technological instrumental disposition on the territory, as already mentioned; allowing the correct evaluation of areas unknown to the planner, having an initial picture of the areas in terms of natural predisposition to certain types of crimes and even allowing a real evaluation of areas where there are no databases on crime distribution. For all these reasons, the authors believe that modelling for urban security purposes is a field to be strongly explored by the scientific community in order to provide tools to help realise liveable and sustainable cities in compliance with the goals of the EU SDGs.

References

1. Van Soomeren, P.: Tackling Crime and Fear of Crime Through Urban Planning and Architectural Design (2013). https://doi.org/10.1016/B978-0-12-411635-1.00012-7
2. Mihinjac, M., Saville, G.: Third-generation crime prevention through environmental design (CPTED). Soc. Sci. 8(182), 1–20 (2019)
3. Maslow, A.H.: A theory of human motivation. Psychol. Rev. 50(4), 370–396 (1943)
4. Ellin, N.: Thresholds of fear: embracing the urban shadow. Urban Stud. 38, 869–883 (2001)
5. Cozens, P., Love, T.: A review and current status of crime prevention through environmental design (CPTED). J. Plan. Lit. 30(4), 393–412 (2015)

6. Armitage, C. J., Ekblom, P.: Rebuilding Crime Prevention Through Environmental Design: Strengthening the Links with Crime Science. 1st Edition Crime Science Series, Routledge, Abingdon (2019)
7. Cutini, V.: La rivincita dello spazio urbano. L'approccio Configurazionale Allo Studio e All'analisi Dei Centri Abitati. Pisa University Press, Pisa (2010)
8. Wortley, R., Townsley, M.: Environmental Criminology and Crime Analysis, 2nd edn. Routledge, Abingdon (2017)
9. Jeffery, C.: Crime Prevention through Environmental Design. Sage, Beverly Hills (1971)
10. Newman, O.: Defensible Space: Crime Prevention through Urban Design. Macmillan, New York (1972)
11. Mayhew, P., Clarke, R.V., Sturman, A, Hough, J.M.: Crime as opportunity. Home Office Research Study. No. 34. London: Home Office (1976)
12. Clarke, R.V., Cornish, D.B.: Modeling offender's decisions: a framework for research and policy. In: Tonry, M., Morris, N. (eds.) Crime and Justice: An Annual Review of Research, vol. 6, pp. 23–42. University of Chicago Press, Chicago (1985)
13. Cornish, D.B.: The procedural analysis of offending and its relevance for situational prevention. Crime Prevent. Stud. 3(1), 151–196 (1994)
14. Cohen, L., Felson, M.: Social change and crime rate trends: a routine activity approach. Am. Sociol. Rev. 44, 588–608 (1979)
15. Brantingham, P.J., Brantingham, P.L.: Environmental Criminology. Sage Publications, California (1981)
16. Wilson, J.Q., Kelling., G.L. Broken windows: the police and neighbourhood safety. Atlantic Month. 2, 9–38 (1982)
17. Goldstein, H.: Problem-Oriented Policing. McGraw-Hill, New York (1990)
18. Barton, M.S., Weil, F., Jackson, M., Hickey, D.A.: An investigation of the influence of the spatial distribution of neighborhood violent crime on fear of crime. Crime Delinq. 63(13), 1757–1776 (2017)
19. Franklin, T.W., Franklin, C.A., Fearn, N.E.: A multilevel analysis of the vulnerability, disorder, and social integration models of fear of crime. Soc. Just. Res. 21, 204–227 (2008)
20. Hillier, B., Hanson, J.: The Social Logic of Space. Cambridge University Press, Cambridge, UK (1984)
21. Hillier, B., Burdett, R., Peponis, J., Penn, A.: Creating life, or, does architecture determine anything? Architect. Behav. Architect. et Comportement 3, 233–250 (1987)
22. Penn, A., Hillier, B., Banister, D., Xu, J.: Configurational modeling of urban movement networks. Environ. Plann. B. Plann. Des. 25, 59–84 (1998)
23. Hillier, B.: Specifically architectural theory: A partial account of the ascent from building as cultural transmission to architecture as theoretical concretion. Bartlett School of Architecture. UCL (1999)
24. Turner, A., Penn, A., Hillier, B.: An algorithmic definition of the axial map. Environ. Plann. B. Plann. Des. 32, 425–444 (1993)
25. Turner, A.: From axial to road-centre lines: a new representation for space syntax and a new model of route choice for transport network analysis. Environ. Plan. B Plan. Design 34, 539–555 (2007)
26. Turner, A., Doxa, M., O'sullivan, D., Penn, A.: From isovists to visibility graphs: a methodology for the analysis of architectural space. Environ. Plann. B. Plann. Des. 28(1), 103–121 (2001)
27. Tandy, C.R.V.: The isovist method of landscape survey. In: Murray, H.C. (ed.) Symposium: Methods of Landscape Analysis. Landscape Research Group, London (1967)
28. Benedikt, M.L.: To take hold of space: isovists and isovist fields. Environ. Plan. B 6, 47–65 (1979)

29. Mara, F., Cutini, V. Digital city-surveillance models and urban security: integrating isovist and space syntax in realising adaptive decision support systems. In: Gervasi, O., Murgante, B., Misra, S., Rocha, A.M.A.C., Garau, C. (eds.) Computational Science and Its Applications – ICCSA 2022 Workshops. ICCSA 2022. LNCS, vol. 13377. Springer, Cham (2022). https://doi.org/10.1007/978-3-031-10536-4_24

30. Koutsolampros, P., Sailer, K., Varoudis, T., Haslem, R.: Dissecting Visibility Graph Analysis: the metrics and their role in understanding workplace human behaviour. In: Proceedings of the 12th International Space Syntax Symposium, vol. 12. International Space Syntax Symposium (2019)

31. Penn, A., Turner, A.: Space syntax based agent simulation. Springer-Verlag (2002)

32. López Baeza, J., et al.: Modeling pedestrian flows: Agent-based simulations of pedestrian activity for land use distributions in urban developments. Sustainability 13(16), 9268 (2021)

33. Ericson, J.D., Chrastil, E.R., Warren, W.H.: Space syntax visibility graph analysis is not robust to changes in spatial and temporal resolution. Environ. Plan. B Urban Anal. City Sci. 48(6), 1478–1494 (2021)

34. Mara, F., Altafini, D., Cutini, V.: Urban design, Space Syntax and Crime: an evidence-based approach to evaluate urban crime geographical displacement and surveillance efficiency. In: Proceedings of the 13th International Space Syntax Symposium, forthcoming (2022)

35. Hillier, B., Penn, A., Hanson, J., Grajewski, T., Xu, J.: Natural movement: or, configuration and attraction in urban pedestrian movement. Environ. Plann. B. Plann. Des. 20(1), 29–66 (1993)

36. Hillier, B., Iida, S.: Network effects and psychological effects: a theory of urban movement. In: van Nes, A. (ed.) Proceedings of the Fifth International Space Syntax Symposium. Techne Press, Delft (2005)

37. Turner, A.: Angular analysis. In: Proceedings of the 3rd International Symposium on Space Syntax, vol. 30, pp. 30–11. Georgia Institute of Technology, Atlanta, GA (2001a)

38. Turner, A.: "Depthmap: a program to perform visibility graph analysis". In: Proceedings of the 3rd International Symposium on Space Syntax, p. 9 (2001b)

39. Turner, A. Depthmap 4: A Researcher's Handbook (2004)

Digital Data in Support of Innovation for Urban Practice: Women-Inclusive Walkable Cities–Naples, a Case Study

Gerardo Carpentieri[1] , Carmen Guida[1]([✉]) , Andrea Gorrini[2] ,
Federico Messa[2] , Lamia Abdelfattah[2] , and Tonia Stiuso[1]

[1] TeMA Lab, Department of Civil, Architectural and Environmental Engineering,
University of Naples Federico II, Naples, Italy
carmen.guida@unina.it
[2] Fondazione Transform Transport ETS, Milan, Italy

Abstract. Urban planning is increasingly focused on solutions for sustainable urban mobility, including the achievement of "walkability", i.e. friendliness to walking, in criteria such as availability of nearby services, street connectivity, and comfort of public spaces. Although city administrations in some countries, partially as a response to the Covid-19 pandemic, have adopted short or long-term plans for reassignment of vehicular space in favour of cyclist and pedestrian infrastructures, traditional approaches to urban planning, tend to overlook urban users in terms of their individual characteristics, which can significantly impact their perceptions of level of walkability for public spaces. Women in particular face harassment, aggression and other safety concerns that can inhibit their mobility in public spaces, especially at night. Despite robust research on other aspects of walkability in cities, there is a lack of knowledge at the intersection between mobility and gender. Addressing the need for further investment in qualitative, and particularly in quantitative analysis, the current contributions proposes and reports on the use of GIS-based methodology, with data collected directly from women in urban contexts, and other open-access location-based data, producing analyses that can support decision-makers concerning policy for walkability in urban environments. In particular, the contribution summarizes the first product of a new, replicable methodology, focused on urban planning and gender inclusion, applied to the city of Naples, Italy.

Keywords: Urban Planning · Gender Inclusion · GIS · Naples

1 Introduction

In current times, urban planning for sustainable urban mobility is crucial. The concept is that of guaranteeing walkable urban environments, through the availability of services, street connectivity and provision of safe public spaces. The perceived levels of urban walkability, however, depend to a significant extent on the individual characteristics of the users, which tend to be overlooked in traditional approaches to urban planning.

© The Author(s), under exclusive license to Springer Nature Switzerland AG 2023
O. Gervasi et al. (Eds.): ICCSA 2023 Workshops, LNCS 14110, pp. 244–255, 2023.
https://doi.org/10.1007/978-3-031-37123-3_19

In particular, urban and transport planning have long neglected the issue of the intersections between gender and urban mobility, with severe consequences, among which inequitable accessibility to different parts of the city, with reduced opportunities for the female gender. Several studies have shown that, in fact, there are differences between men and women in mobility behaviour. In the Italian context, for instance, women in are one and a half times more likely to walk on their daily trips than men, and are generally more diverse in their choices of transport mode [1]. At the same time, still in Italy, only one in twelve women say they feel safe and comfortable walking at evening or night, while for men the ratio is three times higher [2]. These data on the Italian scenario are consistent with studies in other nations [3–5]. Walkable environments, featuring populated and well-lit walkways, can increase women's sense of safety. Research has shown that women with access to walkable neighbourhoods are more likely to engage in regular physical activity, have better mental health, and feel more connected with their community. Additionally, walkable urban environments facilitate social interactions among neighbours, and support local business operations. On the other hand, poor walkability can limit mobility for the female gender; increase dependence on cars both for women and more generally, and negatively affect access to vital services and resources. For trips under a certain distance, walking will obviously be the primary mode of transportation, but it is also a crucial component of longer journeys using private cars or public transport. Given all this, when generating urban mobility plans, it becomes essential to devote close attention to the nexus of gender and walkability, and meet gender-specific requirements. As emphasized by Golan et al. [6], Andersdotter Fabre et al. [7], and Sethi and Velez-Duque [8], males and females experience the urban environment differently, partly because women are more concerned about harassment, aggression, and general personal security. The experience of personal safety is a significant element in the transportation experience, in turn impacting transportation decisions. The constraints for woman, arising from the sense of vulnerability, from the real or perceived risk of violence or other harm, especially at night, give rise to precautionary measures and avoidance behaviours, among which delaying or completely avoiding walking trips, thus significantly hindering their mobility in public spaces [9–13].

However, the knowledge regarding the needs and expectations of women while walking remains shallow, challenged by the limited availability of relevant data from public authorities [5, 14–17]. Most data and statistics on transport are very simply categorized, for example treating gender as a binary male/female variable, without relation to age, ethnicity, disability, caring responsibilities, etc. But gender-related needs in mobility are not homogenous across all women, who cannot be considered a uniform cohort experiencing a sole set of needs. First of all, gender is a multi-dimensional and intersectional construct [5]. The concept of "intersectionality" as proposed by Kimberlé Crenshaw [18] in her critique of antidiscrimination doctrine, highlights the overlapping effects of different social identities, such as race and class, on shaping women's subjective experiences. This naturally includes the mobility experiences of women in the city, not dictated by gender alone, rather differing depending on intersecting social identities, which for "doubly-disadvantaged" persons, could raise still further barriers.

Our research aims to analyse how women perceive urban environments, and to assess their sense of safety as an indicator of various urban factors, including physical, functional, socio-economic, and environmental elements. More specifically, the objective of the current contribution is to evaluate the impact of these factors on the walkability for women in different urban zones and at different times of day.

The experimental work represents a first "delving" into to the use of data collected by a mobile app, which suggests the safest walking journey for women, based on the comments and assessments of the female users themselves. The assessments and comments are usually made by younger adult women, and for this factor and others, the nature of the collected data prevents a comprehensive overview of women's perception of the urban environment. The research strategy has also included surveys designed to gain the views of a broader population, but these results too could be influenced by a heterogeneity of age not sufficiently reflective of the larger population of women. In any case, even though a first attempt at collecting data via such a digital platform, and using it for assessments in planning in the area of urban safety, the research still addresses a prominent data gap and advances innovative methodologies in doing so. The methodology, described in the next section, has first been applied to the city of Naples, Italy, and the case study and results from this application are described in the subsequent sections.

2 Methodology

Various methods have been developed for the measurement of walkability in urban environments, usually considering several factors, among which the availability of public services in close proximity, the overall comfort level and the sense of safety in the spaces, as experienced by pedestrians, as well as the appeal of their architectural design and social context. Only a few scientific methods have delved into gender issues in connection with assessment of walkability, and in fact, in spite of the investigations and potential proofs on the theoretical side, there has been little empirical demonstration of the relationships between gender and perceived safety of urban environments.

The current study introduces a quantitative methodology to compute an index of safety, based on women's experiences, for the investigation of connections between urban space and gender issues.

The index of safety is based on data collected through the mobile app "W-her".[1] W-her is a publicly available mapping application that supports women in urban walking journeys by offering a navigator function that considers the opinions of other users in suggesting secure routes. The app, developed by Italian researchers, is now maintained and operated by the Walk21 Foundation, an England-Wales registered charity.[2] The app solicits data from women on their perceptions of safety in urban spaces in terms of three ranked options (*Go easy, Be careful, Avoid*), relative to three times of day (*Day, Evening, Night*). Users are encouraged not only to rate streets and spaces, but also to provide comments that could help others walk the city safely.

The methodology presented in this contribution is the early product of a comprehensive research project delving into gender-based issues, among which the relationships

[1] For more information visit https://Wher.com/.
[2] For more information visit https://walk21.com/.

between gender and urban environments. The spatial analysis is conducted using a Geographic Information System (GIS) to link W-her data with reference spatial units. The most detailed reference unit is the "census tract" as mapped by the Italian National Institute of Statistics (ISTAT), to which are related the relevant social and economic data on the resident population (ISTAT, 2011).

Figure 1 shows the methodological workflow.

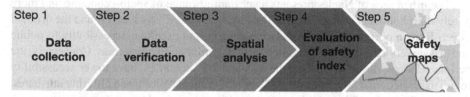

Fig. 1. GIS methodology for the evaluation of the summary Index of Safety

The first stage is that of data collection, using two investigative instruments: the W-her app and a questionnaire. The design and application of the questionnaire are aimed at gaining information on areas where coverage in the Where database is insufficient, with a view to collating the information from the two sources.

The second stage involves checking the sufficiency of the data coverage from the two sources, and their merging.

In stage three, the data on perceived safety data are harmonized with the GIS spatial units corresponding to census tracts, and from there related to the administrative level spatial units, with the aim of usefully informing the decision-making of local authorities.

$$i_s = \left(\frac{L_1}{L_{Tot}} \cdot S_1 \right) + \left(\frac{L_2}{L_{Tot}} \cdot S_2 \right) + \left(\frac{L_3}{L_{Tot}} \cdot S_3 \right) \tag{1}$$

The fourth methodological stage is the measurement of the summary Index of Safety (i_s), which considers the safety perception of women experiencing urban spaces according to formula (1). The i_s is calculated for the ISTAT census tract. The L_1, L_2 and L_3 correspond to the length of the streets within the census tract, classifiable in terms of the three ranks of safety. The total value of length of streets for each census tract is L_{Tot}, while S1, S2 and S3 correspond with the safety ranks *Avoid*, *Be careful* and *Go easy*, which are respectively set equal to 0, 0.5 and 1.

The product of the fifth and final stage is the categorization and illustration of the different safety levels for women, in GIS maps. Our approach, aimed at providing an accurate representation of the safety levels in the reference area, involves the application of the Natural Breaks (Jenks) methodology, thereby computing the safety values in terms of five categories, from Level 1 (*Avoid*) to Level 5 (*Go Easy*). Apart from immediate service to users, the representation of safety ratings for streets and other urban spaces will also serve in further statistical and spatial analyses for the investigation of gender-based issues in mobility.

The methodology is validated through application in a case study in the country of Italy, as reported in the following section.

3 Case Study

The selection of Naples for the purposes of case study considers a number of factors, first of all its rank as third in population size among Italian cities, and fifth in population density. With 913,462 inhabitants (ISTAT, 2022) distributed over an area of 119.02 km², the average population density is slightly over 7,600 persons per km². The city is divided into thirty administrative neighbourhoods, grouped in turn into ten municipalities.

The urban area of Naples presents a substantial range of socio-economic and more purely morphological characteristics. The "historic centre", focused around the original Greco-Roman port, has a high population density and excellent accessibility to public and private services, including commercial and administrative functions. Conversely, the peripheral areas, developed during the 19th and 20th centuries, have lower accessibility to urban services and are primarily residential. On the basis of these differing attributes, the Neapolitan urban fabric can be categorised into three fundamental types, or "zones": Central, Semi-Central, and Peripheral (Fig. 2).

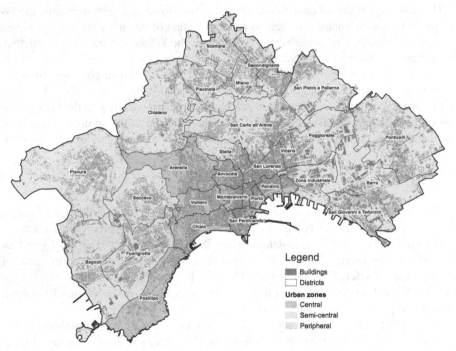

Fig. 2. City of Naples: thirty administrative districts, classified in three urban zones

The residents of Naples include 474,264 female persons, comprising 51% of the total population (data from ISTAT 2022). Figure 3 shows the distribution of females by tract and zone (data from ISTAT 2011 census). The distribution of the female population is: 153,491 in the Central zone, 175,448 in the Semi-Central and 176,967 in the Peripheral zone.

This descriptive analysis of the females present in Naples does not account for non-residents who work or engage in other activities within the city, on which no data is currently available. It should be noted that data on worker gender, from the national census of labour activities, are not accessible. Although the lack of this data represents a critical limitation, affecting the reliability of the results and conclusions of the current study, the method of gaining insight into the safety perceived by women in Naples still provides insight and understanding of the complex interplay of socio-cultural factors affecting their experiences of the urban space, and can support policymakers and urban planners in the design of more inclusive and safe cities for everyone.

Since 2019, data on safety issues in Naples have been collected under a partnership between the coordinators of the W-her app and the researchers of two institutions: the Laboratory of Land-Use, Mobility and Environments (TeMA Lab) of the Department of Civil, Building and Environmental Engineering of the University of Naples 'Federico II', and the non-profit Transform Transport Foundation, based in Milan.

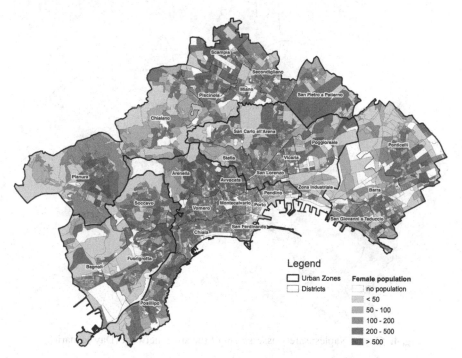

Fig. 3. City of Naples: distribution of female population (ISTAT, 2011).

The W-her app (https://W-her.com/.) was first used for data collection on the safety of streets and spaces with university students, then with women both resident in Naples and present as non-resident users of city streets and spaces, such as for work. The data collected from more than 3,000 assessments referred to over 45% of the city street network. On-site interviews were also conducted with women present in city streets, focused in particular on collecting information on their perceptions of safety for spaces in areas of lesser data from the W-her app, and also aimed at obtaining responses from women not typically participant in "app based" projects. Table 1 summarizes the data collected through interviews (Fig. 4).

Table 1. Summary of interviews

	Residents	Non-residents
N° of interviews	560	253
Avoid [%]	52.1	25.9
Be careful [%]	13.5	26.3
Go easy [%]	35.4	48.8

Fig. 4. City of Naples: safety assessment of the street network (Day scenario)

3.1 Results

This section presents the numerical values obtained by measurement of (i_s) for each census tract of the study area, under the three scenarios, *Day, Evening, Night*, Fig. 5 provides the mapping of the Index of Safety, by census tract, for the Day scenario. The map reveals the presence of perceptions of greater safety for the Central zone and some adjoining residential areas, for example in the western part of the city (Semi-Central), versus perceptions of lower safety in the Peripherical zones. Looking in more detail, women tend to consider almost all parts of the Central zone secure, with only two of its census tracts, both near its outer edges, classified as Level 1 (Avoid). In contrast, in the Peripheral districts, women view few tracts as secure, and where tracts are mapped as Level 5 (Go easy) or Level 4 (the two "green" levels), these coincide with the most historically established and densely populated census tracts.

The districts with the perception of highest safety during the Day scenario (Fig. 5), but also at Evening and Night, are Posillipo, Vomero and Chiaia,

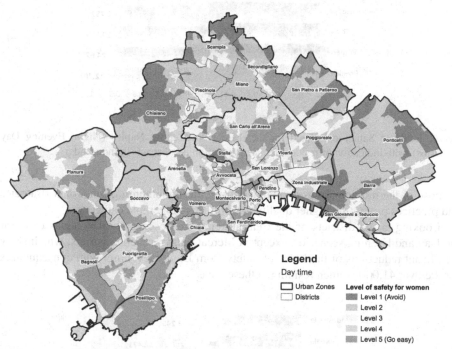

Fig. 5. City of Naples: map of safety perceived by women (i_s) for each census tract (Day scenario).

The proposed methodology can be used to gain deeper understanding of women's perceptions of safety by comparing, at the district level, the calculations of Index of Safety at the three times of day, also considering the female population resident in the different districts.

Figures 6, 7 and 8 present the results obtained, for the Index of Safety for the urban districts, respectively, of the Central, Semi-Central and Peripheral zones, at the three different times of day. In all urban zones the results demonstrate a significant reduction of perceived in the night scenario, with this reduction most pronounced in some residential districts of Peripheral zone. At the right side of each figure, we show the values of female population for the respective districts, in illustration of the direct impact of perceptions of safety for women, measured by Index of Safety. This type of reporting, relating data on female population with values of i_s can support decision-makers and authorities, such

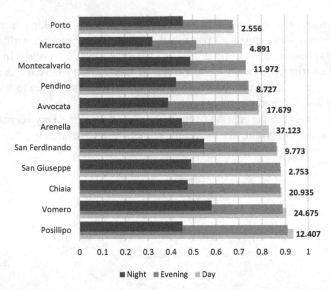

Fig. 6. Index of Safety calculated for the districts of Central Naples (Night, Evening Day scenarios), with indication of resident female population per district (in thousands)

as those of the municipalities and police forces, in implementing functional strategies and practices promoting higher qualityoflife for this vulnerable category.

Looking at the districts of the Central zone, we observe similar values of i_s for the Day and Evening scenarios, except in Mercato and Arenella districts, which show significant reductions of the Index of Safety from Day to Evening, with consequences for the over 41,000 women residing in these areas.

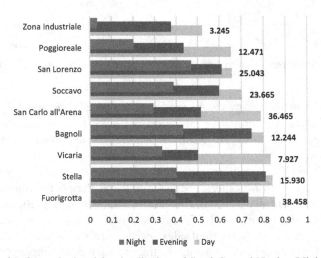

Fig. 7. Index of Safety calculated for the districts of Semi-Central Naples (Night, Evening Day scenarios), with indication of resident female population per district (in thousands)

The results obtained for Semi-Central districts (Fig. 7), similarly to the Central districts, in general show a halving of the values of i_s from the Day scenario to that for Night. Moreover, there is a significant reduction in the index from Day to Evening, for the districts of Vicaria and Poggioreale. The San Lorenzo district show the index values that are most similar across the three scenarios.

In Fig. 8, presenting results for the Peripheral zone, we see that the most populated districts (Pianura and Secondigliano) suffer a great reduction of i_s values safety from the Day to the Night scenario, indicating that there would be particularly significant impacts on freedom of life and movement for women present in the urban spaces of these districts. The Ponticelli district presents a value for the "Day" Index of Safety that is typical for the Peripheral Zone, but with only minimum differences to the index values for Evening and Night.

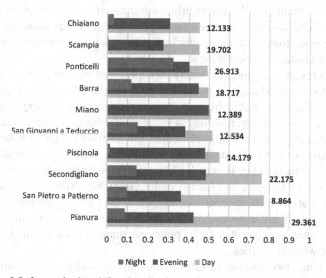

Fig. 8. Index of Safety calculated for the districts of Peripheral Naples (Night, Evening Day scenarios), with indication of resident female population per district (in thousands)

4   Planning Applications, Conclusions

United Nations Sustainable Development Goal 11 states is "about making cities and human settlements inclusive, safe, resilient and sustainable" (UN, 2015). To ensure equitable and safe access to mobility and city services for all, the conception and planning for sustainable urban mobility must consider the gender dimension. The lack of safe mobility options for women in urban areas not only restricts their access to essential services, but also their participation in economic and social activities. Women's choices concerning mobility are significantly impacted by factors such as time of day, frequency of public transit, and the contributions of other infrastructure to safety. Examples would be that women, as users of public transit, in considering the choices of moving at certain times the day, would need to factor in expectations of overcrowded and unsafe conditions; or in considering entry into certain urban areas, would choose not to go at any time of day, over safety concerns.

Gender-related violence is in fact a critical concern for women in urban areas, and the fear of harassment or assault can significantly restrict their mobility. To mitigate the greater risk of violence, women will be more willing than men to modify their behaviour, travel routes, and avoid certain public spaces, and these choices will impact their overall quality of life.

Urban planning must take up a gender-responsive approach, prioritizing the needs and experiences of women. Policies on infrastructure investment, outreach programs, and other targeted strategies can ensure that women achieve equitable access to safe, reliable, and affordable options of mobility, with consequent reductions in gender inequalities, but more in general, leading to more sustainable, inclusive, and thriving cities for all.

Women face unique challenges in urban environments, with impacts on mobility experiences and choices, however traditional approaches to urban planning often fail to address the intersections between gender and urban mobility, resulting in inequitable accessibility and reduced opportunities.

The current research explores the safety perceptions of women in urban areas, applying an innovative methodology of collecting data via the W-her app, used on mobile devices. The results presented in this contribution represent the first experimental product of a comprehensive research project delving gender-based issues in the contexts of urban environment. The methodology presented derives from the know-how of the ongoing research project "STEP UP-Walkability for Women in Milan", submitted under the call for proposals "Inequalities Research–Generating new knowledge to reduce inequalities" of Fondazione Cariplo, and funded under Grant No. 2022-1643. The STEP UP project is aimed at: identification of challenging areas and neighbourhoods in Milan, considering the needs and expectations of women while walking; serving as an analytical testbed for development of a set of policy recommendations aimed at enhancing walkability for women in cities.

By prioritizing environments of safety, connectivity, and access to public services, and thereby walkability, policy makers can contribute to the empowerment of women and, in general, promote the development of more equitable and sustainable cities. Addressing gender inequality in urban mobility is crucial to achievement of the United Nations Sustainable Development Goals and the development of more inclusive and liveable cities for all.

References

1. AitBihiOuali, L., Graham, D.J.: The impact of the MeToo scandal on women's perceptions of security. Transp. Res. Part A: Policy Pract. **147**, 269–283 (2021). https://doi.org/10.1016/j.tra.2021.02.018
2. ISTAT: BES 2022. Il Benessere equo e sostenibile in Italia (2023). https://www.istat.it/it/files//2023/04/Bes-2022.pdf. ISBN 978-88-458-2100-4
3. Sansonetti, S., Davern, F. Expert, I.: Women and transport, EPRS: European Parliamentary Research Service. Belgium (2021)

4. Fiorello, D., Zani, L.: EU Survey on Issues Related to Transport and Mobility. Publications Office of the European Union, Luxembourg (2015)
5. Hail, Y., McQuaid, R.: The concept of fairness in relation to women transport users. Sustainability **13**(5), 2919 (2021). https://doi.org/10.3390/su13052919
6. Golan, Y., Henderson, J., Wilkinson, N.L., Weverka, A.: Gendered walkability: building a daytime walkability index for women. J. Transp. Land Use **12**(1), 501–526, (2019). https://www.jstor.org/stable/26911279
7. Andersdotter Fabre, E., Julin, T., Lahoud, C., Martinuzzi, C.: Her city. A guide for cities to sustainable and inclusive urban planning and design together with girls. United Nations Human Settlements Programme (UN-Habitat), Kenya (2021). https://unhabitat.org/sites/default/files/2021/03/02032021_her_city_publication_low.pdf
8. Sethi, S., Velez-Duque, J.: Walk with women: gendered perceptions of safety in urban spaces. Leading Cities: Boston, MA, USA (2021)
9. Loukaitou-Sideris, A.: Fear and safety in transit environments from the women's perspective. Secur. J. **27**, 242–256 (2014). https://doi.org/10.1057/sj.2014.9
10. Hille, K.: 'Gendered exclusions': women's fear of violence and changing relations to space. Geogr. Ann. Ser. B Hum. Geogr. **81**(2), 111–124 (1999)
11. Pain, R.: Place, social relations and the fear of crime: a review. Prog. Hum. Geogr. **24**(3), 365–387 (2000)
12. Vera-Grey, F.: The right amount of panic: how women trade safety for freedom (2018)
13. Whitzman, C.: Women's safety and everyday mobility. In: Building Inclusive Cities, pp. 51–68. Routledge (2013)
14. Lecompte, M.C., Pablo, B.S.J.: Transport systems and their impact con gender equity. Transp. Res. Procedia **25**, 4245–4257 (2017). https://doi.org/10.1016/j.trpro.2017.05.230
15. Pollard, T.M., Wagnild, J.M.: Gender differences in walking (for leisure, transport and in total) across adult life: a systematic review. BMC Pub. Health **17**(1), 1–11 (2017). https://doi.org/10.1186/s12889-017-4253-4
16. Carpentieri, G., Guida, C., Fevola, O., Sgambati, S.: The Covid-19 pandemic from the elderly perspective in urban areas: an evaluation of urban green areas in 10 European capitals. TeMA-J. Land Use Mobility Environ. **13**(3), 389–408 (2020). https://doi.org/10.6092/1970-9870/7007
17. Carpentieri, G., Gargiulo, C., Guida, C.: I data e gli strumenti digitali a supporto delle politiche di governo del territorio orientati alla post-car city. Urban@ it Centro nazionale di studi per le politiche urbane, 95–102 (2023)
18. Crenshaw, K.: Demarginalizing the intersection of race and sex: a black feminist critique of antidiscrimination doctrine, feminist theory and antiracist politics. u. Chi. Legal f., 139 (1989)

Measuring the Potential for Meaningful Usability of Spaces: The Case Studies of Two Social Housing Districts in Cagliari, Italy

Alfonso Annunziata[1] [iD], Chiara Garau[1]([envelope]) [iD], and Aynaz Lotfata[2] [iD]

[1] Department of Civil and Environmental Engineering and Architecture, University of Cagliari, 09129 Cagliari, Italy
cgarau@unica.it
[2] School Of Veterinary Medicine, Department of Veterinary Pathology, University of California, Davis, USA
alotfata@ucdavis.edu

Abstract. The ongoing debate on the adaptation of urban environments in the context of climate alterations and the COVID-19 pandemic underlines the need for an organization of urban spaces and structures that promote active mobility, socialisation, sports, and recreational activities. This emerging need intersects with the broader issue of the built environment's impact on individuals' quality of life. This study examines the centrality of positive emotions in determining quality of life and introduces the concept of meaningful usability to conceptualize the potential of built environment factors to promote positive emotional responses. The study aims to answer two questions: first, what are the components and qualities of public spaces that influence individuals' positive emotional responses? Second, how can a set of metrics be defined to measure relevant environmental conditions that are conducive to meaningful usability? The case study focuses on the districts of Is Mirrionis and Mulinu Becciu in the Metropolitan City of Cagliari (MCC). The study contributes to the field of urban studies by developing a procedure that measures access to urban services, Green amenities, Public transit, distance form the urban centre and diversity of functions to structure a cognitive foundation for the development of urban regeneration strategies. The analysis demonstrates the validity of spatial and configurational metrics in identifying vulnerable areas, criticalities in terms of access to services and urban quality and defining the objectives of urban regeneration strategies.

Keywords: Configuration · Morphology · Vitality · Urbanity

This paper is the result of the joint work of the authors. 'Abstract', 'Methodology', and 'Results' were written jointly by the authors. Alfonso Annunziata wrote 'Literature Review: factors impacting users' emotional response.'. Chiara Garau wrote the 'Introduction' and "Selection of the areas of Study". Aynaz Lotfata wrote 'Discussion and Conclusions'. Chiara Garau coordinated and supervised the paper.

© The Author(s), under exclusive license to Springer Nature Switzerland AG 2023
O. Gervasi et al. (Eds.): ICCSA 2023 Workshops, LNCS 14110, pp. 256–273, 2023.
https://doi.org/10.1007/978-3-031-37123-3_20

1 Introduction

The emerging need for the adaptation of cities to the post-pandemic scenarios re-proposes the issue of the relation between the built environment (BE) and quality of life. Strategies for the post-Covid 19 scenario focus on a re-organisation of cities, including the adaptation of built form, the re-organization of services and amenities, the transformation of mobility and transport systems and the re-configuration of the public space [1–5]. Moreover, the pandemic altered the influence of distinct aspects of cities on specific life domains [6]. This study focuses on a specific aspect of quality of life, emotional response, and investigates the impact of built environment components on individuals' emotional response. Previous studies tend to focus of residents' perceptions of specific aspects of the built environment. This study considers the emotional response of residents and non-residents and investigates the potential influence of distinct aspects of the built environment on users' satisfaction. The districts of Is Mirrionis and Mulinu Becciu, in the Metropolitan City of Cagliari (MCC), in Italy, are selected as the area of study. The study introduces the concept of meaningful usability to denote the latent or potential influence of built environment macro-scale factors on residents' satisfaction and develops a set of metrics for the evaluation of determinants of built environment's meaningful usability. The proposed method can guide practitioners, planners, and policy makers in the construction of the cognitive base propaedeutic to the development of projects for the adaptation of the urban environment in the post-pandemic scenario. The article is articulated on six sections. After the introduction an extensive literature review on quality of life, emotional response and the built environment is presented in Sect. 2. Section 3 describes the method and data of the study. The Results are presented in Sect. 4 and the implications of the findings are summarised in the final section.

2 Literature Review: Factors Impacting Users' Emotional Response

The analysis of the literature focuses on two distinct issues: i) the conceptualisation of quality of life and the relevance of positive emotions resulting from momentary experience; ii) the identification of built environment objective and perceived factors that elicit specific emotions. Quality of life is a central concern of urban policies. Quality of life is formalised and measured in terms of subjective well-being (SWB). Yet, Distinct interpretations of good living can be identified. SWB is interpreted as a trait, a predisposition of individuals to focus on positive stimuli and to engage in positive and protective memory bias [8], or as a state, resulting from eudemonic aspects, including sense of purpose, satisfaction of central needs and the realization of one's potential [9], and to hedonic aspects related to positive emotions and life satisfaction. Moreover, the evolutionary perspective reflects on the relevance of positive emotions in developing one's personal resources, thus underlining the enduring influence of emotions on quality of life. A conceptualization of quality of life as a combination of eudemonic and hedonic aspects can be identified in urban studies. Mouratidis identifies eudaimonia, happiness, life satisfaction, and emotional well-being as central components of subjective well-being [7, 10, 11]. Alternative conceptualisations of quality of life focus on concepts of hedonic happiness [12], urban happiness [13] and life satisfaction [14]. Moreover, Mouratidis develops a conceptual model, that identifies a set of interdependent factors, including travel, leisure, work, social relationships, residential well-being, emotional responses, health, as variables that mediate the influence of the built environment on distinct aspects of SWB. This model thus recognises satisfaction and emotions elicited by the built environment as relevant aspects of quality of life. A similar focus on the individuals' immediate experience of the built environment is observed in studies investigating pedestrians' satisfaction [15, 16], residential satisfaction [17–20], emotional response to environmental stimuli [21–23] and basic emotions. The latter are defined as emotions that present a biological basis, and are influenced by constraints resulting from evolution [24–27]. Lastly, studies on the emotional response to the built environment propose distinct set of emotional states. Mouratidis identifies as relevant emotional responses, contentment, pleasure, and fear. Birenboim [28] conceptualises emotional responses to the built environment in terms of momentary experiences, resulting from discrete emotions, including sense of security, comfort, happiness, and annoyance. An analogous conceptualisation of emotional response is found in Perrée, Dane and Van Den Berg [21]. Lastly, Resch et al. [29] focus on a set of discrete emotions including happiness, sadness, fear, anger/disgust. The third issue concerns the identification of built environment factors that elicit positive and negative emotions.

The analysis of the literature focuses on articles retrieved from the Scopus database via multiple queries containing the terms "emotion*" or "subjective well-being" or "happiness" and "walkability" or "public space*" or "urban". A comparative content analysis is conducted to identify the aspect of built environment experience considered as the dependent variable and the built environment factors identified as relevant independent variables. Among the factors influencing individuals' satisfaction, Land use diversity is co-related to positive emotional response [11, 12, 16, 23] and to pedestrian satisfaction [16]. Land use density, conceptualised as a condition for access to urban functions, is co-related to emotional response [11, 23] and to pedestrian and residential satisfaction [17–19, 33]. Interestingly, a negative co-relation to neighbourhood happiness is observed in Oslo by Mouratidis and Yiannkou [33]. Built-up areas factors have a limited relevance in eliciting satisfaction and positive emotional response. Density, in particular, is observed to be negatively related to residential and pedestrian satisfaction and to individuals' emotional response [23, 33]. However, Mouratidis observes that density, if relevant urban problems - including noise, perceived unsafety and signs of neglect - are mitigated, can be positively associated to SWB [10, 11]. Built environment (BE) factors relevant in terms of influencing the emotional state of users include access to natural and semi natural areas, trees coverage, safety, and intrinsic, compositional qualities of public spaces. Access to green infrastructure is positively related to emotional response in 11 out of 20 selected studies [11, 12, 14, 17–120]. An important factor is also trees coverage of public spaces, as observed in five studies on quality of life, emotional response to the BE and residential satisfaction [11, 13, 15, 16, 22]. Contrasting results are found by Mouratidis and Yiannakou, in their study on residents' satisfaction and contentment in Thessaloniki, Greece, and Oslo, Norway [33]. Safety emerges as a central determinant of satisfaction and positive emotional response [10, 11, 13, 16–118]. Moreover, safety is frequently formalised as a perceived condition [10, 17, 18, 33, 41]. Gim et al. [35]

conceptualise safety as a condition resulting from satisfaction related to specific built environment factors including rest and green areas, noise, pollution, crime, cleanliness and parking areas. Moreover, specific built environment components are identified as factors conducive to perceived safety: Sepe [13] identifies the presence of road lamps and the design of spaces conducive to multiple practices as determinants of perceived safety. Bivina and Gupta [16] formalise safety and security in terms of presence of police operators, presence of road lamps and presence of road signs. Lastly, several studies [37–42] build on the Broken Window Theory (BWT) to relate perceived safety to the absence of signs of neglect. The BWT, in fact, investigates the impact of urban disorder and anti-social practices on the perception of safety and the probability of future criminal activities [43]. This study introduces the concept of meaningful usability and defines it as the potential of built environment macro-scale factors to increase residents' satisfaction. Based on the scientific literature, the relevant macro-scale determinants of meaningful usability include density of services, diversity of services, access to natural and semi-natural areas, access to public transit, distance to central areas. The set of metrics developed to evaluate these built environment factors is presented in the sub-sequent section.

3 Methodology

The study is articulated on stages: i) Definition of macro-scale factors influencing built environment meaningful usability; ii) Selection of the area of study and construction of a spatial database related to the selected macro-scale factors; iii) definition of the unit of analysis; iv) Definition of a set of spatial, configurational and statistical metrics to measure built-environment factors; v) Indicators' calculation and visualization of results. In particular, the relevant macro-scale factors influencing residents' satisfaction include density of services, diversity of services, access to natural and semi-natural areas, access to public transit, and distance from central areas. Services are grouped in seven categories, including healthcare facilities, educational facilities, cultural services, subsistence services, retail activities, recreational functions, and public services. Each category of services is divided in two sub-categories, based on the frequency of fruition of individual services. Each sub-category of services is represented by a point vector layer. Points of interest, related to individual services, are retrieved from the Google Maps web service. The spatial structure of the area of study is represented by a segment map. A segment map represents a spatial system as a set of lines, delimited by consecutive intersections, that intersect all the convex spaces comprised in a spatial layout. The segment map is created using the road center line (RCL) map obtained from the Open Street Map database. Residential buildings and public transit stops are represented by point vector layers, retrieved from the Territorial Information System of the Sardinia Region. More precisely, points representing residential buildings correspond to the centroids of buildings' ground projection. The census tract is selected as the spatial unit of analysis for developing a detailed quantitative description of the spatial variation of determinants of residents' satisfaction. The census tracts' polygons are retrieved from the Open database of the Italian Institute for Statistics (ISTAT) and refer to the 2011 National census. The 2011 census tract is, in fact, the spatial unit related to the most complete available information on population and buildings at the sub-district scale. Density of services is calculated as the weighted average of measures of proximity of the i-th census tract to services of the j-th category (Table 1). Proximity is measured as the number of points of interest of the j-th category, located within a predefined distance from each census tract, weighted by the distance via an attenuation function. Proximity is calculated via the Attraction Reach (AR) function of the Place Syntax Toolkit (PST). The radius is set at 800 m, a distance relevant for pedestrian movement, equivalent to a 10-min trip. The weights of the AR metrics are calculated using a pairwise comparison matrix that represents the importance of the i-th variable relative to the k-th indicator. The procedure is based on the Analytical Hierarchy Process introduced by Saaty [44–46].

Land use diversity is measured by the Simpson's diversity index, via the Eq. (1):

$$D = 1 - \frac{\Sigma n(n-1)}{N(N-1)} \tag{1}$$

where:

n = number of points of interest of land use category k-th;
N = total number of points of interest.

The considered categories of urban functions include the categories of services considered for the calculation of the indicator density of services and the residential buildings category. The number of points of interest of the k-th category, is calculated via the AR function of PST, by counting the number of potential destinations comprised in the k-th category and located within a 800 m radius from each census tract. Similarly, the indicators access to natural and semi-natural areas and access to public transit, are calculated via the AR function, as the number of destinations within a 800 m radius, weighted by the distance. Lastly, the distance of the i-th census tract from the centre of the urban area, is measured as the topological distance from the i-th census tract to the urban centre. The topological distance refers to the number of turns along the route from an origin point to a destination point, and it is measured via the Attraction Distance function of PST.

The urban centre is identified as the cluster of census tracts presenting optimal access to urban services. The indicators are normalised via a range standardisation function. The indicators values are thus converted into values comprised in the 0–1 interval, where 0 indicates a negative condition and 1 an optimal condition.

An aggregate indicator of Meaningful Usability is then calculated as the weighted average of the metrics related to individual built environment macro-scale factors (Table 1 and Eq. 2).

$$I_{MEUS} = I_{SER} * (0.341) + I_{DIV} * (0.128) + I_{TR} * (0.128) + \\ I_{DCC} * (0.054) + I_{UGA} * (0.341) \tag{2}$$

These metrics are calculated for two districts of the Metropolitan City of Cagliari (MCC), the Is Mirrionis and the Mulinu Becciu districts, which are described in the sub-sequent section.

Table 1. Indicators of macro-scale determinants of meaningful usability

Indicator	Description of the Indicator	Weight
I_SER	**Access to Urban Services**	**0.341**
AR_REC	Access to recreational services	0.074
AR_CUL	Access to cultural Services	0.074
AR_RET	Access to Retail Activities	0.074
AR_BAS	Access to Subsistence Services (Grocery Stores, Pharmacies)	0.289
AR_HEA	Access to Healtcare services	0.221
AR_EDU	Access to educational services	0.221
AR_GEN	Access to General Services (Financial Services, Post Office)	0.033
I_DIV	**Diversity of Functions**	**0.128**
I_TR	**Access to Public Transit**	**0.128**
AR_BUS	Access to Bus Stops	0.552
AR_BEU	Access to Regional Bus Stops	0.095
AR_MET	Access to Tram Stations/ Stops	0.247
AR_TRN	Access to Train Stations	0.095
I_UGA	**Access to natural and semi-natural areas**	**0.341**
I_DCC	**Distance from the urban centre**	**0.054**

3.1 Selection of the Areas of Study

The selected areas of study are the Is Mirrionis and Mulinu Becciu districts in the city of Cagliari, Italy (Fig. 1). Cagliari is the capital city of the Sardinia Region and the core of the MCC, a polycentric urbanised territory that comprises 17 municipalities [30–32]. The MCC presents an isotropic structure, consisting of the compact centres of ancient formation, integrated into a system of scattered settlements that colonise and fragment the rural landscape.

The configuration, land use pattern, and density gradient of the metropolitan structure are determined by both the radial configuration of the transport infrastructure and the structure of geomorphological, pedological, hydrographical, and botanical systems. The Is Mirrionis and Mulinu Becciu districts are two social housing districts built in the 60s and 70s as part of distinct programs of public policies aimed at regulating the urbanisation processes and at addressing the housing emergency resulting from the destructions produced by the 1943 air bombing campaign and the migration of population from rural areas, determined by the economic development, based on industrial production, of urbanised areas. The areas of study are located in the northern periphery of the urban area of Cagliari, along major road infrastructures. The Is Mirrionis district was completed in 1962 and represents the last intervention promoted by the INA Casa Plan. The Mulinu Becciu district, on the other hand, was included in the Plan for Social Housing adopted by the City Council of Cagliari in 1962. The Plans for social housing

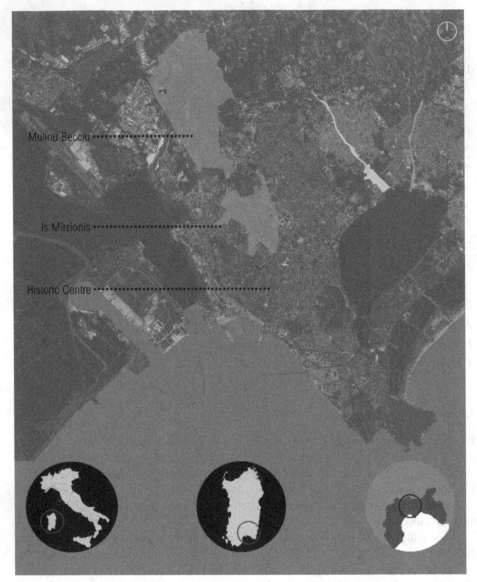

Fig. 1. The City of Cagliari and the districts of Is Mirrionis and Mulinu Becciu (authors' elaboration).

represent the last significant direct intervention of public institutions in the organisation and development of urbanised areas. These social housing districts present a distinctive urban form, resulting from a unitary design and from the experimentation of functional and spatial configurations that reflect the investigation on the organisation of the contemporary city and of its parts. In particular, in the MCC, these districts emerge as peripheral centralities, characterised by the plurality and variety of functions, by articulated spatial, functional and perceptual relations with the environmental dominants, and represent significant nodes of the polycentric system that structures the metropolitan area. Therefore, these districts constitute a fundamental component of the urban landscape and, consequently, a central dimension for defining strategies of urban transformation aimed at building resilient, inclusive, sustainable urban systems.

4   Results

The analysis underlines the significant diversity of the areas of study in terms of macroscale factors conducive to meaningful usability. In particular, the indicator density of services underlines an adequate condition of access to urban functions in the census tracts of the Is Mirrionis district, contiguous to spaces integrated at both the local (radius equal to 800 m) and at the global scale.

A similar condition is observed in the Mulinu Becciu District. Tracts contiguous to a set of segments integrated at the global scale present a more relevant presence of services. In general terms the values of the indicator density of services are comprised in the range 0.365–0.596 in the Is Mirrionis district and range from 0.071 to 0.403 in the Mulinu Becciu district (Fig. 2). The mean and the median are equal to 0.493 and 0.506 in the Is Mirrionis District and to 0.258 and 0.257 in the Mulinu Becciu area. In particular, the mean and median values observed in the Is Mirrionis district is superior than the values measured for the entire Urban core of Cagliari, which are equal, respectively, to 0.461 and 0.472. The indicator diversity of functions, present a significant internal variation in the investigated areas. Areas presenting functional diversity are located along roads integrated at the global scale in both districts. In the Is Mirrionis district the diversity of function ranges from modest, equal to 0.168, to adequate, equal to 0.399 (Fig. 3). A more relevant variation is observed in the Mulinu Becciu district. The values of the indicator diversity of functions are comprised in the 0.000–0.643 interval. The mean and the median values are, respectively, 0.306 and 0.312 in the Mulinu Becciu district, and 0.277 and 0.271 in the Is Mirrionis area. The level of integration of distinct functions of the areas of study is thus comparable to the average condition observed in the urban core of Cagliari. The measure of central tendency measured for the entire urban area, in fact, are equal to 0.321 (mean value) and to 0.258 (median value). A distinctive aspect of the areas of study is the proximity to natural and semi-natural areas, constituting significant nodes of the metropolitan ecological infrastructures (Fig. 4).

In particular, the Is Mirrionis district presents values of the indicator access to urban green areas comprised in the 0.313–0.644 interval, thus denoting adequate to good conditions of access to natural and semi-natural areas (Fig. 4). A greater variation and limited conditions of access to urban green areas is observed in the Mulinu Becciu area. The values range from 0.029 to 0.377, and the inter-quartile range, equal to 0.164, underlines the disparities, in terms of access to urban green amenities, between the denser part of the district, and the sparser census tracts, contiguous to the remains of the agricultural areas.

The mean values, equal to 0.228 for the Mulinu Becciu district and to 0.477, compared to the values measured for the urban core of Cagliari, equal to 0.499, underline conditions

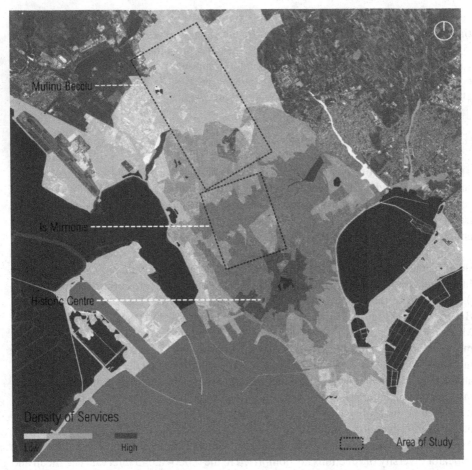

Fig. 2. Variation of the Density of services in the area of study (authors' elaboration).

of proximity to natural and semi-natural areas in line with the city average in the Is Mirrionis area, and inferior in the Mulinu Becciu district. Conditions of access to public transport are inadequate and reflect a distribution similar to that of density of services. In the Is Mirrionis district values range from 0.007 to 0.376 in areas contiguous to segments of secondary and tertiary roads integrated at the global scale. The mean value is 0.246 and the median is equal to 0.257.

In Mulinu Becciu district the level of access to public transport range from 0.000 to 0.433, indicating an adequate condition of proximity to public transit stops limited to census tracts contiguous to the G. Brotzu Hospital (Fig. 4). The mean and the median values are respectively 0.184 and 0.195. Conditions observed in the areas of study are lower than the average level of access observed in the urban core of Cagliari. The mean and the median for the entire urban core are, in fact, equal to 0.282 and to 0.264. Moreover, the mean topological distance from the urban centre is equal to 32 for the Is Mirrioinis district, and to 48 for the Mulinu Becciu district.

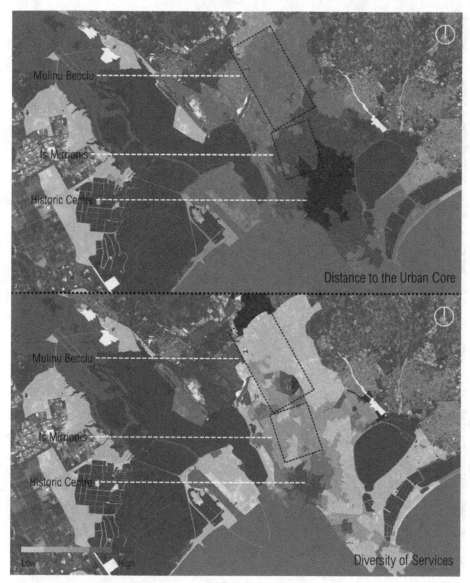

Fig. 3. Distribution of the conditions of diversity of services and distance to the urban core (authors' elaboration).

The indicator of meaningful usability (I_{MEUS}) underlines the limited potential of macro-scale factors to elicit residents' satisfaction in the Mulinu Becciu district (Fig. 5). The values of the aggregated indicator are comprised in the 0.071–0.394 interval, with a mean equal to 0.255 and a median equal to 0.253. In the Is Mirrioinis area, vice versa, present a more favourable condition, in terms of macro-scale qualities conducive to

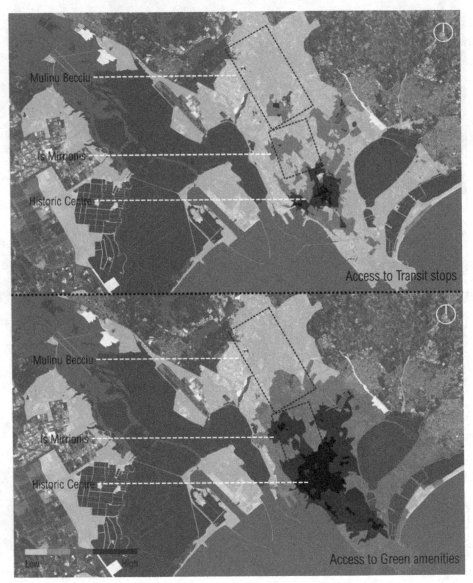

Fig. 4. Conditions of access to public transit and to green amenities in the area of study (authors' elaboration).

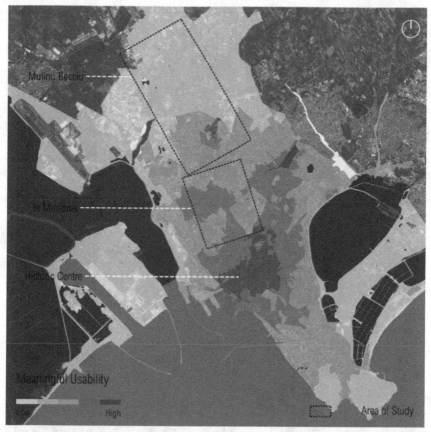

Fig. 5. Distribution of the values of the synthetic Index of Meaningful Usability (authors' elaboration).

residents' satisfaction. The values of the I_{MEUS} indicator, in fact, range from to 0.324 to 0.533, with a mean value of 0.436 and a median of 0.441.

Compared to the average condition of the Urban area of Cagliari (mean equal to 0.444, median equal to 0.432), the values observed in the Is Mirrionis area underlines the integration of the district into the urban structure and its emergence as an eccentric centrality, defined by good conditions of density of services, access to public transit, and proximity to natural and semi-natural areas.

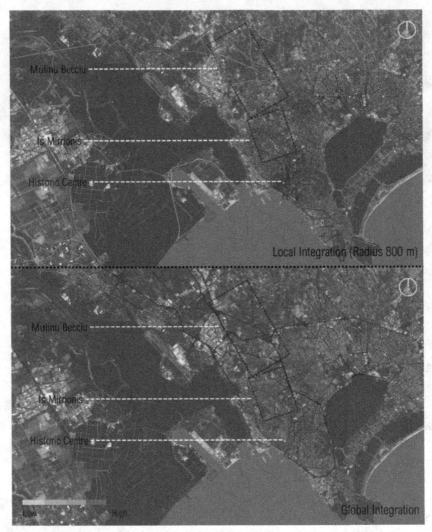

Fig. 6. Distribution of conditions of integration at the local and at the global (metropolitan) scale (authors' elaboration).

5   Discussion and Conclusions

The results presented in the previous section underline a configuration of access to services, contiguity to the ecological infrastructure, and of functional diversity, specific to each district. In particular, the study demonstrates the emergence of the Is Mirrionis district as an eccentric centrality, a pole of local and urban scale services, and, consequently, as a node of metropolitan structural relations aimed at integrating the ecological infrastructure, the production landscape, services and residential areas. Vice versa, the Mulinu Becciu district presents a stronger internal variation of conditions of density and diversity of services and of proximity to the ecological infrastructure. In particular, the denser census tracts delimited by Via Peretti, an important distributor road, contiguous to the G. Brotzu hospital, and by the 554 National Road, present a more significant potential to elicit residents' satisfaction as a consequence of macro-scale built environment factors. The values of the indicator of meaningful usability, in fact, ranges from 0.141 to 0.394 (mean equal to 0.270 and median equal to 0.281). Nevertheless, in general terms, the Mulinu Becciu area presents levels of density and diversity of services and of access to public transit and urban green areas inferior than the Is Mirrionis district. The analysis of the configuration of the spatial structure and of the urban form underlines several structural aspects that can be related to the partial deprivation of the Mulinu Becciu district. Both areas are intersected or are contiguous to road segments integrated and central at the metropolitan scale yet, on average, the Mulinu Becciu district presents minor level of local (radius 800 m) angular integration. The mean value of angular integration of segments in the Is Mirrionis area is equal to 155.54 and to 74.31 in the Mulinu Becciu district (Fig. 6). Moreover, the spatial structure of the Is Mirrionis district is more permeable. Permeability, measured in terms of road intersection density, normalised via a range standardisation function, is equal to 0.113 in the Mulinu Becciu district and to 0.389 in the Is Mirrionis district. The density of road intersections is an indicator of the availability of multiple alternative routes, a condition that favours the distribution of pedestrian movement among spaces, increasing opportunities for social interaction and the availability of suitable locations for economic activities [41, 47]. As a result, the minor integration at the local scale, and the minor permeability of the spatial structure, can be related to the minor density and diversity of urban functions in the Mulinu Becciu area. A relevant aspect concerns the urban form. The is Mirrionis district presents a more compact and dense structure than the Mulinu Becciu area, as indicated by values of the Ground Surface Index (GSI) (the mean value is equal to 0.264, compared to the value of 0.123 measured in the Mulinu Becciu area) and of the Floor Area Ratio (FAR) metric (mean equal to 0.189 in the Is Mirrionis district and to 0.087 in Mulinu Becciu area). The values of the GSI and the FAR metrics are normalised in the 0–1 interval and measure, respectively, the ratio of the ground projection surface of buildings to the total area of the census tract, and the ratio of the total floor area of buildings to the surface area of the census tract. Lastly, a relevant consideration concerns the building typology. A qualitative evaluation of the street space underlines that the most frequent building typology in the Mulinu Becciu area is represented by the isolated building, separated from the public space. As a consequence, the public space is not delimited by a continuous and active street frontage, a fundamental condition for the location of economic activities, for their profitability and, consequently, for urban vitality. As a result, the study underlines two aspects: first, the transformation of the compact, integrated, social housing district of Is Mirrionis into an eccentric centrality of the metropolitan area, thus overturning the stereotype of the degraded suburb, often associated with social housing districts [48, 49]. Second, urban regeneration policies, aimed at improving macro-scale factors conducive to residents' satisfaction, require interventions focused on increasing permeability and integration of the spatial structure, the density of the built-up area and the formation of continuous active street frontages. The future development of this research will be focused on two aspects: i) the investigation of the impact of space configuration on macro-scale factors relevant to residents' satisfaction [50]; and ii) the definition of a set of metrics for evaluating micro-scale factors of public spaces, related to users' emotional response, so as to broaden the notion of meaningful usability [51–53]. The aim is the development of a set of tools that can support informed decisions in the formulation of urban regeneration strategies by public agencies, in particular in relation to four aspects: i) The identification of vulnerable areas; ii) Identification of criticalities in terms of configuration of the spatial structure and access to specific services; iii) Definition of targeted strategies of urban regeneration, based on the identified criticalities of deprived areas; iv) Evaluation of alternative scenarios and v) Evaluation of the impacts of policies of urban regeneration. Thus, the expected result is the definition of information-based processes that can increase the transparency of policies of urban regeneration and their impact in terms of improvement of quality of life and of sustainability, resilience and inclusivity of cities.

Acknowledgements. This study was supported by the MIUR through the project "WEAKI TRANSIT: WEAK-demand areas Innovative TRANsport Shared services for Italian Towns (Project code: 20174ARRHT /CUP Code: J74I19000320008), financed with the PRIN 2017 (Research Projects of National Relevance) programme. This paper is also supported by Cagliari Accessibility Lab, an interdepartmental centre at the University of Cagliari (Rector's Decree of 4 March 2020. https://www.unica.it/unica/it/cagliari_accessibility_lab.page). This study was conducted within the "e.INS – Ecosystem of Innovation for Next Generation Sardinia" funded by the Italian Ministry of University and Research under the Next-Generation EU Programme (National Recovery and Resilience Plan – PNRR, M4C2, INVESTMENT 1.5 – DD 1056 of 23/06/2022, ECS00000038). This manuscript reflects only the authors' views and opinions, neither the European Union nor the European Commission can be considered responsible for them.

References

1. Barbarossa, L.: The Post Pandemic City: Challenges and Opportunities for a Non-Motorized Urban Environment. An Overview of Italian Cases. Sustainability 12 (2020). https://doi.org/10.3390/su12177172
2. Lai, K.Y., Webster, C., Kumari, S., Sarkar, C.: The nature of cities and the Covid-19 pandemic. Current Opinion in Environmental Sustainability. **46**, 27–31 (2020). https://doi.org/10.1016/j.cosust.2020.08.008
3. Annunziata, A., Desogus, G., Mighela, F., Garau, C.: Health and Mobility in the Post-pandemic Scenario. An Analysis of the Adaptation of Sustainable Urban Mobility Plans in Key Contexts of Italy. In: Computational Science and Its Applications–ICCSA 2022 Workshops: Malaga, Spain, July 4–7, 2022, Proceedings, Part VI, pp. 439-456. Springer International Publishing, Cham (2022)
4. Campisi, T., et al.: A New Vision on Smart and Resilient Urban Mobility in the Aftermath of the Pandemic: Key Factors on European Transport Policies. In: Gervasi, O., et al. (eds.) ICCSA 2021. LNCS, vol. 12958, pp. 603–618. Springer, Cham (2021). https://doi.org/10.1007/978-3-030-87016-4_43
5. Campisi, T., Garau, C., Acampa, G., Maltinti, F., Canale, A., Coni, M.: Developing Flexible Mobility On-Demand in the Era of Mobility as a Service: An Overview of the Italian Context Before and After Pandemic. In: Gervasi, O., et al. (eds.) ICCSA 2021. LNCS, vol. 12954, pp. 323–338. Springer, Cham (2021). https://doi.org/10.1007/978-3-030-86979-3_24
6. Nathan, M.: The city and the virus. Urban Studies. 00420980211058383 (2021). https://doi.org/10.1177/00420980211058383

7. Mouratidis, K.: How COVID-19 reshaped quality of life in cities: A synthesis and implications for urban planning. Land Use Policy **111**, 105772 (2021). https://doi.org/10.1016/j.landus epol.2021.105772

8. Diener, E., Ryan, K.: Subjective well-being: A general overview. South African journal of psychology. **39**, 391–406 (2009)

9. Ryff, C.D., Singer, B.: Psychological Well-Being: Meaning, Measurement, and Implications for Psychotherapy Research. Psychother. Psychosom. **65**, 14–23 (1996). https://doi.org/10. 1159/000289026

10. Mouratidis, K.: Compact city, urban sprawl, and subjective well-being. Cities **92**, 261–272 (2019). https://doi.org/10.1016/j.cities.2019.04.013

11. Mouratidis, K.: Urban planning and quality of life: A review of pathways linking the built environment to subjective well-being. Cities **115**, 103229 (2021). https://doi.org/10.1016/j. cities.2021.103229

12. Pfeiffer, D., Cloutier, S.: Planning for Happy Neighborhoods. null. **82**, 267–279 (2016). https:// doi.org/10.1080/01944363.2016.1166347

13. Sepe, M.: The role of public space to achieve urban happiness. Urban Regen. Sustain 364 (2016)

14. Ambrey, C., Fleming, C.: Public greenspace and life satisfaction in urban Australia. Urban Studies. **51**, 1290–1321 (2014). https://doi.org/10.1177/0042098013494417

15. Kim, S., Park, S., Lee, J.S.: Meso- or micro-scale? Environmental factors influencing pedestrian satisfaction. Transp. Res. Part D: Transp. Environ. **30**, 10–20 (2014). https://doi.org/10. 1016/j.trd.2014.05.005

16. Bivina, G.R., Gupta, A., Parida, M.: Walk accessibility to metro stations: an analysis based on meso- or micro-scale built environment factors. Sustain. Cities Soc. **55**, 102047 (2020). https://doi.org/10.1016/j.scs.2020.102047

17. Wang, D., Wang, F.: Contributions of the usage and affective experience of the residential environment to residential satisfaction. Null **31**, 42–60 (2016). https://doi.org/10.1080/026 73037.2015.1025372

18. Cao, X. (Jason), Wang, D.: Environmental correlates of residential satisfaction: an exploration of mismatched neighborhood characteristics in the Twin Cities. Landscape and Urban Planning **150**, 26–35 (2016). https://doi.org/10.1016/j.landurbplan.2016.02.007

19. Cao, J., Hao, Z., Yang, J., Yin, J., Huang, X.: Prioritizing neighborhood attributes to enhance neighborhood satisfaction: An impact asymmetry analysis. Cities **105**, 102854 (2020). https:// doi.org/10.1016/j.cities.2020.102854

20. Kourtit, K., Nijkamp, P., Wahlström, M.H.: How to make cities the home of people – a 'soul and body' analysis of urban attractiveness. Land Use Policy **111**, 104734 (2021). https://doi. org/10.1016/j.landusepol.2020.104734

21. Weijs-Perrée, M., Dane, G., van den Berg, P.: Analyzing the relationships between citizens' emotions and their momentary satisfaction in urban public spaces. Sustainability **12** (2020). https://doi.org/10.3390/su12197921

22. Zhao, Y., van den Berg, P.E.W., Ossokina, I.V., Arentze, T.A.: Individual momentary experiences of neighborhood public spaces: results of a virtual environment based stated preference experiment. Sustainability **14** (2022). https://doi.org/10.3390/su14094938

23. Su, L., Zhou, S., Kwan, M.-P., Chai, Y., Zhang, X.: The impact of immediate urban environments on people's momentary happiness. Urban Studies. **59**, 140–160 (2022). https://doi.org/ 10.1177/0042098020986499

24. Ekman, P., et al.: Universals and cultural differences in the judgments of facial expressions of emotion. J. Pers. Soc. Psychol. **53**, 712 (1987)

25. Ekman, P., Friesen, W.V., Ellsworth, P.: Emotion in the human face: Guidelines for research and an integration of findings. Elsevier (2013)

26. Ekman, P.: Are there basic emotions? (1992)
27. Ekman, P.: Basic emotions. Handbook of cognition and emotion. **98**, 16 (1999)
28. Birenboim, A.: The influence of urban environments on our subjective momentary experiences. Environment and Planning B: Urban Analytics and City Science. **45**, 915–932 (2018). https://doi.org/10.1177/2399808317690149
29. Resch, B., Summa, A., Zeile, P., Strube, M.: Citizen-centric urban planning through extracting emotion information from twitter in an interdisciplinary space-time-linguistics algorithm. Urban Planning **1**(2), (2016). Volunteered Geographic Information and the City (2016). https://doi.org/10.17645/up.v1i2.617
30. Garau, C., Desogus, G., Maltinti, F., Olivo, A., Peretti, L., Coni, M.: Practices for an Integrated Planning Between Urban Planning and Green Infrastructures for the Development of the Municipal Urban Plan (MUP) of Cagliari (Italy). In: Gervasi, O., et al. (eds.) ICCSA 2021. LNCS, vol. 12958, pp. 3–18. Springer, Cham (2021). https://doi.org/10.1007/978-3-030-870 16-4_1
31. Torrisi, V., et al.: Modelling of Interactions Between Pedestrians and Vehicular Traffic to Promote Active Mobility: The Case of San Benedetto Neighbourhood in Cagliari (Italy). In: Computational Science and Its Applications–ICCSA 2022 Workshops: Malaga, Spain, July 4–7, 2022, Proceedings, Part IV, pp. 453-468. Springer International Publishing, Cham (2022)
32. Pellicelli, G., et al.: Sustainable mobility and accessibility to essential services. An assessment of the san benedetto neighbourhood in cagliari (Italy). In: Computational Science and Its Applications–ICCSA 2022 Workshops: Malaga, Spain, July 4–7, 2022, Proceedings, Part VI, pp. 423–438. Springer International Publishing, Cham (2022, July)
33. Mouratidis, K., Yiannakou, A.: What makes cities livable? Determinants of neighborhood satisfaction and neighborhood happiness in different contexts. Land Use Policy **112**, 105855 (2022). https://doi.org/10.1016/j.landusepol.2021.105855
34. Zhang, Y., Van den Berg, A.E., Van Dijk, T., Weitkamp, G.: Quality over quantity: contribution of urban green space to neighborhood satisfaction. Int. J. Environ. Res. Public Health **14** (2017). https://doi.org/10.3390/ijerph14050535
35. Gim, T.-H.T.: Comparing happiness determinants for urban residents. International Review for Spatial Planning and Sustainable Development **9**, 24–40 (2021). https://doi.org/10.14246/irspsd.9.2_24
36. Mouratidis, K.: Neighborhood characteristics, neighborhood satisfaction, and well-being: the links with neighborhood deprivation. Land Use Policy **99**, 104886 (2020). https://doi.org/10.1016/j.landusepol.2020.104886
37. Annunziata, A.: Spazi urbani praticabili. FrancoAngeli, Milano, Italy (2020)
38. Annunziata, A., Garau, C.: A Literature Review on Walkability and its Theoretical Framework. Emerging Perspectives for Research Developments. In: Gervasi, O., et al. (eds.) ICCSA 2020. LNCS, vol. 12255, pp. 422–437. Springer, Cham (2020). https://doi.org/10.1007/978-3-030-58820-5_32
39. Garau, C., Annunziata, A.: Supporting children's independent activities in smart and playable public places. Sustainability **12**, 8352 (2020)
40. Annunziata, A., Garau, C.: A Literature Review on the Assessment of Vitality and Its Theoretical Framework. Emerging Perspectives for Geodesign in the Urban Context. In: Gervasi, O., et al. (eds.) ICCSA 2021. LNCS, vol. 12958, pp. 305–322. Springer, Cham (2021). https://doi.org/10.1007/978-3-030-87016-4_23
41. Garau, C., Annunziata, A.: A method for assessing the vitality potential of urban areas. The case study of the Metropolitan City of Cagliari, Italy. City, Territory and Architecture **9**(1), 1–23 (2022). https://doi.org/10.1186/s40410-022-00153-6
42. Garau, C., Annunziata, A., Yamu, C.: A walkability assessment tool coupling multi-criteria analysis and space syntax: the case study of Iglesias, Italy. European Planning Studies 1–23 (2020). https://doi.org/10.1080/09654313.2020.1761947

43. Wilson, J.Q., Kelling, G.L.: Broken Windows: The Police and Neighbourhood Safety, Atlantic Monthly **2**, 9-38 (1982)
44. Saaty, T.L.: How to make a decision: the analytic hierarchy process. Eur. J. Oper. Res. **48**, 9–26 (1990). https://doi.org/10.1016/0377-2217(90)90057-I
45. Saaty, T.L., Fornman, E.N.: The Hierarchicon. RWS Publishing, Pittsburgh, United States (1993)
46. Saaty, T.L., Vargas, L.G.: The Logic of Priorities. RWS Publishing, Pittsburgh, United States (1991)
47. Jacobs, J.: The death and life of great American cities. Vintage, New York, United States (2016)
48. Gazzola, A.: Intorno alla città. Problemi delle periferie in Europa e in Italia. Liguori Editore, Napoli, Italy (2008)
49. Saiu, V.: L'ultimo capitolo della Città Pubblica. I Quartieri 167 e la costruzione delle periferie metropolitane. LISt Lab, Milano, Italy (2018)
50. Garau, C., Desogus, G., Barabino, B., Coni, M.: Accessibility and Public Transport Mobility for a Smart (er) Island: Evidence from Sardinia (Italy). Sustain. Cities Soc. **87**, 104145 (2022)
51. Nicoletta, R., et al.: Accessibility to Local Public Transport in Cagliari with Focus on the Elderly. In: Gervasi, O., et al. (eds.) ICCSA 2020. LNCS, vol. 12255, pp. 690–705. Springer, Cham (2020). https://doi.org/10.1007/978-3-030-58820-5_50
52. Garau, C., et al.: A methodological framework for assessing practicability of the urban space: the survey on conditions of practicable environments (SCOPE) procedure applied in the case study of Cagliari (Italy). Sustainability **10**(11), 4189 (2018)
53. Pinna, F., Garau, C., Annunziata, A.: A Literature Review on Urban Usability and Accessibility to Investigate the Related Criteria for Equality in the City. In: Gervasi, O., et al. (eds.) ICCSA 2021. LNCS, vol. 12958, pp. 525–541. Springer, Cham (2021). https://doi.org/10.1007/978-3-030-87016-4_38

Smart and Sustainable Island Communities (SSIC 2023)

Environmental and Economic Analysis of Using Recycled Concrete Aggregates in Composite Steel-Concrete Slabs

Flavio Stochino[1] , Alireza Alibeigibeni[1(✉)] , Alessandro Milia[1], Marco Zucca[1] ,
Luisa Pani[1] , and Marco Simoncelli[2]

[1] University of Cagliari, 09123 Cagliari, CA, Italy
alireza.alibeigibeni@unica.it
[2] Politecnico Di Milano, 32, Milan, PL, Italy

Abstract. The needs to reduce the environmental impact of concrete buildings is gaining more importance. In particular the consumption of natural aggregates requires the opening of new quarries and represent an environmental problem. A good solution for the latter is the use of concrete recycled aggregates obtained from construction and demolition waste. Composite slabs offer many advantages over traditional reinforced concrete slabs, including increased strength and stiffness, improved fire resistance, faster and easier installation, and greater environmental friendliness. Thus, the use of composite slabs with concrete recycled aggregates represents a promising strategy to reduce the constructions environmental impact. The aim of this paper is to analyze the environmental impact and the economic aspects of the use of concrete with recycled aggregates for composite steel-concrete slabs with variable spans from 2.5 m up to 8 m and different service loads. In particular, the amount of carbon dioxide saved by replacing natural aggregates with recycled ones has been evaluated considering 30%, 50%, up to the total of 100% replacement percentages. In addition, the construction costs have been estimated, always comparing the use of ordinary concrete with natural aggregates and the use of recycled ones. Results show that using recycled aggregates reduces the environmental impact of composite slabs with a very little economic cost reduction.

Keywords: Composite slab · Concrete · Recycled Aggregate · Sustainable design

1 Introduction

The concrete industry has a significant environmental impact in terms of energy consumption, CO_2 emissions, and land use. In fact, it is responsible for approximately 5% of global carbon dioxide emissions [1]. According to the European Commission, the construction sector alone accounts for 40% of the primary energy demand in the EU and 36% of greenhouse gas emissions. In Italy, the entire building sector requires up to 27.9% of the energy demand and emits up to 24.2% of climate-changing emissions.

© The Author(s), under exclusive license to Springer Nature Switzerland AG 2023
O. Gervasi et al. (Eds.): ICCSA 2023 Workshops, LNCS 14110, pp. 277–288, 2023.
https://doi.org/10.1007/978-3-031-37123-3_21

Regarding the impact on the environment due to the demand for building materials, there are over 4,000 authorized quarries and more than 14,000 disused ones in Italy. Every year, over 29 million cubic meters of sand and gravel are extracted, along with more than 26 million cubic meters of limestone required for cement production [2].

In concrete constructions, 90% of the energy required for their construction is consumed during the production phase of raw materials, particularly clinker, while only the remaining 10% is related to concrete packaging, transport, and on-site use [3].

Literature review [4–11] shows that concretes made with recycled aggregates are suitable for structural use even for high percentages of replacement of natural aggregates with recycled ones. Indeed, the reduction of mechanical performance at material scale is compensated by the structural behavior at structural scale.

Literature review [4–11] shows that concretes made with recycled aggregates are suitable for structural use even for high percentages of replacement of natural aggregates with recycled ones. Indeed, the reduction of mechanical performance at material scale is compensated by the structural behavior at structural scale.

Thus, the use of recycled aggregates allows reducing carbon dioxide emissions into the atmosphere without increasing construction costs for construction companies, provided that there is a network of facilities for the treatment and recycling of construction and demolition waste appropriately spread throughout the territory.

Composite slabs [12], see (Fig. 1), are a combination of steel and concrete and have become increasingly popular for use in building constructions in recent years. This is because they offer many benefits over traditional reinforced concrete slabs. One of the primary advantages of composite slabs is their increased strength and stiffness. By combining the tensile strength of steel with the compressive strength of concrete, the resulting composite slab is much stronger than either material used alone. This means that it can support heavier loads without experiencing excessive deflection, making it ideal for use in structures with high service loads. Composite slabs are also faster and easier to install than traditional reinforced concrete slabs. This is because they are typically prefabricated off-site and then transported to the construction site for installation. This reduces the amount of time required for on-site construction, making the construction process more efficient and cost-effective. Last and not least, composite slabs are also more environmentally friendly than traditional reinforced concrete slabs. This is because they require less concrete, which is a significant source of carbon dioxide emissions. In addition, composite slab can be re-used in different constructions [13] and the components of the slab (both steel and concrete [14]) are often made from recycled materials, further reducing its environmental impact.

This paper will analyze the environmental impact and the economic aspects of the use of concrete with recycled aggregates for composite steel-concrete slabs. After this introduction Sect. 2 will present the adopted models while the results are shown in Sect. 3. Finally, some conclusive remarks are drawn in Sect. 4.

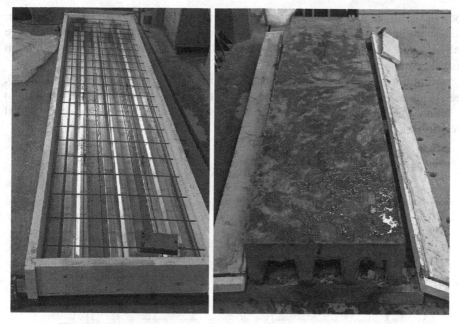

Fig. 1. Composite slabs before (left) and after concrete casting (right).

2 Methods

The composite slabs were designed in accordance with Eurocode 4 [15], considering three types of service loads (2, 4, 6 kN/m) and varying span lengths between 2.5 m and 8 m. The chosen width of the composite slab is 15 m. For ultimate limit states (Flexural strength, Shear resistance, Bonding resistance), and service limit states (Deformability) assessments, simply supported beam scheme have been considered under a uniformly distributed load.

Concrete with strength class C30/37 was utilized, and three different mix designs were taken into account, featuring replacement percentages of recycled aggregates at 30%, 50%, and 100%, see Table 1. The mixture that does not contain any recycled aggregates, referred to as ordinary concrete with aggregates derived solely from natural

Table 1. Mix design for the considered concrete mixes. NA denotes the natural aggregates, while RA represents the recycled ones. The additive is a common fluidizing additive.

Id	W/C	Cement (kg)	Water (kg)	Fine NA (kg)	Coarse NA (kg)	Fine RA (kg)	Coarse RA (kg)	Additive (kg)
M 0–0	0,51	366,27	185,00	893,33	893,33	0,00	0,00	3,31
M_30	0,51	366,27	185,00	536,00	536,00	223,33	223,33	3,31
M_50	0,51	366,27	185,00	370,00	370,00	400,00	350,00	3,31
M_100	0,51	366,27	185,00	0,00	0,00	700,00	700,00	3,31

sources, is utilized as a benchmark for the final values of CO_2 emissions and cost. The environmental and economic costs have been evaluated for the construction stage only assuming that composite slabs are built in Sardinia and that material transportation distances are in average 30 km.

Two different profiles of corrugated sheet were considered: S 55/600–750 and S 110, see [16] and (Fig. 2). The thickness of the sheet metal used varies from 0.8 mm up to 2.75 mm. The concrete slab has been reinforced with a B450C steel [17] electro-welded mesh 150x150 mm with 6 mm diameter.

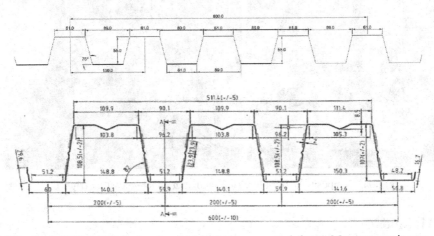

Fig. 2. S 55/600–750 (bottom) and S 110 (top) corrugated sheets. Measures are in mm.

In order to simplify the problem, given that the critical limit state is the bonding resistance and the influence of the mechanical properties of concrete for this resistance is negligible, for this reason the mechanical performance of concrete mixtures containing variable recycled aggregate replacement rates (30%, 50% and 100%) has been considered equal to the one of ordinary concrete class C30/37. For technological reasons, the total thickness of the composite slab cross section must not exceed 355 mm.

To determine the quantities of carbon dioxide released into the atmosphere in the construction of these slabs, the following unit values reported in the following Table 2 have been considered:

The environmental costs (in terms of CO_2 emissions) related to the production of concrete were taken from [8, 18, 19].

To calculate the total carbon dioxide emissions released, the values were multiplied by the total amount of steel mass and concrete volume obtained from the design of the composite slabs considering different span length and service loads. These calculations were used to obtain the total emissions of carbon dioxide released into the atmosphere.

To determine the CO_2 emissions per unit of built area, the total emissions were divided by the respective composite slab area.

The economic costs of materials necessary for the composite slabs were taken from the price list of the Sardinia Region [20] assuming that the composite slabs will be built in Sardinia (Italy), see Table 3. Furthermore, the cost of recycled aggregates, corrugated

Table 2. Carbon dioxide emitted by the materials constituting the composite slabs.

Material	Equivalent CO_2 produced (kg/tonn)
Cement	693
Natural Coarse Aggregates	33
Natural Fine Aggregates	33
Recycled Coarse Aggregates	12
Recycled Fine Aggregates	12
Steel for corrugated sheets	2320
Steel for rebars	1380

sheet and electro-welded mesh were evaluated considering the average prices offered by different stakeholders. In order to simplify the problem difference in materials cost of transportation and labor cost are not considered. These costs are kept constant for both recycled and natural aggregates.

Table 3. Economic costs of the materials constituting the composite slabs.

Material	Economic Costs	Units
Cement	0.29	kg/€
Natural Coarse Aggregates	25	m^3/€
Natural Fine Aggregates	28	m^3/€
Recycled Coarse Aggregates	18	m^3/€
Recycled Fine Aggregates	18	m^3/€
Corrugated sheets	75	m^2/€
Steel for rebars	0.48	kg/€

Also in this case, to calculate the total cost of the composite slabs, the values were multiplied by the total amount of steel mass and concrete volume necessary for the designed composite slabs considering different span length and service loads. In any case the pursuit of the minimum amount of materials have been developed, thus a general optimization of economic costs of composite slabs cross sections have been obtained.

3 Results and Discussion

3.1 Environmental Costs

Figure 3 reports the environmental impact in terms of $\frac{kg\,CO_2}{m^2}$ of composite slabs for a service load $Q_{k1} = 2\frac{kN}{m^2}$ considering different span lengths. It is interesting to highlight that the trend is not monotonically increasing, but a clear oscillation is present between the span length of 5.5 m and 6.5 m. The latter oscillation is caused by the bonding resistance limit state, which cannot be achieved with the S 55/600–750 sheet that with a span length of 6 m. Therefore, it is necessary to use the S 110 sheet, which has better mechanical performances. Furthermore this sheet requires less concrete to satisfy ultimate and serviceability limit states, resulting in reduced carbon dioxide emissions due to the smaller amount of material needed. Furthermore, it can be observed that the CO_2 emissions of the 2.5 m and 3 m span length slabs are identical. This is because the design requirements mandate a concrete slab with a minimum thickness of 50 mm, which is necessary in both cases resulting in the same cross section.

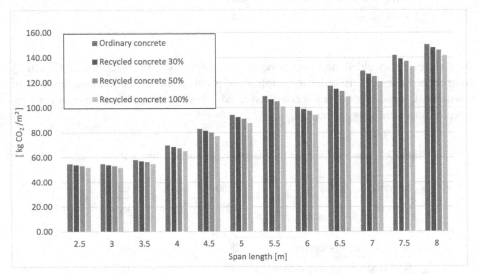

Fig. 3. CO_2 emissions of residential slabs as a function of span length, service load $Qk_1 = 2kN/m^2$

Figure 4 shows that the amount of carbon dioxide saved depends on the replacement percentages of recycled aggregates. For instance, compared to normal concrete composite slabs, the savings range from 0.85 kg/m^2 for a 2.5 m slab that uses 30% recycled aggregates, to a maximum of 9.07 kg/m^2 for an 8 m span length slab that completely replaces natural aggregates with recycled materials (100%).

Furthermore, considering the case of a composite slabs with span length equal to 5.5 m (generally the most used size), there is a saving of CO_2 respectively of 2.43 kg/m^2 in the case of 30% replacement percentage, 4.05 kg/m^2 for 50% and 8.10 kg/m^2 for 100%.

Figure 5 depicts a nearly linear relationship between CO_2 emissions and span length for the case of service load equal to 4 kN/m^2. When compared to an ordinary concrete composite slabs, the amount of CO_2 saved varies from 0.85 kg/m^2 to 10.34 kg/m^2. Always considering the case of a composite slab with span length of 5.5 m, there is a saving of CO_2 respectively of 2.05 kg/m^2 in the case 30% recycled aggregate replacement, of 3.41 kg/m^2 for 50% and 6.82 kg/m^2 in the case of total replacement.

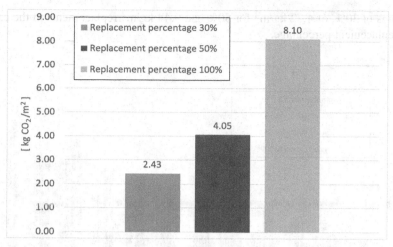

Fig. 4. CO_2 savings for composite slabs with span length equal to 5.5m realized with recycled aggregates in comparison with normal concrete composite slabs.

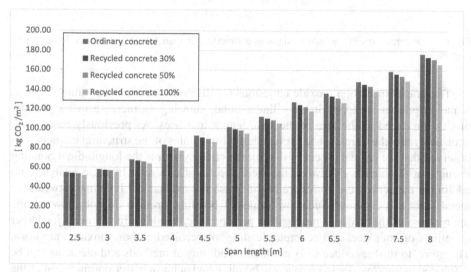

Fig. 5. CO_2 emissions of composite slabs as a function of span length for service load $Qk_1 = 4 \text{ kN/m}^2$

Figure 6 presents the relationship between CO_2 emissions and span length for the case of service load equal to 6 kN/m². Compared to the composite slab made with ordinary concrete, the amount of carbon dioxide saved varies from a minimum of 0.85 kg/m² for a 2.5 m slab with a replacement rate of recycled aggregates of 30%, up to a maximum of 10.33 kg/m², in the case of 8 m span and with the complete replacement of aggregates (100%). Considering the case of a composite slab with a length of 5.5 m, there is a saving of CO_2 respectively of 2.83 kg/m² in the case of concretes with replacement of recycled aggregates of 30%, of 4.72 kg/m^2 for 50% and 9.44 kg/m^2 replacements in the case of 100% replacement percentage.

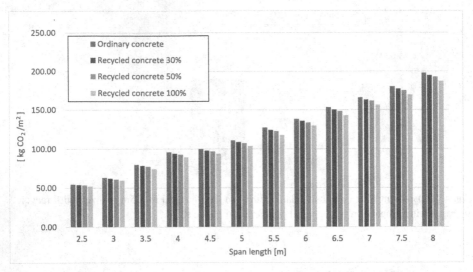

Fig. 6. CO_2 emissions of composite slabs as a function of span length for service load $Qk_1 = 6$ kN/m^2

The graphs of carbon dioxide emissions for different service load values (Figs. 3, 5 and 6) present an approximately linear trend, showing an increase in the amount of CO_2 produced as the size of the span length increases. As previously mentioned, upon analyzing the ultimate and serviceability limit states of the structural element, it is observed that the critical aspect of this construction system is the longitudinal bonding strength at the interface between the steel sheet and concrete. In these analyses, no additional elements were considered to increase the mechanical bonding between the metal sheet and concrete. Such low values of bonding strength do not allow for the optimal use of the material mechanical performance, resulting in the need for larger quantities of both steel and concrete, leading to increased carbon dioxide emissions. Therefore, to further reduce CO_2 production, additional methods and elements can be employed to improve the steel-concrete bonding and achieve better optimization of the composite section's performance.

3.2 Economic Costs

The economic costs of the composite slabs have been evaluated for different loading conditions and span length. As explained before the design have been developed minimizing the quantities of materials necessary to satisfy all the ultimate and serviceability limit states required by Eurocode 4 [15].

Figure 7 presents the economic costs of composite slabs as a function of span length for service load equal to 2 kN/m^2. It should be noted that there are very small variations between the cost composite slab made with ordinary concrete and the ones realized with recycled aggregates. The cost reductions using recycled aggregates varies from a minimum of 0.1 €/m² for a 2.5 m slab with replacement percentage of 30%, up to a maximum of 1.1 €/m², in the case of 8 m span and with 100% replacement percentage.

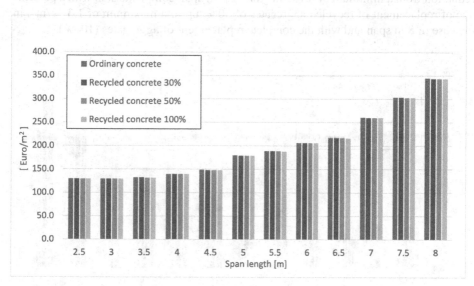

Fig. 7. Economic costs of composite slabs as a function of span length for service load $Qk_1 = 2$ kN/m²

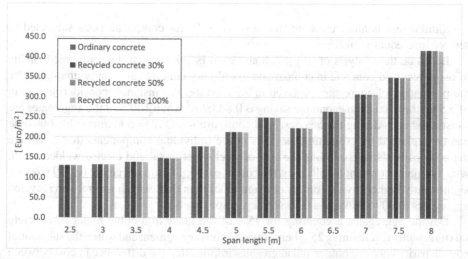

Fig. 8. Economic costs of composite slabs as a function of span length for service load $Qk_1 = 4$ kN/m²

Figure 8 presents the variations of specific economic costs of composite slabs subjected to 4 kN/m² for different span length. Also, in this case there is an oscillation between 5.5 and 6.0 m span lengths due to the changing of the metal sheets necessary to optimize the costs followed by a usual increasing trend. Compared to the composite slab made with ordinary concrete, the construction costs of composite slabs present a small reduction from a minimum of 0.1 €/m² for a 2.5 m span composite slab with a percentage of replacement of recycled aggregates of 30%, up to a maximum of 1.3 €/m², in the case of 8 m span and with the complete replacement of aggregates (100%).

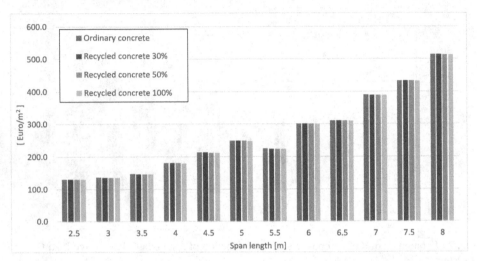

Fig. 9. Economic costs of composite slabs as a function of span length for service load $Qk_1 = 6 \text{ kN/m}^2$

Similar results and trends are shown by (Fig. 9) for composite slabs subjected to service load equal to 6kN/m².

Based on the analysis of (Figs. 7, 8 and 9), it is evident that the economic benefits of using recycled concrete in comparison to ordinary concrete are nearly unaffected by the percentage of aggregates replaced in the mixture. For instance, considering a span of 5.5 m, the maximum economic saving is 0.80 €/m² when 100% of the aggregates are substituted considering the heaviest load configuration $Qk_1 = 6 \text{ kN/m}^2$. This outcome can be explained by examining the costs of the individual components that constitute the composite slabs. Excluding the cost of steel sheet metal and electro-welded mesh, which remains constant for all cases, the cost of each kilogram of cement (0.279 €/kg) is significantly higher (by two orders of magnitude) than that of both natural and recycled aggregates (0.0096 €/kg and 0.0082 €/kg, respectively).

Despite aggregates accounting for 75% of the mass in a cubic meter of concrete mixture, with the remaining 25% being divided between cement and water, the substantial cost disparity between binder and aggregates implies that the difference in cost between constructing the same composite slab with ordinary concrete versus recycled concrete is minimal, even for 100% replacement percentage. Indeed, the difference in price between natural and recycled aggregates is only 0.0014 €/kg. Furthermore, the majority of the cost of concrete is attributed to cement and labor, while the cost of aggregates has a negligible impact on the final expense.

4   Conclusion

This paper analyzed the environmental impact and the economic aspects of the use of concrete with recycled aggregates for composite steel-concrete slabs.

Previous researches [4–11] proved that recycled aggregates can be used in structural concrete, even at high percentages of replacement of natural aggregates, reducing carbon dioxide emissions without increasing construction costs for companies. However, a network of plants for the treatment and recycling of construction and demolition waste must be appropriately spread throughout the territory otherwise transportation costs can become important.

With regards to sustainable development, the findings of this work suggest the following observations to reduce concrete impact on the environment:

- Using recycled aggregates in concrete for structural purposes reduces carbon dioxide emissions by more than 10 kg/m^2, which could lead to significant benefits if applied on a large scale.
- An update of the international standard is necessary to use of mixtures containing higher percentages of replacement of recycled aggregates.
- Encouraging the spread of treatment and recycling plants for waste materials from demolition and construction is crucial for having recycled aggregates available on the market at competitive prices.
- In steel-concrete composite structures, particularly in the construction of slabs, maximizing the bonding resistance is essential to obtain the best performance of the two materials and thus obtain reduced sections and lower CO_2 emissions.

References

1. Faleschini, F., Mariano Angelo, Z., Carlo P.: Environmental impacts of recycled aggregate concrete. In: Italian Concrete Days – Giornate AICAP Congresso CTE, Roma, Italy, 27–28 (Oct 2016).
2. Zanchini, E., Nanni, G.: Rapporto cave 2021, legambiente (2021). https://www.legambiente.it/wp-content/uploads/2021/07/Rapporto-Cave-2021.pdf. Accessed 05 Apr 2023
3. Kurth, H., Winter, K.H., Pospíchal, V.: Ecological requirements for concrete construction. App. Mech. Mater. **796**, 111–118 (2015)
4. Lima, C., Caggiano, A., Faella, C., Martinelli, E., Pepe, M., Realfonzo, R.: Physical properties and mechanical behaviour of concrete made with recycled aggregates and fly ash. Constr. Build. Mater. **47**, 547–559 (2013)
5. Pani, L., Francesconi, L., Rombi, J., Mistretta, F., Sassu, M., Stochino, F.: Effect of parent concrete on the performance of recycled aggregate concrete. Sustainability **12**(22), 9399 (2020)
6. Le, H.-B., Bui, Q.-B.: Recycled aggregate concretes–a state-of-the-art from the microstructure to the structural performance. Constr. Build. Mater. **257**, 119522 (2020)
7. Evangelista, L., Jorge de, B.: State-of-the-art on the use of fine recycled aggregates in concrete production. In: 2nd International RILEM Conference on Progress of Recycling in the Built Environment, pp. 175–183. RILEM Publications SARL (2011)
8. Nedeljković, M., Visser, J., Šavija, B., Valcke, S., Schlangen, E.: Use of fine recycled concrete aggregates in concrete: a critical review. J. Build. Eng. **38**, 102196 (2021)

9. Pani, L., Francesconi, L., Rombi, J., Salis, M., Stochino, F.: Circular economy strategy in the construction sector: the use of recycle aggregates in the sardinian island. In: Gervasi, O., et al. (eds.) ICCSA 2021. LNCS, vol. 12958, pp. 33–43. Springer, Cham (2021). https://doi.org/10.1007/978-3-030-87016-4_3

10. Francesconi, L., Pani, L., Stochino, F.: Punching shear strength of reinforced recycled concrete slabs. Constr. Build. Mater. **127**, 248–263 (2016)

11. Ajdukiewicz, A.B., Kliszczewicz, A.T.: Comparative tests of beams and columns made of recycled aggregate concrete and natural aggregate concrete. J. Adv. Concr. Technol. **5**(2), 259–273 (2007)

12. Ahmed, S.M., et al.: Prediction of longitudinal shear resistance of steel-concrete composite slabs. Eng. Struct. **193**, 295–300 (2019)

13. Brambilla, G., Lavagna, M., Vasdravellis, G., Castiglioni, C.A.: Environmental benefits arising from demountable steel-concrete composite floor systems in buildings. Resour. Conserv. Recycl. **141**, 133–142 (2019)

14. Lv, J., et al.: A new composite slab using crushed waste tires as fine aggregate in self-compacting lightweight aggregate concrete. Materials **13**(11), 2551 (2020)

15. UNI EN 1994-1-1:2005 – Eurocode 4 – Design of Composite Steel and Concrete Structures

16. Spinelli, metal sheets catalog. https://www.spinellisrl.eu/catalogo/lamiere-grecate-ondulate/, Accessed 05 Apr 2023

17. per le Costruzioni, Norme Tecniche. "Norme tecniche per le costruzioni." Decree of the Minister of the Infrastructures 14 (2008)

18. Hossain, M.U., Poon, C.S., Lo, I.M., Cheng, J.C.: Comparative environmental evaluation of aggregate production from recycled waste materials and virgin sources by LCA. Resour. Conserv. Recycl. **109**, 67–77 (2016)

19. Juarez, R.I.C., Stephen, F.: The environmental impact of cement production in Europe: a holistic review of existing EPDs. Cleaner Environ. Syst. **3**, 100053 (2021)

20. Prezziario Regionale per le opere pubbliche in Sardegna 2022. https://www.regione.sardegna.it/prezzario/2022, Accessed 05 Apr 2023

Tourism Governance for Reaching Sustainability Objectives in Insular Territories – Case Study Dodecanese Islands' Complex, Greece

Dionisia Koutsi(✉) 🆔 and Anastasia Stratigea 🆔

Department of Geography and Regional Planning, School of Rural,
Surveying and Geoinformatics Engineering,
National Technical University of Athens, Athens, Greece
koutsi.dionisia@gmail.com, stratige@central.ntua.gr

Abstract. The steadily increasing number of people, travelling around the world for leisure purposes, has raised concerns as to their impacts on sustainability of destinations, affecting the quality of life of local population and the quality of visitors' experience. The higher the volume/seasonality/mass type of tourist flows and fragility of the destination the greater the impacts these flows cause, leading – under certain circumstances – to the "overtourism" phenomenon, i.e. surpass of destinations' carrying capacity in environmental, social, cultural, etc. terms. This phenomenon appears recently as a noticeable trend in several Mediterranean insular destinations; and calls for tourism governance – both horizontal and vertical – and policy interventions that: prioritize long-term sustainability objectives to the benefit of islands' communities and visitors; and engage local communities as integral parts and safeguards of destinations' assets. In this context, this paper explores the potential for sustainable tourism practices to grow in the Greek islands' ecosystem, using as a case study the Dodecanese Islands' complex. Towards this end, it draws upon an innovative methodological approach that integrates quantitative / qualitative research and policy analysis, while cross-cutting all spatial levels. Through this study, weaknesses of tourism governance structure in Greece are highlighted, while challenges and opportunities faced at the local level are also unveiled.

Keywords: Islands · Tourism governance · Sustainable tourism and regional development · Dodecanese islands' complex

1 Introduction

Tourism, as a means for leisure and experience gaining, has so far been part of the human nature and has evolved through time serving life purposes and goals' achievement; while significantly contributing to local, regional and national economies [1]. Nevertheless, the ever-increasing number of travellers willing to explore the world has, in many cases, led to tourism surges that go beyond the carrying capacity of hosting destinations [2]. This phenomenon is currently identified as 'overtourism' and is defined as *"the impact of*

© The Author(s), under exclusive license to Springer Nature Switzerland AG 2023
O. Gervasi et al. (Eds.): ICCSA 2023 Workshops, LNCS 14110, pp. 289–306, 2023.
https://doi.org/10.1007/978-3-031-37123-3_22

tourism on a destination, or parts thereof, that excessively influences perceived quality of life of citizens and/or quality of visitors' experiences in a negative way" [2: 4]; or the state where "hosts or guests feel that there are too many visitors concentrated to a destination and that the quality of life in the area or the quality of the tourist experience has unacceptably deteriorated" [3]. According to the aforementioned definitions, over-tourism is clearly a matter strongly related to destinations' carrying capacity and fragility as well as the type of tourism; and has apparently negative impacts on the natural and social environment as well as the tourism experience itself.

Overtourism can be of critical concern when it comes to the highly attractive but also extremely fragile and spatially confined Mediterranean islands, i.e. top-rating world destinations, endowed by an outstanding natural and cultural wealth [4]. In fact Mediter-ranean islands act as magnets that attract, in most cases, excessive tourist waves that overcome carrying capacity constraints. This is *"the paradox of tourism in the islands"* [5: 133], where arrival of consistent tourist flows could alter their fragile ecological equilibrium, negatively affecting those natural and cultural resources that have initially aroused tourists' interest.

The overtourism phenomenon, especially in the fragmented insular contexts, is a complex and multifaceted issue, recently gaining the attention of the academic and policy community [6–11]. Thus concerns are raising as to the severe environmental (strain of the natural environment, leading to e.g. water scarcity, pollution, and damage to local ecosystems) and socio-cultural (e.g. breaking up of social cohesion, cultural degradation and identity loss, overcrowding, real estate disturbances) repercussions, rendering islands' sustainability objectives at stake.

Response to these challenges calls for the articulation of sustainable tourism path-ways that prioritize long-term well-being of islands' hosting communities, while serving visitors' unique experiences [12–14]. This, in turn, implies adoption of holistic and inte-grated, place-based and community-centric planning approaches that address environ-mental protection, economic prosperity and social justice objectives in insular contexts [15–17]. Such objectives, although are at the forefront of discussion and a building block of tourism for more than two decades – e.g. Agenda for a sustainable and com-petitive European tourism [18]; European Agenda for tourism 2030 [19] – they still remain relevant. Thus planners and policy makers are still in need of confronting with such a "wicked" planning problem, i.e. sustainable tourism, particularly in fragile island compartments; and conceptualizing proactive and socially-innovative approaches that harness tourism benefits, while meeting challenges of the rapidly transforming tourism scenery in insular contexts.

In seeking to achieve sustainable tourism objectives, *tourism governance* seems to be a key dimension [20–23]. In fact tourism governance, within the frame of sustainability, is perceived as the set of processes, rules and stakeholders' empowerment and engagement in support of cooperatively sketching and implementing future tourism pathways of a destination in order for collective goals to be met [22].

Within such a context, this research work attempts to highlight *complexity* of tourism governance in seeking to achieve sustainable, culture-led tourism in insular regions. As a case study, the Dodecanese islands' complex in South Aegean Region, Greece is selected, namely an area of geopolitical importance, remarkable natural and cultural beauty, diverse island-based tourism profiles as well as a quite distinct – in terms of tourism dynamism – and fragile insular territory of the Greek state.

Tourism governance issues in the specific Dodecanese islands' complex are explored in this work by means of the following research questions (RQ):

- RQ1: Does tourism governance at the national, regional and local level promote sustainable culture-led tourism practices? Or, stated differently, are relevant policies at the national, regional and local level coherent and coordinated towards a sustainable tourism perspective in this area?
- RQ2: What is the currently promoted Dodecanese islands' tourism model and how this conforms to sustainability objectives?
- RQ3: What is the real potential of those islands in support of a more people-centric and integrated tourism narrative, serving sustainability objectives?

In seeking to address these questions, this paper is structured as follows: in Sect. 2 the methodological approach is presented; Sect. 3 sketches the study region; Sect. 4 elaborates on the distinct methodological steps of this work; while finally in Sect. 5 results are discussed and conclusions are drawn.

2 The Methodological Approach

By focusing on the Dodecanese islands' complex, this research work aims at responding to the aforementioned research questions. In this respect, it attempts to shed light on *tourism governance* aspects at both the vertical – the Greek tourism policy context as a whole – and the horizontal (local) level. The former is carried out by policy analysis; the latter is grasped through the perceptions of representatives of the Dodecanese insular municipalities. In addition, the already visible social and environmental impacts of the aforementioned tourism governance model in the study region are explored in an effort to realize the linkages between these impacts and tourism governance failures.

More specifically, a blended *quantitative and qualitative* research approach is adopted, built-up as a 3-Component (3-C) methodological process (Fig. 1). This approach: highlights the context of the hierarchical multi-level – national, regional, local – tourism policy environment currently in force in Greece; explores the tourism potential of each single Dodecanese island for setting up more sustainable, culture-led, place-based and people-centric tourism narratives, as perceived by the representatives of local municipalities; and presents the social and environmental impacts of the prevailing tourism model, identified at the municipalities' level in Dodecanese islands. To this end are used policy analysis and quantitative and qualitative research methods, including a web-based questionnaire that is addressed to municipalities' representatives of Dodecanese islands.

In more detail:

- In *C1*, an overview of the currently in force policy documents, related to the tourism sector in Greece – national, regional and local level – is presented, highlighting challenges in tourism governance that can hinder or even promote decision-making and practices towards a sustainable tourism model; and demarcating the way these have affected the tourism model, featured in the Dodecanese islands' complex.

- In *C2*, is attempted a deeper insight into the current local practices forwarded by the Dodecanese islands' municipalities by elaborating on data collected through a *web-based questionnaire*. This aims at illuminating decision-making processes as well as nature/culture-related future alternative tourism practices that target more sustainable tourism outcomes.
- Finally, in *C3 a set of quantitative and qualitative indicators* is used to map the tourism profile of the Dodecanese islands' complex in particular, placing emphasis on issues related to the negative environmental and social impacts over these fragile insular spatial entities. Indicators used relate to tourism flows, tourism density, quality of life etc., in reference to local population and island size, in the effort to sketch the impacts of tourist flows on each single island of the Dodecanese complex.

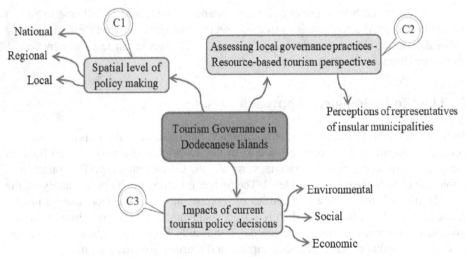

Fig. 1. Steps of the methodological approach, Source: Own elaboration

Realization of the aforementioned steps can shed light on key obstacles and issues that can either endorse or prevent steps towards sustainable tourism practices that set preservation of the local natural/cultural capital as well as local identity and social cohesion at the epicenter of the Dodecanese tourism narrative.

3   The Dodecanese Islands' Complex in Numbers

The case study area consists of a cluster of 15 inhibited islands and numerous smaller islets at the southeastern edge of the South Aegean Region. Dodecanese islands fall into the most distant ones from the mainland; are located next to the Turkey boarders and constitute a 'bridge' between Europe and the East, thus acquiring a certain geopolitical importance; display a diversifying tourism pattern far from their counterpart, i.e. Cyclades islands' complex as also part of the South Aegean Region; while also lag behind in terms of spatial and social cohesion.

Due to the geopolitical importance and the diverse roles Dodecanese Islands have played through centuries as part of the Mediterranean ancient sea routes as well as the prevailing commerce and intercultural exchange pattern, traces of different civilizations are still noticeable in these islands as remnants of cultural importance, e.g. by Ionians, Romans, Byzantines, Venetians, Ottomans and Italians [24]. As a result, a rich cultural heritage, with numerous archaeological sites, medieval castles, and churches is left behind which, in combination with the scenic natural environment, strengthens tourism attractiveness of these islands. Tourism is thus a major economic sector, displaying, however, significant interregional differences in both tourism demand and supply [6]. Rhodes and Kos are by far the most touristic islands of the Dodecanese complex, while islands like Leros, Astypalaia and Symi demonstrate a more relaxing, less crowded, and locally-adjusted tourism profile.

Table 1. Basic information of Dodecanese islands' complex – Population and tourist flows refer to the Municipality level, Source: Own elaboration from [25, 26].

Municipalities of Dodecanese	Population (provisional data 2021)	Size (km^2)	Population Density	Island Category	Total arrivals (plane/boat) (2019)
Agathonisi	203	14,5	15,04	Very small	3201
Astypalaia	1399	96,4	14,45	Small	22612
Chalki	476	26,99	16,92	Very small	0
Kalymnos	17797	111,1	160,51	Medium	98751
Karpathos	6416	324,1	21,30	Medium	121357
Kasos	1224	66,42	18,55	Small	5207
Kos	36986	287,2	127,41	Medium	1312054
Leros	7988	54,05	150,86	Medium	40827
Lipsoi	788	15,84	49,31	Small	13310
Nisyros	1043	41,2	25,19	Small	8097
Patmos	3217	34,14	94,48	Small	58099
Rhodes	124851	1401	89,30	Medium	2675365
Symi	2495	57,86	42,94	Small	185752
Tilos	745	61,49	11,86	Very Small	17179
Megisti	584	9.13	63.96	Very Small	4169

In more detail, the islands included in the Dodecanese complex and their main attributes in terms of size, population and tourism arrivals are presented in Table 1. Taking into account Spilanis and Kizos [27] categorization, distinguishing islands into: Very small (≤750 inhabitants), Small (750–5000), Medium (5000–50,000), Large (50,000–500,000), and Very large (≥500,000), in the Dodecanese cluster a percentage of 40% represents Small islands, 33% Medium-sized ones, while about 27% fall into Very Small islands (draft data on population in 2021) [25]. In terms of tourism arrivals, reference to international and domestic tourists' travelling by boat and plane are used for the 2019 year (a year most representative of tourism flows before the pandemic outburst). According to those numbers, it is evident that all Dodecanese islands receive diverse, but also significant tourism volumes, compared to their size and population (Table 1).

4   Assessing Effectiveness of Tourism Governance in the Dodecanese Islands' Complex

In the following, results obtained out of the implementation of the aforementioned 3-c research methodology (Fig. 1) are presented.

4.1   The Greek Tourism Governance System (C1)

Tourism governance in Greece is the result of a multilevel spatial and developmental policy-making system, which determines the quality of the national tourism policy directions with regard to tourism sustainability and growth, including concerns related to remote, insular and peripheral regions. Decisive role in this governance system plays the Ministry of Tourism, being in charge of the tourism policy and development in Greece. The Ministry sets forward tourism legislation, approves the State's strategic tourism marketing plan, stimulates tourist investments, and focuses on the rise of quality and competitiveness of tourism products of Greece [28]. In doing so, it works in close collaboration with other interested Ministries (e.g. ministry of Environment and Energy); and tourism bodies, such as the Greek National Tourism Organization (GNTO) as the leader of the tourism marketing policy in Greece. Downscaling of tourism policy at the regional and local level is implemented through regional and municipal developmental and spatial plans, programmes and activities, following the national guidelines and being approved by both the Ministry of Tourism and the GNTO.

At the *national level*, GNTO's Marketing Plan 2019–2020 follows a region-based approach, showcasing the hidden attractions of each region and raising awareness of both domestic and inbound visitors in order for an even distribution of tourism flows in Greek regions throughout the year to emerge [28]. Despite the successful outcomes of tourism marketing campaign [29], however, the very essence of tourism planning at the national level seems to face significant challenges, mainly due to the fact that tourism policy directions are outdated at all spatial planning policy levels. This is mainly due to bureaucratic procedures, rendering reviewing and updating of current spatial policies a time-consuming process. In addition, a concrete and comprehensive insular policy is lacking, thus exacerbating sustainability and insularity concerns of respective areas.

In more detail, the current General Framework for Spatial Planning and Sustainable Development (GFSPSD) [30], already institutionalized since 2008, gives a rough direction towards the need to diversify the Greek tourism model, by emphasizing the role of *cultural heritage* towards this end. This, currently outdated, Framework is complemented by a set of sectoral spatial frameworks, including the one for tourism. The latter is under review since 2009, a fact that results in the lack of an effective, nationally-driven spatial and developmental tourism policy in the Greek scenery. In addition, an attempt to establish a Special Framework for Coastal and Insular regions has failed to reach an institutional legitimization. A more optimistic flavour is added to the arsenal of the Greek tourism policy through recent legislations (Law 4582/2018 [31]; Law 4688/2020 [32]), addressing the development of thematic tourism products in alignment with contemporary tourism trends; and aiming at reducing acute seasonality. These recognize sea, spa, health, sports, rural, religious and MICE (Meeting, Incentive, Congress, Event activities) as key tourism growth opportunities. In addition, Law 4770/2021 [33] introduces an integrated maritime policy that favours Greek islands as unique and closely related to marine world places; and reflects on the particular social, economic and environmental challenges introduced by insularity.

Moving downward to the regional/local level, according to Law 3852/2010 [34], these administrative entities are in charge of planning and implementing regional and local developmental plans, funded by Regional Operational and Thematic Programs.

At the *regional level*, and more specifically the South Aegean Region, in which the Dodecanese islands' complex is incorporated, tourism planning is the outcome of the Regional Development Programme (RDP) 2021–2027 [35] and the, outdated since 2003 and currently under review, Regional Framework for Spatial Planning and Sustainable Development (RFSPSD) [36]. RDP is the most important funding mechanism when it comes to tourism policy at this level. According to currently funded projects, the focus is on cultural tourism that promotes more experienced-based, digital, green and inclusive tourism products, addressing already famous and of high importance island entities of both Cyclades and Dodecanese Island complexes [37]. The RFSPSD is the policy document that defines the spatial distribution of regional activities and land uses of the region, tourism included. According to RFSPSD's latest version [36], social and territorial cohesion objectives are of high importance. Achievement of such objectives calls for a place-based approach and locally-driven planning efforts. This is in line with the Shapley's [38] view, arguing that islands can create strong trans-island connections, owning to their uniqueness and specific developmental needs. To deal with this challenge, *four developmental units* are proposed in this RFSPSD's strategy, classifying islands into the: Group 1 - small and underdeveloped islands; Group 2 - islands with developing tourism activity; Group 3 - highly attractive touristic islands; and Group 4: islands facing severe demographic barriers and islets. Specific directions are given for each single group, providing guidance towards a sustainable tourism model and culture-oriented activities. In addition, special attention is placed on "overtourism" impacts, especially for islands of Group 3. According to RFSPSD, responsibility for implementing relevant directions is given to the local level, entitling local municipalities to draft action plans and proceed to action.

At the *local (municipality) level*, local administrations, including the insular ones, are endorsed to further elaborate on the guidelines set at the national and regional level through local development plans; and downscale strategic directions for guiding deployment of local tourism development trails in alignment with available resources and expectations/visions of local population. Such an effort is accomplished within the context of municipalities' *5-year Municipal Operational Plans (MOPs),* sketching, among others, pathways to tourism development. MOPs feature permanent internal procedures and planning processes, targeting the detailed recording, monitoring and assessment of projects and actions that are planned and implemented by each Municipality and the legal entities thereof. Their ultimate goal is to achieve local sustainability objectives, in harmony with the directions of developmental planning at the regional and national level.

From this point of view, MOPs are extremely important – if not the most important – tools for achieving the goals of sustainable local development, tourism included. Focusing on the Dodecanese islands' complex, however, research results on MOPs' deployment is not endorsing. In fact, only 27% of the municipalities of Dodecanese islands own a MOP, dated before 2014; 20% of them have reached only the first stage of completing the MOP; and almost 46% of them never had and are not even in the process of developing such a plan. Only one municipality – island of Kos – has published an updated MOP in 2022 [39]. This situation leads to the conclusion that sustainable development plans/directions are not tightly addressed in islands' municipal agendas, raising thus questions as to how the tourism activity is actually planned in these entities and how the decision-making process is directed. Thus, despite the well-defined strategic policy directions at the regional level, local municipal entities seem to lack capacity, knowledge and human resources for deploying concrete action plans in support of a more sustainable, culture-led tourism narrative in Dodecanese islands. Taking into consideration the Greek islands' tourism brand – 3S / Sea, Sun, Sand – such a deficit seems to put sustainability objectives of these islands at risk, rendering those islands crowded destinations or destinations suffering from overtourism. Examples are the medium-sized islands of Rhodes and Kos, owing a distinct tourism identity, where qualitative and quantitative upgrade of the prevailing tourism model is, among others, endorsed, thus questioning carrying capacity constraints of those islands [40].

4.2 Key Insights into Tourism Governance at Dodecanese Islands' Municipal Level (C2)

For further deepening insight into *local governance practices* for initiating culture-led tourism pathways, in the C2 component of the methodological approach a web-based questionnaire survey is conducted, addressed to municipalities of all Dodecanese islands. A high response rate (80%) is reached in this respect, engaging 12 out of the 15 municipalities in total. Missing are the municipalities of Patmos, Megisti and Rhodes Islands. Out of the above 12 islands taking part in this survey, 27.3% fall into the 'Very Small' category, 45.4% in the 'Small' one and 27.3% in the 'Medium'.

Among the various research questions incorporated in this survey, of key relevance for this work are those identifying the:

i) Disposal of a culture-led tourism development plan as part of a local strategic plan and related MOP; and a means for strengthening islands' position in the tourism map as well as the governance procedures followed in the development of such a plan.
ii) Current penetration and future potential of nature- and culture-related tourism forms.

Key results out of this web-based questionnaire research have as follows.

i) *Culture-led tourism plans and related governance scheme in Dodecanese Islands*

Municipalities' representatives have provided feedback as to the existence of an island's culture-led tourism plan as well as the governance scheme adopted in articulating this plan, i.e. engagement of local administration, community and stakeholders in such a process. In addition, they expressed their statement as to the popularity of respective islands as tourism destinations. Out of the 12 islands engaged in the web-based research, 9 islands fall into the category of "Popular Tourism Destinations"; while 3 of them (Agathonisi, Tilos and Kasos) are considered by the local representatives as less popular ones.

Table 2. State of tourism attractiveness, disposal of cultural/tourism plan and community engagement in Dodecanese islands, Source: Own elaboration based on e-questionnaire responses

Popular/Touristic Destinations	Culture-led tourism plan and governance scheme			
Yes	Own a Cultural/Touristic Plan			
	Yes		No	
	44.4%		55.6%	
	Community engagement			
	Yes	No	-	-
	75.0%	25.0%	-	-
No	Own a Cultural/Touristic Plan			
	Yes		No	
	100.0%		-	
	Community engagement			
	Yes	No	-	-
	100.0%	0%	-	-

From islands falling into the popular tourism destination category (Table 2), more than half of them (55.6%) do not dispose a concrete culture-led tourism plan, implying that the tourism pattern in these islands lacks a holistic, integrated and strategic developmental view for properly downscaling policy directions provided at the national/regional levels, while meeting local visions and expectations. The rest of them (44.4%) dispose such a plan, with 25% of such plans being the product of a 'top-down' approach, lacking thus concern about community engagement in relative planning processes; while 75% of them is the outcome of a 'bottom-up' approach. Quite interesting are results relative to less popular Dodecanese islands where, surprisingly, all of them dispose a culture-led tourism plan, being additionally a product of community engagement. This fact is interpreted as an effort to establish a more strategic tourism planning approach to gain a position in the Dodecanese tourism map.

In order to deepen insight into the substance and the means of community engagement in culture-led tourism participatory planning processes, respective information is requested by municipalities' representatives. Relevant responses reveal two diverse and of high importance issues, namely: i) a significant knowledge deficit as to the meaning and the very essence of participation and co-creation in cultural tourism planning, being rather confused with citizens' participation in local cultural events; ii) adoption of a more passive community engagement model by use of consultation procedures, in alignment with established processes at the national level, lacking however the more active – co-design and co-decide – dimensions of participation. Worth mentioning is that only 2 out of 12 island Municipalities, namely Symi and Karpathos, declare to have "Tourism Boards", acting on a voluntary basis in support of municipality's processes over local sustainable tourism decisions.

ii) *Current and future perspective of alternative forms of tourism in Dodecanese*

Responses of the Dodecanese islands' representatives as to the current state of alternative tourism forms unveil that most of these islands have already undertaken steps towards such tourism pathways. More specifically, in 66.7% of the islands explored, alternative tourism forms are currently integral parts of the local tourism scene. In fact, a wide range of such tourism forms is already in place (Fig. 2), with the most prevailing ones being the: gastronomic tourism (in 21.1% of insular municipalities), cultural tourism (in 13.2%) and nature tourism (in 13.2%). These are also in compliance with already well-established aspects of the Greek tourism narrative, which places the beauty of the Greek landscape, the cultural wealth and the local gastronomy at the heart of the tourism product. However, the abundance of natural and cultural resources of Dodecanese islands [36] demonstrates much wider opportunities than the current penetration of such tourism forms witnesses. That said, the share of cultural tourism in insular municipalities is perceived rather low (13.2%), compared to the real potential of these islands, both in land and at sea. In fact cultural tourism is currently present in small island municipalities, like Agathonisi, Karpathos and Kalymnos, namely islands already acknowledged for their qualitative tourism offer. On the contrary, mass tourism and crowded Dodecanese island destinations, such as Kos, prioritize conference and gastronomic tourism, i.e. alternative forms that best fit to the accommodation and transportation facilities that the larger, mass tourism destinations display. However, there is still enough room for these islands as well for promoting more peaceful, alternative tourism forms in the less crowded parts of their territory, a choice that also offers a means to relieve overwhelmed places of these islands.

Municipal representatives' aspirations as to the future potential of alternative forms of tourism are also requested in the web-based questionnaire research. In this respect, representatives' responses fully converge towards a visionary future end state of their islands, serving sustainable, all year round and resilient tourism forms. They consider alternative tourism forms a highly relevant option for serving sustainability objectives in insular contexts. Cultural tourism, as well as the gastronomic one, namely a form closely related to local food culture and traditional production, seems to be the prevailing forms, gathering 20.9% and 18.6% of responses respectively (Fig. 2). In fact, future aspirations of those participated in the web-based questionnaire research as to the preferable tourism forms are tightly interwoven with the natural and cultural wealth of insular regions. This is also endorsed by the predominance of fishing tourism (14.0%), closely linking

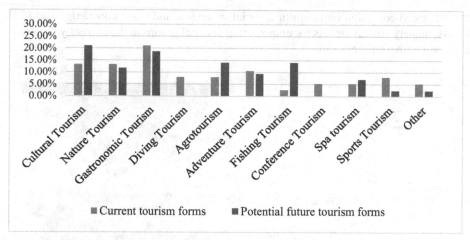

Fig. 2. Current and potential future tourism forms according to local representatives' views in Dodecanese insular municipalities, Source: Own elaboration, based on responses of municipality representatives through e-questionnaire research

the islands' spectacular natural environment and proximity to the marine one; and the agrotourism (14.0%), reflecting acknowledgement of the local agricultural traditional schemes and values.

4.3 Impacts of Tourism on the Dodecanese Islands' Complex (C3)

South Aegean Region, in which the highly acknowledged Dodecanese and Cyclades island complexes administratively belong, possesses a distinguished position in the Greek tourism geography. This is also witnessed through statistical data, displaying the share of this region in hotel beds, owning the highest percentage among the Greek regions in 2019 (26.1%) [26]. That said, South Aegean Region lies in the heart of the tourism activity in Greece, a position that seems to steadily keep in the future as well [41]. Due to this position, South Aegean Region owes the 2nd largest Gross Domestic Product (GDP)/capita in 2019 – following the Attica Region – rising to 18.655 €/capita, also larger than the national rate of that year (17.092 €/capita) [42]. The contribution of tourism is remarkable in this respect. However, having in mind the prevailing mass pattern of the tourism model, critical concerns are raised as to the social and environmental impacts of the Region's developmental profile. Such concerns are clearly demonstrated by the European Social Progress Index for the year 2020 [43], assessing the social progress of European regions at the NUTS2 level. This is calculated by use of twelve components (Fig. 3a) incorporating a total of fifty-five comparable social and environmental indicators, purposefully excluding economic aspects. According to this Index, South Aegean Region performs significantly low, namely it belongs to the ones displaying the lowest performance (highlighted with light purple in Fig. 3b); and scoring with the lowest grade (51.31) both in Greece (country average: 56.5) and the Mediterranean regions as a whole. A deeper insight into indicators composing the European Social Progress Index reveals the low performance of the South Aegean Region in e.g. advanced education opportunities, social inclusion, and basic knowledge and ICT access, namely critical aspects for empowering societal groups in the currently dynamic and competitive environment.

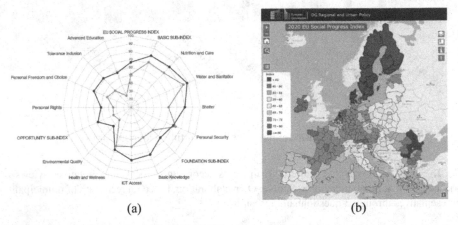

(a)   (b)

Fig. 3. EU Social Progress Index in EU NUTS2 regions: a) Indicators' scoreboard showing performance in the EU (in blue) and South Aegean (in red) regions; b) Mapping of the spatial distribution of the index in all EU regions, Source: [43]

These deficits in the social and environmental realm are also confirmed by the Regional Policy Monitor Report [44], indicating the region's performance towards Sustainable Development Goals (SDGs). In fact, South Aegean Region has so far failed to achieve nine SDGs (namely SDGs 1, 2, 3, 4, 6, 9, 10, 11 and 16); with more than 30% of its inhabitants being at risk of poverty or social exclusion. Minor challenges are also reported in the achievement of two more SDGs before 2030 (namely SDGs 8 and 15), while a better performance is noticed as to the SDG 14.

Considering the significant interregional inequalities among islands of the South Aegean Region as well as the different profiles and tourism load of the island destinations this region incorporates, an effort to identify impacts of tourism on each specific island is carried out. Towards this end, a set of indicators are used (see Table 3) for assessing – directly or indirectly – the social and environmental impact of tourism activity on each single island of the Dodecanese complex.

In more detail, indicators used have as follows:

- *Tourism Intensity* [Total tourist accommodation (beds) / resident]. Tourist accommodation reflects the actual bed capacity of each island, including both commercial (hotel beds, camping spots) as defined by the Greek National Statistic Service 2019 data [26] and Airbnb beds capacity, using the most recent data (2022) from the Inside Airbnb Platform [45]. This number is divided by the permanent population (2021 provisional data by ELSTAT) to implicitly show societal pressure emanating from tourism activity on all Dodecanese islands. The higher the score the highest the impact and the more overcrowded the destination.

Table 3. Data about the tourism reality of the Dodecanese Island complex, Source: [25, 26, 45]

Municipalities of Dodecanese Islands	A. Tourism Intensity	B. Tourism Density	C. Tourists / residents ratio	D. Population density adjusted to tourism flows	E. Change in population density due to Tourism (%)
Agathonisi	0.21	3.19	16.77	252.15	1577
Astypalaia	1.68	24.22	17.16	247.92	1616
Chalki	1.25	21.19	1.00	16.92	0
Kalymnos	0.23	36.81	6.55	1051.12	555
Karpathos	1.45	30.96	19.91	424.24	1891
Kasos	0.22	4.03	5.25	97.47	425
Kos	1.72	219.29	36.47	4647.37	3547
Leros	0.32	48.37	6.11	921.91	511
Lipsi	0.82	40.30	17.89	882.23	1689
Nisyros	0.55	13.77	8.76	220.77	776
Patmos	1.46	137.50	19.06	1800.76	1806
Rhodes	1.03	91.65	22.43	2002.90	2143
Symi	0.74	31.76	75.45	3240.05	7445
Tilos	1.52	18.02	24.06	285.28	2306
Megisti	0.70	44.91	11.51	736.36	1051

- *Tourism Density* (Total tourist accommodation (beds) / island's surface). This indicator is calculated as the actual number of bed capacity in each island, including both commercial (hotel beds, camping spots) [26] and Airbnb beds capacity (2022) [45] divided by the island's surface (area in km^2) [26]. Its value is used as a proxy for the environmental impact of tourism activity on the island (e.g. expansion of the built environment due to tourist accommodation and other infrastructure), representing land consumption for serving tourist activities. This indicator becomes particularly important in case of insular municipalities, taking into consideration scarcity of the land resource.
- *Tourist / resident ratio.* This indicator is the ratio of the total number of tourist arrivals (plane and boat - 2019 data) divided by the total permanent 2021 population [25]. Its value reflects the pressure exerted on local infrastructures, natural and cultural resources, local identity and cohesion, built environment, etc.
- *Population density adjusted to tourism flows.* This indicator is featured by the sum of the total tourist arrivals (2019 data) plus the local population (2021 provisional data), divided by the island's size [26]. It provides a "population density adjusted to tourism flows" figure, which reflects the impact of tourism on the rising of population density.

- *Change in population density due to tourism.* This change is calculated by subtracting from the "Population Density adjusted to tourism flows" the island's "Population Density" (see Table 1). It displays the actual change of population per square kilometer in the timespan of a whole year; useful for realizing the potential strain that tourism can put on local resources and infrastructures, as well as the environmental and cultural impacts that may arise from high tourism volumes.

Interpretation of the values presented in Table 3 leads to the following conclusions:

- *Tourism Intensity:* small islands like Astypalaia (1.68), Tilos (1.52), Karpathos (1.45) and Chalki (1.25), although less known destinations of South Aegean Region, display high scores. Small island's size and population show that tourism activity can severely impact the natural/cultural resources and the social structure.
- *Tourism Density:* a totally different outcome is presented when it comes to this indicator, where the pressure on the natural environmental and landscape by the deployment of tourism accommodation (beds) is assessed. In fact, already famous Dodecanese tourism destinations are leading the scores, e.g. Kos (219.29), Patmos (137.50) and Rhodes (91.65), reflecting the outcome of their mass tourism profile.
- *Tourist / resident ratio:* this is an estimate of how many times the population of the island increases due to tourism over the timespan of a whole year. Through this indicator, the pressure exerted on the island's infrastructure becomes apparent, e.g. increase in water demand, pressure on drainage and waste management systems, to name but a few. A quite unique and of high concern example is the island of Symi, with its annual population being increased by around 75 times due to tourism arrivals. Next follows the island of Kos (score 36.47), followed by the islands of Tilos, Rhodes, Karpathos and Astypalaia (scoring approx. around 20). It is interesting to see that scores of top tourism large islands like Rhodes that incorporate large settlements, services, airport etc., are similar to those of the (very) small islands of Tilos and Astypalaia, which apparently cannot deal with that kind of tourism pressure.
- *Change in population density due to tourism:* calculation of this indicator is more effective for interpreting the impacts of tourism on island contexts. According to its values, Symi seems to suffer from an excessive population density change due to tourism (74.45%), testing durability in societal an environmental terms. Same holds for the island of Tilos, where performance in this indicator confirms concerns as to the impact of tourism on very small islands of the Dodecanese complex.

5 Discussion and Conclusions

Good governance is considered as the "missing link" in order for sustainable tourism outcomes to be attained, by: moving forwards from policy directions to real actions [46]; and downscaling from the national to the local level. Having this in mind, in this paper the multi-level tourism governance in Greece is sketched, exploring linkages at both the vertical – interactions among the national, regional and local policy making – and the horizontal level – interactions among stakeholders within the island context. Such an exploration aims at assessing whether current governance structures act in a supporting or demoralizing manner in insular regions in their effort to pursue a sustainable tourism model; and is accomplished in this work by a combination of qualitative and quantitative research. The former gets insight into a range of policy documents currently in force; while the latter attempts to quantify social, environmental and economic impacts of the prevailing tourism model in the Dodecanese islands' complex, as a rough proxy of the effectiveness of the present tourism governance structure.

Results obtained show that tourism governance in Greece follows a hierarchical – top-down – structure, with the Greek state owning a dominant role and displaying rather weak bonds with the regional and the local level in articulating the national tourism policy. At this level, a strong tourism marketing campaign is shaped, empowering the Greek islands' position in the international competitive tourism arena. However, the lack of nation-wide updated developmental and spatial plans as a means to embed contemporary challenges (e.g. climate change, overtourism) to specific strategic tourism directions as well as the absence of monitoring schemes for regularly adjusting these directions in alignment with the type, volume and distribution of tourism flows, renders most Greek destinations, islands included, quite fragile against uncontrolled tourism development and highly vulnerable to contemporary risks. The well-established mass model – the 'myth of Greece' – for many decades, as witnessed by the island municipalities of the Dodecanese complex, has placed a remarkable burden on the local level. Islands' local administrations, being in charge of implementing strategic tourism choices in their territory lack, in most of the cases, relevant capacity and human resources; and thus fail to articulate local developmental and spatial plans embedding tourism and properly specializing state's strategic policy directions. As a result, tourism development in those islands is currently formed in a fragmented and transient manner, mainly driven by private initiatives that focus on economic benefits and leave aside sustainability and resilience objectives.

Both the web-based questionnaire (C2) and the quantitative research (C3) show a rather uncontrolled tourism development stream that has already negative repercussions on social and environmental dimensions of the Dodecanese islands' complex. Indicators used to assess economic and mainly social and environmental impacts reveal that highly-rated island tourism destinations, e.g. Kos, Patmos and Rhodes, but also very small islands, e.g. Chalki, Astypalaia, Tilos, Symi, although quite different in terms of tourism attractiveness, all score pretty high in tourism density and intensity. This reveals a certain vertical governance deficit, coupled with barriers applying to horizontal governance schemes at the local (islands) level. The latter is featured by the lack of a collaboratively-built, strategic tourism plan, seeking to conform to sustainability concerns and contemporary challenges of tourism development. Such deficits in insular contexts can definitely result in cultural deterioration, social disruption, loss of community identity and a sense of disconnection between local residents and visitors.

Last but not least, culture, as a currently driving force for competing in the tourism arena and a comparative advantage of insular regions, is integrated into Dodecanese islands' tourism products in a rather traditional way, lacking the leading role this should have in these land compartments [47]. The value of culture as a key pillar in Dodecanese islands' branding is however realized by municipalities' representatives; and forms a main part of the future vision of tourism in their islands. Cultural tourism forms, as well as alternative tourism products, promoting islands' connection with the maritime world (e.g., fishing tourism), are given priority in this vision. However, capacity constraints in terms of human resources, both in quantitative and qualitative terms; power relationships, serving economic interests of tourism to the detriment of social and environmental concerns; incomplete implementation of developmental and spatial tools; and, most importantly, lack of a commonly-shared and cooperatively built future vision of islands as peaceful and inclusive destinations seem currently to be the main barriers that need to be overcome. Successful confrontation of these barriers implies the necessity for tourism governance improvements at both the vertical and especially the horizontal level, rendering island communities the 'key actors' in shaping a desirable future development of their land, within which tourism follows a fair and sustainable pattern and spreads its benefits sectorally, spatially and temporally.

References

1. World Tourism Organization and United Nations Development Programme: Tourism and the Sustainable Development Goals – Journey to 2030. UNWTO, Madrid (2017)
2. World Tourism Organization (UNWTO), Centre of Expertise Leisure, Tourism & Hospitality; NHTV Breda University of Applied Sciences, NHL Stenden University of Applied Sciences: 'Overtourism'? – Understanding and Managing Urban Tourism Growth beyond Perceptions, Executive Summary. UNWTO, Madrid (2018). https://doi.org/10.18111/9789284420070
3. Responsible Tourism: OverTourism. www.responsibletourismpartnership.org/overtourism. Accessed 2 Apr 2023
4. Andolina, C., Signa, G., Tomasello, A., Mazzola, A., Vizzini, S.: Environmental effects of tourism and its seasonality on Mediterranean islands: the contribution of the Interreg MED BLUEISLANDS project to build up an approach towards sustainable tourism. Environ. Dev. Sustain. 23(6), 8601–8612 (2020). https://doi.org/10.1007/s10668-020-00984-8
5. Hall, C.M.: Changing paradigms and global change: from sustainable to steady-state tourism. Tour. Recreat. Res. 35, 131–143 (2010). https://doi.org/10.1080/02508281.2010.11081629
6. Ruggieri, G., Calò, P.: Tourism dynamics and sustainability: a comparative analysis between mediterranean islands—evidence for post-COVID-19 strategies. Sustainability 14(7), 4183 (2022). https://doi.org/10.3390/su14074183
7. Briguglio, L., Avellino, M.: Has Overtourism Reached the Maltese Islands? Occasional Papers on Islands and Small States, 2019/01 (2019). ISSN 1024-6282
8. Cruz, M.S., Zaragoza, M.P.P.: Analysis of the accommodation density in coastal tourism areas of insular destinations from the perspective of overtourism. Sustainability 11(11), 3031 (2019). https://doi.org/10.3390/su11113031
9. Dlabaja, C.: Caring for the Island city: venetians reclaiming the city in times of over-tourism: contested representations, narratives and infrastructures. Shima 15(1), 166–185 (2021). https://doi.org/10.21463/shima.117
10. Majdak, P., de Almeida, A.M.M.: Pre-emptively managing overtourism by promoting rural tourism in low-density areas: lessons from madeira. Sustainability 14(2), 757 (2022). https://doi.org/10.3390/su14020757
11. Constantoglou, M., Klothaki, T.: How Much Tourism is Too Much? Stakeholder's Perceptions on Overtourism, Sustainable Destination Management during the Pandemic of COVID-19 Era in Santorini Island Greece. Tour. Hosp. Manag. 9(5), 288–313 (2021). https://doi.org/10.17265/2328-2169/2021.05.004
12. Varga, P., Terrier, A.: Is There a Solution to Overtourism? Lessons from Boracay Island, The Philippines. EHL Insights (2019)

13. Koutsi, D., Stratigea, A.: Unburying hidden land and maritime cultural potential of small islands in the mediterranean for tracking heritage-led local development paths. Heritage **2**(1), 938–966 (2019). https://doi.org/10.3390/heritage2010062
14. Koutsi, D., Stratigea, A.: Sustainable and Resilient Management of Underwater Cultural Heritage (UCH) in Remote Mediterranean Islands: A Methodological Framework. Heritage **4**, 3469–3496 (2021). https://doi.org/10.3390/heritage4040192
15. Olsen, D.H.: Cultural heritage and tourism in the developing world: a regional perspective. J. Heritage Tour. **5**(3), 251–252 (2010). https://doi.org/10.1080/17438731003737539
16. Dłużewska, A., Giampiccoli, A.: Enhancing island tourism's local benefits: a proposed community-based tourism-oriented general model. Sustain. Dev. **29**(1), 272–283 (2021). https://doi.org/10.1002/sd.2141
17. Terkenli, T.S., Georgoula, V.: Tourism and cultural sustainability: views and prospects from cyclades. Greece. Sustainability **14**(1), 307 (2022). https://doi.org/10.3390/su14010307
18. COM(2007)621 final: Agenda for a Sustainable and Competitive European Tourism, Commission of the European Communities, Brussels 19.10.2007
19. 15441/22: The European Agenda for Tourism 2030, Council of the European Union, Brussels, 1.12.2022
20. UNEP-UNWTO: Making Tourism More Sustainable – A Guide for Policy Makers. UNWTO, Madrid, Spain, ISBN: 92-807-2507-6 (UNEP) (2005)
21. Dos Anjos, F.A., Kennell, J.: Tourism Governance and Sustainable Development. Sustainability **11**(16), 4257 (2019). https://doi.org/10.3390/su11164257
22. Roxas, F.M.Y., Rivera, J.P.R., Gutierrez, E.L.M.: Mapping stakeholders' roles in governing sustainable tourism destinations. Tour. Hosp. Manag. **45**, 387–398 (2020). https://doi.org/10.1016/j.jhtm.2020.09.005
23. Dangi, T.B., Petrick, J.F.: Enhancing the role of tourism governance to improve collaborative participation, responsiveness, representation and inclusion for sustainable community-based tourism: a case study. Int. J. Tour. Cities. **7**(4), 1029–1048 (2021). https://doi.org/10.1108/IJTC-10-2020-0223
24. Region of South Aegean: https://www.aegeanislands.gr/el/aegean-place/geographic-information/. Accessed 22 Mar 2023
25. ELSTAT: 2021 Provisional Population and Infrastructure Data (2023). https://www.statistics.gr/2021-census-res-pop-results. Accessed 9 Apr 2023
26. Spilanis, I.: Tourism in the Aegean, the Tourist Activity, its Results and Effects in the Regions and Islands of the South and North Aegean. Aegean Sustainable Tourism Observatory (2021). https://tourismobservatory-n.ba.aegean.gr/index.php/ektheseis/ (in Greek). Accessed 30 Mar 2023
27. Spilanis, I., Kizos, T.: Atlas of the Islands. University of the Aegean, Mytilene, Greece (2015). ISBN 9789608803114
28. OECD: Greece (2020). https://www.oecd-ilibrary.org/sites/f3180e03-en/index.html?itemId=/content/component/f3180e03-en. Accessed 30 Mar 2023
29. Visit Greece: https://www.visitgreece.gr/islands/. Accessed 28 Mar 2023
30. General Framework for Spatial Planning and Sustainable Development (GFSPSD): 128A/03.07.2008
31. Law 4582/2018: Thematic Tourism – Special Forms of Tourism – Arrangements for the Modernization of the Institutional Framework in the Field of Tourism and Tourism Education - Support for Tourism Entrepreneurship and other Provisions. 208/A/2018
32. Law 4688/2020: Special Forms of Tourism, Provisions for Tourism Development and Other Provisions. 110/A/2020
33. Law 4770/2021: Integrated Maritime Policy in the Island Area, Provisions for Compliance with International Navigation Obligations and the Upgrade of the Hellenic Coast Guard and Special Arrangements for Digitization and Aid in General. 15/A/2021

34. Law 3852/2010: New Architecture of Local Government and Decentralized Administration - Kallikratis Programme. 87/A/2010
35. C(2022) 6252 final: Regional Developmental Programme (RDP) 2021–2027. https://pepna.gr/sites/default/files/sfc2021-PRG-2021EL16FFPR018-1.2.pdf (in Greek). Accessed 25 Mar 2023
36. ENVIPLAN: Evaluation, Revision and Specialization of the Regional Framework for Spatial Planning and Sustainable Development (RFSPSD) of the South Aegean Region. Stage B1 (2020). shorturl.at/otFQU. Accessed 4 Mar 2023
37. South Aegean Region's Managing Authority: https://pepna.gr/el/pep-notio-aigaio-2021-2027/programma-me-mia-matia-entagmenes-praxeis. Accessed 25 Mar 2023
38. Sharpley, R.: Island Tourism or Tourism on Islands? Tour. Recreat. Res. **37**(2), 167–172 (2012). https://doi.org/10.1080/02508281.2012.11081701
39. Municipality of Kos: Municipal Operation Plan (2022). shorturl.at/hlqGO (in Greek). Accessed 2 Apr 2023
40. INSETE: South Aegean Region | Dodecanese. https://insete.gr/greektourism2030/perifereia-notiou-aigaiou-dodekanisa/ (2022). Accessed 25 Mar 2023
41. GTP: South Aegean Regions Greece's Tourism Champ in 2021 (2022). https://news.gtp.gr/2022/04/04/south-aegean-region-greeces-tourism-champ-in-2021/ (in Greek). Accessed 25 Mar 2023
42. ELSTAT: Gross Domestic Product for the Year 2019 and Revised Figures for the Years 2012–2018 (2022). https://www.statistics.gr/documents/20181/c50afbab-cb2e-8627-8f6f-be718c393dc5 (in Greek). Accessed 25 Mar 2023
43. EU Social Progress Index 2020: https://ec.europa.eu/regional_policy/information-sources/maps/social-progress/2020_en#chart. Accessed 30 Mar 2023
44. Regional Policy Monitor: The Progress of the Greek Regions in relation to the Sustainable Development Goals (SDGs) (2022). shorturl.at/jvKN2. Accessed 30 Mar 2023
45. Inside Airbnb Platform: Data for South Aegean. insideairbnb.com/south-aegean. Accessed 31 Mar 2023
46. Torres-Delgado, A., López Palomeque, F.: The growth and spread of the concept of sustainable tourism: the contribution of institutional initiatives to tourism policy. Tour Manag Perspect. **4**, 1 (2012). https://doi.org/10.1016/j.tmp.2012.05.001
47. Poulios, I., Touloupa, S.: Tourism, Cultural Management, Local Society and Sustainable Development. https://www.citybranding.gr/2016/02/blog-post_22.html (in Greek). Accessed 2 Apr 2023

Public Participation Project
for the Sustainability of the Greek Island Gavdos

Eleni Mougiakou[1,2]($\boxtimes$) (iD) and Emmy Karimali[1]

[1] Commonspace Coop, Akakiou 1 - 3 and Ipirou 60, 10439 Athens, Greece
mougiakou@commonspace.gr
[2] Agricultural University of Athens, Iera Odos 75, 11855 Athens, Greece
https://www.commonspace.gr, https://www.participatorylab.org

Abstract. The "Public Participation Planning Project for the Sustainability of Greek Island Gavdos" is a multidisciplinary approach designed for a small island located under Crete, in Greece. This work seeks to deal with the decreasing population, lack of job/social opportunities, and inadequate infrastructure through public involvement. The sustainable development plan aims to create communities by including inhabitants, actors, and agents interested in participating in the Cultural, Local, Energy, Production, Research, and Visitors' Communities. The implemented toolkit includes interactive and participatory workshops, digital applications, tailor-made questionnaires, and innovative handcrafted models (such as the spatial SWOT analysis). The participation is surprisingly vivid by any relevant actor during the workshops, the mapping events, and brainstorming meetings. This paper is focused on the methodology, phases, and step-by-step knowledge to organize and implement participatory planning processes in sustainable development projects of the island, mountainous and isolated municipalities. At the same time, it can be used as a methodological guide for practitioners and institution that plan public space, development opportunities, measures, and actions, to promote participation and engagement in public projects.

Keywords: Participatory planning · community building · public participation · local communities · Gavdos island · participatory workshops · participatory tools · sustainability · local development

1 Introduction

The southernmost European point is a small island facing double insularity, geographically and politically isolated [1], dependent on and located under Crete island (Greece) (Fig. 1).

Gavdos island is a top-rated alternative touristic destination with a magnificent natural environment facing threats of depopulation and degradation of the natural environment. In 2017, the Municipality of Gavdos[1], in collaboration with the Management

---

[1] https://gavdos.gr/.

© The Author(s), under exclusive license to Springer Nature Switzerland AG 2023
O. Gervasi et al. (Eds.): ICCSA 2023 Workshops, LNCS 14110, pp. 307–320, 2023.
https://doi.org/10.1007/978-3-031-37123-3_23

Fig. 1. The location of Gavdos island, the southernmost point of Europe.

Organization Unit for Development Programs (MOU),[2] took the initiative to set the goals for the first "Public Participation Planning Project for the Sustainability of Greek Island Gavdos", an ambitious project innovative for Greek standards. Our team[3] works as an expert group in participatory planning and community engagement. Our role is to support the drafting of the development plan like an expert at the required participatory planning methods, tools, and techniques; the final scheme of the development plan and the funding are carried out by a state organization (MOU). Through experience and expertise, we concluded that the starting line and the most crucial prerequirement for elaborating the suggested plan is adopting democratic and open processes. We seek the participation of the local community in the co-production of public policy from the beginning of the planning process. Therefore, the aim of the project is the formation and development of an integrated, holistic, and inclusive approach, the growth of knowledge and abilities of the locals and other stakeholders, the coordination and support of the local community, and in general, the development of a local-oriented activity and participation plan. The essential innovation -and at the same time, the challenge- of the plan is the interrelation between local, regional, and national development goals for an isolated, small, and island community such as Gavdos.

Remote small island and mountainous areas, characterized by difficulties of accessibility and transport encountering geographical isolation, often prove advantageous for implementing integrated sustainable development programs and for applying participatory planning methods and procedures, which small-scale favors. However, practitioners and public authorities need more comprehensive, place-based, topic-related methodological steps.

This paper illustrates the concept of participatory planning and distinguishes it from typical consultation processes. It describes the methodological steps of participatory planning, which is multifaceted and not limited to the inhabitants of each study area, nor just to the public in general. The paper highlights the process of identifying the subject of the participatory actions as a necessary step, and by no means self-evident, for the organization and implementation of participatory planning for sustainable development. In addition, participatory planning methods, techniques, and tools are developed in detail

---

[2] https://www.mou.gr/en/pages/default.aspx.

[3] COMMONSPACE (CS), https://en.commonspace.gr/gavdos-communities.

and in phases to include all its dimensions. This paper is also a toolkit for participatory research in remote areas and covers the broadest range of possible uses.

2 Methodology of Participatory Planning and Community Building Procedure

In this paper, the main focus is on the methodological approach established for this project and the different steps followed. The proposed methodology is place-based and community-based, whereas the Landscape Democracy approach is adopted [2].

The following diagram[4] (see Fig. 2) shows the main methodological steps of the Participatory Planning & Community Building Procedure. The participatory process consists of three phases:

- Phase 1 (2017) - Preliminary work: Agenda setting, framing the problem, mapping the terrain, gathering input and ideas, drafting the pillars of sustainable development vision
- Phase 2 (2018) - Participatory plan and initial steps: State goals and objectives, start stakeholder analysis, create working groups and teams, draft participation plan and communication strategy, and branding. Online questionnaire/SWOT to update preliminary input.
- Phase 3 (2019) - Participatory workshops: Organize and implement participatory processes. Evaluate and update. Disseminate results and raise awareness.

Essential Elements of the Project. To achieve a sustainable development plan for Gavdos based on the visions, interests, and needs of its residents, current, and future, the critical elements are:

- Recognition and understanding of place, landscape, and history. Recording current problems and future opportunities. Using complementary digital tools, like the Public Participacion WebGIS platform (ppGIS, ppWebGIS).
- Extensive stakeholder analysis: residents, agents, visitors, researchers, producers, and potential new residents.
- Develop a strategic communication, public awareness campaign, and participatory plan.
- Perform participatory workshops producing an action plan for the sustainable development model of Gavdos.
- Ongoing assessment and consultation of the evolution of the process. A process parallels the overall plan.

---

[4] Created with Miro app – Mind map.

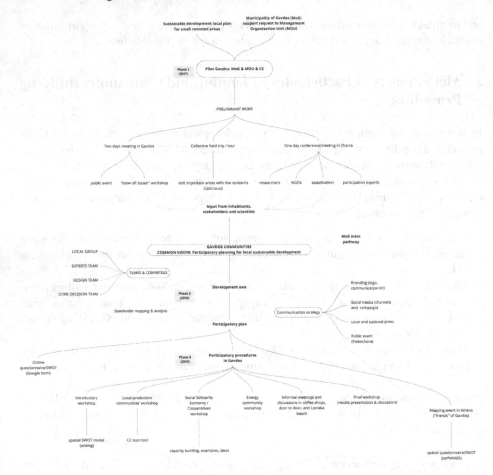

Fig. 2. The methodological scheme of participatory procedures for sustainable development of small remote areas.

Public Interest and Public Involvement. The scheme that describes the extent of the Public Participation Spectrum [3] to plan actions appropriately is studied. As an outcome, the five levels of participation for this project are:

1. Public information
2. Feedback from the public
3. Inclusion of the public
4. Cooperation with the public
5. Empowering the public, wherein the case of Development Plans for isolated areas is the implementation stage after planning.

The following paragraphs describe the participatory methods and tools and highlight the main results.

2.1 Development Goals and Participation Objectives

The next step is to set the public participation objectives concerning each development goal (Table 1). The goals of the sustainable development plan emerged from the results of all the preliminary participatory procedures and were refined at the first meetings of the core team. Each goal of the sustainable development plan corresponds to a set of public participation procedures' objectives.

Table 1. Goals of the sustainable development plan and the objectives of public participation.

Sustainable development plan goals	Public participation objectives
Goal 1: Retention of Existing Population	• Involve residents in development planning • Inform them at every step of decision making • Formulate alternatives • Build the communities
Goal 2. Population growth, attraction of new residents	• Identify potential new residents • Map their skills and desires • Keep up to date on the development plan procedures • Participate in the final consultation
Goal 3. Energy autonomy, creation of energy communities	• Map the energy needs of residents, infrastructure, visitors, and businesses • Jointly envision energy autonomy • Design the energy agenda together and keep everyone informed of developments • Build energy communities and develop synergies with other productive activities
Goal 4. Protection of the landscape and the environment	• Map the social values of the landscape and the environment • Increase awareness and awareness of the island's protection, both for residents and businesses and for visitors • Provide continuous and thorough information on protection zones, legislation, forestry, etc
Goal 5. Increase cooperation, collectivity, co-management, the feeling that the development plan is public ownership	• The enduring goal of the sustainable development plan and the participatory processes

2.2 Selection of Methods and Techniques

The aim is to create a methodology with interconnected tools that provide information relevant to all aspects of sustainable development [4]. Qualitative and quantitative [5] information is collected through digital questionnaires (GETSDI platform, Google forms, GIS-CLOUD spatial form). The required tools [6, 7] used to support the abovementioned goals are shown in the following table (Table 2).

Table 2. Required tools for the accomplishment of the goals.

Goals 1–5	Social media Fieldwork Newsletter Press release Online questionnaires
Goals 1,3,5	Public hearing Focus Groups Questionnaires and interviews Spatial questionnaires (interactive maps)
Goals 1–5	Thematic workshops Design workshops Citizens' Advisory Committee
Goals 1–5	Coordination Committee Committee of experts

2.3 Analysis of Involved Actors, Their Contribution, and Their Responsibility

People and agents can be involved, receive information, and participate in consultations and planning processes in different ways. Four groups of actors have been selected in order to target and then input a Stakeholder Plan:

- The inhabitants of Gavdos
- The municipality, the prefecture, and other public agencies
- The scientists and the academic community in general
- The island's 'friends' and visitors

The Stakeholder Plan [8], adapted to the local needs, is a double input matrix that contains information about the degree of influence and impact of each stakeholder and the engagement and tracking strategy for who is involved and therefore called upon, contributing to the efficient implementation and communication of the campaign.

2.4 Program and Communication

During this process, the detailed timetable and programming, the communication campaign, and the evaluation of the work done are designed. The timetable had to determine the exact steps assigned to specific dates, which had undoubtedly been modified during the project. The communication campaign was conducted through the Media (Newspapers, TV), Facebook, Instagram, Twitter, mailing lists, Facebook events, posters on the island, meetings, and phone calls to inform, attract and empower the potential participants.

3   The Toolkit

Given the particularities of the case, we have selected from a palette of options some general techniques that could help us understand the broad context of participatory planning. The most important are dialogue techniques, exercises, case studies, role-playing, brainstorming, and field trip.

3.1   Determination of the Issue

During the first field trip, a visit was made to all the island's main areas. This tour was the first stage of participatory planning, referring to study area identification and brainstorming. This method is essential for the experts, study and research teams, and residents. The residents re-identify their place and spatially identify problems and challenges through this process. For this tour, a digital tool (giscloud) was used to record collective narratives. The working group members could record geotagged notes, photographs, recordings, and sounds from the points of interest during the tour. These geotagged data were collected through a cloud-form, organized by sector (Primary, Secondary, Services, Natural Environment), and flagged as Positive / Negative or as Idea / Problem.

3.2   Spatial SWOT

The spatial SWOT [9, 10] is an interdisciplinary new tool that was applied/used during the introductive workshop. We introduced two different spatialized SWOT models handcrafted by the workshop participants. After they cogitated on maps and exchanged ideas, they altogether created two models. The first was a spatial SWOT analysis model that concerned critical economic sectors (Fishery, Agriculture, Livestock, Tourism, and Culture). The second model concerned the environment: Energy, Infrastructure, and Natural Environment/Landscape. This tool's main principle was allocating every remark to its specific location. This mechanism provides detailed information, such as the opportunity for touristic development on a beach or the inadequate infrastructure facilities in a particular island settlement. We chose sticks in four colors representing each category of SWOT and papers in different colors representing each economic sector and environment subdivision. Then the stick and the paper were attached as a flag to flag the remarks of the participants, who were impressively creative and enthusiastic during the operation. The following picture (Fig. 3) is the outcome.

All analog data were digitized on GIS and integrated into the spatial questionnaire/digital spatial SWOT results. Those integrated data resulted in helpful information used in the Islandscape Character Assessment study, which is contacted in parallel and collaboration with the main participatory procedures [11].

3.3   Participatory Workshops

In thematic participatory workshops, the goal is to outline the functional space for those involved through design, brainstorming, and information and transfer of expert knowledge. These are in-depth designing workshops (on maps or text, depending on the

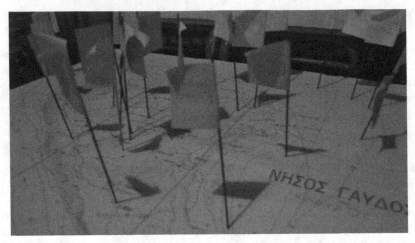

Fig. 3. The (analog) spatial SWOT model.

subject) of the individual themes. In order to have meaningful participation of people, some insight for each topic of discussion and through presentations of the necessary information is provided.

Between March 28 and April 1, 2019, Gavdos' residents actively participated in workshops taking place at the primary school of the island. The high participation and the vivid interest in recording the island's issues, problems, and opportunities led to the successful completion of the third phase (see Fig. 2) of the Sustainable Development Plan based on Participatory Planning techniques. The locals reflected their ideas, opinions, and concerns regarding the future of the island following (and constructing) a democratic process and productive dialogue. Five participatory workshops are organized: the introductive one, one about local production communities; one about social solidarity economy; one about energy communities; and the concluding (final) one gathering all results.

The Introductory Workshop. The introductory workshop initiated the procedure with presentations from the facilitators, the mayor, and representatives from the state organization. The workshop aimed to discuss in groups the strengths and weaknesses, opportunities and threats, and through group work, to rig the (analog) spatial SWOT of the island, as described above. The involvement of the locals was very dynamic not only in terms of their number but also regarding the participation of each individual. For four whole hours, people of all ages and backgrounds were divided into groups and sat around tables to capture their opinions, concerns, and ideas about the future of their island. By prolonging the foreseen time of the workshop, they went beyond what was required, laying the foundations for an entirely democratic process and a constructive dialogue that offered organizers and designing team of the development program information that could not otherwise be obtained. Through the introductory workshop, the locals noted the strong points of the island to be the natural environment and the serenity that the island offers; as weak points, the isolation and the problems with waste management and water supply; as opportunities, the restoration of the old settlements and alternative tourism. Finally, as threats emerged - among others - hydrocarbon mines, the conversion of farmland into forests, and free grazing.

The Local-Production Communities' Workshop. In the Local-production communities' workshop, all participants assessed the production opportunities using a tool oriented toward Community Capital assessment (Community Capital Scan-tool) [12]. Additionally, they wrote and presented their suggestions about the potential productive plans for Gavdos and their involvement in them. This process created the basis for identifying possible synergies between different sectors and actors locally and regionally (Fig. 4).

Fig. 4. Participants discussing and assessing on Community Capital Scan-tool.

The Workshop for the Social Solidarity Economy (SSE). The workshop for the Social Solidarity Economy (SSE) consisted of two presentations. The first presentation explained SSE and cooperatives, while the second gave examples of good practices in Greece and abroad. It was mainly focused on agriculture, tourism, and energy.

The Workshop for the Energy Community. The workshop for the energy community started with an introductory presentation regarding the content and the core of energy communities and the new legal framework for them. The main discussion concerned the possibility of founding such a community in Gavdos, with the participation of the local authorities and several local agents. The pros and cons, as well as the opportunities and constraints, were analyzed in detail with the help of free dialogue and brainstorming technics.

The Final Workshop. During the final workshop, locals attended a presentation summarizing all the information the previous workshops produced. They had the opportunity to be informed about all the results from the analysis, along with some essential themes and ideas that emerged throughout all the workshops. At the same time, there was space and time for synthesis and collective brainstorming regarding future steps. Furthermore, as shown in Fig. 5, the local citizens filled out the Stakeholders' matrix diagram [13] and assessed some of the final proposals for the sustainable development plan.

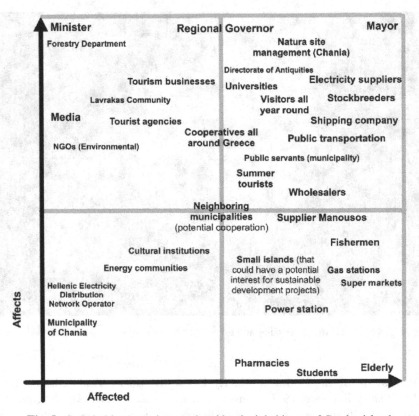

Fig. 5. Stakeholders' matrix completed by the inhabitants of Gavdos island.

3.4 Digital Tools

A crucial step is gathering the people's opinions, both locals and visitors, through interactive maps and digital questionnaires.

Collective Field Trip and Data Collection Form. A collaborative field trip/tour was organized preliminary (2017) with the residents. An online spatial form was created,[5] capturing geotagged notes, photos, and audio. The input concerned the main sectors (production of goods and services, nature, culture, etc.), and the information was categorized as "positive/negative" and "Idea/Challenge."

Online Questionnaire/SWOT. Following (2018), appropriate questionnaires were distributed online during the initial steps (Google form) of the second phase (see Fig. 2).[6] Their answers provided us with helpful material about the characteristics of the island, together with the threats it faces. A similar questionnaire is distributed to the Experts Group. The results of the online SWOT are used as an opening presentation to the inhabitants of Gavdos during the Introductory Workshop. That is a good starting point to frame the discussion.

Spatial Questionnaire/ppGIS. An innovative participatory technique based on a GET-SDI[7] portal is also created (digital spatial SWOT). The participants are invited to follow four simple steps to provide input through a user-friendly software application. Each participant visits the application webpage[8] and logs-in[9], giving their name and e-mail. Then is invited to define the island's important or interesting points[10], routes[11], and areas[12] on an interactive map accompanied by comments or any other data/file (upload function) (Fig. 6).

3.5 Mapping Event - Brainstorming Meetings

Besides digital tools, public consultation is achieved through participatory events. Informative presentations and digital tools are promoted through mapping events organized in central venues of Athens, where inhabitants and 'friends' of Gavdos island came and participated in the spatial questionnaires. This way, they get informed, share ideas and thoughts, and help others to participate online after the gathering.

During the visit to the island, two brainstorming sessions were organized at the cafe and bakery, where people came and talked with the design team about their concerns and additional ideas through freestyle conversations. After the visit to the island, a

---

[5] GISCloud data collection form.

[6] Preliminary online questionnaire: https://docs.google.com/forms/d/1sZxRryPtjVPgNn2Kh 3vRlwPlln4HCmMz-Fm93MqO_YU/viewform?edit_requested=true&fbclid=IwAR2kHSl F7kEllKaO30lEQqtHulZjiSZ9hKG-U2kipepuHkSkSE6d0BJROBw.

[7] https://www.getmap.eu/products/open-source/get-sdi-portal/.

[8] https://gavdos.commonspace.gr/.

[9] Tutorial for log-in: https://www.youtube.com/watch?v=v983Ga1ERUQ.

[10] Tutorial for inserting an interesting point: https://www.youtube.com/watch?v=HulA56dnaXE.

[11] Tutorial for inserting an important route: https://www.youtube.com/watch?v=81qg7J9q7xE.

[12] Tutorial for inserting a challenging area: https://www.youtube.com/watch?v=HVFrASvzqGg.

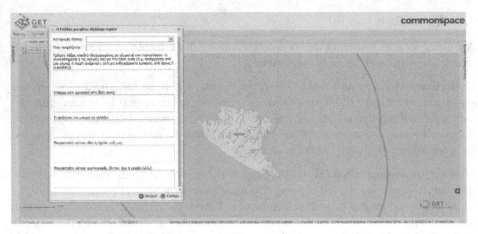

Fig. 6. Screen-shot of the spatial questionnaire.

presentation was held in Paleochora (Crete) informing the citizens of South Crete (in fact, the villages of the southern part of the Chania region) about the process of "Public Participation Planning Project for the Sustainability of Greek Island Gavdos." The aim of informing the neighboring and interested municipalities is their active inclusion and involvement in the development of the sustainability plan.

4   Conclusions

Participatory processes are essential for sustainable development plans following a well-constructed methodology by using a specific toolkit coming from participatory planning and Integrated Spatial Development approaches. Instead of being ostensibly performed, participatory processes should contribute to the abilities and knowledge growth of the citizens and the local actors and empower the locals' active involvement in the decision and policymaking. For that reason, visits were also conducted in the inhabitants' houses who could not join the workshops, also at the remote beach of Lavrakas, where we discussed with the community living there the problems they face and their needs.

The main challenges of small remoted islands include limited access to resources, high costs of goods and services due to dependence on imports, limited economic opportunities, and a small population which can lead to social and cultural isolation. Other challenges include vulnerability to natural disasters, difficulty accessing healthcare and education, and limited political representation [1]. As a permanent characteristic of remote and small islands, the island particularity should be encountered through a tailor-made strategy for local development [13]. The unique characteristics of this small community consisted of 80–100 inhabitants on a very remote island facing transportation difficulties that affected this project a fruitful experience.

We were setting the conditions for emerging cooperation and networks and cultivating a 'participatory culture' for the common benefit [14]. The methodological steps and tools are successful, but the procedure proved more time-consuming than other projects due to remoteness and brutal weather conditions. Significant gaps between the different phases are a negative factor in the participants' creativity and enthusiasm and should be avoided in future projects. The islanders were not exposed to such a previous process; however, they participated actively and passionately, overcoming issues and conflicts among themselves.

Unfortunately, the subsequent phases, the consultation and the implementation of the final sustainable development plan, are postponed due to changes to the political agenda (local and national elections of 2019). This fact can be demoralizing and counterproductive to future participatory procedures.

Acknowledgments. The authors wish to thank all the participants the local inhabitants, visitors and friends of Gavdos for sharing their enlightening knowledge and experience. Thanks are also due to Ms Elena Reizidou at the Management Organisation Unit of Development Programmes and Ms Gelli Kalinikou, former mayor of Gavdos, for their participation in the core/design team and for providing valuable inputs. The participatory program was funded by the Management Organisation Unit of Development Programmes of the Greek Ministry of Development and Investments.

Authors' Contributions. Mougiakou E. devised the main conceptual ideas of the participatory project, conceived the methodological framework and steps, and made the final selection of methods and tools. In collaboration with Karimali E. they designed and organized the participatory procedures of the project. Karimali E. drafted the first version of the manuscript. Mougiakou E. prepared the final document and the figures included in this publication. All authors provided feedback and reviewed the final manuscript.

References

1. Deidda, M.: Insularity and economic development: a survey. Int. Rev. Econ. **63**(2), 107–128 (2015). https://doi.org/10.1007/s12232-015-0238-8
2. Egoz, S. (ed.): Defining landscape democracy: a path to spatial justice. EE ǀ Edward Elgar Publishing, Cheltenham, UK ; Northampton, MA (2018). ISBN: 978-1-78643-833-1
3. International Association for Public Participation AP2 International Federation. Public participation spectrum. Retrieved April, 2023 from: https://cdn.ymaws.com/www.iap2.org/resource/resmgr/pillars/Spectrum_8.5x11_Print.pdf (2018)
4. COMMONSPACE. Online Guide for Spatial, Urban and Environmental Participatory Planning for Climate Change Adaptation (in Greek). Retrieved April, 2023 from: https://repository.participatorylab.org/dataset/avaqopa-njektpov1kou-odnyou (2021)
5. Nogué i Font, J., Sala i Martí, P., Grau i Oliveras, J.: The landscape catalogues of Catalonia: methodology. Landscape Observatory of Catalonia, Olot (2016). ISBN 978-84-617-7800-3
6. Slocum, N.: Participatory Methods Toolkit. A practitioner's manual. United Nations University – Comparative Regional Integration Studies (UNU/CRIS). Retrieved December 3, 2019, from: http://archive.unu.edu/hq/library/Collection/PDF_files/CRIS/PMT.pdf. ISBN 90-5130-447-1 (2003)
7. Roniotes, A., Malotidi, V., Virtanen, H., Vlachogianni, T.: A handbook on the Public Participation Process in the Mediterranean. A tool for achieving Sustainable Development. Retrieved April, 2023 from: https://mio-ecsde.org/wp-content/uploads/2016/08/book_PPP_final.pdf. ISBN: 978-960-6793-20-2
8. Tools 4 dev. Stakeholder Analysis Matrix Template. December 3, 2019 from: http://www.tools4dev.org/resources/stakeholder-analysis-matrix-template/ (2015)

9. Bouma, G., Duijn, M.: Participatory SWOT-analysis for the spatial impact study Railway Zone Breda- a case study. The 45th ERSA Congress, (Amsterdam, Netherlands) (2005)
10. Comino, E., Ferretti, V.: Indicators-based spatial SWOT analysis: supporting the strategic planning and management of complex territorial systems. Ecol. Ind. **60**, 1104–1117 (2016). https://doi.org/10.1016/j.ecolind.2015.09.003
11. Gkoltsiou, A., Mougiakou, E.: The use of Islandscape character assessment and participatory spatial SWOT analysis to the strategic planning and sustainable development of small islands. The case of Gavdos. Land Use Policy **103**, 105277 (2021). https://doi.org/10.1016/j.landusepol.2021.105277
12. Ferguson G.: Capacity Building Seminar on Cooperatives, Social and Solidarity Economy and Community Economic Development (Athens, Greece). Retrieved from the seminar's presentation (2016)
13. Koutsi, D., Stratigea, A.: Releasing cultural tourism potential of less-privileged island communities in the mediterranean: an ICT-enabled, strategic and integrated participatory planning approach. In: Pedro M.R., Melo, A. I., Santos Natário, M.M., Biscaia, R. (eds.) The Impact of Tourist Activities on Low-Density Territories: Evaluation Frameworks, Lessons, and Policy Recommendations, Springer, pp. 63–93, ISBN 978-3-030-65524-2 (2020)
14. Creighton, J.L.: The Public Participation Handbook: Making Better Decisions through Citizen Involvement. Wiley, San Francisco (2005)

Building Island Communities of Practice for Achieving Local Sustainable Cultural Tourism Objectives

Dionisia Koutsi[1]([✉]) [iD], Giulia Desogus[2] [iD], Kilian Flade[3] [iD], Chiara Garau[4] [iD], Hayal Gezer[4], Sonja Hörster[2], Eleni Mougiakou[1] [iD], Marina Neophytou[4] [iD], Christoforos Pissarides[4] [iD], and Sofia Tsadari[1] [iD]

[1] Commonspace coop, Akakiou 1 - 3 and Ipirou 60, 10439 Athens, Greece
koutsi.dionisia@gmail.com
[2] Department of Civil and Environmental Engineering and Architecture (DICAAR), University of Cagliari, via Marengo 2, 09123 Cagliari, Italy
[3] Cocreation Foundation, Frankfurter Tor 6, D-10243 Berlin, Germany
[4] Centre for Sustainable Peace and Democratic Development (SeeD), 14, Michalakopoulou Street, 1075 Nicosia, Cyprus

Abstract. The prevalence of a series of megatrends and challenges such as climate change, overtourism and health crisis, have demonstrated even more the necessity to shift from the current mass and overcrowded, spatially concentrated tourism models to less crowded, more spatially dispersed, and secure environments. This tendency pushed island destinations to rethink their tourism profiles. Nonetheless, the majority of island communities depend on tourism for their economic well-being, which requires rethinking the highly appreciated island tourism destinations' strategies towards more sustainable models. According to European policies and academics, alternative forms of tourism, such as cultural tourism, seem to be the solution for achieving this objective, also by including participatory practises in local communities. Starting from these considerations, this work presents the ongoing ISL project (Forming interdisciplinary Island Communities of Practice operating for sustainable cultural tourIsm models). This paper describes a general overview of the ISL Project which purpose is to offer innovative high quality participatory tools to (i) promote awareness and mobilise local communities and stakeholders on their cultural identity, cultural awareness and their social and historical heritage and (ii) support social and territorial cohesion of island communities at a local and trans-island/transnational level by promoting participatory cultural tourism schemes.

Keywords: Sustainable Cultural Tourism; Participatory Practices · Islands Communities · Terrestrial Cohesion · Local Development · Governance

1 Introduction

The sustainable tourism movement has steadily entered the international policy agendas during the 60's and 70's as an immediate response against the impacts of overtourism during the post-was period. Nowadays sustainable tourism seems to be one of the top

© The Author(s), under exclusive license to Springer Nature Switzerland AG 2023
O. Gervasi et al. (Eds.): ICCSA 2023 Workshops, LNCS 14110, pp. 321–333, 2023.
https://doi.org/10.1007/978-3-031-37123-3_24

priorities of the international and European policy scene, as the concept that covers the complete tourism experience, including concerns for economic, social and environmental issues as well as attention to improving tourists' experiences and addressing the needs of host communities [1]. Today, the emergence of a set of megatrends, such as climate change, overtourism, and the pandemic health crisis have emphasised even more to the urgent need to transform tourism options into this sustainable, and resilient model [2–8]. To promote environmental protection, cultural preservation, economic prosperity as well as public health safety, it has become clear that the prevailing mass and overcrowded tourism model needs to change to a less crowded and more spatially dispersed model [9–12].

These trends introduced island destinations [13, 14] to the center of attention for two significantly different reasons: (i) peripheral island entities are emerging as safe, isolated, attractive tourism alternatives competing with already established touristic islands; and (ii) as the majority of the island communities' prosperity is dependent on the tourism activity, highly appreciated island tourism destinations need to rethink and reorient their strategies towards the future.

According to different academics and policy statements, alternative forms of tourism, such as cultural tourism, may offer a solution to this problem [15–24]. Cultural tourism places a high emphasis on participatory practices [25–30], which are essential for recognising the value of cultural heritage and transmitting it to future generations, as has already highlighted by the Faro Convention [[31], Article 2b] and for ensuring citizen participation in decision making and management relating to the cultural and tourism field [32].

Despite the prevalence of participatory practices in development plans, local island community stakeholders still lack the knowledge and expertise essential to effectively plan for a sustainable future for their islands. For these reasons, this paper describes the experience of the project "ISL - forming interdisciplinary island communities of practice operating for sustainable cultural tourism models"; aspiring to promote bottom-up initiatives for island communities, as well as empower and form interdisciplinary groups of local actors to co-design sustainable tourism futures for their own islands. In particular, the paper explores how the following objectives may be achieved through the ISL project:

- To strengthen the capacity of partners to collaborate transnationally and through participatory practises.
- To provide islands new, high-quality participatory tools to promote active European citizenship.
- To promote awareness and engage local communities and responsible stakeholders with regard to their cultural identity, cultural awareness and their social and historical heritage.
- To foster team and community building on island level to co-design and co-create visions over a more sustainable cultural tourism future for their island.

- To support social and terrestrial cohesion of island communities at a local and trans-island/transnational level [33].

The innovative aspect of the ISL project lies on the methodology followed to address those objectives. In particular, participatory practices and the model of managing inter-disciplinary teams is placed at the heart of the project empowering island communities to foster stable working teams to sustain and promote the sustainable place-based develop-ment of their island. In addition, the planned onsite actions and hands-on workshops as an engaging practice is also one of the innovative aspects of the project adding significant value to the actual impact of the proposed methodology.

This paper describes the methodology introduced by the ISL project, as well as the expected results foreseen during its implementation aiming at forming interdisciplinary island communities of practice (ICoPs) operating for sustainable cultural tourism models. Towards this end, the paper begins with a discussion on Sect. 2 about the formation of the Island Communities of Practice (ICoP). Subsequently, Sect. 3 focuses on benefits, impacts and results and finally, in Sect. 4, the results and the research's future directions are discussed.

2 Methodology for the Formation of Island Communities of Practice (ICoP)

The ISL project takes inspiration from Wenger E.'s idea of *"Communities of practice: Learning, meaning and identity"* [34]. According to this reference, Wenger defines these communities as a group of people who share a common interest or enthusiasm in some-thing they do and who learn to cooperate in order to improve their abilities and knowledge through regular interactions.

The ISL project seeks to encourage the promotion of more sustainable tourism prac-tices as the common goal through the promotion of ICoPs. In order to accomplish this objective, the project intends to establish the notion of ICoP and encourage residents to create a variety of such groups in their regions. Figure 1 shows the selected case studies from three Mediterranean countries that will be addressed during the project and act as pilot cases. These islands are:

- *Leros island, Greece.* Leros has faced several challenges throughout history and is today regarded as a less privileged island community. However, there is a growing need for tourism revitalisation towards sustainable, local development.
- *Nicosia, Cyprus.* This case study is located on a country-sized island and is both an attractive tourism destination. Specifically, the case deals with Nicosia, a divided city consisting of many communities, including a majority of Greek Cypriot and Turkish Cypriot communities (OR Greek speaking and Turkish speaking Cypriots). This unique characteristic has given the city a distinct cultural identity, which currently requires more sustainable tourism options after the pandemic.
- *Cagliari, Sardinia, Italy.* Cagliari is an exceptionally attractive tourist destination in the centre of the Mediterranean, and it has been selected as a case study due to

the rising need for alternatives that emphasise local aspirations over prevalent mass tourism methods.

 The ICoP groups are formed by island-based stakeholders active on the aforementioned islands that are able and willing to create interdisciplinary groups and work collaboratively towards a specific objective: to comprehend, appreciate, and envision the cultural tourism sustainable future of their respective islands.

 The ICoPs can be formed by the following groups of stakeholders:

1. Representatives from Island Municipalities representing the decision-making level.
2. Professionals from the hospitality and tourism industry in the private sector.
3. Local cultural organizations, including both public and private entities.
4. Academics who can demonstrate a relationship with the study areas and provide significant research and theoretical background to the group.
5. Local associations and already existing groups that are active in fields related to the cultural tourism profile of their island.
6. Interested individuals of all ages.

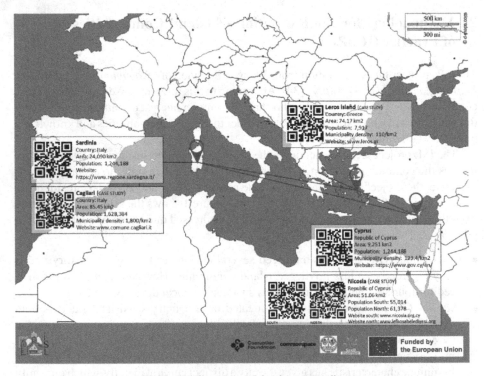

Fig. 1. Mediterranean Islands case studies

 Local stakeholders, that will actively form ICoP groups, have several needs, including broadening the boundaries of democracy and acquiring a more active role in the decision-making process; strengthening cooperation among all the stakeholders in the cultural, tourism, and policy-making fields, and creating an efficient collaboration framework that brings together professionals and citizens from different disciplines. These needs are closely related to the ICoP groups' objectives, which include being involved in decision-making processes, learning how to collaborate effectively, and finding solutions to overcome societal, economic, and environmental challenges arising from various crises, such as the COVID-19 pandemic and the vision of a more sustainable and resilient future for island communities.

ICoPs have a common goal, even though each island may not necessarily have the similar ICoP structure. Each ICoP will have its own distinctive characteristics, such as different kinds of professionals establishing their own methods of cooperation, engagement, and interaction to meet local needs, expectations and governance systems. Some ICoPs may share a common physical workspace or a digital platform, such as communication through smartphones or regular online/physical meeting points.

ICoPs are initiated by four organisations, e.g., the ISL project partners. The selection of the partnership is based on partners' complementarity, experience, and alignment with the ISL project objectives, taking also into account the following criteria:

1. Their motivation to participate in the project and each organisation's goals, methodology, and interest in contributing to a more democratic and participatory decision-making process for the sustainable future of peripheral regions like islands.
2. The competence, expertise, and resources of each partner which contribute efficiently to the project outputs. The partners have strong project specific competencies and skills and dispose of qualified staff who will undertake the implementation of the project.
3. The contacts and the networking of each partner to maximise the impact and the distribution of the project.
4. Their geographic coverage, meaning their connection with island communities, as an asset ensuring a greater impact of the planned activities.

Following this process, partners from Germany (Cocreation Foundation), Greece (COMMONSPACE), Cyprus (SeeD) and Sardinia, Italy (University of Cagliari) form the ISL consortium as shown in Fig. 2.

To reach the project objectives, meet the target groups needs and produce high quality results, the project proposes a two-dimensional participatory scheme; promoting co-design sessions among the partnership members as well as through the active involvement of interested stakeholders that will be informed, participate and finally collaborate to form ICoPs in three countries. Toward this end, participatory workshops (among partners and in collaboration with local island stakeholders) are planned using a set of innovative participatory tools as described in more detail in the following section.

3 Benefits, Impacts and Results of the ISL Project

The ongoing ISL project has already shown great benefits in terms of both the local and transnational nature.

Locally, ISL has already identified informal groups, formal associations, decision making bodies and private entities related to tourism and cultural activities in the local

Fig. 2. The partners of ISL project.

and national level that will be hugely benefited from the ISL results. Practising the co-design process, activating local communities and raising awareness on issues related to more democratic processes is going to ultimately influence the way islanders are taking part in the decision-making process. A distinctive example is the direct involvement of the island Municipality of Leros, Greece, even in the proposal phase ensuring the actual use of the results at an administrative level during and after the end of the project. This action will also provide a valuable research ground from an academic point of view, as well as will inspire the co-design process integration in various fields such as education, environmental policies, etc.

At the transnational level, the ISL project has been a great opportunity for knowledge and expertise transfer and information and ideas exchange, as it comprises experiences from Germany (Cocreation Foundation), Greece (COMMONSPACE), Cyprus (SeeD) and Sardinia, Italy (University of Cagliari). Indeed, the interdisciplinary nature of the project has satisfied the need to shift towards more democratic and participatory decision-making practices. Furthermore, in agreement with EU report on Cultural Governance [35], the project promotes and develops participatory practices by meaningfully involving relevant stakeholders in all phases of the policy cycle from the identification of the problem to policy evaluation and recognising the added value of such engagement. Considering that sustainable tourism practices are a commonly accepted practice being researched and studied in all participating countries trying to overcome the impacts of the pandemic, transnational cooperation seems imperative for good governance choices to be revealed, knowledge exchange and discussions among participating partners and stakeholders to be achieved.

In addition, the methodology of the project and its multidisciplinary dimension is crucial and is meeting the needs of ICoP groups and the goals of the partner organisations:

1. Activating a shared and recognised knowledge on participatory methods.
2. Experience exchange among partners with different back-grounds, coming from different social and geographical contexts (e.g. Central Europe, South Europe).
3. Testing guidelines and good practices them in different contexts.
4. Actively engaging island communities at cross country level.
5. Project activities inspired and reinforced by innovative European practices.

Towards the achievement of the aforementioned goals and aspirations the project is designed in 2 phases, i.e. the pre-workshops' phase and Island workshops' phase. In particular:

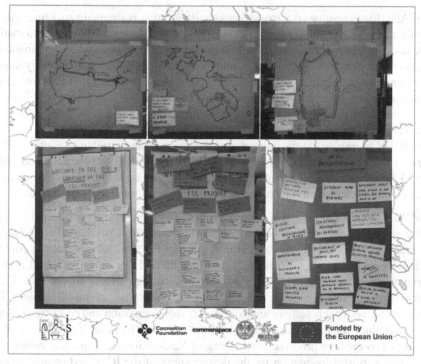

Fig. 3. Internal training session for partners (designed and conducted by the Cocreation Foundation), Berlin, Germany, January 2023

Pre-Workshops' Phase: The objectives of this stage are mainly (i) to support the capacity building process of participating organisations to collaborate transnationally and through participatory practices, (ii) to create a set of innovative high quality participatory tools for islanders to support active European citizenship and the formation of ICoP and (iii) to gather the necessary information on the current situation of the study cases regarding the sustainability status, the cultural and natural reserve and the stakeholder ecosystem. These objectives were achieved during the partners' internal training session held in Berlin in January 2023 (Fig. 3) through a common strategy action was built by the partners, who exchanged experiences, good participatory practices, and field experiences. This co-design session included ice-breaking questions, brainstorming sessions, inspirational walks, etc., which helped the partners to express and feed the discussion with valuable input. In addition, this first stage includes a practical guide on the step-by-step methodology in order ICoPs to be formed in 3 case studies included as pilot cases in ISL project (Leros in Greece, Sardinia in Italy, Nicosia in Cyprus), useful for shaping meaningful and engaging workshops.

This phase of the project, which was organised by the Cocreation Foundation (Germany), was indispensable for gaining significant knowledge on new participatory practices and the idea of co-creation design.

The achieved results of the pre-workshops phase in general are defined as follows:

a) INTANGIBLE results: (i) a stronger and collaborative partnership structure will be facilitated after the joint training session on the implementation and participation methodology enhancing team building and sense of cooperation; (ii) a knowledge base on the current situation of the study cases regarding the sustainability status, the cultural and natural reserve and the stakeholder ecosystem that is active in the area and can be approached in order to form the expected ICoPs for the benefit of the sustainable future of the islands will be obtained offering advantages in the involved partners and groups of participants.

b) TANGIBLE results: (i) an internal partners co-working/ training session will be held; while (ii) an Island Communities of Practice Guide (iii) 3 Participation plans, (iv) 3 Stakeholder environment mapping and analysis and (v) 3 case study analysis representing selected cultural aspects of each study region will be produced.

Island Workshops: The objective of this ongoing activity is strongly connected with the specific objective of the ISL project which aims to form an ICoP that allows islanders to visualize a profile of sustainable cultural tourism for their islands. In this context, this activity includes in total 6 workshops to be carried out in 3 EU island regions (Greece, Cyprus, Sardinia). Three of the four participating partners are connected with island regions and these areas are selected as the 3 case studies of the ISL project. The specific objectives of this activity are: (i) to foster the co-creation and co-design of local policy guidelines for the cultural tourism of the islands; (ii) to raise awareness of the benefits that co-creation processes could bring to the decision-making environment; (iii) to establish a fruitful foundation for the development of the ICoP and inspire them to continue working collaboratively.

The workshops, applied in the 3 participating islands in which the following actions will take place: (i) mapping of the community cultural capital" - evaluation of the existing cultural capital of the island by the participants - collection of empirical knowledge; (ii) building "Island Visions", for which mixed online and participatory tools will be used to carry out brainstorming sessions among the members of the "ICoPs"; finally (iii) 3 summary reports, one for each island, will be the conclusion of this activity. For the realization of each workshop a different set of participatory tools will be used in order to serve local needs and community characteristics. These could include: ice-breaking questions, collective mapping, brainstorming sessions, collective walks, visioning sessions to name a few.

The expected results of this 2nd phase are the following:

a) INTANGIBLE results: (i) islanders will have gained significant knowledge on participatory practices regarding the estimation of the cultural potential of their islands, and the way they can sustainably exploit them towards more resilient cultural tourism choices; (ii) team building among participants of the ICoP will be fostered by learning a way to cooperate and work as teams over common problems and visions not only during the project but also in the future.

b) TANGIBLE results: (i) Island Communities of Practice (one in each country constituted from at least 5 local actors); (ii) 6 local island workshops; (iii) 3 workshop summary reports; (iv) at least 10 stakeholders in each country will participate in the designed island workshops and at least 5 of them will eventually form the local ICoPs; (v) at least 60 participants from 3 different countries in total. In more detail 10 stakeholders in each of the 3 countries will participate in each of the 2 workshops; (vi) high level of satisfaction among the participating stakeholders - evaluated through an after-workshop survey.

At the end of the project, the impact will be evaluated through a set of Key Performance Indicators (KPI) agreed by the ISL consortium measuring the expected results on a partnership and project level; ensuring at the same time the success of the project.

4   Discussion and Conclusions

Considering the goal of the small scale partnerships projects and the first objective of the ISL project set: "building capacity of participating organisations to collaborate transnationally and through participatory practices", the long-term development of the participating entities is of high importance in the project and the implementation of the project is beneficial for the following reasons:

- The international presence and extroversion of all partners endorse the competitiveness of the organisations as well as the significant upskilling towards team spirit, creativity, and innovation for the involved staff.
- The enhancement of participatory practices to be used by the partners not only during the ISL project but also in other activities they are involved in. Exchange of good practices and knowledge through their constant collaboration, training session and co-design of the methodology they will use is a great asset.
- Newcomers (Cocreation Foundation and SeeD) will get familiarised with the Erasmus plus programme and project management in general opening a new field of action having the support of the rest most experienced partners.
- The enhancement of organisations' experience by everyone's involvement in research and documentation practices regarding codesign and sustainable cultural tourism of regional/island regions.

- The development of strong connections with local communities as place-based and community-based actions will ensure better communication and trust-building between the staff involved and the group of stakeholders that will participate in the workshops.

Furthermore, forming ICoPs as the main target of this project is used to offer significant opportunities to people with different backgrounds to participate in democratic life and have a say on the future touristic development of their island. At the same time by emphasising on cultural tourism practices and their sustainable nature, participants are given the opportunity to get familiarised with local cultural identity, cultural awareness, and local social and historical heritage. Moreover, not only participants are engaged in participatory practices but also collaborative sessions among the partners to enhance team building and awareness on such methods are planned in the pre workshops phase.

ISL project enhances social and terrestrial coherence as well as inclusion by focusing on island communities and promoting participation practises of these generally considered inaccessible places, mostly owing to insularity.

People resident in remote regions lack the opportunity to attend co-creation events or such events lack impactful practices in island regions. Through the enrolment of the preparation phase, the implementation of the workshops and the joint dissemination event planned, groups of islanders will have the opportunity to gain appropriate knowledge and capacity to form "ICoPs" through hands-on working workshops; a practice that enhance team and community building through informal learning activities.

The aforementioned challenges also impose a strong barrier for the ISL partnership to ensure the successful creation and continuation of the proposed ICoPs as well as their sustainability in the future. To endorse this success ISL partners will provide support to the ICoPs' members, through constant awareness, guidance and support as well as the reassurance to promote further initiatives related to the support proposal ideas related to ISL context and the ICoPs' needs already established in all three island cases.

Additionally, ISL initiates an innovative educational aspect to all participating actors, including the partners and the target group, providing a co-creation scheme that will empower them to increase their capacity to think critically and creatively, to explore new ways of acting and making informed and adequate decisions.

Finally, the activities take place to secure the sustainability of the project are the following:

- The partners will continue promoting the project after its end through their sites.
- The partners will continue informing anyone interested about the project, after its end.
- The results of the project will be uploaded on partners' website; especially the results of the activities will be promoted and used in the future since their format and digital content can prerequisite it; project results will be also uploaded in the Participatory Lab Repository [36] developed by Commonspace (Greece).
- All project's digital means will form an important element of the project both during the development phases and beyond. Social media platforms are also now accepted as fit-for-purpose and robust communication channels with target groups and between target groups.

- All participants have agreed to continue the project as a large-scale partnership further developing and capitalising on the ISL results, involving more partners and island regions around the EU and beyond aiming at establishing ICoP as a methodology to give islanders the potentiality to form their sustainable future in their own terms; ensuring resilience against the unexpected crisis.

Currently the ISL project is in its initial phase haven't yet produce concrete results. The next steps include the implementation of all planned island workshops in all participating countries; ensuring at the same time the extended dissemination of the project context and results. Finally, steps to further elaborate on the project idea and results to projects corresponding to a larger scale as well as to a wider context of spatial distribution is already into place.

Acknowledgements. This study was supported by the project "ISL - Forming interdisciplinary Island Communities of Practice operating for sustainable cultural tourIsm models", small scale Erasmus+ project (KA210-ADU-6B12071A), DE02 - Nationale Agentur Bildung für Europa beim Bundesinstitut für Berufsbildung. This study was also supported by the project "ISL+, People-oriented, place-based and locally driven planning approach supporting island cultural tourism development", Erasmus+ project (KA220-ADU - Cooperation partnerships in adult education), DE02 - Nationale Agentur Bildung für Europa beim Bundesinstitut für Berufsbildung (Project under evaluation).

Authors' Contributions. Koutsi D. devised the main conceptual ideas of the ISL project, and in collaboration with Mougiakou E., and Tsadari, S., structured the methodological steps of the project idea. Hörster S., and Flade K., designed and conducted the co-creation workshop of the project in Berlin. Garau C., and Degosus G., drafted the manuscript and prepared the figures included in this publication. All authors provided feedback and reviewed the final manuscript.

References

1. UNEP, UNWTO: Making Tourism More Sustainable - A Guide for Policy Makers (2005). https://www.unwto.org/sustainable-development. Accessed 4 Apr 2023
2. DIGITAL REPOSITORY: The impact of the COVID-19 pandemic on the tourism sector in Latin America and the Caribbean, and options for a sustainable and resilient recovery (2020). https://repositorio.cepal.org/handle/11362/46502. Accessed 27 Mar 2023
3. Seabra, C., Bhatt, K.: Tourism sustainability and COVID-19 pandemic: is there a positive side? Sustainability **14**, 8723 (2022). https://doi.org/10.3390/su14148723
4. D'Orazio, M., Bernardini, G., Quagliarini, E.: Sustainable and resilient strategies for touristic cities against COVID-19: An agent-based approach. Saf. Sci. **142**, 105399 (2021). https://doi.org/10.1016/j.ssci.2021.105399
5. Wibowo, J.M., Hariadi, S.: Indonesia sustainable tourism resilience in the COVID-19 Pandemic Era (Case Study of Five Indonesian Super-priority Destinations). Millennial Asia **0(0)**, (2022). https://doi.org/10.1177/09763996221105143
6. Zhang, S., Sun, T., Lu, Y.: The COVID-19 pandemic and tourists' risk perceptions: tourism policies' mediating role in sustainable and resilient recovery in the new normal. Sustainability **15**, 1323 (2023). https://doi.org/10.3390/su15021323

7. Kumar, P., Ckakrabarty, P.: Greener Recovery from Pandemic Effects: Development of a Sustainable and Resilient Destination Economy. Apple Academic Press (2022). ISBN 9781003283331
8. Traskevich, A., Fontanari, M.: Tourism Potentials in post-COVID19: The concept of destination resilience for advanced sustainable management in tourism. Tourism Planning & Development **20**(1), 12–36 (2023). https://doi.org/10.1080/21568316.2021.1894599
9. Lim, J., Kourtit, K., Nijkamp, P., Stream, C.: Spatial deconcentration of tourism concentrations: a visitors' galaxy impact model of the COVID-19 crisis. Sustainability **14**, 3239 (2022). https://doi.org/10.3390/su14063239
10. Leka, A., Lagarias, A., Panagiotopoulou, M., Stratigea, A.: Development of a Tourism Carrying Capacity Index (TCCI) for sustainable management of coastal areas in Mediterranean islands – Case study Naxos. Greece. Ocean & Coastal Management **216**, 105978 (2022). https://doi.org/10.1016/j.ocecoaman.2021.105978
11. Buitrago-Esquinas, E.M., Foronda-Robles, C., Yñiguez-Ovando, R.: A literature review on overtourism to guide the transition to responsible tourism. Revista De Estudios Andaluces **45**, 71–90 (2023). https://doi.org/10.12795/rea.2023.i45.04
12. Seyhan, B.: The Conceptual Grounding of Overtourism and Overtourism-Driven Change: Olympos Case, 0–0. Advances in Hospitality and Tourism Research (AHTR) (2023). https://doi.org/10.30519/ahtr.1120409
13. Santos-Rojo, C., Llopis-Amorós, M., García-García, J.M.: Overtourism and sustainability: a bibliometric study (2018–2021). Technol. Forecast. Soc. Chang. **188**, 122285 (2023). https://doi.org/10.1016/j.techfore.2022.122285
14. Ruggieri, G., Calò, P.: Tourism dynamics and sustainability: a comparative analysis between mediterranean islands—evidence for Post-COVID-19 strategies. Sustainability **14**, 4183 (2022). https://doi.org/10.3390/su14074183
15. European Commission: Sustainable cultural tourism (2023). https://culture.ec.europa.eu/cultural-heritage/cultural-heritage-in-eu-policies/sustainable-cultural-tourism. Accessed 27 Mar 2023
16. European Commission: Internal Market, Industry, Entrepreneurship and SMEs, Cultural tourism (2023). https://single-market-economy.ec.europa.eu/sectors/tourism/eu-funding-and-businesses/funded-projects/cultural_en. Accessed 27 Mar 2023
17. Georgakopoulou, S., Delitheou, V.: The Contribution of Alternative Forms of Tourism in Sustainable Tourism Development: The Case of the Island of Kalymnos. In: Katsoni, V., Spyriadis, T. (eds.) Cultural and Tourism Innovation in the Digital Era. SPBE, pp. 431–446. Springer, Cham (2020). https://doi.org/10.1007/978-3-030-36342-0_34
18. Du Cros, H., McKercher, B.: Cultural Tourism. Routledge, London (2020). ISBN 1000056449, 9781000056440
19. Stoica, G.D., et al.: Perspectives for the development of sustainable cultural tourism. Sustainability **14**, 5678 (2022). https://doi.org/10.3390/su14095678
20. Coronel, M., Papp-Váry, A.F., Pinke-Sziva, I., Berezvai, Z., Smith, M.K.: Post-Pandemic Re-Positioning in a Cultural Tourism City: From Overtourism to E-Tourism. In: Oliveira, L. (ed.) Handbook of Research on Digital Communications, Internet of Things, and the Future of Cultural Tourism, pp. 430–449. IGI Global, Beijin (2022). https://doi.org/10.4018/978-1-7998-8528-3.ch023
21. Matteucci, X., Koens, K., Calvi, L., Moretti, S.: Envisioning the futures of cultural tourism. Futures **142**, 103013 (2022). https://doi.org/10.1016/j.futures.2022.103013
22. Garau, C.: Perspectives on cultural and sustainable rural tourism in a smart region: the case study of marmilla in sardinia (Italy). Sustainability **7**, 6412–6434 (2015). https://doi.org/10.3390/su7066412
23. Garau, C.: Focus on citizens: public engagement with online and face-to-face participation—a case study. Future Internet **4**, 592–606 (2012). https://doi.org/10.3390/fi4020592

24. Koutsi, D., Stratigea, A.: Releasing cultural tourism potential of less-privileged island communities in the mediterranean: an ICT-enabled, strategic and integrated participatory planning approach. In: Pedro Marques, R., Melo, A.I., Santos Natário, M.M., Biscaia, R. (eds.) The Impact of Tourist Activities on Low-Density Territories: Evaluation Frameworks, Lessons, and Policy Recommendations, pp. 63–93. Springer, Cham (2020). ISBN 978-3-030-65524-2
25. European Union: Sustainable Cultural Tourism Guidelines (2018). https://www.culturalt ourism-network.eu/uploads/5/0/6/0/50604825/sustainable_cultural_tourism_guidelines.pdf. Accessed 27 Mar 2023
26. CBI Ministry of Foreign Affairs: The European market potential for cultural tourism (2021). https://www.cbi.eu/market-information/tourism/cultural-tourism/market-potential. Accessed 27 Mar 2023
27. Interreg Europe: Sustainable tourism: an opportunity for regions to benefit from their cultural and natural heritage. A policy brief from the Policy Learning Platform on environment and resource efficiency (2018). https://www.interregeurope.eu/sites/default/files/2022-01/ Policy%20brief%20on%20cultural%20heritage%20and%20sustainable%20tourism.pdf. Accessed 27 Mar 2023
28. Garau, C.: Citizen participation in public planning: A literature review. International Journal of Sciences **1(12)**, 21–44 (2012). ISSN 2305–3925
29. Garau, C.: Processi di piano e partecipazione. Gangemi Editore (2013). ISBN: 8849226497
30. Garau, C., Desogus, G., Banchiero, F., Mistretta, P.: A Multicultural Tourism for Evaluating the Cultural Heritage: The Case Study of the Region of Sardinia (Italy). In: La Rosa, D., Privitera, R. (eds.) INPUT 2021. LNCE, vol. 146, pp. 551–560. Springer, Cham (2021). https://doi.org/10.1007/978-3-030-68824-0_59
31. Treaty No.199/2005. Council of Europe Framework Convention on the Value of Cultural Heritage for Society. https://www.coe.int/en/web/conventions/full-list?module=treaty-detail&tre atynum=199. Accessed 27 Mar 2023
32. Routes4U Project: Cultural tourism in the EU macro-regions: Cultural Routes to increase the attractiveness of remote destinations (2020). https://rm.coe.int/routes4u-manual-attractiv eness-remote-destination-cultural-tourism/16809ef75a%0A%0A. Accessed 27 Mar 2023
33. Garau, C., Desogus, G., Stratigea, A.: Territorial Cohesion in Insular Contexts: Assessing External Attractiveness and Internal Strength of Major Mediterranean Islands. European Planning Studies, 1–20 (2020). https://doi.org/10.1080/09654313.2020.1840524
34. Wenger, E.: Communities of practice: Learning, meaning and identity. Cambridge University Press, Cambridge (1998). ISBN 052143017
35. Directorate-General for Education, Youth, Sport and Culture (European Commission): Participatory governance of cultural heritage, Report of the OMC (Open Method of Coordination) working group of Member States' experts (2018). https://op.europa.eu/en/publication-detail/-/publication/b8837a15-437c-11e8-a9f4-01aa75ed71a1. Accessed 27 Mar 2023
36. Participatory Lab Repository. https://en.participatorylab.org/repository. Accessed 4 May 2023

The Integrated Project of an Energy and Sustainable Community as an Input for Urban Regeneration and Development

Tanja Congiu[1], Barbara Dessì[2], Paolo Mereu[3], and Alessandro Plaisant[1]([✉])

[1] Department of Architecture, Design and Urban Planning, University of Sassari, Piazza Duomo 6, 07041 Alghero, Italy
{tancon,plaisant}@uniss.it
[2] Egeria S.R.L., Cagliari, Italy
[3] Città Metropolitana di Cagliari, Cagliari, Italy
paolo.mereu@cittametropolitanacagliari.it

Abstract. Today the ways in which urban regeneration and development planning is tackled are an important aspect to reflect on to manage a sustainable urban growth scenario. European impulses to counter the effects of climate change and recent Local Authorities reforms have paved the way for the definition of flexible tools to foster a multi-level governance. This paper presents the policymaking process for the Sustainable Development Agenda of the Metropolitan City of Cagliari (Italy), as a continuous process of contextualisation of the SDGs and discusses the institutional context for promoting integrated projects for sustainability as an opportunity to agree mutual commitments and obligations for their implementation. A decision support tool based on the cognitive mapping technique together with specific selection criteria allow to build several clusters, representative of embryonic forms of integrated projects for sustainability. An integrated project for an energy and sustainable community will be started to test the method, as a starting point for the activation of initiatives of an aggregative nature, starting from subjects who have the ability to operate independently in the field of production and more rationale use of energy: They also can make an important contribution to initiating a broader change in behaviour in the use of spaces and in the management of services.

Keywords: Urban regeneration and development planning · energy and sustainable community · Metropolitan Agenda for Sustainable Development · integrated projects for sustainability

1 Background

An important aspect to reflect on are the ways in which development planning is tackled today. The European institutions have allocated a substantial part of the EU budget for the promotion and development of a common policy for the improvement of cities and social life, as, in the coming years, cities will play a crucial role in responding to

© The Author(s), under exclusive license to Springer Nature Switzerland AG 2023
O. Gervasi et al. (Eds.): ICCSA 2023 Workshops, LNCS 14110, pp. 334–350, 2023.
https://doi.org/10.1007/978-3-031-37123-3_25

the effects of climate change and prevent any kind of emergency [1, 2]. While the S3 Smart Specialization Strategies are being implemented, the upcoming S4 + strategy "Smart Specialization Strategies for Sustainable and inclusive growth" foreshadows a new perspective of urban and territorial growth based on the potential of places [3].

In line with the European Green Deal, the S4+ strategy proposes a model of urban growth that emphasizes sustainability in a socio-environmental context based on the capacity of places to express their potential in terms of benefits, rather than a context with a strict socio-economic characterization, as understood in S3. This model offers strategic perspectives to less developed or central cities and regions throughout Europe, especially to low-density settlement territories, where size and environmental quality are constitutive elements of their organized life. Among the measures of the GDE, the Just Transition Fund, goes precisely in this direction: it will co-finance sustainable initiatives in the most backward and vulnerable regions, those that could suffer huge losses in the transition from obsolete production models to more sustainable ones [4].

The metropolitan one represents the optimal dimension for experimenting with integrated interventions toward sustainability. In 2019, the MAATM (today Ministry of the Environment and Energy Security – MASE) launched a process of collaboration and support to the 14 Italian metropolitan cities for the definition of the Metropolitan Agendas for Sustainable Development[1]. The aim is to implement the Sustainable Development Goals (SDGs) at an urban and metropolitan level and, at the same time, place the interventions in a context made up of several levels of government. The metropolitan Agenda for sustainable development is intended as a device for the orientation and integration of planning and programming tools towards SDGs: this device is functional to "strengthen and qualify the attention towards sustainable development within the Metropolitan Strategic Plans, with a view to full integration of all the dimensions of sustainability in the metropolitan planning, programming and management tools."[2]

In this perspective, the path started by the Metropolitan City of Cagliari (CMCA) for the definition of the Agenda represents a process of experimentation of a modus operandi for the implementation of the sustainability goals and, in this sense, aims at the construction of a model of a sustainable urban growth for the metropolitan area: the sustainable metropolitan infrastructure, as a new urban and territorial organization oriented towards the principles of sustainability. The Agenda translates the SDGs and principles into shared guidelines for urban planning and implementation tools and provides the methodological elements for identifying and promoting integrated projects for sustainability, as an opportunity to agree on mutual commitments and agreements among stakeholders for their implementation.

2   The Policymaking Process

The methodological path that led to the definition of the Agenda is a continuous process of contextualization of the sustainable principles and goals divided in two main moments, according to the following steps (Fig. 1).

---

[1] Art. 34 D. Lgs. 152/2006 e s.s.m.m.i.i.

[2] *Ibid.,* Art. 1 p. 4.

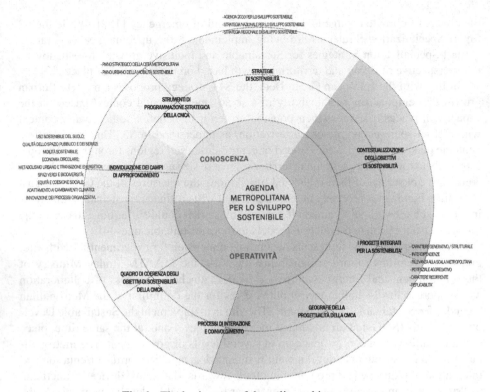

Fig. 1. The basic steps of the policymaking process

2.1 Construction of a Shared Reference Framework for Knowledge Management

The first step aims at the construction of background knowledge from the superordinate sustainability tools and strategies. To this end, a device has been developed with the aim to organize the body of knowledge and allow the single and cross-reading of sources.

For our purposes, we compared extra-territorial and territorial strategies for sustainable development, such as the 2030 Agenda, the National Strategy, the Sardinian Regional Strategy, and the strategic planning tools of the CMCA, such as the Strategic Plan and the Urban Mobility Plan Sustainable. To broaden the spectrum of principles and emerging perspectives on sustainability, the cognitive framework takes into consideration the "Bologna Charter for the environment: metropolitan cities for sustainable development", the Urban Agenda for EU, and other experiences, such as the sustainable development model of Urbanismo Ecosistémico [5] developed and tested in Spain.

However, this analysis aims to return a unitary and homogeneous synthesis of the main contents of the different tools, to overcome the fragmentation, the diversity of scale and terminology of the different tools, programs, and strategies (Fig. 2).

2.2 Construction of the Interpretative Model

The next phase of the work focuses on the construction of an interpretative device that guides the strategic vision of the Agenda.

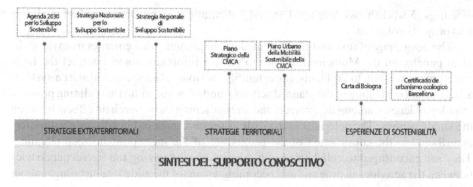

Fig. 2. The reference framework: initiatives, programs and strategies for sustainability

The contents of the cognitive framework, i.e. the set of themes, objectives and related operational guidelines, emerging from extra-territorial and territorial sustainability strategies, have merged into nine "fields of action" which are the operational lens of the methodological device of the Agenda.

Note that the fields of action are to be understood as thematic in-depth areas of supra-municipal and metropolitan interest. They are characterized by resources, uses of space and social practices to which a precise relevance is recognized in relation to a common metropolitan sustainability-oriented strategy. In this sense, the communication and involvement processes of the metropolitan city technostructures and local institutions have been launched around the fields of action.

At the end of this process, 9 thematic in-depth areas are identified to focus on future territorial and urban transformations: *sustainable soil use*; *quality of public space and services*; *sustainable mobility*; *circular economy*; *urban metabolism and energy transition*; *green spaces and biodiversity*; *equity and social cohesion*; *adaptation to climate change*; *organizational process innovations*.

More specifically, through the analysis of the programmatic documents and planning tools in force at local and supra-local level, some "relevant aspects" for the metropolitan city have been identified for each field of action. These relevant aspects, together with some guidelines and lines of action, act as a starting point for the discussion with the (technical/political) delegates of the municipalities and with the different sectors of the Authority. The output is the construction of the CMCA geography of sustainability-oriented urban planning and an initial expression of the contextualized sustainability goals for the metropolitan city.

2.3 The CMCA Geography of Sustainability-Oriented Urban Planning

The participatory process involved local institutions, local stakeholders, and citizens. The activation and dialogue activities were carried out with the delegates of the 17 Municipalities that constitute the Metropolitan City of Cagliari. Each Municipality has identified the participant according to the "field of action" in discussion, identifying the most qualified (technical/political) referent in relation to the local urban planning. 8

meetings (5 workshops) developed around 9 thematic in-depth areas resulted in almost 130 projects collected[3].

The geography of sustainability-oriented urban planning that emerges from the technical panel with the Municipalities aim to collect information and interpret the local structures in relation to problems, opportunities, actions, places, etc. and start a systematization and evaluation of the planned actions, funded or not, aimed at outlining possible interdependencies among the projects and strengthening the synergistic effects between the single actions. The delegates of the CMCA sectors, gathered in a Board Committee, contributed to the construction of the geography of the metropolitan urban planning. They are encouraged to collaborate with the aim of recognizing the interdependencies between the activities in progress and becoming aware of the added value brought about by the synergies.

Therefore, in addition to contextualize the SDGs, the geography of the sustainability-oriented urban planning represents the knowledge basis for the subsequent step of identifying integrated projects for sustainability.

3 A Policymaking Tool: The Integrated Projects for Sustainability

Operationally, through comparison criteria and a policymaking tool, the authors carried out an overall reading of the metropolitan sustainability-oriented urban planning that emerged from the comparison with the delegates of the municipalities and the CMCA sectors. This activity flowed into the identification and representation of some groupings of urban planning actions and projects which were shared and discussed by the CMCA Board Committee. In other words, the groupings of the identified projects are the germs of the integrated projects for sustainability and the inputs for discussion and further exploration through an interaction between experts and stakeholders.

The technique of cognitive maps was used to construct and represent goals, actions, problems, key concepts, options to structure the groupings of projects. For our purpose, the authors have tested cognitive maps technique through a cognitive mapping software. Banxia Decision Explorer®[4] allows to prompt the development of a model[5] by highlighting *values, beliefs, and assumptions an individual has about a particular issue* [6], and so it captures not only knowledge about the background context but also the possible relationships between the concepts and the underlying motivations.

More specifically, a cognitive map is made up by nodes representing constructs - options, facts, goals and so forth, which are also linked to each other by arrows, to form action-oriented chains of argument. Such maps are often structured in a way that identifies values, aspirations, aims and goals at the top, and more detailed options and actions for achieving those goals at the bottom. Moreover, links are inserted between

---

[3] The meetings took place from October 2021 to March 2022 in presence and remotely, in relation to the provisions on the pandemic emergency.

[4] Banxia Decision Explorer Software Decision Explorer (1990), 3.3.0 academic v., Banxia Software ltd., Kendal, UK (web site: <http://www.banxia.com>).

[5] The technique of cognitive maps is based on G. Kelly's "Personal Construct Theory" which maintains that subjects see the world through a clear model formed by "constructs", and the personal construction system constitutes people's "construct space".

constructs to indicate that one construct "causes" or "may lead to" another one. Note that a chain of argument starts with a "tail" concept and ends with a "head" concept. Tail concepts represent triggering events or initial causes or "drivers" of change, such as action possibilities that could lead to more or less desirable outcomes, while head concepts represent "end states" or "aspirations". Moreover, different styles of font, font size and colour are used to distinguish between and display different kind of constructs, such as goals, strategies/issues, options/assertions, agreed actions and analyses results.

Aided by facilitators, participants at the meetings and workshops are prompted to list actions and projects for attaining the sustainable goals related to the "field of action" in argument and discussing some of the cause-effect connections between many of them. This involved asking participants questions like "how?" and "why?", both to elicit the issues and to draw the network of interconnections among them. A "how?" question allows the workshop to explore subjective points of view that are unexpressed and latent, whereas a "why?" question elicits the consequences of a particular action or point of view, along with ends and outcomes. Asking such questions is named process of "laddering". To give an example, with reference to the thematic area "mitigating hydraulic and hydrogeological risk", the "construction of retarding basins" makes it possible to "reduce the run-off time and collect rainwater".

Decision Explorer® software allows to perform several analyses for highlighting key issues in the model, by using for example cluster analysis, domain analysis and centrality analysis[6] [7–9]. Yet, the analysis of the "clusters" allows us to define the areas of interest or thematic areas that emerge from the model.

Afterwards the authors tidied up the maps and built up the model's hierarchy, by identifying and discussing what concepts seem to be actions (blue), goals or objectives (red), what seem to be key issues (yellow/red), and what appear to be the agreed actions to achieve the latter (square) (Fig. 3).

Yet, in the systematization phase, the following criteria guided the definition of the groupings of actions/projects:

– *generative / structural character*: capacity to trigger other projects in the same and/or other fields of action;
– *interdependence with other projects or fields of action*: capacity to establish relationships with other sectors and to produce synergistic and multiplier effects of individual initiatives;
– *relevance on the metropolitan scale*: capacity to pursue sustainability goals in relation to the context;
– *aggregating potential, in terms of social and institutional energies*: capacity to build links and aggregations between stakeholders with widespread interests on relevant issues (water, waste, energy, transport, etc.) starting from local conditions; ability

---

[6] The latter, on the one hand, give an indication of the importance of some fundamental themes within the model and, on the other hand, highlights the necessity of further tests on less represented constructs. Domain analysis gives us an indication on the complexity of each elementary point of view in the whole model, by calculating "density" of links. By contrast, centrality analysis allows to explore the complexity of each theme in the whole model, by calculating how many links it forms with other issues in more than one level from the centre. The higher the score in both analyses the more significance the issue has into the model.

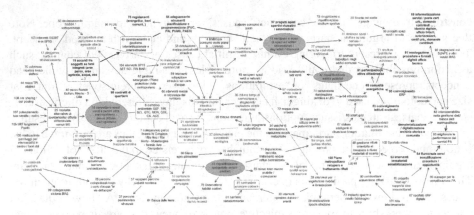

Fig. 3. The cognitive map of the projects expressed by the CMCA municipalities.

to bring out subjects who could act autonomously and who can make an important contribution to the activation of the project;

– *recurring nature*: capacity to be repeated frequently in different territories of the CMCA to respond to widespread problems or offer specific services;

– *replicability*: capacity to be repeated in different territories of CMCA without major modifications.

The first groupings of interventions are embryonic forms of integrated projects for sustainability, organized into thematic areas. The thematic areas allow, on the one hand, to contextualize, spatializing them, the sustainability goals and, on the other hand, they are the inputs for discussion and further exploration through an interaction among CMCA sectors delegates, experts and stakeholders with the aim to define an integrated project for sustainability. Therefore, since the aim of this phase is to reveal the possible interdependencies among projects, the delegates of the CMCA Board Committee were invited to make explicit the ways of acting and the related problems, both from the point of view of procedures and specialist skills, and to identify and exchange good practices and experiences.

The first 5 integrated projects for sustainability are:

1. *Project of connections between green spaces and parks of the Metropolitan City of Cagliari. The interconnected metropolitan park;*
2. *The urban and environmental redevelopment project of the metropolitan coastal system;*
3. *The energy and sustainable community project through the redevelopment of public spaces and buildings;*
4. *The integrated waste cycle project;*
5. *The P.A. performance improvement project.*

In this perspective, the integrated projects for sustainability aim at stimulating collective action between the sectors of CMCA and between CMCA and the Municipalities and, around these, build consensus and the progressive definition of agreements among stakeholders for their implementation, on the example of the River Contracts[7], Agreement Programs[8], *etc.*

They are the fundamental elements of a new urban and territorial organization oriented towards the principles of sustainability, the sustainable metropolitan infrastructure. The next step is to focus the attention on each integrated project for sustainability to define shared guidelines for urban planning and implementation tools.

4   The Integrated Project of an Energy and Sustainable Community in a Pilot Area of the Metropolitan City of Cagliari

The last phase of the planning process proposes to implement the "Integrated project of an energy and sustainable community" in a pilot area of CMCA (Fig. 4). The project arises from the grouping of two main thematic areas. The first thematic area concerns the "Recovery, energy requalification of public buildings and structures", which has as its key objective: "Make public structures and facilities energetically autonomous". It refers to the actions financed by the tender on the energy efficiency of public buildings promoted by the POR FESR 2014–2020[9], which concerns the energy efficiency of municipal buildings and the production of energy from renewable sources and smart grids for energy distribution.

Another action characterized by a high *recurring nature* in the metropolitan area concerns the "Integrated and smart management of public lighting systems", both as regards the arrangement of new lighting fixtures with LED technology (*relamping*), and as regards the renovation of the networks and energy supply infrastructures (*revamping*), promoted by Axis 2 - PON Metropolitan cities 2014–2020. The second thematic area concerns "Social and aggregative renewal and reuse of abandoned, degraded, disused spaces and buildings", and assumes as its key objective "Allocate spaces and structures for social / aggregative use", promoted by specific call for tenders. From the input of the energy efficiency, the integrated project for sustainability outlines a perspective in which single interventions of a punctual nature, considered by the referents themselves to be of strictly local importance, foster the development of new configurations, rules and behaviours. Note that they don't concern only the reduction and the conscious use of energy, but also unfold towards new forms of shared management of spaces and services to be recovered for the community.

4.1   Selection of the Pilot Area: The Terramaini Area

The pilot area is essential for experimenting the effectiveness of the method. The elements that guide the selection of the Terramaini as a pilot area can be summarized mainly for its relevance in the metropolitan area.

Firstly, the strategic importance in term of the environmental landscape is recognized at different scale levels by the special management tools and by the municipal and

---

[7] Art. 68 bis D. Lgs 152/2006.

[8] Art. 205 D. Lgs 152/2006.

[9] Asse Prioritario IV. "Energia sostenibile e qualità della vita" - Azioni 4.1.1.-4.3.1. http://www.sardegnaprogrammazione.it/.

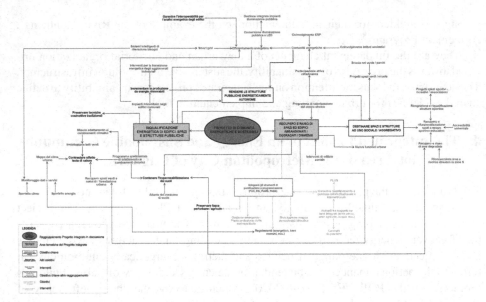

Fig. 4. The cognitive map of the integrated project for a "renewable energy and sustainable community"

metropolitan planning tools. It is, in fact, the "green wedge" defined by the Regional Landscape Plan of Sardinia as a connection system between the north-western bank of the Molentargius Pond, the Municipalities of Cagliari, Pirri and Monserrato up to the agricultural belt. Furthermore, the proximity to the Molentargius-Saline Natural Park, characterized by different levels of protection, suggests integrated policies for the enhancement and a distinct use of the area as a whole: the process starts from the school district and involves gradually other services, including the Terramaini park and the public sports facilities (Fig. 5).

Secondly, the projects planned for this area have a metropolitan relevance with supra-municipal effects in terms of sustainable development: the creation of an energy district, which involves the secondary schools in the area under the jurisdiction of CMCA, and a sports hub, which envisages the creation of a network of paths, watercourses, wetlands and vegetated areas to compose a new park system. These are supported by other projects, such as the "Restoration of the Waterways", which plans the canal navigable and usable with paths and charging stations for electric boats.

Thirdly, this area is a catalyst context for social and institutional energies to test self-organization formulas due to the presence of a highly specialized school complex[10]. Note that various learning communities and numerous sports associations enjoy the use of the area and manage spaces equipped for different sports (hockey, rugby, basketball, padel, football, *etc.*), including a municipal swimming pool and a nautical club. The

---

[10] The school complex is composed of: the "I.T.I. Marconi" Industrial Technical Institute; the "ITC Besta" Commercial Technical Institute; the "Vittorio Emanuele" National Boarding School; the "S. Pertini" Professional Institute for Social Services; the "ITI Scano" Industrial Technical Institute; the "Pietro Martini" Economic Technical Institute - Monserrato Headquarters; the Artistic and Musical High School "F. Fois"; the "Da Vinci" State Technical Commercial Institute.

Fig. 5. The Terramaini pilot area

active involvement of these users in the integrated project for sustainability can be seen in terms of *communities of practice* [10, 11], i.e. different paths linked to practices for experimenting with initiatives useful for satisfying collective needs: at the local level, in terms of communities of users, to define shared contractual regulation formulas for the use and the management of spaces and services and, from these, self-organized formulas for the sustainable use of resources (electricity, water, waste, etc.); at the metropolitan level, in terms of dissemination of good practices.

Finally, the integrated project for sustainability begins with the sharing of energy and extends to the sharing of other sustainability values and resources, triggering regenerative policies with a strong enabling character in terms of cooperation, collaboration and subsidiarity between different subjects. In this sense, it is precisely the local communities and their differences that allow global SDGs to be contextualized.

4.2 The Renewable Energy Communities. Prospects of Activation in the Metropolitan Context

Starting from 2016, as part of the so-called "Clean Energy" package, the European Commission has attributed to energy consumers a central role in the transformation processes of the energy markets. In the current scenario that looks to the reduction of CO2 emissions and control over the elements that govern their price, civil society is urged to participate actively and consciously in rethinking the energy system.

The EU Directive 2018/2001 introduces a governance model defined the "Renewable Energy Communities" (RECs) with the opportunity of energy sharing among its members[11].

Renewable energy communities are defined as legal entities made up of natural persons, small and medium-sized enterprises or local authorities, including municipalities, which on a voluntary basis, through the use of the already existing public distribution network, come together to produce and consume renewable energy. Furthermore, members can actively participate in the various phases of the energy production and management process as well as the economic resources provided by the incentives for the part of shared energy and possibly for the excess which must be minimized in favor of the first. These are based on a decentralized and widespread model in the areas of energy production and consumption.

Some technical requirements are binding for obtaining the incentives but, at the same time, they influence the geography and composition of the RECs. The renewable source plants must not exceed the power of 1 MW and the energy must be shared between plants and energy consumers connected to the same primary transformer station. If, on the one hand, the technical issues define standard constraints and requirements to be considered in the establishment and identification of the RECs, on the other hand, the shared purpose of the members must not be the generation of financial profits but open up new prospects for the territories depending on the diversity and specificity of the community and the places of their actions.

In addition to achieving environmental, economic and social benefits for the members of the Community and local context, RECs must trace a generative trajectory in terms of shared values and objectives. It shows a strict correlation with the concept of community: the "Manifesto of the Energy Communities for an active centrality of the Citizen in the new energy market"[12], promoted by the Energy Center Lab of the Turin Polytechnic,

[11] In Italy, the Directive was implemented with Legislative Decree No. 199 / 2021 and at the end of November 2022 the observations of the Implementation Document were published.

[12] "Manifesto. Le Comunità Energetiche per una centralità attiva del Cittadino nel nuovo mercato dell'energia". Energy Center Lab, Politecnico di Torino, giugno 2021. https://www.energycenter.polito.it/le_comunita_energetiche.

which places the accent on the local aggregation process activated in a REC through the innovation in the way of generating, consuming and managing energy and on the new opportunities for the users of the Community services, citizens and local contexts on which the effects of the activities and projects of the community are experienced.

From the comparison of experiences of RECs already active in Italy and Europe[13], the absence of a standard community model emerges. On the contrary, the diversity of experiences denotes the specificity of the local contexts and the centrality of individual or collective figures who, through awareness-raising and involvement actions, configure themselves as real "community animators". In the constitutive events of the RECs in Italy, as well as in Germany, Great Britain, Spain, *etc.*, these figures often coincide with local administrators, sometimes stimulated by local entrepreneurs or university institutions as in the case of Magliano Alpi, the first Italian energy community.

There is no shortage of cases in which the citizens themselves activate the RECs, involving the municipality in a subordinate position: is emblematic of the experiences of the North Kensington Community Energy (NKCE)[14] made up of 144 members of different ethnic groups. In any case, the local authorities are the key figures in the processes of creation and activation of new subjects. This role is recognized by the different measures and sources of funding at national and regional level, which promote and incentivize the development of ERCs, directing funding to municipalities and public bodies.

In summary, a Renewable Energy and Sustainable Community (RESC) is founded on some Constitutional principles (art. 118 [12]). These are crucial for the activation of the principle of *subsidiarity*, the both vertical and horizontal, which concerns the collaborative relationship between public administrative bodies and citizens, including even private individuals; the principles of *adequacy* and *differentiation* concerning the definition of agreements, contracts, regulations, must take into account the different natures and complexities of the subjects involved, in terms of the roles they can assume and the contribution given for the management of the community, both as support to the territory; the principle of *autonomy* concerning the recognition and enhancement of the free initiative of citizens, especially in the forms of associations, for activities of general interest. In addition, there are conditions that strengthen the sense of community, such as: *mutual trust*, which goes beyond the rules and authorisations; solidarity, inclusion and equity, with particular attention given to disadvantaged subjects and contexts; responsibility, with particular attention given to the subjects who have a coordination and guidance role to support the associative thrusts of the stakeholders.

Starting from these elements, the energy district of the Terramaini area fosters new forms of cooperation, collaboration and subsidiarity between the "activator of the Community" (CMCA) and the users of the surroundings services and facilities of the energy district: the school communities and the sports associations.

---

[13] https://www.interregeurope.eu/sites/default/files/2021-12/Policy%20brief%20on%20rene wable%20energy%20communities.pdf;   https://www.legambiente.it/wp-content/uploads/ 2021//11/Comunita-Rinnovabili-2022_Report.pdf.

[14] https://www.interregeurope.eu/good-practices/community-energy-england.

5   Guiding Requirements for a Sustainability-Oriented Planning by the Integrated Project in the Pilot Area

The integrated project of the Renewable Energy and Sustainable Community of Terramaini makes it possible to further specify the SDGs from the metropolitan context to the specific one, to provide a level of direction and guidance for the actions.

Firstly, the integrated project is articulated through a set of operational key objectives referring to the Terramaini pilot area, which define the reference scenario.

Secondly, the integrated project outlines the types of *actions* to achieve the key objectives. They are divided into *activating* and *complementary actions*, according to their potential in guiding transformations. Yet, the actions are defined in relation to the specificities and uses of the local context. The actions concern: physical spaces, infrastructures and services; usage behaviors and ways of living; methods of collective organization and forms of organized action.

Thirdly, the integrated project focuses on the formulation of context-oriented "*project attentions*", as guidelines useful for guiding actions towards the reference scenario of the RESC. They are expressed in the form of operational and procedural guidelines for the implementation of the actions, which incorporate and pursue sustainability principles and objectives according to the characteristics of the local context (Fig. 6).

Fig. 6. Framework of the integrated project structure

The articulation of the integrated project reveals the will to foster transversal relationships among fields of action for sustainability (from the energy transition to environmental redevelopment, to the regeneration of urban spaces and facilities, to the improvement of their accessibility and usability, to the launch of forms of collaboration for the management of resources and services, *etc.*). Further interdependencies and opportunities can be traced by comparing them with other projects and initiatives in the metropolitan area.

5.1   Activation of an Energy and Sustainable Community in the Pilot Area of Terramaini

The institution of a renewable energy and sustainable community suggests some basic *spatial, technical-infrastructural* and *organizational* requirements. They involve different aspects in relation to energy sharing and technological and infrastructural adaptations, such as: relationships between subjects, procedures, regulations, relationships between planning tools and levels of government.

In the specific case, through the school energy district, the various upper secondary schools of the Terramaini learning district are experimenting with a model of self-consumption and shared management of energy. In other words, this represents the starting point to trigger the broader and more ambitious process of an energy and sustainable community. The integrated project outlines the ways to evolve towards the

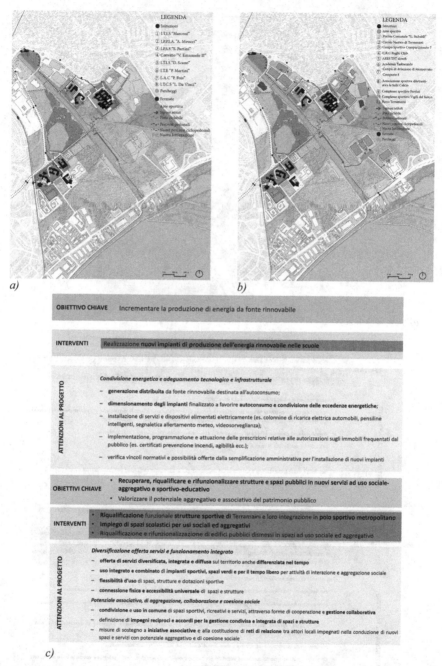

Fig. 7. The multi-scalar and multi-functional process of regeneration of the green wedge of the Terramaini area starts from the school energy district (a) and step by step triggers the complementary actions for involving spaces, services and facilities (b). Examples of context-oriented guidelines (c).

348   T. Congiu et al.

e)

OBIETTIVI CHIAVE	Realizzazione di un sistema integrato e interconnesso di spazi e servizi urbani ed ecosistemici
INTERVENTI	• **Valorizzazione dei cunei verdi come parchi metropolitani** a partire dalla rigenerazione dell'area sportivo-ricreativa di Terramaini • Realizzazione di un **sistema integrato e connesso di spazi pubblici aperti all'interno del tessuto urbano**

ATTENZIONI AL PROGETTO

Connessione, accessibilità e funzionamento integrato

– rafforzamento **connettività fisica e integrazione con tessuto urbano e ambientale circostante attraverso percorsi interni** e collegamenti con l'esterno diretti, sicuri e confortevoli che privilegino i modi di trasporto lenti

– **diversificazione delle possibilità di spostamento** alle diverse scale, verso l'area e al suo interno

– **unitarietà e continuità di spazi e percorsi** e accessibilità universale

– **sicurezza e comfort** degli ambienti

– **flessibilità, complementarietà e varietà di usi** degli spazi pubblici rivolti a molteplici categorie di fruitori

– **permeabilità dei suoli** per contrastare i rischi e gli effetti climalteranti

OBIETTIVI CHIAVE	Preservare le fasce periurbane agricole e recuperare la connettività ecologica dei corridoi fluviali
INTERVENTI	• **Riqualificazione ambientale e valorizzazione attitudine agricola fasce periurbane inedificate** tra Cagliari, Monserrato, Selargius, Quartucciu e Quartu e **loro integrazione con gli spazi attrezzati esistenti** • **Recupero ambientale e rinaturalizzazione corridoi fluviali** Riu Mortu, Riu Saliu, Riu Nou, Rio is Cungiaus, con inclusione delle aree a rischio idraulico

ATTENZIONI AL PROGETTO

Connettività ecologica e fisica e funzionalità ecosistemiche

– **mantenimento dei cunei verdi come spazi inedificati e potenziamento del loro ruolo di servizi ecosistemici**

– **connessione fisica, ambientale e percettiva** attraverso un sistema di percorsi alberati, aree verdi multifunzionali e spazi di relazione

– **recupero aree agricole degradate, ripristino** originaria **vocazione produttiva e funzionalità ecosistemiche suoli**; mantenimento usi agricoli attraverso pratiche colturali compatibili

– **contenimento dispersione insediativa e consumo di suolo con aree verdi multifunzionali**

– ripristino e potenziamento copertura vegetale per contrastare i fenomeni di dissesto: **selezione specie in base a caratteri e qualità del territorio** (suolo, clima, morfologia, idrologia)

– **compatibilità e flessibilità degli usi** nelle **aree a rischio** (per es. come zone urbanistiche S o G)

f)

Fig. 8. The multi-scalar and multi-functional process of regeneration of the green wedge (e). Examples of context-oriented guidelines (f).

condition of a community, extending participation to other public and private entities that share the principles and rules of behavior and involve other spaces, services and facilities.

In this sense, the activating project of the energy district is sustained and implemented by other complementary actions / projects in a multi-scalar process with the aim to enhance the generative role of the green wedge of the Terramaini area (Fig. 7 and 8).

Interdependencies and opportunities can be recognised with actions / projects involving the municipal and private sports facilities, the Terramaini park and the paths along the Terramaini Canal, the existing and new settlements and, on the large scale, the agricultural belt, the urban river channels (Riu Mortu, Riu Saliu, Riu Nou, Rio Is Cungiaus), industrial plants and factories along the main roads, *etc.*

In closing, the integrated project translates the SDGs and principles into shared context-oriented operational and procedural guidelines for urban planning and implementation tools.

6 Conclusions

To summarize, the integrated project of an energy and sustainable community pursues three practical things:

1. The activation of a reference model for urban planning and implementation tools. Starting from the key role of schools this model aims to try out and disseminate new behaviors, both in the production and management of energy, and in the management of their adjacent spaces, the sports facilities and nearby open spaces. These spaces become central for the promotion of opportunities for collective management (between schools and between schools and the city), in addition to be places in which innovative and sustainable forms of energy production and management are experimented.

2. The redevelopment and enhancement of the Terramaini area, confirming and strengthening its value as a green wedge, as a linear system of interconnected open spaces which perform the crucial function of ecosystem services. The green wedge of Terramaini stands out as a place within which the energy transition towards renewable sources takes place: highly natural spaces are connected to each other and made usable by the city, along with fundamental metropolitan services such as the schools, sports and recreation areas. The integrated project represents this area as an integrated and interconnected system of diversified spaces and services within the environmental matrix.

3. A clear and complete information on the distinctive features of an energy community and the technical and procedural steps for its activation and functioning. Last but not least, an opportunity to agree on mutual commitments and agreements among stakeholders for their implementation. In this sense, the integrated project recognizes the Metropolitan City as the most suitable entity to play a role of technical and administrative support through the key objective "to provide support at various levels

(to local authorities, stakeholders, enterprises and citizens) for the establishment of RESCs".

In conclusion, the aggregation potential of the integrated project starts from the sharing of energy and extends to the sharing of sustainability values, including those of inclusion and cohesion, participation and co-management, equity and equalization, supporting to local authorities, businesses, citizens, *etc.* This is the role as well as the objective of the integrated projects for sustainability within the Sustainable agenda of the Metropolitan City.

A fundamental element of the process is the coordination role of the Authority, which exercises the direction of the process, integrating institutional skills, favoring and supporting the associative thrusts of the project communities involved, and eliminating bureaucratic and procedural oppositions along with the transfer of knowledge, information and good practices for the metropolitan area in the medium and long term inspired by the principles and SDGs.

Author Contributions. TC, AP: conceptualization. TC, BD, PM, AP: planning and project investigation. TC, AP: methodology and writing—review and editing. BD: par. 4.2. All authors have read and agreed to the published version of the manuscript.

References

1. World Urbanization Prospects: The 2018 Revision, pp. 9–33. United Nations, Department of Economic and Social Affairs (2019)
2. Leeson, G.W.: The growth, ageing and urbanisation of our world. J. Popul. Ageing **11**(2), 107–115 (2018). https://doi.org/10.1007/s12062-018-9225-7
3. McCann, P., Soete, L.: Place-Based Innovation For Sustainability. Publications Office of the European Union, Luxemburg (2020)
4. Bruxelles, 14.1.2020 COM (2020) 22 final 2020/0006 (COD)
5. Rueda-Palenzuela, S.: El urbanismo ecosistémico. Estud. Territoriales, **51**(202) (2019)
6. Eden, C., Ackermann, F.: Making Strategy: The Journey of Strategic Management. Sage Publications, London (1998)
7. Plaisant, A., Wyatt, R.G., Smith, J.: Using decision-aiding software, and participatory workshops, for better strategic management of a public authority. In: 2004 Congress AESOP Proceedings, Grenoble (2004)
8. Blecic, I., Cecchini, A., Plaisant, A.: Constructing strategies in strategic urban planning: a case study of a decision support and evaluation model. In: Murgante, B., Gervasi, O., Iglesias, A., Taniar, D., Apduhan, B.O. (eds.) ICCSA 2011. LNCS, vol. 6783, pp. 277–292. Springer, Heidelberg (2011). https://doi.org/10.1007/978-3-642-21887-3_22
9. Plaisant, A., Verona, M.M.: Ideas for a better place: e-participation tools supporting decision making process at the local level. In: Planning Support Tools: Policy Analysis, Implementation and Evaluation. FrancoAngeli, pp. 1571–1584 (2012)
10. Wenger, E.: Communities of practice. Communities **22**(5), 57–80 (2009)
11. Brunetta, G., Moroni, S.: Libertà e istituzioni nella città volontaria, Mondadori, vol. 1, pp. 1–164 (2008)
12. Senato della Repubblica: Costituzione della Repubblica Italiana. Retrieved June 28 (2012): 2016

Evaluation of Urban Spaces Through the Integration of Universal Design and Microsimulation: The Case Study of the Marina District in Cagliari (Italy)

Antonio Barbagallo[1] (ID), Giulia Desogus[2] (ID), Chiara Garau[2] (ID), Matteo Ignaccolo[1] (ID), Pierfrancesco Leonardi[1] (ID), and Vincenza Torrisi[3(✉)] (ID)

[1] Department of Civil Engineering and Architecture, University of Catania, Viale Andrea Doria, 6, 95125 Catania, Italy
[2] Department of Civil and Environmental Engineering and Architecture (DICAAR), University of Cagliari, Via Marengo 2, 09123 Cagliari, Italy
[3] Department of Electric, Electronic and Computer Engineering, University of Catania, Viale Andrea Doria, 6, 95125, 95100 Catania, Italy
vincenza.torrisi@unict.it

Abstract. Ensuring safe, functional, and integrated urban environments requires the identification and organisation of qualitative and quantitative analyses to assess the quality of urban spaces, the perceived well-being and by safety the city users, and the interactions between traffic components (e.g., pedestrians and vehicles). Many techniques based on quantitative and qualitative indicators of urban space and transport mobility are offered in literature and this paper provides a methodological approach to perform a comprehensive evaluation of urban spaces and mobility interactions by calculating an Index of Integrated Road Spaces (I_{IRS}) composed of two indicators: the Universal Design Indicator (I_{UD}) and the Service Level Indicator (I_{SL}).This provides the evaluation of Perceived Road Quality (e.g. crossing; visibility; speed limit; road pavement; services), as well as the measurement of network efficiency (e.g. level of service; queue length; number of stops; delay) and environmental impact (e.g. pollutant emissions). The authors applied the merging of the two theoretical approaches of Universal Design and Transport Microsimulation by considering a real case study coinciding with the Marina district in Cagliari (Italy). Future developments of the research will be characterised by a more in-depth analysis, both in terms of spatial extension and number of indicators, useful for performing scenario analysis.

Keywords: VISSIM/VISWALK · Universal Design · Microsimulation · Active mobility · Redesign urban spaces · Level of service · Emissions · Pedestrian evaluation · Smart City

© The Author(s), under exclusive license to Springer Nature Switzerland AG 2023
O. Gervasi et al. (Eds.): ICCSA 2023 Workshops, LNCS 14110, pp. 351–370, 2023.
https://doi.org/10.1007/978-3-031-37123-3_26

1 Introduction

Urban public spaces are essential for the development of cultural, social, economic, and political activities within cities. The quality of public spaces is the first element to characterise a well-organised and safe city, with efficient services able to guarantee fairness and social inclusion [1–7]. These aspects involve a good design and management of transport infrastructures and, in some cases, a redesign of urban environment [8, 9]. To ensure an urban space perceived as safe and functional, it is advisable to pursue an integrated transport-land planning, designing user-centred environments that guarantee a good interaction between transport components within the urban environment [10–13]. There are several models which analyse the transport-territory interactions, both from a conceptual and a methodological point of view. One of the proposed methodologies based to the concept of accessibility focuses on the relationship between transport and land use, by using a synthetic indicator of the organization level of the territory [14]. Another study proposed multi-criteria analysis methods, combining the quantifiable results of traffic microsimulation and AHP multi-criteria optimization method, developing five groups of criteria (functional, safety, economic, environmental, and urban-spatial ones). [15]. Within this context, it can be advisable to combine this research with investigations about the propensity of users to modal shift and other forms of mobility [16–18]. Other work provided operational definitions to assess the road environment through a walkability index useful for later testing significant associations with pedestrian behaviour [19]. More specifically, by using an expert panel assessments five qualities of Universal Design are measured associated with the physical characteristics of the road infrastructures. And their edges: imaginability, enclosure, human scale, transparency, and complexity [20]. As regards the traffic microsimulation modelling, there are many applications that analyse the traffic influence within urban environments. For example, a study focused on a pedestrian crossing and the related indicators have been evaluated. This method allowed the assessment of different scenario and comparative analysis through the calculation of performance indicators related to both private transport and pedestrian users [21]. However, still today, the literature lacks a specific analysis on the integration of dynamic approaches that better define urban mobility management and static approaches that analyse accessibility from the point of view of the user to roads, transit stations or more generally to other public places. Thus, it is necessary to identify a methodology to define measurement, evaluation and monitoring indicators characterizing the relationship between road infrastructures and urban built. In this direction, the authors focus on the integration of two theoretical approaches, a dynamic one and static one. Universal Design is a static design approach that aims to create "products" for all users, e.g., regardless of gender, age, ability to move, prior knowledge, by following the principles of equity, flexibility, and intuitiveness [22]. In the case of urban planning this is linked to the concept of usability which "encompasses an activity component and refers to the extent to which a space, product or service can be meaningfully utilised by users with different individual abilities" [23, p.2]. Therefore, it is a design approach that recognises the diversity of human needs and seeks to satisfy them, avoiding segregating or excluding some users' categories (e.g., vulnerable users). In recent years, the principles of Universal Design have been applied to the built environment, including streets and public spaces, to create more accessible and user-centred environments [24–27].

User-centred design focuses on the needs, capabilities, and preferences of the end user, rather than just technical or engineering considerations. For example, a user-centred approach applied to the road design might include the involvement of users with disabilities or the elderly to understand their needs and designing road infrastructures with appropriate characteristics to meet those needs [28]. This can lead to changes in the physical layout of streets, e.g., wider sidewalks, intersections with interventions to increase pedestrian safety and visibility, as well as to the use of more specific materials, e.g., brightly coloured pavements to improve visibility or tactile markings to guide movements of visually impaired. Furthermore, Universal Design and user-centred design principles have a key role in improving the accessibility of the road environment, promoting social inclusion, increasing physical activity and personal independence, and reducing mobility inequalities.

Starting from these assumptions, the authors intend to develop a methodology that integrates qualitative and quantitative assessments of urban environments. This goal is pursued by identifying an index (composite indicator) of Integrated Road Spaces (I_{IRS}), perceived as the capacity of an urban environment to be comfortable for all user types of and in all its spaces (i.e., infrastructures, streets, pedestrian paths, and services). The paper is structured in five sections: after a brief introduction which states the goal of the paper (Sect. 1), Sect. 2 describes the study area, i.e., Stampace and Marina districts of the city of Cagliari, within which some indicators are analysed. Section 3 presents the methodology used for identifying an index of Integrated Road Spaces (I_{IRS}), being composed of a Universal Design Indicator (I_{UD}) and Service Level Indicator (I_{SL}). Section 4 will report some of the obtained results for the case study and the calculation of the composite indicator through the combination of normalised results of Universal Design and Transport Microsimulation. Finally, Sect. 5 provides conclusions and future work perspectives.

2 Case Study

The selected area is in the historical center of the city of Cagliari in (Sardinia), on the border between the Stampace and Marina districts. This area is characterised by numerous monuments, religious and civil architectures, and archaeological sites. Moreover, there are many for commercial activities and leisure services.

The work focuses on the intersection between Via Roma and Largo Carlo Felice (Fig. 1), one of the most popular meeting places in the city of Cagliari, from which some of the main arteries of the city branch off [29]. The analysis of the area shows that it is one of the busiest in the city, with high rate of pedestrians and vehicular traffic. In addition, it is characterised by the presence of many car parking spaces (Fig. 2), as well as the transit of numerous urban public transport lines. These factors greatly contribute to the increase in the level of congestion within this area. The study area has been analysed within the Sustainable Urban Mobility Plans (SUMPs) of the city of Cagliari [30–33], a tool containing actions and strategies for the promotion of sustainable mobility and the deployment of Information and Communication Technologies (ICT) and Intelligent Transport Systems (ITS) to foster smart cities [34–37]. It represents a critical interchange node both at local and regional level [38–40], from which reference

354   A. Barbagallo et al.

is made for the vehicular flows for the microsimulation methodology. These traffic flows have been obtained from the SUMP General Report of Cagliari, drafted in December 2018.

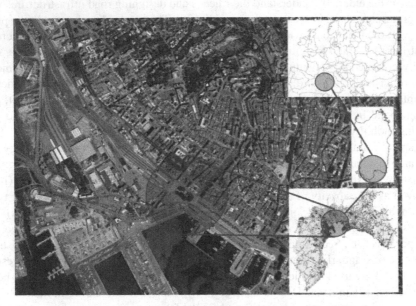

Fig. 1. Study area. Source: Author elaboration from Google Earth

Fig. 2. Study area. Source: Author elaboration from Google Earth

Data recorded refers to the turning manoeuvres at the traffic light intersection, between the main road of Via Roma and Largo Carlo Felice. The traffic data have been counted for one working day for each section, from 7.30 a.m. to 9.30 a.m. and classified by type of vehicle (i.e., car, bike, motorcycle, bus, commercial vehicles, etc.). Simulating a time interval of 3600 s for microsimulation, only data for the time slot 8:30–9:30 a.m. have been considered, with a total of 2,407 vehicles, divided between bikes/motorcycles, cars, light commercial vehicles, heavy goods vehicles, and buses. The table below show the traffic flows for the diagram of the manoeuvres at the intersection (Table 1 and Fig. 3).

Table 1. Traffic Flow

Origin	Destination	Bike/Motorcycle	Car/LCV	HCV	Bus	Total
A	B	1	35	0	10	46
	C	18	165	3	0	186
	D	7	277	0	7	291
	E	0	0	0	12	12
B	A	37	270	0	0	307
	C	61	762	0	1	824
C	A	8	219	0	7	234
	B	14	346	0	0	360
	D	1	84	0	15	100
	E	0	0	0	47	47
Total		**147**	**2158**	**3**	**99**	**2407**

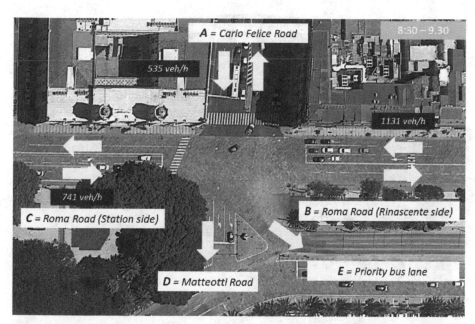

Fig. 3. Intersection with vehicular flows. Source: Author elaboration from SUMP of Cagliari

3   The Methodological Approach.

This methodology is based on the combination of Universal Design indicators and traffic micro-simulation indicators. To compare, the authors adopted a systematic approach [41–43], which results in a specific Index of Integrated Road Spaces (I_{IRS}). Figure 4 schematises the methodological framework characterized by an integrated approach between urban analysis through Universal design which studies spaces that are safe, comfortable, and usable for everyone, regardless of one's physical or cognitive limits, and the Microsimulation approach which simulate the transport network in details and the interactions between transport components and surrounding urban environment.

The Index of Integrated Road Spaces (I_{IRS}) has been defined by use of a geometric mean [44]. Formula 1 shows how the two factors shown in Fig. 4 (Universal Design and microsimulation model) have been combined, once the parameters identified for each key factor were normalised.

$$I_{IRS} = (I_{UD} + I_{SL}) \qquad (1)$$

Universal design is an urban planning strategy that focuses on creating accessible and inclusive public spaces for all people, regardless of their physical abilities, age, gender, ethnic or socioeconomic origin. The main objective of the indicators described in Fig. 4 is to analyse the physical conditions of the spaces around the streets (analysed with the microsimulation approach) to allow people to take full advantage of public spaces and participate in community life.

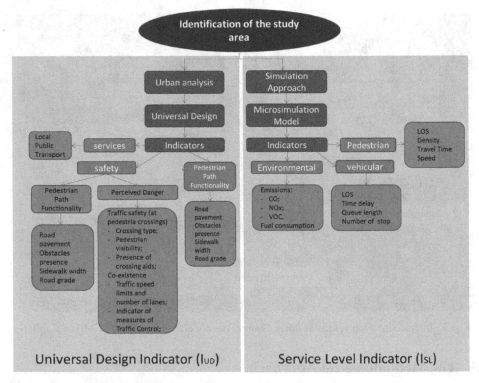

Fig. 4. Methodological framework. Source: authors elaboration.

Micro-simulation shows the movement of individual road users (vehicles, bicycle, and pedestrian traffic) through the traffic network and their interaction with each other.

Microsimulation helps you make the right decisions when it comes to designing and controlling transport infrastructure [45]. Therefore, cities, operating companies and consulting firms rely on software support for planning, evaluating and visualizing traffic measurements.

The analysed indicators for the identification of factors of Universal design (UD) are obtained through (i) google maps (or direct display), (ii) Geographic Information System (GIS) and (iii) regional or municipal laws, in this case Zone30 km/h of the City of Cagliari. In particular, the indicators used define:

1) Safety is a composite indicator that intersects the perception of danger perceived by the user and the functionality of the pedestrian path. In particular, the first is analysed by calculating traffic safety, which describes the type of crossing, pedestrian visibility, presence of crossing aids, and the coexistence between pedestrian and road, i.e., traffic speed limits, number of lanes and control measures traffic). In this way, from a UD perspective, the user's safety describes his perception of the shared space.

2) pleasantness is calculated through the quality of services for the community by making a proportion between the number of activities (Commercial Activities, Food Service, General Services, Recreational Functions) existing in each portion of land and the number of activities accessible to all the types of users. In fact, from a UD perspective, activities accessible to all types of users are important because (i) they guarantee the inclusion of people with disabilities, reducing the risk of discrimination and social isolation, (ii) they improve everyone's quality of life citizens, promoting the use of free time in a healthy and constructive way and (iii) promote social interaction and integration between people, improving the quality of life of all citizens, promoting the use of free time in a healthy and constructive way.

3) Local Public Transport (LPT) services are calculated with a proportion between existing and optimal nodes (understood as LPT stops) (from one node to the other 600 m). The importance of this indicator lies in the fact that the number of stops determines the accessibility of the areas served by the public transport service. The more stops there are along a given line, the greater the spatial coverage of the service and therefore the greater the accessibility to the destinations. This is particularly important for people with disabilities, the elderly, children, and other categories of users who may need an accessible public transport service close to their homes or workplaces.

Table 2 shows for each indicator its normalisation scale from 0 to 1 where 0 represents a poor level of UD and 1 represents an excellent level. The final index of Universal Design is calculated by averaging the resulting values.

The microsimulation indicators of traffic are analysed by modelling the study area using the PTV VISSIM software. VISSIM is a microscopic simulation tool based on simulation behaviour and steps, for modelling urban and suburban traffic as well as pedestrian flows [46, 47].

Indicators can be evaluated for both traffic flows and pedestrian flows and they can be measured at point, link, or node level. For the study area we focus on node evaluations. Node evaluation is used to determine intersection-specific data without having to manually define all sections to derive data.

Table 2. Normalisation classes of UD Indicators

Indicators	Normalisation Values					
	0	0.2	0.4	0.6	0.8	1
a) Safety						
a.1) Perceived Danger						
a.1.1) Traffic safety						
Crossing type	No intersection			Crosswalk		Signalized intersection
Pedestrian visibility	no distancing			Distancing from parking lots	Curb extension	Curb extension (L = 7 m) and raised platform
Presence of crossing aids	No					Yes
a.1.2) Co-existence						
Traffic speed limits and number of lanes	70 km/h	50 km/h (>2 Lanes)	50 km/h (2 Lanes)	50 km/h (1 Lane)	20–30 km/h	
Measures of Traffic Control	None	single speed bump	single raised crossroad		Roundabout; series of speed bumps; chicane	series of raised crossroads; road closure; curb extensions

(continued)

Table 2. (*continued*)

Indicators	Normalisation Values					
	0	0.2	0.4	0.6	0.8	1
a.2) Pedestrian Path Functionality						
a.2.1) Road pavement	path with numerous deformations, cracks, lesions, and grasses that grow on the surface or between the cracks			some deformation, cracks, lesions, and grasses that grow on the surface or between the cracks	good run-in maintenance conditions are such when crack deformations, lesions and grasses growing	excellent maintenance condition course is one with a smooth, stable, continuous, and non-slip surface
a.2.2) Obstacles presence	Yes					No
b) Pleasantness						
b.1) Commercial Activities	(N° TOT_SERV_acc)/(N° TOT_SERV)*					
b.2) Food Service						
b.3) General Services						
b.4) Recreational Functions						
c) Services (LPT)						
c.1) Local Public Transport	NODES/NODES_OCT**					

* N° TOT_SERV_acc = total number of services accessible according to Universal Design parameters; N° TOT_SERV = total number of services in the analysed area.

** NODES = nodes (bus stops) existing in the analysed area; NODES_OCT = optimal nodes (bus stops) calculated with formula (segment length/600)

The calculated indicators at the node level for traffic flows are LOS, time delay, queue length, number of stops:

i) LOS, Level of Service (transport quality): The levels of transport quality A to F for movements and edges, a density value (vehicle units/mile/lane). It is based on the result attribute Vehicle delay (average).

ii) Time delay [s]: Total time delay is determined from the "time lost" per time step. This is determined from the difference between actual speed and desired speed if the pedestrian is slower than desired.

iii) Queue length: Mean of all average queue lengths in a node. Vissim automatically generates queue counters in a node to detect queue lengths. Vissim calculates the average queue length detected by queue counters in a node and then calculates their mean.

iv) Number of stops in the queue: A queue stop occurs when a vehicle that is directly in or upstream of the queue length exceeds the speed defined for the queue conditions in the attribute Start.

In the results of microsimulation at the node level, indicators can be also displayed for exhaust gas emissions and fuel consumption. The data refers to a typical North American vehicle fleet; the node evaluation is used to compare the emissions of different scenarios. These indicators are: (i) Emissions CO: Quantity of carbon monoxide [grams]; (ii) Emissions NOx: Quantity of nitrogen oxides [grams]; (iii) Emissions VOC: Quantity of volatile organic compounds [grams]; (iv) Fuel consumption: Quantity of fuel consumed [US liquid gallon].

The implemented model, based on Helbing or Wiedemann formulations, allows to calculate indicators for the pedestrian simulation, which are: (i) Pedestrian LOS, level of service; Levels of pedestrian movement quality from A to F for displacements and segments, density value. (ii) Pedestrian density in sections [ped/m^2] or [ped/ft^2], depending on the unit selected for short distances. (iii) Travel time [s]: time the pedestrian spent in the section. (iv) Speed: average pedestrian speed in traffic conditions.

4 Application and Results

The indicator for Universal Design is calculated for each segment depicted in Fig. 5, which identifies the study node of the two methodologies: segment 1 and 3 via Roma and segment 2 and 4 Largo Carlo Felice). The right and left sides of each segment were considered, and the indicators were calculated and normalised from 0 to 1 using the formulas and parameters described in Table 2. Table 4 shows the results of the normalisation of each universal design indicator for each segment. In particular: (a) Safety is high as demonstrated by the sub-indicators that calculate Perceived Danger and Pedestrian Path Functionality (which vary in almost all segments from 0.6 to 1). However, the co-existence indicator, and consequently the relationship between different modes of transport and pedestrians, highlights some problems in all the segments analysed, underlining the need to reduce the risks to pedestrian safety and promote safety measures in the community. These safety measures will assist in altering the public's perception of pedestrian safety and enhance the quality of life for all users. Pedestrians must have access to designated secure zones, such as dedicated cycle lanes, footpaths, and pedestrian areas, as well as adequate pedestrian crossings. The high traffic speed of this junction coupled with many lanes poses significant risks to pedestrians when crossing the road. To mitigate this risk, the speed limit should be reduced, and road lanes should be marked accordingly. Additionally, a reduction in speed limits will improve drivers' reaction times and give pedestrians more time to cross safely. (b) The pleasantness of the road is an important aspect in any urban context and is closely linked to the quality of life of citizens. In particular, its evaluation was made through a series of indicators that focus on various aspects, such as the presence of commercial activities, the level of services offered, the quality of the recreational facilities and the availability of food services. The analyses have shown that the commercial activities present along the road contribute significantly to its pleasantness. In fact, all the activities have activated actions against architectural barriers, satisfying the different needs of the local community, making the street a welcoming and inclusive place. In the analysed node there are no General Services and Recreational Functions. (c) The accessibility of local public transport has been implemented effectively and in a targeted manner to meet the needs of all people. This is demonstrated by the values of the Services Indicator (LPT). For those living with disabilities, the accessibility of local public transport is of paramount importance in order to be able to participate fully in community life.

Fig. 5. Study area and calculation segments of the Universal Design Indicator. Source: elaboration by Chiara Garau and Giulia Desogus

The Universal Design Index measures how a product, service, or environment promotes accessibility and inclusion. I On a scale from 0 to 1, the Universal Design Conclusive Index is reported to be 0.61 in Table 4. This means that the studied node scored quite well in terms of accessibility and inclusion. However, there is still room for improvement to ensure greater accessibility and ease of use for people with different abilities. To achieve the goal of designing universal environments, one should adopt a set of universal design principles. These principles include flexibility of use, clarity of information, elimination of physical and cognitive barriers and simplicity of use. Furthermore, as shown in Tables 3 and 4, there should be a constant awareness of the needs of people with disabilities and the challenges they may face, especially in critical design areas as an example in traffic speed limits and number of lanes and measures of Traffic Control.

Table 3. Universal Design analysis results

Indicators	Segment			
	Seg_1	Seg_2	Seg_3	Seg_4
a) Safety				
a.1) Perceived Danger				
a.1.1) Traffic safety				
Crossing type	0.6	0.6	0.6	1
Pedestrian visibility	0.6	0.6	0.6	0.8
Presence of crossing aids	0	1	0	1
a.1.2) Co-existence				
Traffic speed limits and number of lanes	0.2	0.2	0.2	0.2
Measures of Traffic Control	0	0.2	0.2	0.6
a.2) Pedestrian Path Functionality				
a.2.1) Road pavement	1	1	1	1
a.2.2) Obstacles presence	1	1	1	1
b) Pleasantness				
b.1) Commercial Activities	1	1	1	1
b.2) Food Service	1	1	1	1
b.3) General Services	0	0	0	0
b.4) Recreational Functions	0	0	0	0
c) Services (LPT)				
c.1) Local Public Transport	1	1	1	1

As regards the application of the methodology in the study area, this has been modelled within the Vissim software. First, the entire intersection between Via Roma and Largo Carlo Felice was built by modelling the arches with the various lanes and the

Table 4. Universal Design analysis results

Indicators	Average for each indicator	
a) Safety		
a.1) Perceived Danger		
a.1.1) Traffic safety		
	Crossing type	0.7
	Pedestrian visibility	0.65
	Presence of crossing aids	0.5
a.1.2) Co-existence		
	Traffic speed limits and number of lanes	0.2
	Measures of Traffic Control	0.25
a.2) Pedestrian Path Functionality		
	a.2.1) Road pavement	1
	a.2.2) Obstacles presence	1
b) Pleasantness		
	b.1) Commercial Activities	1
	b.2) Food Service	1
	b.3) General Services	0
	b.4) Recreational Functions	0
c) Services (LPT)		
c.1) Local Public Transport		1
UNIVERSAL DESIGN INDICATOR		0.61

relative connectors. Subsequently, the traffic light system that regulates the intersection was implemented (Fig. 6).

Finally, the vehicular flows have been simulated. These have been taken from the General Report of SUMP of Cagliari, as defined in the case study. Once the vehicular flows were entered for each route and for each vehicle category, the simulation for the calculation of the indicator parameters was started. The figure shows how vehicles queue up at traffic lights before crossing the intersection (Fig. 7).

Table 5 shows the results of the simulation in terms of vehicle parameters (Service Level, Time Loss, Queue Length, and number of stops) and environmental parameters (CO, Nox and VOC emissions). Environmental indicators, emission levels and fuel consumption per node were calculated for each crossing manoeuvre in the intersection. Table 5 shows how the average Service Level of the entire intersection is very bad as it appears to have a value of F. In particular, the service level assumes level F for most manoeuvres crossing the intersection, except for some manoeuvres where the level of service assumes values between E and D. As regards time wasters, it is noted that the

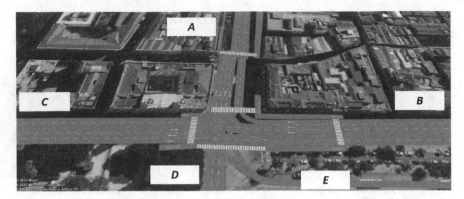

Fig. 6. View of the modelling study area. Source: authors elaboration.

Fig. 7. 3D simulation showing the behaviour of vehicles near the intersection.

Table 5. Output microsimulation

Movement	LOS	VehDelay	Queue Length	Stops	CO [g]	NOx [g]	VOC [g]
A-B	LOS D	47,41	31,91	1,58	305,791	59,496	70,87
A-C	LOS E	76,31	31,91	2,38	87,047	16,936	20,174
A-D	LOS E	67,67	31,91	2,56	570,061	110,913	132,117
A-E	LOS D	45,13	31,91	1,14	9,284	1,806	2,152
B-A	LOS F	211	255,38	10,89	1450,853	282,283	336,249
B-C	LOS F	209,39	255,38	10,52	4304,589	837,517	997,63
C-A	LOS F	85,6	52,35	2,97	616,309	119,911	142,836
C-B	LOS D	54,54	52,35	1,46	697,22	135,654	161,587
C-D	LOS E	70,42	52,35	1,89	158,84	30,905	36,813
C-E	LOS E	76,41	52,35	1,62	78,296	15,234	18,146
Total	**LOS F**	**126,18**	**113,22**	**5,69**	**8312,36**	**1617,283**	**1926,47**

greatest time wasters are found in via Roma in correspondence with arch B, where the value of time wasters exceeds 200 s. This is caused by an excessive flow of vehicles coming from branch B of via Roma. With reference to the length of the queue that forms in the branches near the intersections, in branches A and C, queues are formed on average, respectively about 30 m and 50 m long, while for branch B the length of the queue exceeds, on average, 250 m. Similarly, the number of stops for each vehicle due to traffic lights is approximately 2 for each manoeuvre in branches A and C, while for manoeuvres relating to branch B the number of stops for each vehicle rises to 10. The emission levels relative to the reference node were also calculated. As can be seen from Table 5, the value of emissions increases as the level of service and the number of stops worsen for each crossing manoeuvre. In particular, in manoeuvres coming from branch B, where the number of stop and go is high, there are high values of emission levels. To make a comparison with the Universal Design composite indicator once these values have been determined, the obtained results for vehicle delay, Queue Length, and pauses are normalised on a scale of 0 to 1 (Table 6). After normalisation, the mean value of these three normalised indicators is calculated, resulting in a singular composite indicator. As is evident, the value of this normalised indicator is not particularly high.

Table 6. Microsimulation normalised indicators

Movement	VehDelay	Queue Length	Stops
A-B	0.99	1.00	0.95
A-C	0.81	1.00	0.87
A-D	0.86	1.00	0.85
A-E	1.00	1.00	1.00
B-A	0.00	0.00	0.00
B-C	0.01	0.00	0.04
C-A	0.76	0.91	0.81
C-B	0.94	0.91	0.97
C-D	0.85	0.91	0.92
C-E	0.81	0.91	0.95
Total	0.51	0.64	0.53
SERVICE LEVEL INDICATOR (I_{SL})			

Using Formula 1, the Index of Integrated Road Spaces (I_{IRS}) allows to accurately evaluate the level of integration between the road infrastructure (Service Level Indicator_I_{SL}) and the contour under a Universal Design perspective (Universal Design Indicator_I_{UD}) to improve accessibility and usability general for all people. I_{IRS} is therefore a complex measure of the connectivity and integration of road spaces within both a transport network and a pedestrian network. The I_{IRS} provides a quantitative assessment of the quality and accessibility of road spaces (Table 7), allowing for a better understanding of the fixed transport network and its impact on the community. The I_{IRS} considers several factors, such as the presence of adequate pedestrian spaces, public transport opportunities and the interconnection capacity of the various spaces. A low I_{IRS} (equal to 0.58) indicates that the various street spaces are not well integrated and do not offer easy access to public services, residential and commercial areas, and other parts of the city. This can lead to increased traffic congestion, isolated communities, and increased reliance on private car use.

Table 7. Composite Indicator of Integrated Road Spaces

Indicators	values
UNIVERSAL DESIGN INDICATOR (I_{UD})	0.61
SERVICE LEVEL INDICATOR (I_{SL})	0.56
INDEX OF INTEGRATED ROAD SPACES (I_{IRS})	**0.58**

5 Conclusions and Future Research

This work proposed a methodology to present and evaluate some indicators of two different methodological approaches, namely, those of the Universal Design methodology and those of the traffic microsimulation methodology. Using these two static and dynamic approaches, it was possible to carry out an analysis of the urban environment in the spaces of the road network, within the Marina district of Cagliari.

As regards the Universal Design indicators, the indicators with normalised values of Safety, Services and pedestrian Path functionality obtained with various geolocated IT systems were identified, these were then calculated in the form of a single Universal Design indicator. On the other hand, the traffic microsimulation indicators (service level, number of stops, time wasters and queue length and emission levels) were calculated by modelling the study area within a software, entering data detailed inputs (i.e. number and width of lanes, vehicular flows and routes); in this case, however, in order to make a comparison with the Universal Design indicator, the Vehicle Delay, Queue Length and Stops indicators were normalised and averaged to form a single composite indicator. As the intersection in question is one of the busiest intersections in the city, the results show that the Universal Design indicator has a good value, while the single service level indicator has a modest value. The final goal of this paper was to merge the two indicators of Universal Design and level of service into the composite Indicator of Integrated Road Spaces (I_{IRS}) to obtain a complex measure of connectivity and integration of road spaces within both a transport network and a pedestrian network. The deepening of the research work moves in this direction, which foresees the expansion of the study area and the calculation of more indicators for both methodologies to represent an important decision support tool for administrations and planners in the evaluation of different strategies and actions for the redevelopment of pedestrian and vehicular urban spaces and their mutual interactions.

Acknowledgements. This work started and developed as a result of a project proposal within the doctoral course "Smart and Sustainable Cities (3rd edition)" held at the University of Cagliari coordinated by C. Garau (https://dottorati.unica.it/dotticar/smart-and-sustainable-cities-3-edizione/). This study was also supported by the MUR through the project WEAKI TRANSIT: WEAK-demand areas Innovative TRANsport Shared services for Italian Towns (Project code: 20174ARRHT), financed with the PRIN 2017 (Research Projects of National Relevance) programme. This work is also partially supported by the project of V. Torrisi "SAMOTHRACE (ECS00000022) -" under the programme "European Union (NextGeneration EU) – MUR-PNRR). The work has been partially financed by the project "TETI – innovative technologies for control, monitor and safety at sea" CUP: B45F21000050005 under the programme "PON Ricerca e Innovazione 2014 – 2020". This study was also supported by the Technical-Scientific Collaboration Agreement "PON METRO 2014–2020 ASSE 6 – Action CA6.1.1.b – Cagliari smart city: Integration of urban governance with the mitigation of urban heat islands (CA_UHI)" stipulated between Municipality of Cagliari and the Department of Environmental Civil Engineering and Architecture of the University of Cagliari, (DICAAR_UNICA), This study was developed within the Interdepartmental Center of the University of Cagliari "Cagliari Accessibility Lab".

Authors' Contributions. This paper is the result of the joint work of authors. 'Abstract', 'Introduction', 'Case study', 'Conclusions and future research' were written jointly by the authors. AB, VT and GD wrote 'Methodological approach' and 'Application and Results'. In particular, AB and VT wrote parts on microsimulation and GD wrote parts on Universal Design. CG and MI and VT supervised the article.

References

1. Mouratidis, K.: Urban planning and quality of life: a review of pathways linking the built environment to subjective well-being. Cities **115**, 103229 (2021)
2. Kalakou, S., et al. (2023) Citizens' attitudes towards technological innovations: The case of urban air mobility, Technological Forecasting and Social Change, 187
3. Doğan, E., Jelinčić, D.A.: Changing patterns of mobility and accessibility to culture and leisure: Paradox of inequalities. Cities **132**, 104093 (2023)
4. Camporeale, R., Caggiani, L., Ottomanelli, M.: Modeling horizontal and vertical equity in the public transport design problem: a case study. Transp. Res. Part A: Policy Pract. **125**, 184–206 (2019)
5. Torrisi, V., Ignaccolo, M., Inturri, G.: Innovative transport systems to promote sustainable mobility: developing the model architecture of a traffic control and supervisor system. In: Gervasi, O., et al. (eds.) ICCSA 2018. LNCS, vol. 10962, pp. 622–638. Springer, Cham (2018). https://doi.org/10.1007/978-3-319-95168-3_42
6. Garau, C., et al.: A methodological framework for assessing practicability of the urban space: the survey on conditions of practicable environments (SCOPE) procedure applied in the case study of Cagliari (Italy). Sustainability **10**(11), 4189 (2018)
7. Garau, C., Annunziata, A.: Public Open Spaces: connecting people, squares and streets by measuring the usability through the Villanova district in Cagliari, Italy. Transport. Res. Procedia **60**, 314–321 (2022)
8. Ignaccolo, M., et al.: How to redesign urbanized arterial roads? The case of Italian small cities. Transport. Res. Procedia **60**, 196–203 (2022). https://doi.org/10.1016/j.trpro.2021.12.026
9. Campisi, T., Caselli, B., Rossetti, S., Torrisi, V.: The evolution of sustainable mobility and urban space planning: exploring the factors contributing to the regeneration of car parking in living spaces. Transport. Res. Procedia **60**, 76–83 (2022). https://doi.org/10.1016/j.trpro.2021.12.011

10. Guida, C., Carpentieri, G., Zacharias, J.: A smart approach for integrated land-use and transport planning—an application to the naples metro station areas. In: Gervasi, O., Murgante, B., Misra, S., Rocha, A.M.A.C., Garau, C. (eds.) Computational Science and Its Applications – ICCSA 2022 Workshops: Malaga, Spain, July 4–7, 2022, Proceedings, Part VI, pp. 395–409. Springer International Publishing, Cham (2022). https://doi.org/10.1007/978-3-031-10592-0_29

11. Pellicelli, G., Caselli, B., Garau, C., Torrisi, V., Rossetti, S.: Sustainable mobility and accessibility to essential services. An assessment of the san benedetto neighbourhood in Cagliari (Italy). In: Gervasi, O., Murgante, B., Misra, S., Rocha, A.M.A.C., Garau, C. (eds.) Computational Science and Its Applications – ICCSA 2022 Workshops: Malaga, Spain, July 4–7, 2022, Proceedings, Part VI, pp. 423–438. Springer International Publishing, Cham (2022). https://doi.org/10.1007/978-3-031-10592-0_31

12. Caselli, B., Rossetti, S., Ignaccolo, M., Zazzi, M., Torrisi, V.: Towards the definition of a comprehensive walkability index for historical centres. In: Gervasi, O., et al. (eds.) ICCSA 2021. LNCS, vol. 12958, pp. 493–508. Springer, Cham (2021). https://doi.org/10.1007/978-3-030-87016-4_36

13. Ortega, J., et al.: An integrated multi criteria decision making model for evaluating park-and-ride facility location issue: a case study for Cuenca city in Ecuador. Sustainability 13(13), 7461 (2021). https://doi.org/10.3390/su13137461

14. Rubulotta, E.: Trasporti e territorio. Il ruolo dell'accessibilità nella pianificazione integrata (Doctoral dissertation, Università degli Studi di Catania). Statista Research Department (2022) (2011). https://www.statista.com/statistics/452345/italy-number-of-registered-passenger-cars/

15. Ištoka Otković, I., et al.: Combining traffic microsimulation modeling and multi-criteria analysis for sustainable spatial-traffic planning. Land 10(7), 666 (2021)

16. Torrisi, V., et al.: Assessing the propensity to car sharing services in university cities: some insights for developing the co-creation process. Travel Tourism Studies Transp. Dev., Commun. 24(3), G1–G14 (2022)

17. Campisi, T., et al.: Factors influencing the implementation and deployment of e-vehicles in small cities: a preliminary two-dimensional statistical study on user acceptance. Transp. Res. Procedia 62, 333–340 (2022)

18. Campisi, T., Cocuzza, E., Ignaccolo, M., Inturri, G., Torrisi, V.: Exploring the factors that encourage the spread of EV-DRT into the sustainable urban mobility plans. In: Gervasi, O., et al. (eds.) ICCSA 2021. LNCS, vol. 12953, pp. 699–714. Springer, Cham (2021). https://doi.org/10.1007/978-3-030-86976-2_48

19. Ignaccolo, M., et al.: A step towards walkable environments: spatial analysis of pedestrian compatibility in an urban context; European Transport; Giordano Editore. European Transport\Trasporti Europei 76(6), 1–12 (2020)

20. Ewing, R., Handy, S.: Measuring the unmeasurable: urban design qualities related to walkability. J. Urban Des. 14(1), 65–84 (2009)

21. Torrisi, V., Garau, C., Barbagallo, A., Leonardi, P., Ignaccolo, M.: Modelling of interactions between pedestrians and vehicular traffic to promote active mobility: the case of san benedetto neighbourhood in Cagliari (Italy). In: Computational Science and Its Applications–ICCSA 2022 Workshops: Malaga, Spain, July 4–7, 2022, Proceedings, Part IV, pp. 453–468. Springer International Publishing, Cham (2022)

22. Bollettino di Legislazione Tecnica: https://legislazionetecnica.it/node/1356667

23. Pinna, F., Garau, C., Annunziata, A.: A literature review on urban usability and accessibility to investigate the related criteria for equality in the city. In: Gervasi, O., et al. (eds.) ICCSA 2021. LNCS, vol. 12958, pp. 525–541. Springer, Cham (2021). https://doi.org/10.1007/978-3-030-87016-4_38

24. Pinna, F., Garau, C., Maltinti, F., Coni, M.: Beyond architectural barriers: building a bridge between disability and universal design. In: Gervasi, O., et al. (eds.) ICCSA 2020. LNCS, vol. 12255, pp. 706–721. Springer, Cham (2020). https://doi.org/10.1007/978-3-030-58820-5_51

25. Maltinti, F., et al.: Vulnerable users and public transport service: analysis on expected and perceived quality data. In: Gervasi, O., et al. (eds.) ICCSA 2020. LNCS, vol. 12255, pp. 673–689. Springer, Cham (2020). https://doi.org/10.1007/978-3-030-58820-5_49

26. Nicoletta, R., et al.: Accessibility to local public transport in Cagliari with focus on the elderly. In: Gervasi, O., et al. (eds.) ICCSA 2020. LNCS, vol. 12255, pp. 690–705. Springer, Cham (2020). https://doi.org/10.1007/978-3-030-58820-5_50

27. Coni, M., et al.: On-board comfort of different age passengers and bus-lane characteristics. In: Gervasi, O., et al. (eds.) ICCSA 2020. LNCS, vol. 12255, pp. 658–672. Springer, Cham (2020). https://doi.org/10.1007/978-3-030-58820-5_48

28. Campisi, T., et al.: Evaluation of walkability and mobility requirements of visually impaired people in urban spaces. Res. Transp. Bus. Manag. **40**, 100592 (2021). https://doi.org/10.1016/j.rtbm.2020.100592

29. Garau, C., Desogus, D., Coni, M.: Fostering and planning a smart governance strategy for evaluating the urban polarities of the Sardinian Island (Italy). Sustainability **11**, 4962 (2019). https://doi.org/10.3390/su11184962

30. Piano Urbano della Mobilità Sostenibile. Città di Cagliari. https://www.cittametropolitana cagliari.it/portale/page/it/pums_focus?contentId=FCS10852. Accessed 27 Apr 2023

31. Adozione del Piano urbano della mobilità sostenibile (Pums). Città di Cagliari. https://www.comune.cagliari.it/portale/page/it/01__adozione_del_piano_urbano_della_mobilita_sosten ibile_pums?contentId=DOC136462. Accessed 27 Apr 2023

32. Garau, C., Desogus, G., Annunziata, A., Mighela, F.: Mobility and health in the smart city 3.0: trends and innovations in Italian context. In: Lytras, M.D., Housawi, A.A., Alsaywid, B.S. (eds.) Smart Cities and Digital Transformation: Empowering Communities, Limitless Innovation, Sustainable Development and the Next Generation, pp. 105–127. Emerald Publishing Limited (2023). https://doi.org/10.1108/978-1-80455-994-920231006

33. Annunziata, A., Desogus, G., Mighela, F., Garau, C.: Health and mobility in the post-pandemic scenario. an analysis of the adaptation of sustainable urban mobility plans in key contexts of Italy. In: Computational Science and Its Applications–ICCSA 2022 Workshops: Malaga, Spain, July 4–7, 2022, Proceedings, Part VI, pp. 439–456. Springer International Publishing, Cham (2022)

34. Torrisi, V., Ignaccolo, M., Inturri, G.: Exploiting its technologies through a traffic supervisor system to support strategies and actions promoting sustainable mobility. In: ICTTE 2018, Belgrade, pp. 1042–1049 (2018). ISBN 978-86-916153-4-5

35. Sturiale, L., Scuderi, A.: Information and communication technology (ICT) and adjustment of the marketing strategy in the agrifood system in Italy. In: CEUR Workshop Proceedings, vol. 1152, pp. 77–872011. 5th International Conference on Information and Communication Technologies for Sustainable Agri-Production and Environment, HAICTA 2011Skiathos, 8 Sep 2011–11 Sep 2011

36. Torrisi, V., Garau, C., Inturri, G., Ignaccolo, M.: Strategies and actions towards sustainability: Encouraging good ITS practices in the SUMP vision. In: AIP Conference Proceedings, vol. 2343, no. 1, p. 090008. AIP Publishing LLC (2021). https://doi.org/10.1063/5.0047897

37. Torrisi, V., Garau, C., Ignaccolo, M., Inturri, G.: "Sustainable urban mobility plans": key concepts and a critical revision on SUMPs guidelines. In: Gervasi, O., et al. (eds.) ICCSA 2020. LNCS, vol. 12255, pp. 613–628. Springer, Cham (2020). https://doi.org/10.1007/978-3-030-58820-5_45

38. Garau, C., Desogus, G., Banchiero, F., Mistretta, P.: Reticular systems to identify aggregation and attraction potentials in island contexts. The case study of Sardinia (Italy). In: Gervasi, O., et al. (eds.) ICCSA 2020. LNCS, vol. 12255, pp. 294–308. Springer, Cham (2020). https://doi.org/10.1007/978-3-030-58820-5_23

39. Garau, C., Desogus, G., Maltinti, F., Olivo, A., Peretti, L., Coni, M.: Practices for an integrated planning between urban planning and green infrastructures for the development of the municipal urban plan (MUP) of Cagliari (Italy). In: Gervasi, O., et al. (eds.) ICCSA 2021. LNCS, vol. 12958, pp. 3–18. Springer, Cham (2021). https://doi.org/10.1007/978-3-030-87016-4_1

40. Garau, C., Masala, F., Pinna, F.: Cagliari and smart urban mobility: analysis and comparison. Cities **56**, 35–46 (2016)

41. Garau, C., Desogus, G.: A preliminary survey for a smart framework for the island contexts. In: Proceedings of the IFAU 2018—2nd International Forum on Architecture and Urbanism, Pescara, Italy, 8–10 Nov 2018

42. Garau, C., Desogus, G., Stratigea, A.: Territorial Cohesion in Insular Contexts: Assessing External Attractiveness and Internal Strength of Major Mediterranean Islands. Eur. Plan. Stud. (2020). https://doi.org/10.1080/09654313.2020.1840524

43. Garau, C., Desogus, G., Stratigea, A.: Monitoring sustainability performance of insular territories against SDGs: the mediterranean case study region. J. Urban Plann. Dev. **148**(1), 05021069 (2022)

44. Garau, C., Masala, F., Pinna, F.: Benchmarking smart urban mobility: a study on italian cities. In: Gervasi, O., et al. (eds.) ICCSA 2015. LNCS, vol. 9156, pp. 612–623. Springer, Cham (2015). https://doi.org/10.1007/978-3-319-21407-8_43

45. Torrisi, V., Ignaccolo, M., Inturri, G.: The microsimulation modeling as a tool for transport policies assessment: an application to a real case study. In AIP Conference Proceedings, vol. 2611, no. 1, p. 060006. AIP Publishing LLC (2022)

46. Fellendorf, M., Vortisch, P.: Microscopic traffic flow simulator VISSIM. In: Barceló, J. (ed.) Fundamentals of Traffic Simulation, pp. 63–93. Springer New York, New York, NY (2010). https://doi.org/10.1007/978-1-4419-6142-6_2

47. Lownes, N.E., Machemehl, R.B.: VISSIM: a multi-parameter sensitivity analysis. In: Proceedings of the 2006 Winter Simulation Conference, pp. 1406–1413. IEEE (2006)

Assessing Tourism Environmental Sustainability in Mediterranean Insular Destinations – Case Study Zakynthos Island

Akrivi Leka(✉), Natalia Tsigarda, and Anastasia Stratigea ⓘ

Department of Geography and Regional Planning, School of Rural, Surveying and Geoinformatics Engineering, National Technical University of Athens (NTUA), Athens, Greece
{akrleka,stratige}@central.ntua.gr, ntsigarda@yahoo.com

Abstract. Attractiveness of tourist destinations relies heavily on the quality of natural/cultural resources, the maintenance of which in such destinations is fraught with difficulties. This is particularly true in Mediterranean islands, i.e., fragmented, naturally- and culturally-endowed territories and globally-acknowledged mass tourism destinations, confronted with severe threats, especially in overcrowded coastal zones. The goal of this paper is to outline a Tourism Environmental Sustainability (TES) approach as a means for assessing and regularly monitoring tourism environmental impacts on Mediterranean insular destinations. TES follows an indicator-based stream, built upon a combined top-down and bottom-up approach for guiding the selection of island-specific tourism sustainability indicators. The top-down one brings on board distributed knowledge on relevant, well-established global/European indicator systems (e.g. UNWTO, ETIS Toolkit); and sets up an enriched indicator pool for assessing tourism environmental sustainability. This is downscaled to the Mediterranean islands' context, and is further elaborated by means of a bottom-up approach, supporting indicators' prioritization on the ground of key attributes/vulnerability of each specific island under study. Implementation of TES in Zakynthos Island, Greece, namely an island currently confronted with severe tourism-related environmental impacts, demonstrates the need for well-documented, of global reach tourism sustainability assessments in alignment with place-specific peculiarities/fragility of the natural environment.

Keywords: Mediterranean islands · Sustainable Tourism · Tourism Environmental Sustainability · Environmental Indicators · Zakynthos-Greece

1 Introduction

Tourism, as a sector with a positive imprint on citizens' well-being [1] and a contributor to economic prosperity, growth and competitiveness lies among the primary developmental levers in the planning and policy discourse. However, despite the critical importance of tourism for many national and local/regional economies around the globe – including Greece – due to its capacity to generate growth, development of the sector can also jeopardize social welfare, natural integrity and economic prosperity when

© The Author(s), under exclusive license to Springer Nature Switzerland AG 2023
O. Gervasi et al. (Eds.): ICCSA 2023 Workshops, LNCS 14110, pp. 371–390, 2023.
https://doi.org/10.1007/978-3-031-37123-3_27

violating sustainability principles [2, 3]. Thus reaping tourism benefits takes for granted a well-established balance between economic growth on the one hand and preservation/sustainable exploitation of natural and cultural resources on the other [4]; while also maintaining quality of life and wealth of host communities [5].

The aforementioned balance has initiated the debate on the limits of growth, including the tourism sector. Actually this debate is not a new one, but dates back at least to the 60s [6]. Up to early 80s, such a debate had at its heart the concept of carrying capacity; while the focus was on identifying and properly managing the adverse effects of tourism by duly reorienting tourism policy [7]. Such an approach, however, was by early '90s replaced by the popular sustainable tourism term, perceived as a concept that fits best to all kind of tourism activities, spatial scales and distinct environmental contexts [6]. Defined by the WTO, sustainable tourism denotes a model that takes full account of its current and future economic, social and environmental impacts; while also addresses the needs of visitors, tourism industry, environment and the host communities [8]. However, as mentioned by Saarinen [6], the concept of carrying capacity occupies a key position in sustainable tourism. In fact, many of the principles of sustainable tourism are founded in the concept of carrying capacity, occasionally interpreted as an application of sustainable tourism [9].

The potential contribution of tourism to sustainability objectives is currently acknowledged at the international level, including UN Agenda 2030 and the Sustainable Development Goals (SDGs). Towards this direction, prioritization of sustainable tourism in SDGs is directly linked to [10]:

- SDG8 on 'Decent work and economic growth', and specifically in Target 8.9, aiming to "devise and implement policies to promote sustainable tourism that creates jobs and promotes local culture and products by 2030";
- SDG12 on 'Sustainable production and consumption patterns', particularly in Target 12.b, aiming to "develop and implement tools to monitor sustainable development impacts for sustainable tourism that creates jobs and promotes local culture and products";
- SDG14 on 'Life below water', Target 14.7 aiming to "increase the economic benefits to Small Island Developing States (SIDS) and Least Developed Countries (LDCs) by 2030 through, among others, sustainable management of tourism".

However, attainment of sustainable tourism seems to be a tricky task. In fact, the current rapid growth and wide geographical expansion of tourist flows, coupled with developments occurring in the highly volatile external environment (climate crisis, economic and health crises, etc.) render the study of tourism and its evolution a "wicked problem'. As such, it calls for a multi- and inter-disciplinary as well as a multi-level approach. In addition, in order for a sustainable tourism outcome to be attained, its growth limits should be in alignment with social and environmental carrying capacity of destinations [11–13], rendering thus compliance with carrying capacity constraints quite critical in framing a sustainable tourism model [14].

As recognized by the WTO [8], progress towards sustainability in tourism has so far been rather slow, in addition to the sector's late start in applying monitoring procedures for assessing its impacts on destinations. Furthermore, despite the long-standing discussion and interest in sustainable tourism as well as the major advances in tourism statistics, there is yet no standardized basis for relevant data collection at either the national or the subnational level. This is a significant *gap*, and one that limits the potential for data-enabled policy development, directed at advancing sustainable tourism goals and monitoring tourism sustainability achievements [15]. Furthermore, sustainability perception, in general, varies across diversifying community actors, grasping tourism development from different angles. Thus, applicability of international assessment toolkits can be questioned; while tailored-made approaches are considered as essential for operationalizing tourism sustainability assessments.

When downscaling at the Mediterranean level, the aforementioned knowledge/data gaps on tourism still remain of key importance and actually a main obstacle in order for policy making processes to be properly fed; and sustainable tourism models, in line with communities' expectations, to be articulated [16]. Such a gap is definitely noteworthy when considering the pivotal role of the Mediterranean world's leading destinations – about 30% of international arrivals in 2015 [17] and 41% of the European arrivals in 2019 [18] – rendering thus sustainable tourism a key driver for reaching sustainability objectives in this globally-acknowledged tourism hot spot area.

Particular significance in the Mediterranean region is gained by insular territories, i.e. fragmented land compartments and highly-rated tourism spots, as well as designated planning and management units due to insularity drawbacks [19]. The confined area of islands, the spectacular natural and cultural resources, and the small size of indigenous populations render them particularly vulnerable to tourism impacts. Thus concern is raised as to these impacts on islands' tangible and intangible identity (e.g. architecture, landscape, traditions, etc.), preservation of local ecosystems, land use change for accommodation and tourism-related infrastructure, etc.; since, in most cases, tourist development in such areas leaves aside issues of scale and surpasses carrying capacity limitations [20]. Tourist intensity and overcrowding in insular territories can undoubtedly increase both social and environmental pressures, a state already witnessed in Greek islands [19, 21]; and call for appropriate assessment tools for quantifying impacts or level of tourism sustainability performance.

Within such a context, the focus of this work is on the development of a methodological approach for assessing Tourism Environmental Sustainability (TES) in fragmented, owing fragile ecosystems, insular areas and is structured as follows: in Sect. 2 the environmental dimension of sustainable tourism is shortly discussed; Sect. 3 presents the methodological approach of this work; Sect. 4 describes the implementation of the proposed methodological framework in Zakynthos Island, Greece; finally, in Sect. 5 results are discussed and key conclusions are drawn.

2 The Environmental Dimension of Sustainable Tourism

Tourism development can definitely benefit a destination (e.g., job creation). However, when superficially planned and managed, such development can also have harmful repercussions on the destination's socio-cultural (e.g., loss of the traditional culture and identity) and natural environment (e.g., soil, air and water pollution, ecosystem degradation) [22]. Planning for sustainable tourism development, in this respect, serves the ultimate goal of providing directions towards a less resource-intensive tourist model. This implies a wise balance among economic, social, cultural and environmental objectives, paying noteworthy attention to the integrity and adequacy of resources. The key principles of sustainable tourism include [23]:

- Environmental sustainability, promoting a tourism model that is compatible with and endorses ecological processes, biological diversity and destinations' natural resources.
- Social sustainability, supporting a tourism development form that is in alignment with and further reinforces community's traditional principles.
- Cultural sustainability, ensuring that the tourist model pursued respects community's cultural values, while also strengthening community identity itself.

When it comes to the natural environment, tourism affects in a direct and/or indirect way the environmental state of destinations, thus gradually degrading the key resources upon which the sector is founded. In order to minimize the adverse impacts of tourism on nature, careful planning is essential, bringing on board the concept of carrying capacity. This according to WTO, is defined as *"the maximum number of people that can visit a tourist destination at the same time, without causing destruction of physical, economic or sociocultural means and an unacceptable reduction in the quality of the satisfaction of visitors"* [5, 24]. That said, a need for particular focus on carrying capacity constraints of destinations is raised, with carrying capacity being tightly interwoven with the sustainable tourism perspective. In fact carrying capacity is a means for framing environmentally-acceptable thresholds up to which tourism can grow; and provides input for more informed and environmentally-solid policy decisions as well as the steady monitoring of outcomes of their implementation [14].

Speaking of insular territories as spectacular natural and cultural ensembles, the issue of carrying capacity acquires significant relevance. This is true especially in the context of tourism, being a major pillar of islands' economic profile, but also a source of severe impacts on sustainability achievements. Early studies on island tourism have mostly raised sustainability concerns, aligned with the impact assessment of tourism development. Thus, Mai and Smith [25] assessed sustainable tourism by use of a system dynamic model, fuelled by indicators as to the number of tourists, investments, tourism infrastructure, waste, pollution and attractiveness. Ng et al. [26] assessed islands' sustainable tourism by means of the Sustainable Ecotourism Indicator System (SEIS), i.e. a system grounded in social, environmental and economic dimensions. Mcelroy [27] used tourism density estimations as a critical input for assessing future scenarios and related environmental degradation, caused by tourism overcrowding. However, worth mentioning is that construction of such indicators is case-specific, depending on the particular geopolitical, climatic, cultural and social conditions [28].

Relevant to the above discussion is the concept of Environmental Tourism Capacity (ETC), comprising all 'fixed' and 'flexible' components of the natural and built-up environment as well as infrastructure. The 'fixed' components refer to the capacity of natural systems, expressed occasionally as ecological capacity, assimilative capacity, etc. These cannot be easily manipulated by human action and, to the extent that their limits can be estimated, they should be definitely respected as such. The 'flexible' components refer primarily to infrastructure systems, e.g. water supply, sewage, electricity, transportation. The capacity limits of these components can rise through investments, organizational-regulatory measures, etc. Therefore, their values cannot be used as a basis for determining carrying capacity, but rather as a framework for orientating decision-making on management options [20]. Speaking of tourism destinations, including insular ones, the challenge at the local level is to maintain the 'fixed' components of ETC, i.e. ensure quantity and quality of natural resources that are vital for both the community and the visitors [29]. Of critical concern in this respect are coastal land, fresh water, agricultural land and marine resources, since the land- and sea-scape and especially the coastal part are the most harshly affected assets by widespread tourism activities and infrastructure.

The concept of TES is further elaborated in the following as a means for assessing tourism sustainability paths in insular territories.

3 Methodology

The methodological approach, developed in this work, follows a combined top-down and bottom-up stream in order for the most relevant indicators for assessing TES at the local level to be selected. The top-down approach elaborates on currently in place, well-established indicator systems for TES assessments. As such are considered the UNWTO Indicators for Sustainable Development of Tourist Destinations [30] and the European Tourism Indicator System (ETIS) [31]. The bottom-up approach indicates the distinct environmental aspects of a destination that are fragile and more vulnerable to tourism, thus significantly impacted by tourism development. The combination of top-down and bottom-up approaches aims at gathering distributed knowledge on TES indicators from the global and the European scenery; and properly downscaling this knowledge to the Mediterranean and particularly the islands' level so that environmental distinctiveness of insular destinations and vulnerability to tourism impacts to be effectively addressed by relevant indicators' selection. In particular, the proposed approach consists of four discrete steps (Fig. 1), namely:

- Step1: Exploration of the conceptual design and content (indicators) of global/European tourism indicators systems (UNWTO and ETIS), considered in the top-down stream.
- Step2: Merging of indicators of the above systems and downscaling at the Mediterranean level – especially insular territories – by highlighting those indicators that are relevant to the prevailing tourism model (hot spots of mainly mass nature) and the peculiar attributes – natural, cultural etc. – of Mediterranean islands.
- Step3: A bottom-up stream that, based on the case study specific attributes (Mediterranean island under study), highlights the most relevant of the aforementioned indicators for Mediterranean islands, thus prioritizing the most important ones for further consideration and/or data collection. Critical at this step is also exploration of objective quantitative (e.g. through legally binding rules) and/or scientifically sound (literature enunciated) thresholds for assessing carrying capacity surpass.
- Step 4: Delineation of case- and goal-specific indicators – based on indicators' prioritization of the previous step – and relevant data collection so that the assessment of the impacts of tourism activity on the environmental dimension of the destination to be accomplished.

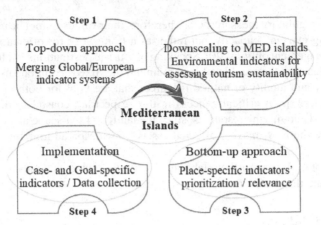

Fig. 1. Steps of the methodological approach, Source: Own elaboration

More specifically, in Step 1, the top-down stream is accomplished by elaborating on two well-documented and widely used indicators' systems, namely the UNWTO and the ETIS. More specifically, the UNWTO 2004 indicators' system is used [30] as one better oriented to planning concerns towards tourism sustainability. This system categorizes indicators into 14 issues (categories) and 42 subcategories. Within each subcategory, descriptive information on the key aspects of relevance is provided, assigning to each of them relevant indicators. The system represents a step-by-step approach, which guides the selection of operational indicators that are practically applicable to a destination. UNWTO system's architecture has formed the ground for developing the proposed, in this work, integrated indicators' system; and assessing TES as a place-based approach in Mediterranean islands.

The ETIS system [31], on the other hand, is a complete tourism management tool, grounded in a set of sustainability indicators. It contains 27 core and a set 40 optional indicators, addressing destination management, social and cultural impact, economic value and environmental impact. To the benefit of this system is that destinations can choose themselves the most relevant indicators in order for their needs, stakeholders' interests and specific sustainability challenges that the destination is confronted with to be met. ETIS provides a comprehensive, flexible and tourism sectoral perspective that intends to serve the specific sustainability expectations at each local destination [31]. Selected indicators out of the ETIS are used for enriching indicators' set of the UNWTO system, by properly merging ETIS indicators into the specific categories and subcategories of UNWTO system, taking into account potential overlapping. In addition, indicators with similar meaning are codified under the same latent category.

In Step 2, a sort of downscaling of the indicators' system produced by merging UNWTO and ETIS indicators to the Mediterranean insular context is carried out. This process takes into account peculiarities of island destinations as distinct land compartments and tourism hot spots. In particular, the selection of categories and subcategories from the previously described system is accomplished so that each one of them to best reflect the range of environmental issues that may arise in a destination that displays the essential attributes of a Mediterranean island, e.g. climate change vulnerability, tourism density and intensity, scarcity of natural resources, extraordinary fragile natural assets. This effort has resulted in a system of 50 indicators, falling into properly selected environmentally-oriented categories/subcategories shown in Table 1 (also in Table I1 in Appendix I, presenting the full list of indicators included).

Table 1. Proposed indicators' system for Mediterranean Islands – Categories and subcategories, Source: Own elaboration from [30, 31]

Category	Subcategory	Source
A. Sustaining Cultural Assets	A1. Conserving built heritage	WTO
	A2. Protecting and enhancing cultural heritage, local identity, and assets	ETIS
B. Managing Scarce Natural Resources	B1. Energy management	WTO, ETIS
	B2. Climate change and tourism	WTO, ETIS
	B3. Water availability and conservation/drinking water quality	WTO
	B4. Reducing Transport Impacts	ETIS, WTO
	B5. Water management	ETIS
C. Limiting Environmental Impacts of Tourism Activity	C1. Sewage treatment	WTO, ETIS
	C2. Solid waste management	WTO, ETIS
	C3. Air pollution	WTO
	C4. Controlling noise levels	WTO
	C5. Managing impacts of tourism & infrastructure	WTO
D. Protection of Valuable Natural Assets	D1. Protecting critical ecosystems	WTO
	D2. Sea water quality	WTO, ETIS
	D3. Beaches	ETIS, WTO
E. Controlling Tourism Activities	E1. Nr of tourists per m^2 of the site and nr of tourists per km^2 of the destination	WTO
	E2. Managing events	WTO

In Step 3, indicators of Table 1 are prioritized according to their importance as to the specific insular territory under study. This is accomplished by means of the bottom-up approach, highlighting potential environmental impacts of tourism in each specific case study context. These impacts can harm, among others, the physical – ecological state of the destination in multiple ways. Indicative impacts per distinct fields are demonstrated in Table 2; while they are also properly linked to subcategories of Table 1 and consequently to a range of respective indicators (see Table I1 for indicators' list) that can be used for assessing environmental sustainability of the tourism sector.

Work carried out in Steps 1 to 3, i.e. a combination of top-down and bottom-up approach, demarcates the necessary indicators that need to be addressed in order for the environmental sustainability of a specific insular destination to be assessed. This is accomplished in the final Step 4, provided that the relevant indicators' information is available. That said, the proposed methodological approach can also be grasped as a means for guiding the selection of indicators and collection of essential data in order for the environmental impacts of tourism in insular destinations to be assessed; and reactive or preventive policy measures for handling these impacts to be featured.

4   Implementation of the Proposed Methodology and Results

Mass tourism development in Greek islands has, for several decades, been the prevailing model and the cornerstone of local socio-economic development. Its role in the national economy is also highly acknowledged, taking into consideration that Greece hosts almost half (50.7%) of the islands located in the Mediterranean Sea [32]; and ranks among the top five tourism destinations in the Mediterranean EU territory [33]. Despite the pivotal role of tourism in the islands and state's economy [19], however, tourist flows in island regions exceed, in most of the cases, the carrying capacity of their fragile and extraordinary natural and cultural environment [14, 19]. Assessing TES of Greek Islands, in this respect, is of high priority for properly guiding policy directions towards a sustainable, resilient and long term flourishing tourist model in these extremely vulnerable land compartments.

Grounded in the previous discussion, the assessment of TES with a focus on the environmental dimension is carried out in this section, having as a case study the Zakynthos Island, Greece, i.e. a Mediterranean island that constitutes a typical example of an insular tourism destination, at least in the Greek context.

4.1   Main Attributes of Zakynthos Case Study Island

Zakynthos is one of the main islands of the Ionian complex (Fig. 2a), owing a surface of $407 \, km^2$ and a coastline of 123 km. It disposes quite distinguishable and fragile natural ecosystems (Fig. 2b), coupled with environmentally-sensitive coastal parts. The island hosts the first institutionalized National Marine Park in Greece that aims at protecting the: nesting beaches of the caretta-caretta turtle, Mediterranean seal, avifauna, terrestrial and coastal flora and fauna, marine ecosystem and fishing stocks.

The island counts for 39,737 inhabitants (2021 provisional Census data). Population displays escalating trends during the last decades and a largely uneven distribution, with the city of Zakynthos – main urban area – hosting about 40% of inhabitants. In addition, the spatial pattern of economic activity follows a polarized pattern, with dominant the eastern coastal part (Fig. 2c); while western coastal settlements are gaining strength to the detriment of the mountainous ones. This polarization is closely related to the intensification of tourism and respective deployment of accommodation/transport infrastructure in the eastern part (Fig. 2d).

Traditional economic sectors – i.e. agriculture/livestock husbandry and processing of primary agricultural products – show signs of decay during the last decade; while a gradual transition towards a tertiarized economy, dominated by the tourism sector, is in

Table 2. Indicative physical – ecological impacts of tourism on islands, Source: Own elaboration from [20]

Fields	Impacts	Subcategory WTO/ETIS
Quality of life	Uncontrolled development	C5. Managing impacts of tourism and infrastructure
	Traffic and congestion	E1. Nr of tourists per m^2 of the site, per km^2 of the destination
	Noise pollution	C4. Controlling noise levels
Infrastructure	Unsustainable waste production	C2. Solid waste management
	Unsustainable pressure on sewage system	C1. Sewage Treatment
Resources	Unsustainable use of water	B3. Water availability and conservation/Drinking water quality
	Unsustainable use of energy	B1. Energy management
	Pollution of fresh water	B3. Water availability and conservation/Drinking water quality
	Marine pollution	D2. Sea water quality
	Air pollution	C3. Air pollution
Natural Environment	Visual degradation of landscape	C5. Managing impacts of tourism infrastructure
	Forest clearance	D1. Protecting critical ecosystems
	Biodiversity loss/disturbance of endangered species	D1. Protecting critical ecosystems
	Damage to natural and cultural heritage	C5. Managing impacts of tourism infrastructure A1. Conserving built heritage
	Erosion (soil/coastal)	C5. Managing impacts of tourism infrastructure
Built Environment	Wear and tear	B2. Climate change and tourism
	Incompatibility/land use conflicts	C5. Managing impacts of tourism infrastructure
	Alteration of historic settlements (urbanization, loss of architectural heritage etc.)	A1. Conserving built heritage

* In each subcategory a number of indicators are incorporated (see Table I1 in Appendix I)

(a) Location of Zakynthos in the
Ionian Islands' complex

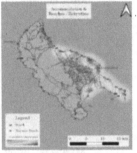

(b) Natural/cultural resources of
Zakynthos Island

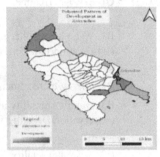

(c) Polarized pattern of development   (d) Tourism accommodation/beaches

Fig. 2. Key attributes of Zakynthos Island, Source: Own elaboration

progress. Such a transition, however, increases environmental pressure on the extraordinary natural ecosystems of the island due to the rapid expansion of the built-up environment and overcrowding (inhabitants and visitors); a situation that appears more intense in the south-eastern part of the island during the peak tourist season.

5   Assessing Environmental Sustainability of Tourism in Zakynthos Island

Minimizing the adverse impacts of tourism on the natural environment demands careful planning, with particular focus on fragile ecosystems and carrying capacity constraints for effectively framing an environmentally-solid ground for sustainable tourism to flourish. Orientation of such a planning exercise calls for identifying potential impacts of tourism on the destination and related indicators for assessing and steadily monitoring these impacts as input to policy action. Following the discussion of previous sections, steps for assessing the TES in Zakynthos Island are presented in Fig. 3.

Speaking about the developmental polarized pattern of Zakynthos Island, the transition towards a tertiarized economy that is driven by the tourism sector and pursues a highly spatially-concentrated pattern is already mentioned (see also Fig. 2). This pattern results in a high stress – in environmental terms – exerted on respective island's compartments, especially the coastal ones. As to the tourism profile, the mass pattern is so

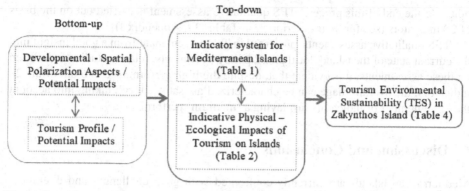

Fig. 3. Steps for assessing tourism environmental sustainability of Zakynthos Island, Source: Own elaboration

far the dominant tourism trail. This profile is sketched by a number of relevant indicators (Table 3) which, as various researchers claim, are indicative of the tourism burden in a destination [34–36].

Table 3. Key attributes of tourism activity in Zakynthos Island (2019), Source: Own elaboration from [35 38]

Indicator	Zakynthos (Ionian Islands)	Value
Tourism density (bed nights/ km^2)	10,865 (10,292 [38])	high
Tourism Intensity (bed nights/inhabitants)	111.3 (116.5 [38])	high
Number of visitors/surface of the island	1,771.34	medium
Number of visitors/local population	18.14	medium

Tourist density and intensity outcomes (Table 3) manifest the high tourist burden of the Zakynthos Island, an outcome considerably aligned with respective values for Ionian Islands as a whole. These values are classified as 'high', comparing to the ones emanating from relative studies with reference to the Greek insular context [36, 38]. Based on these studies as well, the rest two indicators of Table 3 are classified as 'medium'. Nevertheless, the spatial concentration of tourism activities (Fig. 2d), being the main source of the island's polarized developmental pattern (Fig. 3c); and the spatial distribution of natural resources (Natura 2000 regions and natural reserves) (Fig. 2b), clearly demarcate a certain risk to further degradation of natural – coastal and marine – ecosystems.

Following the steps of Fig. 3, in Table 4 the results of the qualitative assessment of the Tourism Environmental Sustainability (TES) of Zakynthos Island are displayed. Categories considered are based on those presented in Table 2, further elaborated in order to adjust to the particularities of Zakynthos Island on the one hand; and fit the categories presented in the pool of categories/subcategories/indicators presented in Table 1 on the other. At the end of this process, TES qualitative assessment is carried out on the basis of 20 indicators (see for their description in Table I1 – Appendix I).

TES qualitative assessments, presented in Table 4, emanate from a good insight into the current state of the island, local plans, policy documents, relative studies, etc. Based on these assessments, it is evident that, despite the high performance in 6 out of the 20 indicators, the overall image can be characterized as 'satisfactory', taking into account the large number of indicators displaying a 'medium' performance.

6 Discussion and Conclusions

Mediterranean Islands are currently confronted with great challenges and dilemmas. Climate crisis, energy crisis, health crisis, economic crisis as well as already visible overtourism trends and their impacts, seem to place those regions and their future sustainable (tourism) development at stake. Most of the above crises, however, are perceived as a two-sided coin, since they carry risks but also present new opportunities ahead for: awareness raising and action undertaking by local stakeholders; assessment and valuation of the services offered by the natural ecosystems to local communities; and a more dedicated effort to the remarkable opportunities offered by the current technological advances for stepping forward towards a more smart, sustainable and resilient future pathway for both insular communities and their visitors. Technological advances, in particular, seem to present a new challenging stream, taking into account the way smart applications can offer solutions to chronic problems – environmental as well – of island regions; and the progress carried out by a number of Mediterranean islands in 'going smart' in various respects.

Tourism, as a major lever for islands' development and a sector that can make a significant contribution to all three sustainable development pillars, needs also to steadily commit to this sustainability journey. The example of Zakynthos Island – being a rather typical one of tourist developed Greek islands – clearly demonstrates the outcome of an irrational, resource-intensive trajectory brought about by the development of tourism; leading also to severe structural changes and a monocultural economic orientation of the local economy. In addition, the currently unsustainable mass tourism model definitely results in a certain overcrowding of the coastal parts, as clearly demarcated in the island's spatial developmental pattern. Concurrently, this pattern places at risk the valuable and abundant land and marine resources. This, in turn, leads to loss of the comparative advantage, upon which tourism attractiveness and related products of the island are built upon. Qualitative assessment of Tourism Environmental Sustainability in Zakynthos Island clearly displays the outcomes of a rather unsustainable model, a situation that is expected to worsen, given the exponential rising of tourist flows around the globe and the position of Mediterranean islands and particularly the Greek ones as important spots in the tourism arena.

Overturning this unsustainable tourism development model calls for a place-based, multi- and inter-disciplinary planning approach, seeking to achieve consensus on well-documented desired future end states and related policy action for their implementation. The proposed TES approach can be a useful tool in this respect, combining well-established, of global reach, tourism indicators' systems – top-down stream – with local

Table 4. Qualitative assessment of Tourism Environmental Sustainability of Zakynthos Island, Source: Own elaboration [estimations by use of 2019 data (before COVID-19 outburst)]

Indicators' Categories and Subcategories		Ranking Indicator	Source	TES qualitative assessment*		
Category	Subcategory / Subvariables			1	2	3
A, Sustaining Cultural Assets	A1. Conserving Built Heritage	I.1	WTO	�		
	A2. Protecting and enhancing cultural heritage, local identity, and assets	I.5	ETIS	▪		
B. Managing Scarce Natural Resources	B1. Energy Management	I.6	WTO		▪	
		I.7	WTO/ETIS			
		I.8	WTO/ETIS		▪	
	B2. Climate Change and Tourism	I.11	WTO/ETIS			
		I.14	ETIS			
	B3. Water Availability and Conservation	1.15	WTO			
	B5. Reducing Transport Impact	I.17	ETIS			
	B6. Water Management	I.20	ETIS			
C. Limiting Environmental Impacts of Tourism Activity	C1. Sewage Treatment	I.23	WTO			
	C2. Solid Waste Management	I.25	WTO			▪
		I.28	WTO			▪
	C5.Managing Impacts of Tourism and Infrastructure	I.38	WTO			
D. Protection of Valuable Natural Assets	D1. Extent of protected area(s)	I.40	WTO	▪		
	D2. Sea Water Quality	I.41	WTO	▪		
		I.42	WTO/ETIS		▪	
	D3. Beaches	I.43	ETIS	▪		
		I.46	WTO/ETIS			
E. Controlling Tourist Activities	E1. Nr of tourists per m² of the site, per km² of the destination	I.47	WTO	▪		

*Note: 1 - High (Best performance); 2 - Medium (Medium performance); 3 - Low (Worst performance)

specificities – bottom-up stream – that highlight particular conditions and fragility of natural resources at each specific island studied. Thus a more focused selection of relevant indicators for assessing and monitoring the impacts of tourism on distinct environmental assets is conducted; and the necessary data collection fields for serving the planning effort are displayed. Provided that the necessary data is available and thresholds related to these assets are given, operationalization of respective indicators; quantification of TES qualitative assessment; regular monitoring/reporting of assessment outcomes; and articulation of relevant proactive and/or remediating policy interventions will be possible for 'filling the gap' of 'nature mistreating'.

Appendix I

See Table I1.

Table I1. Categories and subcategories of global (UNWTO) and European (ETIS) tourism indicator systems used in this work, Source: Own elaboration from WTO, WTO/ETIS, and ETIS

Category	Subcategory	Indicator	Source
A. Sustaining cultural assets	A1. Conserving Built Heritage	I.1 Number and type of new legislation introduced to preserve structures at local, regional, or national level	WTO
		I.2 Number and type of designation under which historic structures, monuments and districts are recognized	WTO
		I.3 Amount of funds allocated to the restoration, preservation, and maintenance of cultural assets on a yearly basis	WTO
		I.4 Percentage/change in the development of the surrounding area to a cultural asset	WTO
	A2. Protecting and enhancing cultural heritage, local identity, and assets	I.5 Percentage of the destination's events that are focused on traditional/local culture and heritage	ETIS
B. Managing scarce natural resources	B1. Energy Management	I.6 Per capita consumption of energy (overall, by tourist sector – per person day)	WTO
		I.7 Percentage of businesses participating in energy conservation programs, or applying energy saving policy and techniques	WTO/ETIS
		I.8 Percentage of energy consumption from renewable resources (at destinations, establishments)	WTO/ETIS
		I.9 Energy consumption per tourist night, compared to general population energy consumption per resident night	ETIS

(*continued*)

Table I1. (*continued*)

Category	Subcategory	Indicator	Source
	B2. Climate Change and Tourism	1.10 Frequency of extreme climate events	WTO
		1.11 Percentage of tourist infrastructure located in vulnerable zones	WTO/ETIS
		1.12 Total CO_2 produced due to the community's energy consumption	WTO
		I.13 Percentage of natural area coverage in the territory of the destination	WTO
		I.14 Percentage of tourism enterprises involved in climate change mitigation schemes, such as CO_2 offset, low energy systems, etc. and adaption responses/actions	ETIS
	B3. Water Availability and Conservation	1.15 Water price per litter or cubic meter	WTO
	Drinking Water Quality	1.16 Percentage of tourism establishments with water treated to international potable standards	WTO
	B4. Reducing Transport Impact	1.17 Percentage of tourists and same-day visitors using different modes of transport to arrive at the destination	ETIS
		I.18 Percentage of tourists and same-day visitors using local/soft mobility/public transport services to get around the destination	WTO/ETIS
		I.19 Average carbon footprint of tourists and same-day visitors travelling from home to the destination	ETIS
	B5. Water Management	I.20 Water consumption per tourist night compared to general population water per resident night	ETIS
		I.21 Percentage of tourism enterprises taking actions to reduce water consumption	ETIS

(*continued*)

Table I1. (*continued*)

Category	Subcategory	Indicator	Source
		I.22 Percentage of tourism enterprises using recycled water	ETIS
C. Limiting environmental impacts of tourism activity	C1. Sewage Treatment	I.23 Percentage of sewage from the destination receiving treated to at least secondary level prior to discharge	WTO
		I.24 Percentage of total waste recycled per tourist compared to total waste recycled per resident per year	ETIS
	C2. Solid Waste Management	I.25 Waste volume produced by the destination (tons)	WTO
		I.26 Percentage of tourism establishments collecting waste separately	WTO/ETIS
		I.27 Percentage of employees informed and trained in the use and disposal of the substances they use	WTO
		I.28 Waste production per tourist night compared to general population waste production per person (kg)	WTO
		I.29 Percentage of total waste recycled per tourist compared to total waste recycled per resident per year	ETIS
	C3. Air pollution	I.30 Number of days exceeding standards	WTO
		I.31 Number of health problems reported by tourists	WTO
		I.32 Cost of repair to buildings and cultural sites	WTO
	C4. Controlling Noise Levels	I.33 Noise levels at site in decibels	WTO
	C5. Managing Impacts of Tourism and Infrastructure	I.34 Total length of roads	WTO
		I.35 Total run of overhead electrical cables	WTO
		I.36 Height of buildings (average and maximum)	WTO

(*continued*)

Table I1. (*continued*)

Category	Subcategory	Indicator	Source
		I.37 Density of buildings per square kilometer	WTO
		I.38 Ridgeline or coastline continuity (percentage of intrusion on ridge and coastline)	WTO
D. Protection of valuable natural assets	D1. Protecting Critical Ecosystems	I.39 Existence of protected areas at the destination	WTO
		I.40 Extent of protected area(s)	WTO
	D2. Sea Water Quality	I.41 Turbidity of water	WTO
		I.42 Level of pollution in seawater per 100 ml (fecal coliforms, campylobacter)	WTO/ETIS
	D3. Beaches	I.43 Percentage of beaches awarded with Blue Flag	ETIS
		I.44 Total km of free beaches relative to total km of beaches	ETIS
		I.45 Percentage of beaches accessible to all	ETIS
		I.46 Number of days per year the beach/shore is closed due to contamination	ETIS/WTO
E. Controlling Tourist Activities	E1. Nr of tourists per m^2 of the site and km^2 of the destination	I.47 Nr of tourists per square meter of the site, per square kilometre of the destination	WTO
	E2. Managing Events	I.48 Number of waste bins (bins/spectators) and number of recycle bins for plastic, aluminium, paper, organic waste	WTO
		I.49 Number of security personnel (as % of spectators), number of incidents (arrests, complaints), number of medical/first aid posts	WTO
		I.50 Area for parking	WTO

References

1. Franzoni, S.: Measuring the sustainability performance of the tourism sector. Tourism Manag. Perspect. **16**, 22–27 (2015). https://doi.org/10.1016/j.tmp.2015.05.007

2. Hall, D., Richards, G.: Tourism and Sustainable Community Development. Routledge Advances in Tourism, London (2000). 0-415-30915-8
3. Coccossis, H., Mexa, A.: The Challenge of Tourism Carrying Capacity Assessment. Routledge, London (2017). ISBN 9780754635697
4. Hunter, C.: Sustainable tourism and the touristic ecological footprint. Environ. Dev. Sustain. **4**, 7–20 (2002). https://doi.org/10.1023/A:1016336125627
5. Da Silva, J., Fernandes, V., Limont, M., Rauen, W.B.: Sustainable development assessment from a capitals perspective: analytical structure and indicator selection criteria. J. Environ. Manage. **260**, 110147 (2020). https://doi.org/10.1016/j.jenvman.2020.110147
6. Saarinen, J.: Traditions of sustainability in tourism studies. Ann. Tour. Res. **33**, 1121–1140 (2006). https://doi.org/10.1016/j.annals.2006.06.007
7. Gössling, S., Hall, C.M.: Uncertainties in predicting tourist flows under scenarios of climate change. Clim. Change **79**, 163–173 (2006). https://doi.org/10.1007/s10584-006-9081-y
8. WTO-UNEP: Making Tourism More Sustainable: A Guide for Policy Makers. World Tourism Organization & United Nations Environment Programme, Madrid (2005)
9. Butler, R.W.: Sustainable tourism: a state-of-the-art review. Tour. Geogr. **1**, 7–25 (1999). https://doi.org/10.1080/14616689908721291
10. United Nations (UN): Global Indicator Framework for the Sustainable Development Goals and Targets of the 2030 Agenda for Sustainable Development. A/RES/71/313 (2017). https://documents-dds-ny.un.org/doc/UNDOC/GEN/N17/207/63/PDF/N1720763.pdf?OpenElement. Accessed 16 Mar 2023
11. Zhao, Y., Jiao, L.: Resources development and tourism environmental carrying capacity of ecotourism industry in Pingdingshan City, China. Ecol. Process. **8**(1), 1–6 (2019). https://doi.org/10.1186/s13717-019-0161-0
12. ESPON: Carrying Capacity Methodology for Tourism – Targeted Analysis – Case Study Annex. Final Report, ESPON (2020). https://www.espon.eu/sites/default/files/attachments/Tourism_final-report_CS-annex.pdf. Accessed 11 Mar 2023
13. Long, C., Lu, S., Chang, J., Zhu, J., Chen, L.: Tourism environmental carrying capacity review, hotspot, issue, and prospect. Int. J. Environ. Res. Public Health **19**, 16663 (2022). https://doi.org/10.3390/ijerph192416663
14. Leka, A., Lagarias, A., Panagiotopoulou, M., Stratigea, A.: Development of a tourism carrying capacity index (TCCI) for sustainable management of coastal areas in mediterranean islands – case study naxos. Greece. Ocean Coastal Manage. **216**, 105978 (2022)
15. Romagosa, F., Fons, J., Schröder, C.: Tourism and the Environment. Towards a Reporting Mechanism in Europe (2018). https://www.researchgate.net/publication/324330475. Accessed 18 Feb 2023
16. Rodriguez, J., Martinez, A.: Measuring Tourism Sustainability in the MED Area. Deliverable n° 3.02.08 (2018). https://planbleu.org/wp-content/uploads/2018/10/1.1.-2nd_thematic_paper_BLEUTOURMED_C3_def.pdf. Accessed 16 Feb 2023
17. UNWTO: Tourism Trends Snapshot: Tourism in the Mediterranean. 2015 edition, eISBN: 978-92-844-1692-9 (2016). https://www.e-unwto.org/doi/epdf/10.18111/9789284416929. Accessed 12 Jan 2023
18. Weston, R., Guia, J., Mihalič, T., Prats, L., Blasco, D., Ferrer-Roca, N., Lawler, M., Jarratt, D.: Research for TRAN Committee – European Tourism: Recent Developments and Future Challenges. European Parliament, Policy Department for Structural and Cohesion Policies, Brussels (2019)
19. Koutsi, D., Lagarias, A., Stratigea, A.: Evidence-based exploration as the ground for heritage-led pathways in insular territories: case study Greek islands. Heritage **5**, 2746–2772 (2022). https://doi.org/10.3390/heritage5030143

20. Coccossis, H., Mexa, A.: Defining, Measuring and Evaluating Carrying Capacity in European Tourism Destinations. B4-3040/2000/294577/MAR/D2, University of the Aegean (2002). https://ec.europa.eu/environment/iczm/pdf/tcca_material.pdf. Accessed 23 Feb 2023

21. Lagarias, A., Stratigea, A.: High-resolution spatial data analysis for monitoring urban sprawl in coastal zones: a case study in crete island. In: Gervasi, O., et al. (eds.) ICCSA 2021. LNCS, vol. 12958, pp. 75–90. Springer, Cham (2021). https://doi.org/10.1007/978-3-030-87016-4_6

22. Zhong, L., Deng, J., Song, Z., Ding, P.: Research on environmental impacts of tourism in China: progress and prospect. J. Env. Manag. **92**, 2972–2983 (2011). https://doi.org/10.1016/j.jenvman.2011.07.011

23. Angelevska-Najdeska, K., Rakicevik, G.: Planning of sustainable tourism development. Procedia Soc. Behav. Sci. **44**, 210–220 (2012). https://doi.org/10.1016/j.sbspro.2012.05.022

24. Mangion, M.-L, Satta, A., Travis, A.S.: Guide to Good Practice in Tourism Carrying Capacity Assessment. UNEP, Priority Actions Programme, Regional Activity Centre (2003). https://www.um.edu.mt/library/oar/bitstream/123456789/99226/1/PAP/RAC%20guide%20to%20good%20practice%20in%20tourism%20carrying%20capacity%20assessment.pdf. Accessed 14 Mar 2023

25. Mai, T., Smith, C.: Scenario-based planning for tourism development using system dynamic modelling: a case study of cat ba island, Vietnam. Tourism Manag. **68**, 336–354 (2018). https://doi.org/10.1016/j.tourman.2018.04.005

26. Ng, S.I., Chia, K.W., Ho, J.A., Ramachandran, S.: Seeking tourism sustainability – a case study of Tioman island, Malaysia. Tourism Manag. **58**, 101–107 (2017). https://doi.org/10.1016/j.tourman.2016.10.007

27. Mcclroy, J.L.: Tourism penetration index in small Caribbean islands. Ann. Tour. Res. **25**(1), 145–168 (1998)

28. Ocampo, L., Ebisa, J.A., Ombe, J., Geen Escoto, M.: Sustainable ecotourism indicators with fuzzy Delphi method – a Philippine perspective. Ecol. Ind. **93**, 874–888 (2018)

29. Moldan, B., Janoušková, S., Hák, T.: How to understand and measure environmental sustainability: indicators and targets. Ecol. Ind. **17**, 4–13 (2012). https://doi.org/10.1016/j.ecolind.2011.04.033

30. UNWTO: Indicators of Sustainable Development for Tourism Destinations – A Guidebook. United Nations & World Tourism Organization (2004)

31. European Commission: The European Tourism Indicator System: ETIS Toolkit for Sustainable Destination Management. Publications Office of the European Union, Luxembourg, ISBN 978-92-79-55249-6 (2016). https://ec.europa.eu/docsroom/documents/21749

32. Stratigea, A., Kyriakides, E., Nicolaides, C. (eds.): Smart Cities in the Mediterranean: Coping with Sustainability Objectives in Small and Medium-sized Cities and Island Communities. Springer International Publishing, Cham (2017)

33. Eurostat: https://ec.europa.eu/eurostat/statistics-explained/index.php?title=Tourism_statistics_-_top_destinations (2019). Accessed 14 Mar 2023

34. Thomas, R.N., Pigozzi, B.W., Sambrook, R.A.: Tourist carrying capacity measures: crowding syndrome in the Caribbean. Prof. Geogr. **57**, 13–20 (2005). https://doi.org/10.1111/j.0033-0124.2005.00455.x

35. Peeters, P., et al.: Research for TRAN Committee – Overtourism: Impact and Possible Policy Responses. European Parliament, Policy Department for Structural and Cohesion Policies, Brussels (2018)

36. Vourdoubas, J.: An appraisal of over-tourism on the island of crete. Greece. Int. J. Global Sustain. **4**(1), 63–77 (2020)

37. INSETE database (Institute of Greek Tourism Confederation): (2019). https://insete.gr/. Accessed 4 Jan 2023
38. Panousi, S., Petrakos, G.: Overtourism and tourism carrying capacity: a regional perspective for Greece. In: Katsoni, V., van Zyl, C. (eds.) Culture and Tourism in a Smart, Globalized, and Sustainable World. SPBE, pp. 215–229. Springer, Cham (2021). https://doi.org/10.1007/978-3-030-72469-6_14

Recycling of Beached Posidonia Oceanica in the Construction Sector

Giovanna Concu[✉] and Luisa Pani

Department of Civil and Environmental Engineering and Architecture, University of Cagliari, Via Marengo 2, 09123 Cagliari, Italy
gconcu@unica.it

Abstract. The paper aims to outline the state-of-the-art related to the possible reuse of the Posidonia Oceanica in the construction sector. The Posidonia Oceanica constitutes an important resource from the point of view of the protection of the marine environment, however the coastal deposits of Posidonia Oceanica, caused by the modification of the sea currents due to the construction of coastal infrastructures, constitute a serious problem for management and tourist perspective. The paper takes stock of the European and Italian regulatory framework and analyzes the results of the studies present in the literature concerning the treatments Posidonia Oceanica should undergo before its reuse in the construction sector, the construction products in which it can be used and the physical-mechanical performance of these products.

Keywords: Posidonia Oceanica · Construction Sector · Recycling

1 Introduction

The Posidonia Oceanica (PO) is a plant that produces flowers and fruits and in optimal conditions colonizes huge portions of the seabed called meadows [1]. The PO meadows represent biocenosis very complex and very well structured that are typical of the Mediterranean Sea. They are characterized by a very high biological variety of species and represent nursery areas for juvenile fish as well as a refuge for many fish. In addition to having this role of protecting biodiversity, the PO meadows provide important ecosystem services: they absorb carbon dioxide, produce oxygen, stabilize the seabed through the rhizomes and therefore protect the coasts from coastal and seabed erosion [2]. The PO meadows are subject to natural exfoliation, the leaves darken and fall and go either towards the open sea forming mulching areas as in the woods, or on the ground forming coastal deposits. In the natural coastal dynamics, winter coastal storms should throw the PO coastal deposits back into the sea, but anthropic works in the coastal areas (constructions of quays, ports, etc.) blocked this natural dynamic [3, 4]. Therefore, huge quantities of PO are deposited along the coasts, with negative consequences to beach qualities, especially in tourist areas. Thus, an invaluable resource for the environment becomes a problem for economic and tourist development. Figures 1 and 2 show PO meadows, beached PO balls and beached PO leaves.

© The Author(s), under exclusive license to Springer Nature Switzerland AG 2023
O. Gervasi et al. (Eds.): ICCSA 2023 Workshops, LNCS 14110, pp. 391–403, 2023.
https://doi.org/10.1007/978-3-031-37123-3_28

Fig. 1. PO meadows and beached PO balls.

Fig. 2. Beached PO leaves.

The management of PO coastal deposits is complex as they are protected by various regulations, and it is not clear whether they are to be considered waste or resources.

At European level, the Barcelona Convention and Amendments [5], the Council Directive 92/43/EEC [6], and the Marine Strategy Framework Directive [7] establish a framework for community action in the field of marine environmental policy.

The legislative framework in Italy is not yet complete and does not appear to be in line with that of the European Community. The Italian Consolidated Act on Environment [8] classifies waste lying on lake shores and on the banks of watercourses as urban waste. The Italian Legislation [9] allows the burying in situ of PO and jellyfish deposited in the beach from the coastal storm without transport. The Italian Law called "Save the Sea" [10], declares that PO coastal deposits could be treated for re-use in other sectors.

In the last ten years, applied research has found interesting solutions for the valorization of PO [11–27]. The PO usage as energy source is difficult due to its low combustible behavior under fire [28], although research is underway on the use of PO as biomass source, e.g. for anaerobic digestion [29], but it can be used as a component of building elements having suitable fire resistance and thermal and mechanical behavior.

At European level, two research projects have been developed aimed at the management of beached PO and its reuse as recycled material. The first is the SEA-MATTER project [30], which aimed to demonstrate the technological and economic feasibility of using coastal algae and seaweed accumulations as raw materials in the composites industry. The goal was to use wet-laid nonwoven textile technology to turn this marine biomass into composite products, in the first instance acoustic panels for buildings. The second is the LIFE REUSING POSIDONIA project [31], which aimed to implement and evaluate alternative construction techniques for a building complex prioritizing the most ecological locally sourced products and demonstrating their economic viability. Specifically, beached Posidonia packed in re-used pallets as insulation material.

In this frame, this paper aims to review the state-of-the-art relating to the use of PO in the construction sector, highlighting the treatments that the material can undergo before being used, the products that have been manufactured so far and the main physical-mechanical performances of such products.

2 Regulatory Framework and Case Studies

The Barcelona Convention and Amendments [5] form the legal framework of the Mediterranean Action Plan (approved in 1975), developed under the United Nations Environment Programme (UNEP) Regional Seas Programme. The key goal of the convention is to *"reduce pollution in the Mediterranean Sea and protect and improve the marine environment in the area, thereby contributing to its sustainable development"*.

The Council Directive 92/43/EEC [6] identifies natural habitat types of community interest whose conservation requires the designation of special areas. According to the habitats hierarchical classification of [32], PO beds are priority habitat types.

The development and implementation of the Marine Strategy Framework Directive [7] should be aimed at the conservation of marine ecosystems. This approach should include protected areas and should address all human activities that have an impact on the marine environment.

The Italian Consolidated Act on Environment [8] classifies waste lying on lake shores and the banks of watercourses as urban waste. This classification is not expected in the European regulatory framework, but it is useful to identify the management authority.

The Italian Legislation [9] declare that *"Without prejudice to the regulations on the protection of the marine environment and the provisions on the subject of by-products, where there are unequivocal elements which suggest that their presence on the shoreline is directly dependent on storm surges or other natural causes, it is permitted to bury the Posidonia and beached jellyfish, provided that this takes place without transport or treatment"*.

The Italian Legislation [33] allows the use of beached PO to produce fertilizers, after the separation of the organic fraction from the sand.

The Italian Legislation [34] is a specific law that aims to classify the materials to be treated and to define their management.

The Italian Law [10] declares that *"In cases where the previous options relating to on-site maintenance or reintroduction into the natural habitat are not possible, these residues are sent to waste management plants, which, using washing technology, allow the effective separation of the sandy component from the vegetable fraction, as well as the separation of man-made waste. The washed sand recovered in the above washing plants is primarily intended for relocation to the original beach. The washed vegetable fraction recovered in the washing plants mentioned above, like other organic material, can be usefully used to produce soil improver in composting plants or valued for re-use in other sectors".*

In the light of the Italian regulatory framework, two important interventions were carried out in Italy aimed at the recovery and reuse of beached PO. The two case studies are explained in the following sections.

2.1 Case Study Respect Your Capital in Marina Di Cecina Tirreno Sea, Italy (2020)

The interventions in Marina di Cecina (Livorno), on the Gorette beach [35], were conceived by Marevivo Onlus and Pramerica SGR with a twofold objective:

1. support the Municipality of Cecina in the operations of cleaning the coast from beached PO, adopting an experimental protocol capable of reducing environmental costs,
2. maintain and document the PO meadow in front of the beach beneficiary of the intervention.

A demonstrative protocol has been implemented in which the PO, once removed from the beach, was transformed into compost, and the recovered sand was relocated to the Gorette beach, thus safeguarding the seabed.

The cost-benefit analysis of the intervention clearly showed that the RESPECT YOUR CAPITAL protocol manages to reduce the environmental costs of the PO removal operations, guaranteeing a social rate of return of 14.2%. This value, which indicates the increase in social welfare induced by the protocol, is particularly high if compared to the reference rate proposed by the European Union and implemented by Italy, which is 3.5%.

The adopted protocol demonstrated that removal costs appear to be slightly lower than those currently in use, and specific parameters able to conduct in-depth analyses in support of marine policy are needed.

It should be noted that, due to Italian regulatory framework, once treated, PO cannot be reused for the formation of dunes to be placed on the beach. Having this possibility would be of great ecological and social importance.

Following the results of the project, the Municipality of Cecina offered an area for the location of a plant for the recovery of beached PO.

The RESPECT YOUR CAPITAL protocol allowed 585 tons of surface layer of the beach to be removed with a system that did not include the presence of weighed vehicles and therefore respectful of the environment. About 150 tons of beached PO were recovered and separated from 320 tons of sand, which was purified from anthropic material (plastics and waste in general, for a total of about 15 tons which were correctly disposed of) and then brought back to the beach, thus reducing the effects of coastal erosion.

2.2   Case Study Beached PO: From Problem to Resource in Port of Sperlonga, Tirreno Sea, Italy (2021)

The Port of Sperlonga (Latina) is inserted in a high-quality environmental context, where the presence of stable and dense meadows of PO is documented. PO deposits are recurrent throughout the stretch coast close to the port area and are transported inland of the port basin itself from storm surges and currents. The sediment to be moved is under a layer of organic debris, about 30–50 cm thick, which appears to be mainly made up of submerged banquettes of PO leaves.

The purpose of the case study [36] was to examine the possible activities to be carried out to deal with the situation in a sustainable way, taking into account the current legislation. The study highlighted the following possibilities for PO treatment:

- disposal in an authorized landfill,
- extraction of active ingredients for medical applications or phytocosmetics,
- production of insulating products, especially for roofs and floors, thanks to PO thermal insulating properties and fire resistance,
- production of biocomposites, natural products obtained coupling different raw materials, to obtain eco-sustainable final products with excellent performance,
- deliver the organic material to recycling plants as input matrix to composting or anaerobic digestion plants for the production of soil improvers.

The case study pointed out that it is advisable to plan a pilot study aimed at achieving the overall feasibility assessment of the interventions and the cost-benefit estimate on the basis of experimental results aimed at defining suitable local contexts, management methodologies, technologies and specific skills that can be structured into production systems and circular economy supply chains.

3   PO Reuse in the Construction Sector

The review of the state-of-the-art relating to the use of PO in the construction sector pointed out that, after proper treatments, PO might be valorised as insulating and reinforcement material in buildings thanks to its positive influence on the physical and mechanical properties of the composites it becomes part of.

3.1   PO Treatments

The analysis of the state of the art concerning PO treatments highlighted several preliminary treatments the collected beached PO goes through before its use as recycled material in the construction sector.

Table 1 reports the main treatments proposed in scientific literature references along with the building product manufactured with recycled PO.

3.2   Mechanical and Thermophysical Characterization of Realized Products

Based on scientific literature references, in Table 2 the main tests carried out on realized products are reported.

Table 1. Main treatments planned for PO and manufactured products.

Ref	Treat	Description	Product
[20]	1°	Milling process using an industrial mill to convert PO and balls PO into short fibres	Fibrous material with high cellulose content. The polymeric matrix to bind the PO fibres was wheat gluten. Composites were made by hot-press moulding by varying the gluten content on composites in the 10–40 wt% range
	2°	Washing stage of short fibres with distilled water, until clean wastewater, to remove sand, soil, and other wastes	
	3°	NaOH (10 wt% in water) treatment for 24 h to remove excessive impurities from the surface of the fibers and made fiber swollen	
	4°	Drying process at 60 °C for 24 h of soaked fibers	
[21]	1°	Cleaning PO in fresh water to remove salt particles and other organic and inorganic debris, which were also manually removed	Polyurethane polymer matrices: resin, treated PO, and pine wood particle for interior lining constructive elements. The resin was poured into the wood-PO mixture, and the mix was stirred by hand until a homogeneous consistency was achieved
	2°	Drying process at 110 °C in an electric oven for 2 h	
	3°	Crushing mechanically to a 1 mm maximum particle size using a cutting mill	
	4°	Sieving to remove all particles lower than 0.3 mm to optimize the particle-resin mixing process, because due to the large specific surface area most of the polymer would be absorbed and the mixture wouldn't be homogeneous	
[22]	1°	Washing and drying under normal conditions (temperature: 20 °C ± 5 °C, humidity: 60% ± 5%)	Ecological loose-fill insulation material to use in the building field
	2°	Soaking in sodium hydroxide solution under different conditions. First treatment T1 consists in emerging fibers in a 2% NaOH solution during 2 h at 80 °C. Second treatment T2 is carried out using 0.75% NaOH solution for 1 h at 100 °C. Last treatment T3 consists in reproducing the T1 treatment to the fibers already treated with this same treatment	

(continued)

Table 1. (*continued*)

Ref	Treat	Description	Product
[23]	1°	Preliminarily treated with tap water to remove salt crystals: an amount of 500 g of PO leaves were weighed and shoved into a 10 l glass vessel. The flow of the tap water was kept at 5.7 l/h, which led to a residence time for the water of circa 105 min	Production of alternative building material in the form of pressed panels
	2°	Valuating salt concentrations using a conductivity meter and the respective calibration curve for salt concentrations	
	3°	Repeating 1° treatment until the conductivity of the outlet water reached the values of the tap water	
	4°	Drying naturally for 24 h	
[24]	1°	Washing with water to remove sand and other impurities	Mixtures composed of plaster and fibers of PO to manufacture an insulating and ecological material
	2°	Drying in an oven at a temperature of 30 °C for 48 h	
	3°	Storing under normal conditions (temperature: 20 °C ± 5 °C, relative humidity RH: 60% ± 5%)	
[25]	1°	Washing and rinsing with distilled water to eliminate sand and other contaminations	Manufacturing of particle boards from beached PO
	2°	Drying at room temperature for about two months	
	3°	Drying at 105 °C to 6.5–7% moisture content	
[26]	1°	Cleaning from sand and debris	PO fibres added to lime mortars to improve their characteristics
	2°	Placing in an air-conditioned room of stable conditions (20 ± 2 °C, 65 ± 3% RH), to attain mean equilibrium moisture content (11.13%)	
	3°	Mechanically crushing into smaller particles in the form of fibres (5–10 mm)	
	4°	Hydrothermal treatment at 140 °C, in an atmosphere saturated with steam, at a pressure of 1.5 atm for 2 h	

(*continued*)

Table 1. (*continued*)

Ref	Treat	Description	Product
	5°	Cooling down in desiccators and afterwards weighed and stored in a climate-controlled room, at 20 ± 2 °C temperature and 65 ± 3% relative humidity	
[27]	1°	Washing	Cement paste reinforced with PO fibers
	2°	Drying	
	3°	Crushing	

Table 2. Tests carried out on realized products.

Ref	Tests
[20]	Standardized flexural tests for evaluating mechanical properties Thermo-mechanical behavior of composites evaluated with dynamic mechanical analysis and determination of heat deflection temperature
[21]	Density, compressive strength, elastic modulus
[22]	Thermal conductivity and diffusivity of samples measured with the Hot-Disk method, and density
[23]	Density, flexural tests, water absorption and swelling properties
[24]	Compressive strength, flexural strength, thermal conductivity, and thermal diffusivity
[25]	Internal bond strength, modulus of rupture and modulus of elasticity, resistance to axial withdrawal of screws and thickness swelling after 24 h and 48 h immersion in water
[26]	Mechanical properties of PO fibres, chemical characterization of fibres, microstructure using scanning electron microscopy, fresh state properties of lime mortars, harden state properties of lime mortars
[27]	Thermal conductivity and thermal diffusivity are measured with the Hot-Disk Transient Plane Source. Density, tensile and compressive strength, and fracture toughness of composite

3.3 Results and Discussions

PO Treatments

In most cases, the treatments are simple and consist of washing, drying, crushing, and sieving. In some cases, to improve the durability of the PO fibres in the alkaline environment of lime/cement mortar and to remove salt crystals (mainly NaCl), PO could be preliminarily soaked in sodium hydroxide solution (solution at 2–6%).

However, their extraction and preparation did not need high technicality.

Mechanical and Thermophysical Characterization of Realized Products
The results obtained from the studies present in the scientific literature are summarized in Table 3.

Table 3. Results from scientific literature.

Ref	Product/composition	Characteristics
[20]	3mm composite sheets PO + wheat gluten protein binder	Flexural strength 22.2–40.8 MPa Flexural modulus 2.35–3.99 GPa Impact energy 0.10–0.11 kJ/m^2
[21]	max 10mm panels PO + pine wood particles + polymer matrice (PU or MDI)	Density 0.629–1.110 g/cm3 Compressive strength 0.99–9.45 MPa Elastic modulus 308.1–1240.9 MPa
[22]	Loose-fill material	Density 17–155 kg/m^3 Thermal conductivity 0.043–0.070 W/mK Thermal diffusivity 0.30–1.06 × 10^{-6} m^2/s Heat capacity 2169–2533 J/KgK
[23]	Composite boards PO leaves + PMDI binder + acetone	Density 308–480 kg/m^3 Flexural strength 2.67–7.94 MPa
[24]	40 × 40 × 160 mm^3 and 270 × 270 × 40 mm^3 specimens PO fibers + Hemi-hydrate gypsum plaster	Density 1.11–0.66 g/cm^3 Flexural strength 4.5–7 MPa Compressive strength 13.8–14.8 MPa Thermal Conductivity 0.11–0.29 W/mK Thermal Diffusivity 2.05–2.9 × 10^{-7} m^2/s
[25]	16 mm single layer particleboards PO leaves + wood chips + urea-formaldehyde resin	Density 0.53–0.55 kg/m^3 Modulus of rupture 1.26–2.83 MPa Modulus of elasticity 279.23–583.29 MPa Internal bond strength 0.03–0.12 MPa Moisture content 9.93–11.41% Thickness swelling 57.42–66.70%
[26]	40 × 40 × 160 mm^3 specimens PO fibres (hydrothermal/alkaline treatment) + lime mortar	Flexural Strength 0.375–0.894 MPa Compressive Strength 0.745–1365 MPa Dynamic modulus of elasticity 3590–7450 MPa Open porosity 33.88–35.09%
[27]	40 × 40 × 160 mm^3 and 44 × 44 × 10 mm^3 specimens PO fibers + Portland cement paste	Density 1613–1761 kg/m^3 Thermal conductivity 0.559–0.718 W/mK Thermal diffusivity 0.298–0.362 × 10^{-6} m^2/s Flexural strength 4.2–4.8 MPa Compressive strength 23–29 MPa

Composites based on PO waste and 10–40 wt% wheat gluten protein as binder [20] show interesting mechanical performance, like some commodity plastics such as polypropylene. Natural fibers are highly hydrophilic, thus composites with natural fibers are highly sensitive to moisture and water uptake. As PO fiber is mainly composed of cellulose and hemicellulose, its sensitivity to water is higher than gluten, so that as the total amount of gluten increases, the water uptake is reduced.

Panels made of a mixture of PO fibers and pine wood particles with two different polymeric matrices (PU-823 – monocomponent PU, and PU-815 – bicomponent PU with MDI isocyanates) as binder [21] show that, in comparison to standard wood particle boards, the mechanical performances do not reach European standards requirements. However, particle boards made of 75% PO and 25% wood particles, and a 20–30% by fibres mass MDI matrix showed the best strength and stiffness to density ratios, being the stiffness even similar to that of a panel made totally in wood and MDI in the same dosage.

The chemical sodium hydroxide (NaOH) treatment can be needed to remove impurities from the fiber's surface [22]. The treatment does not change noticeably the thermal conductivity, the thermal diffusivity, and the heat capacity of PO fibres, which are comparable to those of industrial insulation materials. Therefore, PO fibres could be a promising ecological loose-fill insulation material in the building field.

When PO leaves are bound with polymeric methylene diphenyl diisocyanate (MDPI) to produce leaf boards [23], good flexural strength can be reached, and swelling test results indicate a moisture high resistance. Therefore, it is not suitable to commit PO waste in the landfill, but it could be beneficial to use this biomass in construction.

PO fibres bound with semi-hydrate β plaster realize a plaster with suitable mechanical and thermophysical properties [24]. The addition of PO fibers improves the compressive and flexural strengths and the thermal insulation of the new material.

Particleboards from PO fibres (50%) and wood chips (50%) bound with urea-formaldehyde resin have good performances related to swelling [25].

The use of PO fibres in lime composites improves fresh state (air content, water retention, workable life) and mechanical properties (flexural and compressive strength) [26]. The treatment of PO leaves, both in the presence of NaOH or CaOH, improves the adhesion of the fibres to the lime matrix. In particular, the mechanical properties of the composite were improved by 60% when PO fibres were treated with NaOH.

The reinforcement of cement paste with PO fibers produces the improvement of material insulation properties and compressive and flexural strengths in comparison with cement paste without PO fibres [27]. Incorporating PO fibres in cementitious matrix significantly increases the material ductility and its ability to bridge cracks.

The analysis of the state-of-the-art highlights that the PO can find various uses in the building sector. The research conducted so far is still non-organic, however it highlights the potential of PO as a usable material for the production of composites characterized by increased physical-mechanical properties. Moreover, the ISPRA (Italian Institute for Environmental Protection and Research) report [37] expresses that the accumulations of beached PO on the Italian coasts vary in the range 20 t/year-90 t/year, making clear the economic sustainability of the use of PO in the construction sector.

On the other hand, the analysis of the European and Italian regulatory framework highlights the need for the legislator to definitively clarify that PO beached for natural causes does not constitute waste if treated on site as a natural mass reintroduced into the habitat, or if used as a natural raw material for production purposes, inserting the recovered PO in a circular economy perspective.

Researchers and far-sighted entrepreneurs have focused on the problem of reconciling environmental protection and tourist use of beaches, implementing good practices to transform the problem of managing coastal areas subject to PO accumulation into a series of activities which, on the one hand allow the coast to be preserved (recovery of sand, removal of plastic and waste), and on the other the recycling of PO in other productive sectors such as construction one.

The Italian case studies RESPECT YOUR CAPITAL [35] and BEACHED PO FROM PROBLEM TO RESOURCE [36] and the Spanish projects SEA-MATTER [30] and LIFE REUSING POSEIDONIA [31] are important examples to replicate.

4 Conclusions

The present paper addresses the problem of managing beached Posidonia Oceanica, which affects many areas of the Mediterranean basin, and the transformation of this material from waste to resource through its possible reuse in the construction sector.

To this end, the paper analyzed the state-of-the-art relating to the use of PO as a material for the construction sector, the European and Italian regulatory framework relating to the treatment and reuse of PO, and some case studies to be considered good practices for the management of the problem of beached PO accumulation through its reuse in construction.

The study highlighted the opportunities offered by the reuse of beached PO in the building sector and the need to intervene at a regulatory level to encourage this conversion.

Despite the research conducted so far is still non-organic, the analysis of the state-of-the-art highlighted that PO can be valorized as a building material for the manufacturing of composites characterized by increased physical-mechanical properties. However, for PO recycling and reuse in the construction sector to be followed, it is necessary that the legislation in force in Italy and in Europe classifies PO beached for natural causes not as waste but as natural row material reusable in the context of circular economy.

The possibility of using beached PO in the construction sector constitutes an opportunity to reconcile the need to protect the coastal environment with that of its tourist valorization. This is important especially for the development of territories such as islands, often structurally disadvantaged, for which the implementation of circular economies is beneficial and desirable.

This paper analyzed only the state-of-the-art related to the possible use of PO in the construction sector. Based on the collected data, future research developments aim to carry out experimental activities of beached PO recycling and reuse in buildings on the island of Sardinia (Italy), strongly affected by the presence of PO banquettes.

References

1. Belzunce, M., Navarro, R., Rapoport, H.: Seed and early plantlet structure of the Mediterranean seagrass Posidonia oceanica. Aquat. Bot. **82**, 269–283 (2005)
2. Green, E.P., Short, F.T.: World Atlas of Sea grasses: Present Status and Future Conservation. University of California Press, Berkeley, USA (2003)
3. Duarte, CM.: How can beaches be managed with respect to seagrass litter? In: Borum, J., Duarte, C.M., Krause-Jensen, D., et al. (eds.) European seagrasses: an introduction to monitoring and management Copenhagen: EU project Monitoring and Management of European Seagrass Beds, pp.83–87 (2004)
4. Buia, M.C., Gambi, M.C., Zupo, V.: Structure and functioning of Mediterranean seagrass ecosystems: an overview. Biol. Mar. Mediterr. **7**(2), 167–190 (2000)
5. Convention for the Protection of the Marine Environment and the Coastal Region of the Mediterranean (1976 and 1995). https://www.unep.org/unepmap/who-we-are/contracting-parties/barcelona-convention-and-amendments. Last accessed 24 Mar 2023
6. Council Directive 92/43/EEC: https://eur-lex.europa.eu/legal-content/EN/TXT/?uri=celex%3A31992L0043. Last accessed 24 Mar 2023
7. Marine Strategy Framework Directive 2008/56/EC: https://www.eea.europa.eu/policy-documents/2008-56-ec. Last accessed 24 Mar 2023
8. Italian Legislation D.L. 152/2006: https://www.gazzettaufficiale.it/dettaglio/codici/materiaAmbientale. Last accessed 24 Mar 2023
9. Italian Legislation D.L. 205/2010: https://www.gazzettaufficiale.it/eli/id/2010/12/10/010G0235/sg. Last accessed 24 Mar 2023
10. Italian Law 60/2022: https://www.gazzettaufficiale.it/eli/id/2022/06/10/22G00069/sg. Last accessed 24 Mar 2023
11. Ferrero, B., Fombuena, V., Fenollar, O., Boronat, T., Balart, R.: Development of natural fiber-reinforced plastics (NFRP) based on biobased polyethylene and waste fibers from Posidonia oceanica seaweed. Polym. Compos. **36**(8), 1378–1385 (2015)
12. Khiari, R., Krouit, M., Belgacem, M.N., Mauret, E., Mhenni, M.F.: Preparation and characterization of material composite with Posidonia oceanica. Matériaux Techniques **100**(5), 369–375 (2012)
13. Fortunati, E., Luzi, F., Puglia, D., Petrucci, R., Kenny, J.M., Torre, L.: Processing of PLA nanocomposites with cellulose nanocrystals extracted from Posidonia oceanica waste: innovative reuse of coastal plant. Ind. Crops Prod. **67**, 439–447 (2015)
14. Allègue, L., Zidi, M., Sghaier, S.: Mechanical properties of Posidonia oceanica fibers reinforced cement. J. Compos. Mater. **49**(5), 509–517 (2015)
15. Bettaieb, F., Khiari, R., Dufresne, A., Mhenni, M.F., Putaux, J.L., Boufi, S.: Nanofibrillar cellulose from Posidonia oceanica: properties and morphological features. Ind. Crops Prod. **72**, 97–106 (2015)
16. Puglia, D., Petrucci, R., Fortunati, E., Luzi, F., Kenny, J.M., Torre, L.: Revalorisation of Posidonia oceanica as reinforcement in polyethylene/maleic anhydride grafted polyethylene composites. J. Renew. Mater. **2**(1), 66–76 (2014)
17. Saval, J.M., Lapuente, R., Navarro, V., Tenza-Abril, A.J.: Fire-resistance, physical, and mechanical characterization of particleboard containing Oceanic Posidonia waste. Materiales de Construcción **64**(314), e019 (2014)
18. Garcia-Garcia, D., Quiles-Carrillo, L., Montanes, N., Fombuena, V., Balart, R.: Manufacturing and characterization of composite fibreboards with posidonia oceanica wastes with an environmentally-friendly binder from epoxy resin. Materials **11**(1), 35 (2017)
19. Kuqo, A., Boci, I., Vito, S., Vishkulli, S.: Mechanical properties of lightweight concrete composed with Posidonia oceanica fibres. Zaštita Materijala **59**(4), 519–523 (2018)

20. Ferrero, B., Boronat, T., Moriana, R., Fenollar, O., Balart, R.: Green composites based on wheat gluten matrix and Posidonia Oceanica waste fibers as reinforcements. Polym. Compos. **34**(10), 1663–1669 (2013)

21. Maciá, A., Baeza, F.J., Saval, J.M., Ivorra, S.: Mechanical properties of boards made in biocomposites reinforced with wood and Posidonia oceanica fibers. Compos. B Eng. **104**, 1–8 (2016)

22. Hamdaoui, O., Ibos, L., Mazioud, A., Safi, M., Limam, O.: Thermophysical characterization of Posidonia Oceanica marine fibers intended to be used as an insulation material in Mediterranean buildings. Constr. Build. Mater. **180**, 68–76 (2018)

23. Kuqo, A., Korpa, A., Dhamo, N.: Posidonia oceanica leaves for processing of PMDI composite boards. J. Compos. Mater. **53**(12), 1697–1703 (2019)

24. Jedidi, M., Abroug, A.: Valorization of Posidonia oceanica Balls for the Manufacture of an Insulating and Ecological. Mater. Jordan J. Civ. Eng. **14**(3), 417–430 (2020)

25. Rammou, E., Mitani, A., Ntalos, G., Koutsianitis, D., Taghiyari, H.R., Papadopoulos, A.N.: The potential use of seaweed (Posidonia oceanica) as an alternative lignocellulosic raw material for wood composites manufacture. Coatings **11**(1), 69 (2021)

26. Stefanidou, M., Kamperidou, V., Konstantinidis, A., Koltsou, P., Papadopoulos, S.: Use of Posidonia oceanica fibres in lime mortars. Constr. Build. Mater. **298**, 123881 (2021)

27. Hamdaoui, O., Limam, O., Ibos, L., Mazioud, A.: Thermal and mechanical properties of hardened cement paste reinforced with Posidonia-Oceanica natural fibers. Constr. Build. Mater. **269**, 121339 (2021)

28. Ferrazzini, P.: Matériau agglomeré a haut degreé d'ininflammabilité. Institut national de la proprieté industrielle. 21-06-1985. FR2556738A1. https://patentimages.storage.googleapis. com/52/1d/0d/9a82ae92f6d4c3/FR2556738A1.pdf. Last accessed 5 May 2023

29. Balata, G., Tola, A.: Cost-opportunity analysis of the use of Posidonia oceanica as a source of bio-energy in tourism-oriented territories. The case of Alghero. J. Cleaner Prod. **172**, 4085–4098 (2018). https://doi.org/10.1016/j.jclepro.2017.02.072

30. SEA-MATTER – Revalorization of coastal algae wastes in textile nonwoven industry with applications in building noise isolation. https://webgate.ec.europa.eu/life/publicWebsite/pro ject/details/3520. Last accessed 24 Mar 2023

31. LIFE REUSING POSIDONIA – 14 sustainable dwellings using local resources as Posidonia plants, at the Social Housing Development in Formentera. https://webgate.ec.europa.eu/life/ publicWebsite/project/details/3827. Last accessed 24 Mar 2023

32. Technical Handbook, Volume 1, 73–109, Corine/Biotope/89/2.2, 19 May 1988, partially updated 14 Feb 1989. https://www.eea.europa.eu/publications/COR0-biotopes/file. Last accessed 24 Mar 2023

33. Italian D.L. 75/2010. https://www.gazzettaufficiale.it/eli/gu/2010/05/26/121/so/106/sg/pdf. Last accessed 24 Mar 2023

34. Italian Ministerial Decree 173/2016: https://www.isprambiente.gov.it/it/archivio/notizie-e-novita-normative/notizie-ispra/2016/09/regolamento-recante-modalita-e-criteri-tecnici-per-l2019autorizzazione-all2019immersione-in-maredei-materiali-di-escavo-di-fondali-marini (In Italian). Last accessed 24 Mar 2023

35. Project RESPECT YOUR CAPITAL, https://marevivo.it/attivita/tutela-della-biodiversita/ris petta-il-tuo-capitale/, last accessed 2023/03/24

36. Renzi, M., et al.: A Multidisciplinary approach to Posidonia oceanica detritus management (Port of Sperlonga, Italy): a story of turning a problem into a resource. Water **14**(18), 2856 (2022)

37. Formation and management of Posidonia oceanica banquettes on sandy shores, ISPRA, MLG 55/2010, https://www.isprambiente.gov.it/files/pubblicazioni/manuali-lineeg uida/7077_mlg_55_2010.pdf. Last accessed 5 May 2023

Overtourism as an Emerging Threat for Sustainable Island Communities – Exploring Indicative Examples from the South Aegean Region, Greece

Apostolos Lagarias[1]([✉]) [iD], Anastasia Stratigea[2] [iD], and Yiota Theodora[3] [iD]

[1] School of Engineering, Department of Planning and Regional Development, University of Thessaly, Volos, Greece
lagarias@iacm.forth.gr
[2] School of Rural, Surveying and Geoinformatics Engineering, Department of Geography and Regional Planning, National Technical University of Athens, Athens, Greece
stratige@central.ntua.gr
[3] School of Architecture, Department of Urban and Regional Planning, National Technical University of Athens, Athens, Greece
ptheodora@arch.ntua.gr

Abstract. Tourism is admittedly perceived as a key driver for many national economies, displaying a large share in the GDP of many countries around the globe, including Greece. However, evolving trends of the sector and the noticeable, exponentially rising, tourism density and intensity of certain highly-rated destinations – especially of the vulnerable to overtourism coastal and insular ones – create severe concerns as to their ability to cope with the negative repercussions of tourism in environmental, economic, social and cultural terms; and establish the "overtourism" concept, i.e. the alarmingly surpass of destinations' physical, ecological, social, cultural, economic, psychological, etc. capacity thresholds at certain times and in certain locations. Overtourism, as an already visible threat in several highly-rated urban/insular destinations around the globe that largely affects both habitants' quality of life and tourists' experience, is the focus of this paper, aiming to assess spatial and developmental pressures exerted in selected Greek island destinations, i.e. fragile spatial entities in terms of natural and cultural assets. Towards this end, three distinct case studies in South Aegean are explored, namely Mykonos, Paros-Antiparos, and Kos-Nisyros; while a number of literature-proven key indicators are used for demonstrating the trajectory through time of these destinations and the unsustainable tourism pattern they display, especially in an environmental degradation and climate change era.

Keywords: Island regions · Overtourism risk · Indicators · Spatial planning · South Aegean Region

© The Author(s), under exclusive license to Springer Nature Switzerland AG 2023
O. Gervasi et al. (Eds.): ICCSA 2023 Workshops, LNCS 14110, pp. 404–421, 2023.
https://doi.org/10.1007/978-3-031-37123-3_29

1 Introduction

Tourism is nowadays perceived as the largest and rapidly growing sector in the global economy [1]; and a sector that generates job and income opportunities in many regions around the globe due to its relatively high-income multiplier and inter-industry linkages [2]. As various studies claim [1, 3] the sector's future dynamics seem to be growing at an exponential rate; while international tourist arrivals are predicted to reach 1.8 billion by 2030 [4]. Sustainability concerns are generated by such a growth, seeking to pave the way towards a tourism development model that respects carrying capacity of destinations in ecological, economic, social, cultural, political, etc. terms [5]. Such concerns are justified by the emerging overtourism threat, i.e. an extremely overcrowded tourism pattern, already visible in many world regions.

Overtourism, as a term only recently introduced in the academic and policy discourse, lacks clarity and a clear-cut definition, while is also difficult to operationalize [6]. In fact, systematic research and relative scientific/empirical works are rather limited; while the same holds regarding the ways this can be estimated and its impacts can be assessed. According to Goodwin [7], overtourism is used to describe destinations in which both hosts and guests, i.e. locals or visitors, are suffering from place overcrowding, which affects in an unacceptable manner the quality of life of the former and quality of experience of the latter. García-Buades et al. [8] claim that overtourism is explicitly linked to the adverse impacts of tourism on residents' quality of life and their protests against tourism, tourists, policymakers, and/or tourism stakeholders. Mihalic [9] defines overtourism as the highly accelerating growth of tourism supply and demand, leading to excessive use of destinations' natural assets, destruction of cultural capital and severe socio-economic impacts. Gössling et al. [10] conceptualize overtourism as a psychological reaction to tourism pressure, in which place-person interrelationships are affected and damaged, shifting thus the residents' attitudes towards tourism. Peeters et al. [11] link overtourism with the multiple dimensions of carrying capacity; and claim that overtourism represents a destination's state, where tourism repercussions – at certain times and in certain locations – actually exceed physical, ecological, social, economic, psychological and/or political carrying capacity thresholds. This is closely related to the number of tourists visiting a destination, the type and frame of such a visit, as well as the fragility of the destination [5].

It should be noted here that although overtourism is a newly emerging term in the literature and the policy realm, the phenomenon this expresses is definitely a pre-existing one, dating back to the '70s and highlighting the pressure exerted by an increasing number of tourists in a destination and the surpassing of its saturation levels [12]. That said, overtourism can be interpreted as a repositioning against an already well-grounded debate, framing this debate with the new perceptions of carrying capacity limits and global sustainability concerns, so that constraints to growth and reckless use of resources to be properly stressed [13]. This view lies in the same direction with similar works [e.g. 5, 14], claiming that overtourism is a new term for an old, currently over-exacerbating, problem that emerges from a combination of factors or enablers, responsible for attracting a perfect 'storm of visitors' to specific sites. Among these factors fall the [14]: rise of low-cost carriers and the more affordable travel; growth of cruise tourism; advent of social media and new IT technologies, promoting destinations through online platforms; lack of destination's control over tourist numbers, grounded on proper planning both in type of tourism and in spatial terms; rising of the sharing economy, providing alternative and affordable accommodation; power relationships of tourism stakeholders; etc.

But why overtourism is a worrying or better an alarming phenomenon in the planning and policy discourse? The answer rests upon the impacts of overtourism on sustainability objectives of fragile and of limited carrying capacity territories. Thus, in a longer run, the so far purely 'growth-focused' tourism model definitely renders sustainability objectives of a destination at stake by overcoming carrying capacity limits. Among the various risks overcrowded destinations are confronted with are listed the: devastation of the integrity of cultural and natural assets; decline of the quality of life of local population [15]; loss of authenticity, heritage and local identity as well as sense of place [14, 16, 17]; rising costs of living, largely affecting local population subsistence and causing economic inequalities and social exclusion; damages to the land- and sea-scape [18]; overconsumption of scarce resources, e.g. water, energy; pollution of water reserves [19]; severe alterations in destination's real estate market [20]; traffic congestion and air quality worsening; excessive waste volumes; etc. These, in turn, lead also to the degradation of tourist satisfaction, experience and loyalty to the destination [7, 11, 21]; and, in a longer term, to destination's stagnation or decline. Despite the ominous repercussions of overtourism, however, relevant debate still remains in the first policy-cycle stage of agenda-setting, mainly due to the very recent introduction of the overtourism term in the planning and policy discourse and the, so far, limited number of relevant research works on the topic [11].

An area that rates quite high in tourism preferences around the globe is the Mediterranean Region. Tourism is a major pillar for the local economies of states and regions surrounding the Mediterranean Sea, especially in its coastal zones, rendering these regions top-rated tourist destinations [3, 22]. One distinguishable example of areas, endowed with exquisite tangible and intangible, land and maritime, natural and cultural resources, are Mediterranean islands. Based on their extraordinary resources, some of these islands are by far the most attractive and highly appreciated world destinations [18, 19, 23–25]. Therefore, islands, as fragile and geographically confined land compartments, are perceived among places under considerable and steadily increasing risk to overtourism. Such an ascertainment is verified by various studies, rating coastal areas, islands and rural heritage sites as the most vulnerable to overtourism destinations [2, 11, 26, 27]. Speaking of island regions in particular, severe impacts of overtourism on sustainability are largely associated with the constrained carrying capacity and fragile environment of such land compartments [11]. In fact, high vulnerability of island regions to overtourism rests upon five factors, namely the [9, 27]: limited population number, rendering visitors highly visible in the destination; obstructed area, where tourism facilities/infrastructure consume valuable amount of land; confined natural resources for serving the needs of both population and visitors; lack of control over tourism, being largely dependent on off-island forces and agencies, e.g. international airlines and hotel chains, externally-owned ferry companies, higher levels of government; and geographic location, as a factor enabling accessibility of islands by major close markets.

Within such a context, studies relevant to overtourism risk assessment of Greek islands that integrate sector's growth and its spatial repercussions seem to be quite few. In order to partially fill this gap, the focus of this paper is on illuminating risk to overtourism of three insular case studies, located in the Southern Aegean Region, Greece, taking such an integrated sector's view. The paper is structured as follows: in Sect. 2, a literature review is carried out, aiming to identify sets of indicators that can be of relevance for exploring risk to overtourism conditions; in Sect. 3, data used in this respect and methodological approach are shortly outlined; in Sect. 4, risk to overtourism of the specific case study islands is featured that is based on indicators selected from those identified in Sect. 2 as well additional ones, chosen on the ground of relevance and data availability; in Sect. 5 results are discussed; while, finally, in Sect. 6 some key conclusions are drawn.

2 Assessing Risk to Overtourism – Literature-Based Indicators

Assessment of overtourism per se is a complicated, far from a straightforward, task [28]. In fact, there is neither a commonly accepted set of indicators that can be used in this respect, nor a common approach; while missing are also certain indicator thresholds, beyond which the tourism pattern in a certain destination can be featured as 'overtourism' [5]. Speaking of the approach for assessing overtourism risk, a number of studies attempts to grasp overtourism in an objective and rather quantitative manner, i.e. a set of quantitative indicators, such as tourism density or intensity [11]; while other adopt a more qualitative approach, e.g. by assessing attitudes of local population against tourism/visitors of their place [8], claiming that surveys of residents' or even tourists' perceptions could be more informative in providing the precise image of the number of visitors a destination can bear [29]. Whatever the approach is, however, it is evident that assessment of the overtourism phenomenon and its impacts is strongly linked to the peculiar attributes, as well as the carrying capacity and fragility of a certain destination, i.e. it is a place-based exercise.

This lack of common understanding and approach can definitely hamper a straightforward assessment of destinations that are at overtourism risk or have already entered an overtourism state [11]; while mostly hinders comparison of destinations at risk on a common ground. Realizing the complexity of the overtourism state and its very dependence on destination's attributes, research community is arguing about the establishment of an upper threshold of tourists, beyond which a destination's state is running of overtourism risk.

In seeking to identify risk to overtourism in the case study island regions, a literature review is conducted, leading to the collection of a number of indicators. These are presented in Table 1 and are used for guiding the empirical part of this work.

Table 1. Literature review on indicators for assessing overtourism and/or risk to overtourism

Author(s)	Scope	Literature-based indicators
[11]	Assessing overtourism trends	• Tourism density (bed-nights per km^2) • Tourism intensity (bed-nights per resident) • Share of Airbnb bed capacity • Share of tourism in regional Gross Domestic Product • Air travel intensity (arrivals by air divided by number of residents) • Closeness to airport, cruise ports and UNESCO World Heritage Sites (in km)
[30]	Assessing overtourism trends	• Tourism density (bed-nights per km^2) • Tourism intensity (bed-nights per inhabitant)
[31]	Assessing overtourism trends	• Number of tourists per surface area of the destination • Number of tourists per local population
[32]	Assessing overtourism trends	• Tourism Intensity Index (TII), based on number of tourist arrivals, destination's population, tourism revenues and GDP • Tourism Density Index (TDI), Inbound plus domestic tourism per local population

[27]	Vulnerability to overtourism	• Location
		  – Proximity to markets (1–3 h), Frequent air/sea access, On Cruise ship itineraries
		• Population
		  – Concentrated in few locations, Coastal/urban, Dispersed/rural
		• Island's Size
		  – Small (under 1000 km^2)
		• Resources
		  – Few/limited/agricultural
		• Control
		  – Local or regional power only, No control of means of access

[8]	Indirect overtourism measures	• Tourist / resident ratio • Local government management • Tourist behavior • Attitude of residents / effects on their quality of life
[5]	Territorial aspects of tourism	• Tourism accommodation density (usage of the territorial system for tourism)

3 Data and Methodology

The steps of the methodological approach are presented in Fig. 1 below.

The effort to assess risk to overtourism in the case study islands is capitalizing on former research works and relevant indicators so far implemented (Table 1). From this indicators' list, a certain number is selected, based on data availability as well as reflections on tourism supply and demand side. In addition, two more indicators are added, aiming to quantify density of the built-up environment, a choice that is justified by the fact that built-up areas' expansion and/or dispersion is largely due to developments of the tourist sector and exerts pressure on islands' local assets and landscape [33, 34]. Values of these two indicators, coupled with the distribution of accommodation infrastructure (hotel/guesthouses and Airbnb), are used as a proxy for grasping the territorial/spatial implications of tourism development and the intense coastalization pattern and overtourism risk. Thus ten indicators in total are used (Table 2), aiming to demonstrate tourism growth rates in both supply and demand, tourism density and intensity, as well as the territorial implications of tourism in case study islands.

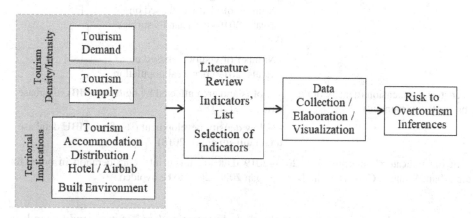

Fig. 1. Steps of the methodological approach, Source: Own elaboration

Data on indicators depicting tourism demand and supply are collected from the INSETE [35] and relate to the time span 2011–2021. However, interpretation of relevant indicators is focusing on the time span 2011–2019 in order for COVID-19-based disturbances to be avoided. Data on Airbnb accommodation (2022 data) is gathered by the Inside Airbnb Platform [36]. As to the territorial dimension, relative data is extracted from the Imperviousness high-resolution set of layers, distributed by the Copernicus Land Monitoring Service [37]. The Impervious Built-up (IBU) 2018 database displays the binary information of 'building' (class 1) and 'no building' (class 0) for the EEA-39 area. Data are provided as a 10 m and 100 m aggregate raster, accounting for the % built-up percentage in each raster cell. In this work, the 100 m raster is used, as it renders possible the differentiation of low density ($1 \leq$ % built-up ≤ 30), medium density ($31 <$ % built-up ≤ 50) and high density built-up areas (% built-up > 50). These data are used

Table 2. Selected indicators for assessing risk to overtourism in the case study islands

View point	Indicators	Data Source
Supply side	- Tourism capacity (Hotel and Guesthouse capacity – number of beds (use of 2021 data)	[35]
	- Airbnb capacity in beds (use of 2022 data)	[36]
Demand side	- % increase of overnight stays[*] 2011–2019 (bed-nights' growth rate)	[35]
	- % increase of arrivals[*] 2011–2019 (tourism arrivals' growth rate)	[35]
	- Number of overnights stays[*] (2019) per surface of the island	[35]
	- Number of overnights stays[*] (2019) per local population	[35]
	- Number of visitors[*] (based on arrivals, 2019) per island's surface (km2)	[35]
	- Number of visitors[*] (based on arrivals, 2019) per local population	[35]
Territorial dimension (density of the built-up environment)	- % of island area affected by built-up structures (2018)	IBU database
	- % low density development (% of total built-up area) (2018)	IBU database

[*] In the indicators' interpretation, 2011–2019 data are taken into consideration in order for disturbances due to COVID-19 in the time span 2020–2021 to be avoided.

in an effort to draw inferences as to the spatial saturation level of case study islands, a state that sets destinations on a downward spiral to exhaustion or degradation [5].

4   Assessing Overtourism Risk in Case Study Islands – Empirical Results

Greece is one of the top-rated tourism destinations in the Mediterranean, with tourism contributing about 27% of GDP in 2017 [37]. Attractiveness of the Greek destinations resulted in record number of visitors in 2019 – 31 million tourists, almost three times the state's population [38, 39] – a number that displays further dynamism in the current year. The three most popular Greek Insular Regions (NUTS2), i.e., Crete, Ionian and South Aegean Regions, account for the 42% of inbound tourism arrivals, 52% of the overnight stays and 60% of total tourism receipts; while they manifest particularly high seasonality peaks during the summer period [32, 40]. However, several Greek destinations, especially insular ones, are featured as quite tourism-saturated places, running the risk of overtourism. In the following section, three distinct examples of island case studies in the Southern Aegean Region are discussed, namely Mykonos, Paros-Antiparos and Kos-Nisyros (Fig. 2), through the 'lens' of overtourism risk.

4.1 Case Study Islands

South Aegean Region consists of the Cyclades and Dodecanese island complexes. The Region is a highly-reputed Mediterranean destination, with a local/regional economy displaying a strong dependence on the tertiary sector (77.8% of total employment in 2011). Tourism development in, among others, the islands of Mykonos, Santorini, Kos, Rhodes and Paros, poses a heavy burden on the natural/cultural and human capital; while gives rise to land use conflicts as well as environmental and landscape degradation. In addition, climate change impacts (heat, extreme wind and storm surges, sea-level rise, drought, etc.) are predicted to strongly affect tourist demand and attractiveness of several destinations of this Region. Finally, signs of overtourism are already visible in certain islands of South Aegean Region, with Santorini and Mykonos being mentioned as distinguishable examples in this respect [11, 40]. In fact, these two islands are, since 2020, subject to temporary banning of new building permits for tourism facilities in areas outside of the settlements' boundaries by the Greek Government, in order for the ongoing environmental degradation to be restrained, until a new spatial plan is accomplished.

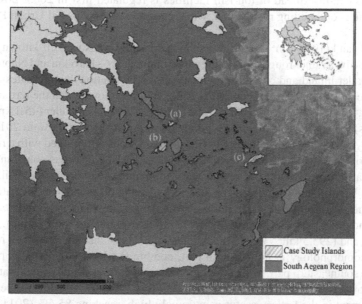

Fig. 2. Islands of the Region of South Aegean (NUTS2) and selected case study islands: (a) Mykonos, (b) Paros-Antiparos, (c) Kos-Nisyros, Source: Own elaboration

Within such a scene, as case study islands for assessing overtourism risk are chosen the islands of Mykonos, Paros and Kos. All three islands are highly acknowledged destinations at the regional, national and international level with high accessibility (ports and airports). These islands witness a steadily rising environmental pressure and urban sprawl [34, 41], calling for a certain control of future tourist development pathways and handling of spatial bottlenecks. Of remarkable value are also the rich natural and cultural resources these case study islands dispose. In fact, Paros and Mykonos are institutionalized as landscapes of outstanding natural beauty, with a great variety of zones (natural, cultural, archaeological) being set under a protection status.

The islands of Paros and Kos in this study are complemented by the smaller ones of Antiparos and Nisyros islands, due to data availability reasons (tourism data are provided by the INSETE database at the regional unit level and not at the level of each single island). Antiparos and Nisyros are smaller islands, exhibiting a less intense tourism development pattern; however, they are functionally, administratively and economically dependent on Paros and Kos core islands respectively.

Mykonos Island (85.5 km^2, 9.802 inhabitants in 2021 Census) is a top-rated tourism destination. Mykonos, along with the nearby islands of Delos (part of the UNESCO World Heritage Sites) and Rineia are featured as a landscape of exceptional natural beauty. The island is endowed by wild life repositories, archaeological sites, settlements under protection due to traditional architecture, etc. Total population displays a certain decrease (3.3%) in the time span 2011–21, while employment in the tertiary sector reaches 75.3% (2011 Census), coupled with a high percentage of employment in the secondary sector (21.8%) that is mostly attributed to the construction sector. The rapidly accelerating spread of tourism facilities is regulated first in 2005, posing several constrains on building regulations; while currently a new Special Urban Plan is in progress.

Paros Island (193.3 km^2, 14,290 inhabitants in 2021) is also a well-known destination, marked by a rather rough morphology, two major ports – Paroikia and Naousa – and several smaller inland and coastal settlements. Total population demonstrates a certain growth rate (4.2%) in the time span 2011–2021, while employment in the tertiary sector reaches 68.4% (2011 Census). Antiparos Island is considerably smaller (45.1 km^2, 1264 inhabitants); however, it also displays a population growth rate of 4.4% in 2011–2021, and employment in the tertiary sector of 67.6% (2011 Census), coupled with a relatively high employment in the primary sector (13%). Paros Island disposes abundant natural and cultural resources (wild life repositories, monuments and archaeological places). A General Urban Plan was adopted in 2012, identifying different types of natural protection zones; and specifying regulatory measures regarding tourism facilities, vacation housing and other land uses, especially in the rather overcrowded coastal part.

Kos Island (295.3 km^2, 36,986 inhabitants in 2021) is characterized by a relatively smooth geomorphology in the northern part, combined with a mountainous protected area in the southeastern part. Total population demonstrates a steady growth rate during the last two decades (9.6% in 2001–2011 and 10.9% in 2011–2021); while the percentage of employment in the tertiary sector is extremely high, reaching 85.4% (2011 Census) and being directly linked to intense tourism activity. The island displays an urbanization pattern, with the major urban area of Kos hosting about 60% of total island population; featured also by a number of smaller inland and coastal settlements. Nisyros Island is much smaller (41.26 km^2, 1043 inhabitants in 2021), demonstrating though a population growth rate of 3.8% in 2011–2021 and a percentage of employment in the tertiary sector of 70.7% (2011 Census). The Kos-Nisyros complex contains three Natura 2000 sites, covering the whole island of Nisyros and most of the southeastern part of Kos; while a total of ten wild life repositories is also reported. Spatial planning in Kos is up to now fragmented and incomplete, covering only certain zones of the island; while environmental and land use pressures from the mass tourism model are particularly high. The island can be characterized as a "hotspot" of international tourism, reaching about 1.3 million arrivals in 2019.

4.2 Pattern of Tourism Activity

Results regarding the tourism pattern (supply, demand, density and intensity, Hotel and Airbnb bed capacity, etc.) are presented in Table 3; while tourism bed-night stays in the time slot 2011–2021 are presented in Fig. 3.

Table 3. Comparative data for tourism activity in the case study islands

Indicator	Mykonos	Paros – Antiparos	Kos – Nisyros
Hotel and Guesthouse capacity in beds	25,010	22,472	62,868
Airbnb capacity in beds	14,375	11,906	2,313
% increase of overnights stays*	219.10	89.0	81.3
% increase of arrivals*	251.90	71.3	104.0
Overnight stays / surface of the island (km^2)	24,115	2,519	25,401
Overnight stays / local population	211.3	39.5	225.7
Number of visitors / surface of the island (km^2)	7,174.2	657.1	3,840.7
Number of visitors / local population	62.9	10.3	34.1
% of island area affected by built-up structures	41.7	15.0	6.2
% low density development (% of total built-up area)	58	75.6	68.8

Inspection of results manifests an incremental growth (peak) in tourism arrivals in all case study islands in the time span 2016–2019; while quite evident are the COVID_19 results in 2020 (Fig. 3). A similar trend is reported in overnight stays, where in the time span 2011–2019: Kos-Nisyros Islands count for 8.58 million overnight stays in 2019, thus presenting an overall growth rate of 89.0%; Mykonos Island exceeds the 2 million overnight stays in 2019 (2.07 million), with an overall growth rate of 219.1%; while Paros-Antiparos Islands display 613.8 thousand overnight stays in 2019 and an overall growth rate rising to 89.0%.

In addition, data show that Mykonos Island scores considerably higher in the visitors/island's surface (km^2) indicator, with 7,174 visitors per km^2; followed by the Kos-Nisyros complex, with 3,840 visitors per km^2. In the Paros-Antiparos complex this indicator is considerably lower, reaching 657.1 visitors per km^2. Similarly, the number

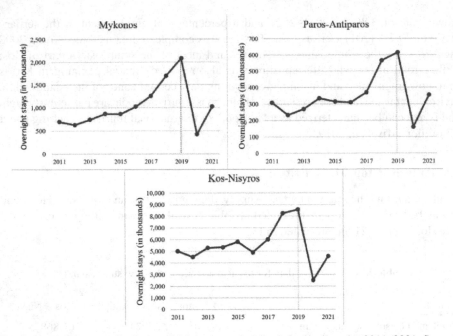

Fig. 3. Overnight stays (in thousands) in case study islands in the time slot 2011–2021, Source: Own elaboration

of visitors per local population in Mykonos is about six times higher than in Paros-Antiparos (62.9 and 10.3 respectively); while the Kos-Nisyros complex appears to be an intermediate case, with 3840.7 visitors per km^2 and 34.1 visitors per local population.

Airbnb and hotel/guesthouse distribution across the case study islands' area is presented in Fig. 4. Since INSETE data lack a spatial reference, the spatial distribution of hotel facilities in case study islands is approximated through the Open Street Map data. These data include a sufficient sample of existing hotel/guesthouse registrations.

Of critical importance is the Airbnb listings/distribution in the case study islands, an issue quite relevant to overtourism risk. In fact, interpretation of Airbnb data demonstrates the following: Mykonos reports 3,927 Airbnb listings in 2022, with a total capacity estimated as 14,375 beds (i.e. almost half of the hotel and guesthouse beds' capacity); and with 88% of the listings being located close to the coast (in the 1km zone from the shore) (Fig. 4). Paros reports 3,617 Airbnb listings in 2022, with a total capacity estimated as 11,906 beds (also half of the hotel beds' capacity), while 82% of the listings are located in the 1 km zone distance from coast (Fig. 4). Thus, the spread of Airbnb in those two islands adds up considerably to the total capacity of tourism accommodation infrastructure, accounting for about 35% of total beds in each case. A different situation is observed in Kos-Nisyros, where Airbnb penetration in tourism accommodation is considerably smaller. More specifically, data shows that 900 Airbnb listings have been registered, with a total capacity of 2,313 beds, corresponding to only 3.5% of total beds' capacity in tourism accommodation facilities; while a different spatial pattern is also displayed, with Airbnb spreading both in coastal and inland areas.

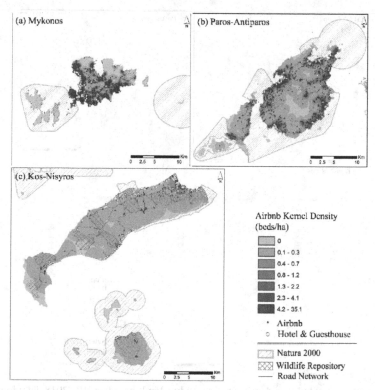

Fig. 4. Distribution of Airbnb in case study islands, overlaid on a Kernel density estimation map (created in ArcMap software), Source: Own elaboration

As inferred from Fig. 4, the coastalization pattern is particularly intense in the case of Paros Island, with tourism facilities forming a relatively dense "ring" along the whole coastline. In Mykonos, only the northern part of the island remains undeveloped, with the south coast displaying a pretty dense tourist development pattern, leading to a high saturation level. In Kos, tourism development appears to be concentrated in specific zones, with hotel and guesthouse facilities spreading mainly along the north-eastern coast, leaving a large part of the central/southern island intact. Airbnb is mainly developing within existing settlements (also inland ones), while the largest concentration is noticed in the port city of Kos.

As estimated by the IBU 100m built-up density database (Fig. 5), 40.5% of Mykonos territory is already affected by built-up structures (as calculated on the 100x100 m raster resolution). In Paros-Antiparos complex, this rises to 15%, demonstrating an intense coastalization pattern, with the central mountainous part remaining largely undeveloped. In Kos-Nisyros, only 6.2% of total area is affected by built-up structures. This small percentage is related to the large size of the island and the concentration of urban and tourism development in specific zones. However, in all case study islands, low density built-up development, related to urban sprawl, appears to be very high. Thus, 58% of

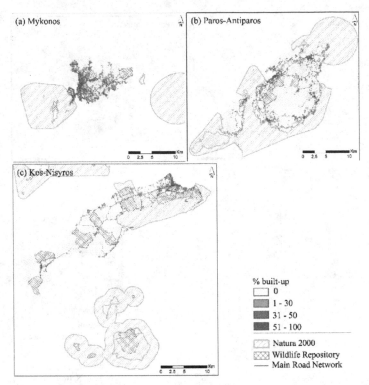

Fig. 5. Distribution of built-up density in case study islands based on IBU 2018 data: low density ($1 \leq$ % built-up < 30), medium density ($31 <$ % built-up ≤ 50) and high density built-up areas (% built-up > 50). Source: Own elaboration

total built-up area in Mykonos, 75% in Paros-Antiparos and 68% in Kos-Nisyros are classified as low-density built-up land.

5 Discussion

Overtourism seems to gain importance in the scientific and the policy discourse [42], being grasped as a source of social and environmental pitfalls that can potentially outweigh economic benefits of tourism for the host communities [2]. Of crucial importance in this respect is the identification of a number of problems that act as barriers in order for the overtourism phenomenon to be fully grasped and assessed; coupled with factors that can act as enablers to further acceleration of overtourism trends.

One of the main barriers relate to data availability at the specific spatial level – island context, in this respect – being a considerable deficit for a place-based approach. This holds true in the case of the present study as well, where tourism supply and demand data are provided at the regional unit level in the INSETE database; this fact resulting to a certain weakness to downscale tourism data to the specific territorial context, namely the islands of Paros and Kos. This data-availability problem, has led the present work to the study of Paros-Antiparos and Kos-Nisyros as island complexes.

A second barrier emanates from the way most tourism destinations are managed. The rather 'growth-based paradigm' [11] seems to value destinations' performance in terms of e.g. number of visitors' arrivals, leaving aside aspects of carrying capacity, fragility of natural and cultural resources, local identity and values, capacity to deal with overtourism repercussions, other policy objectives, etc. However, such an approach seems to ignore the very essence of islands' tourist attractiveness, thus condemning, in a long term, these islands to withering and loss of their social and economic identity, cohesion and ownership of their place. This seems to be the case of Mykonos, taking into consideration its top position in the global tourist market as well as the previous analysis, demonstrating a pattern that goes beyond the island's carrying capacity limits. Same holds for the rest two case studies, which seem to follow a similar trajectory in a rather slower pace.

A third barrier relates to the approach adopted for studying islands' overtourism. Island areas in fact constitute complex, heterogeneous and quite dynamic territorial systems, displaying formal and functional specificities, relevant to their morphological attributes. Thus a 'micro-destination' approach would be more relevant to explore overtourism, focusing on specific islands' compartments [43]. Such an approach could unveil compartments of more homogeneous areas under tourism pressure or overtourism risk. The analysis conducted in this work confirms the need for such an approach, designating coastal parts of case study islands as places that need specific attention, when exploring risk to overtourism. Exceptional examples are the islands of Paros and Kos, where the high tourism infrastructure load is concentrated along the coast. In case of Mykonos, over-saturation of the coastal part features built-up expansion towards the inland zones, further commercializing the island's territory.

An enabler that largely accelerates risk to overtourism, as various studies claim [11, 32, 44], seems to be the development of various platforms, such as Airbnb. Such an enabler brings on board diversifying individual forces, namely non-institutionalized forms of tourism accommodation, which result in overdevelopment of destinations. As noticed in the literature [27, 44], massive proliferation of such – of small scale and privately-owned – properties, hosting part of tourism flows is nowadays immensely escalating, earning thus a large portion of customers, occasionally larger than the one of conventional accommodations (hotels). In addition, these are, many times, the source of failure of sustainable spatial planning of tourism and related policies. This kind of development is noticed in all case study regions of this work, especially in Mykonos and Paros (Fig. 4), further reinforcing the heavy overcrowded coastalization pattern and burdening the fragile coastal land of these islands.

A comparison among the specific case study examples leads to the following conclusions: Mykonos Island stands out as a prominent example of an island territory, exhibiting overtourism signs. Compared to the rest of islands explored, Mykonos scores higher in 'visitors per island's surface', reaching a value of 7.174,2 people/km^2. This, according to other empirical works from Greece [32], is classified as "high". Mykonos Island also counts for the highest value of 'visitors per local population' indicator (62.9). The expansion of the built-up environment affects over 40% of the island, mainly in the form of low-density development; while the spread of tourism facilities, including Airbnb, is very high and tourism demand is accelerating, with over 200% increase in arrivals and overnight stays in the 2010–2019 period.

The Kos-Nisyros complex appears to be an intermediate case. This island complex scores pretty high in indexes related to both tourism supply and demand. 'Visitors per island's surface' indicator reaches a value of 3,840, also classified as "high" [32]; while 'visitors per local population' indicator is also considerably high (34.1). Tourism development, though, appears to be more concentrated in specific zones, and only a minor part of the islands' area is (up to now) affected by built-up structures. However, the over 100% increase in tourism demand (as quantified by the growth in arrivals in the period 2011–2019) clearly connotes a high risk to overtourism, unless specific policy measures are put in place. A micro-destination approach would be quite appropriate for downscaling overtourism risk assessment to specific Kos Island's compartments.

Finally, the Paros-Antiparos complex appears to be in a transitional stage, since most variables examined, such as 'visitors per local population' and 'visitors per island's surface' are considerably lower with respect to the rest case study areas. More specifically, the 'visitors per island's surface' indicator is 657.1, classified as "medium" [32]; while the 'visitors per local population' indicator is relatively low (10.3). Nevertheless, urban sprawl already affects mainly the coastal zone of Paros island, a fact also outlined by other research works [34]. The considerable increase in tourism demand during the past decade in Paros-Antiparos (over 100%) also witnesses that pressures posed on the natural and cultural environment will accelerate in the near future.

6 Conclusions

Insular regions are nowadays confronted with harsh dilemmas and difficult decisions as to their future developmental pathways [45]. This holds even truer in case of Mediterranean islands, i.e. hot spot land parcels in many respects. These regions, as geographically-fragmented and lagging-behind areas due to insularity structural drawbacks, are currently highly specializing and are largely dependent on tourism, namely a quite resource-intensive sector, but also a vulnerable one to various external crises, e.g. climate crisis, COVID-19 health crisis. The commodification of islands' highly appreciated natural and cultural resources and sceneries by the tourism sector has so far been guided by a rather short term and opportunistic 'growth-based' policy view, a view largely grounded on economic profit. This has definitely ignored aspects of islands' identity, historical path and traditions, outstanding landscape as well as natural and cultural qualities; and has, in many cases, led to overtourism pathways. Such pathways, though, violate the 'rights' of both the nature and island communities for a durable development; and leave aside equal rights and opportunities of future generations. Taking also into consideration the confined carrying capacity of islands in ecological, physical, social, economic etc. terms; and the continuously escalating number of tourist flows, concerns as to overtourism and threats to sustainability objectives in that kind of territories are imperatively raised. The role of a multi-level integrated territorial governance for more sustainable spatial planning of tourism is crucial in this respect [46], providing a regulatory framework and related spatial tools for: restraining uncontrolled development; managing the accelerated spread of tourism facilities; handling land use conflicts; and relieving pressures exerted on natural and cultural assets.

As various studies show, overtourism is currently placed high in the academic and policy agenda; and is calling for a paradigm shift in handling the triangle 'tourism, sustainability and carrying capacity' of destinations and their interrelationships. Such a shift is far from one-size-fits-all recipe; while it is also framed by difficulties that are associated with the very nature of tourism and its reliance on factors controlled outside the destinations – e.g. Airbnb, TripAdvisor –, which seem to play a decisive role in triggering or accelerating overtourism trends. That said, there seems to be a dire need to: assess and monitor, in a more systematic, integrated and data-enabled manner the issue of overtourism, with an emphasis on the coastal and marine part as well as the vulnerable to overtourism ecosystems these host; and sketch out of this effort the most proper, place-based and human-centric policy decisions in order for the natural and cultural assets as well as the distinct insular identity to be protected and sustainably managed. Such an effort definitely implies adoption of the quadruple helix approach – decision makers, research community, stakeholders and local communities – in tourism planning processes in order to realize and embed constraints, values, views and expectations in the way local resources and identity are handled; and establish community-driven, qualitative and authentic, long lasting tourism products. In addition, it needs to handle tourism as one sector of a diversified insular economy, which, furthermore, follows a just pattern and spreads its benefits sectorally, spatially and temporally.

References

1. OECD: OECD Tourism Trends and Policies 2020. OECD Publishing, Paris (2020). https://doi.org/10.1787/6b47b985-en, Accessed 6 Feb 2023
2. Briguglio, L., Avellino, M.: Has overtourism reached the Maltese Islands? Islands and Small States Institute University of Malta, MSIDA, Malta, Occasional Papers on Islands and Small States, ISSN 1024-6282, Number: 2019/01. https://www.um.edu.mt/library/oar//handle/123456789/42767 (2019)
3. Lanquar, R.: Tourism in the Mediterranean: scenarios up to 2030. MEDPRO (Mediterranean Prospects). Report no. 1 (2013). http://aei.pitt.edu/58341/1/MEDPRO_Report_No_1.pdf. Accessed 14 Jan 2023
4. UNWTO: Resource Efficiency in Tourism. https://www.unwto.org/sustainable-development/resource-efficiency-in-tourism. Accessed 18 Jan 2023
5. Simancas Cruz, M., Pilar, M., Zaragoza, P.: Analysis of the accommodation density in coastal tourism areas of insular destinations from the perspective of overtourism. Sustainability 11(11), 3031 (2019). https://doi.org/10.3390/su11113031
6. Koens, K., Postma, A., Papp, B.: Is overtourism overused? Understanding the impact of tourism in a city context. Sustainability 10(12), 4384 (2018). https://doi.org/10.3390/su10124384
7. Goodwin, H.: The challenge of overtourism. Responsible Tourism Partnership Working Paper 4. https://haroldgoodwin.info/wp-content/uploads/2020/08/rtpwp4overtourism012017.pdf (2017). Accessed 15 Jan 2023
8. García-Buades, M.E., García-Sastre, M.A., Alemany-Hormaeche, M.: Effects of overtourism, local government, and tourist behavior on residents' perceptions in Alcúdia (Majorca, Spain). J. Outdoor Recreat. Tour. 39, 100499 (2022). https://doi.org/10.1016/j.jort.2022.100499
9. Mihalic, T.: Conceptualizing overtourism: a sustainability approach. Ann. Tour. Res. 84, 103025 (2020). https://doi.org/10.1016/j.annals.2020.103025

10. Gössling, S., McCabe, S., Chen, N.C.: A socio-psychological conceptualisation of overtourism. Ann. Tour. Res. **84**, 102976 (2020). https://doi.org/10.1016/j.annals.2020.102976
11. Peeters, P., et al.: Research for TRAN Committee – Overtourism: impact and possible policy responses. European Parliament, Policy Department for Structural and Cohesion Policies, Brussels (2018)
12. UNWTO: Risks of saturation of tourist carrying capacity overload in holiday destinations. Madrid (1983)
13. Dredge, D.: Overtourism – Old wine in new bottles? (2017). https://www.linkedin.com/pulse/overtourism-old-wine-new-bottles-dianne-dredge/. Accessed 7 Jan 2023
14. Dodds, R., Butler, R.: The phenomena of over-tourism: a review. Int. J. Tourism Cities **5**(4), 519–528 (2019). https://doi.org/10.1108/IJTC-06-2019-0090
15. Mihalic, T., Kuščer, K.: Can overtourism be managed? Destination management factors affecting residents' irritation and quality of life. Tourism Rev. **77**(1), 16–34 (2021). https://doi.org/10.1108/TR-04-2020-0186
16. Adie, B.A., Falk, M.: Residents' perception of cultural heritage in terms of job creation and overtourism in Europe. Tourism Econ. **27**(6), 1185–1201 (2020). https://doi.org/10.1177/1354816620943688
17. Koutsi, D., Lagarias, A., Stratigea, A.: Evidence-Based exploration as the ground for heritage-led pathways in insular territories: case study Greek Islands. Heritage **5**, 2746–2772 (2022). https://doi.org/10.3390/heritage5030143
18. Stratigea, A., Leka, A., Nicolaides, C.: Small and medium-sized cities and insular communities in the mediterranean: coping with sustainability challenges in the smart city context. In: Stratigea, A., Kyriakides, E., Nicolaides, C. (eds.) Smart Cities in the Mediterranean. PI, pp. 3–29. Springer, Cham (2017). https://doi.org/10.1007/978-3-319-54558-5_1
19. Leka, A., Lagarias, A., Panagiotopoulou, M., Stratigea, A.: Development of a tourism carrying capacity index (TCCI) for sustainable management of coastal areas in Mediterranean Islands – Case Study Naxos, Greece. Ocean Coast. Manage. **216**, 105978 (2022). https://doi.org/10.1016/j.ocecoaman.2021.105978
20. Stanchev, R.: The Most Affected European Destinations by Over-tourism. University of the Balearic Islands, Faculty of Tourism (2018)
21. Sæþórsdóttir, A.D., Hall, C.M.: Visitor satisfaction in wilderness in times of overtourism: a longitudinal study. J. Sustain. Tour. **29**, 123–141 (2021). https://doi.org/10.1080/09669582.2020.1817050
22. Lagarias, A., Stratigea, A.: Coastalization patterns in the Mediterranean: a spatiotemporal analysis of coastal urban sprawl in tourism destination areas. GeoJournal **88**, 2529–2552 (2022). https://doi.org/10.1007/s10708-022-10756-8
23. Koutsi, D., Stratigea, A.: Unburying hidden land and maritime cultural potential of small islands in the Mediterranean for tracking heritage-led local development paths – Case study Leros-Greece. Heritage **2**(1), 938–966 (2019). https://doi.org/10.3390/heritage2010062
24. Stratigea, A., Chen, J.: Coping with coastal and maritime sustainability concerns in the Mediterranean. Special Issue, Ocean and Coastal Management (2022). https://www.sciencedirect.com/journal/ocean-and-coastal-management/special-issue/10D695QM9KQ
25. Garau, C., Desogus, G., Stratigea, A.: Monitoring sustainability performance of insular territories against SDGs – The Mediterranean case study. J. Urban Plann. Dev. **148**(1), 05021069 (2022). https://doi.org/10.1061/(ASCE)UP.1943-5444.0000809
26. Jurado, N.E., Damian, I.M., Fernández-Morales, A.: Carrying capacity model applied in coastal destinations. Ann. Tour. Res. **43**, 1–19 (2013). https://doi.org/10.1016/j.annals.2013.03.005
27. Butler, R.W., Dodds, R.: Island tourism: Vulnerable or resistant to overtourism? Highlights Sustain. **1**(2), 54–64 (2022). https://doi.org/10.54175/hsustain1020005

28. Buitrago, E.M., Yniguez, R.: Measuring overtourism: a necessary tool for landscape planning. Land **10**, 889 (2021). https://doi.org/10.3390/land10090889
29. Veríssimo, M., Moraes, M., Breda, Z., Guizi, A., Costa, C.: Overtourism and tourismphobia: a systematic literature review. Tourism **68**(2), 156–169 (2020). https://doi.org/10.37741/t.68.2.4
30. Vourdoubas, J.: An appraisal of over-tourism on the Island of Crete. Greece. Int. J. Global Sustain. **4**(1), 63–77 (2020)
31. Thomas, R.N., Pigozzi, B.W., Sambrook, R.A.: Tourist carrying capacity measures: crowding syndrome in the Caribbean. Prof. Geogr. **57**, 13–20 (2005). https://doi.org/10.1111/j.0033-0124.2005.00455.x
32. Panousi, S., Petrakos, G.: Overtourism and tourism carrying capacity: a regional perspective for Greece. In: Katsoni, V., van Zyl, C. (eds.) Culture and Tourism in a Smart, Globalized, and Sustainable World. SPBE, pp. 215–229. Springer, Cham (2021). https://doi.org/10.1007/978-3-030-72469-6_14
33. Lagarias, A., Stratigea, A.: High-resolution spatial data analysis for monitoring urban sprawl in coastal zones: a case study in crete island. In: Gervasi, O., et al. (eds.) ICCSA 2021. LNCS, vol. 12958, pp. 75–90. Springer, Cham (2021). https://doi.org/10.1007/978-3-030-87016-4_6
34. Tsilimigkas, G., Gourgiotis, A., Derdemezi, E.-T.: Spatial planning incompetence to discourage urban sprawl on Greek Islands. Evidence from Paros, Greece. J. Coast. Conserv. **26**(2), 1–16 (2022). https://doi.org/10.1007/s11852-022-00859-2
35. INSETE (Institute of Greek Tourism Confederation) database: https://insete.gr/. Last accessed 18 Feb 2023
36. Inside Airbnb Platform: http://insideairbnb.com/. Last accessed 18 Feb 2023
37. Copernicus Land Monitoring Service: https://land.copernicus.eu/pan-european/high-resolution-layers/imperviousness. Last accessed 20 Feb 2023
38. INSETE: The contribution of Tourism in the Greek economy in 2017. 1st estimation. https://sete.gr/media/10888/2018_symvolhtourismou-2017.pdf (in Greek) (2018). Accessed 5 Feb 2023
39. UNWTO: UNWTO Tourism Highlights 2020 Edition. World Tourism Organization, Madrid (2020)
40. Karagiannis S., Thomakos D.: Quantitative assessment of the tourism carrying capacity in Greece: a case study of Cyclades. Tourism Today **19**, 36–64 (2020)
41. Tsilimigkas, G., Derdemezi, E.-T.: Unregulated built-up area expansion on Santorini Island, Greece. Eur. Plann. Stud. **28**(9), 1790–1811 (2019). https://doi.org/10.1080/09654313.2019.1687656
42. Milano, C., Cheer, J., Novelli, M.: Overtourism is becoming a major issue for cities across the globe. World Economic Forum. https://www.weforum.org/agenda/2018/07/overtourism-a-growing-global-problem (2018). Accessed 12 Feb 2023
43. Hernández-Martín, R., Simancas-Cruz, M.R., González-Yanes, J.A., Rodríguez-Rodríguez, Y., García-Cruz, J.I., González-Mora, Y.M.: Identifying micro-destinations and providing statistical information: a pilot study in the Canary Islands. Curr. Issues Tourism **19**(8), 771–790 (2016). https://doi.org/10.1080/13683500.2014.916657
44. de la Calle-Vaquero, M., García-Hernández, M., de Miguel, S.M.: Urban planning regulations for tourism in the context of overtourism. Applications in historic centres. Sustainability **13**(1), 70 (2020). https://doi.org/10.3390/su13010070
45. Theodora, Y.: Tracing sustainable island complexes in response to insularity dilemmas _ methodological considerations. In: Gervasi, O., et al. (eds.) ICCSA 2020. LNCS, vol. 12255, pp. 278–293. Springer, Cham (2020). https://doi.org/10.1007/978-3-030-58820-5_22
46. Assumma, V., Bottero, M., Cassatella, C., Cotella, G.: Planning sustainable tourism in UNESCO wine regions: the case of the Langhe-Roero and Monferrato area. Eur. Spatial Res. Policy **29**(2), 93–113 (2022). https://doi.org/10.18778/1231-1952.29.2.06

Smart Transport and Logistics - Smart Supply Chains (SmarTransLog 2023)

Rail Ports as Nodal Gateways in the Sea – Land Connections and the Challenges of Sustainable Globalized Markets: The Case of Adriafer and the Port of Trieste

Giuseppe Borruso[1]([✉]), Maurizio Cociancich[2], Andrea Gallo[1], Alice Scotti[2], Francesca Sinatra[1], Luca Toneatti[1], and Matteo Tredesini[2]

[1] University of Trieste, Via A.Valerio 4/1, 34127 Trieste (TS), Italy
`giuseppe.borruso@deams.units.it`, {`andrea.gallo3,`
`francesca.sinatra`}`@phd.units.it`, `luca.toneatti@dia.units.it`
[2] Adriafer, Magazzino n.53 snc, Porto Franco Nuovo, 34127 Trieste, Italy
{`mcociancich,ascotti,mtredesini`}`@adriafer.com`

Abstract. In recent years rail ports gained a particular attention due to the environmental benefits connected to the freight movement by train of cargo embarked and disembarked from the sea leg. A modal shift from road to rail in fact is more and more considered important in reducing the logistic and transport carbon footprint, complying with the carbon reduction as well as a with many countries' regulations that limit their crossing by road freight transport to reduce the transport-related negative externalities. Countries as Austria and Switzerland in the European continent, in fact, have been introducing road limitations to lorries for years, incentivizing the modal shift and the quest for more sustainable transport.

Shunting and rail operators are key elements in such scenario, easing the sea-land connections and helping a port to enhance and extend its internal connections. The commitment towards the development of cleaner means and ways of fostering rail transport and reducing carbon footprint appears also relevant. On the other side, the reinforcement of rail connections can help also reducing both the road connections, but also allowing relying more on well-connected rail ports instead of choosing different port destinations. Until recent years, in fact, with reference to the European ranges, Northern range ports, although farther to Central Europe markets in terms of maritime distances, won a competition with Mediterranean (i.e., Tyrrenian and Adriatic) ports in attracting freight traffics, due to a higher level of efficiency and efficacy in freight movement and directing to inland destinations. The increase in efficiency of Mediterranean, and Adriatic ports in particular, due to their closer proximity to South-Eastern Asia – Mediterranean routes, the is however making the Mediterranean Ranges gain higher shares of freight movements and importance.

The paper is the result of the joint work of the authors. However, Giuseppe Borruso wrote Sects. 1 and 6, Maurizio Cociancich, Alice Scotti and Matteo Tredesini wrote the Sect. 4.2, Luca Toneatti wrote the Sect. 2.2, Francesca Sinatra wrote the Sect. 2.3 while Andrea Gallo wrote Sects. 2, 2.1, 3, 4.3, and 5. The Sect. 4.1 is the result of a joint effort between Andrea Gallo and Giuseppe Borruso.

© The Author(s), under exclusive license to Springer Nature Switzerland AG 2023
O. Gervasi et al. (Eds.): ICCSA 2023 Workshops, LNCS 14110, pp. 425–441, 2023.
https://doi.org/10.1007/978-3-031-37123-3_30

Little knowledge, however, is still available in terms of the rail routes that can help in reinforcing the inland connections with the destination markets. Indeed, the dynamics of railway freight flows, the major service operators and the aspect related to the final destinations of goods are still poorly explained. Scopes of the present research is therefore that of trying to concretely observe and define the railway connections of the in such a way exploring the existing and potential routes that can be put into the system to increase a – sustainable - market potential and range.

Keywords: Rail Transport · Gateway Ports · Hinterland connection

1 Introduction

The recent changes occurred in intermodal transport and logistics have re-established a considerable importance of gateway ports in enhancing the global flow of goods, commodities and, more in general, value, over global and regional networks [1]. The globalization of supply chain has led to the need for a tight integration of the different logistic segments through their connecting nodes, in order to reduce delays in deliveries, at the same time minimizing warehouse stocks [2].

In time, this has led, first, to the development of the MTO, the Multimodal Transport Operator, a figure capable of managing the best combination of transport means and routes to optimize freight size, times and journeys, and, on the other side and as a consequence, a renewed interest for multi-scope transport nodes where logistics operations are more efficiently carried on [3]. In most recent years an interest towards a renewed interest in gateway nodes, gateway ports in particular, rose, together with the development of dry-ports and inland terminals, as privileged structures where non-strictly port operations are carried on, but, on the contrary, where warehousing, logistics and modal combinations are performed [4].

Rail transport is, in this sense, gaining a paramount importance on managing the medium-to-long range connections, after years of a role squeezed between the increased distances travelled by road transport on the short-to-medium range routes on one side, and maritime transport on the long-to-medium routes on the other side, after years of decline in market shares- this thanks to a growing interest towards intermodality and multimodality, the spreading of different forms of unitized transport, and, in particular, the tighter regulations and social acceptance leading towards forms of more sustainable transport. The transport sector witnessed the raise of an important attention towards environmental issues, particularly since the Nineties of the past century, after 1992 Rio Conference, and the consideration of negative externalities has become of paramount importance when evaluating transport performances [5].

When related to freight transport this led, particularly, to the need to think about alternative transport means along some routes, as, in the case of the European continent, those crossing the Alps and, also, states as Switzerland and Austria, very often just transit areas rather than destinations for traffic flows.

Such a process reinforced the importance of the railway network and operations servicing ports and port-regions and to connect farther port regions in global as well as regional chained networks. The land leg of transport in fact has become more and more connected and vital in supporting the last mile of freight distribution, de facto supporting the maritime component in its geo-economical and geopolitical settings of the international supply chain connections. An increased competition has also risen among rail freight operators, allowing a real market to be set and increasing the choices available to operators in performing rail operations [2].

The widespread adoption of ICT has, nonetheless, increased the performance of operations, thanks to the digitalization of processes and administrative, custom and fiscal aspects, as well as tracking and tracing of many freight components, vehicles and means, thus allowing an increase of the optimization of transport in all of its components. This, however, still holds a drawback in understanding the spatial component and balances of transport systems, particularly in terms of understanding the spatial configuration of the final destinations of journeys and, therefore, goods and freights moved. The real configuration of the port and gateways' hinterlands, as well as a deep understanding of the main to-and-fro of the product categories still appears little known, if not just estimated. Similarly, the planning of the 'best route' or 'shortest path', in economical or in time terms, for freight still remains difficult, if compared to the tools and solutions available to passengers' transport, given a certain widespread lack of the real availability of suitable transport facilities and nodes, as well as suitable tracks for the different cargo and freight types.

In such a sense, there is a need to improve the analytical instruments and methods for tackling this issue and to perform better transport planning for an optimal and environmentally friendly logistic and transport performance.

2 Materials

This section focuses on the definition of the hinterland of a port, particularly considered from the rail system's point of view. This concept is particularly important for understanding the extent of the existing and, more interestingly, the foreseeable connections that can be set. The hinterland can be defined as the area surrounding a port that is directly influenced by the port's operations, in terms of both freight flows and economic activities, or, in similar terms, its port's catchment area. The hinterland of a port can varies in size, depending on factors such as the size of the port, the types of cargo handled, and the transportation infrastructure connecting the port to the surrounding regions. Its delimitation needs to analyze the economic characteristics and performances of the surrounding regions, including the most efficient and effective ways to move goods to and from the port, and the relationship with the port. A thorough identification of a port's hinterland is essential for effective transportation planning and for the sustainable growth and strategic development of the port and the surrounding regions. In the analysis of port hinterlands, however, it must be considered that information regarding the origin and final destination of different freight in transit is usually little known. This, together with the different transport dynamics such as intermediate rail yards, the train structure operations, and the different logistics operators operating the train, represent a system that is as complex as it is poorly identified.

This paragraph will address different considerations about the port's hinterland, the environmental consideration related to the railway transport and about the main actors operating into the multimodal transport. The different aspects covered represent the useful methodological tools to be able to assess the potential drivers of strategic development for a rail port related to unreached markets or in strengthening certain strategic routes.

2.1 Rail Transport in the Dynamics of Intermodal Transport and Sea/Land Relationship

Transportation is an activity that by definition is articulated in its spatial dimension, thus combining various geographic and economic aspects [1]. Logistics infrastructure, nodes and networks play an extremely central role in space and form the basis of a complex spatial [6] system. The development of transport and logistics networks that are increasingly articulated and distributed in their spatial dimension sees the different transport systems integrated into the three geographical dimensions: global, regional and local [2]. The global dimension, in particular, reflects the dynamics of transportation systems on world trade, in which there are key nodes that take on the role of regional gateways (sea-land interfaces) or international hubs [4], which in turn are key nodes in relations at the regional and local scales. Therefore, gateways will find their geographic location in contexts characterized by a strong development of economic activity within their hinterland [7], assuming the role of logistics "clusters," linking maritime and land trade flows through the implementation of an infrastructure that is articulated from the waterfront areas to the inner port areas [8]. Given the current productive environment, articulated along extremely branched production chains, an efficient and well-structured transportation system is a factor of strategic importance, linking different modes of transport (maritime rail and road) and offering intermodal services for the distribution of goods [9].

The growth in global traffic has resulted in the reorganization of freight mobility processes between ports and their hinterlands, leading to rail transport playing a critical role in territorial distribution [10, 11]. This has created an opportunity for horizontal modal integration, with ports serving as modal shift hubs [1]. The gateway inner port areas have logistics infrastructure, such as dry ports or inland terminals, that work as distribution centers for goods in transit by different way of transport [12, 13]. The port function is expanding towards the hinterland and contributing to the creation of a regional distribution network through sea-road transport relationships, leading to a polycentric structure [14]. Rail connections with inland terminals have become crucial for the attractiveness of ports, as they provide benefits like reduced urban port traffic congestion [15], lower transportation costs, faster speed in ports, and lower environmental impact [16]. However, there are also downsides, such as the need for more detailed transportation planning, dependence on economies of scale, higher costs, and longer delivery times over short distances. Creating a well-developed hinterland based on rail connections has the potential to strengthen the maritime transfer segment, increase logistics efficiency, and produce a more sustainable global transport chain [17]. Intermodal rail-water transportation is recognized as one of the transportation methods of the future to be efficient, economical and environmentally friendly [18]. Gateway ports are increasingly becoming multimodal hubs in which rail transport is expected to play a strategic role [6]. Efficient rail operations and connections to and from ports, as well as within the port and directly on the storage areas of the piers, are essential to maximize the use of rail as a sustainable transportation mode.

2.2 The Environmental Impact of the Rail Transportation System

The increasing attention to environmental problems brought to deepen the studies on the primary sources of the different pollutants and emissions to organize and define future actions that must be taken to reduce among others the carbon footprint of human activities. Among these sources, the transport sector plays a central role in CO_2 emissions [19, 20], with different contributions coming from different sectors: maritime, land and air. Every one of these sectors must cope with different challenges to reduce the CO_2 emissions, generated not only by the main engines. For example, cruise ships besides the emissions of the main power system, whose required power level represents the main obstacle, must also reduce the impact of the waste management system [21, 22]. Road transport development follows in each Country different strategies and timing: the European Union's efforts seem to highly push towards an electric conversion of all vehicles starting from the private ones, whilst other Nations have a more conservative approach. Road freight transport is the main responsible for carbon emissions among other transport [23] and several research investigate it, looking for viable innovations to reduce the carbon emission. Mulholland et al. exploit the International Agency's Mobility Model to evaluate temporary actions such as increasing vehicle efficiency, improving logistics, and shifting to less pollutant fuel [24].

In the rail sector, the evolution to zero emissions transport grid is far away from commercial availability, since the innovative technologies, which should substitute internal combustion engines, are not yet implemented and mature to be normally adopted [25]. Electric rail vehicles represent the most common technology to exploit for environmentally friendly and zero-emissions transport, but they need either the electrification of the net, which implies huge economic investment, or the adoption of new systems, such as fuel cells and storage batteries. Since worldwide only about one-quarter of rail lines are electrified [26], several research studied the integration between electrified lines and fuel cells technologies as a viable path to lower the CO_2 emissions: Fedele et al. highlight the role of onboard storage devices integration in rail vehicles to reduce CO_2 emissions, also if "rail is already an efficient and low-polluting transportation sector" [26]. Zenith et al. focused on the economic feasibility of railways electrification with overhead lines, hydrogen, and batteries, highlighting the relevant role played by the battery technology [26]. The research investigates the influence of the costs of the different systems/technologies, as well as the weight of the usage factor of the investigated path: fuel cell and battery technologies should be competitive within the next 10 years. Within this framework, the design process of innovative solutions in the rail sector must carefully consider the path to determine the actual power requirement and to size all the system components, such as batteries, fuel cells, and electric motors [28].

To assess the environmental performances of such integrated systems, which exploit overhead electrified lines and fuel cells, also the production procedure of the hydrogen must be evaluated, but the implementation of the system in a network with a fixed centre, like that used in port operations, allows to foresee good chances for green hydrogen to be exploited since the good storage logistics.

2.3 The Economical Actors Involved in Rail Freight Transport

Rail transport refers to vehicular traffic on guide tracks. Over the years, railways were the most common guideways, but recently thanks to technological developments, monorails and magnetic levitation trains are also available. [2].

A railway company is a public or private enterprise providing rail freight and/or passenger transportation services. Enterprises providing exclusively passenger transport services on metro, tram and/or light rail lines are excluded [29]. Moreover, besides railway companies are public or private they can also vary in size, scope and specialization.

Railway companies shall operate and maintain their trains, railway stations and the infrastructure they need to provide rail transport services. They can also offer support services such as ticket booking, passenger assistance and cargo management.

In many countries, the railway industry is regulated by the government to ensure passenger safety and quality of services. They must comply with government rules and regulations, such as those pertaining to the maintenance of rail infrastructure, the safety of passengers and workers, and the management of the environment.

Also, different railway enterprises can work together to offer integrated transport services, for example through infrastructure sharing agreements, or they can compete with each other to provide better and efficient transport services [30]. Railways companies can provide multimodal transportation services. A Multimodal transport takes place through the use of containers, semi-trailers, and others. Such transport methods are classified as secondary in order to distinguish them from primary ones such as lorry, wagon or ship.

In this scenario, it is possible to identify different stakeholders which are involved in rail transportation: multiservice transport operator (MTO) and logistic operator (LO) [31]. A multimodal transport operator is an intermediary that organises freight transport using multiple modes of transport, such as the combination of rail, road, sea and/or air transport. MTO coordinates all the transport of goods, dealing with all necessary logistics operations, such as loading and unloading of goods, temporary storage, shipping documentation and coordination of transport.

The definition of the Multiservice transport operator (MTO) is referred to the Geneva Convention of 1980 which indicates it as "a person who concludes a multimodal transport contract on his behalf or through the mediation of a third party and who does not act as the agent or agent of the sender or carriers involved in the multimodal transport operations and who assumes responsibility for the execution of the contract".

On the contrary, the role of the logistics operator has gained considerable importance in recent years. The cause is to be found in the exponential growth of e-commerce and in a supply chain whose management becomes increasingly complex. For these and other reasons, the companies often decide to outsource their own logistics. More specifically, LO are companies that supply logistic services to a third part, allowing therefore to other enterprises to outsource their own logistics. For this reason, they therefore rank among suppliers and end customers.

The LO, therefore, takes care of the management of the goods during all the logistic process, from the collection to the delivery. This type of logistics operator can offer services such as goods storage, stock, order processing and labelling, transport coordination and shipment management. Also, they can work in synergy with an MTO, or can manage the logistics of a company independently.

The intermodal services are offered and managed by the MTO, while the LO manages and offers activities for the integrated distribution logistics. In conclusion, the logistics evolution produces a demand for services that guarantee the final delivery of the product left the production chain.

If the physical distribution is limited to the national area, LO may be sufficient. Instead if the supply chain is more complex, reaching or coming from/spread at least on a continental level, with the need for a mix of transport modes and additional services, it creates demand for a Multimodal Transport Operator (MTO) [30].

In both cases, the aim of these stakeholders is to ensure that goods are transported and managed efficiently and safely, reducing costs and improving the accuracy and timeliness of deliveries. Both of these players have revolutionised the rail sector, offering innovative and flexible solutions for freight and passenger management. Thanks to their presence, the railway sector is evolving towards greater efficiency and competitiveness, offering customers a more complete and high quality service.

3 Methods

The research presented here is aimed at gaining a better understanding of the actual pattern of land connections and relations originating from the port of Trieste and connecting it with the major logistic nodes and destinations within the European continent. As highlighted in the previous paragraphs, gaining such a knowledge would allow understanding the real routes followed by freights, allowing also a more detailed estimate of transport emissions and a comparison among different transport routes. Furthermore, by understanding the spatial pattern of production areas, demography and logistic infrastructure, would allow understanding the potential expansion of the market areas from the port itself and, therefore, the expansion of the hinterland itself.

To do that, we start from the standard procedure suggested for the exam of the hinterlands, adapting it to the present railway-based case study, and anticipating the results of the first part of the activity carried on within the research group. The traditional analysis to analyze the catchment area of a port follows different steps, implying:

- the identification of the primary transportation routes and modes used to move freight to and from the port, including road, rail, and waterways,
- an analysis of the cargo flows to and from the port, including the types of cargo, the origin and destination points, and the volumes and frequencies of shipments [2].

The abovementioned points need to be adapted and articulated according to a set of sub-steps, as.

- the analysis of the transport infrastructure surrounding the port, including highways, railways, and waterways,
- the identification of the areas that are directly or indirectly served by these transportation modes,

- the identification of the economic activities that are directly or indirectly influenced by the port's operations, such as manufacturing, warehousing, and distribution [13], both in the area around the port and in proximity of the destinations.
- use of GIS (Geographic Information System) tools and spatial analysis techniques to plot the catchment area of the port, based on the transportation routes, cargo flows and economic activities identified in the previous steps.

The methodology proposed for the port hinterland analysis can then be adapted to try to highlight the dynamics related to rail transport in relation to the catchment area of different port systems. For this reason, the methodology to be used for the rail hinterland analysis of a gateway will follow different steps in order to develop strategies and solutions that can maximize the benefits from the use of rail transportation for port logistics operations while minimizing their negative externalities on the environment and the surrounding communities as presented Table 1 (Table1) [32].

This table could be used as a guide for gathering data and analyzing the factors that contribute to defining the railway hinterland of a port. By completing each step and analyzing the data collected, a clearer picture of the port's catchment area can be developed, also taking advantage of the potential of different GIS software, which can be useful for planning and optimizing transportation and logistics operations. However, it should be noted that in this phase, the research will focus exclusively on the first step, namely the geographical mapping analysis of the main railway flows by origin and destination and part of the transport and logistic infrastructures on the territory.

4   The Case Study

4.1   The Port of Trieste as a Rail Port

The Port of Trieste, located at the Northern end of the Adriatic Sea, represents an extremely important logistical hub for intra-Mediterranean commercial flows and strategic exchange between Central-Western Europe and the Middle Easter, acting as an international port with most of its traffic spread over international routes. In 2022, it was the first Italian port for goods moved, with over 57 million tons of goods (65% of which were liquid bulk products, namely petroleum products). In recent years, the Port of Trieste has been experiencing a phase of growth and intensification of commercial flows, leveraging its traditional geographic advantages (both natural and anthropic), such as the seabed depth of approximately 18 m, the articulated railway network connected to the international hinterland of logistics hubs in Central and Eastern Europe, and the Free Port regime, which provides operational, administrative, financial, and commercial customs advantages [33, 34] both for what concerns the container handling and the Ro-Ro ferries [4]. The Port of Trieste plays an important hub function – with a transshipment share of 32% for pure container transport – as well as a continental gateway, with a significant component of traffic traveling by rail [8, 14]. The intermodal connections of the port of Trieste are represented by the international logistics hubs of Central and Eastern Europe through an efficient and capillary network of connections capable of catalyzing Eurasian traffic with the northern Adriatic ports as deepen presented later. Therefore, due to its strategic location, the port of Trieste is configured as an intermodal logistics platform

Table 1. Overview of the process of analysis of a catchment area of a port. Source: Personal Elaboration of the Authors [2, 18].

	Criteria	Data Collection	Analysis
Step 1: Spatial Analysis	Rail freight flows assessment	Analysis and mapping of the main known railway flows	Plot the different routes with origin and destination of freights on a map
	Geographic proximity	Identify all cities and logistics distribution center and hubs within a certain distance from the port (e.g. 100 km)	Plot the locations of each city/town and hubs on a map
	Designing railway infrastructure	Identify the railways connection from the port to other locations (highlighting any infrastructure constraints)	Plot the infrastructure on the same map as step 1
Step 2: Economic Analysis	Economic activity	Identify major industries and businesses in the area surrounding the port including the analysis of raw materials and semi-finished products used	Categorize the industries by sector and analyze their economical dimension
	Industries transportation need	Comparison between commodity categories handled in ports and demand in adjacent industrial districts	Observe whether there is a correspondence between rail traffic demand and economic activity, to understand their transportation need
Step 3: External Analysis	Competition	Identify other ports within the same geographic region	Analyze their strengths and weaknesses com-pared to the target port
	Logistics operator	Define the routes handled by the various logistics operators	Mapping the area of operation of different logistics operators
	Environmental factors	Identify potential environ-mental impacts of port operations on the surrounding area	Analyze potential mitigation measures

capable of catalyzing commercial flows between the Far East and Central and Eastern Europe [5].

4.2 From Port Shunting Activity Operator to Logistic Operator: The Case of Adriafer

Adriafer is a 100% owned subsidiary of the Port Network Authority of the Eastern Adriatic Sea specialising in the shunting and traction of railway convoys, both incoming and outgoing, within the Enlarged Port District of the Port of Trieste. As the Sole Manager of railway shunting in the port area, Adriafer plays a vital role in the logistics chain centred on the Port, connecting the national railway network managed by RFI to the port terminals. Trieste, in fact, is the most important railway port in Southern Europe, equipped with 70 km of tracks serving all the piers and making it possible to compose trains directly at the terminals.

Adriafer's activity within the District and on the tracks of the railway stations (LDS), managed by RFI, has represented a real turning point for the entire Regional Logistics System, leading to an increase in the potential of the service that can be provided by trains and a reduction in the time required for rail transport, thus leading to a reduction in costs and transit times that have made Trieste a best practice for the modal transition from road to rail. During 2022, in fact, the number of trains moved was 9,536 from about 6,000 in 2015 within the District alone, a number that increases to over 11,000 trains if one widens the view to the port of Monfalcone (also under the control of the Trieste Port Authority), for a total of over 230 trains per week. The area of interest for the Regional Logistics System, it should be underlined, also extends outside the Free Port of Trieste, widening to the back-port areas of Aquilinia, Servola, up to the Italian-Slovenian border at Villa Opicina and the regional freight villages of Fernetti, Cervignano and Gorizia. It is precisely with a view to optimising the port network for the benefit of the various district operators that Adriafer has started to operate on the mainline on short-haul routes. Operations on these routes have been carried out since September 2017, the year in which the National Agency for Railway Safety (ANSFISA) granted the company the Single Safety Certificate to operate the first mainline trains, with the aim of creating a synergic system and improving the competitiveness of the Port System.

The Port of Trieste represents the link between the Mediterranean and the Adriatic Baltic European Corridors, as it is a strategic hub for the flow of goods between the markets of Central and Eastern Europe and the Mediterranean basin.

The rail services available from Trieste in fact reach, with different frequencies, Austria, Germany, Hungary, Croatia, Switzerland, Czech Republic, Poland, Luxembourg, Bosnia and Herzegovina and Slovakia. The Port of Trieste, in terms of freight flows handled by rail, is the first port in Italy and this is also perceived by the railway flows that depart from or arrive at the various port terminals every day. In terms of routes, the Port is connected by rail with 8 major Central European countries, creating a logistical network thanks to the infrastructural articulation with more than 31 different locations distributed throughout the Mitteleuropean region. The largest flows, also due to their geographical position, coincide with Germany, Austria and Italy itself. Every month from Trieste Campo Marzio approximately 42 convoys depart and just as many arrive, resulting in a constant flow of important monthly arrivals/departures, with frequencies of up to 13 convoys per week and 50 per month for the most popular routes.

Although the port of Trieste is the Italian port of call with the greatest international vocation, there have been recent pioneering experiences which have opened up new models for intermodal transport between the North-East and the Centre/South of Italy. This is the first service along the Adriatic railway line, initiated by Sangritana on behalf of Honda Industriale Italia to transport containers in inbound flow from Trieste to the Abruzzo freight village of Manoppello. Launched in January 2023, this new service represents a highly innovative choice because for the first time it extends the area of influence of the port of Trieste as far as the Abruzzo region, and possibly even further, extending into central and southern Italy, an area previously perceived as distant from the Julian port of call.

4.3 Spatial Analysis: The Port of Trieste

The dynamics of commercial flows for the port of Trieste, observing how the share of traffic volumes managed by Northern European ports is the result of the combination of two fundamental factors [31]: the presence of productive districts in inner port areas and the attractiveness of these ports with respect to infrastructure and geographical components. However, it should be emphasized that port systems located in Northern Italy represent an extremely more efficient alternative for all oceanic connections coming from the Far East in transit through the Suez Canal [11]. By using the port of Trieste, four days of navigation (at an average speed of 20 knots/hour) and over 2200 miles of navigation [14] can be saved.

As outlined in the methodology, the aspects that will be prominently focused on in this analysis are those related to the spatial and territorial component: starting from the analysis of freight flows by rail, identifying the main logistics corridors for goods in transit, considering the railway infrastructure present in the territory, and the main distribution centers and logistics hubs in the study area.

The geographic location of the port of Trieste defines it like a gateway to access the markets of Central Europe for this port represents a significant strategic factor in the context of the environmental sustainability of logistics processes. Thanks to its strong international vocation, the port of Trieste channels large volumes of traffic towards the areas of Central-Eastern Europe (Bavaria, Austria, Slovakia, and the Czech Republic) [14].

The main railway connection for the port of Trieste could be summarized in the following table (Table 2), outlined by putting together a previous data collection from institutional sources (Port Authority of Trieste) to the data provided by directly from Adriafer.

Table 2. Summarize of the railway connection for the port of Trieste (Source: Adriafer, internal data given by the company)

National Routes		Distance (km)	International Routes		Distance (km)
IT	Ancona	506	DE	Karlsruhe	847
IT	Cervignano del Friuli	50	DE	Koln	1114
IT	Cremona	347	SI	Koper	78
IT	Milano	393	AT	Lambach	469

(continued)

Table 2. (*continued*)

National Routes		Distance (km)	International Routes		Distance (km)
IT	Padova	179	AT	Linz	269
IT	Manoppello	670	DE	Munchen	508
IT	Pordenone	126	DE	Nuremberg	664
IT	San Martino di Trecate	442	CZ	Ostrava	843
			CZ	Paskov	849
International Routes		Distance (km)			
LU	Bettembourg	1091	SI	Velenje	258
SK	Bratislava	616	AT	Villach	186
HU	Budapest	783	AT	Wels	488
DE	Burghausen	480	AT	Wien	554
HU	Csepel	598	AT	Wolfurt	673
DE	Duisburg	1183	CZ	Mosnov	820
SK	Dunajska	648	SK	Trnava	658
DE	Giengen	712			

However, although the main destinations and origins are known, the mapping and survey work on the analysis of the railway flows for the port of Trieste is still in progress. The proposed objective is to concretely define the catchment area for the port of Trieste.

The thematic cartography presented (Fig. 1) is divided into different layers, in which the main railway connections operated to and from the port of Trieste have been highlighted based on the data given directly by Adriafer company. The extensive railway infrastructure of Central and Eastern Europe is then pushed in evidence, together with the main network of intermodal rail terminals and hubs present in the investigated area. The information presented regarding the intermodal rail terminal network has been developed starting from the interactive map of the European Commission's TENtec, which highlights the main European logistics corridors, freight villages, inland ports and inland waterways (Fig. 2).

For the realization of the cartographic representation of the railway connections and logistic nodes so far highlighted, as well as for inserting the other elements of the analysis as previously mentioned in the 'methods', the research group agreed also to rely on an intermediate product, as a Google MyMaps project, useful, in the present stage, to work concurrently within the research group, gathering in a unique place all the data and information collected and elaborated and capable, once the project is fully implemented, to be used as a dissemination tool for allowing a more general public of users and operators to view and understand the layout of the overall hinterland, including, in its following steps, an evaluation of the flows as well as of the environmental aspects connected to the different routes and destinations.

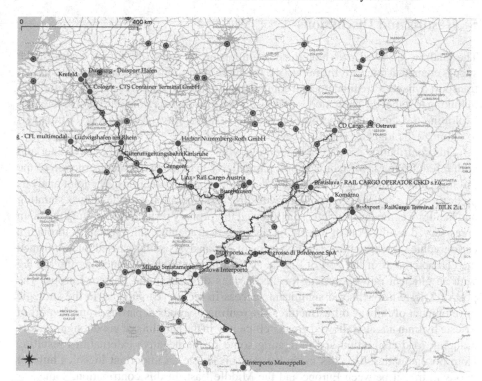

Fig. 1. Rail traffic routes to and from the Port of Trieste. Source: elaboration by A.Gallo from Adriafer internal data and TENtec interactive map[1].

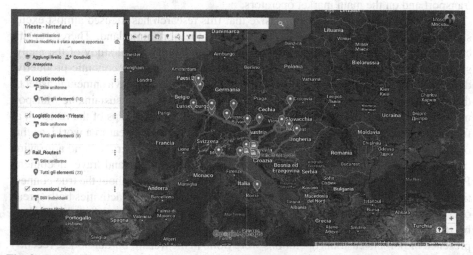

Fig. 2. Rail traffic routes to and from the Port of Trieste. Source: authors elaboration from Port Authority of Trieste, Adriafer, Desk research on main logistic nodes

---

[1] https://ec.europa.eu/transport/infrastructure/tentec/tentec-portal/map/maps.html#Filter_page&ui-state=dialog consulted on 8/05/2023.

5 Results and Discussions

The analysis of a rail port hinterland is important to assess the effectiveness of the supply chain that connects the port to the production and consumption areas. Intermodal transport dynamics are fundamental components for the evaluation of the port hinterland, in linking together different modes of transport to move goods from one point to another, exploiting the strengths, in terms of costs and sustainability, of each mode of transport to optimize the logistics chain.

This contribution provides a general overview of the definition of a port hinterland with reference to railway connections, particularly in terms of the reconstruction of the rail links among the Port of Trieste and its major inland destinations. The joint analysis mode through a desk research coupled with direct collaboration with the railway shunting and handling company (Adriafer) has allowed the primary result of identifying the main areas served by the Port of Trieste, in an analytical manner, but especially through a cartographic representation. The first steps of the analysis so far carried out confirmed the characteristics of the Port of Trieste as an important hub in connecting the sea leg with an efficient railway system for the markets of Central and Eastern Europe. The port of Trieste has achieved significant success in recent years thanks to the strategic development of railway infrastructure. The routing of goods departing from the port of Trieste by train has also allowed greater efficiency in the handling of goods, significantly reducing road congestion and mitigating some of the negative externalities resulting from port activities. This has made the port of Trieste an important logistics hub for goods in transit between Europe and the Middle East. In this contribution, some key dynamics were therefore outlined regarding the role of gateways as main access routes to continental markets, also developing some reflections on the sustainability of freight transport and on the main market operators.

However, it is important to emphasize that this research has focused almost exclusively on the geographical aspects of evaluating the port hinterland. Therefore, this contribution represents a starting point for a thorough and careful study of the analysis of the port catchment area, which also takes into account the economic-productive dynamics of different areas, as well as urban, competitive and environmental aspects, these latter referred particularly to the modal shift towards more sustainable transport means as trains, and the perspective of energy supply. The next steps of the research as foreseen and theorized in this paper are not trivial, as it could appear in a world, as that of transport and logistics, dominated by an important modal integration and a growing importance of ICT in allowing a rapid exchange of information and travel document. Paradoxically, this is, at the same time, allowing little knowledge about the true connections and final destinations of goods, being the custom and tracing activities both spread over a set of different actors and located in different places as those directly involved by transport and logistics operations. As an example, while in the past and with the presence of borders customs operations were done in the transit, border nodes, recently these operations, and the related tracing, are recorded at destinations. Further actions are therefore needed to fill the information gaps so far highlighted in terms of the current pattern of destination nodes from the port of Trieste, as well as in terms of the possible expansion, given a more in depth knowledge of the major production areas.

6 Conclusions

Rail transport is living a renewed importance due to an unprecedented development of intermodalism, that is mainly regarding the integration of maritime and land transport, with particular reference to the role played by Ro-Ro ferries in moving semitrailers and similar unitized freight, and with reference to the port and dry port operations allowing assembling trains for transport over medium-to-long land destinations.

Although this principle is not new, its implementation and proficient operations have been only recently exploited and put in action. This appears particularly true in some gateway ports, as it is the case of Trieste, where the limited amount of space available on the seaside and on its proximity has forced port, freight and rail operators to optimize performances, realising intermodalism either directly on terminals or on port and dry port facilities.

This is enhancing performances both from the economical and environmental points of views, allowing to reduce considerably the number of lorries on roads and motorways. At the same time, the set-up of long and interconnected maritime – land routes allows reaching far destinations well routed into the European continent, de facto extending the international hinterland of the gateway port. Railway connections become therefore particularly important, particularly for an international port as the Port of Trieste, with its historical – and current – positioning as a gateway of Mediterranean and Asian flows on the seaside, and medium-to-long range railway connections well into the European continent. In the present we performed an initial survey of the existing railway connections among the port of Trieste and its major destinations, combining information coming from different research and business data, modelling them in a GIS environment and setting up a methodology for further elaborations of a proper rail hinterland, capable of being scaled and extended to other potential branches and destinations, as well as containing useful tools for evaluating the environmental impacts and benefits in a comparison with alternative transport modes. This can allow scholars and operators, including the main character in the realization of this modal shift revolution, as the local shunting company and rail operator (as Adriafer) to rely on a useful instrument to plan further actions aimed at improving connections, efficiency and environmental sustainability in logistics and transport.

References

1. Vallega, A.: Nodalità e centralità: relais tra teoria regionale e teoria dei trasporti. Studi Marittimi. **6**(19–20), 33–35 (1984)
2. Rodrigue, J.P.: The Geography of Transport System. Routledge, London and New York (2020)
3. Lupi, M., Pratelli, A., Giachetti, A., Farina, A.: Il trasporto ferroviario in Italia: una analisi dei collegamenti ferroviari di trasporto combinato—Rail freight transport in Italy: an analysis of combined transport connections. Ingegneria Ferroviaria **53**(3), 209–245 (2018)
4. Borruso, G.: Port-City relationship in the era of hybridization. A development model. J. Res. Didactics Geogr. **2**, 125–137 (2022)
5. Gallo, A.: The logistic carbon footprint: a dynamic calculation tool for an indicator of the sustainability of logistic processes with a case study on the Port of Trieste. In: Computational Science and Its Applications–ICCSA 2022 Workshops, pp. 109–123, Malaga, Spain, July 4–7, 2022, Proceedings. Springer International Publishing Part V, Cham (2022)

6. Mazzarino, M.: Geografia dell'innovazione logistica nel Nord-Est. EUT Edizioni Università di Trieste (2021)
7. Rodrigue, J.P., Notteboom, T.: Comparative North American and European gateway logistics: the regionalism of freight distribution. J. Transp. Geogr. **18**(4), 497–507 (2010)
8. Sellari, P.: Geopolitica dei trasporti. GLF Editori Laterza (2018)
9. Soriani Stefano: Riorganizzazione del ciclo di trasporto e spazi di influenza portuale. Dinamiche in atto e poste territoriali in gioco, in Salgaro Silvino (a cura di), Scritti in onore di Roberto Bernardi, Bologna, Patron Editore, pp. 165–177 (2006)
10. Vallega, A.: Geografia delle strategie marittime: dal mondo dei mercanti alla società transindustriale. Mursia, Milano (1997)
11. Tadini, M.: Intermodalità ferroviaria e assetto territoriale dei porti gateway: il caso di La Spezia. Rivista Geografica Italiana, CXXVIII **4**, 104–136 (2021)
12. Roso, V., Woxenius, J., Lumsden, K.: The dry port concept: connecting container seaports with the hinterland. J. Transp. Geogr. **17**(5), 338–345 (2009)
13. Notteboom, T.E., Rodrigue, J.P.: Port regionalization: towards a new phase in port development. Marit. Policy Manag. **32**(3), 297–313 (2005)
14. Tadini, M., Borruso, G.: Sea-rail intermodal transport in Italian gateway ports: a sustainable solution? The examples of La Spezia and Trieste. In: Gervasi, O., Murgante, B., Misra, S., Rocha, AMC, Garau, C. (eds), Computational Science and Its Applications – ICCSA Workshops 2022, LNCS, vol. 13381, pp. 156–172, Springer-Verlag, Berlin (2022)
15. Lam, J.S.L., Notteboom, T.: The greening of ports: a comparison of port management tools used by leading ports in Asia and Europe. Transp. Rev. **34**(2), 169–189 (2014)
16. Zhao, J., Zhu, X., Wang, L.: Study on scheme of outbound railway container organization in rail-water intermodal transportation. Sustainability **12**(4), 1519 (2020)
17. Woxenius, J., Bergqvist, R.: Comparing maritime containers and semi-trailers in the context of hinterland transport by rail. J. Transp. Geogr. **19**(4), 680–688 (2011)
18. Ignaccolo, M., Inturri, G., Giuffrida, N., Torrisi, V.: A sustainable framework for the analysis of port systems. Eur. Transp. **78**(8) (2020)
19. Wen, L., Song, Q.: Simulation study on carbon emission of China's freight system under the target of carbon peaking. Sci. Total Environ. **812**, 152600 (2022)
20. Yao, Z., Wang, Y., Liu, B., Zhao, B., Jiang, Y.: Fuel consumption and transportation emissions evaluation of mixed traffic flow with connected automated vehicles and human-driven vehicles on expressway. Energy **230**, 120766 (2021)
21. Toneatti, L., Deluca, C., Fraleoni-Morgera, A., Pozzetto, D.: Rationalization and optimization of waste management and treatment in modern cruise ships. Waste Manage. **118**, 209–218 (2020)
22. Toneatti, L., Deluca, C., Fraleoni Morgera, A., Piller, M., Pozzetto, D.: Waste to energy onboard cruise ships: a new paradigm for sustainable cruising. J. Mar. Sci. Eng. **10**(4), 480 (2022)
23. Breuer, J.L., Samsun, R.C., Stolten, D., Peters, R.: How to reduce the greenhouse gas emissions and air pollution caused by light and heavy duty vehicles with battery-electric, fuel cell-electric and catenary trucks. Environ. Int. **152**, 106474 (2021)
24. Mulholland, E., Teter, J., Cazzola, P., McDonald, Z., Gallachóir, B.P.Ó.: The long haul towards decarbonising road freight–A global assessment to 2050. Appl. Energy **216**, 678–693 (2018)
25. Stobnicki, P., Gallas, D.: Adoption of modern hydrogen technologies in rail transport. J. Ecol. Eng. **23**(3), 84–91 (2022)
26. Zenith, F., Isaac, R., Hoffrichter, A., Thomassen, M.S., Møller-Holst, S.: Techno-economic analysis of freight railway electrification by overhead line, hydrogen and batteries: case studies in Norway and USA. Proc. Inst. Mech. Eng. F J. Rail Rapid Transit **234**(7), 791–802 (2020)

27. Fedele, E., Iannuzzi, D., Del Pizzo, A.: Onboard energy storage in rail transport: review of real applications and techno-economic assessments. IET Electr. Syst. Transp. **11**(4), 279–309 (2021)
28. Fragiacomo, P., Piraino, F.: Fuel cell hybrid powertrains for use in Southern Italian railways. Int. J. Hydrogen Energy **44**(51), 27930–27946 (2019)
29. Glossario, TRASPORTO FERROVIARIO. ANNI 2004–2013, https://www.istat.it/it/files/2015/02/Glossario.pdf. Last accessed 11 Apr 2023
30. L'operatore in trasporto multimodale (MTO) e l'operatore logistico (LO), https://www.confetra.com/it/centrostudi/doc_pdf/quaderni_QUADERNO%20%20N.%2088.2.pdf. Last accessed 11 Apr 2023
31. Notteboom, T.: Concentration and the formation of multi-port gateway regions in the European container port system: an update. J. Transp. Geogr. **18**(4), 567–583 (2010)
32. Wilmsmeier, G., Monios, J.: Counterbalancing peripherality and concentration: an analysis of the UK container port system. Marit. Policy Manag. **40**(2), 116–132 (2013)
33. Roletto, G.: Il porto di Trieste. Zanichelli, Bologna (1941)
34. Borruso, G., Borruso, G.: Capitolo IX-Il Porto di Trieste: analisi del traffico, impatto economico e prospettive di sviluppo. In:Trasporto marittimo e sviluppo economico. Scenari internazionali, analisi del traffico e prospettive di crescita, pp. 235–273. Giannini Editore (2012)
35. Zhao, P., et al.: China's transportation sector carbon dioxide emissions efficiency and its influencing factors based on the EBM DEA model with undesirable outputs and spatial Durbin model. Energy **238**, 121934 (2022)

How the Business Model Impacts on the Sustainability of Fashion Companies

Francesca Sinatra[(✉)] [iD] and Salvatore Dore

DEAMS – Department of Economics, Business, Mathematics and Statistics Sciences "Bruno de Finetti", University of Trieste, 34127 Trieste, Italy
francesca.sinatra@phd.units.it, salvatore.dore@amm.units.it

Abstract. The main contribution of this paper is to understand how fashion companies try to include elements of circularity in their business models since in recent years, the fashion industry is the one that consumes the greatest amount of raw materials and pollutes the environment. Starting from what consumers perceive and as they are interested in the factor of sustainability and ethics in relation to the world of fast fashion and fashion in general, the goal is to understand how these companies move from a linear business model to a circular business model. Then we will analyze the collaboration between H&M-Sellpy. Our empirical investigation aims at gathering knowledge concerning the cocreation mechanisms underpinning the co-creation processes of circular firms and their key co-creating actors. In this scenario, it appear very interesting trying to understand what the attitudes and behaviors of Millennials and Centennials are when they faced with the purchase of luxury and sustainable fashion items. In doing that, a survey questionnaire turned out to be the most suitable tool to conduct such investigation.

Keywords: Circular Business Model · Fashion Industry · Sustainability

1 Introduction

Today, the fashion industry is among the most polluting in the world. In fact, increasing consumer and business awareness has led companies to change their business models. For this reason, this article seeks to provide an overview of what a business model is, especially in reference to circular business models.

Subsequently, a literature review of the transition still taking place today within the fashion world was made: from a linear economic model to a circular one. Moreover, a concrete case has been brought of circularity inside their business model, that is the collaboration between sellpy & H&M to understand which are the advantages for the enterprises.

Furthermore, it was necessary to try to understand what were the variables that affect the choices in buying eco-sustainable luxury products of today's consumers, an empirical survey has been carried out on the attitudes of a chosen target: Millennials & Centennial when they have to buy a sustainable luxury item. Furthermore, it was necessary to try

© The Author(s), under exclusive license to Springer Nature Switzerland AG 2023
O. Gervasi et al. (Eds.): ICCSA 2023 Workshops, LNCS 14110, pp. 442–457, 2023.
https://doi.org/10.1007/978-3-031-37123-3_31

to understand what were the variables that affect the choices in buying eco-sustainable luxury products.

The paper is organised as it follows: Sect. 2 Circular Business Model; Sect. 2.1 Circular Economy; Sect. 3 Linear and Circular Economy in the Fashion Industry; Sect. 3.1 Linear Model in Fashion Industry; Sect. 3.2 Circular Economy in Fashion Industry; Sect. 4 Sellpy and H&M; Sect. 5 Material and Methods and Sect. 6 Conclusions, Limits and Future Research.

2   Circular Business Model

The traditional balance between customers and suppliers has been altered by advancements in the global economy. The emergence of new communication and computing technologies, along with the establishment of more open global trading systems, has provided customers with increased choices. Varied customer needs can now be expressed, and alternative supply options are more transparent. Consequently, businesses must prioritize a customer-centric approach, particularly since technology enables the cost-effective provision of information and customer solutions. These changes necessitate a re-evaluation of the value propositions offered to customers, as the supply-driven logic of the industrial era is no longer viable in many sectors. This evolving landscape also highlights the importance of not only addressing customer needs effectively but also capturing value through the provision of new products and services. Without a well-developed business model, innovators will struggle to deliver and extract value from their innovations, particularly evident in Internet companies where revenue generation can be challenging due to customer expectations of free basic services.

A business model serves to articulate the logic and provide evidence of how a business creates and delivers value to customers. It outlines the revenue, cost, and profit structure associated with the delivery of that value. Various elements need to be determined when designing a business model. The design of a good business model involves interconnected issues that lie at the core of the fundamental question asked by business strategists: How can a sustainable competitive advantage be built to achieve above-average profits? In essence, a business model defines how an enterprise creates and delivers value to customers and converts received payments into profits. To profit from innovation, business pioneers must excel not only in product innovation but also in designing a business model that aligns with customer needs and technological trends. However, developing a successful business model alone is not enough to ensure a competitive advantage, as imitation is often straightforward. It is crucial to establish a differentiated yet effective and efficient business model that is difficult to replicate, thus increasing the likelihood of generating profits. Business model innovation itself can be a pathway to gaining a competitive advantage if the model is distinct enough to discourage replication by both incumbents and new entrants.

The circular economy (CE) is viewed as a development strategy aimed at addressing environmental and economic challenges. Its objective is to decouple the consumption of goods and services from the extraction of raw materials, thereby reducing waste generation and the depletion of natural resources [1, 2]. The concept of CE is often seen as a means to promote sustainable [3, 4]. The most widely accepted definition of CE, as provided by the Ellen MacArthur Foundation, describes it as "an industrial system that is restorative or regenerative by intention and design", with a focus on the principles of reduction, recovery, reuse, and recycling of materials, energy, and waste [3, 5].

The development of CE necessitated a multidisciplinary approach encompassing fields such as ecology, design, economy, and business management, to transition from a linear economy. This shift facilitated the development of eco-innovations that prioritize ecological considerations over anthropocentric perspectives. According to some authors, CE comprises four components: 1) the recirculation of resources, 2) a multilevel approach, 3) its significance for sustainable development, and 4) its close relationship with society. Others highlight the fundamental role of circularity in CE, as papers discussing and defining CE commonly emphasize the circular flow of materials, energy, and nutrients, highlighting the broad range of applications and the importance of CE.

CE presents new business opportunities and encourages the adoption of innovative solutions for sustainable development. For instance, companies can develop business models that fulfill customer needs through product functionality rather than relying solely on the production and sale of physical goods [6]. This approach reduces material costs and enhances resource efficiency [6]. However, effective implementation of CE requires organizations to establish multiple partnerships. These partnerships may involve collaborating with waste collection services for recycling purposes, handling the transportation, sorting, and dismantling of used materials, and mitigating risks and costs [7].

One of the commonly used frameworks for circularity strategies is the 4R framework, consisting of four strategies: Reduce, Reuse, Recycle, and Recover. In this paper, the authors propose the addition of a fifth category, Regenerate, to better accommodate start-ups involved in the development of nature-based solutions. Nature-based solutions aim to enhance the utilization of ecosystem services, which encompass the benefits humans derive from ecosystems. Examples of ecosystem services include green roofs or walls and urban green spaces, which rely on a minimal input of nonrenewable natural resources and prioritize renewable natural processes.

The R-list establishes a hierarchical order for waste management methods, with Regenerate given precedence over Reduce, and so on, as the level of circularity decreases down the list. These strategies can be applied within the two types of material cycles characterizing the circular economy: the biological cycle, which involves the flows of food and biologically-based materials (such as cotton and wood) designed to return to the biosphere through processes like composting or anaerobic digestion, and the technical cycle, which pertains to the flows of inorganic or synthetic materials.

Our consumption behaviors have unprecedented impacts on the natural environment. As a result of these consumption patterns, society, and businesses are faced with a convergence of factors, including environmental degradation, pollution, climate change, social inequity, poverty, and the growing need for renewable energy sources. These factors necessitate a new approach to conducting business. In response, many companies are acknowledging the need for sustainable business practices, and we observe firms like Interface Carpet, Unilever, Nike, and Starbucks incorporating sustainability into the core of their brands. This study reviews the literature on sustainable consumer behavior change and presents a comprehensive psychological framework to guide researchers and practitioners in fostering sustainable behavior.

The Circular Economy is gaining momentum in academia, industry, and policy-making as an alternative model that aims to minimize resource depletion, waste, and emissions. Implementing this concept at the organizational level relies on business models as a crucial leverage point. A body of literature has emerged exploring the notions of circular business models and circular business model innovation. However, there is a significant lack of clarity regarding their theoretical conceptualization. To address this gap and systematize the current state of the emerging field of circular business models and circular business model innovation, we conducted a literature review using systematic database searches and cross-reference snowballing. Our contributions to conceptual clarity include (1) an overview of the history of circular business models and circular business model innovation concepts, (2) a synthesis of definitions of circular business models and circular business model innovation, and (3) an overview and synthesis of conceptual frameworks for circular business models and circular business model innovation [8].

The concept of the circular business model is built upon two fundamental concepts: the circular economy and business model innovation. This section provides a brief introduction to both topics.

2.1 The Circular Economy

The idea of the circular economy draws influence from Boulding's work in 1966, which argued for viewing the Earth as a desirable closed-loop system with the limited assimilative capacity to achieve a balance between the economy and the environment. Stahel and Reday further developed the concept by focusing on industrial economics and introducing the notion of a loop economy. This concept described strategies for waste prevention, regional job creation, resource efficiency, and the dematerialization of the industrial economy [9].

Stahel emphasized the importance of selling utilization rather than ownership of goods as a relevant business model for a loop economy. This approach allows industries to generate profits while reducing costs and risks associated with waste. The contemporary understanding of a circular economy, introduced by Pearce and Turner, incorporates various features and contributions from different concepts that share the idea of closed loops [10]. These concepts include industrial ecology, cradle-to-cradle, laws of ecology, looped and performance economy, regenerative design, biomimicry, the blue economy, and life cycle management and engineering.

The Ellen MacArthur Foundation, supported by McKinsey, played a significant role in popularizing and shaping the contemporary curated form of the circular economy concept through influential reports. Since 2013, the concept has gained increasing attention in academia, resulting in a range of different definitions. For example, definitions highlight the circular flow of materials, the design for restoration, and the aim to keep products, components, and materials at their highest utility and value.

Kirchherr et al., reviewed numerous definitions and proposed a comprehensive definition that describes the circular economy as an economic system based on business models that replace the "end-of-life" concept with reducing, reusing, recycling, and recovering materials. It operates at multiple levels, including the micro, meso, and macro levels, to achieve sustainable development and create environmental quality, economic prosperity, and social equity for current and future generations [3].

However, a previous review of circular economy literature identified shortcomings in this definition, such as oversimplification of the term "end-of-life" and a reduced focus on other lifecycle stages. Therefore, the authors revisited the definitions and adapted a previous definition for this research. For this study, the circular economy is defined as an economic system in which resource input and waste, emissions, and energy leakages are minimized through cycling, extending the lifespan, and maximizing value retention.

The goal of achieving a circular economy involves intensifying and dematerializing material and energy loops. This objective can be accomplished through various means, such as digitalization, servitization, sharing solutions, designing long-lasting products, implementing maintenance and repair practices, and promoting reuse, remanufacturing, refurbishing, and recycling. While achieving a completely closed-loop system is theoretically impossible, our understanding of a circular economy adopts a dynamic perspective of "going circular," acknowledging the ongoing efforts to minimize leakage of materials and energy, rather than aiming for a static state of a fully circular system.

The concept of the business model gained popularity and evolved during the dot-com boom in the 1990s, particularly with the introduction of innovative revenue mechanisms. Initially, the business model concept served as a means to communicate complex business ideas to potential investors within a limited timeframe. Over time, it transformed into a tool for systemic analysis, planning, and communication, as well as a strategic asset for gaining competitive advantage and improving firm performance. The ability to innovate and introduce business models swiftly and effectively can create a significant competitive edge for organizations, especially considering the diminishing returns on technology, increasing complexity, and decreasing cost of capital. The disruption caused by digital transformation further amplifies the importance of business model innovation, as evidenced by the market valuation of relatively new technology conglomerates with innovative digital business models.

Business model innovation capabilities not only have the potential to yield higher returns compared to product or process innovations but can also serve as a "renewable" competitive advantage. These capabilities can trigger a dynamic sustainable competitive advantage for companies, making them crucial for organizational strategy. Additionally, business model innovation plays a critical role in helping organizations fulfill their social and environmental objectives by leveraging effective environmentally, socially, and economically sustainable technologies and solutions.

Business model innovation capabilities not only have the potential to yield higher returns compared to product or process innovations but can also serve as a "renewable" competitive advantage. These capabilities can trigger a dynamic sustainable competitive advantage for companies, making them crucial for organizational strategy. Additionally, business model innovation plays a critical role in helping organizations fulfill their social and environmental objectives by leveraging effective environmentally, socially, and economically sustainable technologies and solutions.

Companies that engage in sustainable business model innovation have the potential to enhance their financial, social, and environmental performance, as well as improve their resilience and ability to manage risks from their operating environment. Academic research on business model innovation has also grown, with numerous reviews and studies conducted on the subject [11–13]. Consequently, various definitions of the concept have emerged, this research adopted a previous definition proposed by the authors, which stems from a comprehensive review of the field [14, 15]. Business model innovation is defined as "the conceptualization and implementation of new business models that may involve the development of entirely novel models, the diversification into additional models, the acquisition of new models, or the transformation from one model to another. The transformation can encompass the entire business model or specific elements related to value proposition, value creation and delivery, value capture, the interconnections between these elements, and the value network" [7, 8, 16].

3 Linear and Circular Economy in the Fashion Industry

3.1 Linear Model in Fashion Industry

Nowadays, the fashion industry is divided in two segments. The first segment involves luxury companies which offer high quality products while the second includes fast fashion enterprises which represents the set of all the brands that follow the new trends by applying affordable prices.

In the last decades, the boundaries of the fashion industry were redefined by fast fashion. Indeed, in the late 80s, the fashion industry was dominated by several retailers, which led to increased competition in the market [17].

To survive this change, fashion retailers have moved from product-oriented distribution channels to buyer-oriented distribution channels, developing alliances with suppliers from different countries with a greater emphasis on the brand. The growth of the sector and strong competition have led to a decrease in mass production and a shift to the structural features of the supply chain.

In this scenario, phenomenon of fast fashion arose. This term refers to "an approach to the production, design and marketing of fashion clothing that emphasizes quickly and economically available fashion trends for consumers" [18].

This new production model led fashion brands to create many styles at the expense of features such as quality and sustainability. This occurs because fast fashion use low-quality raw materials and products with low longevity. In fact, some studies explain and highlight how fast fashion products cannot be worn more than 10 times. Within fast fashion there are cycles in which colors, shapes and styles change continuously, leading consumers to perceive their clothes "out of fashion". This leads to increased profits for brands, as they encourage the purchase of new clothing more frequently, even though those already own by consumers are in excellent condition.

One factor that has accelerated and influenced this new trend are social media, through the promotion of strategies as daily deals, influencers, and others. Using those strategies, companies increased consumption of clothing by consumers, fueled by rapid distribution which has led to increase waste.

In this sector, enterprises usually operate according to the principles of the linear economy, that is a one-way economy based on consumption. Products of such a model are available and are characterized by a short duration and, at the end of their life cycle, end up like waste, generally in landfills. This model does not base production on sustainability models but on mass production models whose products are mainly of poor quality. In addition, mass production and consumption are associated with a consequent depletion of raw materials, energy consumption and waste of resources and products, resulting from all the processes. Such a model is based on the principle of "take-make-dispose", and it is characterized by a large demand of resources and waste production which generate pressures on the natural environment [19].

Despite this, there is now a greater propensity from the consumers to issues as environmental sustainability, so it is clear that this linear model of economic growth no longer reflects the needs of modern society [20].

A clear example of such pressures is given by the fashion industry itself, since the fashion industry is characterized by a high consumption of goods and produces high volumes of waste not only during the production stage but also through all the life cycle [21, 22].

The fashion industry generates revenues for 2 trillion and employs more than 300 million people in the world but is one of the most polluting industries on the planet.

Estimates in recent years have shown that the fashion industry is responsible from 8 to 10% of global annual emissions and the production of one kilogram of cotton requires approximately 10,000 L of water. Just in Europe, 11 kilos of clothes per person per year are thrown away.

The fashion industry consumed from 79 to 93 million cubic meters of water during the year 2015, causing pressure on water supply where scarcity in countries such as China and India is a major problem. Another negative effect produced by the fashion industry on the environment is chemical pollution. In fact, tissue treatment is estimated to cause about 20% of industrial water concern on a global scale.

The main negative aspect is the excessive generation of waste throughout the production chain and the consumption of goods, not considering land use, water, energy and waste and environmental pollution. Furthermore, the fashion industry's linear model has significant social impacts, such as labor exploitation, human rights violations, and unsafe working conditions for factory workers. According to the International Labour Organization, an estimated 170 million children are engaged in child labor, and 70% of the global fashion workforce are women [23–25].

For these reasons, the transition from a linear to a circular economy model is necessary but also challenging, as this transition involves systemic change that affects the entire economy. To address these challenges, the fashion industry is exploring alternative economic models, such as the circular one.

3.2 Circular Economy in Fashion Industry

In a circular economy, resources are kept in use for as long as possible, waste is minimized, natural systems are restored, and materials are regenerated at the end of their life cycle. The circular economy in the fashion industry aims to eliminate the negative impacts of fast fashion, reducing waste and pollution, and promoting sustainable and ethical production practices.

In this model, manufacturers are trying to use recycled materials and produce clothes and products that are more sustainable and easier to repair.

Circular Economy is an emerging concept within the fashion industry which combines aspects such as the circular economy and sustainable fashion. This leads to a distancing from the existing mode, "take-make-dispose".

As we have already said, the linear economic model is based on production and consumption while the circular economic model focuses on concepts such as recycling and reducing waste.

The circular economy in the fashion industry is a model that aims to reduce the waste and environmental impact of industry through recovery, repair, reuse, and recycling of materials. In practice, this means that the actors in the industry need to try to create a virtuous cycle in which materials are not wasted, but are used as much as possible, avoiding ending up in landfills. Nevertheless, improving tissue recycling techniques and encouraging consumers to change their purchasing habits are some of the challenges.

Circular Economy in the apparel and fashion field, is based on three fundamental principles as (1) sustainable design: manufacturers strive to create durable, easy-to-repair and recyclable clothing; (2) reuse: garments that is no longer used is sold or donated to people who need it, rather than being thrown away; (3) recycling: clothing materials that cannot be reused are recycled or transformed into new products.

The circular economy in the fashion industry offers many advantages as the waste reduction which implies the repair, reuse and recycling of materials which reduce resource waste and help preserve the environment. In terms of innovation, we can see how the need to find sustainable solutions for the fashion industry drives research and innovation, with the development of new materials, production techniques and processes. Lastly, reuse and recycling of materials can reduce production costs and increase the profitability of the industry.

The circular economy model for the fashion industry involves designing clothes and accessories with circularity in mind, using sustainable materials, adopting sustainable production practices, and extending the life cycle of products through repair, reuse, and recycling. This approach promotes a shift from a linear model of production, consumption, and disposal to a more circular one that keeps materials in use for longer periods, reducing the environmental impact of the industry.

Textile recycling is an example of a circular economy. The collection, sorting, and processing of used clothing and textiles is part of the recycling process, and this approach helps to reduce waste. According to a report by the Ellen MacArthur Foundation, the textile recycling market could reach $4.9 billion by 2025, creating new job opportunities and economic benefits.

Also, the use of sustainable materials in the fashion industry includes organic cotton, recycled polyester, and bamboo. Cotton and synthetic fibers have a higher environmental impact than these materials. The use of sustainable materials in the fashion industry increased in the last two years by 36% between 2017 and 2019 [26, 27].

Rental and resale platforms have started to be adopted by fashion companies because these platforms allow consumers to rent or buy second-hand clothing, extending the life cycle of garments and reducing waste. According to a report by ThredUp, the resale market is expected to reach $64 billion by 2024, indicating a growing demand for sustainable fashion [28].

Fashion industry is one of the largest and polluting trade worldwide. For this reason, it appears to be the industry with the greatest probability and possibility of damaging the environment, with repercussions on society due to the high use of non-renewable resources. Nevertheless, as already pointed out, companies operating in the fashion industry are trying to implement strategies of circular economy. Dissanayake and Weerasinghe have proposed four types of strategies that can help in the implement of the principles of the circular economy in the fashion industry [29].

These are:

1. Resources efficiency, which is an important aspect of the circular economy in the fashion industry. This means that clothing manufacturers must consider the sustainable use of natural resources during production, such as reducing water use and energy and the use of non-toxic raw materials, to reduce the environmental impact of the fashion industry.
2. Circular design, that is an approach that encourages the creation of products that are designed to last long, be easily repaired and recyclable. This means that apparel manufacturers should try to create high quality products that last long, using durable materials and sustainable designs. In addition, repair and reuse initiatives can be introduced to further extend product life.
3. Product life extension, is a key principle in the fashion circular economy, aimed at reducing waste and maximizing the value of garments. It involves extending the lifespan of a product through various strategies, rather than disposing of it prematurely. By prolonging the use of clothing items, we can minimize the negative environmental and social impacts associated with fashion production and consumption.

End-of-life circularity which is an important strategy of the circular economy in fashion, which aims to ensure that products are disposed of sustainably and that materials can be recovered and recycled to produce new items. So, manufacturers need to think about the end of product life from the design stage, to ensure that materials are easily separable and recoverable [30].

In conclusion, we can see how the use of the circular economy is the basis for the generation of lasting benefits and allowing an economic system to grow and generate income over time.

Although, as we have seen in the previous paragraphs, the fashion industry has always been developed and associated with a high level of consumerism, in recent years sustainability and economic activity have become key issues in the sector.

4 Sellpy and H&M

Sellpy and H&M are two companies operating in the fashion industry. Sellpy is a Swedish company second-hand e-commerce platform founded in 2014. The company has a business model that involves the purchase of used clothes by customers, evaluating garments, cleaning and cataloging products and they provide a marketplace to sell items including clothing, accessories, and home goods. So, in is model, Sellpy takes care of the whole sales process.

Sellpy has obtained investments from major venture capital enterprises, including H&M and Kinnevik, and in 2020 it was acquired by the H&M group.

Instead, H&M is a major Swedish fashion chain that sells apparel for men, women, and children worldwide and was founded in 1947. The company produces and sells new clothing, and it has different store in several countries. H&M's business model involves the production and sale affordable and trendy apparel. However, over the past few year, H&M has focused on sustainability, launching a series of initiatives to reduce the environmental impact of the fashion industry.

Although the two companies have different aim and business models, both are trying to address the growing awareness of the environmental impact of the fashion industry. Indeed, in 2020, Sellpy announced a collaboration with H&M, one of the world's largest fashion retailers.

This partnership came out through the sharing of sustainable development goals and the desire to promote circular fashion. H&M through the acquisition of Sellpy saw a way to expand its business, while Sellpy benefited from the support and resources of a large group like H&M.

The collaboration between Sellpy and H&M is part of H&M's efforts to become more sustainable and reduce its environmental impact. By partnering with Sellpy, H&M aims to encourage its customers to recycle their clothing and make it easier for them to do so. The collaboration also supports H&M's goal to become fully circular and only use sustainable materials by 2030 [31–33].

As part of the collaboration, H&M invested in Sellpy and became a minority shareholder in the company. H&M also provides Sellpy with logistical support, such as access to its warehouses and transportation network. Sellpy benefits from H&M's expertise in logistics, which allows it to scale its operations and expand its reach.

The collaboration between Sellpy and H&M has been successful so far. Sellpy has experienced significant growth since the partnership began, and H&M has seen an increase in sales of its sustainable products. In 2020, Sellpy reported a 60% increase in sales compared to the previous year, and H&M's sustainable products accounted for 27% of its total sales.

Sellpy's collaboration with H&M is part of a larger trend towards sustainable fashion and circular economy. By encouraging people to recycle their clothing and reducing waste, companies like Sellpy and H&M are helping to create a more sustainable future for the fashion industry.

In summary, the collaboration between Sellpy and H&M has several advantages, including promoting circular fashion, providing logistical support, promoting sustainable consumption, and supporting job creation and economic growth [34–37].

5 Material and Method

5.1 Survey on the Attitudes of Millennials and Centennials

As we have said, growing awareness of sustainability among businesses and consumers made necessary the slowdown of the fashion industry production. Also, it is important to pay attention to use sustainable materials in order to reduce the environmental and social impact resulting from the production processes of fashion items. To deepen the knowledge of such phenomenon it has been necessary to investigate consumer attitudes through a quantitative survey using a structured questionnaire.

The main purpose is to highlight whether consumers, without making a distinction between luxury and non-luxury buyers are aware of sustainable luxury items and if they are attracted in buying ethical and sustainable fashion products.

The first step in understanding attitudes and propensity of millennials and Generation Z is to identify the socio-demographic variables of the chosen target. The questionnaire was distributed by 352 individuals, 80 men and 272 women. This result shows a higher percentage of the female sex, equal to 77,3%. The reason for this result probably is strongly linked to the fact that the female gender seems to be most interested and involved in the fashion field. Also, the respondents were also divided into the two age groups corresponding to the two generations studied and the sample is distributed almost equally.

In addition, 49% of respondents were reached for Millennials, compared to 51% for Generation Z. Within the Millennials category there are mainly graduates and workers; while Generation Z consists of students, recent graduates, workers and unemployed.

The sample was then subdivided according to the area of residence.The answers provided by the respondents revealed most individuals living in Southern Italy and the Islands, reaching a percentage equal to 56% of the sample. The last question in the first section of the questionnaire was about the knowledge and the subdivision of this sample in terms of income received within the household during the year 2019. For this variable there was a strong predominance of the band belonging to 0–18,000.00 euro with a percentage equal to 27% of respondents.

From the analysis of the above data, it can be said that luxury purchases are not only made by those with greater purchasing power, but also by individuals with lower incomes. This is presumably due to the fact that such purchases bring numerous benefits to buyers, including high brand symbolic values (Fig. 1).

Increasing awareness in sustainability and ethical practices among businesses and consumers has made it necessary to slow down the production of the fashion industry and increase the focus on the use of sustainable materials in order to reduce the impact environmental and social processes resulting from the production of fashion products. For this reason, the current situation regarding this phenomenon has been thoroughly analysed in the previous paragraphs. The aim assigned to the next section of the questionnaire, called eco-fashion, was specifically to better understand the attitudes and propensity of respondents to this approach.

The section opens with a first important question that is whether the respondents were aware of the recent phenomenon of ethical fashion. A relatively high 38% of the sample indicated that it was not aware of this. On the other hand, 35% of respondents indicated that they were aware of this phenomenon.

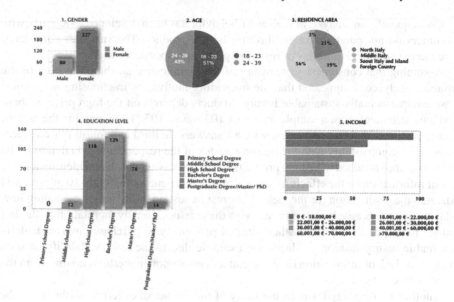

Fig. 1. Socio-demographic area (Author: Sinatra, 2023)

As for the other 28% of respondents, they gave a different answer, "I've heard about it," presumably because they have less in-depth knowledge of ethical fashion.

The study of eco-sustainable fashion ends with a further question regarding the propensity to purchase eco-sustainable fashion products. From the data collected during the survey, it emerged that only a small percentage of respondents, almost all Millennials, purchased eco-sustainable luxury products, recording a percentage equal to 12% of the sample.

The remaining 88% said they had not made a sustainable luxury purchase. This presumably stems from the fact that such a question was addressed to the whole sample, which also includes those who have never purchased luxury products (Fig. 2).

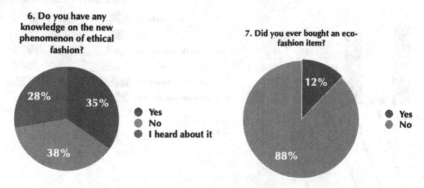

Fig. 2. Eco-Fashion section (Author: Sinatra, 2023)

Consequently, an analysis of consumer behavior has been developed to identify why consumers do not purchase an eco-fashion luxury product. The variables considered were many and the possibilities of response given to respondents wide.

Assuming that consumers were aware of the significance attributed to each of the variables analyzed, it appeared that the overriding motivation in choosing not to purchase environmentally sustainable luxury products depends on the high price of these products, statement from a sample match of 103 out of 193. The second is the lack of information provided by companies, with 84 answers. In third and fourth place respectively, the incompatibility with the personal tastes of the respondents (31) denoting the real importance attached to fashion products in the expression of self and identity and the lack of information on the effects of purchasing such products (46). Only 10 interviewed indicated the justification for the lack of interest in sustainability issues, revealing how today's consumers attach real importance to these issues. Finally, in relation to the last option, 14 respondents justified their limited propensity to purchase environmentally sustainable luxury fashion products, for example due to the low availability of such products or lack of information on the social and environmental effects arising from the use of such goods.

Another area analyzed was on the study of the impact of different attributes on the choices of respondents in not to buying eco-sustainable luxury products. From the data collected, it emerged that the fundamental variable influencing consumers' choices is the price (78 respondents). This result arise probably from an excessive price of environmentally sustainable fashion products, from which it is assumed that both generations are not willing to pay a premium price for obtaining such items.

From the variable analyzed, corresponding "do not follow fashion trends", emerges as a factor that has a lesser impact on the choices of not buying eco-sustainable luxury products for consumers, despite a small percentage have indicated this variable as incisive, presumably because eco-sustainable luxury products are considered less attractive in terms of beauty by today's consumers (Fig. 3).

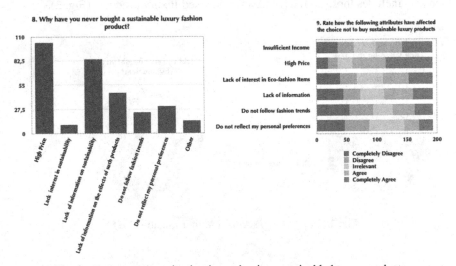

Fig. 3. Consumers' motivation in not buying sustainable luxury products

6 Conclusions, Limits and Future Research

As for the phenomenon of ethical fashion and the purchase of eco-sustainable products, an important fact arises: consumers are aware of this phenomenon but, in fact, a small part of them proceed to purchase such goods. From this it is deduced that, we can hypothesize that people fight for ethical and social causes only to appear on social media, in particular Centennials.

The two generations studied, while presenting points in common, represent different categories of consumers and, as emerged from the survey, the suggest is to fully understand this diversity and try to adapt strategies to each generation.

The inclusion of circularity in companies' business model has become increasingly important in recent years. Circularity can help businesses reduce the environmental impact of their products and services, increase resource efficiency, reduce costs, and improve the company's reputation. Furthermore, circularity can help fashion companies create new commercial opportunities as selling products and services based on recycled materials or repairing and reusing existing products.

So, companies that integrate circularity into their business model can benefit from a number of competitive advantages, such as product differentiation, increase customer loyalty, and reduce resource scarcity risks. Moreover, the inclusion of circularity can help companies meet the needs of increasingly environmentally conscious consumers and respond to the growing demands for transparency and social responsibility.

It is important to underling that this paper several limitations. Firstly, having developed a survey limited only to two categories of consumers (Millennials and Generation Z) has not made it possible to compare and examine in depth differences between other consumers' categories. So, the suggestion for eventual future research is to enlarge the sample.

Secondly, in the future it would be recommended base the research on a more qualitative research model, to better understand motivations and attitudes that lead to certain final purchasing choices.

In conclusion, the inclusion of circularity in their business model can offer numerous opportunities for companies to improve their economic, environmental, and social performance, and to create long-term value for their stakeholders. It is therefore important that companies take the integration of circularity into their modus operandi seriously.

Acknowledgments. This publication was produced while attending the PhD programme in Circula Economy at the University of Trieste, Cycle XXXVIII, with the support of a scholarship financed by the Ministerial Decree no. 351 of 9th April 2022, based on the NRRP – funded by the European Union – NextGenerationEU – Mission 4 "Education and Research", Component 1 "Enhancement of the offer of educational services: from nurseries to universities" – Investment 4.1 "Extension of the number of research doctorates and innovative doctorates for public administration and cultural heritage".

Authors' Contributions. Conceptualization, methodology, formal analysis, materials and resources, data curation and validation: all authors. In particular: Sinatra wrote Sect. 1, Sect. 3, Sect. 3.1, Sect. 3.2, Sect. 4, Sect. 5, Sect. 5.1, Sect. 6; Dore wrote Sect. 2; Sect. 2.1.

References

1. Sauvé, S., Bernard, S., Sloan, P.: Environmental sciences, sustainable development and circular economy: alternative concepts for trans-disciplinary research. Environ. Dev. **17**, 48–56 (2016)
2. Lieder, M., Rashid, A.: Towards circular economy implementation: a comprehensive review in context of manufacturing industry. J. Clean. Prod. **115**, 36–51 (2016)
3. Kirchherr, J., Reike, D., Hekkert, M.: Conceptualizing the circular economy: an analysis of 114 definitions. Resour. Conserv. Recycl. **127**, 221–232 (2017)
4. Velenturf, A.P., Purnell, P.: Principles for a sustainable circular economy. Sustain. Prod. Consum. **27**, 1437–1457 (2021)
5. Geissdoerfer, M., Savaget, P., Bocken, N.M., Hultink, E.J.: The circular economy–a new sustainability paradigm? J. Clean. Prod. **143**, 757–768 (2017)
6. Tukker, A.: Product services for a resource-efficient and circular economy–a review. J. Clean. Prod. **97**, 76–91 (2015)
7. Veleva, V., Bodkin, G.: Corporate-entrepreneur collaborations to advance a circular economy. J. Clean. Prod. **188**, 20–37 (2018)
8. Geissdoerfer, M., Pieroni, M.P., Pigosso, D.C., Soufani, K.: Circular business models: a review. J. Clean. Prod. **277**, 123741 (2020)
9. Stahel, W., Reday, G.: The Potential for Substituting Manpower for Energy (1976)
10. Pearce, D.W., Turner, R.K.: Economics of Natural Resources and the Environment. Johns Hopkins University Press (1989)
11. George, G., Bock, A.J.: The business model in practice and its application for entrepreneurship research. Enterpren. Theor. Pract. **35**(1), 83–111 (2011)
12. Zott, C., Amit, R., Massa, L.: The business model: recent developments and future research. J. Manag. **37**(4), 1019–1042 (2011)
13. Massa, L., Tucci, C.L., Afuah, A.: A critical assessment of business model research. Acad. Manag. Ann. **11**(1), 73–104 (2017)
14. Schallmo, D.: Geschäftsmodell-Innovation. Springer Fachmedien Wiesbaden, Wiesbaden (2013)
15. Foss, N.J., Saebi, T.: Fifteen years of research on business model innovation: how far have we come, and where should we go? J. Manag. **43**(1), 200–227 (2017)
16. Teece, D.J.: Dynamic Capabilities and Strategic Management: Organizing for Innovation and Growth. Oxford University Press on Demand (2009)
17. Barnes, L., Lea-Greenwood, G.: Fast fashioning the supply chain: shaping the research agenda. J. Fashion Mark. Manage. **10**, 259–271 (2016)
18. Merriam-Webster Dictionary: Fast fashion definition. https://www.merriam-webster.com/dictionary/fast%20fashion. Last accessed 22 Feb 2023
19. MacArthur, E.: Towards the circular economy. J. Ind. Ecol. **2**(1), 23–44 (2013)
20. Blum, P.: Circular Fashion: Making the Fashion Industry Sustainable. Hachette, UK (2021)
21. A new textiles economy: redesigning fashion's future. Retrieved from https://www.ellenmacarthurfoundation.org/assets/downloads/publications/A-New-Textiles-Economy_Full-Report_Updated_1-12-17.pdf. Last accessed 2 Mar 2023
22. Vecchi, A.: The circular fashion framework-the implementation of the circular economy by the fashion industry. Curr. Trends Fashion Technol. Textile Eng. **6**(2), 31–35 (2020)
23. Brink, J.V.: Expectations of the Circular Economy in the Fashion Industry, Master's thesis (2018)
24. McNeill, L., Moore, R.: Sustainable fashion consumption and the fast fashion conundrum: fashionable consumers and attitudes to sustainability in clothing choice. Int. J. Consum. Stud. **39**(3), 212–222 (2015)

25. International Labour Organization: Child labour in the fashion supply chain. https://www.ilo. org/global/topics/child-labour/lang--en/index.htm. Last accessed 29 Mar 2023
26. Global Fashion Agenda: Pulse of the Fashion Industry (2019). https://globalfashionagenda. com/wp-content/uploads/2019/05/Pulse-of-the-Fashion-Industry-2019.pdf. Last accessed 16 Mar 2023
27. Textile Exchange: Preferred fiber and materials market report 2020. https://textileexchange. org/wp-content/uploads/2020/11/2020-PFM-Report.pdf. Last accessed 18 Mar 2023
28. ThredUp: 2020 resale report. https://www.thredup.com/resale. Last accessed 22 Mar 2023
29. Dissanayake, D.G.K., Weerasinghe, D.: Towards circular economy in fashion: review of strategies, barriers and enablers. Circ. Econ. Sustain. 2(1), 25–45 (2021). https://doi.org/10. 1007/s43615-021-00090-5
30. Gazzola, P., Pavione, E., Pezzetti, R., Grechi, D.: Trends in the fashion industry. The perception of sustainability and circular economy: a gender/generation quantitative approach. Sustainability 12(7), 2809 (2020)
31. H&M invests in Sellpy, a Swedish secondhand fashion platform. https://hmgroup.com/ media/news/general-news-2020/hm-invests-in-sellpy-a-swedish-secondhand-fashion-pla tform.html. Last accessed 26 Mar 2023
32. Sellpy experiences strong growth after H&M investment. https://fashionunited.uk/news/ business/sellpy-experiences-strong-growth-after-h-m-investment/2020070248368.   Last accessed 26 Mar 2023
33. Circular and sustainable fashion: H&M's new goals and partnerships, https://hmgroup.com/ sustainability/news/general-sustainability-news-2020/circular-and-sustainable-fashion-hms-new-goals-and-partnerships.html. Last accessed 26 Mar 2023
34. H&M Group: Sustainability: https://hmgroup.com/sustainability.ht. Last accessed 29 Mar 2023
35. Fletcher, K., Grose, L.: Fashion & Sustainability: Design for Change. Laurence King Publishing, Hachette UK (2012)
36. Sellpy, il negozio second hand online di H&M, viene lanciato in altri 20 Paesi, https://it. fashionnetwork.com/news/Sellpy-il-negozio-second-hand-online-di-h-m-viene-lanciato-in-altri-20-paesi,1306881.html. Last accessed 30 Mar 2023
37. Sellpy Home page: https://www.sellpy.com/about. Last accessed 30 Mar 2023

RFID and Counterfeiting: An Analysis of Current Trends in the Fashion Industry

Chiara Marinelli[(✉)] [iD] and Francesca Sinatra[iD]

DEAMS - Department of Economics, Business, Mathematics and Statistics Sciences "Bruno de Finetti", University of Trieste, 34127 Trieste, Italy
{chiara.marinelli,francesca.sinatra}@phd.units.it

Abstract. The paper is aimed at providing an overview on Radio Frequency Identification (RFID) technology, focusing more specifically on RFID tags within the fashion industry. Starting with a comprehensive scenario on environmental concerns in the sector, the paper then moves on to focus on the uses of RFID in fashion, from the manufacturing processes up to commercialisation and post-consumption stages. The goal of this paper is to understand how RFID tags can contribute to contrast counterfeiting among other available technologies. In this context, to better understand the counterfeiting phenomenon, at the end of 2020 we submitted a survey questionnaire to a group of Millennials and Centennials. The aim was to explore and interpret consumers' attitudes on counterfeiting issues.

Results show that both Millennials and Centennials are not keen on purchasing fake fashion items. In the last section, the paper provides an overview on future technological perspectives in the fashion and apparel field and summarise the findings of the study.

Keywords: Radio Frequency Identification (RFID) · Fashion Industry · Counterfeiting

1 Introduction

1.1 RFID Technology and Fashion

Several years have passed since the very first creation of Radio Frequency Identification (RFID) tags in 1999, not to talk about RFID technology itself, which was firstly applied during World War II for the purpose of detecting enemy aircrafts [1]. Already since the early 2000s it was indeed possible to attest for a proliferation of academic articles often praising the advantages of RFID tags for a wide range of functions along the entire supply chain. Moreover, several researchers dared to predict the end of the barcode era due to the incredible edges demonstrated by the new applications of the technology. While the entire overhaul of the barcoding system has not occurred yet, after more than 20 years since the very first predictions, it is nonetheless necessary to remark that RFID tags can now claim an extensive variety of applications of which consumers themselves are often unconscious [2].

© The Author(s), under exclusive license to Springer Nature Switzerland AG 2023
O. Gervasi et al. (Eds.): ICCSA 2023 Workshops, LNCS 14110, pp. 458–472, 2023.
https://doi.org/10.1007/978-3-031-37123-3_32

Ranging from pharmaceuticals to virtual payments, from official documents to agri-food systems, RFID tags have been devoted high attention from researchers and managed to adapt to highly different sectors with overall benefits in terms of traceability and identification.

More specifically, RFID tags were soon experimented in the fashion industry, where they have proved their abilities to speed up the entire supply chain processes and improve the efficiency of all stages from production to distribution and consumption. Their positive impacts on management of value chains and sustainability in general are, indeed, widely attested. On the one hand, a wide array of scholars has focused on benefits and technological innovations brought about by RFID; on the other hand, others have highlighted the hindrances related to the implementation of the technology itself and consumers' concerns [3].

Against the versatility of RFID tags in general and within the fashion sector in particular, the present paper concentrates its focus on one of the most important applications of this technology, i.e. in the contrast against counterfeiting. Consequently, in the first section we will offer an overview of the fashion & apparel industry from a sustainability standpoint, thus considering the environmental impact of the sector in general. Then, we will move to generally consider RFID tags applications in fashion, thus restricting the scope to the description of the areas where they are used in the field. Among these, we will then focus on RFID tags against counterfeiting, which is a matter of utmost concern especially for luxury brands in general, but particularly in fashion. Consequently, in the third section we will consider a case study based on a questionnaire investigating attitudes and behaviours of Millennials and Centennials against counterfeiting. We will then conclude with a summary of the paper findings and an overview on the main technological novelties pertaining to RFID and the related Internet-of-Things (IoT).

1.2 Sustainability and the Fashion Industry: An Overview

It is common knowledge that the fashion industry is one of the most polluting sectors all over the world, ranging between the fourth and the second contributing most to environmental pollution worldwide. Some studies argument that the field is responsible for 10% of global worldwide emissions and that 73% of fashion products ends up incinerated or in landfills at the end of their life cycle [4].

The field has worsened its performances also due to the so-called 'fast fashion' phenomenon, which leads to higher amounts of textile products wasted beforehand than their expected lifetime.

The key point is that the entire textile value chain, from raw materials extraction to the production phases up to distribution, consumption and end-use, is unsustainable. Data confirm that not only production and distribution in fashion have an important impact on environment at worldwide level, but post-consumption raises important issues involving reuse opportunities, recycling possibilities, end-users' knowledge and technological development.

The fashion industry raises environmental concerns starting from production processes. First of all, they imply massive energy consumption which often comes from non-renewable sources (especially fossil fuels), since manufacturing is mostly performed abroad in under-developed countries where much less attention is devoted to sustainable practices. Adding to this, textile factories make extensive use of water and natural resources, starting from the cultivation of cotton and natural fibres up to their use during production steps [5].

Procedures such as printing or dyeing also make use of chemical substances whose use has been limited over time, but that still impact on soil, atmosphere and waters due to the release of polluting gases [6].

Not only is environmental sustainability involved, but also social and economic concerns enter the game in the sector. Manufacturing phases are mostly conducted in countries where labour rights are neglected, unsustainable energy sources are implied and the balance between environmental benefits and economic advantages is often unclear to define. Moreover, several supply chain stages are not transparent, thus providing incentives to illicit trafficking and unfair labour conditions in scattered parts of the world, not only during production and distribution but also in after-use stages.

Apart from the amount of waste produced along the supply chain, the post-consumption component needs to be more closely examined. As a matter of fact, the fast fashion trend has changed consumers' habits by shortening retail products life, while at the same time favouring greater chances to reuse, lending and exchange opportunities. For instance, in Italy post-consumption by itself accounted for more than 146 tons of waste in 2019, mainly exiting in storage and material recovery (around 60 tons overall) while 4% ended up incinerated [7].

It is also a matter of concern the lack of knowledge shown by consumers in relation to the different collection modes, reuse and recycle possibilities and final destinations of discarded fashion products, which reveals the need for sensitisation on post-consumption phases [8]. Nonetheless, some studies demonstrate that consumers buying greater amounts of retail items are those also more aware of post-consumption channels to enhance products reuse, reselling and exchange opportunities [9].

Given these premises, it is not surprising that legislative authorities at national and supranational level are striving for regulating the field in direction of circular practices [10]. Particularly, the EU has recently introduced its Strategy for Sustainable and Circular Textiles in order to achieve recyclable, safe, environment-friendly and respectful of labour rights products, so as to allow consumers to benefit from higher-quality items together with repair and reverse logistics services [6]. Extended Producer Responsibility (EPR) is one of the main policies EU authorities will implement in the next few years in this respect, in order to redesign the fashion industry and enhance more sustainable consumption choices.

In this context, the first companies leading the circular transformation of the sector are luxury brands, striving for meeting calls for a more sustainable fashion industry (sometimes even due to emerging scandals on production and labour conditions in the field) as well as consumers' trends towards more sustainable purchases. It is indeed a fact that sustainable labels and targets benefit brand visibility in front of consumers and with respect to competitors.

It is in this scenario that RFID enters the game through its multiple usage possibilities at different stages of the fashion industry, as we will consider in the next section.

1.3 The RFID Technology in the Fashion Industry

The Radio-Frequency Identification (RFID) technology is a non-contact automatic identification technology, whose birth for detection purposes dates back to World War II [11].

However, due to recent technological developments in the fields of information security and network communication, it has been widely applied in several fields ranging from health to agriculture, from housing to mobility in the turn of some decades. As a matter of fact, RFID is one of the components of Internet-of-Things as a new technological model based on interaction and responsiveness between machines and the human world [12].

RFID tags basically consist of small wireless chips with radio circuits where data is encoded. A complete RFID system is made up by three main components: the transponder (or tag), the antenna to communicate with the tag, and the receiver or controller, which controls the antenna, reads the tag and can write the code on it [2]. The main distinction is between active or passive tags (depending on whether they have independent energy sources or not) and the frequency at which they work, ranging from low to very high frequencies. Passive tags are the most common ones in retail and do not possess inner energy, but they respond when interrogated from the antenna and can be read at a limited distance. Another key component is the power of the antenna and, most importantly, of the controller, which affects the reading distance, the identification and writing possibilities with respect to the tag [13].

The implementation of RFID in retail started already in the early 2000s, with some big companies as the retail giant Walmart deciding to revolutionise its supply chain management [14].

RFID tags brought indeed several advantages at all stages of fashion industry, in a context distinguished by simultaneous increase in competitiveness, growth in global demand and complex worldwide supply chains. As a matter of fact, multiple functions can be made more efficient thanks to the uses of RFID in the field, as the technology can benefit all stages of the supply chain from manufacturing to transportation up to distribution and retailing [13].

First of all, the technology can improve efficiency of the production line and enhance 'smart manufacturing' by means of constant monitoring of movement and product aggregation. This can help to free up resources and streamline processes, thus ensuring the accuracy and reliability of inventory and shipping in the production sites as well as tracking equipment maintenance [15].

Moreover, RFID tags can easily fasten logistics processes and ensure reduction of human errors, consequently reducing the risk of lost items, improving reverse logistics and return policies after consumption, which may also be beneficial in light of the future introduction of the Passport for products and EPR policies at EU level [6].

As far as retail is concerned, RFID serves shop operations by favouring inventory management and stock counting, saving or redirecting labour force or improving the visibility and traceability of products. An RFID important contribution in retail consists in improving the purchasing experience by making it faster, easier and potentially customised. Many new applications of RFID technologies in retail imply, for instance, the use of 'smart dressing rooms' providing advice to customers together with 'smart mirrors', 'smart shelves' that ease restocking and reordering of depleting products, as well as anti-theft systems for salespersons [16].

It is possible to selectively adopt RFID only for some stages of the supply chain, although benefits from the technology are enhanced when it is implemented and integrated along the entire process [17].

As a matter of fact, the reduction in human mistakes, the improved efficiency throughout all processes in the supply chain management and better customer services overall ultimately lead to benefits in revenue terms. In particular, this has been the case also for very big retailers as Decathlon, which since RFID implementation has assisted to a reduction in lost resources, increased efficiency in restocking and inventory management and revenues growth. Indeed, the company has already planned not to fire but to redirect personnel to advise and customer services [18].

However, one of the most important uses of the RFID technology is in the contrast against counterfeiting, which is of utmost interest especially for luxury brands. This will indeed be the focus of the next section, which concentrates on the possibilities offered by RFID to prevent and fight against falsification and frauds.

2 Material and Method

2.1 RFID Against Counterfeiting: Possibilities and Applications

In 2016, the Organisation for Economic Cooperation and Development (OECD) estimated the counterfeiting market value to be around 12 billion euros, equal to 4% of Italian import of authenticated items. Moreover, over the same year the global trade market of counterfeited items and imitations of Italian brands reached 32 billion euros, i.e. 3.6% of the value of products sold by the national manufacturing sector [19].

In this context, new technologies are fundamental against counterfeiting as they can help in tracing and contrasting illicit practices. Nonetheless, three key issues are worth remarking in the current fight against counterfeiting through technology [20]:

- Technical problems, as tools and procedures are costly and difficult to spread rapidly on a large scale, while also turning difficult to understand for common consumers;
- Awareness issues, as not many customers understand the importance of not buying fake products and are not aware of actually committing a crime;
- Size factors, given the lack of incentives in the implementation of costly technological anti-counterfeiting devices not only by luxury brands but also by smaller fashion companies.

In this context, actual technologies against counterfeiting can be categorised in four main ways [21]:

- Overt or visible features (manifest);
- Covert or hidden markers;
- Forensic techniques, i.e. legal ones as those making use of chemicals;
- Serialisation or track-and-trace systems.

Similarly, other scholars divide types of anti-counterfeiting systems according to the means of use and their effects, that is to say distinguishing the manifest ones (e.g.

holograms and filigrees), hidden methods such as safety inks and invisible printing, use of chemicals and, in the end, barcodes and RFIDs [17].

In retail, anti-counterfeiting methods can additionally be split according to whether they are fixed to internal supports of the product, attached to the item itself or even inserted in the product or the packaging.

In 2003 the U.S. Food and Drug Administration was the first to propose track-and-trace anti-counterfeiting through RFID in pharmaceutics [22]. RFID tags are, indeed, unique to the associated garments, thanks to the use of PID/UID (Product Identifier or Unique Identifier). Consequently, the tag becomes an identification system that stores the entire history of a product and is able to trace it through the entire value chain [20].

More specifically, some scholars divide anti-counterfeiting systems using RFID into 4 categories, which we will explore in depth [23]:

a) **PUF Based 'Unclonable' RFID ICs and chipless RFID tags for anti-counterfeiting;**
b) **Track and trace anti-counterfeiting;**
c) **Distance-bound control protocols;**
d) **Other types of anti-counterfeiting protocols.**

a) *PUF Based 'Unclonable' RFID ICs and chipless RFID tags for anti-counterfeiting*

Physical Unclonable Functions (PUFs) exploit the physical features of the Integrated Circuits (ICs) manufacturing process, which are distinguishable for every tag, so that copying, cloning or controlling one of them becomes highly difficult [24].

PUFs react to external signals embodied in a physical object through random variables with a different probability distribution which depend on whether the object is a fake or not. Moreover, PUF systems can be further distinguished in:

– Integrated Physical Unclonable Function (I-PUF), i.e. the PUF is connected to a chip preventing communications issues between the anti-counterfeiting system and the product;
– PUF tags, where the technology is directly incorporated into products and the tag acts as a key whereas the inside pattern is the lock.

An alternative way is to use chipless RFID tags, which are not as fully unclonable like the PUF-based unclonable ones due to their manufacturing process but are more low cost, adaptable and more resistant [25].

b) *Track and trace anti-counterfeiting*

This approach has attracted the attention of researchers due to its reliability. This system typically involves an electronic pedigree (e-pedigree) guaranteeing the product visibility and constantly transmits diverse types of data according to the state of the product, so the database is stored in the back-end and forms the pedigree background [21].

Three main steps are involved while using pedigree-generated data:

• Pedigree Data Formatting, which is important for collecting and handling data that facilitate ID generation, item tracking, authentication and monitoring;
• Pedigree Data Processing, which keeps the e-pedigree updated and ensures its integrity;

- Pedigree Transmission Mechanism, which provides access control to the pedigree data, e.g. in the case of internal or external controls.

This anti-counterfeiting system is suitable for supply chain operations where manufacturers, distributors, and retailers are connected in production, selling and transportation of items. Moreover, improvements in imprecise features of the technology have been made, thanks to ultra-high frequency (UHF) tags of 2nd generation which solve critical issues of e-pedigree in diverse stages [22].

c) *Distance-bound control protocols*

This process exploits broadcast and collision techniques to identify RFID cloned tags. As a matter of fact, cloning attacks on RFID tags constitute a non-irrelevant risk in RFID applications [25]. Thus, in this method, each tag is assigned a unique ID and random number which is then stored on a back-end server, the so-called synchronised secret. Tags are interrogated by readers present in the same environment and, in case multiple responses are returned, this means we have at least a cloned tag in addition to the original one.

Consequently, this type of protocols can effectively identify clones and more cheaply than sophisticated cryptographic techniques. Although it is a quick and adaptable method, the adoption of these protocols brings about space limitations, since synchronisation always needs to occur in the same environment.

d) *Other types of anti-counterfeiting protocols*

This category includes different cryptographic protocols. This type of protocols ensures that information retrieved by unauthorised readers is of no interest to attackers, unless they are able to decipher it [11].

Different cryptographic technologies exist, for instance common encryption methods (cheaper, but also more vulnerable) and probabilistic ones. The latter are more complex to decipher as an anonymous ID is provided each time upon interrogation, but are more expensive and difficult to implement on a large scale.

Consequently, some authors proposed a new model composed by two protocols with a unique function. The tag authentication protocol allows the customer to read information stored in the tag, then the database correction protocol corrects it when the status of the read items need to be changed (from unsold to sold) [26].

Although cryptographic protocols involve several computational processes and back-and-forth communications, they result as more flexible and adaptable.

As these techniques show advantages in terms of traceability, effective sorting and circular economy in general, researchers have developed new protocols, i.e. the one exploiting the positive advantages of the combination between QR codes and PUF [1].

While luxury brands were among the first to implement RFID for sustainable and anti-counterfeiting purposes, less well-known fashion companies already successfully adopted this technology several years ago [17].

For instance, this has been the case of an Italian fashion company which has adopted, since 2012, the RFID system using a 22-character alphanumeric code (unique and not reproducible) for each generated tag. This has allowed it to protect its brand and its made-in-Italy production, while ensuring better SCM, distribution and customers' satisfaction overall. Moreover, this has improved relations with customers as the technology allows to check for product authenticity thanks to a mobile app that permits reading of all information stored in the RFID tag. The fact that RFID systems have turned cheaper over time, easing returns on initial investment, has made the adoption of the RFID technology more appealing all along the supply chain and across sectors.

Scholars have contributed to advancing the field by promoting new advancements of this technology, e.g. chipless tags having longer interrogation range that can be used against counterfeiting also for banknotes [27] or active tags that can work in combination with other technologies to ensure higher protection against fraudulent practices [1].

Lastly, additional methods to contrast counterfeiting have been elaborated by researchers, by also taking into account technologies different from RFID. Considering that several companies in the fashion industry have adopted RFID tags for anti-counterfeiting purposes, in the next section we will focus on consumers' behaviour and consumption habits with respect to counterfeited products.

3   Survey on Consumers' Attitudes on Counterfeited Products

In order to deepen the counterfeiting phenomenon in fashion, we conducted a quantitative analysis on a survey concerning behaviour and perceptions of consumers. The survey was realised and administered between September and November 2020 to a selected target of Millennials and Centennials, also named as Generations Y and Z. The former constitutes a group of consumers aged between 24 and 39, while the latter includes people between 18 and 23 years old. The two groups were chosen because of their involvement and proactivity in the fashion field.

The questionnaire aimed at investigating the effective consumption propension of consumers on counterfeited products of 16 luxury brands in fashion. The selected brands were: Luois Vuitton, Gucci, Chanel, Dior, Dolce & Gabbana, Hermès, Rolex, Cartier, Burberry, Yves Saint Laurent, Prada, Lancôme, Faoma, Moët e Chandon Versace and Tiffany & Co. They were chosen due to their popularity among luxury brands and, while some of them concentrate on one field only of the fashion system, others diversify their offer in different fashion sectors.

Thus, we collected a sample of 352 Italian Millennials (24–39, 49% of interviewees) and Centennials (18–23, 51% of the total). These are, indeed, the two main categories of people involved in fashion consumption habits and particularly keen on luxury brands. As for the geographical areas involved, most of the sample was collected in the Southern regions of Italy (56%), while only 3% were abroad at the time of the survey.

Concerning the income, most people presented an average annual income between 0–18,000.00 euro (27% of respondents). This highlights the low purchase power of interviewees (Fig. 1).

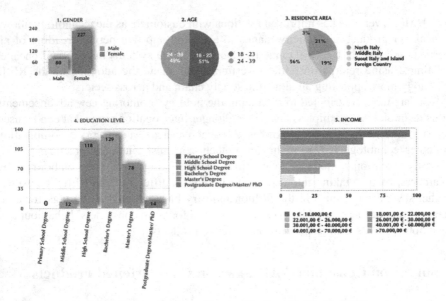

Fig. 1. Socio-demographic area (Author: Sinatra F., 2023)

As a first step, interviewees were asked about the importance they are used to assigning to factors as authenticity, quality, made in and brand. They were demanded whether they ensured about the presence of these factors in the purchase phase. From collected data, it is evident that they assign high importance to the analysed attributes with a particular attention devoted to quality and authenticity. It also emerges the attention devoted to the purchase of luxury products by younger consumers, rather than older generations [28]. Moreover, younger generations assign higher value to the presence of the above-mentioned features in products before making a purchase decision (Fig. 2).

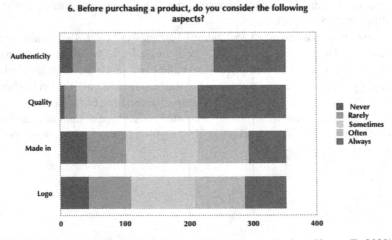

Fig. 2. Factors considered in purchase of luxury items (Author: Sinatra F., 2023)

After that, the survey requested whether they had ever purchased counterfeited products. The label 'counterfeited' does not indeed have negative connotations and simply stands for the copy or unauthorised imitation of luxury products containing similar symbols to the original brands, such as logos or tags. In addition, consumers can be more or less aware of buying counterfeited products. Data show that most of the sampled people had never bought counterfeited products (52%), which led us to think that consumers nowadays are more attracted by ethical practices and understand side backs deriving from the purchase of counterfeited products. 34% of the interviewees declared having purchased counterfeited products at least once and an additional 14% of having done that without awareness of their fake character. Among the latter group, the majority belonged to the Centennials category, which seems to be in line with their lower purchase power and trend not to buy luxury items (Fig. 3).

7. Have you ever bought a fake item?

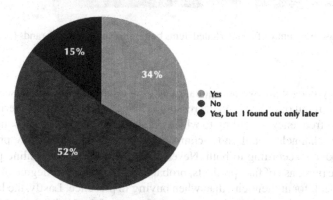

Fig. 3. Purchase frequency of fake items (Author: Sinatra F., 2023)

In case of positive answer to having bought fake items at least once (170 interviewees of the overall sample), the survey proceeded with more specific questions concerning consumers' attitudes on purchase of counterfeited products. The questionnaire went on with questions related to the purchase frequency of counterfeited fashion products of the 16 luxury brands.

Collected answers reveal that most people of both the generations considered in the study never bought counterfeited items of the 16 luxury brands taken into account, mostly because they do not know about their existence (Fig. 4).

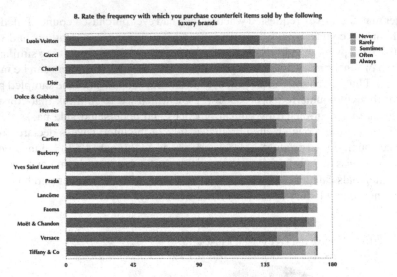

Fig. 4. Purchase frequency of counterfeited items belonging to 16 luxury brands (Author: Sinatra F., 2023)

The survey ends with two additional questions related to the purchase channels of fake products (retail or online) and the reasons conducive to buying counterfeited items.

As for the frequency according to which counterfeited products are bought through the two main channels, retail and e-commerce, there is an overall low propensity to buy fake products according to both. Nevertheless, a wider use of online platforms is attested in the purchase of fake products, probably due to the lower degree of control and chances to check for authenticity than when buying in presence. Lastly, the last question addresses the motivations leading to purchase of counterfeited items and tries to provide an exhaustive answer [29]. Five relevant variables have been taken into account, that is to say low price of fake products, high cost of branded items, social acceptance, personal interest and custom (in the meaning of lower effort required to get fake products). Collected answers reveal that cost-related reasons are the most important ones in purchase choices, particularly for Centennials (Fig. 5).

What overall emerges is a low purchase frequency in relation to counterfeited products of the selected luxury brands, and that consumers (younger ones, too) prefer to buy real items with authenticity features and higher qualitative standards rather than fake ones. The analysis also highlights significant differences on consumption habits of counterfeited products. Consequently, it seems important to try to adapt and diversify strategies to discourage counterfeiting in order to appeal to different consumers' categories.

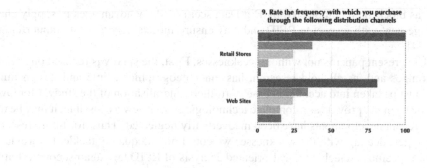

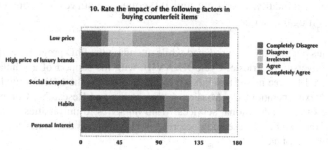

Fig. 5. Purchase channels and influential factors in buying counterfeited items (Author: Sinatra F., 2023)

4 Conclusions

To sum up, the paper focused on RFID tags in the fashion and apparel industry, by providing first an overview of the field to then move to consider the general RFID use. After that, we concentrated the analysis on the technologies against counterfeiting and restricted the scope to RFID use for this purpose. Lastly, we explored consumers' attitudes with respect to counterfeiting in the fashion sector. Results showed that consumers (both Millennials and Centennials) are not used to buying counterfeited products of the 16 selected luxury brands. Moreover, they tend to pay attention to authenticity and quality. What also emerges is that consumption patterns change according to different generations and their purchase power.

Technological development concerning RFID tags has been speeding up a lot since the very birth of IoT, which was initially meant to connect machines with other machines. Nowadays, challenges lie more in perfectioning RFID tags performances, such as making the technology less visible and more adaptable to track people through on- and off-body links [30], for instance through wearable chipless RFID sensors [27] or improving washability in harsh environments [31, 32].

As for the use of RFID tags against counterfeiting, instead, researchers currently focus more on new and safer technologies for data encryption and authentication [11]. However, we need to take stock of the fact that RFID is not anymore a novelty in the fashion sector and that new technologies show promising applications, too. Differently from the early 2000s, researchers now speak more generally of IoT applications and concentrate on the new possibilities it offers [12, 33]. Moreover, other different technologies such as blockchain empowered by Big Data seem to show advantages in supply chain management with respect to RFID and may ensure more safety against counterfeiting, too [34].

The present paper is not without weaknesses. First, the survey is focused on specific age ranges and, as all field research, has inner geographical, time and design limits that must be taken into account in case of further generalisation of the study. Moreover, despite trying to provide as a complete technological overview as possible, it may be that more recent developments have been inadvertently neglected. Thus, for future research we suggest dealing with the weaknesses we could not adequately tackle, by providing a more specific and technological-oriented analysis of RFID tags against counterfeiting and by extending -geographically, over time and in scope- the survey on consumers' perceptions about this illegal practice.

Acknowledgments. This publication was produced while attending the PhD programme in Circula Economy at the University of Trieste, Cycle XXXVIII, with the support of a scholarship financed by the Ministerial Decree no. 351 of 9th April 2022, based on the NRRP - funded by the European Union - NextGenerationEU - Mission 4 "Education and Research", Component 1 "Enhancement of the offer of educational services: from nurseries to universities" - Investment 4.1 "Extension of the number of research doctorates and innovative doctorates for public administration and cultural heritage".

Author Contribution. Conceptualization, methodology, formal analysis, materials and resources, data curation and validation: all authors. In particular: Marinelli wrote Sect. 1, Sect. 1.1, Sect. 1.2, Sect. 1.3, Sect. 2; Sect. 2.1; Sinatra wrote Sect. 3; Marinelli and Sinatra wrote Sect. 4

References

1. Agrawal, T. K., Koehl, L., Campagne, C.: Cryptographic tracking tags for traceability in textiles and clothing supply chain. In: Zeng, X., Lu, J., E Kerre, E., Martinez, L., Koehl, L. (Eds.), World Scientific Proceedings Series on Computer Engineering and Information Science: Volume 10 - Conference on Uncertainty Modelling in Knowledge Engineering and Decision Making (FLINS 2016), pp. 800–805. World Scientific (2016)
2. Nayak, R., Singh, A., Padhye, R., Wang, L.: RFID in textile and clothing manufacturing: technology and challenges. Fashion Text. **2**(1), 1–16 (2015). https://doi.org/10.1186/s40691-015-0034-9
3. Pramatari, K., Theotokis, A.: Consumer acceptance of RFID-enabled services: a model of multiple attitudes, perceived system characteristics and individual traits. Euro. J. Inf. Syst. **18**, 541–552 (2009)
4. Economia circolare applicata. https://circularity.com/economia-circolare-applicata/tessile/. Accessed 07 Mar 2023
5. Denuwara, N., Maijala, J., Hakovirta, M.: Sustainability benefits of RFID technology in the apparel industry. Sustainability **11**(6477) (2019)
6. Textiles in Europe's Circular Economy. https://www.eea.europa.eu/publications/textiles-in-europes-circular-economy/textiles-in-europe-s-circular-economy. Accessed 07 Mar 2023
7. Fondazione per lo Sviluppo Sostenibile, FISE UNICIRCULAR: L'Italia del Riciclo 2021. Italia (2021)

8. Istituto Nazionale di Statistica: Raccolta differenziata dei rifiuti: comportamenti e soddisfazione dei cittadini e politiche nelle città I Anni 2020–2021. Istat, Italia (2022)
9. Woolridge, A.C., Ward, G.D., Phillips, P.S., Collins, M., Gandy, S.: Life cycle assessment for reuse/recycling of donated waste textiles compared to use of virgin material: an UK energy saving perspective. Resour. Conserv. Recycl. **46**(1), 94–103 (2006)
10. ReSet the Trend: EU calls on young people to promote circular and sustainable fashion. https://environment.ec.europa.eu/news/reset-trend-2023-01-26_en. Accessed 07 Mar 2023
11. Oyarhossein, S.: Cryptography and authentication processing framework on RFID active tags for carpet products. In: Proceedings of ICCTA, pp. 26–31. Institute of Electrical and Electronics Engineers (IEEE), Beijing (2009)
12. Prajapati, D., Felix, T.S. Chan, F.T.S., Chelladurai, H., Lakshay, L., Pratap S.: An Internet of Things embedded sustainable supply chain management of B2B E-Commerce. Sustainability **14**(9), 5066 (2022)
13. Sushila, S.D., Singh, S.S.J.: RFID technology in apparel manufacturing. Pharma Innov. J. **8**(2), 669–672 (2019)
14. Stafford, J.: How marks & spencer is using RFID to improve customer service and business efficiency: a case study. In: Kerry J., Butler P. (eds.) Smart Packaging Technologies for Fast Moving Consumer Goods, pp. 197–210. Wiley Online Library (2008)
15. O'Dubhthaigh, D., Borchers, M., Jin, Y., Maropoulos, P.: Implementing smart manufacturing technology into the textile industry. Adv. Manufact. Technol. **35**, 37–44 (2022)
16. Bayraktar, A., Ylmaz, E., Erdem, S.: Using RFID technology for simplification of retail processes. In: Turcu, C. (ed.), Designing and Deploying RFID Applications. IntechOpen, London (2011)
17. Varese, E., Pellicelli, A.C.: The RFID technology for monitoring the supply chain and for fighting against counterfeiting: a fashion company case study. In: Beltramo, R., Romani, A., Cantore, P. (eds.) Fashion Industry - An Itinerary Between Feelings and Technology. InTechOpen, London (2019)
18. Decathlon, come utilizzare al meglio la tecnologia RFID. https://www.alfacod.it/blog-decathlon-come-utilizzare-tecnologia-rfid. Accessed 08 Mar 2023
19. OECD: Il commercio di beni contraffatti e l'economia Italiana: Tutelare la proprietà intellettuale dell'Italia. OECD Publishing, Paris (2018)
20. Meraviglia, L.: Technology and counterfeiting in the fashion industry: friends or foes? Bus. Horiz. **61**, 467–475 (2018)
21. Choi, S.H., Yang, B., Cheung, H.H., Yang, Y.X.: Data management of RFID-based track-and-trace anti-counterfeiting in apparel supply chain. In: The 8th International Conference for Internet Technology and Secured Transactions (ICITST-2013), pp. 265–269. Institute of Electrical and Electronics Engineers (IEEE) (2013)
22. Choi, S.H., Yang, B., Cheung, H.H., Yang, Y.X.: RFID tag data processing in manufacturing for track-and-trace anti-counterfeiting. Comput. Ind. **68**, 148–161 (2015)
23. Khalil, G., Doss, R., Chowdhury, M.: A comparison survey study on RFID based anti-counterfeiting systems. J. Sens. Actuator Netw. **8**(3), 37 (2019)
24. Agrawal, T., Campagne, C., Koehl, L.: Development and characterisation of secured traceability tag for textile products by printing process. Int. J. Adv. Manufact. Technol. **101**(9–12), 2907–2922 (2018). https://doi.org/10.1007/s00170-018-3134-z
25. Bu, K., Liu, X., Xiao, B.: Approaching the time lower bound on cloned-tag identification for large RFID systems. Ad Hoc Netw. **13**, 271–281 (2014)
26. Tran, D.-T., Hong, S.J.: RFID Anti-counterfeiting for retailing systems. J. Appl. Math. Phys. **3**, 1–9 (2015)
27. Behera, S.K.: Chipless RFID sensors for wearable applications: a review. IEEE Sens. J. **22**(2), 11015–11120 (2022)

28. Grossman, G.M., Shapiro, C.: Counterfeit-product trade. Am. Econ. Rev. **78**, 59–75 (1988)
29. Huang, W., Schrank, H., Dubinsky, A.J.: Effect of brand name on consumers' risk perceptions of online shopping. J. Cons. Behav. **4**, 40–50 (2006)
30. Manzari, S., Occhiuzzi, C., Marrocco, G.: Reading range of wearable textile RFID tags in real configurations. In: Proceedings of the 5th European Conference on Antennas and Propagation (EUCAP), pp. 433–436. Institute of Electrical and Electronics Engineers (IEEE) (2011)
31. Moraru, A., Helerea, E., Ursachi, C.: Passive RFID tags for textile items – requirements and solutions. In: International Symposium on Fundamentals of Electrical Engineering (ISFEE), pp. 1–6. Institute of Electrical and Electronics Engineers (IEEE) (2018)
32. Pei, J., Fan, J., Zheng, R.: Protecting wearable UHF RFID tags with electro-textile antenna. IEEE Antennas Propag. Mag. **63**(4), 43–50 (2021)
33. Lemey, S., Agneessens, S., Van Torre, P., Baes, K., Rogier, H. Vanfleteren, J.: Autonomous wearable RFID-based sensing platform for the Internet-of-Things. In: 2017 International Applied Computational Electromagnetics Society Symposium - Italy (ACES), pp. 1–2. Institute of Electrical and Electronics Engineers (IEEE) (2017)
34. Hader, M., Tchoffa, D., El Mhamedi, A., Ghodous, P., Dolgui, A., Abouabdellah, A.: Applying integrated Blockchain and Big Data technologies to improve supply chain traceability and information sharing in the textile sector. J. Ind. Inf. Integr. **28**, 100345 (2022)

Railways Transport Infrastructures for Supporting Tourism: A Bibliometric Analysis

Ema Rahmawati[1,2]($\boxtimes$), Tonny Hendratono[1], Sugiarto Sugiarto[1], Gagih Pradini[3], and Tutut Herawan[1,4]

[1] Sekolah Tinggi Pariwisata Ambarrukmo, Jl. Ringroad Timur No. 52, Bantul, Daerah Istimewa Yogyakarta 55198, Indonesia

[2] PT Gemilang Wisata Persada, Jl. Maninjau Barat No. 18 Sawojajar, Kota Malang, Jawa Timur 65139, Indonesia

[3] Universitas Nasional, Jl. Sawo Manila No. 61, Jakarta Selatan, Daerah Khusus Ibukota Jakarta 12520, Indonesia

[4] AMCS Research Center, Jalan Griya Taman Asri, Yogyakarta 55512, Indonesia

Abstract. In this paper, we present a bibliometric analysis of the Railway Transport Infrastructure model for supporting tourism. We identify the its research evolution for past decade, including; source, document type, journal name, publisher name, topic trends, and author collaborations. Bibliometric analysis was used to analyze 48 articles published from 2013 to 2023. Railway Transport Infrastructure for Tourism is the main keyword used in article titles, abstracts, and keywords to get metadata retrieved from the Scopus database. The tools used in this bibliometric analysis are Harzing's Publish or Perish to extract data from the Scopus database and VoS Viewer for data visualization and further used for citation and metric analysis. The results of this study show that most articles related to railway transport infrastructure for tourism are published in scientific journals, compared to others, where they received the highest citations. Based on network visualization, the most dominant term is tourism development as the key term related to several other issues of railway transport, tourism, transport infrastructure, and economic growth. Meanwhile, when viewed from the overlay visualization, the dominant keywords are transportation infrastructure, data panels, social networks, air transportation, high speed rail, and economic growth. Based on the findings presented in network visualization and overlay visualization, it can be concluded that articles with the topic railway transport infrastructure for tourism have not been widely studied, so they can be used as an interesting keyword for further research.

Keywords: Bibliometric analysis · Tourism · Railways transportation · VoS Viewer · Scopus

1 Introduction

Transportation means moving people and goods from one place to another by land, water, or air. Meanwhile, trains are one of the means of land transportation that moves people in mass. Railway infrastructure as a support for tourism referred to here is the

© The Author(s), under exclusive license to Springer Nature Switzerland AG 2023
O. Gervasi et al. (Eds.): ICCSA 2023 Workshops, LNCS 14110, pp. 473–494, 2023.
https://doi.org/10.1007/978-3-031-37123-3_33

use of railway assets to be used partially or fully to support tourism. According to Severino's research, *et al.* [1] on rail transportation routes related to passenger demand. In the study, it tried to develop a multi-stage model of tourist activities to optimize the development of railway companies. The result of the study is the realization of models that can be developed such as the introduction of tourist routes in accordance with infrastructure and consideration of other income from railway tourism businesses. Wu, *et al.* [2] in their study of people traveling by train and the effect of rail transport infrastructure on passenger consumption and long-term economic growth. The study found that investment in railways and railway infrastructure directly boosts long-term economic development but also indirectly increases tourism. While study of Knežević's, *et al.* [3] on transit tourism in Gorski Kotar. In the study presented the development period of transit tourism, namely the development of carriage traffic in Carolina in 1732 and Lujzijana in 1811 then the railway line in Zagreb-Karlovac-Rijeka which became the main transit line in 1875. Furthermore, it is proven that transit tourism on the railway, brings the greatest economic benefits and lifts supporting service facilities at railway stations. Then Kozłowski, *et al.* [4] examined the innovation of railway transportation companies in Poland related to tourism development. Infrastructure, the organization of transport, as well as economic, social, ecological, and political factors, are the basis for the development of tourism. The results revealed that a rather low level of innovation in the development of railway transport companies in Poland. Different from the research of Ronzoni [5] which revealed that the railway line on the Noto-Pachino line in Syracuse Province, Sicily along 27.5 km was abandoned in 1986. Various types of trains that have been known consist of three types as shown in Fig. 1 below:

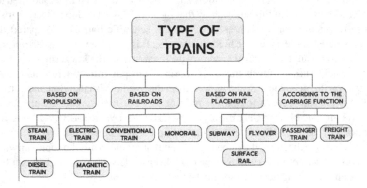

Fig. 1. Type of Trains

In Fig. 1 above, it can be explained that train types are divided into 3 types:

a. By Drive Type consists of steam trains, electric trains, diesel trains, and magnetic power trains
b. Based on the Railway, it consists of conventional rail trains and monorail trains
c. Based on Rail Placement consists of subways, elevated railways, and surface railways

d. By Function The carriages consist of passenger trains and freight trains

Trains are one of the important things in encouraging the growth and development of tourist destinations. This is partly because it is supported by new technological developments in the field of railway transportation which greatly help improve the tourism sector. One of the reasons for this new technological development is the demand for newer, faster, and more efficient modes of travel. According to the study of Masson, et al. [6] on high-speed trains that can be a tourist attraction in Perpignan (France) and Barcelona (Spain), revealed that high-speed fire sledding allows for the reduction of transportation costs as well as can be a tool for tourism development by allowing improvement accessibility. While Lee, et al. [7] conducted a study on the factors that determine the tourist attraction of trains. The study shows that the provision of heritage train attractions, both onboard and offboard, is an important component and adds to the experience of traveling by train. While the smoothness and comfort of travel by train plays a supporting role in improving the determination of tourist attraction. Pagliara, et al. [18] in exploring the interdependence between the rail system of high speed and tourism in Italy. The results showed that the impact of high-speed rail on the number of Italian visitors and the number of nights spent at destinations (tourist) was positive in all cities. While Albalate, et al. [9] conducted a study on whether the relationship between tourism and high-speed rail can increase local visitors in Spain. The evolution of tourism at the local level in Spain. The results showed that the effect of the introduction of high-speed rail corridors on the number of visitors and their total and average stay in some medium-sized cities compared to visitors who did not have such infrastructure.

Most tourism studies on railways define trains to facilitate tourism mobility and railway facilities as supporting tourist comfort [10–20]. In this case, the railway as transportation acts as a link between, on the one hand as a tourist destination center and on the other hand as a tourist generating center [21–25]. Research by Becker, et al. [10] on rapid rail transit and tourism development in the United States. The research highlights the planned development of a rapid transit rail system connecting the continental US and discusses the exploration of the impact of the system on tourism development. Similarly, the study of Su, et al. [11] evaluated the impact of increased accessibility on travelers' travel decisions, as well as experiences in Tibet. The study also discussed the importance of trains for tourists' choice of destinations in Tibet as well as their overall travel experience. Another study from Sun, et al. [12] examines the effect of highspeed rail on individual travel patterns of tourists in Taiwan. The study revealed that highspeed rail has a weak influence on travel distance and length of stay per trip, and a reduction of about 10% in transport carbon emissions through intermodal substitution. Peira, et al. [13] in their study on tourism and tourism, revealed the dynamics of railway heritage recovery, the dynamics of train tourism and the relationship between sustainability and railway tourism. The result of the study is to highlight that the process of railway tourism always comes from railway heritage restoration projects, and to perhaps maintain its authenticity. In the study, it was also found that many tourists are interested in train tourist destinations because they want to feel memorable experiences related to nostalgia.

The works mentioned above focus on trains as a means of tourism mobility in many aspects and places, unfortunately, there has not been much discussion about trains in terms of infrastructure as supporting tourism in bibliometric analysis. The novelty of this work is that, unlike the above work, we explored the VoS viewer as a tool for our analysis. For this, this paper presents a bibliometric analysis of railway infrastructure as a supporter of tourism. In summary, this work made the following contributions:

a. We present a bibliometric analysis of railway infrastructure in support of tourism
b. We explain the comparison of matrices of publications
c. We present the documents types of publications
d. We describe the sources types of publications
e. We present the top 10 cited articles
f. We present 5 publishers which publish articles related to railway infrastructure in supporting tourism
g. We present 5 journals related to railway infrastructure in supporting tourism
h. We present keywords that represent each cluster
i. We present the countries of research location and research domain

The remainder of the paper is organized as follows. In Sect. 2, we describe our proposed research method. Section 3 presents our obtained results and following by complete discussion. Finally, we conclude our work and highlight future work in Sect. 4.

2 Proposed Method

In this paper, we adopt bibliometrics analysis method which are widely used in previous works [26–41]. Our method consisting of six stages as depicted in Fig. 2 below.

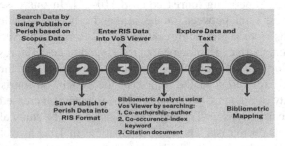

Fig. 2. Flow Chart of the proposed method

3 Results and Discussion

This section describes the results obtained from this work, which includes publications and citations, visualizations, authors and networks, research locations, and research domains.

3.1 Publications and Citations

To determine the comparison of the citation matrix with data taken through Scopus, we create a table in which contains the number of articles, the number of citations, the number of citations per year, the number of authors per year, the H index, the G index, the normal hI, and the annual hI at the beginning of the search and improvement of results. The comparison data matrix in the search for starting results and searching for results after improvement can be seen in Table 1 below:

Table 1. Comparison Matrix

Data	Initial Search Results	Search Results Rcpair
Database	Scopus	Scopus
Year publishing	2013–2023	2013–2023
Year citation	10	10
Number of Articles	48	33
Number citation	359	220
Number Citation per Year	35.90	22.00
Number Authors per Year	2.75	2.91
H index	9	8
G index	18	14
hI Normal	5	4
hI Annual	0.50	0.40

From Table 1 above, it was found that within a period of 10 years i.e., from 2013–2023 there were 48 articles with 359 citations and an average number of authors per year of 2 people. Next, the search is corrected or the results are re-selected by observing one by one articles related to the topic. Articles obtained after improvement and selection obtained as many as 33 articles with a total of 220 citations or an average of 22.00 per year and an average of 2 authors per year. The index for measuring the productivity or impact of work that has been published by scientists or academics (Hirsch's h-Index) is 8. Furthermore, based on the distribution of citations received by publications or research articles (Egghe's g-Index) obtained as many as 14. To find out the year of publication can be seen in Table 2 below which provides a more detailed explanation of Table 1.

From Table 2 above, in 2021 there were the most publications, namely 8 total publications, and in 2020 and 20the 22 most publications were 7 total publications. While the number of most cited articles is in years 2021 and the number of articles least cited is in years 2013, 2015, 2016, and 2023. While the 2014 article did not get any citations. For the total number of citations, the highest were in 2021 and the fewest in 2013, 2015, 2016, and 2023. Furthermore, to find out the description of the publication and citation bar chart can be seen in the chart presented in Fig. 3 below.

Table 2. The Statistics Descriptive of Publication

Year	TP	% (N = 33)	NCP	TC	C/P	C/CP
2013	1	0.03	1	3	3,00	3,00
2014	0	0.00	0	0	0.00	0.00
2015	1	0.03	1	6	6,00	6.00
2016	1	0.03	1	66	66.00	66.00
2017	3	0.09	3	35	11.67	11.67
2018	2	0.06	0	0	0.00	0.00
2019	2	0.06	1	7	3.50	7.00
2020	7	0.21	7	41	5.86	5.86
2021	8	0.24	6	34	4.25	5.67
2022	7	0.21	5	28	4.00	5.60
2023	1	0.03	0	0	0.00	0.00
	33	100%				

Note: TP = total number of publications; NCP = number cited publications; TC = total quotes; C/P = average citations per publication; C/CP = average citation per cited publication

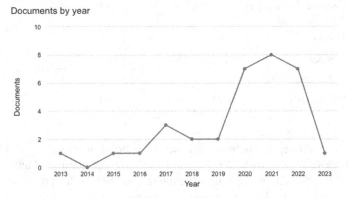

Fig. 3. Publication and Citations Form 2013–2023

It can be seen from Fig. 3 above that the publication and citation bar chart for the 10-year period from 2013–2023 experienced a fluctuating graph. The number of documents annually changes up and down. In 2021 the publication and citation bar increased to reach the top position with the same number of documents, namely on chart number 8. Meanwhile, in 2013, 2015, 2016, and 2023 the publication and citation bars decreased the number of documents in chart 1. In 2018 and 2019 the publication and citation bars are in the same position and center, which is number 2. To see an overview of the document based on its subject field, you can see more clearly in Fig. 4 below.

It can be explained from Fig. 4 above that the subject of Social Science is the subject that plays the most role in writing articles using the keyword Railway Transport Infrastructure for Tourism with a percentage of 35.5%. Next, in second place followed

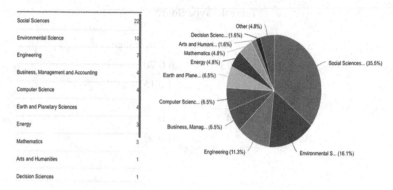

Fig. 4. Documents by Subject Area Form 2013–2023

by Environment subjects with a percentage of 16%. Then in third position is the subject of Engineering with a percentage of 1 1.3%. While the lowest ranks are Arts and Humanities and Decision Sciences with a percentage of 1. 6%. Furthermore, to find out the type of document can be seen from the presentation of the citation matrix of scientific publications related to railway transport infrastructure for tourism in 2013–2023 in Table 3 below.

Table 3. Type Document

Type	Number	Percentage
Article	23	0.70
Conference Paper	7	0.21
Book Chapter	2	0.06
Conference Review	1	0.03
	33	100%

From Table 3 above, From Table 3 above, the types of documents we present are original documents derived from Articles, Conference Papers, Book Chapters and Conference Reviews. We summarize in the description of Table 3 above, the article holds dominance in showing its role with 23 contributions with a percentage of 7 0%, followed by Conference Paper with a total of 7 with a percentage of 21%. Book Chapter occupies the third position with a total of 2 and a percentage of 06%, and in the last position is occupied by Conference Review with a total of 1 and a percentage of 0.3%. Meanwhile, we present in Table 4 below all documents classified into 5 types of publication sources in the form of Journals, Books, Conference Proceedings, and Series.

From Table 4 above, it can be observed that the Journal is the document that has the largest contribution with a total of 23 or equivalent to 70%, followed by Conference Proceedings with total of 5 or equivalent to 15%, followed by the Book Series with a total of 4 or equivalent to 12%, and the last is Book as much as 1 or equivalent to 0.3%.

Table 4. Type Source

Type	Number	Percentage
Journal	23	0.70
Conference Proceeding	5	0.15
Book Series	4	0.12
Book	1	0.03
	33	100%

In presenting this data, we also present a ranking of journals with the names that most often arise from the selection results of the 33 articles mentioned above. To know more details about article citations included in the top 20 list, see table 5 below.

Table 5. Top 20 Cited Articles of Railway Transport Infrastructure for Tourism

Citation	Author	Title	Year	Journal Name	Publisher
66	J.L. Campa, M.E. López-Lambas, B. Guirao	High speed rail effects on tourism: Spanish empirical evidence derived from China's modelling experience	2016	Journal of Transport Geography	Elsevier
32	W. Tang, T. Zhou, J. Sun, Y. Li, W. Li	Accelerated urban expansion in Lhasa City and the implications for sustainable development in a Plateau City	2017	Sustainability (Switzerland)	MDPI
14	A. Severino, L. Martseniuk, S. Curto, L. Neduzha	Routes planning models for railway transport systems in relation to passengers' demand	2021	Sustainability (Switzerland)	MDPI

(continued)

Table 5. (*continued*)

Citation	Author	Title	Year	Journal Name	Publisher
13	X. Li, Z. Wu, X. Zhao	Economic effect and its disparity of highspeed rail in China: A study of mechanism based on synthesis control method	2020	Transport Policy	Elsevier
13	J. Zhang, Y. Zhang	Tourism, transport infrastructure and income inequality: A panel data analysis of China	2022	Current Issues in Tourism	Routledge
9	S. Chen, J. Xi, M. Liu, T. Li	Analysis of Complex Transportation Network and Its Tourism Utilization Potential: A Case Study of Guizhou Expressways	2020	Complexity	Hindawi
8	F. Tian, Y. Yang, L. Jiang	Spatial spillover of transport improvement on tourism growth	2022	Tourism Economics	SAGE
8	C. Wu, N. Zhang, L. Xu	Travelers on the railway: An economic growth model of the effects of railway transportation infrastructure on consumption and sustainable economic growth	2021	Sustainability (Switzerland)	MDPI

(*continued*)

Table 5. (*continued*)

Citation	Author	Title	Year	Journal Name	Publisher
7	D.N. Nguyen, M. Esteban, M. Onuki	Resiliency in tourism transportation: Case studies of Japanese railway companies preparing for the 2020 Tokyo Olympics	2019	International Journal of Disaster Risk Reduction	Elsevier
6	M.K. Anser, M.A. Khan, A.A. Nassani, S.E. Askar, M.M.Q. Abro, K. Zaman, A. Kabbani	The mediating role of ICTs in the relationship between international tourism and environmental degradation: fit as a fiddle	2021	Environmental Science and Pollution Research	Springer
6	P. Coppola, A. Carbone, C. Aveta, P. Stangherlin	Assessing transport policies for tourist mobility based on accessibility indicators	2020	European Transport Research Review	Springer
6	T. Perzyński, A. Lewiński, Z. Łukasik	Safety analysis of accidents call system especially related to in-land water transport based on new telematic solutions	2015	Communications in Computer and Information Science	Springer
5	O.Z. Ouariti, E.M. Jebrane	The impact of transport infrastructure on tourism destination attractiveness: A case study of Marrakesh City, Morocco	2020	African Journal of Hospitality, Tourism and Leisure	Africa Journals

(*continued*)

Table 5. (*continued*)

Citation	Author	Title	Year	Journal Name	Publisher
4	O. Pshinko, T. Charkina, L. Martseniuk, O. Orlovska	Hubs as a Key Tool for Improving the Quality of The Service and Development of Multimodal Passenger Traffic	2022	Transport Problems	Silesian University of Technology
4	J. Procházka, Š. Hošková-Mayerová, D. Procházková	The risks connected with accidents on highways and railways	2020	Quality and Quantity	Springer
3	R. Knežević, R. Grbac Žiković	Changes in the economic importance of transit tourism in Gorski Kotar	2013	Hrvatski Geografski Glasnik	Croatian Geographical Society
3	D. Michniak, M. Więckowski	Changes of transport in cross-border tourist regions in the polish– slovak borderland: An (un)sustainable development?	2021	Transport and Sustainability	Emerald
2	M. Pasetto, G. Giacomello, E. Pasquini, A. Baliello	Feasibility and preliminary design of a new railway line in the dolomites area of veneto region	2017	Transport Infrastructure and Systems - Proceedings of the AIIT International Congress on Transport Infrastructure and Systems, TIS 2017	CRC Press

(*continued*)

Table 5. (*continued*)

Citation	Author	Title	Year	Journal Name	Publisher
2	Z. Liu, F. Wang, P. Xue, F. Xue	Using multi-layer nested network to optimise spatial structure of tourism development between urban and rural areas based on population mobility	2022	Indoor and Built Environment	SAGE
2	Kozłowski, M., Pawełczyk, M., Piotrowska-Piątek, A	Innovativeness of railway transport in the context of the development of tourism in Poland	2020	Quality and Quantitiy	Springer

From Table 5 above, the article written by Campa, *et al.* who studied on the effects of high-speed rail on tourism in Spain derived from the experience of Chinese modeling, published MDPI in 20 16 years has attracted the highest attention of other authors with a total number of citations of 66. Furthermore, an article written by Tang, *et al.* with a study of accelerated urban expansion in Lhasa City and its implications for sustainable development in Highland Cities, was published by MDPI in 2017 with a total number of citations of 32, then an article written by Severino, *et al.* with their studies on route planning for rail transport systems related to passenger demand published by MDPI in 2021 with a number of citations of 14; and followed by articles written by Li, *et al.* who studied on economic effects and disparities about high-speed railways in China was published by Elsevier Ltd in 20 20 years with a total number of quotations of 13. Then to see the results of publishers who are included in the list of the top five that publish articles related to railway transport infrastructure for tourism, can be seen in the presentation Table 6 below.

Table 6. Top Five Publishers on The Related Field

No	Publisher	Number of Articles	Percentage
1	Springer	7	0.37
2	Elsevier	4	0.21
3	CRC Press/Balkema	3	0.16
4	MDPI	3	0.16
5	Routledge	2	0.11
		19	100%

Based on Table 6, the top 5 publishers contributed the most, with a total of 19 articles published. Then we find 7 articles or 37% published by Springer taking the top spot, followed by publisher Elsevier with 4 articles, or 21%. This was followed by publisher CRC Press/Balkema with 3 articles or 1.6%. Fourth position by MDPI publisher with 3 articles, or 1.6%. Then the fifth position 2 articles or 1.1% published by Routledge publishers. Then, to find out the results of the top five journals related to Railway Transport Infrastructure for Tourism can be seen in Table 7 below.

Table 7. Top Five Journals Ranking within Railway Transport Infrastructure for Tourism

No	Journal Name	Number of Articles	Percentage
1	Sustainability (Switzerland)	3	0.38
2	Quality and Quantity	2	0.25
3	Transportation Research Procedia	1	0.13
4	Transport Policy	1	0.13
5	Transport and Sustainability	1	0.13
		8	100%

Based on Table 7 above, it can be presented that the names of the most influential journals in the writing of this journal and found the top 5 with a total accumulation of 8 articles. Sustainability (Switzerland) is the journal that most actively publishes journals related to railways, especially the theme of railway transport infrastructure with 8 articles or equivalent to 3.8%. Then, the journal Quality and Quantity with 2 articles, or 2.5%, followed by Transportation Research Procedia, Transport Policy, and Transport and Sustainability with 1 article or 13% each.

3.2   Visualization Topics Use VoS Viewer

Figure 5 below this show visualization of topic areas using network visualization from VoS Viewer.

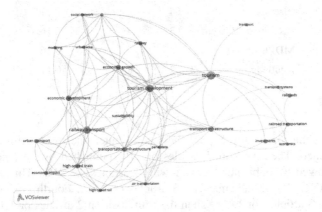

Fig. 5. Visualization Topic Area using Network Visualization

From Fig. 5 above, this study examines the titles and abstracts of documents collected based on the number of occurrences using Vos Viewer. This analysis uses the binary number method in entering data in Vos Viewer. The results of network visualization show that a tourism development is the main term that is the search result related to several other issues, namely railway transport, tourism, transport infrastructure, and economic growth. To see which keywords each cluster represents, we present the results in detail in Table 8 below.

Table 8. Item Number in Clusters

Cluster	Color	Number of Items
1	Red	8
2	Green	8
3	Blue	8
4	Yellow	1

From Table 8 above, it can be said the size at the point indicates the magnitude of occurrence of the item or term, while the line shows the strength of the relationship between items. The color in the visualization shows a cluster of items, where there are 4 clusters of 25 items. Items with cluster 1 have connecting lines and red dots. Cluster 1 has 8 items, cluster 2 is green with a total of 8 items, then cluster 3 is represented in blue with a total of 8 items, then the fourth position is occupied by cluster 4 with a total of 1 item. Furthermore, Fig. 9 below presents a visualization of the topic area based on the overlay visualization. Figure 6 as follow describes the visualization topic area using overlay visualization from VoS Viewer.

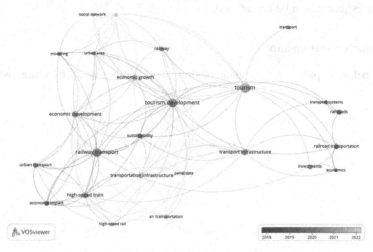

Fig. 6. Visualization Topic Area using Overlay Visualization

From Fig. 6 above, the topic of Railway Transport shows an upward trend. This overlay visualization shows the keyword update with the study year as the research base year, so it can also be seen that the keywords Transportation Infrastructure, Data Panel, Social Network, Air Transportation, High Speed Rail, and Economic Growth are the themes for the current study year. Figure 7 as follow describes the visualization topic area using density visualization from VoS Viewer.

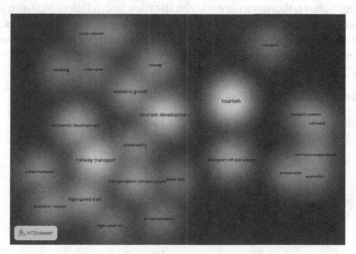

Fig. 7. Visualization Topic Area using Density Visualization

From Fig. 7 above, the brighter color, the more articles published research. Hence, it can be concluded that topics/keywords regarding Transportation Infrastructure, High Speed Train, Sustainability, Air Transport, and High-Speed Rail are keywords with the latest articles/journals to be researched.

3.3 Author's Relationship

Figure 8 below depicts overlay visualization of the author and co-author using VoS Viewer.

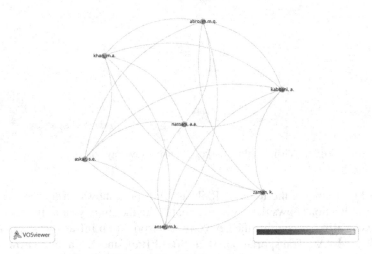

Fig. 8. Visualization of authors and co-authors

From Fig. 8 above, there is a network visualization map relationship from one author to another so that Nassani is the author who collaborated with many co-authors. Research with keywords used and authors with the most recent publication year who write about topics or keywords related to railway transport infrastructure for tourism.

3.4 Research Locations and Research Domains

Figure 9 below depicts the author's country of origin.

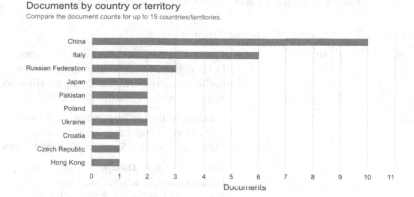

Fig. 9. Country of Origin

Figure 10 below depicts the map of author's country of origin.

Fig. 10. Map of country of origin

From Figs. 10 above, it shows that distribution and distribution by country is related to the writing and publishing of journals related to Railway Transport Infrastructure for Tourism. It is shown that China is the country of origin with the highest number of authors. Then the second author was Italy, and followed by the Russian Federation in third position. Japan, Pakistan, Poland, and Ukraine are the author's home countries in fourth place. All writers from Croatia, Czech Republic, and Hong Kong came in fifth. Table 9 below presents the country of research location and their respective research domain.

Table 9. Country of Location Research and Research Domain

No	Country	Number of Articles	Research Domain
1	China	10	Tourism Development, Tourism, Economic Development, Transportation Infrastructure, Railway Transport, Urban Transport, High-Speed Train, Economic Growth
2	Italy	6	Tourism, Railroads Transportation, Railroads, Investments, Economics, Transportation Planning, Transport Solution, Transport Policy
3	Russia	3	Water Treatment, Transport Systems, Transport Infrastructure, Tourism, Social Impact, Recreational Activities, Railway Tourism
4	Japan	2	Tourism, Tourism Development, Investments, International Tourism, Urban Transport, Railway Tourism, Transport Safety
5	Pakistan	2	Tourism, Sustainable Development Goal, Resource Depletion, Natural Resources, Logistics, International Tourism
6	Poland	2	Wireless Telecommunication Systems, Transportation, Transport Systems, Transport Safety, Tourism Development, Telematic Transport Systems
7	Ukraine	2	Railway Transport, Transportation Planning, Tourist Transportations, Tourism, Profitability, Policy Implementation
8	Croatia	1	Transportation System, Transit Tourism, Tourism Development, The Economic Sustainability, Sustainability
9	Czech Republic	1	Transport, Safety, Risk of Accidents, Investments, Competition
10	Hong Kong	1	Belt And Road Initiative, Community Perceptions, Sustainable Tourism Development

Based on Table 9 above, China is the country with the highest article publication rate with 10 articles, followed by Italy with 6 articles. Then in the next position is the Russian Federation with 3 articles. Next is Japan, Pakistan, Poland, and Ukraine which have the same number of articles, namely 2 articles. Then, was followed by Croatia, Czech Republic, and Hong Kong with 1 article.

4   Conclusion and Suggestion

Studies and research on Railway Transport Infrastructure for Tourism have been studied before, although not widely studied. This paper has successfully presented a bibliometric analysis related to Railway Transport Infrastructure for Tourism. We found that most articles related to the topic were published in scientific journals, compared to other publications. Related articles Railway Transport Infrastructure for Tourism published in scientific journals have received the highest citations compared to others. Based on network visualization, the most dominant term is tourism development as the main or key term that becomes the center of search results related to several other issues of railway transport, tourism, transport infrastructure, and economic growth. Meanwhile, when viewed from the Overlay Visualization, more shows that Transportation Infrastructure, Data Panels, Social Networks, Air Transportation, High Speed Rail, and Economic Growth are themes for the current study year. Based on the findings presented in Network Visualization and Overlay Visualization, it can be concluded that articles with the topic Railway Transport Infrastructure for Tourism have not been widely studied, so they can be used as a gap for further research.

This study has found out the topic of Railway Transport Infrastructure for Tourism, by limiting the year of publication and the relevance of the title to the theme of the journal as well as to find out the latest data on Railway Transport Infrastructure. Based on several previous studies related to journals in the Scopus database, it shows fluctuating movement patterns in the period 2013–2023. This pattern is evidenced by an increase in 2020 years and reaching the highest peak in 2021. However, after that, the trend experienced an initial decline starting in 2022 and 2023 (as of this writing). The data in the articles comes from journals with a total accumulation of 23 articles from a total of 33 articles as references.

This research is focused on publications using the keyword Railway Transport Infrastructure for Tourism, then by using the Scopus database which is one of the largest databases for publishing articles with high quality and is one of the most trusted and quality databases in finding references related to the desired topic. This research will have an impact on further research on Railway Transport Infrastructure for Tourism which will be discussed in future studies. Bibliometric analysis has its own identity and characteristics, which is to use articles that have been discussed to find gaps or find out the research that has been discussed previously to find out the limitations or gaps that you want to find solutions to with this.

This paper still has shortcomings that are expected to be improved in the future so that more accurate data appears and can be used as a measurement for future journals. These shortcomings including Scopus sometimes providing keyword suggestions that do not match the keywords intended. The suggestion given for future research is the need to study Railway Transport Infrastructure more broadly and in depth in the field of tourism, including bibliometric analysis. Since there has not been much researches on Railway Transport Infrastructure for Tourism, this can be used as a gap to propose new research on Railway Transport Infrastructure for Tourism.

Acknowledgment. This research is fully supported by Ambarrukmo Tourism Institute, Yogyakarta, Indonesia.

References

1. Severino, A., Martseniuk, L., Curto, S., Neduzha, L.: Routes planning models for railway transport systems in relation to passengers' demand. Sustainability (Switzerland) **13**(16) (2021), Article number 8686
2. Wu, C., Zhang, N., Xu, L.: Travelers on the railway: an economic growth model of the effects of railway transportation infrastructure on consumption and sustainable economic growth. Sustainability (Switzerland) **13**(12) (2021). Article number 6863
3. Knežević, R., Grbac Žiković, R.: Changes in the economic importance of transit tourism in Gorski Kotar. Hrvatski Geografski Glasnik **75**, 111–130 (2013)
4. Kozłowski, M., Pawełczyk, M., Piotrowska-Piątek, A.: Innovativeness of railway transport in the context of the development of tourism in Poland. Qual. Quant. **54**(5–6), 1691–1703 (2020)
5. Ronzoni, M.: The railway Noto-Pachino as a transport solution for a better tourism. Town and Infrastructure Planning for Safety and Urban Quality. In: Proceedings of the 23rd International Conference on Living and Walking in Cities, LWC 2017. 23rd International Conference on Living and Walking in Cities, LWC 2017; Brescia; Italy; 15 June 2017 through 16 June 2017; Code 220629 (2017)
6. Masson, S., Petiot, R.: Can the highspeed rail reinforce tourism attractiveness? The case of the highspeed rail between Perpignan (France) and Barcelona (Spain). Technovation **29**(9), 611–617 (2009)
7. Lee, C.F., Chen, K.Y.: Exploring factors determining the attractiveness of railway tourism. J. Travel Tour. Mark. **34**(4), 461–474 (2017)
8. Pagliara, F., Mauriello, F., Garofalo, A.: Exploring the interdependences between HighSpeed Rail systems and tourism: some evidence from Italy. Transp. Res. Part A: Pol. Pract. **106**, 300–308 (2017)
9. Albalate, D., Campos, J., Jiménez, J.L.: Tourism and highspeed rail in Spain: does the AVE increase local visitors? Ann. Tour. Res. **65**, 71–82 (2017)
10. Becker, C., George, B.P.: Rapid rail transit and tourism development in the United States. Tour. Geogr. **13**(3), 381–397 (2011)
11. Su, M.M., Wall, G.: The Qinghai-Tibet railway and Tibetan tourism: travelers' perspectives. Tour. Manage. **30**(5), 650–657 (2009)
12. Sun, Y.Y., Lin, Z.W.: Move fast, travel slow: the influence of high-speed rail on tourism in Taiwan. J. Sustain. Tour. **26**(3), 433–450 (2018)
13. Peira, G., Lo Giudice, A., Miraglia, S.: Railway and tourism: a systematic literature review. Tour. Hospit. **3**(1), 69–79 (2022)
14. Rodrigue, J.P.: Transportation Modes, Modal Competition, and Modal Shift. The Geography of Transport System (2020)
15. Stainton, Hayley. 50 types of transport from around the world (2022). tourismteacher.com
16. Liasidou, S., Garanti, Z., Pipyros, K.: Air transportation and tourism interactions and actions for competitive destinations: the case of Cyprus. Worldwide Hospitality and Tourism Themes, (ahead-of-print) (2022)
17. Tang, C., Weaver, D., Lawton, L.: Can stopovers be induced to revisit transit hubs as stayovers? A new perspective on the relationship between air transportation and tourism. J. Air Transp. Manag. **62**, 54–64 (2017)
18. Odilbekovich, S.K., Bekmuratovich, E.A., Islamovna, M.F.: Requirements for a Railway Operation Specialist on Traffic Safety Issues. Pioneer: J. Adv. Res. Sci. Progress **2**(3), 98–101 (2023)

19. Boysen, H.E.: General model of railway transportation capacity. In: 13th International Conference on Design and Operation in Railway Engineering (Comprail), pp. 335–347 (2013)
20. Ghofrani, F., He, Q., Goverde, R.M., Liu, X.: Recent applications of big data analytics in railway transportation systems: a survey. Transp. Res. Part C: Emer. Technol. **90**, 226–246 (2018)
21. Artagan, S.S., Bianchini Ciampoli, L., D'Amico, F., Calvi, A., Tosti, F.: Non-destructive assessment and health monitoring of railway infrastructures. Surv. Geophys. **41**, 447–483 (2020)
22. Macchi, M., Garetti, M., Centrone, D., Fumagalli, L., Pavirani, G.P.: Maintenance management of railway infrastructures based on reliability analysis. Reliab. Eng. Syst. Saf. **104**, 71–83 (2012)
23. Zhang, A., Liu, L., Liu, G.: High-speed rail, tourist mobility, and firm value. Econ. Model. **90**, 108–116 (2020)
24. Albalate, D., Fageda, X.: High speed rail and tourism: empirical evidence from Spain. Transp. Res. Part A: Pol. Pract. **85**, 174–185 (2016)
25. Dileep, M.R., Pagliara, F.: Rail tourism. In Transportation Systems for Tourism, pp. 171–187. Springer, Cham (2023). https://doi.org/10.1007/978-3-031-22127-9_10
26. Ariyanto, A., et al.: A decade analysis of tourism entrepreneurship: bibliometric approach. Int. J. Adv. Technol. Manage. Entrepr. **3**(1) (2022)
27. Güzeller, C.O., Çeliker, N.: Bibliometric analysis of tourism research for the period 2007–2016. Adv. Hosp. Tour. Res. **6**(1), 1–22 (2018)
28. Johnson, A.G., Samakovlis, I.: A bibliometric analysis of knowledge development in smart tourism research. J. Hosp. Tour. Technol. **10**(4), 600 623 (2019)
29. Anggraini, F.D., et al.: A decade analysis of lifestyle tourism analysis: bibliometric approach. Int. J. Adv. Public Health **3**(1) (2022)
30. Donthu, N., Kumar, S., Mukherjee, D., Pandey, N., Lim, W.M.: How to conduct a bibliometric analysis: an overview and guidelines. J. Bus. Res. **133**, 285–296 (2021)
31. Ellegaard, O., Wallin, J.A.: The bibliometric analysis of scholarly production: how great is the impact? Scientometrics **105**(3), 1809–1831 (2015). https://doi.org/10.1007/s11192-015-1645-z
32. Ermawati, K.C., Anggraini, F.D., Ihalauw, J.J., Damiasih, D.: A decade analysis of local wisdom in tourism: a bibliometric approach. Intnal Journal of Advanced Psychology and Human Sciences, 4(4) (2023)
33. Moral-Muñoz, J.A., Herrera-Viedma, E., Santisteban-Espejo, A., Cobo, M.J.: Software tools for conducting bibliometric analysis in science: An up-to-date review. Profesional de la Información **29**(1) (2020)
34. Boyle, F., Sherman, D.: Scopus™: the product and its development. Ser. Libr. **49**(3), 147–153 (2006)
35. Ballew, B.S.: Elsevier's scopus® database. J. Electron. Resour. Med. Librar. **6**(3), 245–252 (2009)
36. MuletForteza, C., Martorell-Cunill, O., Merigó, J.M., Genovart-Balaguer, J., Mauleon-Mendez, E.: Twentyfive years of the journal of travel & tourism marketing: a bibliometric ranking. J. Travel Tour. Mark. **35**(9), 1201–1221 (2018)
37. Widodo, W.I., et al.: A decade analysis on tourism sentiment analysis: bibliometric approach. Int. J. Adv. Data Sci. Intell. Anal. **3**(2) (2023)
38. Palácios, H., de Almeida, M.H., Sousa, M.J.: A bibliometric analysis of trust in the field of hospitality and tourism. Int. J. Hosp. Manag. **95**, 102944 (2021)
39. Leong, L.Y., Hew, T.S., Tan, G.W.H., Ooi, K.B., Lee, V.H.: Tourism research progress–a bibliometric analysis of tourism review publications. Tourism Review **76**(1), 1–26 (2020)

40. Rahmawati, E., Anggraini, F.D., Kastuti, T.I., Ariyanto, A., Hendratono, T., Sugiarto, S.: A decade analysis on luxury transportation in tourism: bibliometric approach. Int. J. Adv. Technol. Manage. Entrepreneurship, **4**(1) (2023)
41. Mulet-Forteza, C., Genovart-Balaguer, J., Mauleon-Mendez, E., Merigó, J.M.: A bibliometric research in the tourism, leisure and hospitality fields. J. Bus. Res. **101**, 819–827 (2019)

Circular Economy and Reverse Logistics: An Analysis of Sustainable Business Models

Salvatore Dore[✉] and Andrea Gallo

University of Trieste, 34127 Trieste, IT, Italy
salvatore.dore@amm.units.it, andrea.gallo3@phd.units.it

Abstract. The present paper aims to investigate circular business models and the key role assumed by reverse logistics in promoting sustainability and the reduction of negative externalities associated with various economic processes. The objective of this paper is to investigate how reverse logistics is integrated within corporate circular business models. The objective is to highlight how the implementation of circular business models depends as much from a management of company production processes as from the optimization of reverse logistics and from an accurate analysis of company location dynamics, aimed at a more effective and efficient use of resources through optimal management of resources by transforming waste into raw materials following the principles of repair, recycling, and reuse. The methodology adopted involves qualitative and inductive analysis starting with the definition of the theoretical framework of circular business process. In this context, it will be essential to analyze and define reverse logistics, assisted by a survey about the geographical location of waste to be processed and industrial production sites.

Keywords: Circular Business Models · Reverse Logistics · Sustainability · Circularity

1 Introduction

The circular economy is a concept that has been gaining popularity in recent years, both nationally and internationally. The goal of the circular economy is to create a sustainable economic system, which not only aims to reduce negative environmental impact, but with a focus on better efficiency in the use of resources, through to an optimal management of waste, where it is transformed into new resource materials, thus going on to reduce environmental impact and ensuring long-term sustainability [1].

We will therefore need to initially introduce the concept of sustainability, where a commonly accepted definition is that provided by the Brudtland report of 1987 [2] "development that meets the needs of the present without compromising the ability of future generations to meet their own needs.". At the World Summit Development in

---

The paper is the result of the joint work of the two authors. However, Salvatore Dore wrote paragraphs 2–3 while Andrea Gallo wrote paragraphs 4–5. The para-graphs 1, 6 and 7 was written together.

© The Author(s), under exclusive license to Springer Nature Switzerland AG 2023
O. Gervasi et al. (Eds.): ICCSA 2023 Workshops, LNCS 14110, pp. 495–511, 2023.
https://doi.org/10.1007/978-3-031-37123-3_34

2002, the concept of the triple bottom line was defined [12], meaning that sustainable growth cannot be separated from its three basic components, People, Profit and Planet. These three factors represent the pillars on which sustainable development is based. With regard to circularity in business models, on the other hand, there are some fundamental concepts [3] that need to be introduced to better define the framework of application [4–6]:

- Design for circularity: designing products, processes and systems that can be used, repaired, remanufactured or recycled efficiently.
- Performance economics: a business model that rewards positive environmental performance instead of relying on the product ownership model.
- Efficient use of resources: reducing the use of finite resources and increasing energy efficiency to reduce negative environmental impact.
- Repair, remanufacture and recycle: increase the useful life of products through repair and remanufacturing, and reduce waste through recycling and the use of recycled materials.
- Creating networks of integrated production systems to develop the circular economy.

This set of concepts will be useful in developing the framework of this paper, where the analysis will focus on the development of circular business models [7], going to examine the relationship that exists in circular business models, reverse logistics [8], and the spatial location component and development network system to maximize the efficiency of these production systems [9].

Reverse logistics, or the management of material flows out of the value chain, is a key element of the circular economy [10], as it focuses on managing the recovery, reuse and recycling activities of products and raw materials. Reverse logistics can have a positive impact on the environment, business competitiveness and the quality of life of local communities [11]. Reverse logistics is an important element of the circularity of the business process, as it focuses on managing the recovery, reuse and recycling activities of products and raw materials [12].

In this study, we will explore the basic principles of the circular economy and reverse logistics with a focus on the geographic and localization aspects, analyzing the role of localization in the implementation of the circular economy and reverse logistics, and analyzing the opportunities and challenges related to its implementation in different geographic contexts.

The information presented through desk research will then be used to develop a SWOT analysis on the sustainability of business processes applied to the case of IKEA, a company that, as we will see, places circularity and sustainability of its processes as key drivers of its strategic development.

2 Literature Review

Increasing attention to environmental aspects assisted by the quest for efficient use of resources has determined that the topic of circular economy and reverse logistics is an extremely central component of production processes [12, 13]. The literature points out that the circular economy and reverse logistics are closely linked and that their implementation can have a significant impact on local communities and the environment [14,

15]. For example, effective management of waste and unused materials can increase the availability of raw materials and reduce costs associated with disposal [16]. In addition, circular economy and reverse logistics can also help create new economic opportunities by following the basic principle of the 3Rs: recycle, reuse, recover [17]. The R-list establishes a clear hierarchy of priorities for waste management methods: the first R (Regenerate) is given priority over the second R (Reduce) and so on, with the degree of circularity decreasing progressively down the list [18, 19]. These strategies can be applied within the types of material cycles characterizing as the biological cycle, which encompasses the flows of food and biologically-based materials (for instance, cotton and wood) that are designed to return to the biosphere through processes such as composting or anaerobic digestion and the technical cycle, which relates to the flows of inorganic or synthetic materials [20].

The importance in managing limited resources and waste in production processes is one of the leading themes within the circular economy [21], however, emphasizing that the goal is to optimize process efficiency by minimizing resource use and waste generation. The literature has also highlighted the importance of reverse logistics for the development of circular business models that also take into account product end-of-life [22, 23]. Reverse logistics represents one of the central elements of circular business processes as widely pointed out in the literature [24, 25], as it aims to reduce waste by enhancing the value of discarded products, thus generating a flow of goods in the opposite direction to the main one [26–28]. Thus, reverse logistics represents the starting point for product recycling aimed at recovering the residual value of discarded products [29]. It is necessary to emphasize the circularity of production processes and optimal reverse logistics management depend on several factors [12, 30]: among them we find the corporate culture oriented toward the sustainability of processes, which can lead to an increase in the company's effort toward the practices of efficient and careful management of reverse logistics, trying to increase the quality of returns and reducing the costs associated with waste management, and a second aspect, related to technological advances [31, 32], so as to optimize different waste material flows [5].

3   The Concept of Circular Business Models

The concept of the Circular Economy is gaining increasing attention and support in academia, industry, and policymaking circles as a viable alternative to minimize resource depletion, waste, and emissions [33]. To effectively implement the Circular Economy at the organizational level, business models play a crucial role as a leverage point. However, the theoretical conceptualization of circular business models and circular business model innovation lacks clarity and consensus.

A comprehensive literature review was conducted to address this gap and provide a systematic understanding of the emerging field of circular business models and circular business model innovation [34].

The concept of the circular business model is built upon two core concepts: the circular economy and business model innovation. This section provides a brief introduction to both concepts. The idea of the circular economy, initially influenced by Boulding's work in 1966, suggests that achieving a balance between the economy and the environment requires viewing the Earth as a closed-loop system with limited capacity for assimilation [35]. This concept encompasses a loop economy, which entails implementing strategies in industries to prevent waste, foster regional job creation, improve resource efficiency, and promote the dematerialization of the industrial sector. A relevant business model for a loop economy involves shifting from ownership to utilization, enabling industries to generate profit while reducing costs and risks associated with waste [36, 37].

The contemporary understanding of the circular economy, introduced by Pearce and Turner in 1989 [38], incorporates various features and contributions from related concepts that emphasize closed loops. These include industrial ecology, cradle-to-cradle design, the laws of ecology, looped and performance economy, regenerative design, biomimicry, the blue economy, and life cycle management and engineering [39, 40]. In 2015, Webster made a significant contribution by promoting the idea that a circular economy should be restorative by design, aiming to maximize the utility and value of products, components, and materials throughout their lifecycles [46].

Kirchherr et al. conducted a comprehensive review of 114 definitions of the circular economy and proposed a new definition based on their analysis [47]. According to their proposal, a circular economy describes an economic system based on business models that replace the concept of "end-of-life" with practices such as reducing, reusing, recycling, and recovering materials in production, distribution, and consumption processes [41, 42]. This system operates at multiple levels, including the micro level (individual products, companies, and consumers), meso level (eco-industrial parks), and macro level (cities, regions, nations, and beyond). The aim is to achieve sustainable development by creating environmental quality, economic prosperity, and social equity for both present and future generations [43].

However, a previous review of circular economy literature has identified several shortcomings in this definition. For instance, it simplifies the term "end-of-life" to "disposal", overlooking the broader interpretation commonly adopted in product development theory [45]. It also places a reduced emphasis on other lifecycle stages, presents a three-tier level system that essentially encompasses all levels, and places an undue focus on sustainability aspects that are not always integral to the circular economy concept [44]. For instance, the existing definition simplifies the term "end-of-life" to "disposal," disregarding the more comprehensive interpretation commonly adopted in product development theory [48]. It also lacks sufficient attention to other stages of the product lifecycle, employs a three-tier level system that essentially encompasses all levels, and places excessive emphasis on sustainability aspects that may not always align with the core principles of the circular economy concept [49]. In this study, we will define the circular economy as an economic system that aims to minimize resource input, waste, emissions, and energy leakages by implementing practices such as cycling, extending, intensifying, and dematerializing material and energy loops. Achieving this objective involves various strategies such as digitalization, servitization, sharing solutions, designing long-lasting products, prom and opting maintenance, repair, reuse, remanufacturing, refurbishing, and recycling [50, 53].

Considering that achieving a completely closed-loop system is theoretically impossible, our understanding of the circular economy adopts a dynamic perspective, focusing on the transition towards circularity rather than envisioning a static state of a fully closed system with no material or energy leakage [51]. It acknowledges the need for continuous improvement and innovation.

The concept of the business model gained popularity and underwent significant evolution during the dot-com boom of the 1990s, characterized by the introduction of innovative revenue mechanisms. Initially, the business model concept served as a means to convey complex business ideas to potential investors within limited time frames [52].

From its fundamental function, the concept of the business model has evolved to serve as a tool for systemic analysis, planning, and communication. Additionally, it has become a strategic asset that contributes to competitive advantage and firm performance [54]. The ability to innovate and introduce new business models can provide organizations with a significant competitive edge, particularly in light of diminishing returns on technology, increasing complexity, and declining costs of capital [55]. This advantage is further amplified by the disruptive impact of digital transformation, as evidenced by the substantial market valuation of relatively new technology conglomerates with innovative digital business models [56]. Furthermore, business model innovation plays a crucial role in enabling organizations to achieve their social and environmental objectives by harnessing environmentally, socially, and economically effective technologies and solutions [49, 57].

Companies that actively pursue sustainable business model innovation have the potential to enhance their financial, social, and environmental performance, as well as strengthen their resilience and ability to navigate environmental risks [59][60].

In this research, we adopt a previously established definition, which is based on a thorough review of the field. Business model innovation is defined as the process of conceptualizing and implementing new business models. This encompasses various possibilities, including the development of entirely new business models, diversification into additional business models, acquisition of new business models, or the transformation from one business model to another. The scope of transformation can vary, ranging from the entire business model to specific elements such as the value proposition, value creation and delivery mechanisms, value capture elements, interrelationships between these elements, and the overall value network [58].

4   Reverse Logistics and Circular Business Models

Reverse logistics refers to the process of moving products in the opposite direction from the typical forward flow in order to recover their value or dispose of them properly [61]. Reverse flow can occur through a number of channels, including an organization's traditional channels, separate channels, or a combination of both. It is important to note that reverse flow is not necessarily a mirror image of forward flow. When reverse logistics is introduced to recover value from finished goods, the goods enter a closed-loop network, which is more complex than traditional open-loop networks because it must handle both forward and reverse logistics [62].

In recent years, many companies have begun to introduce reverse logistics into their supply chains as a means of increasing profitability. This trend has been driven, in part, by the fact that organizations are increasingly being held accountable for their actions along the supply chain. This accountability stems from both legal and social applications and has generated multiple pushes for companies to adopt reverse logistics, finding economic, social and environmental sustainability to be its key pillars [63].

From an economic point of view, companies can benefit significantly from returned products. According to), the costs of recovering returned products are often lower than the expenses associated with raw materials [64], which can help reduce the high production costs of new products. Companies adopt reverse logistics not only for the direct profit derived from it [61], but also as a strategic decision to improve their competitiveness and prepare for future legislation. Reverse logistics can help companies establish their brand as sustainable, generating a positive green image and increasing sales as environmental issues are becoming increasingly important [65].

Legislation can also provide economic incentives to support the circular economy through reverse logistics. In Sweden, for example, a lower tax rate on repairs of some products was introduced in 2017 to increase economic incentives for customers to choose repairs over new products. The tax rate was reduced from 25 percent to 12 percent for the repair of products such as bicycles, shoes, and textiles [66]. This measure aims to create greater demand for repair services and make it more attractive for companies to offer such services [8].

Reverse logistics is essential for improving resource utilization by circulating products and materials and reusing, repairing, remanufacturing, or recycling them instead of generating waste and filling landfills. By adding reverse logistics to advanced logistics, we can close the cycle of production and consumption, thereby reducing waste and conserving resources (Ellen MacArthur Foundation and Material Economics, 2019). The benefits of implementing reverse logistics go beyond economic incentives, as it also supports sustainability and helps reduce our environmental impact.

Bernon et al. (2018) [67] highlight the critical role of "tone from the top" in promoting the circular economy, meaning that top management should align company values with circular economy principles and integrate them into strategic directives. This implies a greater emphasis on second-hand products and a decrease in sales of new products. To achieve this, circular economy values should be incorporated throughout the organization and reflected in performance measures [28]. By implementing reverse logistics, products and materials can be reused, repaired, remanufactured, or recycled, reducing waste and landfill and improving resource utilization. Reverse logistics can close the cycle of production and consumption, thus facilitating the transition to a circular economy [15]. The benefits of a circular economy include reducing environmental impact, improving resource efficiency, and promoting sustainable economic growth. Companies can also gain a competitive advantage by developing a positive reputation as a sustainable brand, increasing sales and customer loyalty [35]. Therefore, it is critical for companies to adopt a circular economy approach through the integration of reverse logistics and circular economy values into their operations, starting from top management to the entire organization [42].

To achieve a circular economy, the value of second-hand products and the reduction of new product sales should be integrated into strategic directives and permeate the entire organization, reflected in performance measures. Reverse logistics is a crucial aspect of achieving this goal, as it allows products and materials to be reused, repaired, remanufactured, or recycled instead of being discarded and landfilled [5]. The reverse logistics process involves several activities, including collection, inspection, separation, reprocessing, and redistribution. Figue 1 shows the steps that a product follows as part of the management of a reverse logistics flow for product companies.

Collection is the initial activity involving the purchase, transportation and storage of returned products [14]. Inspection is the subsequent activity in which returned products are inspected and product quality is measured through disassembly, crushing, and testing. In the separation activity, products are selected according to the different characteristics determined by the previous inspection activity. Separation is used to make the most profitable and suitable decision for disposal and includes sorting and storage. Reprocessing refers to product recovery and includes reuse, repackaging, repair, refurbishment, remanufacturing and recycling, depending on the inspection and separation [3]. Finally, redistribution involves the reintegration of reusable products back into the market through sale, leasing, transportation, storage, and marketing [22].

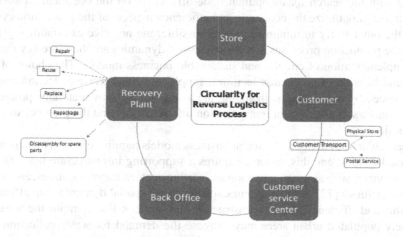

Fig. 1. Scheme of the circularity for reverse logistics process (Source: Author's elaboration on Fleischmann, M., Bloemhof-Ruwaard, J. M., Beullens, P., & Dekker, R. (2004) [79].

5 Circular Economy and Geographical Localization

A key component of circular business models is represented by the locational considerations of waste treatment plants in reference sites of supply of raw materials to be treated. In fact, the accurate management of reverse logistics, i.e., the flow of materials and products back to the production cycle, requires special attention to their origin and route [68, 79]. Locational choices of production facilities must be evaluated very carefully both in terms of reverse logistics and the final destination of flows leaving industrial sites after being processed [69]. The choice of the geographic location of production facilities and supply sites is a critical factor in the effective management of reverse logistics and the success of a circular business model [9, 70]. The circularity of the economic system is based on reducing the consumption of prime raw materials and using those already present in the production cycle [72]: in this context, it seems clear that raw material treatment plants, therefore, represent the key elements of the circularity of the business model as they allow the recovery and reuse of waste materials and transform them into new raw materials to be introduced in new production processes [71].

Consequently, the geographical location of plants is a key aspect of environmental and energy economic efficiency: the proximity of treatment plants to raw material supply sources can reduce transportation costs and improve the quality of recovered materials. In addition, locating treatment plants near urban areas can reduce the environmental impact of transporting materials for recycling [59]. At the same time, however, it is imperative to also consider the environmental, economic, and social impacts on the territory and regions adjacent to industrial plants, highlighting the negative externalities inevitably generated during these processes [14]. Locational choices will therefore be faced with the search for an optimal trade-off, where on the one hand an attempt will be made to optimize the economic and efficiency aspects of the production cycles and on the other to try to minimize, where possible, the negative externalities generated by the production processes. Locational spatial dynamics are therefore key factors in the implementation of circular and sustainable business models. The choice of the geographic location of production facilities, supply sites, and waste collection centers are influenced by many factors, including the availability of raw materials, proximity to outlet markets, availability of transportation infrastructure, and the presence of local communities.

In particular, the adoption of circular business models requires efficient management of reverse logistics, and this, in turn, requires a supporting infrastructure network and specific services, such as waste collection and sorting centers, transfer stations, and waste treatment facilities [72]. It thus becomes apparent how spatial dynamics can affect the availability and efficiency of such infrastructure and services. For example, the presence of densely populated urban areas may increase the demand for waste collection and sorting services, but at the same time may make traffic and transportation management more complex [35]. Conversely, the presence of rural or remote areas may make reverse logistics management more expensive due to the greater distance and lack of adequate infrastructure [11].

The issues and perspectives of circular economy recall some of the main points related to the more traditional location theories as studied in geographical research. Recently, geographers and planners started from the traditional Weber's theory of industrial location proposing a modified model capable of hosting a circular model instead of a linear one, involving, as important places to be considered in location decisions, not only the raw materials places, but also those dedicate to treating and managing waste and second raw materials [76], here, as Balletto, Borruso and Mei point out, considering circularity in the construction and demolition sector can have important implications on the spatial consequences of the new activities put in place in the treatment leg. In this specific interpretation of the locational issues within the experience of the MEISAR project, in fact, led to considering the Construction and Demolition Waste (CDW) as secondary raw materials, whose locations, in terms of places of origin of waste, as well as treatment plants, become important places influencing, potentially, producing plant location decisions [77, 78]. The extended, modified model, in particular, is focused on the dynamics of spatial localization of the different production sites called upon to regenerate waste materials in order to generate new raw materials can also be considered in light of Weberian localization theory in its linear simplification. The above cited authors in fact starts from the original Weber theory in its simplified version to embed new locations dedicated to the treatment and processing activities, with a consequent re-organization of the entire locational process.

In the hereby proposed research we can recall the basic principles of Weber's theory, where it is hypothesized that there are two fixed locations, identified as the raw material extraction site (RM) and the final market (FM) [74].

According to Weber's theory of optimal localization, optimal localization occurs at the point where total costs are minimized. Based on these considerations, it will therefore be necessary to find the point of cost minimization for transportation by deciding on the spatial localization of the materials treatment plant according to three different options: adjacent to final markets, near sources of raw materials, or at an intermediate point [75].

We can consider the total cost of transportation to be minimized according to the following formula:

$$TTC = t \cdot q_{RM} \cdot d_{RM} + t \cdot q_{FM} \cdot d_{FM} \qquad (1)$$

The total cost of transportation (TCC) will be equal to the unit transportation cost (t) multiplied by the quantity demanded (q) and the distance (d) both for the component from the extraction site of raw materials to the productive plant (dRM) and for the distance between productive plant and final markets (dFM) [76].

Therefore, we can graphically outline the different choices of spatial localization for production sites following the linear simplification of the Weberian model, presented in the following figure (Fig. 2).

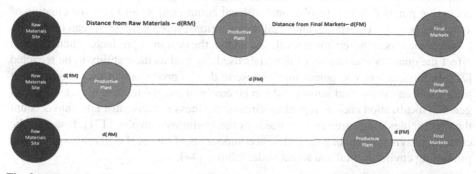

Fig. 2. Schematization of Weber's model of a location on a line. Source: Personal elaboration based on [76].

Therefore, the different companies will adopt a localization choice between the site where raw materials (RM) are located and the final market (FM). This location will depend on the weight of the raw materials compared to the final product, using an indicator introduced by Weber called MI (Materials Index), which is the ratio of the weight of raw materials to the weight of the final product.

In the case where MI > 1, the optimal site location will be close to the raw material site to minimize waste transportation costs (third case in Fig. 2). In the case where final products are mainly produced through perishable resources, we will be in the second case highlighted in Fig. 2 (Fig. 2).

In the case where MI is equal to 1, then the industrial localization of the production site should be exactly halfway between the raw material markets and the final markets (first case in Fig. 2) [76].

The above mentioned theory represents the starting one in the simplified Weber's model. As anticipated, a possible extended model [76] foresees the possible, best locations of treatment plants as important elements in location decisions.

In a further extension of the Weber model adapted to the circularity concepts of production processes, it would be useful to also conceptualize the dynamics of reverse logistics to consider the flows of returned goods. In such terms, there would be the needs to insert different variables within the model, including, as a matter of example, considerations about the locations in space that will be involved in the reverse location process itself, as well as the costs and distances related to the transport means involved. This will be the object of future research in such sense.

The localization choices for structuring circular business models can be multiple and must balance the specific needs of enterprises with the characteristics of available territories, infrastructure, and services [70].

In implementing circular business models, therefore, several spatial planning decisions will have to be made, which could represent key performance indicators such as the choice of locating production facilities close to outlet markets or sources of supply, where these two places are unlikely to coincide: choices regarding transportation management, a critical factor for the efficiency of circular business models [72]. In this context, companies may choose to use environmentally friendly means of transportation, such as rail or ship, or to reduce the distance between production and material collection points [73, 75]. Involvement of local communities can foster the creation of synergies between enterprises and local organizations, promoting the spread of circular business models at the territorial level, and finally, the design of products, where this can affect the quantity and quality of materials used, as well as their ability to be recycled [72]. In this context, companies may choose to design products that use materials that have a low environmental impact and can be easily disassembled and recycled [71]. In general, localization choices regarding circular business models must take into account the specificities of the area and the needs of the businesses involved [71], fostering the creation of synergies among the different components of the local economic system and promoting environmental and social sustainability [44].

6 Assessing a SWOT Analysis for the Circularity of Business Models: The Cases of IKEA

Building on the information previously discussed on circular business processes and the notions of reverse logistics. This section proposes to analyze the circularity of business models for IKEA company, through an initial screening of the analytical characteristics, using in particular the information presented in the company's sustainability reports, and then by elaborating a SWOT analysis on the sustainability of business models for the two companies.

Ikea is a multinational company specializing in the production and sale of furniture and furnishings present in over 62 countries worldwide and with over 460 stores. We will first focus on the reverse logistics operations followed by IKEA, and then analyze in more detail the strategies adopted by the Swedish company to try to mitigate the negative externalities generated along its supply chain [84].

Returns are managed by local IKEA stores, which have an area where returned items are sold at a reduced price [82]. The Customer Service Center (CSC) at each store handles all returns, and saleable products are either returned to the warehouse or sold directly in the store. Unsaleable items are sent to the recovery department, where some products are sold directly in an As-Is area, while others undergo a recovery process, where them could be disassembly or repair. While IKEA lacks data on the percentage of unsaleable products recovered [84], they claim that approximately 70% of products can be sold as-is after recovery [80].

Each IKEA store has a salvage department, which considers factors such as complexity, time, resources, and space when deciding whether to salvage a product. In the recovery department, products can be disassembled for use as spare parts, and the main activities include repackaging and integrating products with spare parts. Repackaged, repaired, and reconditioned products are then sold as-is or as new, depending on the extent of the recovery process and the product's condition [81]. Most recovered products are sold as-is due to regulations and the difficulty of ensuring quality and safety [83]. However, if a product only needs repairs and can be sold as new, it offers significant financial advantages because it takes less time and has a higher price margin [82].

Regarding the circularity of its business processes, IKEA takes action across various components of its production chain to minimize waste production from its operations. This includes using recycled materials for packaging, generating more electricity from sustainable sources than it consumes, and incorporating environmentally friendly materials into its production lines [84].

Around 70% of the materials used to create IKEA products are derived from natural fibers such as wood and paper, with a smaller percentage of plastic and metal materials used (only 5% for plastic).

By transitioning to recycled and renewable materials like recycled wood and plastic, promoting lightweight construction, and encouraging renewable energy in raw material production processes, IKEA can significantly reduce its ecological footprint and other environmental impacts. This approach also supports the group's economic sustainability [84].

Therefore, is possible to outline the SWOT analysis for the circularity of IKEA business processes, aimed at highlighting the strengths, weaknesses, opportunities, and threats in this particular area of application. In particular appear clear that corporate development activities have been aimed for years at improving the company's environmental sustainability processes, however we can highlight some strengths how IKEA has implem,ented various initiatives to reduce its carbon footprint, such as using renewable energy self-produced, and cutting off the total usage of fossil fuel energy consumption, designing products that are easy to recycle and improving its waste management policy [80, 83].

For what concern the weaknesses: appears clear that the complexity of the supply chain could makes difficult to monitor and control environmental and social impacts, and also considering the geographical localization of the production plant and the global dimension of the final distribution markets, seems clear that the management of the materials flows are difficult to manage and to implement under an environmental point of view [81, 84].

IKEA proposes to achieve complete sustainability of its production processes by 2030, it seems clear that this is an extremely difficult challenge to face as it requires a total and complete rethinking of the production line, of the logistics inherent in the distribution of goods in the different sales on a global scale. The greater development opportunities in this case are highlighted by a focus on the use of recyclable materials, through an optimization of logistics and the physical movement of people through greater use of virtual reality to make the physical store superfluous, through an increase expenditure on research and development and finally through a consumer education policy [83, 84].

As far as threats are concerned, although IKEA currently holds a position of market leader, the presence of intense competition on the furniture production market represents a problem for the company which must be able to implement its environmental efficiency policies without however giving up operating margins in terms of economy [80, 84].

7   Conclusions

The aim of this paper is to highlights the importance of circular business models in promoting sustainability and reducing negative externalities associated with various economic processes. In this context, reverse logistics plays a crucial role in facilitating circularity by managing the recovery, reuse, and recycling activities of products and raw materials. The implementation of circular business models depends on the optimal management of resources [38]. It is possible to emphasizes the need to create networks of integrated production systems to develop the circular economy, where efficient use of resources and performance economics are rewarded [5].

The present study underscores the importance of analyzing the role of geographic and localization aspects in the implementation of circular business models and reverse logistics, and the opportunities and challenges related to their implementation in different geographic contexts, in fact the transportation dynamic related to the row materials, final product and reverse logistics represent one of the first challenge when we consider the mitigation of the negative externalities for the different business models. This paper provides a valuable contribution to the field of sustainability and circular economy, highlighting the importance of reverse logistics in facilitating circularity and promoting sustainable economic growth [46]. It is important to note that the implementation of circular business models and reverse logistics requires a fundamental shift in the way companies approach resource management. This shift involves moving away from the linear "take-make-dispose" model towards a circular model that prioritizes resource efficiency and waste reduction [10].

To successfully implement circular business models, companies must adopt a holistic approach that considers the entire product life cycle, from design to end-of-life management. This approach involves designing products and processes that can be used, repaired, remanufactured, or recycled efficiently, and creating closed-loop systems where waste is transformed into new resource materials. Moreover, the implementation of circular business models and reverse logistics can bring numerous benefits, such as reducing negative environmental impacts but also for improving business competitiveness, and enhancing the quality of life of local communities: for this reason we decided to elaborate a focus on IKEA company, that represent the ideal case study in term of circularity for the attention and the effort that the company puts in all the consideration related to the sustainability, starting from the production, where they used only energy derived from renewable sources, related to the waste management where the refuse are minimum reduced and considering all the other initiatives to bring IKEA as a model in the field of sustainability and the circularity [83].

The theoretical considerations presented on the circularity of business processes and the need for careful planning of reverse logistics to achieve sustainability goals in terms of carbon neutrality and net zero impact represent a first step towards analyzing the sustainability of the business processes involved. The theoretical framework presented serves as a starting point for reflections that take into account, on one hand, how reverse logistics represents a key element in achieving the objectives of sustainability for business processes, and on the other hand, aims to highlight how spatial localization dynamics of companies. Recalling recent revivals of the traditional location theories from geographers and planners (see model discussed in literature by Balletto, Borruso, and Mei [76]), location and location theories represent a strategic factors to be studied and implemented for waste flow management in terms of the localization of waste treatment and regeneration plants, also considering the geographical localization dynamics of such facilities as place of origin of secondary raw materials obtained from waste regeneration.

As a consequence, the implementation of circular business models and reverse logistics is a critical step towards achieving a more sustainable economic system that, now more than ever, depends on the implementation of extremely careful and accurate reverse logistics to be embedded within companies' business models.

References

1. Morseletto, P.: Targets for a circular economy. Resources, Conservation and Recycling, 153 (2020)
2. Imperatives, S.: Report of the world commission on environment and development: our common future, 1–300 (1987). Accessed 10 Feb 1987
3. Ogunmakinde, O.E., Sher, W., Egbelakin, T.: Circular economy pillars: a semi-systematic review. Clean Technol. Environ. Policy 23(3), 899–914 (2021). https://doi.org/10.1007/s10 098-020-02012-9
4. Geissdoerfer, M., Pieroni, M.P., Pigosso, D.C., Soufani, K.: Circular business models: a review. J. Clean. Prod. 277, 123741 (2020)
5. Lieder, M., Rashid, A.: Towards Circular Economy implementation: a comprehensive review in context of manufacturing industry. J. Clean. Prod. 115, 36–51 (2016)

6. Masi, D., Day, S., Godsell, J.: Supply chain configurations in the circular economy: a systematic literature review. Sustainability **9**(9), 1602 (2017)
7. Nußholz, J.L.: Circular business models: defining a concept and framing an emerging research field. Sustainability **9**(10), 1810 (2017)
8. Ćwiklicki, M., Wojnarowska, M.: Circular economy and industry 4.0: one-way or two-way relationships? Eng. Econ. **31**(4), 387–397 (2020). https://doi.org/10.5755/j01.ee.31.4.24565
9. Murphy, P.R., Poist, R.F.: Management of logistical retro movements: an empirical analysis of literature suggestions. J. Transp. Res. Forum **29**(1), 177–184 (1998)
10. Julianelli, V., Caiado, R.G.G., Scavarda, L.F., Cruz, S.P.D.M.F.: Interplay between reverse logistics and circular economy: critical success factors-based taxonomy and framework. Resour. Conserv. Recycl. **158**, 104784 (2020)
11. Ding, L., Wang, T., Chan, P.W.: Forward and reverse logistics for circular economy in construction: a systematic literature review. J. Cleaner Prod. **388**, 135981 (2023). https://doi.org/10.1016/j.jclepro.2023.135981
12. Agrawal, S., Singh, R.K.: Analyzing disposition decisions for sustainable reverse logistics: triple bottom line approach. Resources, Conservation and Recycling, 150 (2019)
13. Biancolin, M., Capoani, L., Rotaris, L.: Relazione tra logistica inversa ed economia circolare: una rassegna bibliografica. Rivista di economia e politica dei trasporti, 2021(2), 1–28 (2022)
14. Govindan, K., Soleimani, H.: A review of reverse logistics and closed-loop supply chains: a journal of cleaner production focus. J. Clean. Prod. **142**, 371–384 (2017)
15. Masudin, I., Fernanda, F.W., Jie, F., Restuputri, D.P.: A review of sustainable reverse logistics: approaches and applications. Int. J. Logist. Syst. Manage. **40**(2), 171–192 (2021)
16. Bocken, N.M., Ritala, P., Huotari, P.: The circular economy: exploring the introduction of the concept among S&P 500 firms. J. Ind. Ecol. **21**(3), 487–490 (2017)
17. Yang, Q.Z., Zhou, J., Xu, K.: A 3R implementation framework to enable circular consumption in community. Int. J. Environ. Sci. Dev. **5**(2), 217 (2014)
18. Bocken, N.M., Short, S.W., Rana, P., Evans, S.: A literature and practice review to develop sustainable business model archetypes. J. Clean. Prod. **65**, 42–56 (2014)
19. Soleimani, H., Govindan, K., Saghafi, H., Jafari, H.: Fuzzy multi-objective sustainable and green closed-loop supply chain network design. Comput. Ind. Eng. **109**, 191–203 (2017)
20. Aminoff, A., Valkokari, K., Antikainen, M., Kettunen, O.: Exploring disruptive business model innovation for the circular economy. In: Campana, G., Howlett, R.J., Setchi, R., Cimatti, B. (eds.) SDM 2017. SIST, vol. 68, pp. 525–536. Springer, Cham (2017). https://doi.org/10.1007/978-3-319-57078-5_50
21. Krstić, M., Agnusdei, G.P., Miglietta, P.P., Tadić, S., Roso, V.: Applicability of industry 4.0 technologies in the reverse logistics: a circular economy approach based on comprehensive distance based ranking (COBRA) method. Sustainability **14**(9), 5632 (2022). https://doi.org/10.3390/su14095632
22. Pokharel, S., Mutha, A.: Perspectives in reverse logistics: a review. Resour. Conserv. Recycl. **53**(4), 175–182 (2009)
23. Ferguson, N., Browne, J.: Issues in end-of-life product recovery and reverse logistics. Prod. Plann. Control **12**(5), 534–547 (2001)
24. Bernon, M., Tjahjono, B., Ripanti, E.F.: Aligning retail reverse logistics practice with circular economy values: an exploratory framework. Prod. Plann. Control **29**(6), 483–497 (2018)
25. Esposito, M., Tse, T., Soufani, K.: Reverse logistics for postal services within a circular economy. Thunderbird Int. Bus. Rev. **60**(5), 741–745 (2018)
26. Cruz-Rivera, R., Ertel, J.: Reverse logistics network design for the collection of end-of-life vehicles in Mexico. Eur. J. Oper. Res. **196**(3), 930–939 (2009)
27. Murphy, P.: A preliminary study of transportation and warehousing aspects of reverse distribution. Transp. J., 12–21 (1986)

28. Blackburn, J.D., Guide, V.D.R., Jr., Souza, G.C., Van Wassenhove, L.N.: Reverse supply chains for commercial returns. Calif. Manage. Rev. **46**(2), 6–22 (2004)
29. Carter, C.R., Ellram, L.M.: Reverse logistics: a review of the literature and framework for future investigation. J. Bus. Logist. **19**(1), 85 (1998)
30. Milios, L., Matsumoto, M.: Consumer perception of remanufactured automotive parts and policy implications for transitioning to a circular economy in Sweden. Sustainability. **11**(22), 6264 (2019)
31. Garrido-Hidalgo, C., Olivares, T., Ramirez, F. J., Roda-Sanchez, L.: An end-to-end internet of things solution for reverse supply chain management in industry 4.0. Comput. Ind. **112**, 1031127 (2019)
32. Chileshe, N., et al.: Factors driving the implementation of reverse logistics: a quantified model for the construction industry, Waste Manage. **79**, 48-57 (2018)
33. Winans, K., Kendall, A., Deng, H.: The history and current applications of the circular economy concept. Renew. Sustain. Energy Rev. **68**, 825–833 (2017)
34. Lewandowski, M.: Designing the business models for circular economy—towards the conceptual framework. Sustainability **8**(1), 43 (2016)
35. Boulding, K.E.: Economics and ecology (1966)
36. Stahel, W., Reday, G.: The Potential for Substituting Manpower for Energy. Technical report, Geneva Research Centre: Geneva, Switzerland (1976)
37. Stahel, W. R.: The product life factor. An inquiry into the nature of sustainable societies: the role of the private sector (Series: 1982 Mitchell Prize Papers), NARC, 74–96 (1982)
38. Pearce, D.W., Turner, R.K.: Economics of natural resources and the environment. Johns Hopkins University Press (1989)
39. Graedel, T.E., Allenby, B.R.: Matrix approaches to abridged life cycle assessment. Environ. Sci. Technol. **29**(3), 134A-139A (1995)
40. McDonough, W., Braungart, M.: Design for the triple top line: new tools for sustainable commerce. Corp. Environ. Strateg. **9**(3), 251–258 (2002)
41. Commoner, B.: Economic Growth and Ecology-A Biologist's View. Monthly Lab. Rev. **94**, 3 (1971)
42. Lyle, J. T.: Regenerative design for sustainable development. John Wiley & Sons (1996)
43. Benyus, J.M.: Biomimicry: Innovation inspired by nature (1997)
44. Pauli, G.A.: The blue economy: 10 years, 100 innovations, 100 million jobs. Paradigm publications (2010)
45. Niero, M., Hauschild, M.Z.: Closing the loop for packaging: finding a framework to operationalize circular economy strategies. Procedia Cirp. **61**, 685–690 (2017)
46. Webster, K.: The circular economy: a wealth of flows (2015)
47. Kirchherr, J., Reike, D., Hekkert, M.: Conceptualizing the circular economy: an analysis of 114 definitions. Resour. Conserv. Recycl. **127**, 221–232 (2017)
48. Javed, H., Fazal Firdousi, S., Murad, M., Jiatong, W., Abrar, M.: Exploring disposition decision for sustainable reverse logistics in the era of a circular economy: applying the triple bottom line approach in the manufacturing industry. Int. J. Supply Oper. Manage. **8**(1), 53–68 (2021)
49. Skene, K.R.: Circles, spirals, pyramids and cubes: why the circular economy cannot work. Sustain. Sci. **13**(2), 479–492 (2017). https://doi.org/10.1007/s11625-017-0443-3
50. Wirtz, B.W., Pistoia, A., Ullrich, S., Göttel, V.: Business models: origin, development and future research perspectives. Long Range Plan. **49**(1), 36–54 (2016)
51. Doleski, O. D.: Integrated Business Model: applying the St. Gallen Management concept to business models. Springer (2015). https://doi.org/10.1007/978-3-658-09698-4
52. Casadesus-Masanell, R., Ricart, J.E.: From strategy to business models and onto tactics. Long Range Plan. **43**(2–3), 195–215 (2010)

53. Magretta, J.: Why business models matter. Harvard business review (2002)
54. Chesbrough, H.: Business model innovation: it's not just about technology anymore. Strat. Leadership **35**(6), 12–17 (2007)
55. Christensen, C.M., Overdorf, M.: Meeting the challenge of disruptive change. Harv. Bus. Rev. **78**(2), 66–77 (2000)
56. Parker, L.D.: Australian universities in a pandemic world: transforming a broken business model? J. Account. Organ. Chang. **16**(4), 541–548 (2020)
57. Boons, F., Lüdeke-Freund, F.: Business models for sustainable innovation: state-of-the-art and steps towards a research agenda. J. Clean. Prod. **45**, 9–19 (2013)
58. Geissdoerfer, M., Savaget, P., Bocken, N.M., Hultink, E.J.: The circular economy–a new sustainability paradigm? J. Clean. Prod. **143**, 757–768 (2017)
59. Nidumolu, R., Prahalad, C.K., Rangaswami, M.R.: Why sustainability is now the key driver of innovation. Harv. Bus. Rev. **87**(9), 56–64 (2009)
60. Freeman, R.B., Medoff, J.L.: What do unions do. Indus. Lab. Rel. Rev. **38**, 244 (1984)
61. Tibben-Lembke, R.S.: The impact of reverse logistics on the total cost of ownership. J. Market. Theory Pract. **6**(4), 51–60 (1998)
62. Tibben-Lembke, R.S., Rogers, D.S.: Differences between forward and reverse logistics in a retail environment. Supply Chain Manage.: Int. J. **7**(5), 271–282 (2002)
63. De Brito, M.P., Dekker, R.: A framework for reverse logistics. Springer Berlin Heidelberg, 3–27 (2004). https://doi.org/10.1007/978-3-540-24803-3_1
64. Akdoğan, M.Ş., Coşkun, A.: Drivers of reverse logistics activities: an empirical investigation. Procedia Soc. Behav. Sci. **58**, 1640–1649 (2012)
65. Fleischmann, M.: Reverse logistics network structures and design. Available at SSRN 370907 (2003)
66. Malmgren, K., Mötsch Larsson, K.: Reverse Logistics in the Transition towards Circular Economy-A Case Study of Customer Returns at IKEA. (2020)
67. Balletto, G., Borruso, G., Mei, G., Milesi, A.: Strategic circular economy in construction: case study in Sardinia, Italy. J. Urban Plann. Dev. **147**(4), 05021034 (2021)
68. Acar, A. Z., Önden, İ., Kara, K.: Evaluating the location of regional return centers in reverse logistics through integration of gis, ahp and integer programming. Int. J. Ind. Eng. **22**(4) (2015)
69. Sarkis, J., Helms, M.M., Hervani, A.A.: Reverse logistics and social sustainability. Corp. Soc. Responsib. Environ. Manag. **17**(6), 337–354 (2010)
70. Schultmann, F., Zumkeller, M., Rentz, O.: Modeling reverse logistic tasks within closed-loop supply chains: an example from the automotive industry. Eur. J. Oper. Res. **171**(3), 1033–1050 (2006)
71. Petit-Boix, A., Leipold, S.: Circular economy in cities: reviewing how environmental research aligns with local practices. J. Clean. Prod. **195**, 1270–1281 (2018)
72. Gravagnuolo, A., Angrisano, M., Fusco Girard, L.: Circular economy strategies in eight historic port cities: criteria and indicators towards a circular city assessment framework. Sustainability **11**(13), 3512 (2019)
73. Fusco Girard, L., Nocca, F.: Moving towards the circular economy/city model: which tools for operationalizing this model? Sustainability **11**(22), 6253 (2019)
74. Weber, A.: Über des standort der industrien. Part. I. Reine theorie des standorts, Tübingen.Trad ingl. Alfreds weber's theory of location of industries (C.J. Friedrich), The University of Chicago press (1909/1922)
75. Isard, W.: The general theory of location and space-economy. Q. J. Econ. **63**(4), 476–506 (1949)
76. Balletto, G., Borruso, G., Mei, G.: Location theory and circular economy. Demolition, constructions and spatial organization of firms–an applied model to Sardinia Region. The case

study of the New Cagliari Stadium. In: Computational Science and Its Applications–ICCSA 2019: 19th International Conference, Saint Petersburg, Russia, July 1–4, 2019, Proceedings, Part III. Springer International Publishing, 535–550 (2019). https://doi.org/10.1007/978-3-030-24302-9_38

77. Materiali per l'Edilizia e le Infrastrutture Sostenibili: gli Aggregati Riciclati (MEISAR) cluster Top-Down finanziato dalla Regione Autonoma della Sardegna attraverso: POR Sardegna FESR 2014/2020 - asse prioritario i "ricerca scientifica, sviluppo tecnologico e innovazione" Azione 1.1.4

78. Pani, L., Francesconi, L., Lopez Gayarre, F.: Properties of precast hollow concrete blocks using recycled concrete aggregates. In: Sardinia 2015 15th International waste management and Landfill Symposium, pp. 1–10. CISA, Coop. LibrariaEditrice (2015)

79. Fleischmann, M., Bloemhof-Ruwaard, J. M., Beullens, P., Dekker, R.: Reverse logistics network design. Reverse logistics: quantitative models for closed-loop supply chains, 65–94 (2004)

80. Cosmo, D.E., Yang, K.: A further strategic move to sustainability-a case study on IKEA. J. Strateg. Innov. Sustain. 12(2), 39–47 (2017)

81. Laurin, F., Fantazy, K.: Sustainable supply chain management: a case study at IKEA. Trans. Corpor. Rev. 9(4), 309–318 (2017)

82. Luu, M.: Developing the implementation of green warehousing at IKEA Finland (2016)

83. Gbanabila, Y.: Effects of corporate sustainability on established brand: the case of IKEA (2014)

84. Ingka Holding B.V.: Ingka group annual summary & sustainability report FY19. Retrieved from Leiden: Ingka Holding B.V (2020)

**Ports of the Future - Smartness
and Sustainability (SmartPorts 2023)**

Methodologies for Sustainable Development of TEN-T/RFC Corridors and Core Ports: Economic Impacts Generated in Port-Related Areas

Francesco Russo[ID] and Giuseppe Musolino[✉][ID]

DIIES, Università Mediterranea di Reggio Calabria, 89100 Reggio Calabria, Italy
giuseppe.musolino@unirc.it

Abstract. Container ports were born with the container revolution in the last decades of the 20th century. Their evolution is represented by the third-generation ports, playing a crucial role in the global supply chain, becoming generators of value added. One of the measures that facilitates the increase of value added in a third-generation ports is the Special Economic Zone (SEZ). The economic impacts of SEZs is amplified in smart ports, where the three pillars of smartness (ICT, Transport and Energy) are present, and in a core ports connected to TEN-T/RFC corridors. The paper describes the method and the application to quantify the indirect and induced economic impact of a SEZ inside a third generation port in terms of employment by means of an aggregated model. A case study is reported considering a SEZ in an undeveloped UE region. The results are obtained from a comparative analysis of representative case studies of port impact studies, estimated by means of a specific class of econometric (input-output) models.

Keywords: Sustainable ports · Smart ports · TEN-T corridors · RFC corridors · special economic zone · indirect and induced economic impact · port of Gioia Tauro

1 Introduction

Ports are the gate for the exchange of freight and people. As far as concerns commercial ports, they may be classified according to the generation criterion (see [1–3]; and the references included). The first-generation ports were built close to the cities: the *city-port* was the dominant model for centuries. The second-generation port, or the *industrial port*, was built during the industrial revolution of the 20th century close to industrial plants to support the supply of raw materials and final products. The third-generation ports, as an upgrade of the *container port*, were born with the container revolution, in the last decades of the 20th century. Containerization allows the globalization of the economy. Ports are nodes of a global supply chain, becoming generators of value added [4, 5]. The fourth-generation port, or the *cooperative port*, was born after the 2000s when ports shifted from competition to cooperation with closer ports. Nowadays the fifth-generation port, the *digital port*, introduced massively the emerging ICT in facilitating the horizontal and vertical interactions among port actors [6].

© The Author(s) 2023

O. Gervasi et al. (Eds.): ICCSA 2023 Workshops, LNCS 14110, pp. 515–526, 2023.
https://doi.org/10.1007/978-3-031-37123-3_35

Third-generation ports have been widely explored in scientific literature, as far as concerns two main elements: the port areas, which are important for freight handling and transportation operations; the port hinterlands, which are important for increasing the added value of goods in transit through ports. A detailed study concerned an important hub container port. The limits and weaknesses of the port area and the general actions to be implemented to reduce the costs of a third-generation port were identified. The relationship with the hinterland and, in particular, with the research centers have been studied and the main industrial sectors connected with a third-generation port, which are logistics, mechanics and agri-food, were analyzed (see [7] and references included).

One of the measures that could facilitate the increase of added value in third-generation ports are Special Economic Zones (SEZs). The existing literature on economic impacts of SEZs shows that they boost economic activities in port-related areas in line with sustainable development of ports. Recent studies examined different elements connected to the activation of a SEZ in a hub container port, which is a core port connected to a TEN-T and RFC corridor, such as territorial attractiveness, the aggregate economic impact and the disaggregated one, the system of higher education and research. The positive effects of a SEZ may be amplified when the port is a smart port, where the three pillar of smartness (ICT, Transport and Energy) are present (see [8, 9] and references included).

An analysis presented in [10] showed that higher times are necessary to export goods in many developed countries. The study presented in [11] showed relevant differences between export/import times of goods in countries having similar technical-administrative structures and belonging to the same economic-political area. The European countries present high variances in times connected to the export of goods respect to an average value of ten days. According to [11], the Italian Prime Ministry presented an analysis of times connected to export issues, disaggregating them into documentation times, customs times, handling and transport times [12]. The results showed that customs times are similar for all countries, while documentation and handling times are considerably different. These times are important as they are connected to the export capacities of a country. It is worth noting that the documentation and customs times depend on the administrative organization of the country and not on the ports' organization.

The paper describes the methods to quantify the indirect and induced economic impact of a SEZ given the aggregated quantity of direct impact. The model and the parameters are obtained from a comparative analysis of representative case studies of port impact studies, estimated by means of a specific class of econometric (input-output) models. A test case in terms of employment is reported, considering the port of Gioia Tauro in Southern Italy.

The following part of the paper is articulated into four sections. Section 2 deals with the theoretical background and the backbone of the modelling framework (input-output models) of the port impact studies. Section 3 reports some examples of port impact studies executed by the input-output modelling framework. Section 4 presents the results of the modelling estimation of the aggregate indirect and induced impact of employment generated by the activation of the SEZ in Calabria (Italy), as part of a more general modelling framework. The last section reports the conclusions and the further developments.

The proposed work is of interest for the technical managers of ports and SEZs and for the politicians of public bodies, who have to plan investments in areas with a slow development. The work is also useful for researchers because it allows to apply a synthetic method for the study of specific transport-territory interaction problems, for which the results are known in many real cases.

2 Economic Impact Estimation: Input-Output Models

In the behalf of literature on port impact studies, the Input-Output (IO) model ([13, 14], and included references) allow the estimation of the direct, indirect and the induced impacts of port through the identification of interactions among the port firms.

The basic principle underlying the IO model is the production-consumption one (Fig. 1), according to which firms, in order to produce some outputs needs some inputs.

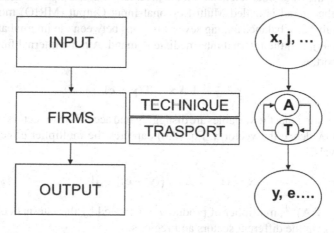

Fig. 1. Production-consumption principle underlying the IO model

The basic principle is to equate the products generated (internally produced and imported) and the products consumed (transformed into other products, internal consumed and exported).

The mechanism of production-consumption is regulated by the technique of transformation (matrix of technique, **A**), and by the amount of trade among regions (matrix of trade, **T**).

The basic equation of the IO model simulates inter-dependencies between economic sectors through technical coefficients belonging to matrix **A**. Equation (1.a) establishes a balance inside an (open to import and export) region between the internal and external production, $\mathbf{x} + \mathbf{j}$, and the internal intermediate demand, $\mathbf{A}\,\mathbf{x}$, the final demand, $\mathbf{y}$, and the export, $\mathbf{e}$:

$$\mathbf{x} + \mathbf{j} = \mathbf{A}\,\mathbf{x} + \mathbf{y} + \mathbf{e} \qquad (1.a)$$

where:

x, vector of internal production;
j, vector of import;
y, vector of internal production;
e, vector of export.

It is worth noting that the variables are disaggregated according to sectors. By putting in evidence the vector **x**, Eq. (1.b) captures the multiplier effects at sector level:

$$\mathbf{x} = (\mathbf{I} - \mathbf{A})^{-1}[(\mathbf{y} + \mathbf{e})] - \mathbf{j} \qquad (1.b)$$

where:

B = $(\mathbf{I} - \mathbf{A})^{-1}$ is the multiplier of production (or Leontief matrix) activated by the internal consumption, **y**, and by export, **e**;

I is the identity matrix.

The IO model able to reproduce a spatial representation of economy is obtained by introducing the trade coefficients to locate production-consumptions across regions. In this case, the model is called Multi-Regional-Input-Output (MRIO) model. Equation (2.a) establishes a balance among several regions between the internal and external production, **x** + **j**, and the internal intermediate demand, **Ax**, the internal final demand, **y**, and the export, **e**:

$$\mathbf{x} + \mathbf{j} = \mathbf{T}\mathbf{A}\mathbf{x} + \mathbf{T}(\mathbf{y} + \mathbf{e}) \qquad (2.a)$$

It is worth noting that the variables are disaggregated according to sectors and regions. By putting in evidence the vector **x**, Eq. (2.b) captures the multiplier effects at sector and region levels:

$$\mathbf{x} = (\mathbf{I} - \mathbf{T}\mathbf{A})^{-1}[(\mathbf{y} + \mathbf{e})] - \mathbf{j}] \qquad (2.b)$$

with **B'** = $(\mathbf{I} - \mathbf{T}\mathbf{A})^{-1}$, multiplier of production activated by the internal consumption, **y**, and export, **e**, in the different sectors and regions.

The financial flows expressed by means of IO and MRIO models are related with the physical flows of goods (and passengers). The physical flows may be estimated by means of Transport System Models (TSMs), which are generally composed by a transport supply model, a travel demand model and a supply-demand interaction model (see [15], and references included).

3 Port Impact Studies

The major challenge in port impact studies is the identification of the port firms and of the degree of port dependency of these firms with the port hinterland [16]. According to classification of literature [12, 16], port firms may be subdivided into:

- *port-required* which activities rely directly to the operation of port facilities;
- *port-attracted*, dependent on port-required ones and that are attracted because the presence of the port generates higher value added than value added generated in other ports;

- *port-induced*, which expand their markets by means of the presence of the port.

For each of the above category of firms, it is possible to associate three categories of economic impacts (see Fig. 2):

- *direct impact*, generated by port-required firms directly involved in the supply of the port operations;
- *indirect impact*, generated by port-attracted firms which provide labour, services, materials, and other items to port-required firms;
- *induced impact*, generated by port-induced firms that comes from household purchases of goods and services made possible because of wages generated by activities of port-attracted and port-attracted firms.

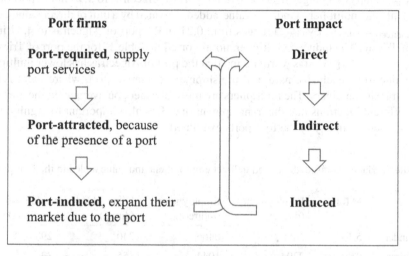

Fig. 2. Relationships between port firms and categories of impacts.

Several port impact studies have been presented in the literature based on the use of IO framework. The existing studies may be grouped into two categories according to the level of disaggregation of the representation of port firms and of their interactions with the local economy [17]. The first group of studies identify the structural factors in the port and simulate the port-city interactions, according to a Land Use Transport Interaction (LUTI) process [18, 19]. In this case, the land use variables, such as land consumption, are endogenous inside the IO model. The second group of studies represents the port in more aggregate terms and simulate the interactions between the port and the national economies, according to a National Economic Transport Interaction (NETI) process [20, 21]. In this case, the variables considered have a financial nature and the IO model estimates the impact of changes in transport networks and in spatial economies on interregional, and even in international, trade patterns.

The paper reports a description of four port impact studies concerning four European ports: Antwerp (Belgium), Trieste (Italy), Santander (Spain), and Algeciras (Spain).

The economic impact study of the port of Antwerp is based on microeconomic data related to the port firms and between port firms and the Belgian economy in year 2000 [22]. The economic impact of the port of Trieste was estimated with a IO table of year 2007, and having as reference the port sectors [23]. The economic impact study of port of Santander allowed to obtain the direct impacts using accounting information about the port firms and indirect and induced impacts by means of the Spanish IO table [24]. The economic impact of the port of Algeciras was obtained as result of a survey and of accounting data analysis of port firms, as far as concerns the direct impact. The indirect impact was obtained from data about goods and services purchased by port firms [25].

The data about the direct and indirect value added and employment generated are reported in Table 1, which also reports the handled traffic. It emerges that the multiplier of indirect employment activated by a unit of direct employment ($m_{emp\text{-}indirect} = emp_{indirect}/emp_{direct}$) ranges from 0,46 in the port of Algeciras to 3,96 in the port of Trieste; while the multiplier of indirect value-added activated by a unit of direct value-added ($m_{va\text{-}indirect} = va_{indirect}/va_{direct}$) ranges from 0,21 in the port of Algeciras to 4,37 in the port of Trieste. The induced multiplier, not reported in Table 1, for the port of Trieste is $m_{va\text{-}induced} = 1.46$ [23]. It is worth noting that the port of Algeciras has lower multipliers values due to its exclusive nature of transhipment container port, where there is high rate of transit containers. The multipliers are more elevated, on average, in the ports that have different functions that the transhipment one. It is also important to highlight that no SEZ operates in any of the four ports examined.

Table 1. Handled traffic, direct and indirect employment and value added in the four ports

Port	MTonn	Employment (direct)	Employment (indirect)	Value added (direct)	Value added (indirect)
Santander	5,13	2458	6466	240	298
Algeciras	91	2294	1044	155	32
Antwerp	190	63080	89551	9342	8361
Trieste	56,6	2890	11443	182	796

(sources: [22–25])

The port of Algeciras has a similar structure of the port of Gioia Tauro, as both ports mainly handle container traffic. The handled traffic, the direct and indirect employment and value added of the port of Algeciras is reported in Table 2. The handled containers are sub-divided into containers in transit through the port and containers in import/export to/from the country. The data of Table 2 show that the value of multiplier for employment, $m_{emp\text{-}indirect}$, is similar for transhipment and import/export operations; while the value of multiplier for value-added, $m_{va\text{-}indirect}$, ranges from 0,19 for transhipment to 0,30 for import/export operations.

4   Test Case of SEZ Based on Gioia Tauro Core Port

The first comprehensive law about SEZs in Italy was forwarded to the Italian Parliament in September 2015 by the Calabria Regional Council, on the basis of the proposal of the Regional Government. The proposal, as result of intense work carried out with EU, was verified by the Italian Government during 2016. Having considered its potential benefits and its juridical consistency, the Italian Parliament decided to extend the law to all Regions of Southern Italy. The Prime Minister Gentiloni and the Minister for Southern Italy De Vincenzi emanated the Decree Law n.91 of June 2017, which establishes the SEZs in Italy and the Regulation was emanated on 25 January 2018 (DPCM n.12). The DPCM regulates the procedures and conditions for the establishment of the SEZs, which are defined as geographically delimited and clearly identified areas, located within the Italian border, also composed of not-physically adjacent areas but presenting a functional-economic connection. Furthermore, the DPCM identified the role of the Port Authority by setting up a Steering Committee headed by the President of the Authority, strengthening the role of the President. The first brick towards the creation of the SEZ in Italy was crated, in order to reduce the gap in export times that separate Italy from the main European competitors, recalled in the introduction.

Table 2. Handled traffic, direct and indirect employment and value added in port of Algeciras

Algeciras	MTEUs	Direct employment	Indirect employment	Direct value added	Indirect value added
Transit	2,517	1792	809	132,00	25,00
Import/Export	0,148	502	235	23,00	7,00

(source: [25])

The SEZ in Calabria was planned to facilitate physical and functional integration of ports and airports and industrial areas of the region, according to the indications of the DPCM. The fulcrum of the SEZ is the port of Gioia Tauro, which is a core port of the TEN-T corridor 5 and RFC corridor 3. The port of Gioia Tauro needs to complete its full transition towards a third-generation port, boosting settlement of industrial activities in the large industrial agglomeration existing in its hinterland.

According to the strategic development plan of SEZ, the SEZ should attract mechanical and agri-food firms, transport and logistics companies in the hinterland of the port of Gioia Tauro and in the industrial areas of Calabria region.

4.1   Indirect Impact of SEZ

This section reports the calculation of the expected indirect and induced impacts of the establishment of the SEZ related to the port of Gioia Tauro.

The general estimation of the effects of the studied SEZ is conducted through a framework composed of six models: aggregated direct impact [8]; land capacity constraint; economic-functional link; settlement of firms; incentives; aggregated indirect and induced impacts.

The model "indirect and induced impact" allows to estimate, in aggregate terms at regional level, the indirect and induced impacts on employment generated by the activation of SEZ.

The indirect impacts are related to the employment generated by firms that are economically interdependent from the firms directly beneficiaries of the SEZ, or are indirectly beneficiaries of the SEZ. In the case of the SEZ area close to the port of Gioia Tauro, the beneficiaries of the SEZ are port-attracted firms that can increase their activities due to the presence of the port.

The induced impacts are related to the employment generated by firms for the purchase of goods and services by households whose members are employed in firms directly and indirectly beneficiaries of the SEZ.

The methodology used to estimate the indirect and induced impacts is based upon the methods reported in Sect. 3. Hereby it is reported the aggregate estimations for all economic sectors of the indirect and induced impacts on employment generated by direct employment.

The indirect impacts on employment are estimated by means of the following equation:

$$emp_{SEZ(indirect-10)} = m_{emp-indirect} \times emp_{SEZ(direct-10)}$$

with

- $emp_{SEZ(indirect-10)}$, total indirect employment generated by SEZ in Calabria ten years after the starting year (in the hypothesis of a full activation of the SEZ, with complete availability of financial resources and decrees for simplification, at the starting year);
- $m_{emp-indirect}$, indirect multiplier, or total indirect employment generated by total direct employment;
- $emp_{SEZ(direct-10)}$, total direct employment generated by SEZ in Calabria ten years after the starting year.

The induced impacts on employment are estimated by means of the following equation:

$$emp_{SEZ(induced-10)} = m_{emp-induced} \times (emp_{SEZ(direct-10)} + emp_{SEZ(indirect-10)})$$

with

- $emp_{SEZ(induced-10)}$, total induced employment generated by SEZ in Calabria after ten years from the starting year (see definition above);
- $m_{emp-induced}$, induced multiplier, or total induced employment generated by total direct and indirect employment.

According to the comparative analysis reported in Sect. 3, the following results have been obtained:

- the estimated value of the indirect multiplier of employment generated by SEZ Calabria should range from 0.6 in a worst-case scenario to 1.0 in a best-case scenario: $m_{emp-indirect} \in [0.6-1.0]$

- the estimated value of the induced multiplier of employment generated by SEZ Calabria should range from 0.2 in a worst-case scenario to 0.6 in a best-case one; $m_{emp-ind} \in [0.2–0.6]$.

The above estimated ranges lead to the definition of a base-line scenario where the indirect and induced multipliers are assumed respectively equal to $m_{emp-indirect} = 0.8$ and $m_{emp-induced} = 0.4$.

Figure 3 reports the estimated indirect and induced employment in the three above scenarios activated by the direct employment generated by the SEZ. The value of direct employment had been estimated by means of the aggregated impact model presented in [8].

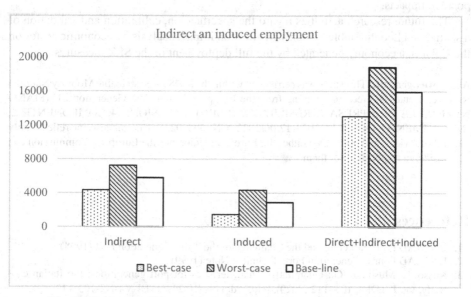

Fig. 3. Estimated indirect and induced employment by the activation of SEZ.

5 Conclusions

Third-generation ports were born after the container revolution, in the last decades of the 20th century. They play a crucial role in the global supply chain, becoming generators of value added. One of the measures that facilitates the increase of value added in third-generation ports is the Special Economic Zone (SEZ). The economic impacts of SEZs is amplified in smart ports, where the three pillar of smartness (ICT, Transport and Energy) are present, and in a core port connected to TEN-T/RFC corridors. The paper presented a methodology to quantify the indirect and induced economic impacts in terms of employees of a SEZ starting from the knowledge of the direct impacts.

SEZ in Calabria was conceived to operate in several existing industrial areas of the region, having its fulcrum around the transhipment hub port of Gioia Tauro, which is a core port, connected to a TEN-T/RFC corridor. The main objectives of the SEZ were to reduce the gap in export times that separate Italy from the main European competitors; to facilitate physical and functional integration of ports and airports and industrial areas of the region; to complete the full transition of Gioia Tauro towards a third-generation port, in order to become a value-added generator.

The paper described a test application to a planned SEZ in the Calabria region. The results are obtained from a comparative analysis of representative case studies of port impact studies, estimated by means of a specific class of econometric (input-output) models.

The results of the modelling estimation of the aggregate indirect and induced impact of employment generated by the activation of the SEZ in Calabria showed relevant positive impacts.

The future research activities regard the specification, calibration and validation of a spatialized Leontief table, which will allow an impact analysis by economic sector on the Calabrian economy generated by the full deployment of the SEZ measures.

Acknowledgement. This study was carried out within the MOST – Sustainable Mobility National Research Center and received funding from the European Union Next-Generation EU (PIANO NAZIONALE DI RIPRESA E RESILIENZA (PNRR) – MISSIONE 4 COMPONENTE 2, INVESTIMENTO 1.4 – D.D. 1033 17/06/2022, CN00000023). This manuscript reflects only the authors' views and opinions, neither the European Union nor the European Commission can be considered responsible for them.

References

1. UNCTAD Port Marketing and the Challenge of the Third Generation Port (1994)
2. UNCTAD Fourth-Generation Port: Technical Note (1999)
3. Russo, F., Musolino, G.: Quantitative characteristics for port generations: the Italian case study. Int. J. TDI **4**, 103–112 (2020). https://doi.org/10.2495/TDI-V4-N2-103-112
4. Troch, F., Meersman, H., Sys, C., Van De Voorde, E., Vanelslander, T.: The added value of rail freight transport in Belgium. Res. Transp. Bus. Manag. **44**, 100625 (2022). https://doi.org/10.1016/j.rtbm.2021.100625
5. Russo, F., Musolino, G., Assumma, V.: Ro-Ro and Lo-Lo alternatives between Mediterranean countries: factors affecting the service choice. Case Studies on Transport Policy **11**, 100960 (2023). https://doi.org/10.1016/j.cstp.2023.100960
6. Russo, F., Musolino, G.: The role of emerging ICT in the ports: increasing utilities according to shared decisions. Front. Future Transp. **2**, 722812 (2021). https://doi.org/10.3389/ffutr.2021.722812
7. Russo, F., Chilà, G.: Structural factors for a third-generation port: actions and measures for Gioia Tauro, Italy. In: The Regional Transport Plan. In Proceedings of the Urban and Maritime Transport 2021, WIT Transactions on the Built Environment, vol. 204, pp. 17–30. WIT Press, 16 June 2021
8. Musolino, G., Cartisano, A., Fortugno, G.: Special economic zones planning for sustainable ports: aggregate economic impact of port of Gioia Tauro. In: Gervasi, O., Murgante, B., Misra, S., Rocha, A.M.A.C., Garau, C. (eds.) Computational Science and Its Applications – ICCSA 2022 Workshops. LNCS, vol. 13381, pp. 60–71. Springer, Cham (2022). https://doi.org/10.1007/978-3-031-10548-7_5. ISBN 978-3-031-10547-0

9. Musolino, D.A., Panuccio, P.: Special economic zones planning for sustainable ports: the test case of territorial attractiveness and urban planning in Calabria Region. In: Gervasi, O., Murgante, B., Misra, S., Rocha, A.M.A.C., Garau, C. (eds.) Computational Science and Its Applications – ICCSA 2022. LNCS, vol. 13381, pp. 72–84. Springer, Cham (2022). https://doi.org/10.1007/978-3-031-10548-7_6. ISBN 978-3-031-10547-0

10. Pellicanò, D.S., Trecozzi, M.R.: Special economic zones planning for sustainable ports: general approach for administrative simplifications and a test case. In: Gervasi, O., Murgante, B., Misra, S., Rocha, A.M.A.C., Garau, C. (eds.) Computational Science and Its Applications – ICCSA 2022. LNCS, vol. 13381, pp. 47–59. Springer, Cham (2022). https://doi.org/10.1007/978-3-031-10548-7_6. ISBN 978-3-031-10547-0

11. International Finance Corporation Doing Business 2014: Understanding Regulations for Small and Medium-Size Enterprises (2013)

12. Presidenza del Consiglio dei Ministri Iniziativa Di Studio Sulla Portualità Italiana (2014)

13. Barna, T. (ed.): Structural Interdependence and Economic Development. Palgrave Macmillan, London, (1963). ISBN 978-1-349-81636-1

14. Kockelman, K.M., Jin, L., Zhao, Y., Ruíz-Juri, N.: Tracking land use, transport, and industrial production using random-utility-based multiregional input-output models: applications for Texas trade. J. Transp. Geogr. **13**, 275–286 (2005). https://doi.org/10.1016/j.jtrangeo.2004.04.009

15. Cascetta, E.: Transportation Systems Engineering Theory and Methods. Springer, New York (2013). https://doi.org/10.1007/978-1-4757-6873-2. ISBN 978-1-4757-6873-2

16. Davis, H.C.: Regional port impact studies: a critique and suggested methodology. Transp. J. 61–71 (1983)

17. Russo, F., Musolino, G.: A unifying modelling framework to simulate the spatial economic transport interaction process at urban and national scales. J. Transp. Geogr. **24**, 189–197 (2012). https://doi.org/10.1016/j.jtrangeo.2012.02.003

18. De la Barra, T.: Integrated Land Use and Transport Modelling: Decision Chains and Hierarchies, 1st ed. Cambridge University Press, Cambridge (1989). ISBN 978-0-521-24318-6

19. Echenique, M.: Econometric models of land use and transportation. In: Hensher, D.A., Button, K.J., Haynes, K.E., Stopher, P.R. (eds.) Handbook of Transport Geography and Spatial Systems, pp. 185–202. Emerald Group Publishing Limited (2004). ISBN 978-0-08-044108-5

20. Cascetta, E., Nuzzolo, A., Biggiero, L., Russo, F.: Passenger and freight demand models for the Italian transportation system. In: Proceedings of the 7th World Conference on Transport Research; Vol. II

21. Bachmann, C.: Calibrating and applying random-utility-based multiregional input–output models for real-world applications. Netw. Spat. Econ. **19**(1), 219–242 (2019). https://doi.org/10.1007/s11067-019-9444-3

22. Coppens, F., et al.: Economic impact of port activity: a disaggregate analysis - the case of Antwerp. SSRN J. (2007). https://doi.org/10.2139/ssrn.1687569

23. Danielis, R., Gregori, T.: An input-output-based methodology to estimate the economic role of a port: the case of the port system of the Friuli Venezia Giulia Region Italy. Marit. Econ. Logist. **15**, 222–255 (2013). https://doi.org/10.1057/mel.2013.1

24. Mantecón, I.M., Millán, P.C., Castro, J.V., González, M.Á.P.: Economic Impact of a Port on the Hinterland: Application to Santander's Port. IJSTL **4**, 235 (2012). https://doi.org/10.1504/IJSTL.2012.047487

25. Coronado Guerrero, D., et al.: Economic Impact of the Container Traffic at the Port of Algeciras Bay. Springer, Heidelberg (2006). https://doi.org/10.1007/3-540-36789-6. ISBN 978-3-540-36789-5

Open Access This chapter is licensed under the terms of the Creative Commons Attribution 4.0 International License (http://creativecommons.org/licenses/by/4.0/), which permits use, sharing, adaptation, distribution and reproduction in any medium or format, as long as you give appropriate credit to the original author(s) and the source, provide a link to the Creative Commons license and indicate if changes were made.

The images or other third party material in this chapter are included in the chapter's Creative Commons license, unless indicated otherwise in a credit line to the material. If material is not included in the chapter's Creative Commons license and your intended use is not permitted by statutory regulation or exceeds the permitted use, you will need to obtain permission directly from the copyright holder.

Sustainable Development of Railway Corridors: Methods and Models for High Speed Rail (HSR) Demand Analysis

Francesco Russo⦿, Domenico Sgro⦿, and Giuseppe Musolino(✉)⦿

DIIES, Università Mediterranea di Reggio Calabria, 89100 Reggio Calabria, Italy
giuseppe.musolino@unirc.it

Abstract. The realization of High Speed Rail (HSR) lines generates different type of effects that have been observed and studied in the scientific literature in last decades. The paper focuses on the travel demand models to estimate the effects of HSR on passenger mobility. The HSR travel demand may be segmented into three main components: diverted demand from other modes, or from other rail services, to HSR; induced demand, which can be direct and indirect; economy-based demand growth. The aim is to analyse and highlight the actual trend of scientific publications on the HSR demand analysis, thus identify the existing research gaps and the needs inside this trend, so the necessary future directions of research.

Keywords: High Speed Rail (HSR) · travel demand models · sustainable development · railway corridors · state-of-the-art

1 Introduction

According to the Union International des Chemins de Fer [1], there are more than 100,000 km of planned and operative High-Speed Rail (HSR) lines in the world: 52,484 km in operation, 11,960 km under construction, 11,383 km planned, and 28,586 km planned over the longer term. The largest network today is in China (35,388 km), followed by Spain (3330 km), which has overtaken Japan (3041 km) and then France (2734 km). The HSR network in Italy includes less than 1000 km in operation and about 120 km under construction.

Historically, the first HSR has been implemented in Japan with Shinkansen technology since 1975: an infrastructure characterized by the presence of slab tracks and not of ballast. Afterwards, HSR spread to Europe and almost every country developed its own technology: TGV in France since 1981, Pendolino in Italy since 1988 and AVE in Spain since 1992. In the last decades, HSR lines spread worldwide; and today China is the global leader in HSR, given his primacy in extension of railway lines.

The construction of HSR lines generate potential effects that have been studied and analysed in the scientific literature. They may be grouped into: *transportation*, such as infrastructures, services and demand; *socio-economic*, such as economic growth,

© The Author(s) 2023

O. Gervasi et al. (Eds.): ICCSA 2023 Workshops, LNCS 14110, pp. 527–538, 2023.
https://doi.org/10.1007/978-3-031-37123-3_36

accessibility, equity; and *environmental*, such as energy saving and decarbonization. In more general terms, HSR effects may be brought back to some of the 17 Sustainable Development Goals of United Nations [2]. Goal 9 can be recalled: "Build resilient infrastructure, promote sustainable industrialization and foster innovation". Goal 9 includes Target 9.1 "Develop quality, reliable, sustainable and resilient infrastructure, including regional and transborder infrastructure, to support economic development and human well-beings, with a focus on affordable and equitable access for all". Hence, Goal 9 determine direct impacts on industry, innovation, and infrastructure, however, there are also indirect impacts on climate health. Goal 13: "Take urgent action to combat climate change and its impacts. Climate change is a real and undeniable threat to our entire civilization. The effects are already visible and will be catastrophic unless we act now. Through education, innovation and adherence to our climate commitments, we can make the necessary changes to protect the planet. These changes also provide huge opportunities to modernize our infrastructure which will create new jobs and promote greater prosperity across the globe." The pursuit of goal 13 is essential for sustainable development. HSR is the mode/service of transport that competes directly with air transport for passenger mobility considering the economic and social components. The existing research shows that HSR is the mode/service with the lowest carbon footprint per passenger/Kilometer, while air transport is the mode with the highest carbon footprint. Therefore, in conditions of economic and social parity, HSR allows a strong pursuit of the environmental component expressed by goal 13 [2].

The paper focuses on the travel demand models to estimate the effects of HSR on passenger mobility. In the current scientific literature, the HSR travel demand is commonly segmented into three main components: *diverted* demand from other modes, or from other rail services, to HSR; *induced* demand, which can be direct and indirect; *economy-based* demand growth. The objective of the paper concerns the review of the current scientific literature on HSR travel demand analysis and assessment, by means of existing and methods and models. Thus, the aim is the identification of the existing gaps in the state of the art, in order to identify possible future directions of research. Thereby, the remaining part of the paper is articulated as follows. Section 2 contains some HSR definitions, reported in the main reference documentation of EU and international association. Section 3 is subdivided into two parts: the first part describes the HSR demand variables and the second part describes the main papers reporting case studies of application of passenger travel demand models for HSR. Finally, the research perspectives are discussed in the last section.

This work is aimed to support transport planners and decision-makers in the evaluation of future investment in HSR lines by means of methodological and modelling tools to assess the potential travel demand.

2   HSR Definitions

This section reports the main definitions of HSR existing in the technical literature, which may be classified as definitions based on the characteristics of the railway infrastructure, such as the maximum speed, and definitions based on the characteristics of the railway services, such as the use of the railway infrastructure by the different services.

As far as concerns railway infrastructure, it is necessary to recall the four main advancements regarding the HSR definitions in EU.

EU introduced in 1996 [3] some definitions of HSR associated to the maximum speed that trains could reach while travelling on a specific track segment. According to EU, the term "High Speed Rail" indicates a system "composed of the railway infrastructures comprising lines and fixed installations, of the trans-European transport network, constructed or upgraded to be travelled on at high speeds, and rolling stock designed for travelling on those infrastructures.". The EU Directive 48/1996 established that high speed infrastructure comprises three types of lines:

- "specially built high-speed lines equipped for speeds generally equal to or greater than 250 km/h";
- "specially upgraded high-speed lines equipped for speeds of the order of 200 km/h";
- "specially upgraded high-speed lines which have special features as a result of topographical, relief or town-planning constraints, on which the speed must be adapted to each case."

European Rail Infrastructure Managers in 2008 [4] classified railway lines according to the different demand segments, and infrastructure performances (axle load). Among the identified classes, the characteristics of the following railway networks are reported below (see Table 1):

- High-Speed (HS) passenger network with speeds higher than 250 km/h;
- Conventional High-Speed (CHS) passenger network with speed up to 250 km/h;
- Heavy Freight (HF) network with 100 km/h and up to 35 tons for axle load; and
- High-Speed/Logistical Freight (HS/LF) network with speeds up to 250 km/h.

A strategic vision for the above railway networks at year 2035 has been also proposed; in particular, a maximum speed of 360 km/h was foreseen for the HS network, taking into account the business needs of potential travellers (Table 1).

Table 1. Vision for some railway networks at 2035 [4]

	Railway network	2006/2007		2035	
		Speed (km/h)	Axle load (tons)	Speed (km/h)	Axle load (tons)
Pax	H.S.(*)	300	18	360	18
	C.H.S.(**)	200	20	250	18
Freight	H.F.(−)	100	25	100	Up to 35
	H.S./H.F.(°)	160	20	Up to 250	18

(*)High Speed; (**)Conventional High Speed; (−)HF: Heavy Freight; (°)HS-HF: High Speed-Heavy Freight.

EU directive of European Parliament and of the Council of 11 May 2016 [5] integrated the criteria for identifying HSR lines introduced in [3]:

- specially built high-speed lines equipped for speeds generally equal to or greater than 250 km/h;

- specially upgraded high-speed lines equipped for speeds of the order of 200 km/h;
- specially upgraded high-speed lines which have special features as a result of topographical, relief or town planning constraints, to which the speed must be adapted in each case. This category includes interconnecting lines between high-speed and conventional networks, lines through stations, accesses to terminals, depots, etc. travelled at conventional speed by 'high-speed' rolling stock.

Finally, UIC released a directive in 2018 [1], consistent with the EU standards, where "High speed rail (HSR) encompasses a complex reality involving many technical aspects, such as infrastructure, rolling stock and operations, as well as strategic and cross-sector issues including human, financial, commercial and managerial factors". Moreover, UIC states that "HSR is still a grounded, guided and low grip transport system: it could be considered to be a railway subsystem". The most important change comes from the speed: "HSR means a jump in commercial speed and this is why UIC considers a commercial speed of 250 km/h to be the principal criterion for the definition of HSR.". A secondary criterion is admitted on "average distances without air competition, where it may not be relevant to run at 250 km/h, since a lower speed of 230 or 220 km/h or at least above 200 km/h is enough to catch as many market shares as a collective mode of transport can do."

As far as concerns railway services, Campos et. al., (2009) [6] introduced an economic definition of the HSR service, which is defined as "the relationship of HSR with existing conventional services, and the way in which the use of infrastructure is used". They identified four exploitation models:

1. *exclusive exploitation* model, when a complete separation exists between high speed and conventional services, each one with its own infrastructure (model adopted in Shinkansen technology in Japan);
2. *mixed high-speed* model, when high speed trains run either on specifically built new lines or un upgraded segments of conventional lines (model adopted in TGV technology in France);
3. *mixed conventional* model, where some conventional trains run on high speed lines (model adopted in AVE technology in Spain);
4. *fully mixed conventional* model, where both high speed and conventional services can run (at their corresponding speeds) on each type of infrastructure.

Campos et al. [5] categorized the Italian railway network as "Fully Mixed Conventional", just for the Rome-Florence line. Particular attention has been given to the study of the Southern Italy railway system, with a focus on the experimental studies about the introduction of services using the conventional and HSR networks. A model has recently been proposed in order to analyse the services, defined as "hybrid", which operate on two different networks [7], proposing the formalization of the optimal timetable project model with unchanged infrastructural resources [8].

3 Travel Demand Models

The travel demand models presented in this paper have their theoretical background in Transport Systems Models (TSMs) framework [9–13]. TSMs simulate a transport system through a process, in which transport supply and travel demand interact generating the flows and the performances of the transport system. TSM is composed of three main elements. The transport supply model simulates the utilities of users deriving from the use of transport infrastructures and services; The travel demand model simulates user choices based on the performance of transport infrastructures and services. The supply-demand interaction model simulates the interaction between the user's choices and the performance of the infrastructures and the services.

Travel demand models may be broadly classified into two main approaches: *aggregate* models and *disaggregated* models.

Aggregated models may be segmented into three categories:

- *statistical-descriptive* models which estimate the levels of demand throughout relationships with attributes belonging to the level-of-service and socio-economic class;
- *time series* models which use historical data to forecast demand flows with given characteristics (e.g. origin-destination relationship);
- *partial-share* models, which simulates the user choice method through a procedure of partial sequential choices, or steps; the most common case is constituted by multi-stage models, including trip generation, trip distribution, time choice (arrival/departure), service choice, route/run choice.

Disaggregated models are theoretically and operationally more complex in relation to the difficulty of finding data on user choice behaviour. They can be based on the theory of discrete choice model [9, 14, 15]. The discrete choice model has been specified with different formalization of alternatives and linked perceived utility random utility [9, 14, 15], fuzzy utility [16, 17], or quantum utility [18, 19].

Generally, the random utility models differ according to the perceived utility function, which can be specified by considering different functional relationships between the levels of choice (hierarchical or factorial), different hypotheses on structure of choice set of alternatives, and different hypotheses about the distribution of random residuals. The different hypotheses about the distribution of the random residuals lead to two main categories of models:

- models with choice probabilities expressed in closed form (e.g. multimodal logit, nested logit);
- models with simulated choice probabilities (e.g. probit, mixed logit).

As far as concerns the partial share models, the models associated to the main trip choice dimensions of travellers are reported in the following, according to [9, 11, 12].

The *trip generation* model estimates the number of trips from an origin o, given the purpose and the temporal interval (sh):

$$d(o/sh) = d(\mathbf{x_G}, \beta_G) \qquad (1)$$

where: $\mathbf{x_G}$ is the vector of attributes and β_G is the vector of generation parameters.

The *trip distribution* model estimates the percentage/probability of trips undertaken by travellers to a destination d, given the origin, the purpose and the temporal interval (osh):

$$p(d|osh) = p(\mathbf{X_D}, \beta_D) \qquad (2)$$

where: $\mathbf{X}_D$ is the matrix of attributes and $\boldsymbol{\beta}_D$ is the vector of distribution parameters.

The *mode-service choice* model estimates the transport mode-service m chosen by the travellers given the origin, the purpose, the temporal interval and the destination (oshd):

$$d(m/oshd) = d(\mathbf{x}_M,\ \boldsymbol{\beta}_M) \tag{3}$$

where: $\mathbf{x}_M$ is the vector of attributes and $\boldsymbol{\beta}_G$ is the vector of mode-service parameters.

The *route, or run, choice* model estimates the route, or run, r chosen by travellers given the origin, the purpose, the temporal interval, the destination and the mode-choice (oshdm):

$$d(r/oshdm) = d(\mathbf{x},\ \boldsymbol{\beta}_R) \tag{4}$$

where $\mathbf{x}_R$ is the vector of attributes and $\boldsymbol{\beta}_R$ is the vector of route, or run, parameters.

4   HSR Travel Demand Variables and Models

4.1   Framework of Classes of Demand

The transport demand generated by HSR services is sub-divided in the scientific literature into three classes [20]:

- Diverted demand:

  - from other modes (e.g., car, air, and bus) to HSR, and
  - from other rail services to HSR;

- Induced demand:

  - direct (e.g., changes in trip frequency)
  - indirect (e.g., increase in mobility due to changes in lifestyle and/or land use;

- Economy-based demand growth (Table 2).

Diverted demand is a shift of demand, or diversion, towards HSR services. This diversion may occur either from other modes, as in the case of a shift from airplane/car to HSR services, or from other rail services, as in the case of shift from intercity to HSR services. The diverted demand could depend on several attributes, endogenous to the transport system, such as the location and the number of railway stations, the location of airports, the ticket price, the service frequency.

Existing studies show that entity of diverted demand towards HSR from other modes could be different in relation to HSR in-vehicle travel times. The revealed user behaviours concerning the diversion towards HSR mode-service from air mode show the following elements [1, 21]:

- when HSR travel times are less than 2.5 h, travellers' choices are oriented almost totally to HSR alternative (train is the dominant mode);

Table 2. Classification of demand generated by HSR services [20].

Diverted	From other modes	Shift from air/auto to HSR	Endogenous factor
	From other rail services	Shift from Intercity to HSR	
Induced	Direct	Changes of trip frequency, destination or related activity pattern	
	Indirect	Increase of mobility due to changes in activity patterns and land use	Exogenous factor
Economy-based		Decrease/increase of mobility due to economy trends	

- when HSR travel time is about 3.5 h, travellers' choices are equally distributed between train and air;
- when HSR travel times are higher than 5 h, travellers' prefer air mode.

Induced demand depends on [20]:

- directly on travel behaviour in terms of frequency, destination, or organization of activities, and it is characterized by factors which are endogenous to the transport system,
- indirectly on changes in land use, or in lifestyle of travellers, and it is characterized by factors which are exogenous to the transport system.

Economy-based demand is characterized by national and international economic trends, considering that higher-income users travel more. This component of demand is a function of additional attributes, such as: accessibility and regional equity, and thus of exogenous factors [20].

Some before-after studies present in the literature concern mainly the observation of the diverted demand component. There are fewer cases where the induced component has been explicitly quantified, while in any case the demand generated form the economic growth was reported separately. The studies show, in general, positive effects in the terms of diverted demand towards HSR services both from other modes and from conventional rail services [21–23]. In Italy the opening of HSR line from Turin to Salerno in 2009 generated an increment of railway traffic from 15 million of pax/year in 2009 to 43 million of pax/year in 2018 [24], of which 7 million have been diverted from conventional railway services, 19 million have been diverted from private car, buses, and air modes, and 17 million constitute the component of induced demand.

4.2 Models

This section contains a description of existing publications mainly focusing on models estimating the diverted demand towards HSR, classified according to the country of application of the model.

The selected publications, in some cases, are more general dealing with the presentation of a general framework for estimation of the HSR demand components described in the previous paragraph. As matter of fact, it is worth to recall the study of [25], that defined a general modelling framework for the evaluation of the three components of the HSR travel demand and their reciprocal interactions. The authors further analysed the case of the entering of a new private HSR company in the Italian railway market, that generated a competition between private and public railway companies, and airline companies, on long-distance inter-city trips [26].

The modelling of the HSR diverted demand is treated in several contributions of literature concerning different countries.

In Italy, Cascetta et al., (2011) [27] presented a study of the impacts of the HSR service operating along the Italian Rome-Naples relationship. The authors analysed the diverted demand towards HSR service from other transport modes and from other rail services (e.g., Intercity, Eurostar services). They built a discrete choice model on the dimensions of mode-service-company-run for "home-based trips" and "non-home-based trips" purposes. Cascetta and Coppola (2012) [28] calibrated a discrete choice model on the dimensions of mode-service-run for different travel purposes (e.g., business, and other purposes). The specified model was a multi-level nested logit model, where the different levels were transport modes, rail services, HSR companies and service class. Cascetta E. and Coppola P. (2014) [29] analysed the effects of the entering of a single public HSR operator in the Italian railway market from 2005 to 2012; and the effects of the entering of a second private HSR operator from 2012. The authors developed an integrated modelling system to forecast the effects of competing timetables-services-prices between the HSR and air companies, auto, conventional railway mode-services. Borsati and Albalate (2020) [30] empirically studied the effects of the opening of HSR services in Italy on the total distances travelled by light vehicles along motorways during the period 2001–2017 and the entity of these effects after the opening of on-track competition between two HSR Italian companies.

As far as concerns France, Zembri (2010) [31] provided an empiric study on the rail-air competition between HSR services, called TGV, and air services in France, and on the conditions resulting in the success of HSR service in terms of demand diverted. Behrens and Pels (2012) [32] calibrated a nested (and mixed) multinomial logit models of HSR-air passenger demand traveling along the London-Paris relationship and estimated the direct elasticity of passenger demand with respect to frequency for business and leisure purposes. They considered the competition between a combination of four airports (Heathrow, Gatwick, Luton, London City) and four airline companies (Air France, British Airways, British Midland Airways, EasyJet) and the HSR service operated by Eurostar. Direct and cross elasticities are estimated with respect to travel time, frequency, and fare per each alternative, year, and trip purpose by means of a multinomial logit model.

The Spanish country was studied in some publications. Roman et al. (2009) [33] analysed the extra-urban rail demand, considering the potential competitors to the HSR service, diverted by other modes of transport (air, private car and bus). A nested logit model is specified and calibrated, and the direct and cross elasticities are estimated. Roman and Martin (2014) [34] simulate passenger choices between two transport alternatives: HSR rail and air services. Two models have been specified and calibrated: multinomial logit and mixed logit. Cross elasticity is introduced, but not calculated.

As far as concern China, Cheng (2010) [35] examined the impact of HSR on the intercity transportation market in Taiwan. When HSR entered in operation the generated traffic was mainly diverted from air mode, conventional railway, and buses. It is worth noting that air transportation almost exited the market. Li and Sheng (2016) [36] studied the diverted demand between two choice alternatives, air and HSR, along the Beijing-Guangzhou corridor (China). They conducted a stated preference survey to estimate the parameters of multinomial logit-based discrete choice models. Zhang et al. (2017) [37] used panel data of air passenger demand from 2010 to 2013 to analyse the effects of HSR on the main airlines in China. According to the authors, HSR services had relevant negative impacts on the air demand, as it became much more elastic after the introduction of competing HSR services. Ren et al. (2019) [38] analysed the impact of HSR services on intercity travel behaviour along the Chengdu-Chongqing corridor (China), with a focus on the diverted demand towards HSR services.

In Japan, Yao and Morikawa (2005) [39] specified a multi-level discrete choice model on the dimensions of mode/service/run. The alternatives considered were bus, car, airplane. Clever and Hansen (2008) [40] focused on competition between air and HSR modes in Japan, analysing the trade-offs between accessibility, frequency, and speed of the two services.

Hensher (1997) [41] specified and calibrated a discrete choice model in the dimensions of mode, service and run estimating the diverted demand to HSR from other modes in Australia. The direct and cross elasticities have been introduced and calculated.

5 Final Remarks

The paper deals with travel demand models to estimate the effects of HSR services on the passenger mobility at country level, focusing on the inter-city trips. According to the literature, the HSR travel demand may be segmented into three main components: diverted demand, induced demand, economy-based demand.

Literature studies focused mainly on the development of models for the estimation of the diverted demand towards HSR in the countries where high investments were allocated for the realizations of HSR lines. The proliferation of these publications was mainly due to the attempt of capturing the demand diversion from the air mode, which was the main macroscopic effect in the market generated by the opening of HSR lines.

Publications specifically dealing with models to estimate induced demand are less numerous in the literature. It is worth to recall the publication [29], where trip generation and trip distribution models have been specified and calibrated in order to estimate the demand induced by the activation of HSR service in Italy; and the publication [38], which reports the spatial variations of travel demand through a comparison of trip intensity indices of different origin-destination (OD) pairs in China.

The travel demand generated by the economic growth may be estimated as the result of the specification and application of Spatial Economic Transport Interaction (SETI) modelling frameworks (see [42], and the references included), as in [10], where the authors developed an integrated macro-economic and transport system of models for passenger and freight demand estimation at country level.

In general, from the literature review it emerges that it is possible to associate to each of the three HSR demand components one (or more) partial share model(s) simulating one (or more) trip choice dimension(s), presented in Sect. 3 (see Table 3).

The diverted demand may be estimated by means of mode-service-company-run choice models, presented respectively in Eqs. (3) and (4). The induced demand from changes of trip frequency and trip destination may be estimated by means of trip generation and trip destination models, presented respectively in Eqs. (1) and (2). The estimation of induced demand by the modification of passengers' activity patterns and of land use, and of the demand generated by the economy growth, implies the building of SETI modelling frameworks able to capture the two-way relationship between spatial economic and transport systems (see [42], and the references included).

Future research will concern a more comprehensive and detailed classification of literature on HSR travel demand models according to the HSR demand model characteristics in terms of specified attributes and calibrated parameters.

Table 3. HSR demand components and trip choice dimension models.

HSR demand component	Model	Type
Diverted	Mode-service/route(run)	Travel demand
Induced	Trip generation/distribution	
	Activity generation/location	SETI[*]
Economy-based	Production-consumption generation/location	

[*] Spatial Economic Transport Interaction model, [42]

Acknowledgements. This study was carried out within the MOST – Sustainable Mobility National Research Center and received funding from the European Union Next-Generation EU (PIANO NAZIONALE DI RIPRESA E RESILIENZA (PNRR) – MISSIONE 4 COMPONENTE 2, INVESTIMENTO 1.4 – D.D. 1033 17/06/2022, CN00000023). This manuscript reflects only the authors' views and opinions, neither the European Union nor the European Commission can be considered responsible for them.

References

1. Leboeuf, M.: UIC High Speed advisor, High Speed Rail fast track to sustainable mobility, UIC Passenger Department, pp. 1–76 (2018)
2. UN Homepage (2023). https://www.un.org/sustainabledevelopment/. Accessed 31 Mar 2023
3. European Union: Directive (UE) 96/48/EC of 23 July 1996 on the interoperability of the trans-European high-speed rail system. Off. J. Eur. Communities **L235**(6), 1–3 (1996)
4. EIM: European Railway Technical Strategy Technical Vision to Guide the Development of TSIs. European Rail Infrastructure Manager; German Marshall Fund of the United States, (ed.) German Marshall Fund of the United States: Washington, DC, USA (2008)
5. European Union: Directive (UE) 2016/797 of the European Parliament and of the Council of 11 May 2016 on the interoperability of the rail system within the European Union (recast), L 138/44 (2016)

6. Campos, P., De Rus, G., Barron, J.: A review of HSR experiences around the world. In: De Rus (ed.) The Economic effects of high-speed rail investment. BBVA Foundation, Bilbao, pp. 19–32 (2009). https://econpapers.repec.org/bookchap/fbbreport/2012126.htm. Accessed 3 Jan 2023

7. Di Gangi, M., Russo, F.: Potentiality of rail networks: Integrated services on conventional and high-speed lines. WIT Trans. Built Environ. **213**, 101–112 (2022). https://doi.org/10.2495/cr220091

8. Di Gangi, M., Russo, F.: Design of hybrid rail services on conventional and high-speed lines. International Journal of Transport Development and Integration (2023)

9. Ben-Akiva, M., Lerman, S.R.: Discrete choice analysis: theory and application to travel demand, p. 1984. MIT Press Series in Transportation Studies, Cambridge (1984)

10. Cascetta E., Biggiero L., Nuzzolo A., Russo F.: Passenger and freight demand models for the Italian transportation system. In: Proceedings of the 7th World Transport Research. Volume 2: Modelling Transport Systems (1996)

11. Ortuzar, J., Willumsen, L.G.: Modelling transport (Third Edition), John Wiley and Sons, Chichester (2001)

12. Cascetta E.: Transportation Systems Analysis, models and application. Springer Optimization and its Application. Springer, NY (2009). https://doi.org/10.1007/978-0-387-75857-2

13. Cascetta E., Nuzzolo A., Biggiero L., Russo, F.: Passenger and freight demand models for the Italian transportation system. In: Proceedings of 7th World Conference on Transport Research, vol. 2 (1995)

14. Manski C.F., McFadden D.: Alternative estimators and sample designs for discrete choice analysis (1981)

15. Train K.: Discrete choice methods with simulation, 2nd ed.Cambridge University Press: Cambridge; NY, USA (2009); ISBN 978–0–521–76655–5 (2009)

16. Russo, F.: Fuzzy theory in transportation field: fuzzy sets for simulating path choice behaviour. In: Advances in Intelligent Systems, pp. 279–283 (1997)

17. Quattrone, A., Vitetta, A.: Random and fuzzy utility models for road route choice. Transp. Res. Part E Logistic Transp. Rev. **2011**(47), 1126–1139 (2001)

18. Vitetta, A.: Quantum utility model for route choice in transport systems. Travel Behav. Soc. **2016**(3), 29–37 (2016)

19. Di Gangi, M., Vitetta, A.: Quantum utility and random utility model for path choice modelling: specification and aggregate calibration from traffic counts. J. Choice Model. **2021**(40), 100290 (2021)

20. Cascetta, E., e Coppola, P.: High speed rail (HSR) induced demand models. Procedia- Soc. Behav. Sci. **111**, 147–156 (2014)

21. Givoni, M., e Dobruszkes, F.: A review of ex-post evidence for mode substitution and induced demand following the introduction of high-speed rail. Transp. Rev. **33**(6), 720–742 (2013)

22. Givoni, M.: Development and impact of the modern high-speed train: a review. Transp. Rev. **26**(5), 593–611 (2006)

23. Beria, P., Grimaldi, R., Albalate, D., Bel, G.: Delusions of success: costs and demand of high-speed rail in Italy and Spain. Transp. Policy **68**, 63–79 (2018)

24. Cascetta, E., Coppola, P.: Evidence from the Italian high speed rail market Competition between modes and between HSR operators. High-Speed Rail and Sustainability: Decision-Making and the Political Economy of Investment, pp. 66–79 (2017)

25. Russo, F.: Which high-speed rail? LARG approach between plan and design. Future-Transp. **1**, 202–226 (2021). https://doi.org/10.3390/futuretransp1020013

26. Ben-Akiva M., Cascetta E., Coppola P., Papola P., Velardi V.: High speed rail demand forecasting in a competitive market: the Italian case study, pp. 1–9 (2009)

27. Cascetta, E., Papola, A., Pagliara, F., Marzano, V.: Analysis of mobility impacts of the high-speed Rome-Naples rail link using within-day dynamic mode-service choice models. J. Transp. Geogr. **19**, 635–643 (2011)

28. Cascetta, E., Coppola, P.: An elastic demand schedule-based multimodal assignment model for the simulation of high-speed rail (HSR) systems. Assoc. Eur. Oper. Res. Soc. **2012**(1), 3–27 (2012)
29. Cascetta, E., e Coppola, P.: Competition on fast track: an analysis of the first competitive market for HSR services. Procedia - Soc. Behav. Sci. **111**, pp. 176–185 (2014)
30. Borsati, M., Albalate, D.: On the modal shift from motorway to high-speed rail: evidence from Italy. Transp. Res. Part A **137**, 145–164 (2020)
31. Zembri, P.: New objectives of the French high-speed rail system within the framework of a highly centralized network: a substitute for the domestic air transport market? ERSA Annual Conference, NECTAR, pp. 1–17 (2010)
32. Behrens, C., Pels, E.: Intermodal competition in the London-Paris passenger market: high-speed rail and air transport. J. Urban Econom. **71**(3), 278–288 (2012)
33. Roman, C., Espino, R., Martin, J.C.: Analysing competition between the high speed train and alternative modes. The case of the Madrid-Zaragoza-Barcelona Corridor. J. Choice Model. **3**(1), 84–108 (2009)
34. Roman, C., Martin, J.C.: Integration of HSR and air transport: understanding passengers' preferences. Transp. Res. Part E: Logistics and Transp. Rev. **71**, 129–141 (2014)
35. Cheng, Y.-H.: High-speed rail in Taiwan: new experience and issues for future development. Transp. Policy **17**(2), 51–63 (2010)
36. Li Z.-C., e Sheng, D.: Forecasting passenger travel demand for air and high-speed rail integration service: a case study of Beijing-Guangzhou corridor, China. Transport. Res. Part A, **94**, 397–410 (2016)
37. Zhang, Q., Yang, H., Wang, Q.: Impact of high-speed rail on China's big three airlines. Transp. Res. Part A **98**, 77–85 (2017)
38. Ren, X., et al.: Impact of high-speed rail on intercity travel behavior change: the evidence from the Chengdu-Chongqing passenger dedicated line. J. Transp. Land Use **12–1**, 265–285 (2019)
39. Yao, E., Morikawa, T.: A study of on integrated intercity travel demand model. Transp. Res. Part A: Policy. Pract. **39**(4), 367–381 (2005). https://doi.org/10.1016/j.tra.2004.12.003
40. Clever, R., Hansen, M.: Interaction of air and high-speed rail in Japan. Transp. Res. Rec. **2043**, 1–12 (2008)
41. Hensher, D.A.: A practical approach to identifying the marker potential for high-speed rail: a case study in the Sydney-Canberra corridor. Transp. Res. **31–6**, 431–446 (1997)
42. Russo, F., Musolino, G.: A unifying modelling framework to simulate the spatial economic transport interaction process at urban and national scales. J. Transp. Geogr. **24**, 189–197 (2012)

Open Access This chapter is licensed under the terms of the Creative Commons Attribution 4.0 International License (http://creativecommons.org/licenses/by/4.0/), which permits use, sharing, adaptation, distribution and reproduction in any medium or format, as long as you give appropriate credit to the original author(s) and the source, provide a link to the Creative Commons license and indicate if changes were made.

The images or other third party material in this chapter are included in the chapter's Creative Commons license, unless indicated otherwise in a credit line to the material. If material is not included in the chapter's Creative Commons license and your intended use is not permitted by statutory regulation or exceeds the permitted use, you will need to obtain permission directly from the copyright holder.

Methodologies for Sustainable Development of TEN-T/RFC Corridors and Core Ports: Settlement Capacity of Industrial Firms in Port Related Areas

Francesco Russo[1]($\boxtimes$) [iD], Giovanna Chilà[2], and Clara Zito[3]

[1] DIIES Reggio Calabria University, Feo di Vito, 80125 Reggio Calabria, Italy
francesco.russo@unirc.it
[2] Department of Public Works Municipality of Motta San Giovanni, Motta San Giovanni, RC, Italy
[3] Reggio Calabria, Italy

Abstract. The issue of industrial areas with specific rules and incentives, identified as Special Economic Zones has become increasingly important for undeveloped European regions. On a world level, the SEZs have allowed the significant development of the territories concerned. The main experiences are in the area of ports. It is possible to model some main developments that the SEZ can achieve on the basis of international results. It is modeled the maximum potential increase in employment due to the establishment of a SEZ, subject to land constraints. A test case is proposed referring to the TEN-T core node of Gioia Tauro in the Southern of Italy.

Keywords: Sustainable Ports · Smart Ports · TEN-T · Special Economic Zone · Port of the future · Network in SEZ · Land constraints

1 Introduction

The industrial areas with specific rules and incentives identified as SEZs, are the fundamental elements of the development of ports and allows their future development. The ports supplying goods to these industrial areas, constitute the decisive element for the development of the SEZs. In a general view, with SEZ, it is possible identify the special industrial zone around the port if it is of a third-generation port following UNCTAD indications [1, 2]. In this case the literature reports different studies relative to the economic impacts [3–11].

In the world there are about 4000 SEZs (special economic zone), with the aim of attracting foreign investment through measures such as incentives, tax breaks and regulatory derogations. The best-known examples are those in China and in Dubai; in Europe there are about 90, 14 of which are established in Poland [12–14].

C. Zito—Free Lance Researcher.

© The Author(s) 2023
O. Gervasi et al. (Eds.): ICCSA 2023 Workshops, LNCS 14110, pp. 539–550, 2023.
https://doi.org/10.1007/978-3-031-37123-3_37

The impacts resulting from the establishment of SEZs can be assessed against the three declinations of sustainability in relation to the Agenda 2030 [15]: economic, social and environmental.

Economic sustainability is measurable in terms of an increase in: exports employment and foreign investment.

Social sustainability of the SEZ mainly concern: safety, security, participation, raising working standards; development of human resources with retraining of the workforce and the growth of skills through training.

Environmental sustainability impacts of the SEZ mainly concern: the environmental standards achievable by providing companies with infrastructures and services specifically designed, with the awareness of having to pursue effective management of the environment.

One of the main objectives of the SEZ is the increase in exports: a decisive tool for this objective is to reduce the times to carry out an export, in order to make companies that locate plants in the SEZ competitive. In 2013, the World Bank presented the document "Doing Business 2014", in which it is indicated as essential for the export of a country: the time to carry out an export [16]. This time is divided into: time for preparing documents, time for handling in ports, time for customs. In 2014, the Presidency of the Italian Council, deepening the World Bank document, presented the study "Study initiative on Italian ports" [17], in which the average times for export from different European countries competing on the same markets are compared, obtaining: 19 days for Italy; 9 days for Germany and Belgium; 7 days for Holland.

It is important to study a SEZ area which is directly connected with a port belonging to the main European network. The ports to be studied are those that belong both to the strategic transport infrastructure network, defined as the Trans-European Transport Network (TEN-T), and to the operational and tactical network of freight services, defined as the Rail Freight Corridor (RFC) [18, 19].The development of a SEZ directly connected with a port of the TEN-T network requires that the port has a very high level of ICT and therefore has smart port characteristics, in line with what is defined by the EU for smart cities, ie an integrated presence of ICT, transport and energy [20–22].

The objective of this note is to recall a general system of models that allows to estimate ex ante, starting from input variables, the potentially reliable results with the establishment of the SEZ, and to specify a model that gives the maximum settlement of firms given the land constraints.

Considering the overall model system, it is necessary to move from the model that assesses the potential offered by the presence of available areas within the SEZ, to the model that allows to effectively define which companies can set up and what characteristics they can have. On the one hand it is necessary to study what territorial constraints there are (model already present in the literature), on the other it is necessary to verify which companies can set up. That is, even if the model of territorial constraints shows that there are areas, it is not known if these are suitable for companies, and therefore which companies, given the free areas, can settle. In this way, Sect. 2 presents the overall system of models that can be implemented to estimate the results obtainable from a SEZ and specifies the model estimating the number and type of equivalent companies that can establish themselves, and/or can be the subject of an expansion if already established, in the industrial agglomerations considered following the establishment of the SEZ. A case study is proposed in Sect. 3. The area considered is that of Calabria (Southern Italy) and the SEZ is the one that refers to the intercontinental TEN-T port of Gioia Tauro and the other national ports linked.

2 The Proposed System of Models

2.1 The Considered System of Models

A general system of models is proposed that constitutes an advanced framework from a first proposal given by the authors [23]. The system of models gives as final results the estimates of the expected impacts of the establishment of a SEZ.

The general framework (Fig. 1) includes:

- Aggregated direct impacts;
- Land capacity constraint;
- Economic - functional integration;
- Settlement of firms;
- Incentives;
- Aggregated indirect and induced impacts.

According to an aggregated approach, the proposed general framework allows, on the basis of literature data and of specific database related to the different applications, an estimate of the impacts deriving from the establishment of the SEZ [24].

The impacts must be verified in relation to the constraints deriving from the surface availability and the socio-economic characteristics of the areas analyzed in the Land Capacity Constraint Model, with a disaggregated approach [23].

After having acquired the theoretical surface of the necessary areas, two modeling paths must be developed in parallel. In the first path, the number and type of industries that can establish themselves must be modeled in a disaggregated form, verifying, the surfaces available in each locality where a part of the SEZ is located.

The territorial impacts on material and immaterial components have been studied [25–28]. The feasibility of the hypotheses with respect to possible settlements and upgrades of companies, based on the available surfaces is verified with the settlement of industries model, that is proposed in this note.

In the second path, the integration between the different parts into which a SEZ is divided must be verified, considering the attributes of time and cost and therefore the active and passive accessibility of each part.

Once the results from the two paths have been obtained, if both are accepted independently, it can be move on to the final phase which is given by the study of the quantity of employed generated by SEZ. Leaving from the quantity of direct employees estimated in the aggregated impact model, both the quantity of employees in indirect activities and the quantity of employees in induced activities are therefore studied in the aggregated indirect and induced impacts model [29, 30].

The overall structure of the model thus proposed can be implemented in any other SEC, and in particular in those which present the complexity of being divided into different parts.

542   F. Russo et al.

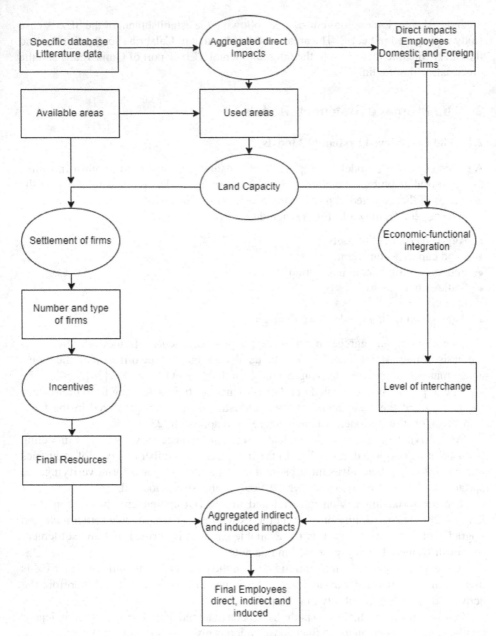

Fig. 1. System of models for SEZ in TEN-T core port

2.2 Land Capacity Constraint Model

In this section, the land capacity constraint model is recalled [23].

The impacts of the SEZ must be estimated by considering a reference decade from year 1 to year 10, considering the characteristic variables measured in the base year of activation of the SEZ indicated with year 0.

The model estimates the increase in employment at each industrial site.

It has the following formulation:

$$\Delta Emp_{SEZ\_Total\_1,10} = \Sigma_i \Delta Emp_{Ai-1,10} = \Sigma_i d_i \cdot \Delta S_{Ai\_1,10} \tag{1}$$

with

- $\Delta Emp_{SEZ\_Total\text{-}1, 10}$ total change in the number of employees;
- $\Delta Emp_{Ai\text{-}1,10}$ change in the number of employees in the single agglomeration A_i in the decade considered;
- $\Delta S_{Ai\_1,10}$ change in the area occupied by new holdings in the individual agglomeration A_i in the decade considered, respect to the base year
- d_i density of employees in the single agglomeration A_i estimated on the basis of the current values recorded in the areas considered in the SEZs.

Compared to the change in the area occupied by holdings in the individual agglomeration A_i, model estimates must be made knowing the area of the SEZ areas that are free and therefore the ones potentially available for the establishment of new companies.

An analysis of the areas in the SEZ is carried out, identifying those free from industrial plants and therefore potentially available for new settlements. For these areas, different development scenarios are hypothesized:

- low, an increase in the occupied area of 50% of the free area is expected compared to the value of year 0;
- high, it is expected an increase in the occupied area equal to 100% of the free area compared to the value of the year zero.

Equation 1 gives as outputs the reference information.

It is also necessary to consider two other elements, in addition to completely free areas: areas to be regenerated, and better use of areas already occupied. The result of the model must then be compared with the result of the aggregate impact model.

The surface already occupied and affected by regeneration is indicated by

$$\Delta^r S_{Ai\_0}$$

The increase in use with the inclusion of new employees in companies already operating can be considered in the model expressed by Eq. 1, multiplying the d:

$$\Delta d = d_{rif} - d_{act}$$

with

d_{rif}: reference density in the scenario considered

d_{rif}: current density of operating enterprises increasing production and labor requirements.

2.3 Settlement of Firms' Model

"Settlement of firms" model estimates the number and type of companies that can establish themselves, and/or can be the subject of an expansion if already established, in the industrial agglomerations considered following the establishment of the SEZ.

The estimate was obtained on the basis of the results obtained from the application of Land Model, which concerns the potential increase in employees according to the surface still available in the industrial agglomerations concerned. It can be considered four holding classes, combining:

- two classes of occupation of free surfaces,
- two classes of density of employees.

Considering the constraints relating to the available surfaces deriving Land Capacity model, as regards the variation of the free surface, it can be considered the 2 classes of possible developments are:

- low, an increase in the occupied area of 50% of the free area is expected compared to the value of year 0;
- high, it is expected an increase in the occupied area equal to 100% of the free area compared to the value of the year zero.

3 The Study Case of SEZ in Gioia Tauro Port

3.1 Land Capacity Model

The area considered in the study is that of Calabria Region where the first Italian SEZ have been proposed [31–36]. The SEZ is the one that refers to the intercontinental TEN-T [18, 19] port of Gioia Tauro and the other national ports and airport located in the region. The Gioia Tauro SEZ is directly connected to the port. The port of Gioia belongs both to the strategic infrastructural network, in particular to the TEN-T 5 corridor, and to the freight services network, in particular to the RFC 3. It is the southernmost port of the Italian peninsula (Fig. 2). In the last 10 years it has always been in the top three positions among container ports in the Mediterranean and among the top 5 at European level.

To implement the model specific characteristics of Calabria region interesting the port, have been considered.

The Land capacity model makes it possible to verify whether the increase in employment can be constrained by the availability of areas, or if the areas are in excess of potential development.

In this phase, it is assumed from the model that the density is homogeneous for all areas and that, in the reference decade, it can assume two possible scenario values:

- $d_1 = 10$ emp/ha, on the establishment of medium-sized enterprises;
- $d_2 = 20$ emp/ha, on the establishment of large enterprises.

The change in the area occupied by holdings in the individual agglomeration has been estimated compared to the base year $Y = 0$.

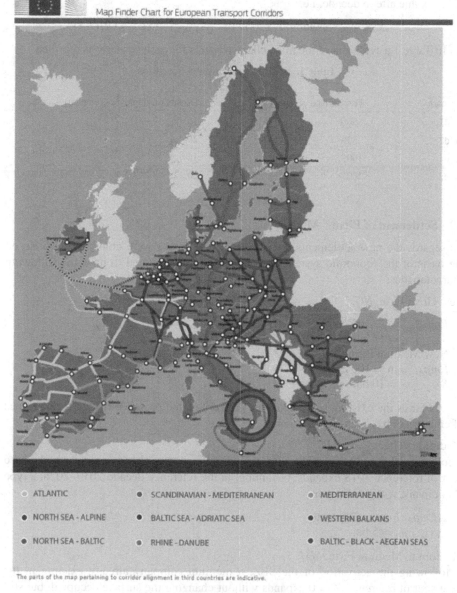

Fig. 2. TEN-T core port of Gioia Tauro

Two possible trend developments were considered:

- low, increase of occupied area equal to 50% of the free area compared to the $Y = 0$ value after a decade, i.e.

$$\Delta S_{Ai\_1,10} = 0,50 \cdot (\Sigma_i\ S_{Ai\_0\_AIL})(SCENARIO\ B);$$

- high, increase in the occupied area equal to 100% of the free area compared to the Y $= 0$ value after a decade, i.e.

$$\Delta S_{Ai\_1,10} variation = 1,00 \cdot (\Sigma_i\ S_{Ai\_0\_AIL})(SCENARIO\ A).$$

In Table 1 a synthesis of the main characteristics for each scenario is reported.

Table 1. Synthesis of different Scenarios

Scenario	Free surface occupation	Density of employees (emp/ha)
B_d1	50%	10
B_d2	50%	20
A_d1	100%	10
A_d2	100%	20

3.2 Settlement of Firms' Models

As regards the new settlements, two types of enterprises were considered which, on the basis of the economic system of Calabria, can be assumed to have the following characteristics:

New Great Firm, NG

- $Emp_{Ai-1,10}n = 300$ emp.;
- $S_{Ai\_1,1,10} = 15$ ha;
  New Medium Firm, NM
- $Emp_{Ai-1,10}n = 100$ emp.;
- $S_{Ai\_1,1,10} = 10$ ha.

As far as the existing settlements are concerned, the presence of two further types of enterprises has been hypothesized:

Medium to Great Firm, MG
if following the activation of the SEZ, a medium company already existing in the base year of reference 2018 expands, becoming, in the reference decade 2019–2028, a type G company, with consequent

- $\Delta Emp_{Ai-1,10}n = 200$ emp.;
- $\Delta S_{Ai\_1,10,} = 5$ ha;

Medium to Medium Firm, MM
if following the activation of the SEZ, a medium company already existing in the base year of reference $Y = 0$ expands without changing the surface occupied, but still undergoing an increase in employees in the reference decade 1–10.

Considering the constraints relating to the available surfaces deriving from Land Capacity model, the hypotheses reported in Table 2 are considered. The hypotheses refer to Land Capacity as regards the variation of the free surface, which envisaged 2 possible developments:

- low, an increase in the occupied area of 50% of the free area is expected compared to the Y $= 0$ value, i.e. $\Delta S_{Ai\_1,10,} = 0,50 \cdot (\Sigma_i\ S_{Ai\_0\_AIL})$ (SCENARIO B);

- high, an increase in the occupied area is expected equal to 100% of the free area compared to the $Y = 0$ value, i.e. $\Delta S_{Ai\_1,10} = 0{,}50 \cdot (\Sigma_i\ S_{Ai\_0\_AIL})$ *(SCENARIO A)*.

The assumptions relating to density, d_1 and d_2, considered in Land Capacity model, are considered through the two types of firms NM/MM and NG/MG, since the first is characterized by a density of type d1 and the second is characterized by a density of type d2.

In Land Model it was assumed that the actual available surface can be considered double the current one.

In this case, the hypotheses relating to the establishment of businesses are those shown in Table 3.

Table 2. Scenario Settlement of firms SEZ (estimated area available in the base year)

		Class of Firm			Total
		NG	NM	MG	
Scenario B	Num of Firms	3	1	2	
	$\Delta Emp_{SEZ\_Calabria}$	900	100	400	1.400
	$\Delta S_{Ai-1,10}$	45	10	10	65
Scenario A	Num of Firms	6	3	4	
	$\Delta Emp_{SEZ\_Calabria}$	1.800	300	800	2.900
	$\Delta S_{Ai-10,10}$(ha)	90	30	20	140

As far as *MM*-type enterprises are concerned, the expansion of 40 existing enterprises is assumed, with an increase in total employees of 1,400 in the ten-year period 2019–2028.

Table 3. Scenario Settlement of firms SEZ (enhanced available area estimates)

		Class of Firm			Total
		NG	NM	MG	
Scenario B	Num of Firms	6	3	4	
	$\Delta Emp_{SEZ\_Calabria}$	1.800	300	800	2.900
	$\Delta S_{Ai-1,10}$	90	30	20	140
Scenario A	Num of Firms	12	6	8	
	$\Delta Emp_{SEZ\_Calabria}$	3.600	600	1.600	5.800
	$\Delta S_{Ai-1,10}$(ha)	180	60	40	280

4 Conclusions

The model "Settlement of firms" refers to the employment in the industrial agglomerations included in the SEZ with assumptions on businesses, evaluated on the basis of the economic context of Calabria.

The establishment of firms is studied considering discrete alternatives. The process followed is of the what if type, analyzing the results achieved for each configuration.

The model provides a result wholly consistent with the results deriving from aggregated impacts models and land constrained model 2, considering the establishment of 12 businesses of type *NG*, 6 of type *NM* and 8 of type *MG* (expansion from type M to type G), as well as the upgrading of *MM* enterprises (existing M-type enterprises to be upgraded. The development of the work can be carried out both with respect to the other SEZs proposed in EU and in Italy directly linked to TEN-T/RFC corridors, and with respect to specific product sectors within the SEZs.

The model discussed in the paper, placed in the context of the modeling system reported in Sect. 2.1, is useful for planners at national and regional level and for port authority technicians. The model is also useful for researchers in fields related to the economic development of ports.

The proposed work can be developed considering different modifications of the occupation density and different modifications of the surface commitment.

Acknowledgement. This study was carried out within the MOST – Sustainable Mobility National Research Center and received funding from the European Union Next-Generation EU (PIANO NAZIONALE DI RIPRESA E RESILIENZA (PNRR) – MISSIONE 4 COMPONENTE 2, INVESTIMENTO 1.4 – D.D. 1033 17/06/2022, CN00000023).

This manuscript reflects only the authors' views and opinions, neither the European Union nor the European Commission can be considered responsible for them.

References

1. UNCTAD: Port Marketing and the challenge of the Third Generation Port. Geneva, Switzerland: Trade and Development Board Committee on Shipping ad hoc Inter-government Group of Port Experts (1994)
2. Russo, F., Musolino, G.: Quantitative characteristics for port generations: the Italian case study. Int. J. Transp. Dev. Integr. 4(2), 103–112 (2020). https://doi.org/10.2495/TDI-V4-N2-103-112
3. Mateo-Mantecón, I., Coto-Millán, P., Villaverde-Castro, J., Pesquera-González, M.Á.: Economic impact of a port on the hinterland: application to Santander's port. Int. J. Shipping Transp. Logist. 4(3), 235–249 (2012)
4. Coronado, D., Acosta, M., Cerbán, M.d.M., López, M.d.P.: Economic Impact of the Container Traffic at the Port of Algeciras Bay. Springer, Heidelberg (2006). https://doi.org/10.1007/3-540-36789-6
5. Coppens, F., et al.: Economic impact of port activity: a disaggregate analysis. In: The Case of Antwerp. Working Paper Document n° 110. National Bank of Belgium (2007)
6. Musolino, G., Chilà, G.: Structural factors for a third-generation port: planning general logistics interventions in Gioia Tauro. WIT Trans. Built. Environ. (2021)
7. Musolino, G., Trecozzi, M.R.: Structural factors for a third-generation port: planning interventions for agri-food logistics in Gioia Tauro. WIT Trans. Built. Environ. (2021)
8. Musolino, G., Cartisano, A., Fortugno, G.: Structural factors for a third-generation port: planning interventions for mechanical logistics in Gioia Tauro. WIT Trans. Built. Environ. (2021)

9. Russo, F., Rindone, C.: Structural factors for of a third-generation port: planning interventions for research and development in Gioia Tauro TENT-T node. WIT Trans. Built. Environ. **204**, 67–78 (2021)

10. Russo, F., Panuccio, P., Rindone, C.: Structural factors for a third-generation port: between hinterland regeneration and smart town in Gioia Tauro. WIT Trans. Built. Environ. **204**, 79–90 (2021)

11. Russo, F., Chilà, G.: Structural factors for of a third-generation port: actions and measures for Gioia Tauro in the regional transport plan. WIT Trans. Built. Environ. **204**, 17–30 (2021)

12. Leong, C.K.: Special economic zones and growth in China and India: an empirical investigation. Int. Econ. Policy **10**, 549–567 (2013). Springer

13. Wang, J.: The economic impact of special economic zones: evidence from Chinese municipalitie. J. Dev. Econ. **101**(2013), 133–147 (2013)

14. Fias: Special economic zones. Performance, lessons learned, and implications for zone development, The World Bank Group (2008)

15. United Nation. UN. Sustainable Development Goals (SDG) (2015). https://sdgs.un.org/goals. Accessed 7 Jan 2023

16. Business, D.: Data Notes. World Bank, Washington, DC (2012)

17. Presidenza del Consiglio. https://ptp.porttechnologylivorno.it/wp-content/uploads/2020/08/Rapporto_portualitx_finale_2014.pdf

18. Regolamento (UE) n. 1315/2013 del Parlamento europeo e del Consiglio, dell'11 dicembre 2013, sugli orientamenti dell'Unione per lo sviluppo della rete transeuropea dei trasporti e che abroga la decisione n. 661/2010/UE. Testo rilevante ai fini del SEE (GU L 348 del 20 dicembre 2013)

19. Regolamento (UE) n. 1316/2013 del Parlamento europeo e del Consiglio, dell'11 dicembre 2013, che istituisce il meccanismo per collegare l'Europa e che modifica il regolamento (UE) n. 913/2010 e che abroga i regolamenti (CE) n. 680/2007 e (CE) n. 67/2010. Testo rilevante ai fini del SEE. (GU L 348 del 20 dicembre 2013), pp. 129–171

20. EC, European Commission, Communication from the Commission Smart Cities and Communities European Innovation Partnership (2012). https://ec.europa.eu/transparency/documents-register/detail?ref=C(2012)4701&lang=en. Accessed 7 Jan 2023

21. European Commission. EC. Strategic Implementation Plan (SIP) (2013). https://smart-cities-marketplace.ec.europa.eu/media/2261. Accessed 7 Jan 2023

22. European Commission. EC. Operational Implementation Plan (OIP): First Public Draft (2014). https://smartcities.at/wp-content/uploads/sites/3/operational-implementation-plan-oip-v2-en2.pdf. Accessed 7 Jan 2023

23. Russo, F., Chilà, G., Zito, C.: Strategic planning for special economic zones to ports of the future: system of models and test case. In: Gervasi, O., Murgante, B., Misra, S., Rocha, A.M.A.C., Garau, C. (eds.) ICCSA 2022. LNCS, vol. 13381, pp. 173–184. Springer, Cham (2022). ISBN 978-3-031-10547-0, https://doi.org/10.1007/978-3-031-10548-7_13

24. Musolino, G., Cartisano, A., Fortugno, G.: Special economic zones planning for sustainable ports: aggregate economic impact of port of Gioia Tauro. In: Gervasi, O., Murgante, B., Misra, S., Rocha, A.M.A.C., Garau, C. (eds.) ICCSA 2022. LNCS, vol. 13381, pp. 60–71. Springer, Cham (2022). ISBN 978-3-031-10547-0, https://doi.org/10.1007/978-3-031-10548-7_5

25. Musolino, G., Cartisano, A., Chilà, G., Fortugno, G., Trecozzi, M.R.: Evaluation of structural factors in a third-generation port: methods and applications. Int. J. Transp. Dev. Integr. **6**(4), 347–362 (2022)

26. Musolino, D.A., Panuccio, P.: Special economic zones planning for sustainable ports: the test case of territorial attractiveness and urban planning in Calabria region. In: Gervasi, O., Murgante, B., Misra, S., Rocha, A.M.A.C., Garau, C. (eds.) ICCSA 2022. LNCS, vol. 13381, pp. 72–84. Springer, Cham (2022). ISBN 978-3-031-10547-0, https://doi.org/10.1007/978-3-031-10548-7_6

27. Rindone, C., Cirianni, F.M.M., Delfino, G., Croce, A.I.: Special economic zones planning for sustainable ports: the role of research and training in the Calabria region. In: Gervasi, O., Murgante, B., Misra, S., Rocha, A.M.A.C., Garau, C. (eds.) ICCSA 2022. LNCS, vol. 13381, pp. 85–97. Springer, Cham (2022). ISBN 978-3-031-10547-0, https://doi.org/10.1007/978-3-031-10548-7_7

28. Pellicanò, D.S., Trecozzi, M.R.: Special economic zones planning for sustainable ports: general approach for administrative simplifications and a test case. In: Gervasi, O., Murgante, B., Misra, S., Rocha, A.M.A.C., Garau, C. (eds.) ICCSA 2022. LNCS, vol. 13381, pp. 47–59. Springer, Cham (2022). ISBN 978-3-031-10547-0, https://doi.org/10.1007/978-3-031-10548-7_4

29. Kochelman, K.M., Ling, J., Zhao, Y., Ruiz-Juri, N.: Tracking land use, transport and industrial production using random utility-based multiregional input–output models: application for Texas trade. J. Transp. Geogr. **13**(3), 275–286 (2005)

30. Russo, F., Musolino, G.: A unifying modelling framework to simulate the spatial economic transport interaction process at urban and national scales. J. Transp. Geogr. **24**, 189–197 (2012)

31. Piano Regionale dei Trasporti: Regione Calabria, adottato, nella sua proposta finale, con DGR n. 503 del 06/12/2016, approvato con DCR n.157 del 19/12/2016 e valutato positivamente dalla Commissione UE, Direzione Generale Politica Regionale e Urbana come comunicato con nota n.1086324 del 01/03/2017 (2016)

32. Pirro, F.: L'industria in Calabria. Un profilo di sintesi. STM-MIT (2017)

33. Banca d' Italia: Economieregionali L'economia della Calabria Aggiornamento congiunturale (2017)

34. Decreto Legge n. 91 del 20 giugno 2017 Disposizioni urgenti per la crescita economica nel Mezzogiorno convertito in legge il 1° agosto 2017

35. DGR. n. 294 del 11/08/2015 Misurestraordinarie per lo sviluppo dell'area di Gioia Tauro DDL per l'istituzione di una Zona Economica Speciale

36. Deliberazione n. 52/2015 Misure straordinarie per lo sviluppo dell'Area di Gioia Tauro - DDL per l'istituzione di una zona economica speciale

Open Access This chapter is licensed under the terms of the Creative Commons Attribution 4.0 International License (http://creativecommons.org/licenses/by/4.0/), which permits use, sharing, adaptation, distribution and reproduction in any medium or format, as long as you give appropriate credit to the original author(s) and the source, provide a link to the Creative Commons license and indicate if changes were made.

The images or other third party material in this chapter are included in the chapter's Creative Commons license, unless indicated otherwise in a credit line to the material. If material is not included in the chapter's Creative Commons license and your intended use is not permitted by statutory regulation or exceeds the permitted use, you will need to obtain permission directly from the copyright holder.

Methodologies for Sustainable Development of TEN-T/RFC Corridors and Core Ports: Estimation of Time-Series Economic Impact

Giuseppe Musolino[1] (✉) (iD), Antonio Cartisano[2], and Giuseppe Fortugno[3]

[1] DIIES, Università Mediterranea di Reggio Calabria, 89100 Reggio Calabria, Italy
giuseppe.musolino@unirc.it
[2] Reggio Calabria, Italy
[3] Italferr S.P.A., Rome, Italy

Abstract. The container revolution in the last decades of the 20th century determined the arise of container ports. They further evolved in the so-called third-generation ports, becoming generators of value added due to the manipulation of goods in transit. The increase of value added in third-generation ports is amplified in core ports connected to TEN-T/RFC corridors, where Special Economic Zones (SEZs) and the three pillars of smartness (ICT, Transport and Energy) are present. The paper deals with time-series models for the estimation of economic impact of a SEZ in an underdeveloped region of EU. The test case is the Calabria region (Italy). SEZ in Calabria has its fulcrum in the industrial area close to the transhipment hub port of Gioia Tauro. The economic impacts of the SEZ were quantified through two variables: exports and employment of industrial firms settled in Calabria. The comparison of two scenarios (Do-Nothing scenario and SEZ) shows relevant positive impacts in the SEZ one. Future developments concern the calibration and validation of multi-variate time-series models from observations provided by worldwide SEZs.

Keywords: sustainable ports · smart ports · TEN-T corridors · RFC corridors · special economic zone · time-series · economic impact · port of Gioia Tauro

1 Introduction

Commercial ports may be classified according to the generation criterion (see [1–3]; and the references included). According to the literature, a third-generation port is a container port, where added value of the goods in transit may be incremented due to the manipulations of freight. Therefore, given a port a and a port b, a port b is more competitive than a port a, if it is verified the following equation:

added value in port b > added value in port a

Third-generation ports have been studied in the scientific literature, both in terms of physical components, such as transport and logistic infrastructures [4]; and in terms of intangible components, such as the research infrastructures of firms, universities and

© The Author(s) 2023
O. Gervasi et al. (Eds.): ICCSA 2023 Workshops, LNCS 14110, pp. 551–562, 2023.
https://doi.org/10.1007/978-3-031-37123-3_38

research centres [5]. A large container hub port belonging to the third-generation and located in an underdeveloped EU region was extensively studied by identifying the limits, the weaknesses and the measures to be implemented to increase value added in a third-generation port [6, 7]. The relationship with the hinterland and, in particular, with the research centres were studied in [8]. The main industrial sectors, such as logistics, mechanics and agri-food, connected to a third-generation port were analysed respectively in [9–11].

Special Economic Zones (SEZs) are one of the measures able to allow the increasing of added value in a third-generation port. In particular, recent studies analysed the effects of the activation of a SEZ in terms of territorial attractiveness [12], aggregate and disaggregate economic impacts [13, 14]. The role of higher education and research and the effects of administrative simplifications for SEZ development are analysed respectively in [15] and [16]. The generation of added value may be further amplified in core ports which are connected to a TEN-T and RFC corridor and where the three pillars of smartness, ICT, Transport and Energy, are present [17].

A recent study [18] reports a comparison of export-import times of goods in countries having similar technical-administrative structures and belonging to the EU area. These countries present high variances in export times of freight in relation to an average value of ten days. After the publication of [18], the Italian Government released an analysis of times components connected to export operations, such as documentation, custom, handling and transport [19]. It emerged that custom times were similar in all countries, while documentation and handling times were considerably different. The documentation and custom times depended on the administration of the country, not on the ports, and they influenced in the export capacities.

The paper deals with time-series models able to estimate the economic impact generated by a place-based measure (as SEZ) in a region, where a European core port connected with a TEN-T corridor is present. The test case concerns a planned SEZ in Calabria region. The main objective of Regional Government of Calabria, defined in the strategic development plan of SEZ of 2018, was to facilitate the settlement of industrial firms in port-related areas of Gioia Tauro in order to increase the added value, according to the paradigm of the third-generation port [3, 20].

The following part of the paper is articulated into three sections. Section 2 sketches the current situation of container traffic in Euro-Mediterranean area in relation to the growth rates of economy of the different regions. Section 3 presents the time-series estimation of export and employment of firms settled in Calabria generated by the implementation of a SEZ. The last section concerns the conclusions and the research perspectives.

The model presented in the paper, in the context of a more general modelling framework, could support planners at national and regional level and for port authorities. The model is also useful for researchers in field related to the sustainable development of ports (see [21–23], and references included).

2 Container Traffic in the Euro-Mediterranean Area

The world economy returned to the pre-crisis levels in 2021 with an increase of +6.1% of GDP and of +10.1% of trade volumes respect to 2020 [24]. The Euro-Mediterranean area showed in the period 2018–2021 an increase of +7.7% in GDP and of +11.6% in consumption. By disaggregating the area into four regions (see Table 1), the growth of the Balkans and Turkey in GDP (+19.5%), and in consumption (+40.4%) emerges. North Africa faced smaller growth both in GDP (+13.2%) and in consumption (+17.4%). The values of GDP and consumption were stable in EU-Med and Middle East regions: + 2.2% of GDP and +0.5% of consumption in EU-Med, and +5.0% of GDP and −2.4% of consumption in Middle East [25].

Table 1. GDP and consumption growth in Euro-Mediterranean area during 2018–2022.

Region	Countries	GDP (%)	Consumption (%)
EU-Med	Italy, France, Spain, Portugal, Greece, Malta, Ciprus	+ 2.2	+ 0.5
Balkans and Turkey	Albania, Bosnia, Croatia, Montenegro, Slovenia, Turkey	+ 19.5	+ 40.4
Middle East	Israel, Lebanon, Syria, Palestine	+ 5.0	−2.4
North Africa	Algeria, Egypt, Lybia, Morocco, Tunisia	+ 13.2	+ 17.4

(source: [25])

The total amount of investments in the Euro-Mediterranean area was 531 billion of US$, equal to the 7.9% of the global investments in the period 2018–2022. As a matter of fact, while the main investors in 2018 in Merger & Acquisition were USA (20% of total operations) and China (11% of total operations), the main investors in 2021 were France, Italy and Spain with the 39% of total operations [25].

Global container throughput reached 802 million TEU in 2019. Similar to the financial crisis of 2008–09, the Covid-19 pandemic caused a negative growth; however, container throughput has exceeded in 2021 pre-pandemic levels, reaching 849 million TEUs.

The centrality of the Mediterranean Sea in the global traffic was still confirmed after the pandemic, as it accounted for 20% of global maritime traffic and for 27% of container traffic in 2021. Several transhipment hub ports operate in the Mediterranean area, some of them handle a throughput greater than 3 million of TEUs/year in the last three years (see Table 2).

The forecasts show that Euro-Mediterranean ports will in general increase their container traffic by 2025, with an expected annual average increase of +4.3%. Despite the Ukraine conflict, the East-Mediterranean ports (in Balkans, Turkey and Middle east areas), mainly due to the performance of ports such as Piraeus, will perform an increment of +4.5% of traffic. Ports of North Africa will perform a traffic increment of +5.4%; while West Mediterranean ports will perform +3.8% of traffic [26].

The container ports generate a relevant economic impact when they are able to fully develop their third-generation nature [3, 4], also due to the development of closer SEZs. The three more dynamic SEZs of the Mediterranean Sea are: Suez Canal (Egypt), Tanger-Med (Morocco), Mersin (Turkey). The SEZ of Suez Canal has four industrial zones and six ports including Port Said. The SEZ generated 100,000 direct jobs and the investments allocated over the last seven years were approximately 18 billion US$. The SEZ of Tanger-Med generated 8.8 billion euro of exports and hosted about 1,000 export-oriented firms, employing some 90,000 people. The SEZ of Mersin employed 9,600 people, with a trade value of 3.8 billion US$ [24].

Table 2. Main transhipment hub ports in Euro-Mediterranean area (period 2020–2022).

Port	2020 [TEUx10^6]	2021 [TEUx10^6]	2022 [TEUx10^6]	Δ20–21 [%]	Δ21–22 [%]
Tanger Med	5.77	7.17	7,59	+24.0	+7,3
Valencia	5.41	5.63	5,05	+4.0	−10,7
Piraeus	5.44	5.32	--	−2.0	--
Algeciras	5.10	4.78	4.80	−6.0	+0,4
Port Said	4.01	3.86	--	−3.6	---
Barcelona	2.96	3.51	3.52	+19.0	+0,3
Gioia Tauro	3.19	3.14	3.47	−1.5	+10,3
Marsaxlokk	2.44	2.97	2.88	+21.7	-3,7
Ambarli	2.88	2.93	--	+2.0	---
Genoa	2.35	2.57	--	+9.0	---

(elaboration from [24])

3 Time-Series Economic Impact of SEZ: Test Case for Calabria

3.1 Time-Series Models

Time-series models are founded on stochastic processes theory, according to which a time-series can be defined as a finite part of a single realization of a stochastic process [27]. Time-series, therefore, is a non-exhaustive partial realization of a stochastic process. Starting from the observed time-series, a stochastic model is assumed in order to determine the process generating the observed data.

A time-series, $\{x_t\}$, with t = 1, 2, ..., n, is an ordered sequence of n real numbers that measures a given phenomenon x_t, observed with regard to its evolution with respect to the time t.

Several types of time-series models have been proposed in the literature. Their classification can be made on the basis of different criteria:

- univariate and multivariate models, according to whether the evolution of time-series is justified in itself or with reference to the evolution of other series;
- models that explicitly or implicitly show the presence of components of the time series.

An elementary time-series model is given by the following equation:

$$x_t = f(t) + \varepsilon_t, \qquad \text{with } t = 1, 2, \ldots, n \tag{1}$$

where:

$f(t)$ is an (explicit) mathematical function of t;
ε_t, residual term.

3.2 Scenarios Definition

The economic impact of SEZ in Calabria, that has the hinterland of Gioia Tauro port as place where the highest concentration of industrial activities is expected, is linked to the growth of export and employment. The industrial settlements inside SEZ will therefore be oriented towards the export of goods on international markets, thus maximizing the benefits of the locating the SEZ close to the port of Gioia Tauro.

Two variables are considered in the estimation of economic impacts of the SEZ:

- *export* of goods and services of industrial firms located in Calabria;
- *employment* of industrial firms located in Calabria with (total or partial) foreign and domestic capital.

Two scenarios have been compared:

- *Do-Nothing*, where export and employment are estimated over a period of seven years ($\Delta Y = 7$) from a starting year (Y = 1), with no SEZ and with the current economic policies;
- *SEZ*, where export and employment are estimated over a period of seven years ($\Delta Y = 7$) from a starting year (Y = 1), with the activation of SEZ by assuming the complete availability of financial resources and decrees for simplification at the starting year.

Two categories of firms are considered in the analysis:

- *firms inside SEZ*, or industrial firms settled in SEZ areas;
- *firms outside SEZ*, or industrial firms settled out of SEZ areas.

The two scenarios and the two categories of firms generate four combinations of growth forecasts concerning export and employment:

- firms inside SEZ in Do-nothing scenario;
- firms outside SEZ in Do-nothing scenario;
- firms inside SEZ in SEZ scenario;
- firms inside SEZ in SEZ scenario.

3.3 Results

The following part of the section reports the yearly growth of export and employment of firms in presence of SEZ activation over a period of seven years ($\Delta Y = 7$) from a starting year ($Y = 1$).

Since the results of the evaluation depend on the starting values of export and employment, the values of a year ($Y = 0$) of firm inside and outside the SEZ were assumed as reference values (see more details in [13]).

The historical time-series of export and employment of industrial firms located in Calabria for a previous period (e.g. the decade 2008–2017) were provided by the Italian Institute of Statistics [38]. The following growth rates have been assumed as average values observed in historical time-series related to a previous period (e.g. the decade 2008–2017) (see Tables 3 and 4):

- Do-Nothing scenario

  - export of Calabria will grow according to a constant growth rate equal to +2.0%;
  - employment of Calabria will grow according to a negative growth rate of −1.2% in foreign-capital firms and a positive growth rate of +2.0% in domestic-capital firms.

- SEZ scenario

  - export of firms outside SEZ will grow assuming a constant growth rate: +2.0%:
  - export of firms inside SEZ and employment (both of domestic and foreign capital firms) have been estimated assuming a variable growth rate equal to the growth rates observed in international SEZs during the six years after their full activation (see [28, 29]).

Table 3. Growth rates of export after the full activation of the SEZ.

	Scenario	Inside SEZ	Outside SEZ	Calabria
Growth rate	Do-nothing	0,02	0,02	0,02
	SEZ	(*)	0,02	(*)

(*) variable growth rate (see [28, 29])

Table 4. Growth rates of employment after the full activation of the SEZ.

	Scenario	Foreign-capital firms	Domestic-capital firms	Firms in Calabria
Growth Rate	Do-nothing	−0,012	0,02	0,005
	ZES	(*)	(*)	(*)

(*) variable growth rate (see [28, 29])

Table 5 presents the time-series of export values of firms operating in Calabria in the Do-nothing and SEZ scenarios. The estimated pattern shows that the increase of export

Table 5. Estimated export yearly values [MEuros] of export inside and outside SEZ.

	Scenario	Do-Noth	Do-Noth	SEZ	SEZ
	Firms	Inside SEZ	Outside SEZ	Inside SEZ	Outside SEZ
Year	1	236	193	503	193
	2	242	198	545	198
	3	248	203	588	203
	4	254	207	646	207
	5	260	213	658	213
	6	266	218	725	218
	7	273	223	929	223

is evident in the firms located inside the SEZ areas where the SEZ measures are effective (SEZ scenario), as expected, rather than the other areas of Calabria.

Table 6 presents the time-series of employment values of domestic and foreign firms in Calabria in the Do-nothing and SEZ scenarios. The pattern that could be observed is the following. The increase of employment is present in in the both domestic and foreign firms, as expected. In the case of foreign firms, the growth changes form a negative rate in the Do-Nothing scenario to a positive rate in the SEZ scenario.

Table 6. Estimated employment yearly values of employment for domestic and foreign firms.

	Scenario	Do-Noth	Do-Noth	SEZ	SEZ
	Firms	Domestic	Foreign	Domestic	Foreign
Year	1	8974	1302	9329	2716
	2	9154	1289	9892	3051
	3	9337	1276	10488	3122
	4	9524	1263	11121	3249
	5	9714	1250	11791	3344
	6	9908	1238	12502	3502
	7	10106	1225	13256	4095

Figure 1 shows the time-series of export of firms in Calabria in the Do-nothing and SEZ scenarios. The pattern that could be observed in the picture is the following. The increase of export after the first year of activation of SEZ measures (Y = 1) is already consistent. The export increases with lower rates in the next five years (from years Y = 2 to Y = 6). The seventh year after the activation (Y = 7) it could be observed an increase with a n higher rate similar to the one of the first year.

Figure 2 shows the time-series of employment of firms in Calabria in the Do-nothing and SEZ scenarios. The pattern that could be observed in the picture is similar to the

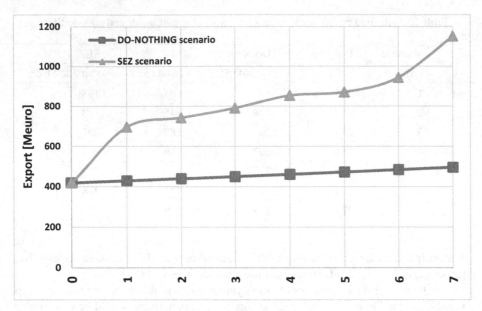

Fig. 1. Time-series of export of firms in Calabria: Do-nothing and SEZ scenarios.

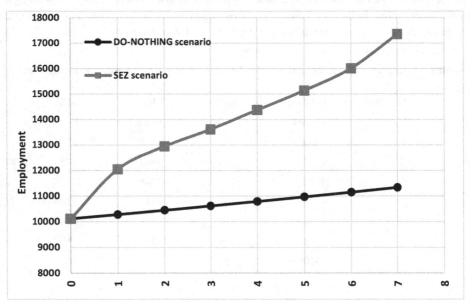

Fig. 2. Time-series of employment of firms in Calabria: Do-nothing and SEZ scenarios.

one observed for the export, as the rates of increase are higher in the first (Y = 0) and in the seventh (Y = 7) years after the activation of SEZ measures.

4   Conclusions

The paper presents a time-series analysis of economic impact generated by a SEZ in the Calabria (Italy). It is expected that the hinterland of the port of Gioia Tauro was the area where the greatest amount of industrial activities should be concentrated. The economic impacts of the SEZ was calculated taking into considerations the yearly growth of export and employment of industrial firms of Calabria. Two scenarios were compared: Do-Nothing, assuming the absence of SEZ; and SEZ, assuming that SEZ fully operates at a starting year (e.g. 2018).

The following final considerations may be reported according to the evaluation reported in the previous section (see Table 7). The export of firms inside SEZ should reach the value of 273 million of Euro after six years after the starting year (e.g. at year 2024) in the Do-nothing scenario; while their export should be equal to 929 million of Euro in the SEZ scenario. The export of firms outside SEZ should be equal to 223 million of Euro after ten years from the starting year (e.g. at year 2024), whatever the scenario will be (Do-nothing or SEZ). The employment of firms inside SEZ should be 1225 in Do-nothing scenario and 4095 in SEZ scenario after six years from the starting year (e.g. at year 2024). The employment of firms outside SEZ should be 10106 after six years from the starting year (e.g. at year 2024) in the Do-nothing scenario and 3256 in the SEZ scenario.

Table 7. Estimated export and employment for each scenario and category of firms.

	Year	Scenario	Firms inside SEZ	Firms outside SEZ	Firms in Calabria
Export [M€]	0(*)	Current	209	209	418
	7(**)	Do-nothing	273	223	496
		SEZ	929	223	1152
Employment	0(*)	Current	1315	8798	10113
	7(**)	Do-nothing	1225	10106	11332
		SEZ	4095	13256	17351

(source: [13]) (*) full activation of SEZ measures; (**) full deployment of SEZ measures

Synthetically, the export should be equal to 496 million of Euro and the employment equal to 11332 workers in Calabria in the Do-nothing scenario; while the export should be equal to 1152 million of Euro and the employment equal to 17332 workers in Calabria in the SEZ scenario. The above values are assumed as reference values of direct impact generated by SEZ in Calabria used for the estimation of indirect and induced impacts.

Future developments are expected as far as concerns the calibration and validation of further specifications of multi-variate time-series models from a more extended set of observed data provided from worldwide SEZ experiences.

Acknowledgements. This study was carried out within the MOST – Sustainable Mobility National Research Center and received funding from the European Union Next-Generation EU (PIANO NAZIONALE DI RIPRESA E RESILIENZA (PNRR) – MISSIONE 4 COMPONENTE 2, INVESTIMENTO 1.4 – D.D. 1033 17/06/2022, CN00000023). This manuscript reflects only the authors' views and opinions, neither the European Union nor the European Commission can be considered responsible for them.

References

1. UNCTAD Port Marketing and the Challenge of the Third Generation Port (1994)
2. UNCTAD Fourth-Generation Port: Technical Note (1999)
3. Russo, F., Musolino, G.: Quantitative characteristics for port generations: the Italian case study. Int. J. TDI **4**, 103–112 (2020). https://doi.org/10.2495/TDI-V4-N2-103-112
4. Musolino, G., Cartisano, A., Chilà, G., Fortugno, G., Trecozzi, M.R.: Evaluation of structural factors in a third-generation port: methods and applications. Int. J. Transp. Dev. Integr. 347–362 (2022)
5. Russo, F., Rindone, C., Panuccio, P.: External interactions for a third generation port: urban and research developments. Int. J. Transp. Dev. Integr. 253–270 (2022)
6. Russo, F., Chilà, G.: Structural factors for a third-generation port: current state, limits and weaknesses of Gioia Tauro, Italy, in The Regional Transport Plan. In: Proceedings of the Urban and Maritime Transport 2021, WIT Transactions on the Built Environment, vol. 204, 16 June 2021, pp. 3–15 (2021)
7. Russo, F., Chilà, G.: Structural factors for a third-generation port: actions and measures for Gioia Tauro, Italy, in The Regional Transport Plan. In: Proceedings of the Urban and Maritime Transport 2021, WIT Transactions on the Built Environment, vol. 204, 16 June 2021, pp. 17–30. WIT Press (2021)
8. Russo, F., Panuccio, P., Rindone, C.: Structural factors for a third-generation port: between hinterland regeneration and smart town in Gioia Tauro, Italy. In: Proceedings of the Urban and Maritime Transport 2021, WIT Transactions on the Built Environment, vol. 204, 16 June 2021, pp. 79–90 (2021)
9. Musolino, G., Chilà, G.: Structural factors for a third-generation port: planning transport interventions in Gioia Tauro, Italy. In: Proceedings of the Urban and Maritime Transport 2021, WIT Transactions on the Built Environment, vol. 204, 16 June 2021, pp. 31–42 (2021)
10. Musolino, G., Rosaria Trecozzi, M.: Structural factors for a third-generation port: planning interventions for agri-food logistics in Gioia Tauro, Italy. In: Proceedings of the Urban and Maritime Transport 2021, WIT Transactions on the Built Environment, vol. 204, 16 June 2021, pp. 43–54 (2021)
11. Musolino, G., Cartisano, A., Fortugno, G.: Structural factors for a third-generation port: planning interventions for mechanical logistics in Gioia Tauro, Italy. In: Proceedings of the Urban and Maritime Transport 2021, WIT Transactions on the Built Environment, vol. 204, 16 June 2021, pp. 55–66 (2021)
12. Musolino, D.A., Panuccio, P.: Special economic zones planning for sustainable ports: the test case of territorial attractiveness and urban planning in Calabria Region. In: Gervasi, O., Murgante, B., Misra, S., Rocha, A.M.A.C., Garau, C. (eds.) Computational Science and Its Applications – ICCSA 2022 Workshops. LNCS, vol. 13381, pp. 72–84. Springer, Cham (2022). https://doi.org/10.1007/978-3-031-10548-7_6. ISBN 978-3-031-10547-0

13. Musolino, G., Cartisano, A., Fortugno, G.: Special economic zones planning for sustainable ports: aggregate economic impact of port of Gioia Tauro. In: Gervasi, O., Murgante, B., Misra, S., Rocha, A.M.A.C., Garau, C. (eds.) Computational Science and Its Applications – ICCSA 2022 Workshops. LNCS, vol. 13381, pp. 60–71. Springer, Cham (2022). https://doi.org/10.1007/978-3-031-10548-7_5. ISBN 978-3-031-10547-0
14. Russo, F., Chilà, G., Zito, C.: Strategic planning for special economic zones to ports of the future: system of models and test case. In: Gervasi, O., Murgante, B., Misra, S., Rocha, A.M.A.C., Garau, C. (eds.) Computational Science and Its Applications – ICCSA 2022 Workshops. LNCS, vol. 13381, pp. 173–184. Springer, Cham (2022). https://doi.org/10.1007/978-3-031-10548-7_13. ISBN 978-3-031-10547-0
15. Rindone, C., Cirianni, F.M.M., Delfino, G., Croce, A.I.: Special economic zones planning for sustainable ports: the role of research and training in the Calabria Region. In: Gervasi, O., Murgante, B., Misra, S., Rocha, A.M.A.C., Garau, C. (eds.) Computational Science and Its Applications – ICCSA 2022 Workshops. LNCS, vol. 13381, pp. 85–97. Springer, Cham (2022). https://doi.org/10.1007/978-3-031-10548-7_7. ISBN 978-3-031-10547-0
16. Pellicanò, D.S., Trecozzi, M.R.: Special economic zones planning for sustainable ports: general approach for administrative simplifications and a test case. In: Gervasi, O., Murgante, B., Misra, S., Rocha, A.M.A.C., Garau, C. (eds.) Computational Science and Its Applications – ICCSA 2022 Workshops. LNCS, vol. 13381, pp. 47–59. Springer, Cham (2022). https://doi.org/10.1007/978-3-031-10548-7_4. ISBN 978-3-031-10547-0
17. Russo, F., Rindone, C.: Smart city for sustainable development: applied processes from SUMP to MaaS at European level. Appl. Sci. **13**, 1773 (2023). https://doi.org/10.3390/app13031773
18. International Finance Corporation Doing Business 2014: Understanding Regulations for Small and Medium-Size Enterprises (2013)
19. Presidenza del Consiglio dei Ministri Iniziativa Di Studio Sulla Portualità Italiana (2014)
20. Cascetta, E., Nuzzolo, A., Biggiero, L., Russo, F.: Passenger and freight demand models for the italian transportation system. In: Proceedings of the 7th World Conference on Transport Research, vol. II
21. Ignaccolo, M., Inturri, G., Giuffrida, N., Torrisi, V.: A sustainable framework for the analysis of port systems. European Transport \ Trasporti Europei (2020). Issue 78, Paper n° 7,
22. Giuffrida, N., Ignaccolo, M., Inturri, G., Torrisi, V.: Port-city shared areas to improve freight transport sustainability. In: Gervasi, O., et al. (eds.) ICCSA 2020. LNCS, vol. 12255, pp. 67–82. Springer, Cham (2020). https://doi.org/10.1007/978-3-030-58820-5_6
23. Ignaccolo, M., Inturri, G., Giuffrida, N., Torrisi, V., Cocuzza, E.: Sustainability of freight transport through an integrated approach: the case of the Eastern Sicily port system. Transp. Res. Procedia **45**, 177–184 (2020). https://doi.org/10.1016/j.trpro.2020.03.005
24. Deandreis, M., Ferrara, O., Panaro, A.: Maritime Scenario in the Mediterranean: Analysis of the Competitiveness and In-Vestments of the Major Logistics Players (2022)
25. Iacovone, D.: Nuova stagione di crescita per la zona Euro-Mediterranena (2023)
26. Panaro, A.: The New Challenges of Logistics and Maritime Economy. Presented at the Annual meeting GSTTA
27. Box, G.E.P., Jenkins, G.M.: Time Series Analysis: Forecasting and Control. In: Revised ed. Holden-Day Series in Time Series Analysis and Digital Processing. Holden-Day, San Francisco (1976). ISBN 978-0-8162-1104-3
28. Wang, J.: The economic impact of special economic zones: evidence from Chinese municipalities. J. Dev. Econ. **101**, 133–147 (2013). https://doi.org/10.1016/j.jdeveco.2012.10.009
29. Leong, C.K.: Special economic zones and growth in China and India: an empirical investigation. IEEP **10**(4), 549–567 (2012). https://doi.org/10.1007/s10368-012-0223-6

Open Access This chapter is licensed under the terms of the Creative Commons Attribution 4.0 International License (http://creativecommons.org/licenses/by/4.0/), which permits use, sharing, adaptation, distribution and reproduction in any medium or format, as long as you give appropriate credit to the original author(s) and the source, provide a link to the Creative Commons license and indicate if changes were made.

The images or other third party material in this chapter are included in the chapter's Creative Commons license, unless indicated otherwise in a credit line to the material. If material is not included in the chapter's Creative Commons license and your intended use is not permitted by statutory regulation or exceeds the permitted use, you will need to obtain permission directly from the copyright holder.

Evaluating the Environmental Sustainability of an Intermodal Freight Logistic Chain Using the GLEC Framework

Gianfranco Fancello⬭, Daniel Mark Vitiello⬭, and Patrizia Serra⁽⊠⁾ ⬭

DICAAR – Department of Civil and Environmental Engineering and Architecture,
University of Cagliari, 09123 Cagliari, Italy
pserra@unica.it

Abstract. In the last years, evaluation of environmental sustainability of supply chains has become central in policies aimed at reducing polluting gas emissions (see, for example, Kyoto protocol, United Nations Framework Convention on Climate Change in Paris, Green Deal: Sustainable and Smart Mobility Strategy). The transport sector is one of the principal causes of global greenhouse gas (GHG) emissions. The sector consumes 25% of total final energy consumption and is responsible for nearly 40% of the emissions from end-use sectors. In 2021, global CO_2 emissions from the sector was about 7.7 Gt CO_2, of which 5.9 Gt CO_2 from road vehicles. In the European Union the transport sector accounts for 20% of anthropogenic GHG emissions. The main objective of the European Commission is to cut emissions by 90% within 2050. In March 2023, the International Standard Organization (ISO) released the ISO 14083 standard that provides requirements and guidance for the quantification and reporting of GHG emissions along the entire transport chains for passengers and freight. It is aligned with the ISO families 14040 and 14060. The ISO 14083 is in line, among the others, with the Global Logistics Emissions Council (GLEC) Framework for Logistics Emissions Accounting and Reporting.

This paper will focus its attention on a land-sea intermodal freight logistic chain, with an application to a real case study. In accordance with the ISO 14083 standard, the GLEC Framework, proposed by the Smart Freight Centre, will be used to calculate the energy consumption and the GHG emissions caused by supply chains.

Keywords: ISO 14083 · GHG emissions · GLEC Framework

1 Introduction

In the last years, the evaluation of environmental sustainability of supply chains has become central in policies aimed at reducing polluting gas emissions (see, for example, Kyoto protocol, United Nations Framework Convention on Climate Change in Paris, Green Deal: Sustainable and Smart Mobility Strategy).

The transport sector (including transport of people, freights, and logistic operations) is one of the principal causes of global greenhouse gas (GHG) emissions. The sector

© The Author(s), under exclusive license to Springer Nature Switzerland AG 2023
O. Gervasi et al. (Eds.): ICCSA 2023 Workshops, LNCS 14110, pp. 563–576, 2023.
https://doi.org/10.1007/978-3-031-37123-3_39

consumes 25% of the total final energy consumption (of which 90% oil) and it's responsible for nearly 40% of the emissions from end-use sectors. Between 2010 and 2019, the transport sector recorded the largest growth in emissions of all end-use sectors due to the increasing demand for passenger and goods mobility. In 2021, global CO_2 emissions from the sector were about 7.7 Gt CO_2, of which 5.9 Gt CO_2 from road vehicles [1].

In the European Union the transport sector accounts for 20% of anthropogenic GHG emissions [2]. In order to become climate neutral, the main target is to cut emissions by 90% within 2050. Furthermore, more than 75% of freight traffic (measured in ton-kilometers) is performed by trucks [3].

For these reasons, the European Commission has presented the Sustainable and Smart Mobility Strategy, part of the European Green Deal, which defines that rail freight traffic should increase by 50% by 2030 and double by 2050, whereas transport by inland waterways and short sea shipping should increase by 25% by 2030 and by 50% by 2050. Moreover, it encourages the diffusion of zero-emission vehicles, vessels and aeroplanes, renewable & low-carbon fuels and related infrastructures (for instance, airports and ports) [4].

This decarbonisation process must necessarily start from the measurement of emissions; hence the standardization of emission calculation methods is fundamental to achieve the global GHG reduction targets and to realize sustainable supply chains [5]. Thus, a common carbon accounting framework is needed.

The objective of this paper is to analyse the evaluate the GHG emissions of a supply chain. We will focus our attention on a land-sea intermodal freight logistic chain, with an application to a real case study. The paper is structured as followed: Sect. 1 introduces the paper's issue; Sect. 2 proposes the main methodologies that are internationally used for the GHG emission calculations. Section 3 illustrates the chosen methodology while Sect. 4 presents the case study. The paper end with Sect. 5 that provides the main results and conclusions.

2 Literature Review

In recent years, many efforts have been made to formalize a new global standard, that could harmonize measurements among stakeholders. The framework should be reliable, transparent, relevant, and accurate to allow consistency and comparability of emissions from all modes of transport. Furthermore, it should facilitate data collection and exchange between the involved partners of the transport chain. Among the others, the Global Logistics Emissions Council (GLEC) has promoted the standardisation of GHG emissions accounting methodologies and reporting standards with the publication of an internationally developed and applicable methodological framework for the calculation of transport chain emissions, the GLEC Framework.

In March 2023, the International Standard Organization (ISO) released the ISO 14083 standard (Quantification and reporting of greenhouse gas emissions arising from operations of transport chains) that, for the first time, provides requirements and guidance for the quantification and reporting of GHG emissions along the entire transport chains for passengers and freight. It covers all modes of transport and includes the operational GHG emissions from hubs [10]. It is aligned with the ISO families 14040 and 14060 and also, among the others, with the Global Logistics Emissions Council (GLEC) Framework for Logistics Emissions Accounting and Reporting.

With the introduction of the ISO 14083 standard, the GLEC Framework becomes a valid support for the implementation of the ISO standard, functioning as guidelines to assist companies in understanding and implementing it.

Environmental characteristics of products are not always communicated to the users. Often the available information is unclear or partial. Furthermore, the comparison between the environmental characteristics can only be performed if the information is of the same type. If no information is provided, common guidelines are necessary to perform evaluations. Therefore, standardization of environmental labels (ecolabels) is needed [6].

Ecolabels and environmental declarations are environmental management tools that communicate specific information about the environmental impacts of a product or a service [7–10]. They are often also proposed as a possible support mechanism in the transition to Circular Economy [11].

The International Organization for Standardization (ISO) provides general definitions and principles and requirements for the establishment of voluntary environmental labels and environmental declarations through the ISO 14020 family of standards [10]. The ISO 14020 family of standards is structured as follows:

- ISO 14020:2022. Core document in the ISO 14020 family of standards; it sets principles and general requirements for all environmental statements. For example, it establishes that ecolabels must consider all relevant aspects of the product's life cycle.
- ISO 14021:2016/Amd 1:2021. Self-declared environmental claims (Type II environmental labelling).
- ISO 14024:2018. Environmental labels known as ecolabels (Type I environmental labelling). It is third-party verified.
- ISO 14025:2006. Environmental product declarations (EPDs) (Type III environmental labelling). It is third-party verified.
- ISO 14026:2017. Principles, requirements and guidelines for communication of footprint information
- ISO/TS 14027:2017. Development of product category rules
- ISO/TS 14029:2022. Mutual recognition of environmental product declarations (EPDs) and footprint communication programs

Sustainability is a complex process that regards not only environmental aspects but social and economic aspects too [12, 13]. Ceschin and Gaziulusoy [14] argue that it is not a property of the individual elements forming systems but rather a property of the system itself. For this reason, Life Cycle Assessment (LCA) is one of the most influential and robust methodologies - along with environmental labelling - to evaluate the environmental impacts of products and services [6]. It is regulated by the international standards ISO 14040 and ISO 14044 [15].

3 Methodology

The GLEC Framework was developed by the Global Logistics Emissions Council (GLEC), a voluntary and independent partnership of companies, green freight programs and industry associations, supported by researchers and experts, led by the Smart Freight Centre [16]. It aims at standardizing the calculation of GHG emission related to freight transport, specifically developed for transport chains, including all transport modes. This methodology focuses on the Kyoto Protocol greenhouse gases listed in Annex A (carbon dioxide, methane, nitrous oxide, hydrofluorocarbons, perfluorocarbons, sulphur hexafluoride) plus nitrogen trifluoride. In particular, carbon dioxide (CO_2) comprises the majority of GHG emissions for logistics activities. For this reason, GHG emissions are expressed in a common standard unit, based on the global warming potential (GWP), called CO_2-equivalent (CO_2e or CO_2eq or CO_2-e) [17].

3.1 The Carbon Accounting Methods

The carbon accounting methods used to develop the GLEC Framework are various. Among the others, it is aligned with the GHG Protocol (World Business Council for Sustainable Development & World Resources Institute) and the Intergovernmental Panel on Climate Change (IPCC) Guidance. Furthermore, it harmonizes numerous other existing methodologies. Table 1 provides the methodologies used for logistics sites, road and sea transport.

Table 1. Carbon accounting methods used to develop the GLEC Framework. Source: authors adaptation from GLEC Framework

Transport mode	Carbon accounting method	References
Logistic sites	Guidance for Greenhouse Gas Emissions Accounting at Logistics Sites	[5]
	Guidance for Greenhouse Gas Emission Footprinting for Container Terminals	[18]
Road transport	European Committee for Standardization EN 16258: Methodology for calculation and declaration of energy consumption and GHG emissions of transport services (freight and passengers)	[19]
	SmartWay Road Carrier Tool	[20]
Sea transport	International Maritime Organization Ship Energy Efficiency Operation Index	[21]

3.2 Scopes

According to the GHG Protocol and the ISO 14064, the GLEC Framework classifies the emissions into three categories called scopes:

- Scope 1: direct emissions from assets that are owned or controlled directly by the reporting company (e.g.: combustion of fuel).
- Scope 2: indirect emissions from the production and distribution of electricity, heat, and steam purchased by the reporting company.
- Scope 3: indirect emissions from the reporting company's supply chain. It also covers the production and distribution of fuels burned in Scope 1.

3.3 Fuel Emissions

As required from the GHG Protocol, all climatic emissions caused by the use of fuels should be included while accounting fuel emissions. For this reason, the Framework takes into account the entire fuel life cycle, known as Well-to-Wheel (WTW) emissions. There emissions are sub-classified in:

- Well–to-Tank (WTT) emissions. They include all the processes between the energy source (well) and the various stages of refining, storage and delivery up to the point of use (tank). They are reported as Scope 3.
- Tank-to-Wheel (TTW) emissions from fuels combusted to power Scope 1 activities. They are reported as Scope 1.

3.4 Calculation Steps

The GLEC Framework suggests the use of three steps for an efficient calculation of logistic carbon accounting. The first step includes the creation of the emission calculation boundaries, the definition of the end goals and the identification of the needed data. The issue of the second step is to calculate Scope 1 and Scope 2 emissions while in the third step Scope 3 is calculated.

Fig. 1. The GLEC Framework's calculation steps. Source: Authors' adaptation

In order to generate a reliable and transparent logistics emissions calculation output, the GLEC Framework highlights the importance of a rigorous methodology, starting from the consciousness of the problem. It suggests to:

- Set the boundaries.
- Think about end goals a use of the results.

- Determine what kind of input data are necessary to our final goal.

For Scope 1 and 2, fuel and electricity data are converted to emissions using a standard fuel or electricity emission factor (GLEC).

In order to calculate Scope 1 direct emissions, it is necessary to primarily know the fuel information that can be gleaned from payment receipts, management systems or annual expenditures. Fuel data should cover the entire journey, i.e. including laden, part-laden and empty trips. Once fuel data is known, it can be converted into emissions. Since each type of fuel emits different amounts of CO_2e it is essential to convert each fuel type separately. In the event that detailed fuel data is not available, the methodology recommends estimating the quantity of each fuel based on the available information. Equation 1 shows how to calculate the fuel emissions for n types of fuel.

$$\text{kg}\,CO_2e = \sum_1^n \left(\text{fuel (kg)} \cdot \text{fuel mission factor} \left(\frac{\text{kg}\,CO_2e}{\text{kg fuel}} \right) \right) \tag{1}$$

Scope 2 indirect emission information can be gathered from electricity bills. The following equation is used to calculate it.

$$\text{kg}\,CO_2e = \sum_1^n \left(\text{electricity (kWh)} \cdot \text{electricity emission factor} \left(\frac{\text{kg}\,CO_2e}{\text{kWh electricity}} \right) \right) \tag{2}$$

The target of step 3 is to evaluate Scope 3 supply chain emissions. The emissions are calculated as the amount of fuel or CO_2e used for moving a certain quantity of freight for a certain distance in a period of one year. The GLEC Framework suggests expressing it in tonne-kilometers.

The calculation for Scope 3 emissions can be carried out following two different approaches, depending on the factor being adopted:

- with a fuel efficiency factor (f.ef.f.):

$$\text{kg}\,CO_2e = \sum_1^n \left(\text{total tkm} \cdot \text{f.ef.f.} \left(\frac{\text{kg fuel}}{\text{tonne} - \text{km}} \right) \cdot \text{fuel emission factor} \left(\frac{\text{kg}\,CO_2e}{\text{kg fuel}} \right) \right) \tag{3}$$

- with a CO_2e intensity factor:

$$\text{kg}\,CO_2e = \sum_1^n \left(\text{total tkm} \cdot CO_2e \text{ intensity factor} \left(\frac{\text{kg}\,CO_2e}{\text{tonne} - \text{km}} \right) \right) \tag{4}$$

4   Case Study

For the application of the GLEC methodology, an intermodal freight logistic company - that operates in the Mediterranean basin - was chosen. This company offers to its customers integrated logistics solutions using its network of warehouses, terminals, and road transport services for last mile distribution. It also offers Ro/Ro and containerized cargo line services. The peculiarity of this company is its ability to operate in Door-to-door mode, managing the entire transport cycle.

The chosen case study for this application is a land-sea intermodal supply chain integrally operated by the company previously mentioned. The phases of the land-sea supply chain that will be taken into account are:

- road transport
- maritime transport
- road transport

Therefore, there is a first phase of capillary collection and positioning of the goods from the single customers to the warehouses first and then to the port. The second phase refers to the maritime transport from the origin port to the destination one. Last, the third phase is yet again a road transport from the destination port to the final client, that can occur with a direct or an undirect delivery. In addition to the transport phases, also operations at the port terminals will be analysed. In fact, in the port terminals, goods are handled and stored in the terminal's warehouses. In this chapter, planning and calculation of emissions for each phase of the supply chain will be presented.

4.1 Planning and Calculation of Emissions for Maritime Transport

Based on the GLEC guidelines, a first preparatory planning phase was carried out, including the selection and collection of data. For each voyage, the data included:

- Consumption of fuel
- Distance
- Volumes of goods transported

The data provided from the company for the volumes of goods were expressed in heterogeneous load units, such as 20 ft, 24.5 ft, 40 ft and 45 ft containers or trailers expressed in linear meters. Subsequentially, these volumes of goods were homogenized in equivalent TEUs (TEUeq). The conversion was accomplished by dividing the total linear meters of containers and trailers by the standard length of 20ft containers, defining a single unit of measurement. This homogenization was necessary since the company operates a mixed type of transport; thus, it did not allow a correct use of the GLEC methodology. Furthermore, the quantities of goods weren't expressed in weight values, attribute that is necessary for the purposes of implementing the GLEC methodology.

In absence of further information, CCWG and EcoTransIT guidelines propose an allocation of an average load between 10 and 14 tonnes per full TEU and 2 tonnes per empty TEU. Therefore, an average load of 12 tonnes per full TEU and 2 tonnes per empty TEU has been allocated. These estimated weights were considered in line with the monthly transported quantities declared by the company.

Once the preparatory phase was defined, we proceeded with the calculation of the emissions of Scopes 1, 2 and 3. GHG emissions were calculated for two different types of fuel used by the ships, namely the HFO (heavy fuel oil), used during navigation and manoeuvring phases and the MDO (marine diesel oil), used during the mooring phases in port.

The evaluation of the emissions generated by the ship is based on Eq. 5, applied both for Scope 1 (TTW) and for Scope 3 (WTT). Table 2 provides the fuel emission factors for both Scopes.

$$\text{kg CO}_2\text{e kg emissions} = \sum_1^n \left(\text{fuel (kg)} \cdot \text{fuel emission factor} \left(\frac{\text{kg CO}_2\text{e}}{\text{kg fuel}} \right) \right) \quad (5)$$

Table 2. Fuel emission factors. Source: authors' elaboration. (*European values)

	WTT	TTW	WTW	WTT	TTW	WTW
	[kg CO$_2$e/ kg fuel]			[kg CO$_2$e/ l fuel]		
Heavy fuel oil (HFO)	0.26	3.15	3.41	0.25	3.06	3.31
Marine diesel oil (MDO)*	0.68	3.24	3.92	0.61	2.92	3.53
Marine gas oil (MGO)*	0.68	3.24	3.92	0.61	2.88	3.49
Diesel*	0.69	3.21	3.90	0.57	2.67	3.24

As regards to the GHG emissions generated by the use of heavy fuel oil during navigation (Scope 1 - TTW emissions), Table 3 provides the total result for the year 2021, calculated as the sum of the single trips. The input data were the quantity of fuel oil, the total travelled distance, the tons of transported freight and the fuel emission factor. GHG emission intensity was also found equal to CO$_2$e per ton-km.

Table 3. Scope 1 - heavy fuel oil (HFO) - TTW. Source: authors' elaboration

Fuel (HFO)	Fuel emission factor	GHG emissions	Voyage distance	Freight
[ton]	[kg CO$_2$e/ kg fuel]	[ton CO$_2$e]	[km]	[ton]
14,428	3.15	45,448	282,266	1,461,477

Scope 3 emissions (WTT emissions) were calculated using a different fuel emission factor that gave a value of about 8,400 kg CO$_2$e per voyage and 7.3 g CO$_2$e per ton-km (see Table 4).

Table 4. Scope 3 - heavy fuel oil (HFO) - WTT. Source: authors' elaboration

Fuel (HFO)	Fuel emission factor	GHG emissions	Voyage distance	Freight
[ton]	[kg CO$_2$e/kg fuel]	[ton CO$_2$e]	[km]	[ton]
14,428	0.26	3,751	282,266	1,461,477

Once the TTW and WTT emissions were calculated, it was possible to calculate the final WTW emissions (see Table 5).

The evaluation of the GHG emissions caused by the marine diesel oil had to necessarily take into consideration that its use does not include transport activities. Therefore, it was not possible to calculate a GHG emission intensity. Table 6 shows the results. The GHG TTW emissions associated to the use of MDO was about 10,500 kg of CO2e.

Table 5. Scope 1 & 3 - heavy fuel oil (HFO) - WTW. Source: authors' elaboration

	GHG emissions
	[ton CO_2e]
TTW	45,448
WTT	3,751
WTW	**49,199**

Table 6. Scope 1 - marine diesel oil (MDO) - TTW. Source: authors' elaboration

Fuel (MDO)	Fuel emission factor	GHG emissions
[ton]	[kg CO_2e/ kg fuel]	[ton CO_2e]
1,129	3.24	3,658

Scope 3 emissions (WTT emissions) were calculated using its fuel emission factor. (see Table 7).

Table 7. Scope 3 - marine diesel oil (MDO) - WTT. Source: authors' elaboration

Fuel (MDO)	Fuel emission factor	GHG emissions
[ton]	[kg CO_2e/kg fuel]	[ton CO_2e]
1,129	0.68	768

Once the TTW and WTT emissions were calculated, it was possible to calculate the final WTW emissions (see Table 8).

Table 8. Scope 1&3 - marine diesel oil (MDO) - WTW. Source: authors' elaboration

	GHG emissions
	[ton CO_2e]
TTW	3,658
WTT	768
WTW	**4,426**

Finally, the emissions derived from the two fuels can be added together to obtain the total GHG WTW emissions. Table 9 summarizes the results.

Table 9. Scope 1&3 - maritime transport phase. Source: authors' elaboration

Type of fuel	TTW GHG emissions	WTT GHG emissions	WTW GHG emissions
[-]	[ton CO_2e]	[ton CO_2e]	[ton CO_2e]
HFO	45,448	3,751	49,199
MDO	3,658	768	4,426
Total	**49,106**	**4,519**	**53,625**

4.2 Planning and Calculation of Emissions in the Port Terminal

To calculate the emissions produced by the port terminal operations, the IML methodology [5] was used. In this case, the database provided by the company was incomplete and data were often aggregated. Hence, the evaluation was brought out considering the total annual consumption of the vehicles operating in both port terminals, 546,120 litres of diesel. The vehicle fleet consists of:

- 20 port terminal tractors
- 10 reach stackers
- 2 forklifts

To calculate the emissions, the following equation was used. In the absence of further detailed information, we have considered the European value of WTW fuel emission factor of diesel (3.24 kgCO_2e/litre). In this case, Scope 1 and Scope 3 emissions are calculated together.

$$\text{kg } CO_2\text{e emission} = \sum_1^n \left(\text{fuel (kg)} \cdot \text{fuel emission factor} \left(\frac{\text{kg } CO_2\text{e}}{\text{kg fuel}} \right) \right) \quad (6)$$

The annual emissions produced by the vehicle fleet amount to about 1,769,400 CO_2e. It can be noticed that the emissions deriving from port logistics operations can be considered negligible compared to the ones associated to the maritime transport phase.

4.3 Planning and Calculation of Emissions for Road Transport

The last step is the evaluation of the emissions related to road transport activities. It is important to notice that this evaluation will be applied only to the freight handled directly by the company. Therefore, only 30% of the total freight transported by sea will be considered in this analysis.

When planning and calculating emissions from road transport, the GLEC Framework considers the standard EN16258, the EcoTransIT method and the CLECAT one. The latter are particularly useful in the event of a lack of specific data regarding transport means and activities.

The data provided by the company include the transport activities carried out during 2021 and include the type of vehicle, the total distances covered, the number of trips and the number of TEUs transported. No specific data about gross weight and fuel consumption were available. For these reasons, in accordance with EcoTransIT and CLECAT, we identified the average default attributes necessary to evaluate GHG emissions. The vehicle fleet consists in thirty-five B-double road trains and ninety semi-trailer trucks. Both types of trucks have a capacity of 2 TEUs per trip. At each TEU was assigned a load of 12 tons. Table 10 describes the input data.

Table 10. Input data for the road transport phase. Source: intermodal freight logistic company

Type of vehicle	Total distance travelled	Number of trips	Average distance per trip	Load factor	Freight	Freight
[-]	[km]	[n.]	[km]	[%]	[TEU]	[ton]
B-double road trains	2,002,514	8,756	229	93.5	16,369	196,428
Semi-trailer trucks	2,310,680	11,392	203	100	22,784	273,408
Total	**4,313,194**	**20,148**	**214**	**1.94**	**39,153**	**469,836**

As for Scope 1 emissions calculation, we have first estimated the total fuel consumption utilising a specific consumption of about 0.34; then the GHG emissions were calculated applying the correct fuel emission factor (see Table 10). Table 11 presents the evaluation of Scope 1 emissions while Table 12 Scope 3 emissions.

Table 11. Scope 1 - road transport - TTW. Source: authors' elaboration

Type of vehicle	Total distance travelled	Specific consumption	Total fuel consumption	Fuel emission factor	GHG emissions
[-]	[km]	[l/km]	[l]	[kg CO_2e/l]	[kg CO_2e]
B-double road trains	2,002,514	0.34	680,855	2.67	1,817,883
Semi-trailer trucks	2,310,680	0.34	785,631	2.67	2,097,635
Total	**4,313,194**	**0.34**	**1,466,486**	**2.67**	**3,915,518**

Table 12. Scope 3 - road transport - WTT. Source: authors' elaboration

Type of vehicle	Total distance travelled	Specific consumption	Total fuel consumption	Fuel emission factor	GHG emissions
[-]	[km]	[l/km]	[l]	[kg CO_2e/l]	[kg CO_2e]
B-double road trains	2,002,514	0.34	680,855	0.57	388,087
Semi-trailer trucks	2,310,680	0.34	785.631	0.57	447,810
Total	**4,313,194**	**0.34**	**1,466,486**	**0.57**	**835,897**

Finally, Table 13 provides the total GHG emissions derived from the road transport phase.

Table 13. Scope 1 &3 - road transport. Source: authors' elaboration

Type of vehicle	GHG emissions
[-]	[kg CO_2e]
Scope 1	3,915,518
Scope 3	835,897
Total	**4,751,415**

5 Results and Discussions

From the results obtained through the implementation of the GLEC methodology it emerges that the evaluation of the GHG emissions caused by the maritime transport phase was the most complete, due to better detailed information provided by the company and a wider literary documentation.

The analysis of the road transport phase was limited to assessing the emissions due to the company's internal operations. Compared with the total freight shipped by sea (1460,000 tons), the share of road freight was under 30% (469,800 tons). Despite this issue, the results highlight the impact of the maritime transport in this specific supply chain. Indeed, if we consider the hole intermodal supply chain, it's easy to notice that the maritime transport phase contributes the most (about 89%) to the total GHG emissions. Table 14 summarizes the main results.

Table 14. Total supply chain GHG emissions. Source: authors' elaboration

Supply chain phase	Scope 1	Scope 3	Total	% on the total
[-]	[kg CO_2e]	[kg CO_2e]	[kg CO_2e]	[%]
Sea transport	49,106,000	4,519,000	53,625,000	89%
Port terminal	–	–	1,769,400	3%
Road Transport*	3,915,518	835,897	4,751,415	8%
Total			**60,145,815**	

The results also highlight the differences between Scope 1 and Scope 3 GHG emissions, with the first resulting highly impactful on the total emissions. In the case of the port terminal's emissions, it wasn't possible to separate the two scopes.

6 Conclusions

From this application it emerged that the GLEC Framework is certainly useful for calculating the GHG emissions of an entire supply chain. However, it should be noted that it does not take into consideration the different types of cargo. The incorrect homogenization of the different units can bring to errors when comparing results with similar situations.

Further studies must be made in order to analyse the application of the Framework to other typical transport chains.

This study was carried out before the publication of the ISO 14083. The authors suggest a comparison between the application of the GLEC Framework and the new ISO standard (Quantification and reporting of greenhouse gas emissions arising from operations of transport chains) that, for the first time, provides requirements and guidance for the quantification and reporting of GHG emissions along the entire transport chains for passengers and freight.

Acknowledgements. This study was carried out within the MOST – Sustainable Mobility National Research Center and received funding from the European Union Next-GenerationEU (PIANO NAZIONALE DI RIPRESA E RESILIENZA (PNRR) – MISSIONE 4 COMPONENTE 2, INVESTIMENTO 1.4 – D.D. 1033 17/06/2022, CN00000023). This manuscript reflects only the authors' views and opinions, neither the European Union nor the European Commission can be considered responsible for them.

References

1. Energy and Air Pollution - World Energy Outlook 2016 Special Report (2016)
2. Haasz, T., et al.: Perspectives on decarbonizing the transport sector in the EU-28. Energy Strategy Rev. **20**, 124–132 (2018). https://doi.org/10.1016/j.esr.2017.12.007
3. Finger, M., Montero-Pascual, J.J., Serafimova, T.: Navigating towards the decarbonisation of European aviation. European University Institute (2021)
4. EC: 'Sustainable and Smart Mobility Strategy – putting European transport on track for the future', COM/2020/789 final (2020)
5. Dobers, K., Rüdiger, D., Jarmer, J.-P.: Guide for Greenhouse Gas Emissions Accounting at Logistics Sites (2019)
6. Ruiz-Méndez, D., Güereca, L.P.: Streamlined life cycle assessment for the environmental evaluation of products in the supply chain. In: Yakovleva, N., Frei, R., Rama Murthy, S. (eds.) Sustainable Development Goals and Sustainable Supply Chains in the Post-global Economy, pp. 115–131. Springer International Publishing, Cham (2019)
7. Bratt, C., Hallstedt, S., Robèrt, K.-H., Broman, G., Oldmark, J.: Assessment of eco-labelling criteria development from a strategic sustainability perspective. J. Cleaner Prod. **19**, 1631–1638 (2011). https://doi.org/10.1016/j.jclepro.2011.05.012
8. Roe, B.E., Teisl, M.F., Deans, C.R.: The economics of voluntary versus mandatory labels. Annu. Rev. Resour. Econ. **6**, 407–427 (2014). https://doi.org/10.1146/annurev-resource-100 913-012439
9. Suikkanen, J., Saarinen, I., Näyhä, A.: Practices and perceptions on ecolabels of Finnish companies with circular economy business models. In: E3S Web Conference, vol. 349, p. 01005 (2022). https://doi.org/10.1051/e3sconf/202234901005
10. ISO (2023). https://www.iso.org. Accessed 11 Mar 2023
11. Meis-Harris, J., Klemm, C., Kaufman, S., Curtis, J., Borg, K., Bragge, P.: What is the role of eco-labels for a circular economy? A rapid review of the literature. J. Cleaner Prod. **306**, 127134 (2021). https://doi.org/10.1016/j.jclepro.2021.127134
12. Purvis, B., Mao, Y., Robinson, D.: Three pillars of sustainability: in search of conceptual origins. Sustain. Sci. **14**, 681–695 (2019). https://doi.org/10.1007/s11625-018-0627-5
13. Payán-Sánchez, B., Labella-Fernández, A., Serrano-Arcos, M.M.: Modern age of sustainability. In: Sustainable Resource Management, pp. 75–98. Elsevier (2021)

14. Ceschin, F., Gaziulusoy, I.: Evolution of design for sustainability: from product design to design for system innovations and transitions. Des. Stud. **47**, 118–163 (2016)
15. Peña, C., et al.: Using life cycle assessment to achieve a circular economy. Int. J. Life Cycle Assess. **26**, 215–220 (2021). https://doi.org/10.1007/s11367-020-01856-z
16. Ehrler, V.C., et al.: Standardization of Transport Chain Emission Calculation – Status Quo and What Is Needed Next (2018)
17. Dehdari, P., Wlcek, H., Furmans, K.: An updated literature review of CO_2e calculation in road freight transportation. Multimodal Transp. **2**, 100068 (2023). https://doi.org/10.1016/j.multra.2022.100068
18. EU Ports European Economic Interest Group. Guidance for Greenhouse Gas Emission Footprinting for Container Terminals (2017)
19. European Committee for Standardization. EN 16258: Methodology for calculation and declaration of energy consumption and GHG emissions of transport services (freight and passengers). (2012).
20. Technical Documentation: United States Environmental Protection Agency. 2018 Smart-Way Truck Carrier Partner Tool (2018)
21. IMO (2023). https://www.imo.org/. Accessed 25 Feb 2025
22. Clean Cargo Working Group. Clean Cargo Working Group Carbon Emissions Accounting Methodology (2015)

A Review of Port KPIs Considering Safety, Environment, and Productivity as the Three Dimensions of Port Sustainability

Patrizia Serra$^{(\boxtimes)}$ ⓘ, Michela Codipietro, Alessandra Melis,
and Gianfranco Fancello ⓘ

DICAAR – Department of Civil and Environmental Engineering and Architecture, University
of Cagliari, 09123 Cagliari, Italy
pserra@unica.it

Abstract. Together with economic growth, ports generate a series of externalities, both social and environmental. The need to minimize environmental externalities while promoting economic growth and addressing societal requirements defines the concept of port sustainability. Undertaking actions aimed at increasing port sustainability requires in parallel the availability of quantitative tools to evaluate and monitor the performance of a port in this sense. Using the critical literature review method, this paper proposes a framework which categorizes port sustainability key performance indicators (KPIs) according to the three lines of sustainability: social, economic, environmental. The ultimate scope is to identify a set of sustainable KPIs that port managers can use to monitor and assess the impact of actions aimed at improving their sustainability.

Keywords: Sustainable Port · KPIs · Port Safety · Port Performance · Port Efficiency

1 Introduction

Ports are catalysts for economic development and are central to the growth of the global economy. Together with economic growth, however, ports also generate a series of externalities, both social and environmental [1]. The need to minimize environmental externalities while promoting economic growth and addressing societal requirements defines the concept of port sustainability (see, a.o., [2]).

The search for port sustainability has accelerated in the last two decades due to increased scrutiny of ports and environmental pressures [3]. Such growing attention towards port sustainability, and above all towards the measures that ports can implement internally to improve their performance in terms of sustainability, finds ample confirmation both in the practice of the port sector and in the relative rich scientific literature of the last decade [4].

Undertaking actions aimed at increasing port sustainability requires in parallel the availability of quantitative tools to evaluate and monitor the performance of a port in

© The Author(s), under exclusive license to Springer Nature Switzerland AG 2023
O. Gervasi et al. (Eds.): ICCSA 2023 Workshops, LNCS 14110, pp. 577–593, 2023.
https://doi.org/10.1007/978-3-031-37123-3_40

this sense. Performance assessment is indeed crucial to effectively supervise and manage logistics systems and is deemed essential for efficient planning and monitoring of activities within the decision-making process [5]. There are many reasons why a port or terminal should measure its performance, among the most relevant:

- it must know how effectively it is operating
- it must know what resources (manpower, equipment, areas, etc.) are needed in relation to its activities
- it must be able to monitor its performance and improvements over time, and compare them with those of its competitors
- it must be able to define a set of goals and compare its performance against those goals, and eventually adjust its goals for the future.

For these and other reasons, it is crucial that ports or terminals measure their performance, set performance targets and then regularly evaluate their performance against those targets.

The key role of performance measures in logistics systems has found large attention in the scientific literature [6–9], and several approaches have been applied to the purpose [10]. These approaches may vary depending on the perspective they adopt to investigate performance (product-oriented, process-oriented or planning level-oriented) or the method they use.

As for the latter, [11] provide an overview of the main methods used for the measurement of logistics performance, even in the port domain. Among the various methods available, the leading role of key performance indicators (KPIs) emerges for their simplicity of use and numerous advantages they offer: they are not predefined, they can be used to measure the performance of a specific process or segment of the system, to monitor its performance over time, to compare its performance with the others, etc.

This document proposes a review of the port sustainability KPIs, i.e. the indicators that can be used to evaluate the performance of a port from a sustainability-oriented perspective. The focus is on internal port sustainability and on the analysis of indicators that can be used to evaluate the sustainability performance of port actions which in turn strongly depend on the performance of the workers who carry them out. Port labor is in fact a key element in the performance of a port. Only in Europe, it is estimated that more than 110,000 regular dockworkers are engaged in loading and unloading ships and in other port-based services [12]. Despite the progressive shift towards the capital-intensive paradigm, the human factor still represents one of the most precious assets in ports [13]. Several scholars have investigated and proved the causal relation between port labor and competitiveness, concluding that port labor affects the final performance of a port [14], even in terms of sustainability.

The paradigm of port sustainability is here understood in its three-dimensional structure [15]. Breaking free from a concept of port sustainability which is still too often associated exclusively with the issue of environmental impact, the objective of the analysis is to investigate port performance indicators in relation to both environmental, economic, and social sustainability.

More specifically, the study involves the three spheres of port sustainability as follows:

- safety of operations, for the social dimension
- productivity of internal port operations, for the economic dimension
- energy consumptions and related emissions of internal port operations, for the environmental dimension.

As for the first sphere, sustainability and safety are two closely interrelated concepts that both concern the conservation of resources. Specifically, safety is about human resources and the safeguarding of human life and well-being. The basic principle is that a port system cannot be sustainable if it is not safe for humans. Port safety can thus be described as not only the measures taken to reduce the risk of port injuries and deaths but also the feeling of being safe in the port system and the reliability that port workers will not be injured or killed in that system. The focus of the analysis will be on active safety and the importance of monitoring operators' fatigue and stress for enhancing work performance while reducing the possibility of accidents.

As for the second sphere, broadly speaking, the term productivity refers to the measure of the efficiency of a production process, given by the ratio between output and input. A port can be considered efficient or highly productive if, for given inputs, it produces a maximum output, or if it uses minimal inputs to produce a given output. Because of the importance they hold for the assessment of the economic sustainability of port operations, productivity-related KPIs have long been a topic of interest to both port managers and academics.

As for the third sphere, international shipping is recognized as one of the largest GHG emitting sectors of the global economy. According to IMO estimates, the share of shipping emissions in global anthropogenic emissions has increased from 2.76% in 2012 to 2.89% in 2018, and emissions are projected to increase from about 90% of 2008 emissions in 2018 to 90–130% of 2008 emissions by 2050 [16]. As for the port area, shipping emissions in ports are substantial, accounting for 18 million tons of CO_2 emissions, 0.4 million tons of NO_x, 0.2 million of SO_x and 0.03 million tons of PM_{10} in 2011. Most shipping emissions in ports (CH4, CO, CO_2 and NO_x) are estimated to grow fourfold up to 2050. This would bring CO_2-emissions from ships in ports to approximately 70 million tons in 2050 [17]. The focus of the analysis will be on environmental KPIs to monitor internal port emissions and energy consumption.

Using the method of critical literature review, this document proposes a framework that classifies port sustainability KPIs according to the three dimensions of sustainability. The ultimate goal is to identify a set of sustainable port KPIs that port managers can use to monitor and evaluate the impact of actions aimed at improving the sustainability of their operations.

The structure of the paper is the following. After this introductory section, Sect. 2 briefly presents the methodology used to perform this critical review, Sect. 3 discusses the proposed framework that classifies port sustainability KPIs according to its three dimensions, finally Sect. 4 concludes.

2 Methodology

This study uses the critical literature review method to answer the following research question: *what are the main quantitative KPIs that can be used to evaluate the sustainability of ports encompassing the triple bottom lines, i.e., the social, economic, and environmental dimensions?*

The main goal of this overview is to categorize the available port sustainability KPIs into three categories:

- port KPIs related to safety of operations, stress and fatigue (social dimension)
- port KPIs related to productivity performance (economic dimension)
- port KPIs related to environmental and energy impact of internal port operations (environmental dimension).

The emphasis is on analyzing data from sufficient established research in the field, without covering all the studies contained in it, but still leading to a combination of different perspectives. Unlike a systematic literature review, which is commonly based only on peer-reviewed academic studies, this review is constructed following the triangulation search approach, which refers to the use of multiple and diverse data sources to develop a comprehensive understanding of the topic under study. To build an overall picture of the complex issue of port sustainability KPIs that considers the three dimensions of sustainability, this research therefore developed on two fronts:

- review of the relevant peer-reviewed academic production
- analysis of the relevant gray literature (chapters of books, proceedings, technical reports of trusted experts, etc.).

The selected studies were collected by searching the Scopus and Google Scholar databases between December 2022 and March 2023. Searching within titles and keywords iteratively used the following keywords: (port OR terminal) AND (Sustainab*) AND (measures OR indicators OR KPI OR performance OR evaluation).

The studies identified through the keyword search were preliminarily filtered by reading the abstracts to understand if they could fall within the scope of the analysis. Additional relevant studies that were not captured by keyword search were identified through the snowball technique and personal knowledge of the authors. In total, the review converges on approximately 40 studies whose contents are used to answer the proposed research question.

It should be noted that this research is not intended to be comprehensive or all-encompassing as there may be several studies that the research performed did not capture. However, it provides a general picture of the state of the art of the main KPIs so far available in the literature to measure port sustainability in its three dimensions.

3 Review of KPIs for Port Sustainability

This section presents the results of the performed review organized into three sub-paragraphs, each relating to a dimension of port sustainability:

- port KPIs related to safety of operations, stress and fatigue (social dimension)
- port KPIs related to productivity (economic dimension)
- port KPIs related to environmental and energy impact of internal port operations (environmental dimension).

3.1 Port KPIs Related to Safety of Operations, Stress and Fatigue

According to the so-called "systemic approach", the port can be seen as a complex and dynamic system made up of three components: vehicles/equipment, infrastructures, and management system. Man is at the centre of this system and can be the recipient of the system design (man-user) or a component of the system itself (man-operator). In such a systemic vision of the port, each component interacts both with the other internal components and with the external environment. In the relationships between the components of the system, safety arises as a design area whose impact can fall - depending on the objectives - on the man-user or on the man-operator. In this regard, two different areas of study can be identified:

- passive safety, which deals with limiting the negative effects of the accident
- active safety, which deals instead with studying the measures useful for reducing the risk of an accident occurring.

Focusing on the performance of the operator, and therefore of the man-operator, the focus in this section will be on active safety and on the importance of monitoring operator fatigue and stress to improve work performance by reducing the possibility of accidents. Fatigue is multidimensional as it affects both the physical and psychological bodies. Operating while fatigued is associated with longer and more delayed reactions in response to changing demands, fewer steering corrections, reduced galvanic skin response, increased body movements, and increased irritability [18]. In addition to accidents, there are a number of work-related health problems associated with dock work (for example, musculoskeletal disorders, whole-body vibration effects, noise-induced hearing loss, accidental intoxication from chemical exposure and harmful biological substances, etc.). Furthermore, activities that require high levels of production and fast turnaround times, such as the loading and unloading of container ships, can lead to psychosocial health problems such as stress and fatigue which, in addition to making workers ill, also lead to which increase the risk of accidents. From the analysis of the state of the art it can be stated that there are not many studies on the safety and health conditions of port workers inside a port.

The literature seems to deal mainly with technical design and mathematical modelling problems with reference to the risk analysis techniques adopted for specific ports [19]. Analyzing the impacts that containerization has had on worker safety, [20] state that several factors can influence the frequency of occupational accidents, in particular economic factors, technologies used (e.g. low automation, discontinuous operation), work organization (e.g. execution of a specific task, availability of adequate equipment for this task), environmental conditions (e.g. weather conditions, time of day, day of the week, etc.) and human factors (e.g. age, work experience, education). In this regard, it has been shown that technological advances can lead to improvements in productivity and occupational health and safety, but not necessarily simultaneously.

The scientific literature on port worker stress and fatigue is not extensive. Among the analyzed studies related to stress and fatigue in the port environment, we can mention [21–23]. According to these authors, human error is one of the main factors influencing port safety. Indeed, in ports, 80–90% of accidents occurring on the docks are caused by human error. Therefore, despite the high degree of automation achieved in ports and container terminals, the operator continues to play a very important role. The growing level of specialization, especially required of crane operators, has also been accompanied by a growing level of stress and consequently by an increased risk of serious accidents. Studies on stress and fatigue fall within the scope of active safety. Active safety includes both the study of human factors and the areas of ergonomics and anthropometry. In general, the factors that cause work stress can be divided into:

– physical factors: environmental (heat, cold, noise, vibrations, etc.) and physiological (lack of sleep, dehydration, muscle fatigue, etc.)
– mental factors: cognitive (too much or too little information, judgment difficulties, etc.) and emotional (pressure, frustration, boredom/inactivity, etc.).

[24] propose a set of indicators to be applied in port areas related to health, safety and occupational safety starting from the indicators used by the ports and then implementing them on the basis of the proposals of the interested parties. The final list of selected occupational health indicators includes:

– the number of deaths from accidents at work in a period
– the number of full calendar days in which the operator is unable to work due to an accident at work
– the number of occupational accidents in a period.

Similarly, [20] propose two indices to analyze the incidence of port workers' injuries in the port of Genoa:

– the frequency index, given by the ratio between the total number of accidents and the number of hours worked
– the accident index, given by the ratio between the number of total accidents and the number of employees.

The study by [25] proposes to use the following port security indicators:

– damages per year or damages per 1000 TEU
– losses per year or losses per 1000 TEU
– damage to dangerous goods (in % of cases)
– total number of injuries per year.

To evaluate the effectiveness of simulator training, the study by [23] uses a series of indicators relating to operator safety, stress and fatigue. These include incorrect positioning of containers, the number of collisions and the stress level of the operators.

The paper by [21] highlights that there are no simple and immediate methods to measure stress and fatigue. The measures adopted so far in the literature concern:

- physiological parameters, used to evaluate tiredness and/or drowsiness (EEG electroencephalogram, ECG electrocardiogram, etc.)
- behavioral parameters, used to measure fatigue. They are mainly based on the frequency of body movements
- parameters of facial behavior, used to evaluate fatigue: changes in facial expression, eye and head movements are all indicators of fatigue. Other parameters such as pupil movement and saccades are indicative of the level of alertness.
- performance parameters: number of errors in carrying out the task, number of near misses, number of collisions, abrupt maneuvers, etc.

However, the data obtained from these measurements, mainly carried out with medical instruments, are not easy to interpret.

Table 1 lists the safety-related indicators analyzed. It should be noted that this analysis is not intended to be exhaustive as it mainly aims to provide a general picture of the state of the art of the main environmental/energy performance indicators used so far in the port sector.

Table 1. Summary of the analyzed safety-related KPIs used in ports

Health, stress and fatigue indicators	Unit of measure	Reference
Frequency rate of fatal work accidents	Accidents/month or year	[24]
Number of fatal work accidents	Fatal accidents/ year	
Near miss	Near miss/month or year	
Frequency index	accidents/h worked	[20]
Injury index	accidents/employees	
Number of accidents in ports	accidents/year	[24–26]
Wrong container positioning	n. of events/employee	[23]
Collisions	n. of events/employee	
EEG, ECG	*instrumental detection*	[21]
Number of body movements recorded during task performance		
Changes of facial expression		
Eye movements		
Head movements		
Pupil movements and saccades		

Source: authors' own elaboration

3.2 Port KPIs Related to Productivity Performance

Until the end of the 1990s, port efficiency studies mainly focused on partial productivity measures (e.g., vessel turnaround times, crane productivity, etc.), since then, academics have shown an increasing interest in the development of methods that analyze the overall efficiency of the port, especially for container terminals [27]. While looking at the overall productivity of the port seems to be the best solution, in practice it entails a number of problems. The port environment can be considered a dynamic system within which different actors interact (carriers, port operators, stevedores, dock workers, port authorities, shippers, railways, government, etc.). Each actor wants to achieve a certain objective (which often conflicts with the objective of other subjects), and, in pursuing it, it affects the overall productivity of the terminal (or even of the entire logistics system). The various subjects who relate to the terminal evaluate the quality and productivity of the port service with respect to various parameters. By way of example: the average hourly productivity of quay cranes represents an important indicator for the shipping company, while the presence of parking and maintenance areas for empty containers can be useful for the owning company [28].

Because of their importance, port performance indicators have long been a topic of interest to port managers and academics. As early as 1976, UNCTAD proposed a series of port performance indicators divided into two broad categories: financial and operational [29]. The former measured the financial performance of the port in terms of monetary units per ton of cargo, while the latter provided a measure of operational performance including late arrival (ship/day), waiting time (hours/ship), service (hours/vessel), delivery times (hours/vessel), tonnage per vessel (ton/vessel), number of groups per vessel per shift (groups/vessel shift), tons per vessel/hour in port (ton/h), tons per group-hour (tons/gang-h).

The paper by [25] proposes a set of quality and performance indicators for intermodal terminals using the point of view of the terminal customer and the terminal operator, respectively. The first group, called quality indicators, describes the service level of a terminal and provides customers with a correct view of the terminal's performance in terms of waiting times, reliability, accessibility, flexibility, security, services in general and frequencies. The second group, called performance indicators, describes the productivity of a terminal and its processes.

According to [30], the productivity of a container terminal depends on the efficient use of manpower, equipment and land, therefore productivity measurement serves to quantify the efficiency of these three resources. The authors list the elements of the terminal which - according to them - influence productivity and for each element they define productivity factors and productivity measures. The measure of gross crane productivity can be expressed in movements/gross group or crane hours, while the net productivity of the crane is measured in movements/gross group or crane hours - idle time. The measure of gross labor productivity is given by the number of movements/man/hour. It must be assumed that there are limits to the throughput of the terminal and such limits can be imposed by different factors (institutional, physical, economic, etc.) [31].

Table 2. Summary of the analyzed productivity KPIs used in ports

Productivity KPIs	Unit of measure	Bibliographic reference
Vessel service time	hours/ship	[29]
Tons per ship hour at berth	tons/hour-ship	
Tons per gang-hour	tons/gang-hour	
Throughput	TEUs/day or week or year; TEUs/year-hectare; TEUs/year-employee	[a.o., 25, 21, 23]
Total number of transhipped TEU/loading units per hour	TEUs/hour	
Tranhipment capacity	TEUs/day or week or year	
Labour productivity	TEUs/year-employee	
Crane rate	TEUs/hour-crane	
Crane load	total annual throughput/n. of cranes	
Crane productivity	moves/hour-crane	[21, 30, 32]
Gross labour productivity	moves/man hour	
Equipment productivity	moves/hour-machine	
Single move time	time/move, average time/move, max time/move	[23]
Wrong container positioning	n. of events/day or month or year	
Extra container moves	n. of extra moves/ day or month or year	

Source: authors' own elaboration

Following a similar approach, [32] identifies among the various key productivity measures the following:

– crane productivity, calculated per crane and expressed in gross and net values
– productivity of the equipment, expressed as the number of container movements performed per hour of work
– labor productivity, calculated per man-hour in a given period.

Regarding labor productivity, the study by [21] analyzed the performance of dockside crane operators. In this study, the productivity and performance of dockside crane operators is measured in terms of containers moved per hour. The objective of the investigation was to construct experimentally performance curves for ship-to-shore gantry crane operators according to the Yerkes-Dodson model. The authors found that low workload translates into poor performance, because as the workload increases, the level of performance increases, until it reaches its peak. From there on, performance degrades as the workload increases. However, it has been observed that, if the operator is skilled, it is possible to maintain high levels of performance even under high workloads. This means that it is possible to intervene on the productivity of quayside cranes through the training and updating of quayside crane operators. In this regard, an interesting study on the use of the simulator as a training tool in container terminals can be found in [23]. To evaluate the effectiveness of simulator training, the authors quantify the performance of dockside crane operators using the following measures:

- number of moves per unit of time
- average and maximum travel time
- single movement time
- wrong container placement number
- number of extra container movements.

Table 2 summarizes the productivity indicators discussed in this section.

3.3 Port KPIs Related to Environmental and Energy Impact of Port Operations

There are estimates according to which berthing activities contribute to emissions of up to 69% of the total ship activities at the container port [33], but they are not the only emissions at hand. However, the percentage of CO_2 emissions to be specifically attributed to port activities has never been quantified, though it is widely recognized that since maritime trade will increase, in the absence of adequate measures, these emissions will also increase [34, 35]. In 2022, climate change has become, for the first time, the top environmental priority of European ports [36].

Analyzing the port system, GHG emissions are attributable to the following components:

- vessels
- port operations
- land transport.

Taking the Port of Los Angeles as an example, about 80% of total port emissions are generated by their customers (ships, trucks, and trains) while only 20% is attributable to port equipment [37]. In the literature, most of the studies have focused mainly on the emissions produced by ships at the quay and on those generated by land transport while very few articles have addressed the issue of CO_2 emissions from the point of view of port operations [38]. Among them, the study by [34] analyzes the policies that ports implement to reduce GHG emissions and, in particular, the technical and operational measures that the various "port polluters" (maritime operators, ports and land transport) should adopt. The measures identified for the reduction of GHG emissions in ports are the following:

- information measures, essential for monitoring emissions and energy consumption and establishing a baseline
- equipment, involving the physical change of emission sources in order to get newer, cleaner and more energy efficient engines
- energy measures, to provide cleaner energy, other than fossil fuels
- energy efficiency measures, to reduce the energy consumption of port equipment, buildings, vehicles, warehouses, and berthing vessels

- port operational measures such as digitalization, intelligent logistics, container terminal automation, green purchasing and procurement, circular economy, port city integration, etc.

Some authors have examined the environmental impact generated by the different equipment of a container terminal. Trucks (or tractor trailers or yard tractors), rubber gantry cranes and quay cranes are the main sources of CO_2 emissions. This has led researchers and terminal operators to focus on the study of appropriate energy efficiency measures in port terminals [39].

On the seaside, the main source of port pollution is the quay crane. To accommodate the phenomenon of naval gigantism and the growth of maritime trade, the market offers increasingly larger cranes with ever greater handling productivity, in order to minimize the permanence of ships in port. On the one hand, this has led to growing needs for electrical power (up to 4 MW for operating a crane) and, on the other hand, has increased the gap between technical productivity (crane cycles/h) and productivity achieved operationally, making this equipment unsustainable [40].

As regards the connection between the seaside area and the yard, CO_2 emissions generated by trucks have been shown to be one of the main sources of pollution in maritime transport [41]. Among the proposed solutions is the conversion of terminal tractors from diesel to more sustainable energy sources [42], or the replacement of traditional trucks with automated guided vehicles, which run smoother and more efficiently by being driven with controllable speeds and accelerations [40]. As with traditional trucks, optimization of consumption can be achieved through a driving style characterized by low accelerations and decelerations and a better synchronization of operations (see, among others, [43]). As regards the stacking of containers in the yard, some authors address the problem of choosing the most sustainable equipment [40] while others analyze to what extent the scheduling of yard cranes can optimize lifting operations thus reducing energy consumption [44].

What emerges in all cases is the need to monitor the phenomenon through the quantification of quantitative and measurable quantities. Environmental and energy efficiency indicators can thus be used to evaluate and monitor how a port is performing in this regard using scientific evidence and quantifiable measures.

However, despite the growing awareness of ports on the importance of using environmental and energy efficiency indicators, there is no common approach regarding which indicators can be adopted.

The paper by [45] identifies a comprehensive set of environmental performance indicators used in the port sector distinguishing between management indicators (which provide information on management efforts affecting the environmental performance of the port), operational indicators (which provide information on the environmental performance of port operations) and environmental indicators (which provide information on environmental conditions). Martinez-Moya et al. [42] analyze the energy efficiency and CO_2 emissions of the Valencia terminal and propose an estimate of the diesel consumption of the terminal's engines expressed both in TOE (tonnes of oil equivalent) and in liters/TEU, and the corresponding emission in $kgCO_2$/TEU. The authors also propose an estimate of the electricity consumption and CO_2 emissions of quay cranes expressed respectively in KWh or KWh/TEU, and in $kgCO_2$/TEU.

Table 3. Summary of the analyzed environmental and energy efficiency KPIs used in ports

Environmental/Energy KPIs	Unit of measure	Bibliographic reference
Resources consumption	–	[45]
Diesel fuel consumption of yard tractors	TOEs (tonnes of oil equivalents)/year	[42] [35]
	liters/TEU	
Electrical consumption of STS cranes	KWh/year	
	KWh/TEU	
GHG emissions	tons/week	
CO_2 emissions of yard tractors and STS cranes	kg of CO_2/TEU	
Consumption of diesel-mechanically driven tractor trailers	liters/hour	[40]
Amount of energy per container visit (container passage through the terminal)	–	
Fuel consumption of the truck as acceleration varies	liters/second	[43]
Energy consumption per load unit	KJ / KW per load unit	[25]

Source: authors' own elaboration

The study by [40] proposes to use the amount of energy per container visit to quantify the sustainability of a terminal. Following a similar aggregated approach, in which containers are viewed as energy consumers during handling, the paper by [25] defines a set of performance indicators for intermodal terminals which include energy consumption per load unit expressed in Kj/Kw. In [43], the energy consumption of diesel trucks used to transport containers within the terminal is analyzed using distance as the main factor.

Table 3 summarizes the environmental and energy efficiency indicators analyzed.

4   Discussion and Conclusion

This document presented a framework that classifies port sustainability KPIs according to the three dimensions of sustainability: safety of operations (social dimension), productivity (economic dimension), environmental and energy impact of inland port operations (environmental dimension).

As far as the safety dimension is concerned, the indicators analyzed seem to be attributable to two main groups: KPIs that monitor the number, frequency, severity and cost of accidents and KPIs used to monitor the onset of stress and fatigue in port operators to reduce the likelihood of recurring accidents. If the first can be extremely useful for monitoring the port's performance over time in terms of safety and promptly identifying any critical issues that require timely intervention, the second can allow not only to establish for which workload values port workers can work in safety, but also to objectively verify the effects that safety-oriented measures and initiatives can have in terms of increasing safety or reducing risk. For example, to reduce the onset of stress and fatigue, port workers need to be sufficiently trained for the workload they will be subjected to. Indeed, port stakeholders typically advocate high standards of training to ensure safe and efficient operations in ports [46]. The analyzed indicators can then be used to evaluate the effectiveness of port training courses and the application of health and safety standards in a port or terminal. Since in the real world it can be difficult to measure the level of fatigue and stress of the operators, these analyzes are often carried out in a virtual environment using simulators assisted by electromedical devices for the detection of the physiological parameters linked to the onset of fatigue and stress.

As far as the productivity dimension is concerned, there is a wide range of KPIs that can be traced back to the evaluation of port performance, these indicators vary enormously according to the point of view adopted but have in common the fact that they can all be traced back to three fundamental elements: labour/workforce, port equipment and port infrastructure. Depending on the level of aggregation used in the estimation, these KPIs provide a measure of terminal productivity which can sometimes refer to a single piece of equipment, a single worker or team, a given unit of time (work hour, year, etc.) or infrastructural entity (linear meter of quay, square, etc.), sometimes to the entire port/terminal.

As for the port's environmental and energy sustainability KPIs, despite the growing awareness of ports on the importance of using these indicators, from the analysis carried out there does not seem to be a common approach on which indicators should be adopted. Most studies focus on emissions from port vessels and land transport, and very few articles address emissions from a port operations perspective. The analyzed energy/environmental KPIs can be classified into two large groups according to the approach on which they are based. The first group is based on an aggregated approach and provides a quantitative estimate of the amount of energy and/or pollutant emissions per container visit or per unit load. These aggregate KPIs consider containers, or more generally load units, as consumers of energy and producers of emissions during handling. The second group, on the other hand, adopts a disaggregated approach to provide an estimate of energy consumption and environmental impacts relating to the individual equipment used in carrying out port operations. These indicators mostly provide an estimate of energy consumption and related emissions as a function of the distance traveled or the reference time unit.

What emerges by observing the KPIs and the three dimensions of sustainability analyzed is that they are strongly correlated. Although a subdivision of the indicators analyzed within the three sustainability areas has been proposed, the same indicator can often be attributable to more than one area, and it is sometimes even difficult to understand which is the primary area of its impact. Some examples can help to understand the strong correlation that exists. Although the economic KPIs are mainly used to evaluate the profitability of the port, they also have implications in terms of both environmental and social sustainability. Similarly, improving the efficiency of port operations can reduce energy consumption and related CO_2 emissions. The productivity of the worker can depend on that of the equipment on which he works but also on the safety procedures adopted in the terminal and can in turn be both an indicator of safety, productivity, and cost-effectiveness. Consider, for example, the indicator related to the number of incorrect container placements or the number of extra container movements. This single indicator finds immediate space in all three dimensions analyzed as it can provide at the same time a measure of social sustainability (a high number of errors is usually related to high levels of fatigue and tiredness, low levels of training, a greater number of accidents), economic sustainability (unproductive maneuvers lead to a slowdown in the operating cycle and additional costs), environmental sustainability (extra movements mean higher energy consumption and extra emissions). These elements make it clear how much the evaluation of port sustainability must go through the evaluation of different elements, it must not be reduced to the use of single indicators but rather foresee their combined and integrated use.

Using the method of critical literature review, this paper has proposed a framework that classifies port sustainability KPIs according to the three dimensions of sustainability. The identified sets of sustainable port KPIs can help port policy makers and industry operators monitor and evaluate the impact of actions aimed at improving the sustainability of their operations and make reliable decisions for a wider implementation of sustainability. Looking in particular at the importance that advanced training practices are acquiring in the port environment for the improvement of sustainable performance, the quantification of the value assumed by the relevant indicators before and after the training period will allow port managers to evaluate the impact of the training on the three spheres considered. The ultimate goal is to make available to those who work in the port and logistics sector a series of tools that can help make operations safer, more efficient and more sustainable by acting directly on the advanced training of the human capital.

Acknowledgements. This study was carried out within the MOST – Sustainable Mobility National Research Center and received funding from the European Union Next-GenerationEU (PIANO NAZIONALE DI RIPRESA E RESILIENZA (PNRR) – MISSIONE 4 COMPONENTE 2, INVESTIMENTO 1.4 – D.D. 1033 17/06/2022, CN00000023). This manuscript reflects only the authors' views and opinions, neither the European Union nor the European Commission can be considered responsible for them.

References

1. Acciaro, M., Vanelslander, T., Sys, C., Ferrari, C., Roumboutsos, A., Giuliano, G., Kapros, S.: Environmental sustainability in seaports: a framework for successful innovation. Marit. Policy Manage. **41**(5), 480–500 (2014)
2. Cheon, S.: The economic–social performance relationships of ports: roles of stakeholders and organizational tension. Sustain. Dev. **25**(1), 50–62 (2017)
3. UNCTAD: Review of maritime transport 2021. In: United Nation Conference on Trade and Development, Geneva, Switzerland (2021)
4. Alamoush, A.S., Ballini, F., Ölçer, A.I.: Ports' technical and operational measures to reduce GHG emission and improve energy efficiency - a review. Mar. Pollut. Bull. **160**, 111508 (2020)

5. Neely, A., Adams, C., Crowe, P.: The performance prism in practice. J. Measuring Bus. Excellence **5**(2), 6–13 (2001)
6. Fancello, G., Schintu, A., Serra, P.: An experimental analysis of Mediterranean supply chains through the use of cost KPIs. Transp. Res. Procedia **30**, 137–146 (2018)
7. Shepherd, C., Günter, H.: Measuring SC performance - current research and future directions. Int. J. Prod. Performance Manage. **55.3**(4), 242–258 (2006)
8. Agami, N., Saleh, M., Rasmy, M.: Supply chain performance measurement approaches - Review and classification. J. Organ. Manage. Stud. 1–20 (2012)
9. Fadda, P., Fancello, G., Mancini, S., Pani, C., Serra, P.: Design and optimisation of an innovative two-hub-and-spoke network for the Mediterranean short-sea-shipping market. Comput. Ind. Eng. **149**, 106847 (2020)
10. Gunasekaran, A., Kobu, B.: Performance measures and metrics in logistics and supply chain management - a review of recent literature (1995–2004) for research and applications. Int. J. Prod. Res. **45**(12), 2819–2840 (2007)
11. Serra, P., Fancello, G.: Performance assessment of alternative SSS networks by combining KPIs and factor-cluster analysis. Eur. Transp. Res. Rev. **12**(1), 1–24 (2020)
12. Van Hooydonk, E.: Port Labour in the EU: Labour Market, Qualification and Training, Health and Safety. European Commission, Brussels (2014)
13. Satta, G., Maugeri, S., Panetti, E., Ferretti, M.: Port labour, competitiveness and drivers of change in the Mediterranean Sea: a conceptual framework. Prod. Plan. Control **30**(13), 1102–1117 (2019)
14. Serra, P., Fadda, P., Fancello, G.: Evaluation of alternative scenarios of labour flexibility for dockworkers in maritime container terminals. Marit. Policy Manag. **43**(3), 371–385 (2016)
15. Gimenez, C., Sierra, V., Rodon, J.: Sustainable operations: their impact on the triple bottom line. Int. J. Prod. Econ. **140**(1), 149–159 (2012)
16. Faber, J., et al.: Fourth IMO GHG Study. London, UK (2020)
17. Merk, O.: Shipping Emissions in Ports. International Transport Forum, Paris (No. 2014–20). France, Discussion Paper (2014)
18. Cardoso, M., Fulton, F., Callaghan, J.P., Johnson, M., Albert, W.J.: A pre/post evaluation of fatigue, stress and vigilance amongst commercially licensed truck drivers performing a prolonged driving task. Int. J. Occup. Saf. Ergon. **25**(3), 344–354 (2019)
19. Walters, D., Wadsworth, E., Bhattacharya, S.: What about the workers? Experiences of arrangements for safety and health in global container terminals. Saf. Sci. **121**, 474–484 (2020)
20. Fabiano, B., Currò, F., Reverberi, A.P., Pastorino, R.: Port safety and the container revolution: a statistical study on human factor and occupational accidents over the long period. Saf. Sci. **48**(8), 980–990 (2010)
21. Fancello, G., Errico, G.M., Fadda, P.: Processing and analysis of ship-to-shore gantry crane operator performance curves in container terminals. J. Marit. Res. **5**(2), 39–58 (2008)
22. Bruzzone, A.G., Fadda, P., Fancello, G., D'Errico, G., Bocca, E., Massei, M.: A vibration effect as fatigue source in a port crane simulator for training and research: spectra validation process. In: Proceeding of I3M Conference-International Conference on Harbour, Maritime and Multimodal Logistics Modelling and Simulation 2009, vol. 1, pp. 77–86 (2009)
23. Bruzzone, A.G., Longo, F.: 3D simulation as training tool in container terminals: the TRAINPORTS simulator. J. Manuf. Syst. **32**(1), 85–98 (2013)
24. Antão, P., Calderón, M., Puig, M., Michail, A., Wooldridge, C., Darbra, R.M.: Identification of occupational health, safety, security (OHSS) and environmental performance indicators in port areas. Saf. Sci. **85**, 266–275 (2016)
25. Siciliano, G., Vaghi, C., Ruesch, M. and Abel, H.: Indicatori di qualità e performance per i terminal intermodali europei. SIET VIII Riunione Scientifica, Trieste (2006)

26. Fadda, P., Fancello, G., Frigau, L., Mandas, M., Medda, A., Mola, F., Pelligra, V., Porta, M., Serra, P.: Investigating the role of the human element in maritime accidents using semi-supervised hierarchical methods. Transp. Res. Procedia **52**, 252–259 (2021)

27. Pallis, A.A., Vitsounis, T.K., De Langen, P.W., Notteboom, T.E.: Port economics, policy and management: content classification and survey. Transp. Rev. **31**(4), 445–471 (2011)

28. Benacchio, M.: L'utilizzo del fattore produttivo spazio nei terminal container: linee di evoluzione (2001). https://www.openstarts.units.it/bitstream/10077/8113/1/M_Benacchio_Trasporti_2001_85.pdf. Accessed 3 Apr 2023

29. UNCTAD: Port Performance Indicators (1976). https://unctad.org/system/files/official-document/tdbc4d131sup1rev1_en.pdf. Accessed 25 Mar 2023

30. Dowd, T.J., Leschine, T.M.: Container terminal productivity: a perspective. Marit. Policy Manag. **17**(2), 107–112 (1990)

31. Lim, S., Pettit, S., Abouarghoub, W., Beresford, A.: Port sustainability and performance: a systematic literature review. Transp. Res. Part D **72**, 47–64 (2019)

32. Esmer, S.: Performance measurements of container terminal operations. Dokuz Eylül Üniversitesi, 1 (2008). Accessed 3 Apr 2023

33. Budiyanto, M.A., Habibie, M.R., Shinoda, T.: Estimation of CO_2 emissions for ship activities at container port as an effort towards a green port index. Energy Rep. **8**, 229–236 (2022)

34. Alamoush, A.S., Ballini, F., Ölçer, A.I.: Revisiting port sustainability as a foundation for the implementation of the United Nations Sustainable Development Goals (UN SDGs). J. Ship. Trade **6**(1), 1–40 (2022)

35. Serra, P., Fancello, G.: Towards the IMO's GHG goals: a critical overview of the perspectives and challenges of the main options for decarbonizing international shipping. Sustainability **12**(8), 3220 (2020)

36. ESPO: Environmental Report (2022). https://www.espo.be/media/ESP-2959%20(Sustainability%20Report%202022)_V8.pdf. Accessed 21 Mar 2023

37. Chen, G., Govindan, K., Golias, M.M.: Reducing truck emissions at container terminals in a low carbon economy: Proposal of a queueing-based bi-objective model for optimizing truck arrival pattern. Transp. Res. Part E Logistics Transp. Rev. **55**, 3–22 (2013)

38. Serra, P., Fadda, P., Fancello, G.: Investigating the potential mitigating role of network design measures for reducing the environmental impact of maritime chains: the Mediterranean case. Case Stud. Transp. Pol. **8**(2), 263–280 (2020)

39. Drungilas, D., et al.: Deep reinforcement learning based optimization of automated guided vehicle time and energy consumption in a container terminal. Alex. Eng. J. **67**, 397–407 (2023)

40. Rijsenbrij, J.C., Wieschemann, A.: Sustainable container terminals: a design approach. In Handbook of terminal planning, pp. 61–82. Springer, New York (2011)

41. Yu, H., Ge, Y.E., Chen, J., Luo, L., Tan, C., Liu, D.: CO_2 emission evaluation of yard tractors during loading at container terminals. Transp. Res. Part D Transp. Environ. **53**, 17–36 (2017)

42. Martínez-Moya, J., Vazquez-Paja, B., Maldonado, J.A.G.: Energy efficiency and CO_2 emissions of port container terminal equipment: evidence from the Port of Valencia. Energy Policy **131**, 312–319 (2019)

43. Eglynas, T., et al.: Evaluation of the energy consumption of container diesel trucks in a container terminal - a case study at Klaipeda port. Sci. Progress **104**(3), 1–25 (2021)

44. He, J., Huang, Y., Yan, W., Wang, S.: Integrated internal truck, yard crane and quay crane scheduling in a container terminal considering energy consumption. Expert Syst. Appl. **42**(5), 2464–2487 (2015)

45. Puig, M., Wooldridge, C., Darbra, R.M.: Identification and selection of environmental performance indicators for sustainable port development. Mar. Pollut. Bull. **81**(1), 124–130 (2014)

46. Turnbull, P.: Training and qualification systems in the EU port sector: setting the state of play and delineating an ETF vision. Cardiff: European Transport Workers' Federation (2009). https://www.etf-europe.org/wp-content/uploads/2018/08/Training-and-qualification-systems-in-the-EU-port-sector-EN.pdf. Accessed 20 Apr 2023

The Port - City Relations in the Era of Hybridization

Giuseppe Borruso[1]([⊠])[iD] and Ginevra Balletto[2][iD]

[1] DEAMS - Department of Economics, Business, Mathematics and Statistics "Bruno de Finetti", University of Trieste, via A. Valerio 4/1, 34127 Trieste, Italy
giuseppe.borruso@deams.units.it
[2] DICAAR - Department of Civil, Environmental Engineering and Architecture, University of Cagliari, via Marengo, 2, Cagliari, Italy
balletto@unica.it

Abstract. Ports play an important role as interfaces among sea and land, elements of organization of the coastal space, with important influences on the cities and regions they are inserted in. A wide attention and consideration has been put in time by scholars from different disciplines on the relationships between ports and cities on the waterfront, following the different stages of maritimization and the evolution of the roles of ports and cities. In particular, during this evolution, ports become more and more hybrid in their roles and characters, changing continuously their shapes and functions, and, consequently, the relationship they have with their surrounding areas, cities in particular, being the most proximal elements to ports. In research and planning, however, little attention has been put towards dry ports and inner harbors, as the new areas important for ports, hosting vital operations for linking ports and their hinterlands in order to keep quays free for freight handling on the seaside. In this paper we put the attention on the process of hybridization of ports in time, focusing in particular on the new challenges coming out from the evolution of port activities into inner areas and, therefore, observing the interaction these have with peri-urban and peripheral areas. Analyzing some theoretical and real world cases, a matrix of interactions is proposed to evaluate the positive/negative interactions and the correspondence of planning instruments in tackling the issues of the port and city development.

1 Introduction

Ports represent important interfaces in the connections between sea and land, namely between the maritime routes and the terrestrial ones, connecting distant production sites with local, coastal and internal markets.

Their role is multiple in scale, as ports can be relevant nodes in an international, global context, and/or in a national one, but they are relevant at regional levels [1, 2] and, as is the

---

The paper is the object of the common reflection of the two authors. However, the organization of the paper can be split among the authors as it follows. Ginevra Balletto wrote paragraphs, 3 – except the paragraph "The case of Trieste" and 4,while Giuseppe Borruso wrote paragraphs 1 and 2 and the paragraph "The case of Trieste". Paragraph 5 was jointly written by the two authors.

© The Author(s), under exclusive license to Springer Nature Switzerland AG 2023
O. Gervasi et al. (Eds.): ICCSA 2023 Workshops, LNCS 14110, pp. 594–607, 2023.
https://doi.org/10.1007/978-3-031-37123-3_41

main focus of the present paper, also locally, particularly in the city-port relationship [3]. This has evolved in the years, also in terms of the changing role of industrial production and development. Only relatively recently have we witnessed the specialization of port and industrial areas, particularly in the so-called third generation ports [4]. While more recently the requalification and redevelopment of the old waterfronts toward urban uses took place. In the development of ports and of the city-port relationship, the current period of time and stage can be defined as an hybrid one, where a wide application of the concept of hybridization can be observed. Transport modes, in fact, mix in port operations on the shorelines and in the inland terminals. Also, city and port functions mix on waterfronts, but also in more internal and peripheral areas, following urban sprawl and the port-related function of inner relocation. In this we recall a revision of the Anyport model [5, 6], in light of the on-going changes, as well as a reflection on the changes occurred in the MIDAs – Maritime Industrial Development Areas around ports, proposing a method of study and examination of the city-port relations in the evolution of these systems. The occasion is that of reflecting on the overall changing set of relationships that occur between port and its different components and dimensions. This in particular follows the growing needs for efficient urban logistics and for the consequent needs to the new locations necessary from the widespread diffusion and importance of the last mile in the door-to-door urban distribution. In this sense, the new inner harbor spaces deserve particular attention, where logistic functions supporting port activities are mixed and confused with the urban ones, often without proper coordination. Furthermore, operations traditionally carried out in ports now find most efficient locations farther from the shoreline, leaving space on quays for freight movement, management and temporary storage. Pressures are put on waterfronts and peripheries following the evolution of cities and their ports. In Italy, however, the port-city system has specificities given by the proximity of the ports to the cities, what influenced both urban and port planning, with positive and negative externalities [7]. The urban form of several ancient port cities, in fact, was influenced by the location and role of the ports themselves, determining relationships that are still visible today. Port cities holds also a strong identity based on the historical stratification of the union of urban culture and maritime culture and multiculturalism is a strong characterizing component [8]. Port cities are also united by a functional-organizational project that in relation to the different reference scales of the urban and port attractiveness [9]. The port-city relationship, in its complexity, also the sum of the stratification of historical relationships, is at the center of a set of contradictions and problems of contemporary planning, even in the context of global competition. In fact, the city-port relationship intertwines multiple aspects: from its scalar dimension and security to the most suitable funding and planning tools [10]. In this sense, the transformation of port cities and urban waterfronts highlights how the relationship between the city and the port is not conceived without a zoning approach (homogeneous space), but rather of diversity (hybrid space) [11, 12]. In Italy, in particular, the waterfront policy focuses on the regeneration of the city-port contact space, a place immediately behind it that has non-merchant functions.

The regeneration of the city-port contact aims to make the waterfront accessible with slow and sustainable mobility (walk and bike, local public transport and e-mobility) and attractive with services (museums, refreshment and conference centres, etc.) [2, 13, 14].

The regeneration of the waterfronts has been an important opportunity for urban planning in the - maritime state property - which, although characterized by complex legislation, has opened up replicable scenarios which, however, yet often homogenized by the public space [15, 16]. Furthermore, some research and applications of the last 10 years have demonstrated the important role of the connectivity of ecological networks through green spaces, where port and mobility infrastructures have interrupted the ecological continuity of the coastal system. Green infrastructures, in fact, are able to face a wide range of challenges: from the conservation of biodiversity, adaptation to climate change, support for the blue and green economy [17], improvement of social cohesion and participation integrated into the urban functions of the waterfront [13, 18, 19].

Such elements represent the framework from which the research question originates. The aim of the paper is to investigate port-city relations with particular reference to the transition from specialization to the hybridization of port-city functions, highlighting and proposing methods for analysing the city-port relationship and to address the potential conflicts on land use. The paper is organized as follows. In Sect. 2 Materials and Methods are presented. Section 3 hosts the Methods, where a framework for analysing the port - city relationship in a hybridized environment is proposed. Section 3.2 is focused on two case studies applied to different ports, as the Ports of Cagliari and Trieste (Italy). Results and discussion follow in Sect. 4, and Conclusions and a future research agenda are presented in Sect. 5.

2   Materials

2.1   From Specialization to Regionalization of Ports

The continuous specialization of port functions, over time, has in fact moved the port core away from the urban center and developing port infrastructures and services further away from the urban nucleus unlike in the past. The origin of the specialization of the port and therefore of the relations with the city can be summarized as an initial port site with small quays very close to the city center and warehouses in close proximity. Technological innovation and the progressive growth of the port and naval dimensions, as well as the movement of goods, led to the progressive removal of docks and docks from the city center and in particular from the business centre, with a consequent specialization of the terminals.

Following Bird, as recently resumed in Notteboom [20] a typical port, in its evolution, passes through three major stages as originally proposed in the Anyport model of development. These can be summarized in setting, expansion and specialization [21].

Setting. A port set up is highly related to geographical elements, particularly related to sail ships, and there is a tight relationship with its city and its economy, as a port city is oriented to port-related activities as trading, shipbuilding quays in close proximity of the center, fishing activities, with, in the pre-industrial era, port-related activities based on wholesaling and warehousing. The spatial and social mix of port and urban activities is strong.

Expansion. The city-port relationships evolved dramatically with the exploitation of the industrial revolution, that brought several changes, including the expansion of quays, the growing amount of freight and passengers moved, the increase of ships' size and, consequently, the need for adequate, bigger warehouses and proper, wider docks, as well as deeper waters to host new ships. The industrial revolution brought industrial activities in close proximity to the waterfront to gain economies of scale and location, helped by the development of railways and a wider integration of the port towards a wider regional area. Maritime Industrial Development Areas (MIDAs) started to be realized [22]. The port expansion started towards external areas in search of deeper waters.

The specialization of port functions is a consequence of the evolution of freights and the growth of volumes handled. Unitization in particular, led to a consequent need to rely on dedicated terminals, that need to be specialized and dedicated to handle differentiated freights, with different techniques for handling, storage and movement. Containers - together with other unitized freight as semi trailers and swap bodies - need wide spaces and dedicated intermodal facilities (i.e., cranes and railways). Ores, grain, petroleum and coal require dedicated warehouses and handling. A closely related element is naval gigantism in all sectors, implying dredging, greater depths, longer and wider quays. Facilities closer to the urban center become rapidly obsolete and their activities need to be moved out from the urban core, in search for wider space for freight management, handling and storage. Older, central, urban obsolete port facilities start to be reconverted towards urban uses (i.e., residential activities, retail, services, urban parks, etc.).

Notteboom et al. (2022) [23] and Rodrigue et al. (2020) [24], commenting on the evolution of ports, introduces a further stage, as that of regionalization of ports, coming out from the important changes introduced by unitization - and containerization in particular - with the development of a wide network of satellite terminals and inland terminals connected to the port facilities themselves. This regionalization of ports implies the capacity of a port to transform its surrounding territory, extending the port-related functions to the entire region of influence of the port itself.

2.2   The Hybridization of Ports and Cities

The historical relationship among cities and ports seems living a renewed season in a further hypothesized stage of hybridization. Together with regionalization of ports, cities also have been expanding in other parts of their territories.

Important related changes in transport and logistics, as containerization, globalization, naval gigantism, etc., led to specialization of ports and terminals with a separation of functions and activities and a regionalization of major port systems, that, according to most of the authors cited, occupied an important share of the end of the twentieth century and beginning of the twenty-first century. Further changes are however on-going, in line with the specialization of terminals and regionalization of ports, and such a concept could be defined as Hybridization, to be observed at different scales and according to different points of views.

The growth of specialized maritime traffic then favored the formation of the "inner harbor" and intermodal terminal for freight, including both road and rail modes, and often other areas with sorting and distribution functions. The main function is the decongestion of port areas by storing goods a few - or even hundreds - of kilometers away from the port itself.

This allows to manage efficiently the entire transport cycle, including handling, storage and warehousing, as well as the intermodal break of bulk [25].

Not only ports changed their role and expansion in space and time. The urban areas in their different periods witnessed a process of expansion in space is aimed to gain spaces farther from their original locations, in peripheral and semi-peripheral areas. Such evolution of the city has been studied by authors in the years, leading to theories and models of urban expansion, well known in urban geography theory, that led to phenomena such as suburbanization, disurbanization and/or ri-urbanization [26–34]. In any case cities have been extending their areas in their territories, with phenomena of urban residential - as well as logistic and retail - sprawl and sprinkling. This is very often coupled, at least in Western countries, with ageing and decline of population. The key element and consequence in that is an increased difficulty in meeting the needs of an increasingly dispersed population and to provide central, urban services. Urban density reduction and urban extension represent therefore two sides of the same coin, as the origin of the main spatial challenges connected to cities.

Similarly, ports have been expanding in other 'dry' parts of the territory, as well as playing differentiated roles and functions in the areas not always proximal to quays. These two processes are to-date converging in different parts of the city-port dyad, not only and not always in central locations, but also, and what is even more challenging, in peripheral and semiperipheral areas. The competition for land use is therefore moving out, both from the central city and from the traditional quays of the port, to invest other and different territories, whose social challenges are more and more characterizing and putting at risk a smooth transformation of our cities.

3   Method and Study Area

3.1 Methodology

The methodological proposal fits into this synthetic framework aimed at analyzing the complex relationships involving urban areas, waterfronts, peripheries, semi periph- eries, suburbs and port areas. The aforementioned concept of hybridization repre- sents a premise to propose methods, instruments and tools for valuably analyze such relationships.

Such a descriptive overview needs to be integrated by a different set of analysis, implying a survey and methodological organization of the different planning tools - at strategic and urban levels -, together with those related to the organization of the industrial and logistic aspects. Our approach involves the consideration of different aspects as:

- The planning tools available for managing spatially-related aspects;
- Their state of development and/or approval;
- Their spatial dimension (urban, metropolitan);
- Their main realm of application (i.e., industrial, urban, port, etc.).

These elements are summarized in a matrix useful to analyze the co-existence of planning instruments and the level of integration or potential conflicts among different uses of port and urban areas.

The above mentioned approach can be summarized in the matrix as in Fig. 1 (Fig. 1), that can represent in perspective a useful tool for evaluating the urban-port performances [24], together with an overall harmonization of the set of the strategic and planning tools.

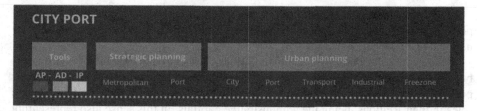

Fig. 1. City Port: Analysis matrix

From the planning point of view, we On one side there is the need to organize and analyse the approved (AP), adopted (AD) or in progress (IP) strategic and planning tools to understand to what extent they area able to in terms of their capacity to tackle together the aspects related to the different land uses at urban and peri-urban levels, therefore observing the effects on urban and port centres. Generally speaking, when dealing with If we can observe that strictly urban and port planning tools, these are generally coordinated and interrelated, given the use and habit of having representative of both port authorities and municipalities involved in the planning decisions within the municipal urban plans as well as within the port plan. Thing change this is not always true when we consider transport and industrial planning tools, as well as when we consider the 'spontaneous' behavior of de-facto logistic operators, whose location in space can be non-structured and referred to traditional standard industrial and retail locations, but with logistic-like impacts in space.

The methodology proposed at the basis of the matrix is divided into the following phases:

1. Desk analysis: Assessment of the state of the art of strategic and planning tools - approved (AP), adopted (AD) or in progress (IP);
2. Cartographic analysis Assessment of the main industrial areas/free zones/transport systems;
3. Field survey on the existing logistic and logistic-related activities on the territory;
4. Overlay of the different levels of information

The above mentioned methodology is applied to a sample of Italian cities and ports for a first overview of their characters. In particular in the present research a first set of analysis was focused on the first stage of the analytical framework hereby described.

3.2 The Study Area

In Italy the city-port system has specific characteristics compared to the international context. In particular, Italian ports are associated with urban systems and have developed operational relationships with the territory and with the logistics hubs. However, despite the centrality, functionality and/or specialization especially in the South Italy, ports are affected by the multitude of subjects who have an institutional role in planning-management, which fragments operations - Region, Municipalities, Port System Authorities, etc.

The research started from the local cases of Cagliari and Trieste as examples of port-cities relations, to extract analytical and research points for further evolutions on national and international cases.

These ports were chosen for some similarities characterizing their urban environment but also in terms of the differences that, nonetheless, characterize particularly their port systems. From the urban point of view, both cities hold important administrative roles in their Regions, being the administrative capitals, in this sense also representing hierarchically higher order centres a là Christaller, concentrating a wide set of higher order services, including administration, health, education and, more recently, tourism. Similarly, they have also deindustrialization in common, as a decline of the traditional manufacturing sector, towards an economic system more oriented to services. Also, they both represent the major urban areas at regional level. In the case of Cagliari, a metropolitan area is set, therefore with functions played at a wider level and providing services for a considerable number of citizens and city users (around 400.000 considering the 17 Municipalities). In the case of Trieste, the former Province - now re-established from an administrative point of view but still not yet operational - is limited in the numbers of Municipalities included (six) but at the same time Trieste represents a compact and densely inhabited area, with a catchment area that counts for around 240,000 inhabitants.

From the maritime and port point of view, the port cities of Cagliari Trieste were chosen because of the Northern route with origin from the Suez Canal, the Western and Eastern sides respectively. However, their characteristics as ports are conceptually and functionally rather different one to each other.

These ports, however, present very different cargo and passenger movements (Table 1), as well as different roles in their respective ranges.

Cagliari used to play a role as an important international transshipment port in the Western Mediterranean, before the changes in route choices from shipping companies. Internal demand is mainly served, on the contrary, by other ports (as Olbia) specialized in Ro-Ro, Ferry cargo. The port of Trieste is mainly an international one, with a role of gateway for international destinations within Central Europe, with important synergies with other inner harbours in the European continent. Both ports play an important role in liquid bulk cargo - particularly oil - and in hosting free zones on - at least part of - terminals, whose performances have not been yet fully implemented.

Similarities and differences are also in the passenger traffic. Both cities and ports host cruise ships in proximity of their urban waterfront, with lower figures of cruise passengers in the case of Cagliari, although highly compensated by ferry passenger traffic, and higher ones in the case of Trieste. The competition with other ferry ports in the case of Cagliari on one side, and the presence of Venice in proximity to Trieste on the other side, are all elements to be further considered when observing the two ports.

These considerations are particularly important with reference to the relations occurring among the strictly urban areas and the ones dedicated to port and port-related functions, including the industrial ones.

The Case of Cagliari. The port system of Cagliari consists of two main areas: the historic or old port, which extends over 5,800 m of quays and is dedicated to freight and passenger traffic, including Ro-Ro, passenger and cruise ships (with a dedicated

Table 1. Port movements 2022 (System Authorities and Ports of Trieste and Sardinia – Cagliari)

Port Movements	Liquid and Solid Bulk (ton)	TEU Total	Ro-Ro Unit	Pax	Cruise Pax
East Adriatic Port Authority	61,437,302	879,766	392,337	544,391	532,935
Port of Trieste	57,591,813	877,805	320,337	462,288	437,336
Sardinia Port Authority	43,888,126	140,216	572,521	6,025,499	220,595
Port of Cagliari	30,766,400	140,216	170,457	345,421	151,977

Source: Assoporti, Autorità di Sistema Portuale - Movimenti Portuali
https://www.assoporti.it/media/12508/adsp_movimenti_portuali_annuale_2022.pdf

terminal), the channel port, which extends over 1,600 m and offers five berths for transshipment and Ro-Ro traffic. A dedicated facility is located to the West of the channel port, - in the Municipality of Sarroch - with oil terminals and one huge petrochemical plant, with moorings for seventeen ships, a service of one of the most important national refineries (Fig. 2).

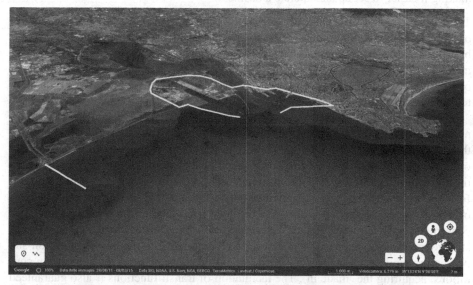

Fig. 2. The Port of Cagliari. https://www.adspmaredisardegna.it/cagliari/

The entire waterfront of Cagliari stretches for about 12 km from the Santa Gilla lagun in Sant'Elia with the new marina under construction (2022). The seafront, with singular places of historical and environmental value that alternate with abandoned spaces or spaces intended for port or industrial activities, is involved overall in the transformation and redevelopment process, animated by multiple public actors. The design theme of the city-port interface can be summarized as a redefinition of the relationship between the "historical" city and the seafront, with the aim of integrating the sea-city. The goal that everyone agrees is given by the connections of long and short, fast and slow networks.

The complex network of relationships between the parts and elements of the water-front and the city offers a progressive redevelopment of empty spaces and abandoned sites, responding to the needs of the metropolitan city. The interface is thus configured to give rise to the different types of relationship between the urban and port systems. In this sense, In Sardinia, a Special Economic Zone (SEZ) was established in 2019 and covers three areas: the Port of Cagliari, the Port of Porto Torres (for total 1700 ha), and the area surrounding the Sardinia International Airport. The SEZ of Cagliari aims to attract foreign investment and promote economic development in the region, focusing on strategic sectors such as logistics, manufacturing, and tourism, offering a wide range of incentives and benefits for companies that invest in the area, including tax breaks, simplified administrative procedures, and access to state-of-the-art infrastructure. Some of the key features of the SEZ of Cagliari include modern infrastructure and strategic location, particularly for companies involved in logistics and transport. Tax incentives are also available, as companies investing in the SEZ area of Cagliari can benefit from a range of tax incentives, including a reduced corporate tax rate of 24% and a full exemption from property tax for up to 15 years; Simplified administrative procedures: The ZES offers streamlined administrative procedures for companies that invest in the area, making it easier to set up and operate a business.

The Case of Trieste. The port of Trieste is located in close proximity to the Northeastern border of Italy with Slovenia, and at the crossroads of the main international routes between the Mediterranean and central Europe. It occupies about 2.3 million square meters, around 1.8 million square meters of free zones. The quays cover a total length of 12 km with 58 operational moorings, and maximum depths of up to 18 m (container terminal - Pier VII in particular), and served by a total length of 70 km of railway tracks.

The Port of Trieste is a unique case on the national scene, especially for the international Free Port regime, sanctioned after the end of the Second World War, and after the long definition of the northeastern border of Italy. This regime, recently regulated in order to adapt to the transformation of national ports within the Port System Authorities, provides in particular for customs relief, and port development as a transit hub and for the development of local economic activity. In particular, the free points of the port of Trieste are considered as a duty-free territory from the custom point of view, with consequences, in particular, linked to simplifications in terms of introduction of goods, storage, processing, deferred payments, as well as relative to the possibility of on-site processing while maintaining the origin, or, on the contrary, according to certain conditions, acquiring the 'made in'. The facilitation of transit functions is also guaranteed by free rail access, with the opening of access for all rail carriers to free points, and the exemption of fixed rights on the movement of vehicles, with the liberalization of the transport of goods in transit. The strong development of the Port of Trieste as the first Italian railway port, as well as the most connected to an international hinterland, and the strong presence of traffic, especially Ro-Ro, are elements that can certainly be connected to this regulatory situation which, in perspective, can orient the port and local economic development towards the definition of free zones. The evolution that has taken place in recent years, starting from January 2016, has led to a potential changing and changed relationship between the port and neighboring areas or areas linked to the urban context. From that moment, in fact, the free zone regime, up to that moment unchangeable in its locations, was able to be 'moved' and assigned to areas where it could more readily and fully be exploited: in particular, from the Punto Franco Vecchio, a large part, in fact, of port structures dating back to the Austro-Hungarian period, the area of which is now destined for a 'traditional' redevelopment as an urban waterfront, towards other locations, such as the new FreeEste logistics center, part of Interporto Trieste (Fig. 3).

Fig. 3. The Port of Trieste and the two inner ports of Fernetti and Bagnoli https://www.porto.tri este.it/

4   Results and Discussion

The aforementioned framework, as well as previous preliminary research carried on considering a similar topic and city-port relations represent the important framework for analyzing more in depth the areas of conflict or coexistence (Figs. 4 and 5).

Ad hoc matrices were therefore developed. The first stage of analysis has been followed and applied to the two cases and the analytical matrix was filled for the two cities and ports. In particular, the overall planning tools insisting on the different areas of the port-city dyads were considered, together with the different territorial contexts where these can be applied. The planning tools considered are those connected to urban and port planning, the mobility plans and the industrial ones. Also, the metropolitan level of planning is mentioned, as well as the consideration of the presence and operation of Free Zones (SEZ or similar).

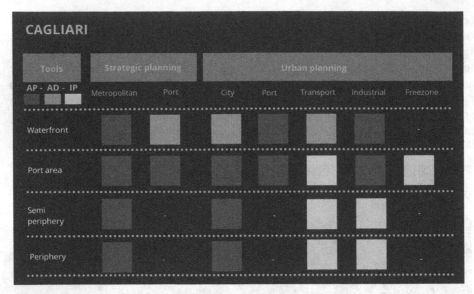

Fig. 4. Cagliari matrix

Fig. 5. Trieste analysis matrix

Considering the different levels of adoption of instruments, it was possible to observe the differences in the cities and ports' performances in terms of the availability of usable planning instruments for fulfilling urban and port planning. In such sense, the city and port of Trieste are at present fitted with a wealth of instruments that can be used and applied and therefore produce effect over territories, and considering the different levels, as centre, port areas and extensions, semi-periphery and periphery. Only periphery appears still little covered by the ordinary urban planning tools for transport issues.

In the case of Cagliari, the wide presence of a proper metropolitan area and city, as well as delays in the realization and put in operation of the Free Zones in particular, are characterizing the city and the neighbouring area. The presence of a vast area, in terms of population, manufacturing and services, make it more difficult to tackle the aspects related to peripheral and semi-peripheral contexts in particular, with the planning attention still concentrated on central urban and port facilities. At the same time, delays in the full implementation of the industrial component under dedicated custom regimes still seems to represent a potential obstacle to future development.

5 Conclusion and Future Developments

The recent evolutions of ports, between specialization and regionalization, are leading towards a renewed relationship with the cities connected to them and, to a wider extent, to the regions hosting them. The present stage can be considered as that of hybridization, where 'hybrid' situations can be observed in different contexts of the port and of the port-city evolutions. Port-city functions mix in waterfronts on central locations and in peripheral contexts, due to the extension of port-related functions out from the shoreline. Transport and logistic functions mix more and more with industrial ones, thanks, also, to the development of free zones in proximity of port areas. The same terminals, from highly specialized ones, are becoming dedicated to multiple kinds of freights, as the multipurpose platforms capable of hosting both containerized, ro-ro and other freight types. The same ports are being hybridized in their roles, minimizing a conceptual distinction between pure gateways and hubs, with both nodes assuming, more and more, mixed roles.

In some ways, this new stage has brought a city and its port closer than it happened in the recent past, with the port and city economics even closer, as it was in the pre-industrial revolution era, where the port emporium functions were shared with those of the related city. Such a post-specialization stage is leading to a blurring of port and city functions, particularly following two similar processes followed by ports and cities in their expansions out from their original nuclei. Cities in fact have been characterized in the post-war decades by urban sprawls of residential and retail activities out from their centres. Ports have also expanded and occupied portions of land far from their shores, due to the increased need of space on quays and in their proximity for port operations, leaving other functions as warehousing, some multimodal and intermodal transport and logistic operations, custom and document exchange, to dry or inland ports. These twofold expansions towards internal locations.

In conclusion and in perspective, therefore, in addition to greater coordination between the plan initiatives already in place at the urban and logistical-port level, it becomes possible and necessary to map the logistical and distribution nodes, whether linked to the already existing and planned dedicated infrastructures, both those managed by private operators, also for micro-distribution and storage functions, in order to be able to evaluate the development areas of these activities more precisely and high-light possible interactions and criticalities in urban interactions, including periphery and margin.

There will be the need to apply and map properly the areas of presence and potential interface of the different urban and port uses, particularly in those margin areas where, today, the major challenges are put to ports. These regards surely the quays and the waterfronts, but also, and more and more, those peripheral and semi peripheral areas that, still, are not always adequately considered in the implementation of urban plans. On the contrary they are or can become the realm of the evolution and implementation of transport and logistic-related functions, a situation in which potential conflicts with marginal and, sometimes, deprived communities are located.

References

1. Vigarié, A.: Le navire, le port e la ville. Transport et mutationes actuelles, 71–114 (1983)
2. Hoyle, B.S.: Global and local change on the port-city waterfront. Geogr. Rev. **90**(3), 395–417 (2000)
3. Hoyle, B.S.: The port-city interface: trends, problems and examples. Geoforum **20**, 429–435 (1989)
4. Pardali, A.: The port industry facing the challenges of the globalized economy. In: International Scientific Conference. Globalization: Illusions and Reality, Piraeus (2001)
5. Bird, J.: The Major Seaports of the United Kingdom. Hutchinson University Library, London (1963)
6. Bird, J.: Seaports and Seaport Terminals. Hutchinson University Library, London (1971)
7. Musso, E., Benacchio, M., Ferrari, C.: Ports and employment in port cities. Int. J. Marit. Econ. **2**, 283–311 (2000)
8. Mah, A.: Port cities and global legacies: Urban identity, waterfront work, and radicalism. Springer (2014)
9. Debrie, J., Raimbault, N.: The port–city relationships in two European inland ports: a geographical perspective on urban governance. Cities **50**, 180–187 (2016)
10. Borruso, G., Balletto, G., Milesi, A., Ladu, M.: Cartography and security. port security: trends and perspectives. In: Computational Science and Its Applications–ICCSA 2021: 21st International Conference, Cagliari, Italy, September 13–16, 2021, Proceedings, Part X 21, pp. 252–261. Springer International Publishing, Cham (2021)https://doi.org/10.1007/978-3-030-87016-4_19
11. Balletto, G., Borruso, G., & Campisi, T.: Not only waterfront. The Port-City relations between peripheries and inner harbors. In: Gervasi, O., Murgante, B., Misra, S., Rocha, A.M.A.C., Garau, C. (eds.) Computational Science and Its Applications–ICCSA 2022 Workshops: Malaga, Spain, July 4–7, 2022, Proceedings, Part V, pp. 196–208. Springer International Publishing, Cham (2022). https://doi.org/10.1007/978-3-031-10548-7_15
12. Borruso, G.: Port-city relationship in the era of hybridization. a development model. J-READING J. Res. Didactics Geo. 2 (2021)
13. Pirlone, F., Spadaro, I., Sabattini, M., De Nicola, M.: Sustainable urban regeneration in port-cities. A participatory project for Genoa waterfront. TeMA-J. Land Use Mob. Environ. **15**(1), 89–110 (2022)
14. Konvitz, J. W.: Cities & The Sea: Port City Planning in Early Modern Europe. JHU Press (2020)
15. di Venosa, M., Manigrasso, M.: Coste in movimento: Infrastrutture ambientali per la rigenerazione dei territori. Donzelli editore (2022)

16. Pittaluga, P.: Progetto e resistenza: il progetto dello spazio come azione critica. Progetto e resistenza, 1–137 (2020)
17. https://oceans-and-fisheries.ec.europa.eu/system/files/2022-05/2022-blue-economy-report_en.pdf
18. Wu, X.: Research on urban waterfront landscape design based on ecological urbanism. In: E3S Web of Conferences, vol. 283, p. 02040). EDP Sciences (2021)
19. Di Pierto, L., Sciuto, G., Ronsivalle, D.: La costruzione di connessioni longitudinali e trasversali sul waterfront centrale di Catania: applicazione del concetto di infrastruttura verde per la rigenerazione urbana. URBANISTICA DOSSIER, 67–72. (2022)
20. Notteboom T., Pallis A. and Rodrigue J. P.: Port Economics, Management and Policy, Routledge, London (2022)
21. The model can be found summarized at this link https://bit.ly/Anyport
22. Vallega, A.: Geografia delle strategie marittime. Dal mondo dei mercanti alla società transindustriale, Milano, Mursia (1997)
23. Notteboom, T., Pallis, A., Rodrigue, J.P.: Port Economics, Management and Policy. Routledge, London (2022)
24. Rodrigue, J.P.: The Geography of Transport System. Routledge, New York (2020)
25. Hao, L., Jin, J.G., Zhao, K.: Joint scheduling of barges and tugboats for river–sea intermodal transport. Transp. Res. Part E Log. Transp. Rev. **173**, 103097 (2023)
26. Hall, P.: Cities of Tomorrow: An Intellectual History of Urban Planning and Design Since 1880. Wiley, London (2014)
27. Landini, P.: Urban Structure, Territorial Structures and Regionalization Processes, 197–214; Dematteis, G., Guarrasi, V.: Eds.; Urban Networks. Pàtron: Bologna, Italy (1995)
28. Gemmiti, R.: Il concetto di periurbanizzazione. Specificità concettuale e rilevanza operativa di un vecchio neologismo. Geotema 11 (1998)
29. Dematteis, G.: Il Fenomeno Urbano in Italia: Interpretazioni, Prospettive, Politiche; FrancoAngeli: Milano, Italy (1992)
30. Indovina, F.: Dalla città all'arcipelago metropolitano. FrancoAngeli, Milano, Italy (2009)
31. Dematteis, G.: Polycentric urban regions in the Alpine space. Urban Res. Pract. **2**, 18–35 (2009)
32. Morelli, V.G., Rontos, K., Salvati, L.: Between suburbanisation and re-urbanisation: Revisiting the urban life cycle in a Mediterranean compact city. Urban Res. Pract. **7**, 74–88 (2014)
33. Fielding, A.: Counterurbanisation in Western Europe. Prog. Plan. **17**(1), 1–52 (1982)
34. Van den Berg, L., Drewett, R., Klaassen, L.H., Rossi, A., Vijverberg, C.H.T.: Urban Europe: A Study of Growth and Decline. Pergamon Press, Oxford (1982)

Methodologies for Sustainable Development of TEN-T/RFC Corridors and Core Ports: Workers Mobility between Urban and Port-Related Areas

Corrado Rindone[1]($\boxtimes$) (iD), Paola Panuccio[2] (iD), and Domenico Sgro[1] (iD)

[1] DIIES, Università Mediterranea Di Reggio Calabria, 89100 Reggio Calabria, Italy
corrado.rindone@unirc.it

[2] PAU, Università Mediterranea Di Reggio Calabria, 89100 Reggio Calabria, Italy

Abstract. This paper concerns the passenger mobility generated by a SEZ area near to a core port connected to Trans European Network-Transport (TEN-T) and Rail Freight Corridors (RFC). The SEZ area and the port represent the places where workers perform their daily activities. Transport connections between the port and the corridor can be a bottleneck that produces externalities for the areas around. This paper examines spatial and temporal connections identifying strategies to achieve sustainability according to the UNs Agenda 2030.

Keywords: Smart ports · TEN-T corridor · RFC corridor · SEZ · passenger mobility · sustainability

1 Introduction

According to UNCTAD classification, ports evolve towards different generations. The first generation includes ports inside the cities. The second generation includes the industrial ports. The third one includes container ports with increasing levels of added value (AV) produced by the freight movements and transformations processes [1, 2]. Industrial areas near to the third-generation port contribute to increase the AV [3, 4]. A specific typology of industrial area is the Special Economic Zone (SEZ) that supports the production of added value (AV) linked with economic activities [5]. SEZs are regulated by special conditions for operating enterprises [6]. Accessibility and smartness, in terms of integration between transport, energy and ICT [7–9], are the main SEZ's characteristics to contribute to increase the production of AV [10], linked with economic activities [11, 12].

This research concerns the ports belonging to the Trans European Network (TEN-T) and their bottlenecks that could constitute a limit for freight and passenger mobility. In relation to freight mobility, bottlenecks regard physical barriers and/or administrative obstacles, that produce inefficiency on the free flow of goods, people, and information, with reference to the gateway ports [13]. For instance, in Italy in 2014, the average

© The Author(s) 2023
O. Gervasi et al. (Eds.): ICCSA 2023 Workshops, LNCS 14110, pp. 608–621, 2023.
https://doi.org/10.1007/978-3-031-37123-3_42

times for export are 19 days that are greater than for Germany and Belgium (9 days) and Holland (7 days) [14].

At the same time, the SEZ and the port area generate workers mobility because they represent the job daily activities' places. The problem regards the interactions between transport and economic systems [15]. The paper produces more insights about the workers mobility deriving from the interactions between port and the external territory. Urban and transport planning can regulate these interactions individuating solutions at short and long terms, with the aim to increase the sustainable people mobility according to the UN's sustainable Development goals [16]. Transit Oriented Development (TOD) [17] and Mobility as a Service (MaaS) are possible solutions for improving sustainable transport connections. In this context, the paper offers two kinds of research's contributions:

- an analysis of the phenomenon related to external interactions between a port and the surround area, focusing on the people mobility component;
- a methodology to analyse and improving spatial and temporal connections of third generation ports with a transit network.

The specific case study is the Gioia Tauro port in the south of Italy, a core node of TEN-T inside the Scandinavian – Mediterranean Corridor (TEN-T 5) and a gateway for the Rail Freigth Corridor (RFC) 3 with a SEZ area. The port has different potentialities, but it presents some limitations in the spatial and temporal connections with TEN-T and around territories. The proposed methodology can support port authority and, more in general, public and private decision makers involved in the development process of a third port generation.

After this introduction, the paper has three sections. Section 2 recalls the general problems related to the territorial and mobility interactions, with a specific reference to the case SEZ areas near to a port of international relevance. Section 3 describes the methodological approach followed in this paper for studying spatial and temporal connections. Section 3 reports the main results obtained from the methodology's application for the connection of Gioia Tauro port with Scan Med TEN-T and RFC3 Corridors. Section 4 discusses the results with final remarks and further developments of this research.

2 Territorial Activity and Mobility

This paper focuses the territories characterized by the presence of a port of third generation belonging to the TEN-T and with a SEZ. The specific case regards ports located outside of an urban area (Sect. 2.1). The working activities produce AV but, at the same time, they generate daily mobility between residential and port related areas (Sect. 2.2) (Fig. 1).

2.1 Urban and Port Related Activities

The study context is a particular case of the general spatial economic transport interaction (SETI) process [18]. The economic activities are performed in the port related areas. The workers, living in residential areas distant from the port, performs daily trips that use available transport connections.

The SETI process implies the necessity to individuate urban planning solutions, including urban regeneration, new town, or smart city approaches [19]. Urban planning regulates the equilibrium between the economic sustainability, measured with the increasing of the AV, and social/environment components for workers and inhabitants [20]. Strengths related to the presence of the port and SEZ areas have to be considered with weakness of the hinterland [21]. Transport infrastructures and services connections can be considered a first step of the regeneration process.

Fig. 1. People mobility generated by port-territory interactions.

In this specific context, an integrated transport-territory planning could balance the advantages, related to the generation of added value (AV) for the entire area [19] and disadvantages, related to externalities produced by workers' mobility. This means to achieve the following objectives: 1) to enhance the competitivity of the port in the international supply chain; 2) to improve efficiency of the productive processes inside the SEZ and their potentialities for export; 3) to limit the effects produced by the potential urban sprawl due to the distances between the residential and port related areas. Urban regeneration is a possible way for defining spatial and temporal connections that facilitate freight and people mobility.

2.2 Workers Mobility

Sustainable mobility actions have a decisive role to improve workers mobility [22]. Optimal passenger's mobility services increase connections and therefore accessibility allowing people to perform their daily activities with the minimum quantity of economic resources (time, energy, monetary costs,…).

A high level of accessibility is a necessary condition to increase the quality of life in the city. A possible planning tool aimed at increasing the accessibility of the urban territory is the SUMP [7, 23, 24]. The SUMP defines a set of integrated (material and immaterial) infrastructural and managerial measures to pursue sustainability objectives. The indications about the transport system can be accompanied by urban regeneration solutions in terms of (Fig. 2):

- material infrastructures, including the regeneration of the urban environment, production facilities and business services;
- immaterial infrastructures, including the redefinition of urban technologies supporting for civil uses (ICT, energy, waste, water, …);

- management and services, including organizational aspects related to mobility, energy and sustainable monitoring.

This paper focuses on the management and services issues with an attention to mobility services for people's mobility. In the following chart, this issue is named "urban mobility regeneration".

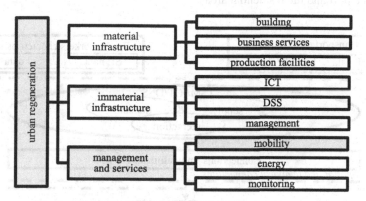

Fig. 2. Urban mobility inside the urban regeneration process.

Urban regeneration renews the passenger mobility services, improving spatial and temporal connections between the port, the SEZ area and the TEN-T corridor. It can be considered a trigger of the entire urban regeneration process.

Transit Oriented Development (TOD) is a possible short-term solution to start the urban mobility regeneration process. It is a consolidated approach to improve territorial-transport interactions around a transport node [17, 25, 26]. It consists of matching urban places (buildings, and public space) and people's needs generated by their daily activities (e.g., jobs activities in the port). At medium – long term, the TOD approach must be integrated with the Mobility as a Service (MaaS) concept [27–29] that combines emerging ICT potentialities and Transport System Models (TSM). ICT technologies allows the collection of data and information about mobility needs. According to the paper's focus, TOD and MaaS are integrated to respond the current and future people mobility needs generated by the port's activities. By considering the options that produces the minimum level of externalities, MaaS evolves towards the Sustainable Mobility as a Service concept [30, 31].

3   The Proposed Methodology

Urban regeneration process can be implemented following the proposed methodology, specified for analyzing and improving people's mobility of between the SEZ area and the surrounding territory. The methodology is organized into two steps (Fig. 3):

- the first step analyses the current performance level of spatial and temporal connections between the port and the surrounding territory, in relation to the workers mobility needs (Sect. 3.1).

• with the results of the first step, the second step defines urban regeneration strategies inside a sustainable mobility planning (Sect. 3.2).

3.1   Spatial and Temporal Connections

This step is aimed at analyzing the current level of space and temporal connections between the port and the residential areas.

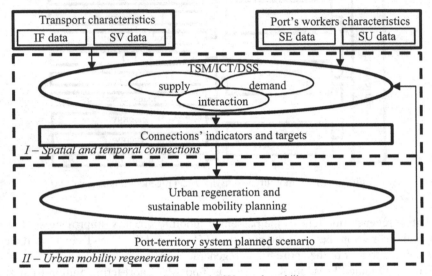

IF: Infrastructures; SV: Services; SE: Socio Economic; SU: people mobility survey
TSM: Transport System Models; ICT: Information and Communic. Technol.; DSS: Decision Support System

Fig. 3. Methodology to improve port-territory workers mobility.

Spatial connections are constituted by the road and railway infrastructures that link in the space the core port with transport network. Often, a spatial connection is a necessary but not sufficient condition to ensure the port's accessibility and the sustainable mobility. It is necessary to analyze and improve the temporal connections ensured by the collective transport services and their characteristics (in Fig. 3 SV data). Transport network design models can be used integrating data obtained from ICT [32], Transport System Models (TSM) and Decision Support System (DSS) [33, 34] (Fig. 3).

Monitored data must include socioeconomic characteristics (residential uses, SE data) of the and habits of port's workers (origins, desired arrival/departure times, modes, SU data) [31] aimed at individuating the travel choices of port's users.

3.2   Urban Mobility Regeneration

Step 1's results (Sect. 3.1) identify accessibility gaps and sustainability issues related to passenger mobility generated by the port terminal and SEZ activities.

TSM support the transportation planning process [24] aimed at individuating interventions for removing bottlenecks and improving spatial and temporal connections [35]. The interventions have different temporal horizons.

At short term, it is possible to modify transit services (e.g., new itineraries and schedules), with the same level of transport infrastructures, according to the temporal demand profiles. This requires the integrated use of ICT and TSM, by adopting a Sustainable Mobility as a Service (S-MaaS) in terms of transport network design [36] to consider the user's behavior [33], transport supply [34] and their mutual interactions [30]. Typical examples of interventions are integrated electronic ticketing system, information systems and demand management.

At long term, it is necessary to consider the interventions that modify the material asset of transport infrastructures. Each intervention produces direct and indirect effects on transport and territorial systems that can be estimated and compared with the indicators and relative targets defined by the Agenda 2030 [16].

4   Case Study

The methodology presented in Sect. 3 has been applied for Gioia Tauro, the core port of the Scan-Med core corridor (Fig. 4). This is a third-generation port with a SEZ instituted by the Italian Government [37]. SEZ zone covers an area of 402 hectares where it is possible to perform industrial and service functions [3, 38, 39]. The port location implies workers daily mobility around the territories of the Calabria region, in the south of Italy.

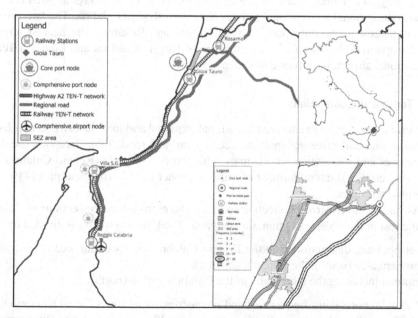

Fig. 4. The study area: main infrastructures belonging to TEN-T Scan Med Corridor.

In the current configuration, the port produces container movements with a limited AV. This is due also to the lack of services and transport connections. The port is located near a territorial area characterized by a high rate of unemployment [40]. The study area is near to the territory named "piana di Gioia Tauro", inside the metropolitan city of Reggio Calabria. The nearest urban areas are Gioia Tauro, Rosarno and San Ferdinando. Port and SEZ areas have great economic potentials to improve export processes and for economic development of the Calabria region [41–43].

The port amounts around 4,000 workers that daily operate inside the terminal area [44]. In the future, the port's activities and relative production processes could increase. The "piana" territory is characterized by an urban sprawl that produces accessibility problems. The economic development of the SEZ area will generate a major number of workers (about 7,000) and then a greater number of daily trips between the port and the surround residential areas.

The following sections illustrate the application of the proposed methodology (Sect. 3). The analyses of the current situation (step 1, Sect. 4.1) support the definition of interventions at short and long terms (step 2, Sect. 4.2).

4.1 Spatial Connections

As far as road connections are concerned, the Scan Med corridor includes the highway A2 Salerno-Reggio Calabria, with the main junctions Rosarno and Gioia Tauro. Others relevant road infrastructures are the SS18 for north-south connections, the transversal motorway SS682 that link the SEZ area with the Jonic side of Calabria region, thus the SS 106 Reggio Calabria – Taranto. Concerning rail connections, the Scan Med corridor includes the national conventional railway Salerno – Reggio Calabria. The two railway stations nearest to the core port are Gioia Tauro and Rosarno. The nearest airports are "Aeroporto dello stretto", in the province of Reggio Calabria and Lamezia Terme International airport, in province of Catanzaro).

4.2 Temporal Connections

Temporal connections are analyzed at national, regional and local levels, and in relation to considering collective transport services by rail and road. Table 1 reports the daily frequencies and connecting travel times with the two airports (Reggio Calabria and Lamezia Terme). The total number of railway services is 27. The great part (74%) has a regional relevance.

As far as concerns road collective services, the extra-urban connections of "piana" and the rest of the Calabria region are analyzed. The Calabria region is divided in:

- metropolitan, distinguished in the Reggio Calabria metropolitan area into "piana", southern area (south), the Jonian area (east);
- regional including the other parts of the Calabria region (north).

Table 2 reports daily frequencies and connecting travel times for all Calabria territories. The total number road collective services are 39, regarding metropolitan services (90%), connecting the south territory (41%), the "piana" (31%) and the east territories (18%). Travel time related to bus mode has been estimated with an average speed of

Table 1. Railway connections (source: www.trenitalia.it)

Territorial reference		Number of companies	Daily frequency (bidirectional)	
			n	%
Regional	North	2	4	10%
Metropolitan	Piana	1	12	31%
	South	2	16	41%
	East	2	7	18%
Total			36	100%

RC: Reggio Calabria airport; LT: Lamezia Terme airport; GT: Gioia Tauro port.

90 km/h for Nord and South areas, while an average speed of 60 km/h for the East and Piana side has been assigned. Note that total number of daily road services connecting the area is relevant (Table 2).

Table 2. Road services connections in the study area (Gioia T., Rosarno, San Ferdinando)

Territorial reference	Daily frequency (bidirectional)		Travel times (minutes)	
	n	%	GT-RC	GT-LT
Regional/local	20	74%	53	62
National	7	26%	43	42
Total	27	100%		

Services are available at few stops but located at a not walkable distance from port related areas. In fact, Fig. 5 shows the actual layout of connections and their daily frequencies in a working day. Most part of travel services is along the highway A2 from South territory and on the railway TEN-T network. Note that it exists only a 10% of the total analyzed runs with a stop inside the port area. Besides, frequencies are not specific for port employees' temporal needs; hence, on Sundays are residual (Fig. 3).

4.3 Indicators and Targets

The results of the step 2 are the indicators' values of spatial and temporal connections (Table 3). As regards the spatial connections, Table 3 reports the spatial distances between the port gate and railway stations, road junction, bus stops. Moreover, it is reported the distance between the port terminal and Reggio Calabria and Lamezia Terme airports. It is specified that the distances between port gate and bus and train stops are longer than, respectively, 400 m and 800 m which represent the targets indicated by the national SUMP Italian guidelines [37].

As far as concerns the temporal connections quality, depends on the differences between transit timetables and port employees' temporal needs. The highest values of

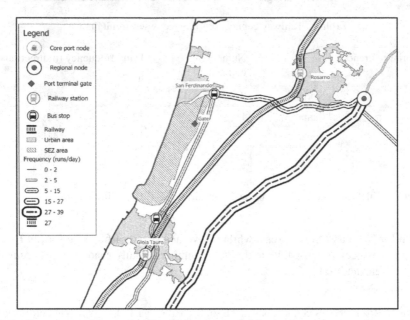

Fig. 5. Current quantities and territorial distribution of the spatial and temporal connections

Table 3. Distances between the port's gate and nearest stops for each mode (km)

	Rail	Road	Bus	Air
Gioia Tauro	12	10	4	–
Rosarno	7	10	4	–
San Ferdinando	–	14	–	–
RC, LT airports	–	–	–	77

daily frequencies reported in Table 1 for rail and road connections are scheduled in stops distant from the port's terminal.

Demand analysis shows that only 5% of workers declare that they choose railway mode. Consequently, it is clear that the interaction demand-supply is unbalanced.

4.4 Urban Mobility Regeneration

The current limits support the individuation of material, immaterial and organizational interventions. Figure 6 reports the three above mentioned intervention areas aligned to the classes reported in Fig. 2 for a long-term scenario (Sect. 2.2).

Material interventions at short term regard cycling and walking paths for improving last mile connections; at long-term, collective transport green infrastructures for connecting residential (Gioia Tauro, Rosarno and San Ferdinando) and port related areas and TEN-T corridor.

Management interventions at short term concern optimization of existing transit services. At long term, it is possible to integrate management and immaterial interventions implementing the S-MaaS approach and electrification mobility. All the solutions above described will have to be on target with guidelines and provided rules specified in the Sect. 3.2.

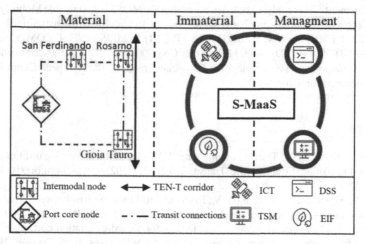

Fig. 6. Long term scenarios for spatial and temporal connections

5   Discussion and Final Remarks

The analyses presented in this paper show the necessity to further investigate the issue related to transport connections between nodes and links of TEN-T network, by focusing on the passenger mobility. The goal is to better understand the phenomena that produce negative impacts produced by the presence of a terminal dedicated to the movement of large quantities of goods in a territory.

This paper has focused on core ports, SEZ areas and hinterland relations. These specific territories represent a pole of attraction for the people's mobility because they constitute the workplaces of a significant number of employees who work in the port and in the SEZ area. The port interacts with the external territories and, in some cases, produces negative externalities in terms environmental impacts.

The results of the analyzed case study show that the growth of the port of Gioia Tauro has not been accompanied by mobility management policies aimed at guaranteeing the accessibility of the port in a sustainable way.

The people's mobility is unbalanced on private modes, and this produces congestion and negative impacts. According to the research's objective of this paper, the proposed methodological approach supports the investigation of the disconnection level between the core port and TEN-T corridors by means collective transport services.

The quantitative analysis of disconnections produces inputs for defining mobility management policies, within a wider transport planning process aimed at increasing sustainability.

The paper has limitations related to a more detailed analysis of the mobility needs of the people who interact with the port. Two main research directions are possible: to enhance the estimation of effects deriving from the territory-transport planning at short and long terms; to evaluate the realization of new high capacity transport line that connect urban and port related areas.

Acknowledgement. This study was carried out within the MOST – Sustainable Mobility National Research Center and received funding from the European Union Next-GenerationEU (PIANO NAZIONALE DI RIPRESA E RESILIENZA (PNRR) – MISSIONE 4 COMPONENTE 2, INVESTIMENTO 1.4 – D.D. 1033 17/06/2022, CN00000023). This manuscript reflects only the authors' views and opinions, neither the European Union nor the European Commission can be considered responsible for them.

References

1. Russo, F., Musolino, G.: The role of emerging ICT in the ports: increasing utilities according to shared decisions. Front. Future Transp. **2**, 722812 (2021). https://doi.org/10.3389/ffutr.2021.722812
2. Russo, F., Musolino, G., Assumma, V.: Ro-ro and lo-lo alternatives between Mediterranean countries: factors affecting the service choice. Case Stud. Transp. Policy **11**, 100960 (2023)
3. Musolino, G., Trecozzi, M.R.: Structural factors for a third-generation port: planning interventions for agri-food logistics in Gioia Tauro Italy. WIT Trans. Built Environ. **204**, 43–52 (2021)
4. Musolino, G.; Cartisano, A.; Fortugno, G.: Structural factors for a third-generation port: planning interventions for mechanical logistics in: Gioia Tauro, Italy. WIT Trans. Built Environ. **204**, 55–66 (2021)
5. Russo, F., Chilà, G., Zito, C.: Strategic planning for special economic zones to ports of the future: system of models and test case. In: Gervasi, O., Murgante, B., Misra, S., Rocha, A.M.A.C., Garau, C. (eds.) Computational Science and Its Applications – ICCSA 2022 Workshops. ICCSA 2022. LNCS, vol. 13381, pp.173–184. Springer, Cham (2022). https://doi.org/10.1007/978-3-031-10548-7_13
6. Pellicanò, D.S., Trecozzi, M.R.: Special economic zones planning for sustainable ports: general approach for administrative simplifications and a test case. In: Gervasi, O., Murgante, B., Misra, S., Rocha, A.M.A.C., Garau, C. (eds.) Computational Science and Its Applications – ICCSA 2022 Workshops. ICCSA 2022. LNCS, vol. 13381, pp. 47–59. Springer, Cham (2022). https://doi.org/10.1007/978-3-031-10548-7_4
7. Russo, F., Rindone, C.: Smart city for sustainable development: applied processes from SUMP to MaaS at European level. Appl. Sci. **13**(3), 1773 (2023)
8. Comi, A., Russo, A.: Emerging information and communication technologies: the challenges for the dynamic freight management in city logistics. Front. Future Transp. Sec. **3**, 887307 (2022). https://doi.org/10.3389/ffutr.2022.8873079
9. Russo, F., Musolino, G.: Quantitative characteristics for port generations: the Italian case study. Int. J. TDI **4**, 103–112 (2020). https://doi.org/10.2495/TDI-V4-N2-103-112
10. Musolino, G., Cartisano, A., Fortugno, G.: Special economic zones planning for sustainable ports: Aggregate economic impact of port of Gioia Tauro, pp. 60–71 (2022). https://doi.org/10.1007/978-3-031-10548-7_5
11. Musolino, G., Peda, G., Russo, F.: Emerging ICT and port community systems: a survey of scientific literature. WIT Trans. Built Environ. **212**, 123–135 (2022). https://doi.org/10.2495/UMT220111

12. Rindone, C., Cirianni, F.M., Delfino, G., Croce, A.I.: Special economic zones planning for sustainable ports: The role of research and training in the Calabria Region. In: Computational Science and Its Applications–ICCSA 2022 Workshops: Malaga, Spain, July 4–7, 2022, Proceedings, Part V, pp. 85–97. Springer International Publishing, Cham (2022)
13. Tongzon, J.L., Oum, T.H.: The role of port performance in gateway logistics. In Proceedings of the 1st International Conference on Gateways and Corridors (2007)
14. CIPE. Iniziativa di studio sulla portualità italiana. Luglio (2014)
15. Cascetta, E.: Transportation Systems Engineering: Theory and Methods, vol. 49. Springer Science & Business Media (2013)
16. Russo, F.: Sustainable mobility as a service: Dynamic models for agenda 2030 policies. Information (Switzerland), **13**(8), 355 (2022). https://doi.org/10.3390/info13080355
17. Acampa, G., Contino, F., Grasso, M., Ticali, D.: Evaluation of infrastructure: application of TOD to Catania underground metro station. In: AIP Conference Proceedings, vol. 2186, no. 1, p. 160010. AIP Publishing LLC (2019)
18. Russo, F., Musolino, G.: A unifying modelling framework to simulate the spatial economic transport interaction process at urban and national scales. J. Transp. Geogr. **24**, 189–197 (2012). https://doi.org/10.1016/j.jtrangeo.2012.02.003
19. Russo, F., Panuccio, P., Rindone, C.: Structural factors for a third-generation port: between hinterland regeneration and smart town in Gioia Tauro, Italy. WIT Trans. Built Environ. **204**, 79–90 (2021). https://doi.org/10.2495/UT210071
20. Russo, F., Rindone, C., Panuccio, P.: External interactions for a third generation port: from urban sustainable planning to research developments. Int. J. Trans. Dev. Integr. **6**(3), 253–270 (2022)
21. Musolino, D.A., Panuccio, P.: Special economic zones planning for sustainable ports: the test case of territorial attractiveness and urban planning in calabria region. In: Gervasi, O., Murgante, B., Misra, S., Rocha, A.M.A.C., Garau, C. (eds.) Computational Science and Its Applications – ICCSA 2022 Workshops. ICCSA 2022. Lecture Notes in Computer Science, vol. 13381, pp. 72–84 (2022).https://doi.org/10.1007/978-3-031-10548-7_6. ISBN 978–3–031–10547–0
22. Panuccio, P.: Smart planning: from city to territorial system. Sustainability **11**(24) (2019). https://doi.org/10.3390/su11247184
23. European Commission. EC. Guidelines for developing and implementing a Sustainable Urban Mobility Plan. Second edition (2019). https://www.eltis.org/guidelines/sump-guidel ines. Accessed 07 Jan 2023
24. Russo, F., Rindone, C.: Regional transport plans: from direction role denied to common rules identified. Sustainability **13**(16), 9052 (2021)
25. Papa, E., Bertolini, L.: Accessibility and transit-oriented development in European metropolitan areas. J. Transp. Geogr. **47**, 70–83 (2015). https://doi.org/10.1016/j.jtrangeo.2015.07.003
26. Loo, B.P.Y., Chen, C., Chan, E.T.H.: Rail-based transit-oriented development: lessons from New York City and Hong Kong. Landsc. Urban Plan. **97**(3), 202–212 (2010). https://doi.org/10.1016/j.landurbplan.2010.06.002
27. Hensher, D.A., Mulley, C., Ho, C., Wong, Y., Smith, G., Nelson, J.D.: Understanding Mobility as a Service (MaaS): Past, Present and Future. Elsevier (2020)
28. Canale, A., Tesoriere, G., Campisi, T.: The MaaS development as a mobility solution based on the individual needs of transport users. In: AIP Conference Proceedings, vol. 2186, no. 1, p. 160005. AIP Publishing LLC (2019)
29. Le Pira, M., Tavasszy, L.A., de Almeida Correia, G.H., Ignaccolo, M., Inturri, G.: Opportunities for integration between mobility as a service (MaaS) and freight transport: a conceptual model. Sustain. Cities Soc. **74**, 103212 (2021)

30. Vitetta, A.: Sustainable mobility as a service: framework and transport system models. Information **13**(7), 346 (2022)
31. Musolino, G., Rindone, C., Vitale, A., Vitetta, A.: Pilot survey of passengers' preferences in mobility as a service (MaaS) scenarios: a case study. Transp. Res. Procedia **69**, 328–335 (2023)
32. Musolino, G., Cartisano, A., Fortugno, G.: Special economic zones planning for sustainable ports: aggregate economic impact of port of Gioia Tauro. In: Gervasi, O., Murgante, B., Misra, S., Rocha, A.M.A.C., Garau, C. (eds.) Computational Science and Its Applications – ICCSA 2022 Workshops. ICCSA 2022. Lecture Notes in Computer Science, vol. 13381, pp. 60–71 Springer, Cham (2022). https://doi.org/10.1007/978-3-031-10548-7_5. ISBN 978–3–031–10547–0
33. Musolino, G.: Sustainable mobility as a service: demand analysis and case studies. Information **13**(8), 376 (2022)
34. Rindone, C.: Sustainable mobility as a service: supply analysis and test cases. Information **13**(7), 351 (2022)
35. Garau, C., Desogus, G., Barabino, B., Coni, M.: Accessibility and public transport mobility for a smart (er) Island: evidence from Sardinia (Italy). Sustain. Cities Soc. **87**, 104145 (2022)
36. Musolino, G., Rindone, C., Vitetta, A.: Models for supporting mobility as a service (MaaS) design. Smart Cities **5**(1), 206–222 (2022)
37. Italian Government (2019). Decreto Ministeriale n.396 of 28/08/2019. https://www.mit.gov.it/normativa/decreto-ministeriale-n-396-del-28082019. Accessed 31 Mar 2023
38. Musolino, G., Cartisano, A., Chilà, G., Fortugno, G., Trecozzi, M.R.: Evaluation of structural factors in a third-generation port: methods and applications. Int. J. Trans. Dev. Integr. **6**(4), 347–362 (2022)
39. Musolino, G., Chilà, G.: Structural Factors for a third-generation port: planning transport interventions in Gioia Tauro, Italy. WIT Trans. Built Environ. **204**, 31–42 (2021)
40. Russo, F., Chilà, G., Zito, C.: Strategic planning for special economic zones to ports of the future: system of models and test case. In: Gervasi, O., Murgante, B., Misra, S., Rocha, A.M.A.C., Garau, C. (eds.) Computational Science and Its Applications – ICCSA 2022 Workshops. ICCSA 2022. LNCS, vol. 13381, pp. 173–184 . Springer, Cham (2022). ISBN 978–3–031–10547–0
41. Russo, F., Chilà, G.: Structural factors for a third-generation port: current state, limits and weaknesses of Gioia Tauro, Italy, in the regional transport plan. WIT Trans. Built Environ. **204**, 3–15 (2021). https://doi.org/10.2495/UT210011
42. Russo, F., Chilà, G.: Structural factors for a third-generation port: actions and measures for Gioia Tauro, Italy, in the regional transport plan. WIT Trans. Built Environ. **204**, 17–30 (2001)
43. Russo, F.; Chilà, G.: Structural factors for a third-generation port: current state, limits and weaknesses of Gioia Tauro, Italy, in the regional transport plan. WIT Trans. Built Environ. **204**, 3–15 25 August 2021
44. Calabria Region (2018). Piano di sviluppo strategico Zona Economica Speciale Calabria (2018). https://www.agenziacoesione.gov.it/zes-zone-economiche-speciali/zes-cal abria/. Accessed 31 Mar 2023

Open Access This chapter is licensed under the terms of the Creative Commons Attribution 4.0 International License (http://creativecommons.org/licenses/by/4.0/), which permits use, sharing, adaptation, distribution and reproduction in any medium or format, as long as you give appropriate credit to the original author(s) and the source, provide a link to the Creative Commons license and indicate if changes were made.

The images or other third party material in this chapter are included in the chapter's Creative Commons license, unless indicated otherwise in a credit line to the material. If material is not included in the chapter's Creative Commons license and your intended use is not permitted by statutory regulation or exceeds the permitted use, you will need to obtain permission directly from the copyright holder.

Methodologies for Sustainable Development of TEN-T/RFC Corridors and Core Ports: The Role of Governance in the Export Time Optimization

Francesco Russo(✉) and Domenica Savia Pellicanò

Mediterranea University of Reggio Calabria, 89124 Reggio Calabria, Italy
francesco.russo@unirc.it

Abstract. Ports are a key element of the economic development of a country but have to face with many problems of different nature, above all, linked to the governance process. In particular, some ports, due to a slow and complex bureaucracy, find difficult to become competitive on a European and international level.

The paper investigates the critical issues related to port nodes and proposes a model that allows to understand which variables at governance level, can be modified to intervene in order to improve the competitiveness of a port and therefore encourage the economic development of his country. A European comparison is presented in which the individual components of the costs are analyzed.

Keywords: Sustainable port · Smart port · Core port · Export time port optimization · Port governance · Special Economic Zones · TEN-T network · RFC

1 Introduction

Ports are a key element of the economic development of a country; for many years they represented the main point of access to territories and cities and were *the gateway for the exchange of freight among cities* due to the lack of land connections [1].

In recent years, ports have been a key component of the supply chain. The port is a resource that allows his country to compete on an international level with decisive impacts on productivity and therefore on the economy.

Ports have been the topic of many classifications. It is possible to refer to a classification proposed by UNCTAD [2] according to which ports are divided into first, second and third generation [3–5].

First generation ports gave birth to cities; they not only represent a symbol of the city but are also its development engine. Second generation ports developed thanks to the industries of the 20th century. The port was built to serve the industrial system and for this reason the structure was organized in relation to industrial needs. Third-generation ports were created for the containers transport and therefore have well-defined characteristics

© The Author(s) 2023
O. Gervasi et al. (Eds.): ICCSA 2023 Workshops, LNCS 14110, pp. 622–634, 2023.
https://doi.org/10.1007/978-3-031-37123-3_43

and functions in relation to the type of cargo unit transported. Unlike previous generation ports, these ports represent a crucial and strategic node of the supply chain capable of generating added value [6–13]. UNCTAD [14] proposed the definition of fourth and fifth generation ports on which the debate is still open [15–17].

To be competitive, today, a port has to produce added value; it has to be a third-generation port and certain conditions have to be met. The first condition in EU concerns the connection with the TEN-T and RFC networks. The TEN-T networks are a set of linear (railway, road and river) and nodal (urban nodes, ports, freight villages and airports) infrastructures considered relevant at a Community level; these networks constitute the priority of Community strategies and policies and have the objective of ensuring the continuity of the Corridors, creating the missing connections, ensuring connections among the different modes of transport, eliminating the existing bottlenecks [18, 19]. The Rail Freight Corridors (RFC) are oriented to the international market services in EU, established to strengthen cooperation among infrastructure managers on key aspects such as the assignment of paths, the diffusion of interoperable systems and the development infrastructure; find the right balance between freight and passenger traffic along the rail freight corridors, allocating adequate capacities and priorities for freight transport in line with market needs and ensuring the achievement of the common punctuality objectives for freight trains; promote intermodality among rail and other modes of transport by integrating terminals in the management and development of corridors [20].

Furthermore, a port has to be smart [21, 22], in terms of integration of ICT, transported energy factors to pursuit sustainable development goals of Agenda 2030 [23] considering the three pillars related to society, economy and environment [24–29]. Emerging information and communication technologies (ICT), involved in horizontal interactions among different decision makers could reduce the generalized costs of port operations (for example, times) [1]. ICT modify horizontal interactions through a more advanced level of communication and have to be integrated and interconnected with transport and the energy sector for a port to be smart [21].

The observance of these conditions increases the competitiveness of a port which can become of third generation if it produces added value thanks to the presence of industrial areas.

In recent years, many Special Economic Zones (SEZs) have been established, especially in underdeveloped EU regions, with the aim of generating added value in the ports, attracting investments and increasing exports [30–34]. The main purpose of the SEZ is financial and fiscal support and bureaucratic simplification.

A study proposed by the World Bank [35] shows how export times in some European ports, such as Italy and Greece, are almost double those of Holland, Germany and Belgium.

How can SEZ produce added value in a port that has to face challenges of a different type and, above all, of a bureaucratic nature? How can the competitiveness of a port be expressed and what are the main components on which it is possible to intervene? Sect. 2 of the paper investigates the critical issues related to ports and proposes a model that allows to understand which variables to intervene in order to improve the competitiveness of a port and therefore encourage the economic development of a country. A European comparison is recalled in which the components of the costs are analysed. The case of

Italy, located in the centre of Mediterranean area, is introduced; Italy is crossed by four of the nine TEN-T corridors (Mediterranean, Rhine Alps, Baltic Adriatic, Scandinavian-Mediterranean); it has many core ports that risk compromising competitiveness due to slow and complex bureaucracy.

How can a port be competitive if export times are long? How can a port be third generation if it has long export times? What is the advantage for companies of remaining within a SEZ area connected to a port that has longer export times than in other European contexts? The paper proposes an application in which the case of Italy is presented where, as stated by the World Bank [35], the average export times are around 19 days, almost double that of other European countries such as Germany and Belgium (9 days) and Holland (7 days).

2 General Model

A third-generation port is a port in which added value is created with consequent optimization of costs and benefits. The cost optimization problem can be expressed as:

$$min(C) \tag{1}$$

where C represents the generalized cost of transportation that can be minimized by increasing port efficiency.

The benefit optimization problem can be expressed as:

$$max(U) \tag{2}$$

where U represents the utility that can be maximized by introducing the added value in the products into the port.

To make a port strongly competitive it is therefore necessary that the utility linked to the added value of the goods in a port is greater, in absolute value, than the costs:

$$|U| > |C| \tag{3}$$

Assuming that the utility is equal, with zero value for all ports, the main goal is to minimize the generalized cost of transportation, C_E, which, in the case of ports, can be expressed in relation to export costs given by:

$$C_E = \beta_1 \cdot C_m + \beta_2 \cdot T \tag{4}$$

where:

C_m: is the monetary cost of export which represents the ticket to be paid in order to carry out the shipment, expressed in dollars;

T: is the time necessary to complete the export operations, expressed in days;

β_1, β_2: are parameters of homogenization or parameters of mutual substitution.

Assuming that the monetary cost is constant in each country.

The export time is defined by the World Bank as the time, recorded in calendar days, necessary to comply with all procedures required to export goods [35] considering all the waiting times between the start of the procedure (packing of the goods in the container) until its completion (departure of the container from the port).

The export time is the sum of three main components: documental time, time for customs activities and handling time in port. Each time will be analysed below.

The export involves a procedure that requires the compilation of many documents that must be verified and approved in order to finalize the shipment. These activities also provide for the interface with several entities located in different places in the area. The documentary phase is therefore divided into a lot of processes which, in most cases, cannot be developed simultaneously since the approval of the documents envisaged in the previous step is required to start the next step with a different decision-maker.

The procedural process relating to export also includes customs operations. In particular, this phase begins with the electronic presentation of the customs declaration and if this is accepted, the risk analysis for tax and security purposes follows. Once these obligations have been fulfilled, the freight are subjected to checks before they can be completely released.

Before leaving the port, the goods to be exported undergo a series of handling and transfers within the node; the cargo that arrives at the port on trucks or on trains is moved to a collection area where it is checked and validated. The freight is then stored waiting to be combined with any loads with the same destination and subsequently, when the ship is ready in the port, the containers are loaded.

The export time can therefore be divided into three components linked to the: document procedure T_D, customs operations T_C and handling in port T_H:

$$T = T_D + T_C + T_H \tag{5}$$

It is possible to represent the trend of the cost function C and of the utility function U (Fig. 1). Neglecting the component linked to the monetary cost, the cost for each country is a function of the export time T.

Assuming that the utility has a constant value of reference for all the EU countries, for which its trend is similar to a straight line parallel to the x axis and there is an average cost (identical to U in absolute value) for the whole EU continent T^*.

The intersection between the average time function and the time function in each country determines an equilibrium point u^* for which the utility is equal to the cost ($T^* = T$).

Countries on the right u^* are characterized by higher costs than utility; are non-competitive countries, while the countries on the left are the competitive ones with higher utilities than costs.

The problem is understanding how countries can become competitive, what actions need to be taken to make countries move to the left of u^*. It is possible to intervene in two ways: increase of the utility (increase of straight-line $y = T^*$), or reduction of the export time. Utility is linked to the added value of the freight. To reduce export costs, it is necessary to analyse their cost components and identify the critical issues that produce slowdowns in export procedures.

Assuming the trends of the time components as shown in Fig. 2. To reduce the total time, it is necessary to intervene on the components that significantly affect the total value. While the time related to customs operations T_C is negligible, the time related to the handling of goods T_H and the time for documentation T_D play a significant role. T_H can be reduced by optimizing node activities. How is it possible to intervene to reduce T_D and therefore move the countries to the left of u^* by increasing their competitiveness of ports?

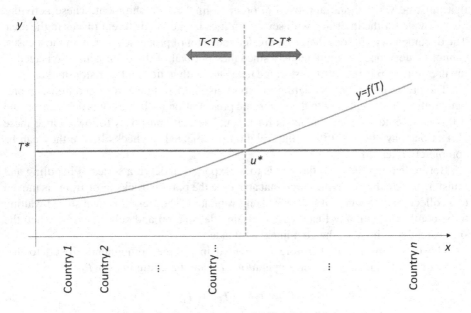

Fig. 1. Trend of cost and utility functions

From a disaggregated point of view, the solution is to organize operations in ports in the best possible way. From the aggregate point of view, it is possible to intervene on the management of the SEZ area where the companies that have to create added value are located. The SEZs were born with the goal of procedural simplification that cannot be pursued due to delays produced by the sequence of the activities and by the fragmentation of the decision-making activities.

If the cost function is expressed in terms of time, in the present case (a):

$$Ta = \sum_{i=1}^{N} (t_i + R_i) \tag{6}$$

where:
  t_i is the time necessary to complete the i-th procedure;
  R_i is the delay related to the i-th procedure;
  N is the number of decision makers involved.

Referring to the graph of administrative procedures in Fig. 3 [32], where the nodes represent the decision-makers involved in the process, the links represent the relationships among them. Each company to have an authorization, from the origin to the final node, is forced to cross a multiplicity of nodes (a) which translates into losses in terms of time and costs.

To simplify the procedures, one could intervene by eliminating some nodes (solution b) but this could lead to problems of a different nature.

A first result can be given by the grouping of some nodes in a single interface which allows the performance of several operations (solution c).

In the latter case the total time can be expressed as (6) but the total value decreases because the number of authorities involved N decreases.

Solution c could be further improved by considering parallel activities within a single authority (solution d, Fig. 4).

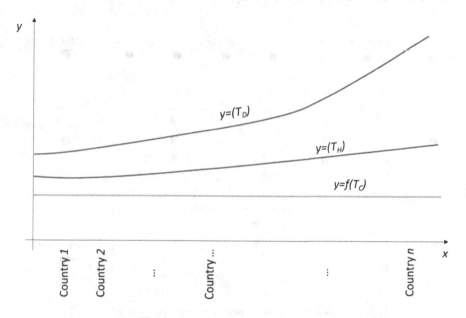

Fig. 2. Export time components trend

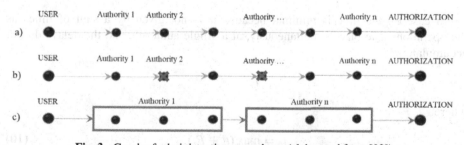

Fig. 3. Graph of administrative procedures (elaborated from [32])

The optimal solution would be to have a single governance of the SEZ and the activities were in parallel and not in series; in this way, the times linked to the documentary procedures would be reduced and consequently the export time would be reduced with the possibility for the State to be competitive (solution e, Fig. 4).

In case d) the time function would become:

$$T_d = \sum_{i=1}^{N} t_d^i \qquad (7)$$

where:

$$t_d^i = \max_i (t_i + R_i) \qquad (8)$$

where i refers to the single generic authority.

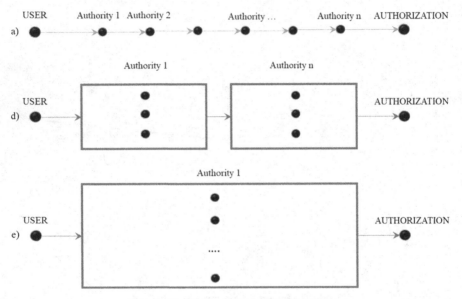

Fig. 4. Graph of administrative procedures

In case e), the time is minimal because it is not given by a sum of times as the operations take place simultaneously, at a single authority, and the delays do not accumulate:

$$T_e = t_e \qquad (9)$$

where:

$$t_e = \max_i (t_i + R_i) \qquad (10)$$

The reduction of the number of authorities allows to pass from Eq. (6) to (7) and in the optimal case, with single authority, to have a time expressed by (9).

3 Application

3.1 The Dataset

Starting from the data provided by the World Bank [35] it is possible to draw the experimental trend of the cost by reporting the export time for each country, as shown in Fig. 5.

The values of the export time are considered, elaborated at a national level [36], according to an increasing scale starting from the Netherlands for which T is 6 days up to Italy with T equal to 19 days.

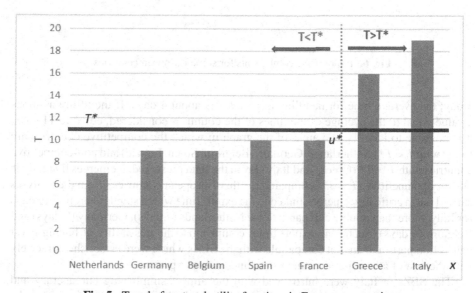

Fig. 5. Trend of cost and utility functions in European countries

It is possible to compare the three components of export time for each port of origin. In particular, from Fig. 6, it can be seen that the time T_D for customs operations is almost constant and assumes a value of 1 day for all the countries considered except for Italy which is 2. The weight of T_D on the time export is minimal. The handling time T_H is relevant for some countries such as Belgium and France for which it covers over 50% of the total time; for Germany it has the same value of the documental time T_D equal to 3 and 4 days respectively. For the Netherlands, Spain, Greece and Italy, $T_H < T_D$ occurs.

Documentary time plays an important role for all countries except Belgium for which it is 3 days (33.3% TE). In particular, it covers more than 50% of T for the Netherlands (57.1%), Spain (50.0%), Greece (68.8%), Italy (57.9%).

3.2 Results

The average values of the time components have been calculated. The average time for document procedure T_D is 6 days; the average time for customs operations T_C is about

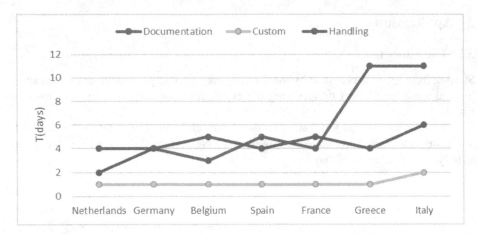

Fig. 6. Export time components for some European countries

1 day; the average time for handling in port T_H is about 4 days. If the utility assumes a value equal to the average of the times of the countries considered, equal to 11 days, it is possible to identify two areas of the graph in which the competitive countries are found with $T < T^*$ (Netherlands, Germany, Belgium, Spain, France) and non-competitive countries with $T > T^*$ (Greece and Italy).From the data presented, it emerges that Italy is not very competitive ($T > T^*$) compared to other European countries. From the analyses carried out, a criticality emerges linked to the export time which stands at around 19 days for Italy, more than double compared to the Netherlands (7 days), Germany (9 days) and Belgium (9 days). Such long export times compromise the possibility of having latest generation ports and are not compatible with the SEZs which were established precisely with the aim of attracting investments and increasing exports.

The SEZs in Italy were introduced with the aim of simplifying bureaucracy and reducing the number of entities involved; in fact, initially the port authority was the only entity identified with the power of initiative and decision-making. The unique and central role of the Port Authority would have improved the country's competitiveness, affecting the times associated with documentary activities and therefore the export time.

Subsequently, loans managed by Entities other than the Port Authorities are made available to the Italian SEZs. Thus, the number of nodes in the bureaucratic graph is not reduced but is increased; the process becomes complex.

Another entity in the governance of the SEZ (Government Commissioner) is also identified, eliminating the unification of the decision-making responsibilities of the process times within the SEZs, and therefore also of the times of exports.

To ensure Italy's competitiveness, it is necessary to move the country to the region with $T < T^*$; it is necessary to reduce the export times which are affected by the component linked to document activities. To reduce T_D it is necessary to centralize governance under a single entity and carry out all activities simultaneously so that the delays of each phase are not reflected in the entire process.

4   Conclusions

The port is a resource that allows countries to compete on an international level with decisive impacts on productivity and therefore on the economy. For this reason, there are specific strategies aimed at optimizing port processes with the main goal of improving the efficiency of the port and making it as competitive as possible, well integrated with the other components of the global distribution network. The paper has investigated the critical issues related to port nodes and proposed a model that allows to understand which variables at governance level, can be modified to intervene in order to improve the competitiveness of a port and therefore encourage the economic development of a country. A European comparison has been presented in which the costs in the individual components are analyzed.

The paper has proposed an application that analyzes the components of the export time for Italy.

Acknowledgement. This study was carried out within the MOST – Sustainable Mobility National Research Center and received funding from the European Union Next-GenerationEU (PIANO NAZIONALE DI RIPRESA E RESILIENZA (PNRR) – MISSIONE 4 COMPONENTE 2, INVESTIMENTO 1.4 – D.D. 1033 17/06/2022, CN00000023). This manuscript reflects only the authors' views and opinions, neither the European Union nor the European Commission can be considered responsible for them.

References

1. Russo, F., Musolino, G.: The role of emerging ICT in the ports: increasing utilities according to shared decisions. Front. Future Transp. **2**, 722812 (2021)
2. UNCTAD: Port marketing and the challenge of the third generation port. Trade and Development Board Committee on Shipping ad hoc Intergovernment Group of Port Experts (1994)
3. Russo, F., Musolino, G.: Quantitative characteristics for port generations: the Italian case study. Int. J. Transp. Dev. Integr. **4**(2), 103–112 (2020)
4. Bichou, K., Gray, R.: A critical review of conventional terminology for classifying seaports. Transp. Res. Part A **39**, 75–92 (2005)
5. Beresford, K.C., Gardner, B.M., Pettit, S.J., Wooldridge, C.: The UNCTAD and WORK PORT models of port development: evolution or revolution? Marit. Policy Manag. **31**(2), 93–107 (2004)
6. Musolino, G., Cartisano, A., Fortugno, G.: Structural factors for a third-generation port: planning interventions for mechanical logistics in Gioia Tauro, Italy. In: Passerini, G., Ricci, S. (eds.) Urban and Maritime Transport XXVII, WIT Transactions on the Built Environment, June 16–18, 2021, Proceedings, vol. 204, pp. 55–66 (2021)
7. Musolino, G., Chilà, G.: Structural factors for a third-generation port: planning transport interventions in Gioia Tauro, Italy. In: Passerini, G., Ricci, S. (eds.) Urban and Maritime Transport XXVII, WIT Transactions on the Built Environment, June 16–18, 2021, Proceedings, vol. 204, pp. 31–42 (2021)
8. Musolino, G., Trecozzi, M. R.: Structural factors for a third-generation port: planning interventions for agri-food logistics in Gioia Tauro, Italy. In: Passerini, G., Ricci, S. (eds.) Urban and Maritime Transport XXVII, WIT Transactions on the Built Environment, June 16–18, 2021, Proceedings, vol. 204, pp. 43–54 (2021)

9. Russo, F., Chilà, G.: Structural factors for a third-generation port: current state, limits and weaknesses of Gioia Tauro, Italy, in the regional transport plan. In: Passerini, G., Ricci, S. (eds.) Urban and Maritime Transport XXVII, WIT Transactions on the Built Environment, June 16–18, 2021, Proceedings, vol. 204, pp. 3–15 (2021)

10. Russo, F., Chilà, G.: Structural factors for a third-generation port: actions and measures for Gioia Tauro, Italy, in the Regional Transport Plan. In: Passerini, G., Ricci, S. (eds.) Urban and Maritime Transport XXVII, WIT Transactions on the Built Environment, June 16–18, 2021, Proceedings, vol. 204, pp. 17–30 (2021)

11. Russo, F., Panuccio, P., Rindone, C.: Structural factors for a third-generation port: between hinterland regeneration and smart town in Gioia Tauro, Italy. In: Passerini, G., Ricci, S. (eds.) Urban and Maritime Transport XXVII, WIT Transactions on the Built Environment, June 16–18, 2021, Proceedings, vol. 204, pp. 79–90 (2021)

12. Musolino, G., Cartisano, A., Chilà, G., Fortugno, G., Trecozzi, M.R.: Evaluation of structural factors in a third generation port: methods and applications. Int. J. Transp. Dev. Integr. **6**, 347–362 (2022)

13. Russo, F., Rindone, C., Panuccio, P.: External interactions for a third generation port: urban and research developments. Int. J. Transp. Dev. Integr. **6**(3), 253–270 (2022)

14. UNCTAD Secretariat: Fourth-generation port: Technical note. Ports Newsletter 19, 9–12 (1999)

15. Lee, P.-W., Lam, J.S.L.: Developing the fifth generation ports model. In: Lee, P.-W., Cullinane, K. (eds.) Dynamic Shipping and Port Development in the Globalized Economy, pp. 186–210. Palgrave Macmillan UK, London (2016). https://doi.org/10.1057/9781137514233_8

16. Flynn, M., Lee, P.T.W., Notteboom, T.: The next step on the port generations ladder: customer-centric and community ports. In: Notteboom, T. (ed.) Current Issues in Shipping, pp. 497–510. Ports and Logistics, University Press Antwerp, Brussels (2011)

17. Paixão, A.C., Bernard Marlow, P.: Fourth generation ports – a question of agility? Int. J. Phys. Distrib. Logist. Manag. **33**(4), 355–376 (2003)

18. European Union: Regulation (EU) No 1315/2013 on guidelines for the development of the trans-European transport network (2013)

19. European Union: Regulation (EU) No 1316/2013 of the European Parliament and of the Council of 11 December 2013 establishing the Connecting Europe Facility, amending Regulation (EU) No 913/2010 and repealing Regulations (EC) No 680/2007 and (EC) No 67/2010 (2013)

20. European Union: Regulation (EU) No 913/2010 of the European Parliament and of the Council (2010)

21. Russo, F., Rindone, C.: Smart city for sustainable development: applied processes from SUMP to MaaS at European level. Appl. Sci. **13**(3), 1773 (2023)

22. Battino, S., del Mar Muñoz Leonisio, M.: Smart ports from theory to practice: a review of sustainability indicators. In: Gervasi, O. et al. (Eds.) Computational Science and Its Applications – ICCSA 2022 LNCS, vol. 13381, pp. 185–195. Springer, Cham (2022). https://doi.org/10.1007/978-3-031-10548-7_14

23. United Nations: Transforming our world: the 2030 Agenda for sustainable development (2015)

24. Balletto, G., Borruso, G., Campisi, T.: Not only waterfront. the port-city relations between peripheries and inner harbors. In: Gervasi, O. et al. (Eds.) Computational Science and Its Applications – ICCSA 2022 Workshops, Malaga, Spain, July 4–7, 2022, LNCS, vol. 13381, pp. 196–208. Springer International Publishing, Cham (2022). https://doi.org/10.1007/978-3-031-10548-7_15

25. Fancello, G., Serra, P., Vitiello, D.M., Aramu, V.: Investigating the competitive factors of container ports in the mediterranean area: an experimental analysis using DEA and PCA. In: Gervasi, O., et al. (eds.) Computational Science and Its Applications – ICCSA 2022 Workshops, Malaga, Spain, July 4–7, 2022, LNCS, vol. 13381, pp. 124–139. Springer International Publishing, Cham (2022)

26. Serra, P., Mancini, S., Fancello, G., Sollai, F., Fadda, P.: Port clusters as an opportunity for optimizing small-scale LNG distribution chains: an application to the mediterranean case. In: Gervasi, O., et al. (eds.) Computational Science and Its Applications – ICCSA 2022 Workshops, Malaga, Spain, July 4–7, 2022, LNCS, Part V, vol. 13381, pp. 140–155. Springer International Publishing, Cham (2022)

27. Braidotti, L., Mazzarino, M.: A study on ports' emissions in the Adriatic Sea. In: Gervasi, O., et al. (eds.) Computational Science and Its Applications – ICCSA 2022 Workshops, Malaga, Spain, July 4–7, 2022, LNCS, Part V, vol. 13381, pp. 98–108. Springer International Publishing, Cham (2022)

28. Gallo, A.: The logistic carbon footprint: a dynamic calculation tool for an indicator of the sustainability of logistic processes with a case study on the port of trieste. In: Gervasi, O., et al. (eds.) Computational Science and Its Applications – ICCSA 2022 Workshops, Malaga, Spain, July 4–7, 2022, LNCS, vol. 13381, pp. 109–123. Springer International Publishing, Cham (2022)

29. Tadini, M., Borruso, G.: Sea-rail intermodal transport in italian gateway ports: a sustainable solution? the examples of La Spezia and Trieste. In: Gervasi, O., et al. (eds.) Computational Science and Its Applications – ICCSA 2022 Workshops, Malaga, Spain, July 4–7, 2022, LNCS, vol. 13381, pp. 156–172. Springer International Publishing, Cham (2022)

30. Musolino, D.A., Panuccio, P.: Special economic zones planning for sustainable ports: the test case of territorial attractiveness and urban planning in Calabria region. In: Gervasi, O., et al. (eds.) Computational Science and Its Applications – ICCSA 2022 Workshops, Malaga, Spain, July 4–7, 2022, LNCS, vol. 13381, pp. 72–84. Springer International Publishing, Cham (2022)

31. Musolino, G., Cartisano, A., Fortugno, G.: Special economic zones planning for sustainable ports: aggregate economic impact of port of Gioia Tauro. In: Gervasi, O., et al. (eds.) Computational Science and Its Applications – ICCSA 2022 Workshops, Malaga, Spain, July 4–7, 2022, LNCS, vol. 13381, pp. 60–71. Springer International Publishing, Cham (2022)

32. Pellicanò, D., Trecozzi, M.R.: Special economic zones planning for sustainable ports: general approach for administrative simplifications and a test case. In: Gervasi, O., et al. (eds.) Computational Science and Its Applications – ICCSA 2022 Workshops, Malaga, Spain, July 4–7, 2022, LNCS, vol. 13381, pp. 47–59. Springer International Publishing, Cham (2022)

33. Rindone, C., Cirianni, F.M.M., Delfino, G., Croce, A.I.: Special economic zones planning for sustainable ports: the role of research and training in the Calabria Region. In: Gervasi, O., et al. (eds.) Computational Science and Its Applications – ICCSA 2022 Workshops, Malaga, Spain, July 4–7, 2022, LNCS, vol. 13381, pp. 85–97. Springer International Publishing, Cham (2022)

34. Russo, F., Chilà, G., Zito, C.: Strategic planning for special economic zones to ports of the future: system of models and test case. In: Gervasi, O., et al. (eds.) Computational Science and Its Applications – ICCSA 2022 Workshops, Malaga, Spain, July 4–7, 2022, LNCS, vol. 13381, pp. 173–184. Springer International Publishing, Cham (2022)

35. World Bank Group: Doing Business 2014. Understanding Regulations for small and medium-size enterprises (2014)

36. Dipartimento per la Programmazione e il Coordinamento della Politica Economica: Iniziativa di studio sulla portualità italiana (2014)

Open Access This chapter is licensed under the terms of the Creative Commons Attribution 4.0 International License (http://creativecommons.org/licenses/by/4.0/), which permits use, sharing, adaptation, distribution and reproduction in any medium or format, as long as you give appropriate credit to the original author(s) and the source, provide a link to the Creative Commons license and indicate if changes were made.

The images or other third party material in this chapter are included in the chapter's Creative Commons license, unless indicated otherwise in a credit line to the material. If material is not included in the chapter's Creative Commons license and your intended use is not permitted by statutory regulation or exceeds the permitted use, you will need to obtain permission directly from the copyright holder.

Methodologies for Sustainable Development of TEN-T/RFC Corridors and Core Ports: Public Incentives for Industrial Activities Location in Port Related Areas

Domenica Savia Pellicanò[1](✉) 🄳 and Maria Rosaria Trecozzi[2]

[1] DIIES - Mediterranea University, 89124 Calabria, Reggio, Italy
domenica.pellicano@unirc.it
[2] Calabria Region, 88100 Catanzaro, Italy

Abstract. The Special Economic Zone (SEZ) is a regulated area where industrial activities are facilitated and have many incentives in order to become more competitive and attractive. The establishment of a SEZ is the responsibility of the national government which provides a model based on specific measures to attract investment. The local administrations have to define a plan, according to the national model, for the development of the SEZs in order to respect and enhance the peculiarities of each area. The goal is to push the strategic connection among logistics, industry and ports through incentive packages, including fiscal and non-fiscal ones, in order to have strong repercussions on economic development.

The impacts of the SEZs can be assessed in terms of sustainability: social, environmental and economic. In relation to economic sustainability, the paper proposes a general model developed to estimate the financial burdens borne by the regional and national administrations deriving from the establishment of the SEZ. The paper introduces a test case of Calabria Region to estimate the financial burdens necessary for the SEZ establishment in the Gioia Tauro macro-node, into the TEN-T core network and the RFC.

Keywords: Special Economic Zones · Economic development · financial model · public incentives · industrial activities location · TEN-T corridors · RFC corridors · sustainable ports · smart ports

1 Introduction

A port can be classified in relation to its generation [1] defined on the basis of quantitative characteristics [2]. A third-generation port is strategic node in the supply chain able of generating added value [3–10]; it requires the creation of a high level of services also through the implementation of continuous innovation processes. A third-generation port can be pursued through the creation and upgrading of industrial areas. Nowadays, the SEZs are established, representing a type of industrial areas capable of generating added value.

© The Author(s) 2023
O. Gervasi et al. (Eds.): ICCSA 2023 Workshops, LNCS 14110, pp. 635–646, 2023.
https://doi.org/10.1007/978-3-031-37123-3_44

The SEZ *represents a powerful tool for the development of a region thanks to the presence of adequate financial, fiscal, simplification and bureaucratic support* [11].

The SEZ is therefore a tool for sustainable development which, within a global economic growth strategy, allows to increase exports, foreign investments and employment levels; it also provides an efficient control of companies through adequate services [11–15]. The pursuit of sustainable development is the main goal already set in 1987, in the Brundtland report [16]. The main components of the sustainability are economy, society and environment that are important and independent but closely connected.

The concept of sustainable development then evolved over time and in 2015, thanks to the 2030 Agenda, was broken down into 17 goals [17]. Each goal refers to a general issue, the goals 9 and 11 are attributable for important parts to the transport sector [18].

The SEZ is a tool for sustainable development of a port, therefore it generates added value, only if some conditions, necessary but not sufficient, are verified (Fig. 1). The first condition requires that the port, in which the SEZ is established, belongs to the TEN-T network [19, 20]; the SEZ must be closely linked to the major European transport infrastructures. Moreover, the port must be smart in which transport, energy and ICT components are integrated and interconnected [21–23]. The last necessary condition for the SEZ to work is that there are incentives; these incentives derive from the transport and logistics sector which are highly monitored activities and therefore respectful of all the constraints and agreements established at European level. The incentives must allow the achievement of objectives of common interest [24], in accordance with the Treaty of Lisbon (2007) [25], and must not lead to distortions of competition. Incentives can be given if some critical issues that hold back the development of a port are resolved, such as export time; some studies conducted by the World Bank [26] showed that some European countries, such as Italy and Greece, have export times almost double as the Netherlands, Germany and Belgium.

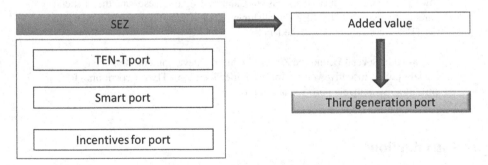

Fig. 1. Necessary conditions for SEZ

The impacts deriving from the establishment of the SEZ can be evaluated with respect to the three aspects of sustainability.

Economic sustainability has to be understood as efficiency and effectiveness, considering specific objectives ranging from the reduction of costs borne by users and the production costs of services with an increase in production efficiency and product effectiveness, to raising the quality of services and of labour, the processes of liberalization and regulation which can constitute a tool. The impacts in terms of economic sustainability of the SEZ mainly concern the export growth through the acceleration of economic growth and diversification of the export sectors; the growth in employment levels in relation to the availability of areas for the settlement of new activities and the growth of those already in the SEZ; the growth of foreign capital investments by offering companies adequate services and infrastructures; industrial upgrading and technology transfer through the implementation of basic research lines functional to economic activities, promotion of start-ups and spin-offs, training and retraining of the workforce; the financial statements through the tax policies envisaged by current legislation to companies.

Social sustainability includes the prevention (reduction) of accidents related to the mobility of citizens and goods (safety) with the consequent reduction of the related social costs, and as protection from criminal acts (security), and understood not only as a cost, but as a prospect of technological, industrial and economic growth. Social sustainability also includes participation that is the form of both accessibility and reliability of services for all citizens, passenger rights and participation in decisions relating to mobility systems. The impacts in terms of social sustainability of the SEZ mainly concern the raising working standards by implementing safety development lines both through the introduction of new technologies and the verification of work organization methods, considering that safety is not a cost, but a resource and an opportunity for growth for the entire economic system; the development of human resources both in term of retraining of the workforce and the growth of skills.

Environmental sustainability is divided into different specific objectives relating to anthropized and non-anthropized areas. Some topics concern the increase in energy efficiency and environmentally friendly propulsion; the reduction of environmental pollution with particular reference to air quality; the reduction of visual intrusions and noise pollution in urban and non-urban areas. The impacts in terms of environmental sustainability of the SEZ mainly concern the environmental standards that can be achieved by providing companies with specifically designed infrastructures and services, in the awareness that effective management of the environment is a key point for optimizing the resources used by investors.

In the scientific literature, there are many researches focusing on the incentives related to the SEZ area. Some studies delve into the structure of incentives in some countries [27, 28], others evaluate the impacts deriving from such incentives [29, 30]; there is no model that unequivocally clarifies how these incentives can be estimated.

The aim of the paper concerns the analysis of the impacts of the SEZ from an economic point of view. In particular, an incentives model is proposed which makes it possible to estimate the financial charges deriving from the establishment of the SEZ.

The paper is addressed to technicians, politicians, researchers etc. who are interested in knowing the frame of incentives necessary for the establishment of a SEZ.

The paper is structured in four sections including the introduction (Sect. 1) and the conclusions (Sect. 4). In the Sect. 2, after a general framework that allows to define a structure of models for the evaluation of the impacts of the SEZ, the paper presents the formulation of an incentives model. In the Sect. 3, an application to a real context is proposed by presenting the case of the Calabria SEZ. Calabria SEZ has its center in the port of Gioia Tauro, a core port of the TEN-T network and constitutes a southern gateway to Europe. The port of Gioia Tauro is crossed by the Scan-Med corridor and ScanMed RFC which are the axes that connects Finland and Sweden in the north, up to the island of Malta in the south, crossing Denmark, Germany, Austria and Italy. The regions along these corridors constitute the most important socio-economic area of the EU.

Gioia Tauro, as an Italian port, is affected by the critical issues related to export times which make the node uncompetitive compared to other European countries. According to data provided by the World Bank [26], export times in Italy are 19 days, more than double compared to the Netherlands, Belgium and Germany.

2   An Incentives Model

2.1   A System of Experimental Models for the SEZ

The impacts produced by the SEZ can be quantified through the use of experimental models. These models are of a different nature and allow for different outputs; they are part of a general system which, through a "trial and error" procedure, will have the SEZ model as its final output.

The models can be structured as: Aggregated Direct Impacts; Land Capacity Constraint; Economic - Functional Integration; Settlement of Firms; Incentives; Aggregated Indirect and Induced Impacts.

The Aggregated Direct Impacts model allows, on the basis of literature data, an aggregate estimate of the impacts deriving from the establishment of the SEZ; these impacts are consistent with the constraints deriving from the surface availability and the socio-economic characteristics of the areas analyzed in Land Capacity Constraint model, with a disaggregated approach. The economic-functional link between the areas is estimated using Economic-Functional Integration model, based on the origin-destination matrix among the areas and a gravity model including service level attributes expressed in terms of distances and travel times. The feasibility of the hypotheses with respect to possible establishments and expansions of companies, on the basis of the available surfaces, and the need for resources is verified with Settlement of firms and Incentives models. Finally, Aggregated Indirect and Induced Impacts model allows to estimate impacts in terms of direct and induced employment.

2.2   The Formulation

The incentives model allows to estimate the financial burdens deriving from the establishment of the SEZ.

The incentives derive from the transport and logistics sector which are highly monitored activities and therefore respectful of all the constraints and agreements established at European level. The incentives have to allow to achieve objectives of common interest as services of general economic interest, social and regional cohesion, employment, research and development, sustainable development, promotion of cultural diversity, etc., in accordance with the Treaty of Lisbon (2007) [25], and must not lead to distortions of competition.

It is possible to define different types of financial burdens [31]: incentives for investments; operating incentives for small and medium companies (SMEs); additional incentives.

The incentives for investments F^I will be granted to companies that start an investment program in the SEZ, within the limits of the established resources and in compliance with the community regulations on incentives for regional purposes and in particular on the basis of the provisions of Regulation 651/2014 [32]. These incentives, expressed in Gross Grant Equivalent (GGE), can be used by the company up to the value of the grant granted. Furthermore, the beneficiary companies must maintain their activity in the SEZ area for at least five years from the completion of the investment covered by the grant, under penalty of retroactive revocation of the benefits granted.

Incentives for investments can only be recognized for:

- creation of a new establishment or for the expansion of the capacity of an existing establishment;
- diversification of the production of an existing plant to obtain products never manufactured before;
- fundamental change to the overall production process of an existing plant.

Operating incentives for small and medium companies (SMEs) F^{SME}, based on European legislation, can only be recognized to reduce a company's current expenses not linked to an initial investment. Such expenses include costs for personnel, materials, contracted services, communications, energy, maintenance, rent, administration, but not depreciation and financing costs if these have been included in the eligible costs when the incentives for investments have been granted. Operating incentives for SMEs, unlike incentives for investments that can be activated without notification pursuant to Regulation no. 651/2014, are bound to the express authorization of the European Commission which will have to evaluate the reasons why a Member State requests it.

Additional incentives F^{ADD} are a faculty of the Region that can institute such forms of incentive considering that the regulatory provisions do not produce any expenditure automatism, as the capital account charges in question are of an eventual nature.

The estimated financial burdens depend on the expected scenario of SEZ. In particular, the expected scenario of SEZ is defined leaving from the Settlement of Firms model that gives:

- the number and type of equivalent companies that can settle, and/or can be under expansion if already settled, in the industrial agglomerations of the SEZ;
- increase in the occupied area.

In particular, the estimated financial burdens can be expressed as:

$$F = \sum_t I_t \cdot w_t \qquad (1)$$

where I_t is the total unitary incentive for the t type of company and w_t is the number of companies of t type obtained from the Settlement of Firms model.

The financial burdens F can be expressed as the sum of its three components as follows:

$$F = F^I + F^{SME} + F^{ADD} = \sum_t \left(I_t^I + I_t^{SME} + I_t^{ADD} \right) \cdot w_t \qquad (2)$$

This formulation defines the complete framework of the incentives that a company can request to establish itself within a SEZ. The components of incentives model include all contributions that can be granted to companies; not all companies request for or can receive the whole package of incentives, but some rates can be requested or granted.

3 Application

The proposed model has been applied to a real case, the SEZ established in Calabria, in the Gioia Tauro macro-node. Gioia Tauro is one of the main commercial hubs in Italy specialized in container transhipment operations. In 2020, it was one of the few ports that increased the container traffic, + 26%, respect to 2019 [4]; in 2021, it handled around 1.15 million TEUs [33]. Gioia Tauro is also specialized in Ro-Ro services [34, 35]; as regards the import/export traffic, the volumes of vehicles were respectively about 0.28 in 2018 and 0.21 million in 2019 [33]. It has a strategic location in the centre of the Mediterranean; it is a core port of the TEN-T network also crossed by the RFC.

3.1 Incentives for Investments

The estimated incentives for investments depend on the regional aid map which sets limits on the intensity of investment aid in the different regions. For the Calabria Region, which is positioned among those areas with a GDP between 65% and 75%, the maximum aid intensities are envisaged: 25% for large companies; 35% for medium companies; 45% for small companies.

As regards the new settlements, two types of companies have been considered which, on the basis of the economic system of Calabria, can be assumed to have the following characteristics: NG Type (15 ha of occupied surface, 300 employees); NM Type (10 ha of occupied area, 100 employees).

As far as the existing settlements are concerned, the presence of two further types of companies has been hypothesized:

- MG Type, if after the establishment of the SEZ, a company already existing in the base year of reference 2018 expands, becoming, in the reference decade 2019–2028, a NG type company, with consequent increase of 5 ha of occupied area and increase of 200 employees;
- MM Type, if after the establishment of the SEZ, a company already existing in the base year of reference 2018 expands without changing the surface occupied, but still undergoing an increase in employees in the reference decade 2019–2028.

In relation to the previous ceilings, it should be noted that for major projects, involving investments of more than 50 million euro, the ceiling in GGE (Gross Grant Equivalent, unit of measurement that is used to calculate the amount of economic aid in relation to the entire amount of the investment) is calculated as:

$$Maximum\ aid = max(GGE)\% \cdot [50 + (0.5 \cdot B) + (0.34 \cdot C)] \qquad (3)$$

where $max\ (GGE)\%$ is the ceiling in GGE or investments, equal to 25% for large companies; B is the cost between 50 and 100 million euro and C is the cost exceeding 100 million euro.

Large projects mean the establishment of NG companies.

The real intensity of the benefit is progressively reduced with respect to the ceiling for amounts exceeding 50 million euro.

For the estimation of the financial endowment, it can be hypothesized to set a spending ceiling. Specifically, if the recognition of the benefit is assumed for a baseline scenario defined by *Nc, Tc* and *GGE* that correspond to:

- 4 NG type companies setting up in the territory, with a ceiling of 25% in GGE for investments up to 50 million euro;
- 4 existing NM type companies, with an average ceiling of 40% GGE for investments up to 3 million euro.

In this scenario, an annual financial allocation for incentives for investments of 54,800 million euro is estimated, for a total of 164 million euro over the three-year period.

3.2 Operating Incentives for Small and Medium Companies

The operating incentives, in compliance with European legislation, only for SMEs operating in the SEZ and for a duration not exceeding three financial years of the same SMEs, can be disbursed according to the *de minimis regime*, with a maximum allowable plafond equal to 200 million euro for each company.

For the estimation of the operating incentives, it can be hypothesized to set an amount for the *de minimis regime*. Specifically, can be the recognition of the benefit is assumed for a baseline scenario defined by *Nc* and *Tc* that correspond to:

- 100,000 euro for the 50 SMEs already established;
- 200,000 euro for 4 new SMEs settling in the area.

In this scenario an annual financial allocation for operative incentives of 5,8 million euro is estimated.

3.3 Additional Incentives

The additional incentive can be estimated on the basis of estimates referring to SMEs with an intensity of subsidy referring to the similar administrative program implemented by the Calabria Region with the ISP call (Integrated Subsidy Packages) of 2010, relating to the realization of technical feasibility studies, research and development projects technology and projects for companies innovation and competitiveness.

The maximum amount of the contribution cannot, in any case, exceed:

- 22,500.00 euro for each Technical Feasibility Study;
- 500,000.00 euro for each Research and Technological Development Project (industrial and pre-competitive);
- 50,000.00 euro for each Innovation and Technology Transfer Service.

In this scenario an annual financial allocation for additional incentives of 4.18 million euro is estimated.

3.4 Framework of Incentives

It is possible to summarize all the financial burdens for the scenario hypothesis considered. For each type of burden, Table 1 shows the economic nature of the expenditure, the temporal nature of the expenditure and the expected amount of expenditure.

Table 1. Financial burdens

Type	Economic nature	Temporal nature	Expected amount (Million euro)
Investment incentives	I	P	164
Operating incentives	C	P	5.8
Additional incentive measures	I	P	4.18
Total			173.98

C: current expenditure; I: investment expenditure; A: annual; P: multi-year

3.5 Incentives for Different Scenarios

The incentives estimation procedure can be performed on the basis of the results of Settlement of Firms model relating to the quantification of the number of companies and scenarios A and B based on the surface area available at the base year.

In particular, in Calabria, considering the constraints relating to the surfaces available throughout the SEZ, it's possible to hypothesize two development scenarios respect to an increase in the occupied area:

- Scenario A - high, an increase in the occupied area of 100% of the free area is expected compared to the 2018 value.
- Scenario B - low, an increase in the occupied area of 50% of the free area is expected compared to the 2018 value.

Table 2 reports the estimates incentives for investments for scenarios A and B based on the area available in the base year. Table 3 shows the estimates incentives for investments for scenarios A and B based on the upgraded area, in which it is also hypothesized that the actual available surface can be considered double.

Considering the upgraded surface area and scenario A, a cost of around 308 million euro is obtained; in the hypothesis that there is an additional financial support of 100 million euro to be allocated to NM-type companies, an overall cost of the SEZ equal to 400 million euro can be estimated.

Table 2. Estimates incentives for investments based on available area at base year

Scenario	Companies (Number)	Type	Amount of incentives (Million euro)	Maximum aid intensities	Total/year (Million euro)	Total/year (Million euro)
A	6	NG	360,000	25%	90,000	154,000
	3	NM	60,000	40%	24,000	
	4	MG	160,000	25%	40,000	
B	3	NG	180,000	25%	45,000	73,000
	1	NM	20,000	40%	8,000	
	2	MG	80,000	25%	20,000	

Table 3. Estimates incentives for investments based on upgraded area

Scenario	Companies (Number)	Type	Amount of incentives (Million euro)	Maximum aid intensities	Total/year (Million euro)	Total/year (Million euro)
A	12	NG	720,000	25%	180,000	308,000
	6	NM	120,000	40%	48,000	
	8	MG	320,000	25%	80,000	
B	6	NG	360,000	25%	90,000	154,000
	3	NM	60,000	40%	24,000	
	4	MG	160,000	25%	40,000	

4 Conclusions

A SEZ is a regulated area where industrial activities are facilitated and have many incentives in order to become more competitive and attractive. The aim is to push on the strategic link among logistics, industry and ports to have strong impacts on economic development working on sustainability terms.

To evaluate the impacts from the SEZ, starting to the analysis of the specific characteristics in which the SEZ is established, such as economic and legislative ones, it's possible to use of experimental models which develops on several levels. One of these levels concerns the estimate of financial burdens to make the SEZ operational. The paper has proposed a model for technicians, politicians, researchers etc. in order to evaluate the incentives necessary for the establishment of a SEZ.

The model has been applied to a real context of the Calabria SEZ. In Calabria, the package of incentives necessary for the SEZ has been estimated assuming a scenario based on the availability of areas and the type of industry. The expected amount is about 174 million euro for investment, operating and additional incentives.

Two scenarios have also been considered in relation to the increase in occupied area (high and low). The model has allowed to estimate the incentives for the two scenarios also considering a doubling of the available surface.

In the best scenario, which foresees an increase in the occupied area of 100% of the free area (compared to 2018) and a doubling of the current available area, the investment incentives are estimated at around 400 million euro.

Acknowledgement. This study was carried out within the MOST – Sustainable Mobility National Research Center and received funding from the European Union Next-GenerationEU (PIANO NAZIONALE DI RIPRESA E RESILIENZA (PNRR) – MISSIONE 4 COMPONENTE 2, INVESTIMENTO 1.4 – D.D. 1033 17/06/2022, CN00000023). This manuscript reflects only the authors' views and opinions, neither the European Union nor the European Commission can be considered responsible for them.

References

1. UNCTAD: Port marketing and the challenge of the third generation port. Trade and Development Board Committee on Shipping ad hoc Intergovernment Group of Port Experts (1994)
2. Russo, F., Musolino, G.: Quantitative characteristics for port generations: the Italian case study. Int. J. Transp. Dev. Integr. 4(2), 103–112 (2020)
3. Musolino, G., Cartisano, A., Fortugno, G.: Structural factors for a third-generation port: planning interventions for mechanical logistics in Gioia Tauro, Italy. In: Passerini, G., Ricci, S. (eds.) Urban and Maritime Transport XXVII, WIT Transactions on the Built Environment, June 16–18, 2021, Proceedings, vol. 204, pp. 55–66 (2021)
4. Musolino, G., Chilà, G.: Structural factors for a third-generation port: planning transport interventions in Gioia Tauro, Italy. In: Passerini, G., Ricci, S. (eds.) Urban and Maritime Transport XXVII, WIT Transactions on the Built Environment, June 16–18, 2021, Proceedings, vol. 204, pp. 31–42 (2021)
5. Musolino, G., Rosaria Trecozzi, M.: Structural factors for a third-generation port: planning interventions for agri-food logistics in Gioia Tauro, Italy. In: Passerini, G., Ricci, S. (eds.) Urban and Maritime Transport XXVII, WIT Transactions on the Built Environment, June 16–18, 2021, Proceedings, vol. 204, pp. 43–54 (2021)
6. Russo, F., Chilà, G.: Structural factors for a third-generation port: current state, limits and weaknesses of Gioia Tauro, Italy, in the regional transport plan. In: Passerini, G., Ricci, S. (eds.) Urban and Maritime Transport XXVII, WIT Transactions on the Built Environment, June 16–18, 2021, Proceedings, vol. 204, pp. 3–15 (2021)
7. Russo, F., Chilà, G.: Structural factors for a third-generation port: actions and measures for Gioia Tauro, Italy, in the regional transport plan. In: Passerini, G., Ricci, S. (eds.) Urban and Maritime Transport XXVII, WIT Transactions on the Built Environment, June 16–18, 2021, Proceedings, vol. 204, pp. 17–30 (2021)
8. Russo, F., Panuccio, P., Rindone, C.: Structural factors for a third-generation port: between hinterland regeneration and smart town in Gioia Tauro, Italy. In: Passerini, G., Ricci, S. (eds.) Urban and Maritime Transport XXVII, WIT Transactions on the Built Environment, June 16–18, 2021, Proceedings, vol. 204, pp. 79–90 (2021)
9. Musolino, G., Cartisano, A., Chilà, G., Fortugno, G., Trecozzi, M.R.: Evaluation of structural factors in a third generation port: methods and applications. Int. J. Transp. Dev. Integr. 6, 347–362 (2022)

10. Russo, F., Rindone, C., Panuccio, P.: External interactions for a third generation port: urban and research developments. Int. J. Transp. Dev. Integr. **6**(3), 253–270 (2022)
11. Pellicanò, D., Trecozzi, M.R.: Special economic zones planning for sustainable ports: general approach for administrative simplifications and a test case. In: Gervasi, O., et al. (eds.) Computational Science and Its Applications – ICCSA 2022 Workshops, Malaga, Spain, July 4–7, 2022, LNCS, Part V, vol. 13381, pp. 47–59. Springer, Cham (2022)
12. Musolino, D.A., Panuccio, P.: Special economic zones planning for sustainable ports: the test case of territorial attractiveness and urban planning in calabria region. In: Gervasi, O., et al. (eds.) Computational Science and Its Applications – ICCSA 2022 Workshops, Malaga, Spain, July 4–7, 2022, LNCS, Part V, vol. 13381, pp. 72–84. Springer, Cham (2022)
13. Musolino, G., Cartisano, A., Fortugno, G.: Special Economic zones planning for sustainable ports: aggregate economic impact of port of Gioia Tauro. In: Gervasi, O., et al. (eds.) Computational Science and Its Applications – ICCSA 2022 Workshops, Malaga, Spain, July 4–7, 2022, LNCS, Part V, vol. 13381, pp. 60–71. Springer, Cham (2022)
14. Rindone, C., Cirianni, F.M.M., Delfino, G., Croce, A.I.: Special economic zones planning for sustainable ports: the role of research and training in the Calabria Region. In: Gervasi, O., et al. (eds.) Computational Science and Its Applications – ICCSA 2022 Workshops, Malaga, Spain, July 4–7, 2022, LNCS, Part V, vol. 13381, pp. 85–97. Springer, Cham (2022)
15. Russo, F., Chilà, G., Zito, C.: Strategic planning for special economic zones to ports of the future: system of models and test case. In: Gervasi, O., et al. (eds.) Computational Science and Its Applications – ICCSA 2022 Workshops, Malaga, Spain, July 4–7, 2022, LNCS, Part V, vol. 13381, pp. 173–184. Springer, Cham (2022)
16. World Commission on Environment and Development: Report of the World Commission on Environment and Development: Our Common Future (1987)
17. United Nations: Transforming our world: the 2030 Agenda for sustainable development (2015)
18. Russo, F., Pellicanò, D.S., Iiritano, G., Petrungaro, G., Trecozzi, M.R.: From global goals to local development: the role of regional plan for sustainable urban mobility. Eur. Transp.\Trasporti Europei **85**(4), 1–15 (2021)
19. European Union: Regulation (EU) No 1315/2013 on guidelines for the development of the trans-European transport network (2013)
20. European Union: Regulation (EU) No 1316/2013 of the European Parliament and of the Council of 11 December 2013 establishing the Connecting Europe Facility, amending Regulation (EU) No 913/2010 and repealing Regulations (EC) No 680/2007 and (EC) No 67/2010 (2013)
21. Russo, F., Musolino, G.: The role of emerging ICT in the ports: increasing utilities according to shared decisions. Front. Future Transp. **2**, 722812 (2021)
22. Musolino, G., Peda, G., Russo, F.: Emerging ICT and port community systems: a survey of scientific literature. WIT Trans. Built Environ. **212**, 123–135 (2022)
23. Russo, F., Rindone, C.: Smart city for sustainable development: applied processes from SUMP to MaaS at European level. Appl. Sci. **13**(3), 1773 (2023)
24. Russo, F., Fortugno, G., Merante, M., Pellicanò, D.S., Trecozzi, M.R.: Updating national air passenger demand from traffic counts: the case of a secondary airport in an underdeveloped region. Sustainability **13**(15), 8372 (2021)
25. Union, E.: Treaty of Lisbon, amending the Treaty on European Union and the treaty establishing the European Community. Official J. Eur. Union, OJ C **306**, 1–271 (2007)
26. World Bank Group: Doing Business 2014. Understanding Regulations for small and medium-size enterprises (2014)
27. Aijaz, U., Hassan Daud Butt, D., Bano, S., Hayat, A., Raees, M. B., Mazhar, M.: Dynamics of SEZs a comparative analysis of incentive packages for special economic zones of Pakistan, Bangladesh & Vietnam. J. Positive Sch. Psychol. **6**(11), 1247–1269 (2022)

28. Jusoh, S., Abd Razak, M.F.: Special economic zones in ASEAN: the cases of Lao PDR, Malaysia, and Myanmar. In: Handbook of Research on Special Economic Zones as Regional Development Enablers. IGI Global, pp. 92–108 (2022)
29. Liotti, B.F., Ndubai, J.W., Wamuyu, R., Lazarov, I., Owens, J.: The treatment of tax incentives under Pillar Two. Trans. Corporations **29**(2), 25–46 (2022)
30. Mbogo, J.N.: The Impact of Tax Incentives on Foreign Direct Investments in Kenya. PhD Thesis. University of Nairobi (2022)
31. Calabria Region Council: Deliberazione N. 52 del 25 settembre 2015 - Presentazione al Parlamento ai sensi dell'articolo 121 della Costituzione e dell'articolo 16 dello Statuto regionale di proposta di legge statale, recante: "Misure straordinarie per lo sviluppo dell'Area di Gioia Tauro – DDL per l'istituzione di una zona economica speciale (ZES)" (2015)
32. European Union: Commission Regulation (EU) No 651/2014 of 17 June 2014 declaring certain categories of aid compatible with the internal market in application of Articles 107 and 108 of the Treaty (2014)
33. Assoporti. https://www.assoporti.it/media/10681/adsp_movimenti_portuali_annuale_2021.pdf. Accessed 03 Apr 2023
34. Russo, F., Musolino, G., Assumma, V.: Ro-ro and lo-lo alternatives between Mediterranean countries: factors affecting the service choice. Case Stud. Transp. Policy **11**, 100960 (2023)
35. Russo, F., Musolino, G., Assumma, V.: An integrated procedure to estimate demand flows of maritime container transport at international scale. Int. J. Shipping Transp. Logist. **6**(2), 112–132 (2014)

Open Access This chapter is licensed under the terms of the Creative Commons Attribution 4.0 International License (http://creativecommons.org/licenses/by/4.0/), which permits use, sharing, adaptation, distribution and reproduction in any medium or format, as long as you give appropriate credit to the original author(s) and the source, provide a link to the Creative Commons license and indicate if changes were made.

The images or other third party material in this chapter are included in the chapter's Creative Commons license, unless indicated otherwise in a credit line to the material. If material is not included in the chapter's Creative Commons license and your intended use is not permitted by statutory regulation or exceeds the permitted use, you will need to obtain permission directly from the copyright holder.

Author Index

© The Editor(s) (if applicable) and The Author(s), under exclusive license
to Springer Nature Switzerland AG 2023
O. Gervasi et al. (Eds.): ICCSA 2023 Workshops, LNCS 14110, pp. 647–648, 2023.
https://doi.org/10.1007/978-3-031-37123-3